PRESIDENTIAL TIMBER

PRESIDENTIAL TIMBER

A HISTORY OF NOMINATING CONVENTIONS, 1868-1960

HERBERT EATON

⌊*Fp*⌋

THE FREE PRESS OF GLENCOE
COLLIER-MACMILLAN LIMITED, LONDON

For Alice Eaton

PREFACE

Presidential Timber is neither a history of American presidential politics, nor is it a history of presidential campaigns. It is an account of how and why thirty-two men have, since 1868, received their parties' nominations for the presidency of the United States. All material is subordinated to the specific events leading to nomination in national convention, and issues and political events have been considered primarily for their bearing on the nominations. Naturally, certain conventions are discussed at greater length than others. Conventions in which the presidential nominations were foregone conclusions or in which delegates had gathered merely to ratify renomination of incumbents have been dealt with briefly.

For the major conventions—those in which there were great clashes of men and issues—I have relied heavily on anecdotal material, believing that men and issues may often be illuminated more clearly by personal anecdote, sometimes minor and sometimes comic, than by all the party platforms and formal speeches, which are usually as empty and as unhuman as a public monument. It is, I think, all too often forgotten that politics, especially presidential nominating politics, involves human beings preoccupied, more often than not, with the very human problems of securing patronage, thwarting one's opponents, and getting oneself re-elected—whether it be to Congress, a State House, or a county sheriff's office. It is the rare convention delegate or candidate's manager who sees himself participating in those great impersonal forces of history that are so popular today in explaining the events of the past. By considering the participants in these conventions as men who can be seen and understood through personal details and actions, a realistic picture can be drawn of the processes of presidential nomination.

It has also been my intention in this book to lay to rest, wherever possible, the many popular myths surrounding certain nominations. I believe that the nomination of a candidate for the presidency of the United States is sufficiently dramatic without the embellishment of folklore or the distortion of myth. It is sometimes hard to give up cherished fantasies, but frequently the actual events are more fantastic than the popular myths that surround many nominations.

It has been my hope that an account of how presidential candidates have been nominated in the past will lead to a greater understanding of contemporary nominating politics. There has been, I think, too little attention given to the process of choosing candidates to fill what is now the most powerful elective office in the world. In the past, that selection have often been made for selfish or what would now seem trivial reasons, and men have sometimes been chosen to represent their parties almost by accident. An awareness of these facts may help to prevent such accidents in the future.

I wish to express my thanks to Harcourt, Brace & World, Inc., for permission to quote from *Behind the Ballots* by James A. Farley; to Mr. William Jennings Bryan, Jr., and the estate of Mrs. Ruth Bryan Rohde for permission to quote from *Memoirs* by William Jennings Bryan; and to William L. White for permission to quote from *Politics the Citizen's Business* by William Allen White. Selections from *Random Recollections of an Old Political Reporter*, by William C. Hudson, are reprinted by permission of Cupples & Leon Co. I have, in researching and writing this book, received valuable assistance from many individuals. I should like to give particular acknowledgment to Mr. Thomas M. Storke of Santa Barbara, California; Governor Alfred M. Landon; Governor Robert F. Bradford; Senator Harry F. Byrd; Mr. John D. M. Hamilton; Chief Justice Raymond Baldwin; and Senator Edward Martin, all of whom were kind enough to clarify various points. Also my grateful thanks to Alan Hislop of the University of California, who saved me from many pitfalls of grammar and style. Finally, my gratitude to Ronald L. Pratt, whose editorial judgment was invaluable. The assistance was theirs. The errors of fact and judgment are mine.

Herbert Eaton

BERKELEY, CALIFORNIA
March 10, 1964

CONTENTS

Chapter 5

Chapter 6

Chapter 7

Chapter 8

Chapter 9

Chapter 10

Chapter 21

Chapter 22

Chapter 23

Chapter 24

"There is something about national conventions as fascinating as a revival or a hanging."

—*H. L. Mencken*

CHAPTER 1

"Pity me, Harvey, pity me"

THE TENTH DEMOCRATIC NATIONAL CONVENTION
New York, July 4, 1868

The battle for the Democratic presidential nomination in 1868 was fought on one major issue—the "greenback question," on which the Democratic Party was sharply divided. Should government bonds be redeemed from private investors in gold or in the depreciated paper currency that had been issued to meet the demands of the war? The principal holders of government bonds, the eastern financial interests, opposed any scheme that would depreciate the bonds' value. There was popular support in the West for the "Ohio plan," under which the obligations of the national government would be paid in greenbacks in all cases where the authorizing acts did not specifically provide for redemption in gold. To the farmers and shopkeepers of the West, hard pressed by taxation and poor prices for crops, it was an attractive proposal. "The same currency for the bond-holder and the plough-holder" became a slogan that rallied the debtor West and alienated the creditor East.

The Democrats judged their prospective candidates according to their support for or opposition to the Ohio plan. Only George H. Pendleton of Ohio supported it. He soon found himself alone against the field.

"Gentleman George" Pendleton was, at forty-three, the undisputed leader and idol of the Ohio Democracy. A congressman

1

from 1857 to 1865, he had been the Democratic candidate for vice-president in 1864. In Congress, he had stood between the Copperheads and the "War Democrats," building a record for guarding the principles of the Democratic minority without ever being simply an obstructionist. Pendleton announced his support of the Ohio plan in July, 1867, and was immediately assailed by the eastern Democrats. As often happens to wealthy men who espouse theories unpopular with the rich, Pendleton was denounced as a traitor to his class and accused of demagoguery. When charged with having abandoned the traditional Democratic "hard money" position, he replied that he preferred hard money to soft but believed that, as long as greenbacks remained legal tender, they should be used for all obligations, including bond payments.

The race for the nomination was primarily a contest between Pendleton and the leaders of the eastern Democracy. Pendleton needed enough pledged delegates to overcome the combined opposition of the other candidates. The East needed only to keep at least one-third of the delegates out of Pendleton's camp.

August Belmont, Chairman of the Democratic National Committee, made the first moves against Pendleton. The wealthy banker, who had come to America thirty years before as a representative of the Rothschilds, pressured the National Committee into selecting New York City, far removed from the main sources of Pendleton's strength, as the convention site. Next, he set July 4 as the opening date, in defiance of many party leaders who wanted a May convention. A late convention, Belmont believed, would dissipate much of the early enthusiasm for Pendleton.

The traditional two-thirds rule was the most ominous obstacle in Pendleton's path. Were the rule to be enforced, 205 out of a total of 317 votes would be required to nominate. With slightly more than a hundred votes controlled by the eastern states, it would be virtually impossible for Pendleton to win unless the two-thirds rule were abandoned or a stampede could be begun in his behalf.

A western candidate of more conservative financial views was Senator Thomas A. Hendricks of Indiana. One of the most distinguished figures in the party, he was, at forty-seven, making the difficult transition from politician to statesman. Hendricks was popular in the East as the man who might stop Pendleton. The Indiana Senator's views on money were appealing to easterners, who planned to use him to divide the western forces. The Pendleton supporters, knowing that Pendleton had the greater support in the West, thought it akin to treason for another westerner to break what should be a united front. Unless Hendricks could overcome the implacable hostility of Pendleton's forces, his candidacy would be nothing more than a pawn in eastern hands.

The most prominent eastern candidate was Salmon Portland Chase, Chief Justice of the Supreme Court. Portly, pompous, and awesomely lacking in humor, Chase had held throughout his lifetime an exalted belief in his own importance. He had been a Free-Soil senator whose vigorous defense of abolition took him into the Republican Party in 1855. In the same year, he had been elected governor of Ohio. An active contender for the presidential nomination in 1856 and 1860, he had been named Secretary of the Treasury by Lincoln.

Chase had angled frantically to replace Lincoln as the Republican candidate in 1864 and, after the collapse of his candidacy, had offered one of his frequent resignations. To his surprise, it was accepted. Some months later Lincoln elevated Chase to the Chief Justiceship, in the belief that he was putting a perpetual candidate in the one office that would silence ambition. Lincoln underestimated his man.

For a time after the war, Chase, a member of the Radical wing of the party, was a leading candidate for the Republican nomination, but his growing uneasiness over the excesses of the Radical leaders, combined with the strength of Grant's candidacy, estranged Chase from the Republicans. The impeachment trial, over which Chase presided with a fairness and impartiality that infuriated the impeachers, completed the break.

He could not be nominated by his own party, but there were other parties and other nominations. The presidency burned feverishly in Chase's mind, and he would take any road that led there. In 1868, the stately Chase, physically the epitome of a dignified jurist, could be seen scrambling for the Democratic nomination in a manner anything but dignified.

Chase began his campaign among the Democrats by admitting

that, if the party should accept his doctrines of "suffrage for all; amnesty for all; good money for all; security for all its citizens at home and abroad against governmental invasion," he could not refuse the use of his name. The Democratic Party, however, was not interested in accepting the doctrine of suffrage for all, and Chase realized he would have to abandon either aspiration or principle. It took him only three months to turn his back on the cause for which he had labored for thirty years. By July, he was insisting that questions of suffrage should be left to the tender mercies of the individual states, without federal interference.

As for his party affiliation, Chase considered himself a Democrat, in spite of the differences between himself and the party on matters of principle. He would accept the party's nomination if the party would accept his principles. It was a forthright stand, but the capacity for self-delusion among politicians is infinite. When it became obvious that his principles were unacceptable, he reframed them to the satisfaction of the Democrats. On July 1, he permitted a fifteen-point platform to be circulated among Democratic leaders. It was a masterpiece of compromise and evasion. On the three most important points—Negro suffrage, Reconstruction, and the greenback question—the Chief Justice managed to be on both sides of the issue. He advocated the principle, if not the practice, of universal suffrage and repudiated the Radical Reconstruction program, while endorsing the use of troops to maintain the carpetbaggers. The greenback plank ("The public debt should be honestly paid but creditors are not entitled to special favors in the interpretation of the laws. The courts should decide cases of conflicting interest") meant everything or nothing. Chase had joined the party instead of the party joining Chase.

A second Republican who sought the Democratic nomination was Andrew Johnson. His opposition to the congressional Radicals had won him, at first, much admiration from the Democrats. But the ineptitude with which he waged his battle, his growing political isolation, and the stubbornness that antagonized even his friends lost him much of the support he had originally commanded. Still, he would be able to count on substantial southern support in the convention.

Two military candidates were Winfield Scott Hancock of Penn-

sylvania and Frank Blair, Jr., of Missouri. Major-General Hancock
had been appointed in 1866 to command the Department of Louisiana and Texas. He soon came into conflict with the Radical Congress, which removed him from command—in itself enough to
recommend him to the Democrats.

Hancock had, before the convention, three specific sources of
strength. His home state, although nominally pledged to railroad
magnate Asa Packer as a favorite son, was for him. He had wide
support among the war veterans, and a Soldiers' and Sailors' Convention was organized to meet in conjunction with the Democratic
National Convention to work for his nomination. Support also
came from the South, which had been favorably impressed by the
fairness with which he had commanded the Fifth Military District.
Howell Cobb, General Nathan Bedford Forrest, and newspapers
in Memphis, Charleston, Macon, and Mobile all urged his
candidacy.

While Hancock was a professional soldier whose life had been
devoted to the career of arms, Frank Blair, Jr., was a political
general. The forty-seven-year-old son of Francis Preston Blair—
editor, member of Jackson's Kitchen Cabinet, and elder statesman
—and brother of Montgomery Blair, Lincoln's Postmaster General,
Frank Blair had a long record of political service in the cause of
abolition. He had been the only Free-Soil congressman elected
from a southern state and had, along with his father and brother,
joined the Republicans in 1860. Leaving Congress in 1862 for military service, he rose to the rank of major-general and served with
Sherman on the march to the sea. After the war, the course of the
Radicals drove the Blair family back to the Democratic Party.

For many years the elder Blair and Montgomery had labored
to educate and groom Frank for the presidency. They began, in
the spring of 1868, a canvass of political leaders. Response was
friendly but noncommittal. Many were well disposed to Blair, but
no one offered pledged delegates. Although not averse to going
along with Blair if everyone else did, none of the party leaders
wished to be the first to declare in his favor. The Blair candidacy
remained largely a family affair.

Like Chase, Blair issued a platform before the convention.
Blair's strategy was to hold off from an early drive for the nomi-

nation. He hoped, by letting Missouri go to Pendleton on the first few ballots, eventually to inherit the Pendleton strength. To increase his chances of being second choice of the Pendleton forces, Blair announced his platform in a letter to Colonel James O. Brodhead, chairman of the Missouri delegation. Where Chase's platform had been ambiguous and straddling, Blair's was blunt, specific, and explosive.

Blair believed the only issue before the country was Reconstruction. He considered it imperative to overthrow the Radical program and the carpetbag governments. Blair suggested that this policy could be accomplished only by presidential action. He proposed that the President declare the Reconstruction Acts null and void and "compel the army to undo its usurpations at the South, disperse the carpetbag State governments, and elect Senators and Representatives." Blair was confident that the Democrats could gain control of the House; the Democratic majority could then admit the southern representatives "elected by the white people of the South." Then, with concerted action, the President and the House could compel the Senate to follow their lead in destroying the Radical program. "It is idle to talk of bonds, greenbacks, gold, the public faith and the public credit. What can a Democratic President do in regard to any of these with a Congress in both branches controlled by carpetbaggers and their allies?"

Blair's platform stirred a great outcry in the North. The Radicals denounced it as reviving the specter of civil war, and his threat to use the army to crush the carpetbaggers frightened many northerners. The New York *Tribune* dubbed his doctrine "Revolution, plain and simple—an appeal from the decision of the ballot box to force and violence." When Radicals cried that Blair spoke for the real policies of the Democratic Party, conservatives agreed.

The final candidate, albeit a highly reluctant one, was Horatio Seymour of New York. As a former governor of his state the fifty-eight-year-old Seymour was the leader of the eastern Democrats. Slender, reserved, but kindly, Seymour looked like the scholar and gentleman he was. His devotion to the serenities of private life was excelled only by his passionate devotion to the party. He was popular with Democrats of all sections, and it was said that no one who knew him could be his enemy. A fear of possible emotional instability—his father had committed suicide after financial reverses in the panic of 1837—contributed to Seymour's reluctance to serve too actively in public life. But his sense of duty always outweighed his private inclinations. He was elected governor of New York in 1852 and was defeated for re-election two years later.

In 1860, he refused to be a candidate for the presidential nomination. He loyally supported the Union cause when he was returned to the governorship in 1862. He presided over the Democratic National Convention of 1864 and lost his bid for re-election as governor the same year. No other northern Democrat since the death of Douglas was more deserving of the name "statesman" than was Horatio Seymour in 1868.

There were, however, certain weaknesses in Seymour's record. He had, in his gubernatorial races, run consistently behind his ticket, and he had been defeated three out of the five times he had made the race. Never having held national office, his career, if not his fame, was wholly associated with New York. His greatest handicap was the general opinion that he had played a Copperhead role in the New York City draft riots of 1863. The actual riots had been grossly exaggerated, and Seymour's role in helping to control them had been straightforward and decisive. But the accusation had been made, and it left an unjust and unwarranted stain on his public record. For that reason, as well as for his unswerving party regularity, he did not have much attraction for conservative Republicans or War Democrats.

Seymour was mentioned early for the nomination. In late November, 1867, a newspaper in Oneida County, New York, suggested him as the proper candidate for 1868. Seymour reacted promptly. He wrote the paper's editor, stating emphatically that he was not and could not be a candidate for the presidency.

His refusal attracted attention and protests. Republicans doubted his sincerity, and Democrats questioned his judgment. In order to halt all speculation, Seymour wrote a second letter for publication in January, 1868: "I assure you I am not a candidate for the office of President. In my letter, I said what I meant; and I am annoyed to find that it is looked upon by some as a strategic movement." This second refusal quieted much of the discussion of his availability, and Seymour was not generally considered an active candidate before the convention.

In June, George Pendleton revived the Seymour candidacy by endorsing him for the nomination. "I would rather trust him than myself with the delicate duties of the next four years. . . . You know I am sincere. . . . I am ready, anxious to give up the nomination to anybody who can get one single more vote than myself." The letter was written for circulation among the delegates. Pendleton apparently hoped either to divide and confuse the eastern forces by promoting a candidate who would refuse the nomination, or he planned to effect the New Yorker's nomination in order to keep out Hendricks or Chase.

On July 2, the New York delegation assembled in caucus. It was moved that they should offer the former Governor as their candidate and invite other states to support him. Seymour protested and, for the third time, explicitly refused to allow his name to go before the convention. The delegates had no choice but to accede to his wishes. It was decided to support Sanford E. Church as a favorite son until the strength of the major candidates was known and an alternative candidate to Seymour could be selected.

The Democratic National Convention met on July 4, 1868, in the newly constructed Tammany Hall on 14th Street near Union Square. The weather was hot, "too hot for the warm work on hand here," as Chief Justice Chase was informed by his daughter, Kate Chase Sprague. But the heat in no way diminished the enthusiasm of the resurgent Democracy. Triumphal arches of evergreen, flags, and bunting with portraits of Jackson and Jefferson were thrown across 14th Street, while bands and marching demonstrators crowded the city. The most active demonstrations were provided by the Pendleton men, who, the day before the convention, paraded three hundred strong, clad in linen dusters and caps, wearing counterfeit greenbacks as badges, and carrying a great banner that read: "The people demand payment of the bonds in greenbacks and equal taxation. One currency for all. Pendleton the people's nominee." Brevity was considered neither the soul of wit nor the source of political advantage. The Pendleton enthusiasts put on a noisy show, but they were soon overwhelmed by the normal bustle and noise of New York and lost to view.

The Chase forces centered their activities around Chandler House—where the Committee of One Hundred, a Philadelphia group pledged to Chase, dispensed liberal hospitality to delegates on their way to Tammany Hall across the street—and the mansion of the wealthy Kate Chase Sprague. The Chief Justice's daughter was the wife of millionaire Senator Sprague of Rhode Island. A beautiful, ambitious, willful woman, she had been the reigning belle of Washington society during the Lincoln administration. Never satisfied to be a guest in the White House, she passionately desired to be its mistress. Her zeal for the nomination surpassed her father's, and many believed that Chase was in the race more for his daughter's sake than for his own. Keeping open house at 94 Fifth Avenue, the regal Kate, who dazzled delegates with her charm and wit, was a formidable asset to the Chief Justice's campaign.

While the Soldiers' and Sailors' Convention was meeting to recommend General Hancock to the Democrats, keen interest was aroused by the Confederate delegates to the convention. The southerners, with their long hair, slouch hats, Confederate gray clothing, and courtly manners, presented a sight not recently seen in the North. Among the defeated generals gathered to nominate a presidential candidate were Wade Hampton, Nathan Bedford Forrest, Sterling Price, and John B. Gordon. They were joined by such political leaders as former Senator James B. Chestnut of South Carolina and Benjamin Hill of Georgia.

The delegates were described by one, admittedly unfriendly, observer as "a rough lot—hirsute, porky creatures, in linen 'dusters,' with badges in their buttonholes. They sally forth from the Astor House, the St. Nicholas, and other hotels in squads of a dozen, and invade the already occupied omnibus. 'Here's a seat, Governor.' 'Hello, Senator, is that you? You sit in my lap.' 'I reckon we'd better stop at the New York Hotel and licker up,' and so on."

The buses at last were emptied, the bar at the New York Hotel abandoned momentarily, and—at twelve noon, Saturday, July 4— August Belmont called the National Democratic Convention to order. When Henry L. Palmer of Wisconsin took the chair as temporary chairman, the first of many conflicts developed. It was necessary to adopt temporary rules to serve until the Committee on Permanent Organization had reported. The Ohio delegation moved the adoption of the rules of the House of Representatives, which did not contain a two-thirds rule. Knowing that the temporary rules would be reported as the permanent rules of the convention, the anti-Pendleton forces countered by moving to adopt the rules of the last Democratic convention, including the crucial two-thirds rule. The motion to adopt the rules of the previous convention carried by voice vote, and the Pendleton forces suffered their first major setback.

On the second day, Horatio Seymour was named President of the Convention. He was escorted to the chair by Governor Bigler of Pennsylvania and Governor Hammond of South Carolina. The choice of escorts was not lost upon either the delegates or the country at large. The picture of New York and Pennsylvania walking arm in arm with South Carolina offered striking proof of the reunification of the Democratic Party.

The Pendleton forces were now able to achieve a victory that did much to offset their defeat on the two-thirds rule. By a vote of 189½ to 90½, the convention moved to adopt a platform before nominating a candidate. If the greenback position were included in the platform, it would assist the selection of a greenback candidate. Some states that did not favor Pendleton himself were in favor of a greenback plank. If such a plank could be placed in the platform, it would be a considerable deterrent to the nomination of a hard-money candidate.

The platform, presented on the third day, was a resounding victory for the western and out-and-out Democrats. It endorsed the greenback position and condemned the Radical Reconstruction program. Negro suffrage was called a matter of state control, and a revenue tariff was proposed. Although an appeal was made for conservative support, the espousal of greenback doctrines made the document one likely to drive the conservatives back to the Republicans.

After the adoption of the platform, Seymour had the two-thirds rule read to the convention. He clarified the point that a vote of two-thirds of the entire Convention, not merely two-thirds of those present and voting, was needed for nomination. It was ruled that 212 votes out of a total of 317 would be necessary for nomination.

Nine candidates were placed in nomination: Governor James E. English of Connecticut, General Hancock, George H. Pendleton, former Governor Joel Parker of New Jersey, Sanford E. Church of New York, Asa Packer of Pennsylvania, President Andrew Johnson, and Senator James R. Doolittle of Wisconsin. Neither Chase, Blair, nor Hendricks was placed in nomination. Their supporters preferred to await developments.

On the first ballot, as expected, Pendleton led with 105 votes. Surprisingly enough, Andrew Johnson placed second with 65. The other totals were Church 34, Hancock 33½, Packer 26, English 16, and Parker and Doolittle with 13 each. Three candidates who had not been nominated were Reverdy Johnson with 8½, Hendricks with 2½, and Blair with ½.

Pendleton, whose vote had come primarily from the Middle and Far West, also received support from Delaware, Kentucky, Maine, Maryland, Massachusetts, and West Virginia. Johnson's 65 votes, with the exception of a single vote from Maine, came from the South.

On the second ballot, Pendleton lost 1 vote. Johnson lost 13— 6 of his Texas votes switched to Hancock, who stood third with 40½. Johnson's 10 Virginia votes went to Blair who stood at 10½.

Pendleton gained 15½ votes on the third ballot for a total of 119½. His new strength came from the change of Virginia from Blair, as well as scattered votes from Nevada, California, South Carolina, and North Carolina. Johnson slipped to 34½, losing Florida, North Carolina, and half of South Carolina. Hancock climbed to 45½. Vermont abandoned English to give Hendricks a total of 9½.

On the fourth ballot, North Carolina cast nine votes for Horatio Seymour. This change was greeted by loud and enthusiastic cheering from the galleries, although the delegates took it somewhat more calmly. Seymour came forward to decline the vote, saying, "I must not be nominated by this Convention, as I could not accept the nomination if tendered, which I do not expect. . . . It

must be distinctly understood, it is impossible, consistently with
my position, to allow my name to be mentioned in this Convention
against my protest." For the fourth time, Horatio Seymour refused
to be a candidate for the nomination.

On the fifth ballot, Pendleton advanced from 118½ to 122,
Hancock from 43½ to 46, Hendricks from 11½ to 19½, and Blair
from 2 to 9½. A new name appeared on the ballot. John Quincy
Adams, son of Charles Francis Adams, received one vote from
South Carolina.

The final ballot of the day, the sixth, saw little change in the
strength of Pendleton and Hancock, but Hendricks moved up
from 19½ to 30. After the sixth ballot, the convention, with a deadlock in prospect, adjourned until the following morning. In six
ballots, Pendleton had increased his strength by only 17½ votes,
while Hancock and Hendricks had also made only minor gains.
The Blair candidacy had not yet developed, and Johnson had lost
all hope for the nomination. Pennsylvania, New Jersey, and New
York, as well as Connecticut and Wisconsin, remained committed
to favorite sons.

The first break in the convention came the following morning.
Indiana placed Hendricks in formal nomination, a minority of the
delegation declaring they would continue to vote for Pendleton
as instructed. Despite the defection of Indiana, Pendleton's strength
increased from 122½ to 137½, most of the new votes coming from
the South. Hendricks stood at 39½; Hancock slipped to 42½.

After the seventh ballot, New York retired for consultation and
returned to change its 33 votes from Church to Hendricks. The
eastern leaders plainly intended to use one westerner to stop the
other. Hendricks rose to 75 votes, but Pendleton also gained new
support, mostly at the expense of Hancock, and rose to 156½. This
total was two votes short of a majority, and the Pendleton men
bitterly contemplated the stranglehold of the two-thirds rule.
Without that insurmountable roadblock, their man would undoubtedly have gone on to victory on this ballot. But New York's switch
marked the beginning of the end for Pendleton. On the ninth
ballot, he fell to 144. Hendricks rose to 80½.

There was little change on the next three ballots. By the twelfth,

Pendleton stood at 145½, Hendricks at 89, and Hancock at 30. On this ballot, two new names appeared. General McClellan, the standard bearer of 1864, received 1 vote from Tennessee to the accompaniment of great cheers and applause from the galleries. Salmon P. Chase was given ½ vote from California. The vote for Chase was arranged by the New York leaders to test the reaction of the convention. The announcement of the Chief Justice's name brought applause, not only from the galleries, but from the delegates as well. As the applause subsided, several hisses were heard, causing a renewal of applause and cheers as a rebuke to the hissers. It was some time before order could be restored. The enthusiasm generated by Chase's name was no doubt partly due to a genuine interest in his candidacy, but it must be admitted that the general high spirits that prevail at national conventions was also a factor. As one reporter observed: It was "partly due to that love of the sensational and surprising among the on-lookers which regarded a vote for him simply as a bold demonstration, a defiance of precedent, and which would have paid the same tribute to a vote for Jefferson Davis or for Horace Greeley." At any rate, the demonstration satisfied the Chase advocates, although they felt the time to press his candidacy had not yet arrived.

On the next ballot, the Chase vote did not increase, and a single vote from Tennessee was cast as a compliment to Franklin Pierce. Pendleton declined to 134½, Hendricks to 81. Hancock gained 18½ votes for a total of 48½. The fourteenth ballot continued the deadlock. On the fifteenth, another major break occurred.

It was evident that the candidate from Indiana had been successful in stopping the candidate from Ohio. Now it was time to build up a third candidate to stop both westerners. Consequently, Pennsylvania abandoned its favorite son, Asa Packer, and cast 26 votes for Hancock. With this increase, Hancock stood at 79½, Pendleton at 129½, and Hendricks at 82½.

The switch to Hancock, unlike the previous swing to Hendricks, created wild excitement. On the next ballot, Arkansas, Georgia, Louisiana, Maryland, Mississippi, Kansas, and Missouri brought new strength to the Pennsylvania general. Hancock took the lead with 113½ votes to 107½ for Pendleton and 70½ for Hendricks. The

seventeenth ballot increased the momentum of the Hancock bandwagon. He rose to 137½; Pendleton fell abruptly to 70½. Chase reappeared with the same ½ vote from California, and Nebraska
made a bewildering move and cast 3 votes for John T. Hoffman,
Grand Sachem of Tammany Hall.

Hancock picked up another 7 votes on the eighteenth ballot,
and another ballot might very well have clinched his nomination,
but that was not part of New York's strategy. Hancock was supposed to eliminate Pendleton and Hendricks, not win the nomination for himself. It was a desperate moment for the New Yorkers,
but quick action by Seymour prevented a Hancock victory.

At the conclusion of the eighteenth ballot, a dispute arose in
the Illinois delegation over the unit rule. The delegation, after
voting for Pendleton for sixteen ballots, had gone to Hendricks on
the eighteenth. A delegate loudly insisted that, unit rule or no, his
vote should go to Pendleton. The argument spread to other delegations, and a general fight was threatening when a delegate from
Massachusetts moved for adjournment. The question was put. The
voice vote in favor of the motion was very light. The negative vote
was thunderous. Seymour nevertheless declared the motion carried,
adjourned the convention, and promptly left the chair to avoid
argument. The Hancock bandwagon had been stopped in its tracks.

The prelude to the final act of the convention was now ready
to begin. Pendleton had been eliminated; the Hancock boom had
been stopped for the moment. It was now time for the opposing
forces to make their final plans. The key delegations were Ohio
and New York. The Empire State controlled the eastern Democracy; any action on the part of New York would have a decisive
effect on the deadlocked convention. Ohio, although unable to
secure the nomination for Pendleton, could, at least, veto the other
candidates. In these two delegations, plans were laid on the night
of July 8 to present a mutually satisfactory candidate to the Democracy of the country.

New York had been casting its vote for Hendricks to prevent
the nomination of either Pendleton or Hancock. The real preference
of the delegation, at the urging of Horatio Seymour, was Chief
Justice Chase. As soon as Hendricks stalemated Hancock, New

York would switch to Chase. This switch, followed, it was hoped, by the support of Ohio, would be sufficient to stampede the convention for the Chief Justice.

This strategy had two question marks. Would Ohio follow New York into the Chase camp? Clement L. Vallandigham, the firebrand Copperhead leader, and several other Ohio delegates were active in Chase's support, but other Ohio delegates, as well as Pendleton, were opposed to his nomination. Could Vallandigham deliver Ohio? On the night of July 8, the delegation held a stormy caucus. Vallandigham was absent. After considerable debate, the delegates were swayed by a drunken harangue from an Iowa delegate who persuaded them to pass a resolution that they would not under any circumstances support the Chief Justice.

The second question mark was the attitude of the chairman of the New York delegation, Samuel J. Tilden. As a close associate of Seymour, Tilden was, apparently, a Chase supporter. Privately he preferred his friend Seymour and went along with the Chase strategy only so long as it suited him. There are conflicting reports of Tilden's activities on the night of July 8, but the sequence seems to have been: First, Tilden met in a private dining room at Delmonico's with several Pendleton leaders, among them Allen G. Thurman; Washington McLean, editor of the Cincinnati *Enquirer;* and General George W. McCook. In this singularly elegant "smoke filled room," they concocted a scheme whereby Ohio would the next day retire for consultation during the balloting and return to the hall to present Seymour's name. The conspirators met again the following morning at the Fifth Avenue Hotel to complete the details. The plan was worked out in absolute secrecy and kept from the rank and file of both the Ohio and New York delegations. The plan was also kept from Horatio Seymour.

After dinner at Delmonico's, Tilden next joined Seymour, Abram S. Hewitt, New York industrialist; and John Kelly, Congressman and future Grand Sachem of Tammany, for dinner at the Manhattan Club. There they reached unanimous agreement that Chase was to be nominated on the following day.

Tilden, after his double repast, called a meeting of the New York delegation for Thursday morning, July 9. At this caucus,

Seymour asked the delegation to give up Hendricks and turn to
Chase. After vociferous opposition by several delegates, the delegation agreed by a vote of 36 to 27 to switch to Chase, as soon
as Hendricks's strength began to decline. It was believed that
Hendricks would have to be stopped first to avoid the appearance
that New York was dictating a nominee to the convention.

In other delegations, which were unaware of the plots of the
previous night, support for Chase was gathering. A minority of
the Ohio delegation, led by Vallandigham, pledged themselves to
the Chief Justice, and a considerable portion of the Pennsylvania
delegation agreed to support him if Hancock should lose ground.
Wisconsin was expected to abandon Doolittle and second Chase's
name, while Massachusetts, Michigan, Tennessee, Rhode Island,
Georgia, Maine, and New Jersey were said to be waiting to follow
the lead of New York.

When the convention was called to order on July 9, the delegates knew that momentous decisions had been made. The first
move of the day was the formal nomination of Frank Blair, who,
unaware that events had already passed him by, had high hopes
of emerging as the compromise candidate. Next, California offered
its own compromise in Justice Stephen J. Field of the Supreme
Court, but this nomination was received with little interest. Vallandigham then approached the platform and read a letter from
Pendleton formally withdrawing from the contest. His remaining
delegates were now free to vote for other candidates.

The nineteenth ballot showed that the enthusiasm for Hancock
had indeed been checked by adjournment. His vote fell from 144½
to 135½. Hendricks gained 20½ votes, mainly from released Pendleton delegates, to reach 107½, the highest vote he had yet received.
Ohio cast her 21 votes for Asa Packer in an effort to confuse and
split the Pennsylvania delegation between two favorite sons. Blair
received 13½ votes, and 15 went to Field. Four votes were cast for
Governor Thomas H. Seymour of Connecticut, as a result of delegates' confusion about where to turn.

On the twentieth ballot Hancock rose to 142½, while Hendricks
picked up 13½ votes for a total of 121. Hendricks increased to 132
on the twenty-first ballot. Hancock slipped to 135½. Hancock

had been stopped, but the convention was preparing to turn to Hendricks.

The time had come for final action. The Hancock and Hendricks managers met and agreed that, in return for his support, Hancock would be given the vice-presidential nomination on a Hendricks ticket. Before the bargain could be executed, Ohio decided to move.

Vallandigham, still loyal to Chase, rushed to Tilden and begged him to switch on the next ballot. Tilden refused, arguing he could not effect the change to Chase until Hendricks began to lose strength. Vallandigham thereupon went to Seymour to warn him that Ohio would present his name on the next ballot unless Tilden immediately swung New York to the Chief Justice. Seymour flatly stated that he would refuse the nomination. Vallandigham returned to Tilden and again asked him to present Chase. Tilden again refused. Fearful of a Hendricks victory unless immediate action were taken, Vallandigham admitted defeat for Chase and returned to the Ohio delegation to await the results of the plan to present Seymour.

As the twenty-second roll call proceeded, Hendricks continued to gain support. When Ohio was called, General McCook arose and formally presented the name of Horatio Seymour. Seymour thereupon came forward and, declaring his name must not be used, instructed the secretary not to record the vote. He then left the platform. Vallandigham rose and insisted the vote for Seymour must stand. From the New York delegation, Francis Kernan emphatically voiced the same opinion. Seymour returned to the platform and started forward, apparently with the intention of nominating Chase. He never made it. Several friends blocked the way; one seized his arm and dragged him from the platform. Seymour, his cheeks wet with tears, met Peter Harvey of Boston in the corridor as he was being rushed from the hall. "Pity me, Harvey, pity me," he cried. The reluctant candidate, still protesting and weeping, was bustled out the back door into a carriage and driven to the Manhattan Club to be held *incommunicado* until the Convention had completed its business.

After Seymour's abduction, the balloting continued with little change. One vote from Tennessee went to Seymour, but the other delegations held firm. Kentucky, Wisconsin, and Massachusetts, however, had been passed. Wisconsin was recognized first and cast its 8 votes for Seymour. Kentucky and Massachusetts quickly followed. Then North Carolina changed its vote from Hendricks to Seymour, and the stampede was on.

The New York *Times* described what happened. "The end had come. Instantly all over the hall the delegations sprang to their feet, every chairman demanding recognition by voice and gesture. The lobbies broke out into tumultuous continuous cheers. Hats, fans, handkerchiefs were waved aloft, delegates seized the silken pennons of their States, and brandished them over the heads of the yelling crowd. The tumult swelled until it became confusion worse confounded. . . . Sovereign States scrambled forward with unseemly haste, and rudely jostled each other in their rush to be the first in changing to SEYMOUR. The end was seen, and the order issued for the battery in Union Square . . . to begin. With the roar of the first gun the crowd within the hall was invigorated, and began again to cheer continuously, lustily. There seemed no limit to their capacity for uproar, nor their endurance in maintaining it. All business and order was swept before the storm, and the officers strove in vain to restore some semblance of order." Out of all this sound and fury, Horatio Seymour, the one man in or out of the convention hall who did not want to be president, was the unanimous choice of the Democratic National Convention to be its standard bearer.

When order was finally restored, the convention moved immediately to the nomination of a vice-presidential candidate. There was some protest at the haste, and motions were made for a recess, but the convention, perhaps fearing to allow Seymour time to return to the hall and refuse the nomination, crushed all attempts to recess and began a roll call for nominations. Frank Blair had just been put in nomination when Governor Bigler managed to interrupt and secure an hour's recess.

General John A. McClernand, Asa C. Dodge, and General Thomas Ewing, Jr., were placed in nomination but withdrew their names. Ex-Confederate Generals William Preston of Kentucky, James B. Steadman of Louisiana, and Wade Hampton seconded

Blair's nomination. Hampton stated it was a gesture of friendship and good will from the South to welcome the nomination of such a distinguished northern general.

Frank Blair was unanimously nominated. This nomination, so hurriedly completed, with little consultation or deliberation, was an act of haste the Democrats would regret as the specter of the letter to Brodhead followed them throughout the campaign. The decision, wise or not, had been made; Seymour of New York and Blair of Missouri were on the Democratic ticket for 1868.

"Sacred as a soldier's grave"

THE FOURTH REPUBLICAN NATIONAL CONVENTION
Chicago, May 21, 1868

Long before the Republicans met in Chicago in May, the party's candidate had been determined. But the path that led Ulysses Simpson Grant from Appomattox Court House to a unanimous nomination for the presidency of the United States had not been without its obstacles. For one thing, it was difficult—as with so many generals who suddenly find themselves involved in politics—to ascertain what Grant's political convictions were or, for that matter, if he had any opinions at all. So vague were his expressions on the political issues of the day that, throughout 1866 and well into 1867, he was considered as likely a candidate for the Democrats as for the Republicans.

Grant was diligently wooed by the Radicals in their fight against President Johnson. As a soldier on active duty, the taciturn Grant carefully refrained from expressing any political opinions; privately, he became an ally of the Radicals. Many of the Radical leaders who were eager to use Grant as a weapon against Johnson —men like Ben Wade, who nursed his own presidential ambitions, and Ben Butler—were less enthusiastic over the prospects of his actually being a presidential candidate. Butler was an especially acrimonious opponent. He lost few opportunities to discredit the General and even hired detectives to investigate Grant in the hope of finding evidence that would ruin his candidacy. Grant's election, Butler sarcastically remarked, would give the nation an opportunity to "see if there is any difference between a drunken tailor and a drunken tanner."

As Grant's popularity increased—despite the coolness of congressional leaders—politicians outside Congress took matters into their own hands. Thurlow Weed of New York, the once powerful king maker, organized a group known as the "Union Republican General Committee" of New York City, which, on June 24, 1867, nominated Grant for the presidency.

To counter charges that Grant was only a tool of the Weed machine, Weed organized another pro-Grant meeting. Carefully hiding his own role, Weed persuaded some of the leading figures of the city, including A. T. Stewart, Moses Taylor, and Cornelius Vanderbilt, to call a mass meeting at Cooper Institute for early December, 1867, for the avowed purpose of taking Grant's nomination out of the hands of the politicians. In an expansive mood as the call went forth, Weed privately boasted that he would handle the campaign for Grant as he had that for Zachary Taylor. Not conceding Grant's reticence as a liability, Weed vowed that, if Grant would make no declarations and write no letters, he would elect him.

By early 1868, the Grant candidacy was accelerating, helped along by the "nonpartisan" nomination at Cooper Institute. The conservative Republicans were, by and large, firmly united behind the General, and the Radicals were won over when Grant publicly broke with Johnson.

The Grant-Johnson break arose over the battle to remove Edwin T. Stanton as Secretary of War. Grant, as *ad interim* head of the War Department, agreed when the Radicals demanded Stanton's reinstatement and turned the office back to Johnson's enemy. A series of name-calling letters ensued between the excitable President and Grant, which goaded the General into siding wholeheartedly with the delighted Radicals. He supported the impeachment proceedings and the entire Radical program. His testimony at the impeachment trial assured his nomination. Even Ben Butler swallowed his pride and made overtures of support to Grant.

The Fourth Republican National Convention met in Chicago

on May 21. Eight thousand people, spectators and delegates, crowded into Crosby's Opera House to cheer the Victor of Appomattox and to damn the Democrats.

Carl Schurz of Missouri was temporary chairman and was followed in the chair by Governor Hawley of Connecticut. Both men defended the Radical cause and pledged the party to a sound fiscal policy. There was officially no greenback sentiment in this convention. Governor Hawley put the party squarely, if rather melodramatically, behind gold payments: "Every bond, in letter and in spirit, must be as sacred as a soldier's grave."

The convention, on the second day, considered and quickly adopted the platform for the campaign. It endorsed the Radical Reconstruction program, guaranteed equal suffrage to all loyal men in the South (leaving the suffrage question in the North to the discretion of the individual states), denounced the greenback doctrine "as a national crime," and promised to reduce the national debt, lower taxes, and provide economy in government.

The eighth plank was, perhaps, the most remarkable statement ever made by a major party. Turning their attention to the man who was, despite their best efforts, still President of the United States, the Republicans declared: "We profoundly deplore the untimely and tragic death of Abraham Lincoln, and regret the accession of Andrew Johnson to the Presidency, who has acted treacherously to the people who elected him and the cause he was pledged to support; has usurped high legislative and judicial functions; has refused to execute the laws; has employed his executive powers to render insecure the property, peace, liberty and life of the citizens; has abused the pardoning power; has denounced the National Legislature as unconstitutional; has persistently and corruptly resisted, by every means in his power, every proper attempt at the reconstruction of the States lately in rebellion; has perverted the public patronage into an engine of wholesale corruption; and has been justly impeached for high crimes and misdemeanors, and promptly pronounced guilty thereof by the votes of thirty-five Senators."

General John A. Logan placed Grant's name in nomination. His brief speech should be an example to all politicians who may be called upon to perform similar duties: "In the name of the loyal citizens, soldiers and sailors of this great Republic of the United States of America; in the name of loyalty, of liberty, of humanity, of justice; in the name of the National Union Republican party; I nominate, as candidate for the Chief Magistracy of this nation, Ulysses S. Grant." The spectators rose to their feet and gave three rousing cheers for the nominee. Handkerchiefs waved in the air, and the band, somewhat prematurely, struck up "Hail to the Chief!" The convention then balloted.

With oratorical flourishes and amid much applause, each state in the roll call cast its vote for Grant. After Wisconsin's vote had been recorded, Governor Hawley declared, "Gentlemen of the Convention, you have six hundred and fifty votes. You have given six hundred and fifty votes for Ulysses S. Grant."

The formality of the presidential nomination out of the way, the convention turned to the vice-presidency. With the example of recent events before them—Johnson's sudden and unexpected rise to power—the Republicans took a greater, possibly even somewhat ghoulish interest in the office of vice-president than was usual in political conventions.

There was no lack of aspirants: Senator Henry Wilson of Massachusetts, Senator Benjamin Wade of Ohio, Speaker of the House Schuyler Colfax of Indiana, Governor Reuben E. Fenton of New York, Governor Andrew G. Curtin of Pennsylvania, and former Vice-President Hannibal Hamlin of Maine, as well as James Harlan of Iowa, John Creswell of Maryland, James Speed of Kentucky, Senator S. C. Pomeroy of Kansas, and Judge William D. Kelly of Pennsylvania were placed in nomination.

Ben Wade, who but for the vote of one Republican senator would have replaced Andrew Johnson in the White House, was the leading candidate, followed by Henry Wilson, one of the senior leaders in the Senate; "Smiler" Colfax, the amiable, light-weight Speaker; and "master spoilsman" Governor Fenton, who was favored by most of the professional bosses within the party.

On the first ballot, Ben Wade led with 147 votes. Fenton was second with 126, followed by Wilson with 119, Colfax 115, Curtin 51, Hamlin 28, Speed 22, Harlan 16, Creswell 14, Pomeroy 6, and Kelley 4.

By the third ballot, the contest had narrowed to Wade at 178 and Colfax at 165. If they deadlocked, there was a possibility that Fenton, with 139 votes, might slip through to victory.

The break came on the fifth ballot. Pennsylvania switched 13 Wade votes to Colfax. Sensing a dramatic turn in the proceedings, Tennessee abandoned Fenton and gave an additional 14 votes to the Speaker, who also picked up 4 new votes from Wisconsin. At the end of the roll call, Colfax led with 226 votes to 207 for Wade, 139 for Fenton, 56 for Wilson, and 20 for Hamlin.

Before the results were announced, Iowa led the rush to Colfax. Pennsylvania, Louisiana, Connecticut, and Massachusetts climbed aboard the bandwagon. The sixth ballot, taken as a formality, gave Colfax 541, Fenton 69, and Wade 38.

The nomination of Colfax came as a surprise to the nation and, perhaps, even to the convention. Wade, Fenton, and Wilson were all stronger candidates. But Smiler Colfax was well named. His bland, genial personality and his ability to win friends had carried the day. He was also helped by the strong backing of the Methodist Episcopal General Conference, which was meeting in Chicago. Colfax was a long-time temperance man, and the Methodists exerted great pressure in his behalf. The convention may also have realized that the teetotaling Speaker would add a much needed air of sobriety to a ticket headed by Ulysses S. Grant.

CHAPTER 2

"Hoist by their own petard"

THE FIRST LIBERAL REPUBLICAN NATIONAL CONVENTION
Cincinnati, May 1, 1872

The saturnalia that followed Grant's inauguration is too well known to bear repeating in detail. With a president who was honest but incompetent, reveling in the lavish gifts pressed upon him by admiring financial pirates, who could expect lesser men to avoid the paths to easy wealth? The railroad magnates, the silver kings, the merchant princes, and the new industrialists flocked to Washington or sent their well provisioned lieutenants, and few came away disappointed. The public trough was open to all who could buy or pressure their way up to it; from lowly congressmen to presidential brothers-in-law, the scramble was on.

The liberals and reformers, choking on the stench of corruption, were driven to despair. Hoping at first to work with and guide the politically inexperienced President, the liberals soon realized that their influence was useless. Inept in his dealings, incapable of and uninterested in understanding the complexities of political life, Grant alienated the liberals and presided with equanimity over the morass of his administration.

It was not long before the independents and liberals took an opposition role. In the Senate, Carl Schurz, elected from Missouri in 1869, was the leading Republican liberal. It was to him that the disillusioned and disaffected turned in the hope of organizing an effective opposition to Grant and the regular Republican machine.

The first successful challenge to Grant's party was in Missouri. A bitter contest developed in 1870 over a state test oath, which barred thousands of whites from participating in politics. The Republican State Convention had split over the issue, and the liberals, who favored abolishing the oath, formed their own party. Calling themselves the Liberal Republicans and led by Carl Schurz, they fielded their own ticket, headed by B. Gratz Brown, against the regular Republican candidates. Grant was furious at this disloyalty and used all available pressures to defeat the new party. The Liberals nevertheless swept the election; the test oath was abolished by a wide margin, and Gratz Brown was triumphantly elected governor. The new party immediately followed up its first victory by electing Frank Blair, who had left the Democrats for the Liberals, to the Senate, in place of a Radical Grant supporter.

The success of the Liberal Republican movement in Missouri encouraged those Republicans who opposed Grant, but an opposition organization had yet to be formed. It was clear to those who wished to replace Grant in 1872 that the courses open to them were three: They could remain in the party and hope to make their influence potent enough to effect the changes they advocated; they could abandon the party and join the Democrats; or they could organize a new party. As Grant's renomination seemed inevitable, the first course was impractical. Joining the Democrats was unthinkable. The Republicans had been too long in opposition to Democratic policies to embrace them now. The third possibility—a new party—appeared, after the Missouri success, the best solution.

It was therefore decided, in January, 1872, to launch the Liberal Republican movement on a national scale. The Missouri Liberal Republicans met in convention and adopted resolutions calling for universal amnesty, a more equitable adjustment of the tariff, reform of the civil service, and the checking of federal encroachments on the rights of the states. A call was issued to all Republicans desirous of securing these reforms to meet in national mass convention on May 1 in Cincinnati.

The response to this call was immediate. Republican reformers flocked to the banner in ever-increasing numbers. A striking feature of the new movement was the number of old Free-Soilers and original founders of the Republican Party who joined the ranks. The surviving members of Lincoln's cabinet—Salmon P. Chase, Gideon Welles, and Montgomery Blair—were early enrollees. Senators Trumbull, Ross, and Fowler, who had voted for acquittal in the impeachment trial, were numbered among the converts, along with Lincoln's managers, Justice David Davis and Leonard Swett; Orville Hickman Browning; Senator Tipton of Nebraska; Gustav Koerner; Charles Francis Adams and his sons, John Quincy and Henry; and General Nathaniel P. Banks. In Illinois, Governor Palmer refused renomination and almost certain re-election on the regular ticket to cast his lot with the Liberals. The old giant of the Senate, Charles Sumner, lent tacit support, and many distinguished journalists—among them Edwin L. Godkin of the *Nation*, Murat Halstead of the Cincinnati *Commercial*, "Marse Henry" Watterson of the Louisville *Courier-Journal*, Horace White of the Chicago *Tribune*, William Cullen Bryant of the New York *Post*, and Samuel Bowles of the Springfield (Mass.) *Republican*—joined the party.

Alongside the impressive ranks of reformers and Republican founders who, from the highest motives, moved into the new party, could be seen recruits of quite a different stripe. Disappointed office seekers, members of broken rings and losing factions, political adventurers of all sorts, looking for spoils. Senator Reuben E. Fenton, the loser in a factional fight with the dazzing Roscoe Conkling, moved boldly into the Liberal Republican camp. Senator Alcorn of Mississippi, Governor Warmoth and his predatory carpetbaggers in Louisiana, the anti-Cameron men in Pennsylvania—including the honest but highly practical Alexander K. McClure—all entered the Liberal ranks. Some were seeking spoils, some to do what mischief they could, and some to advance ambitions thwarted by the Grant administration.

Not surprisingly, one of the first names mentioned as a potential candidate for the Liberal Republican nomination was that quadrennial hopeful, Chief Justice Chase. An independent movement had been worked up for Chase in West Virginia—hardly a king-making state—and in April, 1872, a conference of Liberals and independent Democrats met in Parkersburg to adopt resolutions instructing delegates to the Cincinnati convention to work for Chase's nomination. It is difficult to know whether Chase could have been a serious candidate or whether the interest in his behalf was merely a reflex conditioned by many years of campaigning. It would, after all, hardly seem a presidential year without Chase coming forward for one nomination or another. In 1872, however, Chase was entering his last illness, and the state of his health precluded his making the race. Still, it is touching and rather fitting that, in this last campaign year of his life, the distinguished Ohioan still waited hopefully in the wings.

Charles Francis Adams seemed the ideal candidate. His integrity, liberal views, and wide experience eminently fitted him to lead the new movement. His service as Minister to England during the war had given him an opportunity to serve his country and party without becoming involved in partisan controversy. He was free of both Radical involvements and any suggestion of Copperheadism. Adams, more than any man of his time, stood above party, appealing as strongly to Democrats as to Liberal Republicans.

This appeal was important, because the Liberals hoped their candidate might also become the Democratic nominee. Such a coalition, they believed, would certainly win the election. Adams was the only candidate of Republican antecedents who would not put the Democrats on the defensive. The Democratic New York *World* favored his candidacy, and August Belmont assured Carl Schurz, who was the leader of the Adams forces, that the Democratic Party would willingly support him.

Shortly before the meeting of the Cincinnati convention and before leaving for England, where he was to take up duties as a member of the commission to settle the Alabama claims, Adams wrote David Wells that he did not desire the nomination and was perfectly indifferent to it. Were the nomination given without pledges of any kind, he would not refuse. "If the call upon me were an unequivocal one based upon confidence in my character earned in public life, and a belief that I would carry out in practice the principles I professed, then indeed would come a test of my courage in an emergency; but if I am to be negotiated for, and have assurances given that I am honest, you will be so kind as to draw me out of that crowd." The letter was not written for publication, but Samuel Bowles, believing it would help Adams's candidacy, published it in the Springfield *Republican.* The letter hurt rather than helped. There was dismay at the candidate's indifference to the nomination and ill feeling toward the phrase "that crowd."

Next in strength was David Davis, Associate Justice of the Supreme Court. A huge man, both in body and ambition—he was likened at times to Falstaff for his appearance, wit, and appetites—extremely able and wealthy, Davis was regarded as the candidate of politicians both Republican and Democratic. He was nominally a Republican, but ten years on the Supreme Court had weakened his party convictions. His decisions and dissents indicated a liberal leaning popular with Democrats, especially in the Middle West. A preliminary step for securing the nomination had been made in February, 1872, when Davis was nominated by the national convention of the Labor Reform Party, with Governor Parker of New Jersey, a pronounced Democrat, as his running mate. This convention denounced monopolies and advocated greenback legislation, the payment of the national debt in paper, a low tariff, and a general amnesty. Davis was hardly a typical Labor Reformer. It was understood that he was using this nomination as a stepping stone to success in Cincinnati.

Ironically, the office-seeking fraternity and practical politicians who were the basis of Davis's support formed a major obstacle to his candidacy. Many of his advocates had become active in the cause of reform only after the movement had made considerable headway, which left their sincerity open to question. Furthermore, Davis's and his followers' free dispensation of money appeared to onlookers as an attempt to buy the nomination.

Two minor candidates were Lyman Trumbull of Illinois and B. Gratz Brown. Senator Trumbull had the tacit support of Charles Sumner and the open support of William Cullen Bryant and the New York *Evening Post.* Governor Brown reasoned that the Liberal Republican Party would not have existed without his victory in Missouri. By priority right, if nothing else, he believed himself entitled to the nomination. That his co-founder, Carl Schurz, was not in sympathy with this attitude and believed that Brown had been sufficiently rewarded was already causing major difficulties in Cincinnati.

Finally, there was Horace Greeley. The eccentric editor, whose political ambitions, thus far unsatisfied, were never far below the surface, fancied himself suddenly as a presidential candidate. This unexpected attitude was greeted at first with amusement and later with irritation. Too late the amusement turned to consternation.

Although Greeley's first reactions to the Liberal movement were unfavorable, there were from the beginning certain areas of agreement. He had long approved a policy of magnanimity toward the southern whites and had even gone so far as to provide the bail bond for Jefferson Davis, an act of particular courage. He had never shown much interest in civil-service reform, however, and he was utterly opposed to tariff revision. A strong advocate of high protection, he considered Schurz and Brown to be little better than free-traders, which, in his opinion, made them enemies of the nation. If Horace Greeley were to enlist in the Liberal crusade, something would have to be done about the tariff reformers who marched under the Liberal banner.

As the Liberal movement grew and as friends hinted that Greeley not only belonged in the new party but at the head of its ticket, the attitude of the *Tribune* and its editor began to change. By the winter of 1871, Greeley was not only demanding universal amnesty and denouncing the corruption in Washington, he was also demanding civil-service reform with a fervency possible only to a recent convert to the faith. Greeley was even beginning to suggest, cautiously and timidly, to be sure, that perhaps, after all, the tariff was a local issue, to be decided on the local level.

In January, 1872, Greeley laid down his terms for joining the Liberal Republicans. In a favorable review of the history of the new movement, he declared that the Cincinnati convention would never nominate Grant. Rather than accept the President for another term, the Liberals would bolt the party. Would the *Tribune* also bolt? Probably not, was the reply, since free trade would be a plank in the Liberal platform. Greeley's price for entering the new party would be the abandonment of tariff revision as a principle.

He suggested that the tariff question be referred to the voters of each congressional district for a referendum. What such a proposal would accomplish, beside chaos, is open to question, but it provided a means by which the Liberals and Greeley could come to terms without embarrassment on either side. By the end of March, the Liberals were willing to accept Greeley's terms, and he accepted an invitation to participate in the Cincinnati convention.

When he abandoned his high-tariff stand for the local-option plan, Greeley became one of the stock candidates in editorial speculations. Including his name along with Adams, Davis, Trumbull, and Brown was more of a polite gesture toward his eminence on the national scene than a serious consideration of his candidacy. But while most of the leaders scoffed, Greeley was quietly building support for himself in the West and South.

That this most brilliant and partisan of editors, this man who had castigated the conservatives and the Democrats and exalted the Radicals should bolt the party he had helped to found and had blindly supported with an almost religious fervor seemed unreasonable enough; but that he should also become the leader of the bolters seemed utterly ridiculous. How could the Democrats, whom he had savagely attacked for so many years, be expected to accept such a candidate? Beside, his appearance and temperament conflicted with all previous ideals about the occupant of the White House. Greeley simply did not look like a president. This man, with his round, pink, cherubic face fringed with a straggling white beard, who dressed in a white linen duster, the pockets of which were crammed with notes, pencils, and papers, his head crowned with a large white hat, seemed an unlikely presidential image. Obviously, it was another of Horace's harebrained schemes, less amusing, perhaps, than his vegetarianism or his campaign against women's corsets. The leaders would let him play his game and indulge his vanity only so long as it did not interfere with the serious business of the convention.

There were some, however, who saw Greeley's candidacy as

something more than a joke. Many western delegates, who had long been influenced by *Tribune* policy, offered their support. To some politicians, Greeley appeared eminently suitable as a running mate for Davis. Greeley was inclined toward taking second place on such a ticket, although he ruled out the possibility of a deal. When Alexander K. McClure, who backed Davis, told him that he could not win the nomination, Greeley replied, "Well, if they won't take me head foremost, they might take me boots foremost."

The delegates who gathered in Cincinnati during the last week of April, 1872, represented perhaps the most diverse elements ever assembled for the purpose of nominating a presidential candidate. The malcontents, the lofty idealists, the close-mouthed manipulators, the impeccable, and the disreputable all flocked to Cincinnati. "Anything to beat Grant" was the battlecry. The civil-service reformer, Carl Schurz, was registered at the same hotel as the master spoilsman, Reuben Fenton. Free-trade doctrinaires like David Wells and Edward Atkinson stood beside such high protectionists as William Dorsheimer and Whitelaw Reid, while fiery-eyed old abolitionists like Josiah B. Grinnell came face to face with "a motley array of Southerners of every sort," not the least of whom was that prince of carpetbaggers, Governor Warmoth of Louisiana. Yet the delegates were, for the most part, dedicated, honest men. Newspapermen abounded. So many newspapers sent reporters that Henry Watterson recalled, "One might have mistaken it for an annual meeting of the Associated Press."

On the eve of the convention, the practical politicians had already decided on a Davis-Greeley ticket, while most of the reform group, with the approval of the conservative eastern Democrats, backed Adams, with a prominent middle-western Liberal like Trumbull or Governor Palmer as his running mate.

The Davis forces, led by Leonard Swett, Senator Fenton, and Alexander K. McClure, planned to take the convention by storm on the first day and push through a nomination before the Adams forces could rally. To bolster this plan, the Justice's managers provided, at an estimated cost in excess of $40,000, free transportation for everyone they could persuade to go to Cincinnati to support their candidate. Several hundred supporters from Davis's home state of Illinois made the excursion. Their function was to pack the galleries and work on the delegates to stampede the convention as soon as it began.

Along with Carl Schurz, four newspaper editors were Adams's chief managers, and they would have a decisive effect on the outcome of the convention. Murat Halstead, Samuel Bowles, Horace White, and Henry Watterson met with Schurz the night before the convention, in the sitting room between Watterson's and the Senator's bedrooms in the St. Nicholas Hotel, to draw up a plan to control the convention. Calling themselves the Quadrilateral, the four editors agreed to limit the contest to Adams and Trumbull, either of whom was, as they saw it, acceptable to the Liberal movement.

The Davis candidacy, promoted by politicians of questionable virtue and paid for by seemingly limitless funds, was to these editors a complete travesty of the reforms for which they were working. The Quadrilateral disposed of Davis by dispatching to their respective newspapers blistering editorials exposing the Justice as a politician out to buy and scheme his way to the nomination. In this curious convention, such news was enough to kill his chances. Fenton admitted that the opposition of the independent editors was fatal. He promptly returned to Washington, and the Davis boom collapsed even as his managers were enjoying a pre-victory dinner. "The earth seemed to have arisen and hit him amidships," Watterson related. "The incoming delegates were stopped and forewarned. Six months of adroit scheming was set at nought, and little more was heard of 'D. Davis.'"

The easy victory of the Quadrilateral over Davis brought over-confidence. These amateurs in politics, intoxicated by the heady atmosphere of power, believed that other candidates would topple as easily as Davis. Thinking the battle won even before the convention met, they began a series of miscalculations that eventually defeated their own plans as effectively as they had defeated Davis's.

As soon as the news of the editorial cabal was abroad, Henry Watterson was approached by Whitelaw Reid, Greeley's second-in-command at the *Tribune*. Reid—sent to Cincinnati to look after

Greeley's interests—wanted to know why, in a newspaper combine, the *Tribune* had been left out. Watterson admitted that it had been an oversight and instructed his colleagues to admit Reid to their councils. The others at first demurred, but Watterson won them over. "Now, gentlemen, in this movement we shall need the New York *Tribune*. If we admit Reid we clinch it. You will all agree that Greeley has no chance of a nomination, and so by taking him in we both eat our cake and have it." The chief Greeley manager was therefore admitted to the inner council of the Adams forces, privy to all their strategy.

The second serious mistake was to allow Carl Schurz to preside as permanent chairman of the convention. Schurz, as a member of the Missouri delegation, had been instructed to vote for Brown, but he preferred to take the chairmanship so that he would not have to vote. He would have been of much greater value to Adams working on the floor, even if it meant casting his vote for Brown, but he and the Quadrilateral were so confident that they did not think his presence on the floor would be necessary.

On May 1, the delegates gathered in the huge Exposition Hall —a frame structure with two wooden towers and the internal appearance of a "whitewashed depot." More than 7000 spectators jammed into the building, overflowing into the musicians' gallery and the press boxes. Beneath galleries lined with shields representing each state, the Liberal Republicans prepared to overthrow the Grant regime.

The convention adopted the rules of the House of Representatives, precluding the unit and two-thirds rules and, on the second day, installed Carl Schurz as Permanent Chairman.

During the evening of May 2, two new figures appeared in Cincinnati: Governor Brown and Frank Blair. The Missouri delegation had been subjected to extreme pressure by Schurz to abandon Brown and switch to Adams. When Governor Brown and his manager Blair were informed in St. Louis, they immediately boarded a train for Cincinnati, furiously determined either to win the nomination or to prevent Adams from doing so.

There was immediate consternation among the Adams forces at the unexpected arrival of the Missourians. Colonel Grosvenor, chairman of the Missouri delegation, was the first to react. He ran through the corridors of the Burnet House, pounding on doors and shouting, "Get up! Blair and Brown are here from St. Louis." Several Adams and Trumbull men gathered in the rotunda of the hotel, but even though they remained there in uneasy expectation until after two in the morning, they could obtain no information about the Missouri Governor's plans.

The platform was expected on the third day. The only controversy was over the tariff. The two extremes of opinion on the platform committee were represented by the free-traders and the Greeley supporters. The debate was long and bitter. At one point, the committee considered reporting to the convention that no agreement could be reached. This plan was rejected for fear it might initiate a bolt. A compromise was finally worked out in an all night session. Most of the delegates, more concerned with the southern problem and civil service than with tariff matters, agreed to accept Greeley's formula for leaving the question of tariff revision to local option. The meaningless plank simply established that the delegates had agreed to disagree.

The remainder of the platform presented no problems, embodying, as it did, the main planks of the Missouri platform. Many of the planks had been written by Charles Sumner—especially those on equality before the law and the acceptance of the war amendments—and sent to Cincinnati from Washington. Not yet publicly declared for the Liberal movement, Sumner was keeping his hand in, preparing for the moment when he would join the cause.

The convention proceeded to the balloting for the presidential nomination. Adams was still the strongest candidate, but there were hidden weaknesses in his position. No one was sure what Blair and Brown intended to do, although Colonel Grosvenor had been predicting that Brown would withdraw in favor of Greeley. The collapse of the Davis boom left many delegates in doubt about their future course. Davis's main strength lay in the Illinois delegation, which was divided between him and Trumbull, and there was much anti-Adams sentiment in the delegation. When Davis men predicted that Grant would carry Illinois by 50,000 votes over Adams, many western delegates questioned the wisdom of supporting Adams.

Adams led on the first ballot, however, He received 205 votes out of a total of 714, with 358 necessary to nominate. Greeley surprised everyone by placing second with 147 votes. Next were Trumbull with 110, Brown with 95, Davis with 92½, Andrew G. Curtin of Pennsylvania with 62, and Chase with 2½.

After the roll call of the states was completed but before the results could be announced, the plot Colonel Grosvenor had so gloomily predicted came to light. Governor Brown, although not a delegate, sent a note to Schurz asking to be allowed to address the convention. Visibly disconcerted, Schurz hesitated over whether or not to invoke the parliamentary rule against such a request. As the chairman hesitated, Brown appeared upon the platform and Schurz, facing his antagonist before the whole convention, nervously permitted him to speak. Brown, his red beard aflame in the sun streaming in from the upper windows, withdrew his name and urged his delegates to support Horace Greeley.

It was the hardest blow he could strike against his former friends. The Adams forces were dismayed. For some inexplicable reason, they were not prepared for this switch. Confusion, which Schurz was unable to control, broke out on the floor. For a few tense moments it appeared that a stampede to Greeley would occur on the second ballot. The Adams forces finally rallied, and order was restored. Schurz begged the Missouri delegation not to go to Greeley, and all but one-third agreed to vote for Trumbull for the time being. Pennsylvania had retired for consultation, and, upon returning to the hall, McClure withdrew Curtin's name. A majority of the delegation followed McClure into the Adams camp, but eighteen votes bolted to Greeley.

The rallying of Pennsylvania to Adams prevented a stampede on the second ballot. Adams gained 38 votes to stand at 243, but Greeley rose by 92 for a total of 239. Trumbull, benefiting from the reluctance of some delegates to back either of the front-runners, increased to 148, a gain of 38. Davis slipped to 81, Brown received 2 votes, and 1 vote went to Chase. Before the results were announced, California changed 6 votes from Davis to Greeley. The official results of the second ballot put Greeley ahead of Adams by 2 votes.

It looked, on the third ballot, as if the strategy to stampede the convention to Greeley had failed. The editor gained only 13 votes for a total of 258, while Adams again took the lead with 264, the 21 new votes coming from Davis men. Trumbull also picked up some Davis votes for a total of 156. Davis received 44, Brown 2.

The fourth ballot indicated a deadlock. Greeley lost 7 votes, while Adams gained 15. Trumbull lost 15, and Davis picked up 7. Although Adams had gained, he was still 79 votes short of nomination, and Greeley, despite a minor setback, was holding firm. If the Trumbull votes held, it was quite possible that neither Adams nor Greeley could be nominated, which, of course, was exactly what the Trumbull forces hoped for. Pressure was exerted on the 21 Davis men from Illinois to give Trumbull a united delegation, in the hope of starting a swing away from the front-runners, and Governor Palmer telegraphed to Cincinnati calling for a swing to Trumbull.

The Trumbull forces began to crumble on the fifth ballot. Adams rose to 309, while Greeley remained relatively stationary at 258. Davis dropped to 30, Brown kept his 2 votes, and Chief Justice Chase suddenly reappeared with 24 votes that had previously gone to Trumbull. The Trumbull total fell to 91.

The sixth ballot was taken amid great confusion. The first break came when Georgia gave Greeley an additional 4 votes. Then 7 Trumbull votes from Indiana went to the New Yorker, along with 1 Adams vote. The shift to Greeley continued and, although several votes were switched to Adams, it was too late to prevent a sudden rush to the editor. At the end of the roll call, Adams had risen to 324, but Greeley had picked up 74 votes to take the lead with 332. Chase rose to 32, and the other candidates stood: Trumbull 19, Davis 6, and Governor Palmer 1.

Before the results were announced, the politicians working for Greeley realized that the time had come to push ahead to victory. Minnesota changed 9 votes from Trumbull to set off a prearranged demonstration. "The Hall was filled with a mechanical, preordained, stentorious bellowing. Hoary-haired, hard-eyed politicians, who had not in twenty years felt a noble impulse, mounted their chairs and with faces suffused with seraphic fervor, blistered their throats hurraying for the great and good Horace Greeley. The noise bred a panic. A furor, artificial at first, became real and ended in stampede." From all parts of the hall, changes for Greeley were shouted so rapidly that the clerks were hard pressed to record them. Schurz, stunned by the sudden madness of the convention, ruled that the roll call was defective and a new ballot must be taken. He was shouted down. Schurz so lost control that he had to be reminded that he had forgotten to announce the results of the ballot. Reluctantly he announced 482 votes for Greeley, 187 for Adams. A move to make the nomination unanimous was shouted down, but the Adams men could not alter the fact that Horace Greeley—white hat, linen duster, and all—was the candidate.

After the emotional outpouring of the stampede, a sudden silence settled over the hall. The Adams men sat stunned. Delegates who had been swept off their feet turned to each other in bewilderment. It was as if, given a moment of reflection, they could hardly believe what they had done. Only in the New York delegation and among the Brown men, who were tasting the sweet fruits of revenge, was there rejoicing.

For the vice-presidential nomination, Governor Brown, J. D. Cox, and Senator Trumbull were nominated. The results of the first ballot were: Brown 237, Trumbull 158, George W. Julian 134½, Governor Walker of Virginia 84½, Cassius M. Clay 34, Cox 25, J. M. Scovel 12, Senator Tipton 8. It was moved that Governor Brown be nominated by acclamation, but the Adams forces roared their disapproval.

B. Gratz Brown, in payment for his dramatic withdrawal in Greeley's favor, received the nomination on the second ballot. Trumbull had been withdrawn at his own insistence, and there was no one for the anti-Brown forces to rally to. The final ballot stood: Brown 435, Julian 175, Walker 75, Palmer 8, Tipton 3.

The Quadrilateral, the eager amateurs in politics, had been given a lesson in professional politics. Now they had to pay the price of overconfidence. In the early days of the convention, riding high on a wave of optimism, the Quadrilateral had agreed magnanimously to attend a dinner to be given by Whitelaw Reid after the nominations. What they had believed would be an Adams victory dinner turned into an Adams wake. "Frostier conviviality I have never sat down to than Reid's dinner," wrote Henry Watterson. "Horace White looked more than ever like an iceberg; Sam Bowles was diplomatic, but ineffusive; Schurz was as a death's head at the board; Halstead and I, through sheer bravado, tried to enliven the feast. But they would have none of us, nor it, and we separated early and sadly, reformers hoist by their own petard." Whitelaw Reid, at least, vastly enjoyed the dinner.

"We deny the paternity"

THE FIFTH REPUBLICAN NATIONAL CONVENTION
Philadelphia, June 5, 1872

The Republicans gathered in Philadelphia on June 5 for the formality of nominating Grant for a second term. There was little fervor among the delegates; the decisions had already been made. Their function was to present a united front to the nation. The spirit of the convention was summed up by one delegate who was told that another was not for Grant. "What's he doing here then?" came the astonished reply. The office-holders stayed behind the scenes, and Samuel Bowles, recovered from the shocks of Cincinnati, reported on the delegates. They were "business men, materialists, men of fact and reality—not reformers, not leaders in principles; and those satisfied with the present, who postpone revolution and improvement for another four years."

The highlight of the first session was Oliver Morton's speech. The ruthless, crippled partisan of the Senate wielded his hatchet on the Liberals. "Among several nations of antiquity the idea prevailed that the father had a right to kill off his own offspring, and some men who think they were the fathers of the Republican party have recently set up the claim that on that account they have the right to kill it. As a general thing we deny the paternity."

On the second day, as planned, Grant was renominated unanimously. The energies that could not be expended on a contest were released in a song fest after the nomination. The delegates, given no choice of candidates, were allowed to choose their own songs. After the inevitable campaign song, John Brown's body mouldered once again, and "There was scarcely a dry eye in the assemblage; not a heart that was not thrilled with the sublimity of the moment." The delegates were marching through Georgia, when someone remembered that they had not yet nominated a vice-president. Hearts renewed and eyes dried, the delegates settled to the one contest of the convention.

"Smiler" Colfax would have been the logical choice of the convention, but he had fallen from favor. Before the bolt of the Liberal Republicans, there had been some talk of Colfax as presidential timber. The genial Vice-President was only too happy to listen to the voice of ambition and, in an opening gambit to what he hoped would be a "draft Colfax" movement, announced that he would retire from public life upon the expiration of his term. Grant, disliking office-hungry pretenders in his official family, took him at his word and let it be known that Colfax would, indeed, be retired in 1872.

With Grant's benediction withdrawn from Colfax, Henry Wilson, junior senator from Massachusetts, became the leading contender—primarily because his nomination would be an embarrassment to his colleague Sumner and would reduce the possibility of Sumner's taking Massachusetts into the Greeley camp.

Many delegates, perhaps eager to make a show of independence, supported Colfax's renomination. On the first ballot, Wilson led with 364½—12½ short of nomination—and Colfax received 321½. Sixty-six votes went to five minor candidates. Virginia immediately dropped her favorite son to cast 20 votes for Wilson, and West Virginia and Georgia also switched. The nomination of Wilson was made unanimous without a formal announcement of the final results of the ballots.

*   *   *

All that remained for the Democrats, with Grant and Greeley already in the field, was to acquiesce in the Liberal nomination. It was a bitter potion for the Democrats, who could not forget

Greeley's years of abuse and scorn. Some party leaders, like Senator Bayard of Delaware, could not face the prospect. But to most Democrats, the facts of political life could not be ignored. They knew they could not win without coalition, and coalition meant Greeley. With the choice between possible victory with Greeley and certain defeat without him, the Democrats met in convention in Baltimore on July 9 and accepted the Greeley-Brown ticket and the Cincinnati platform. The Democrats were now the tail of the Liberal Republican dog, and the campaign that was to destroy the Liberal Party could begin.

CHAPTER 3

"That kind of neutral man"

THE SIXTH REPUBLICAN NATIONAL CONVENTION
Cincinnati, June 14, 1876

The presidential contest of 1872 brought re-election to Grant, death to Greeley, and scandal to the nation. The first Grant administration had been a saturnalia; the second brought exposure and ruin. The Crédit Mobilier scandal involved Vice-Presidents Colfax and Wilson and many other Republican leaders; the exposure of the wholesale lootings of the Whiskey Ring dragged the White House through the mud, in the person of the President's private secretary; and the Secretary of War was impeached for corruption. Finally, the Panic of 1873 brought financial ruin and widespread unemployment.

In the midterm election of 1874, the nation reacted to depression and scandal by giving the Democrats control of the House of Representatives for the first time since before the Civil War and by sweeping Republicans out of office in New York, Pennsylvania, and Massachusetts. With the approach of the presidential election of 1876, it seemed likely that a disgusted electorate would institute a thorough housecleaning in Washington.

Where was the man who could see the Republican Party through its travail and lead it to victory? The party's prospects were grim, but there was no shortage of candidates for its nomination. Chief among the contenders were former Speaker of the

House James G. Blaine of Maine; Secretary of the Treasury Benjamin Bristow, who had exposed the Whiskey Ring scandal; the old Radical leader of the Senate, Oliver P. Morton; and the boss of New York, Senator Roscoe Conkling. Not in the forefront of the race but still to be considered were Governors Rutherford B. Hayes of Ohio and John Hartranft of Pennsylvania and Postmaster General Marshall Jewell of Connecticut. Also, Grant himself was making sounds that indicated a third term would not be entirely repugnant to him.

The strongest candidate was the former Speaker. The Man from Maine was at forty-six the most popular Republican in the country. Blaine's admirers—and they were legion—formed not so much a political faction as a cult, and he had, in recent years, risen to such heights of esteem as to overshadow the leading senatorial figures, Morton and Conkling. A large, florid man of commanding presence, Blaine exerted a magnetic hold over all who met him, and even his enemies conceded his personal charm. His great love of theater and opera made him an astute judge of acting, and he put his understanding to shrewd use as the greatest actor on the political scene.

In Congress, Blaine followed a more liberal course than that set by the Radicals but managed to combine a moderate point of view with complete party loyalty. He often opposed Grant, however, and came to lead a faction known as the Half-Breeds in opposition to the Stalwarts, led by Conkling, who were thorough Grant men.

The Blaine-Conkling rivalry stemmed from more than opposing political attitudes. During a bitter debate in the House in 1866, Blaine had referred to Conkling's "overpowering turkey-gobbler strut." The House, whose members had often suffered the lash of the arrogant New Yorker's sarcasm, was delighted with the epithet, and the picture of "Turkey-Gobbler" Conkling caused amusement throughout the country. Conkling, inordinately vain, never forgave Blaine, and their enmity grew more bitter as the years passed.

One of Blaine's liabilities was that he had not had a military record in the war and had not been a vigorous Radical after it was over. The bloody shirt was still a potent weapon in 1876, and both Conkling and Morton were masters at waving it. Blaine corrected this weakness in January, 1876, by rising in the House to launch a vitriolic attack on the Confederates. It was a dishonest speech and a base appeal to cheap emotions, but it was enormously effective. In one stroke, Blaine had stolen Morton's thunder, and the enthusiastic reception of the speech made his nomination seemingly inevitable. The speech shattered his name for magnanimous statesmanship, but it made Blaine a partisan of the first order and, as he well knew, partisanship, not magnanimity, is the high road to the White House.

Blaine's enemy, Roscoe Conkling, was more of a nuisance candidate than an actual one. He was more concerned with preventing the nomination from going to Blaine than with receiving it himself. It was his strategy to keep the rich prize of New York away from any candidate he could not control and to have as many favorite sons as possible on the first ballot. He believed that if Blaine could be kept from a first ballot nomination, he could be prevented from ever achieving the prize. As for Conkling's own chances, he would control the largest delegation in the convention, and he had the tacit support of Grant. As it turned out, the mounting disgust of the country turned the label of "administration candidate" into a decided liability.

Another candidate who met with Grant's favor was Oliver P. Morton. His violent radicalism and implacable hatred of the Old South gave him southern carpetbag and scalawag support. Apart from the South, his only source of delegate support was his home state of Indiana. Morton's greatest handicap was his health. Although he was only fifty-two, an increasing paralysis made the use of crutches necessary at all times. It was feared he would not be able to survive the strain of the presidency. But all the candidates realized that the enmity of this narrow, vengeful man would be a formidable obstacle in the convention, and no one dared count him out of the race so long as he lived.

The only western candidate, apart from Morton, was Rutherford B. Hayes, Governor of Ohio. Hayes lacked the intellectual brilliance of Morton, the forensic ability of Blaine, or the flamboyant personality of Conkling, but he was an astute politician and an honest, able administrator. He had become a national figure by turning back a Democratic tide and winning the governorship in

1875. He had the advantage of being unconnected with the national administration, and he had no political enemies. He had no outstanding virtues and no outstanding faults—and was therefore recognized as an ideal compromise candidate should one be needed.

Senator John Sherman of Ohio; his brother, the hero of Atlanta; and General Phil Sheridan launched the Hayes drive in January, 1876. General Sherman confidently predicted that the winning ticket would include Hayes and William Wheeler, a machine politician from New York. Hayes's only reaction was to write his wife, asking, "Who is Wheeler?"

Hayes realized that he was, at best, a dark horse. His strategy was to wait patiently, offend no one, and watch for the main chance. He was pleasant and noncommittal to the constant stream of visitors who called to discuss the nomination. "I have said the whole talk about me is on the score of availability," he wrote in February. "Let availability do the work then."

Of the leading candidates, Blaine had the support of the rank and file Republicans. Conkling and Morton were the administration candidates, and Morton was, in addition, the candidate of the southerners. Hayes was everybody's favorite second choice. There was one major group of Republicans—the Liberals—who could not accept any of these candidates.

Those Liberals who had returned to the party after the debacle of 1872 resolved this time to present a candidate within the regular party organization. As always, Carl Schurz, still the Liberal leader, was inclined to press for the nomination of Charles Francis Adams, but most Liberals were convinced that Adams could win neither the nomination nor the election and decided to back the Secretary of the Treasury, Benjamin H. Bristow.

Bristow, a native of Kentucky, had been an ardent Unionist and had served gallantly in the Union army. He had been, after the war, solicitor general of the United States and had taken over the Treasury Department in 1874. His exposure of the Whiskey Ring commended him to the Liberals. Here was a man who dared to brave the hostility of Grant and expose malefactors, regardless of party or high connections.

There was, for a time, a possibility that Grant would seek a third term. Grant enjoyed being president. He had, in his years in the White House, acquired a taste for easy, gracious living that he feared he could not afford in private life. In 1875, delicate hints went out that the President just might be persuaded to run again. The response was not quite what Grant expected. In December, 1875, the House, by a vote of 233 to 18, passed a resolution declaring that any attempt to depart from the precedent established by Washington and followed by other presidents "would be unwise, unpatriotic, and fraught with peril to our free institutions." Grant got the point and dropped all thought of being a candidate.

During the spring, the contest for the nomination shaped up with Blaine against the field. State after state fell into line behind the Man from Maine. So bright were his prospects that one day, on being informed that Washington Territory had pledged its delegates in his favor, he could laugh genially, "Well Maine is for me and Washington Territory is for me; the little gap between it is for my friends to fill up!" Blaine would not feel like laughing again for some time to come.

Throughout the scandals of the Grant administration, Blaine had remained uninvolved, and his reputation for honesty had never been questioned. While others' careers crashed in ruins, Blaine stood out as a man of unimpeachable integrity—or so it seemed. In 1875, vague and disquieting murmurs began circulating through Washington and the country at large that perhaps Blaine's record was not quite so clean as had been supposed. In February, 1876, the rumors became more specific. Blaine, it was alleged, had deposited bonds of the Little Rock and Fort Smith Railroad as collateral for a $64,000 loan from the Union Pacific Railroad. The bonds had been presented to Blaine in recognition of certain services he had performed as speaker, and the loan had never been repaid. The complete story of Blaine's transactions with the railroads has never been unraveled, but Blaine had sold, in the role of broker, $125,000 worth of Little Rock and Fort Smith bonds and had received in return $157,500 in bonds from the railroad. When the bonds turned out to be worthless, the Union Pacific Railroad took them off his hands at a handsome profit.

In April, Blaine denied that his dealings with the railroads were anything more than ordinary business transactions, but the Democratic House decided to investigate. On May 31, James

Mulligan of Boston, an employee of the broker through whom Blaine had sold the bonds, testified that Blaine had sold worthless stock to the Union Pacific and that he, Mulligan, had letters written by Blaine that would throw light upon the entire transaction. This statement had a remarkable effect on Blaine, who whispered to the Republican member of the committee to ask for an immediate adjournment.

After the committee adjourned, Blaine went to Mulligan's hotel and asked him to give him the letters. Mulligan refused. Blaine then asked permission to read them, which was granted. He read them over twice and handed them back to Mulligan, who went to his room. Blaine followed, asking to read the letters again. Blaine, once he had the letters in his hand, claimed that, since he had written them, they were his property and refused to give them up. He left the hotel taking the letters with him, and they were never again out of his possession.

This turn of events created a sensation in Washington. What was in the letters? When the committee demanded that Blaine turn the letters over to it, he refused, saying that they were his private property and that the committee had no right to see them. Public opinion turned sharply against Blaine and jeopardized, not only his campaign for the nomination, but his entire career. A master stroke was needed, and Blaine was not long in supplying it.

Blaine announced that he would speak in the House on June 5. The galleries were packed with an expectant audience, which overflowed onto the floor of the House itself. Blaine began by asserting that the investigation was instigated by southern hostility to his "bloody shirt" speech in January and that two former rebels were serving on the subcommittee chosen to hear the evidence. Having established to his own satisfaction that the whole matter was a case of partisan rivalry, he proceeded to defend his right to refuse the letters to the committee. Then he declared that he was not afraid to show the letters. The actor had prepared carefully for this moment. His eyes flashing, his voice vibrant with outraged justice, he suddenly ceased to speak. With all eyes fixed upon him, he made the most of the tense silence. Drawing forth a small package from his pocket, he held it aloft as high as his arm could reach. Then, with a long sweep of his arm, he slammed the

package upon his desk and shouted, "There they are!" The effect
on his audience was electrifying. Adlai E. Stevenson, Congressman
from Illinois, who sat near Blaine, later described the scene as the
most superb piece of acting the House had ever witnessed.

Blaine waited until the pandemonium of applause died down
and said, "With some sense of humiliation, and with a mortification
I do not pretend to conceal, with a sense of outrage which I think
any man in my position would feel, I invite the confidence of
44,000,000 of my countrymen while I read those letters from this
desk." Blaine read the letters, keeping up a running commentary
and defense as he read. But he read them out of chronological
order, omitted passages from some, and omitted several letters
altogether.

As if there had not already been enough dramatics that afternoon, Blaine had one more theatrical stroke prepared. Josiah Caldwell, a director of the Union Pacific, had been requested to cable
from London to Proctor Knott, chairman of the Judiciary Committee, corroborating testimony that Blaine was blameless. Knott
had received the cablegram, but, because he had no way of
ascertaining if it had actually come from Caldwell and because it
added nothing new to the case, he had refrained from presenting
it to the committee. Blaine knew that. After reading the letters,
Blaine asked Knott if he had received a cable from Caldwell.
Knott admitted that he had. Making the most of his histrionic
advantage, Blaine drew himself up to the fullest heights of righteous
wrath and thundered, "I heard that you got a dispatch last Thursday morning at eight o'clock from Josiah Caldwell completely
and absolutely exonerating me from this charge and you have suppressed it." It brought down the house. James Garfield stated, "I
never saw such a scene in the House." Nor had anyone else. "It
was one of the most extraordinary exhibitions of histrionic skill,
one of the most consummate pieces of acting that ever occurred
upon any stage on earth," said the hapless Proctor Knott.

To the mass of Republicans reading the glowing reviews of
Blaine's performance, it was clear that he had won a complete
triumph. To more thoughtful men, there were still some unanswered
questions. He had not read all the letters, and he had omitted
much of those he had read. What was in the other letters? No one

ever knew, because no one ever saw them after that dramatic day in the House.

Blaine had weathered one storm. Another quickly followed. Sunday, June 11, four days before the convention was to meet, was a hot, sultry day in Washington. Relieved of the strain of the recent investigation, Blaine came to the breakfast table in good spirits, carrying two of his children perched on his shoulders. When it was time for church, he decided to walk the mile distance rather than use the carriage. As he was mounting the broad stone steps of the church, he suddenly raised his arm, crying, "My head, my head!" and fell senseless into his wife's arms. Carried home unconscious, he lay in a coma for two days.

Friends flocked to the Blaine house to ascertain the extent of his illness. Word of Blaine's collapse reached Bristow while he was at work in his office, and, although their friendship had been severely strained in recent months, he hurried to the Blaine house. When Bristow arrived, Mrs. Blaine, a woman of spirit and strong opinions who believed that Bristow had been responsible for many of the recent attacks upon her husband, had the door shut in his face. The affronted Bristow believed that Blaine had deliberately insulted him. When word of the incident reached Cincinnati, Bristow's managers decided that, under no circumstances, would they help Blaine.

On Tuesday, the day before the opening of the convention, Blaine's mind cleared. He telegraphed his managers in Cincinnati: "I am entirely convalescent, suffering only from physical weakness. Impress upon my friends the great gratitude I feel for the unparalleled steadfastness with which they had adhered to me in my hour of trial." Reports had circulated that Blaine was dead or dying; his friends were overjoyed to hear he was making a rapid recovery. The Man from Maine had received yet another reprieve from adversity, and, as the delegates gathered to open the convention, he was still the man to beat.

During Blaine's dramatic spring of 1876, Hayes had continued to make himself available. He acquired important support from the Grand Army of the Republic and became, in effect, the unofficial soldiers' candidate. Other support came, perhaps surprisingly, from literary figures in the East. William Dean Howells, Mark

Twain, Bret Harte, and Joaquin Miller lent their names and talented pens to the Hayes campaign.

In his self-sought role as second choice, Hayes made a shrewd move to gain the favor of the Bristow men. In March, he suggested to a friend, "Bristow is a good man and growing in public favor. Why not take him?" So flat a declaration might seem a disavowal of his own candidacy, but Hayes knew that the administration would never allow Bristow to be nominated. He thus put himself in an excellent position to inherit Bristow's strength.

Hayes also hoped to pick up New York and Pennsylvania. Conkling was well disposed, and Pennsylvania was expected to follow his lead. Charles A. Dana declared in the New York *Sun* that Hayes would be the candidate. "Each of the more celebrated aspirants, and their friends with them, would rather have him than either of their immediate rivals. He will be nominated, if such be his fate, as Lincoln was nominated in 1860, or Pierce in 1852, or Polk in 1844. He is that kind of neutral man who is always taken when the powerful chiefs can only succeed in foiling each other."

Interest in the sixth Republican National Convention ran high because, for the first time since 1860, it promised to be an open convention. Lincoln and Grant had dominated the last three conventions, but now the country even forgot for the moment the excitements of the great Centennial Exposition in Philadelphia to concentrate on the struggle in Cincinnati.

Every hotel and rooming house was jammed to capacity, and bands and cheering throngs roamed the streets all day and long into the hot night. At least one delegate was not satisfied with the prospect of overcrowded hotels and noisy throngs. Senator John P. Jones of Nevada solved the housing problem by renting the home of a widow. Paying $2,000 for the brief use of the house, Jones had all the owner's possessions removed to storage and furnished the house completely down to the linen, silver, and dishes to suit his taste and sense of comfort. After the convention, the generous Senator made the good widow a gift of all the furnishings.

Other delegates, less fortunate, stayed at the local hotels. The New York delegation hired the entire Grand Hotel for its headquarters. Arriving with a large orchestra, the New Yorkers paraded the streets wearing bright blue badges and tall silk hats. Also in great number were the Indianians, who flocked to Cincinnati, in trains and steamboats chartered for the purpose, "as thick as mosquitos in blackberry time" and buzzed fervently for Morton.

The hall into which the delegates and spectators crowded on Wednesday morning, June 14, had little to recommend it but its size. According to the New York *Tribune,* the convention hall covered "over four acres, its architecture that of an ambitious and disappointed railroad depot, its decorations those of a country barbecue on a four-acre scale, its rafters innocent of any tint except that of age, and its roof an unsightly mass of beams and rafters."

While Theodore M. Pomeroy of New York, the temporary chairman, and Edward McPherson of Pennsylvania, a Blaine man and permanent chairman, presided over the opening business of the convention, the backstage politicking entered its crucial phase. Hayes's manager was General Edward F. Noyes, the shrewdest of the Ohio politicians. Seeming to be everywhere at once, Noyes maintained contact with all the managers and the most influential delegates. To each group he urged the nomination of Hayes if its own man could not win. So persuasive were his arguments that the Blaine men began to look on the Ohio governor as their most dangerous rival. Noyes was especially successful in wooing the Bristow forces. Stanley Matthews, who was, along with John Harlan, the leading Bristow manager, already inclined toward Hayes. Related to Hayes by marriage and believing that Hayes personally favored Bristow's candidacy, Matthews was more than willing to use his influence in swinging the crusading Secretary's votes to Hayes as a second choice.

The stop-Blaine movement continued to grow. Led by Chester A. Arthur, representing Conkling, and by Don Cameron, representing as always the Camerons, the opposition worked among the uncommitted western and southern delegates. Cameron also put down a threatened revolt in his Pennsylvania delegation. A sizable minority of the delegates wanted to abandon favorite-son Hartranft for Blaine. Cameron cannily proposed that the delegation continue to support Hartranft so long as his vote remained steady or increased. As soon as his vote began to fall, the delegation should vote as a unit for whichever candidate the majority preferred. The Blaine men jumped at the chance. Convinced that Hartranft had no support outside his own state, they were delighted at the prospect of presenting a solid Pennsylvania vote to Blaine. Cameron, having secured the pledge for Hartranft, called in Colonel Holloway, Morton's manager. He explained the situation, and Holloway agreed to provide a few Morton votes on each ballot to keep Hartranft in the field. The Blaine men realized they had been trapped but were powerless to do anything about it.

The Blaine managers hoped to spike the guns of the opposition by stealing the compromise candidate away from them. Convinced that Conkling, Bristow, and Morton could not be nominated, Blaine realized that Hayes would inherit their strength. If, however, Blaine could tempt Hayes by an offer of the vice-presidency, the great coalition would never have a chance. It was, accordingly, suggested to Noyes that Hayes would be welcomed as Blaine's running mate.

Hayes was not taken in. He could read the signs as well as Blaine. The Blaine managers were informed that under no circumstances would Hayes run with Blaine.

A test of strength between the Blaine and anti-Blaine forces developed on the second day. The Alabama delegation was contested. One set of delegates favored Morton, while the other was divided between Blaine and Bristow. By a vote of 375 to 354, the Blaine-Bristow delegation was seated, and Morton suffered the loss of 20 votes.

The next order of business was the platform. Of particular interest were planks favoring the exclusion of Orientals, opposition to public funds for church schools, and abolition of polygamy. In the light of recent events, one plank was most amusing. With a perfectly straight face, the framers of the platform declared: "We rejoice in the quickening conscience of the people concerning political affairs, and will hold all public officers to a rigid responsibility, and engage that the prosecution and punishment of all who betray official trusts shall be swift, thorough, and unsparing."

The platform, after reminding the country once again who had won the Civil War, was not above a few judicious threats. "We sincerely deprecate all sectional feeling and tendencies. We therefore note with deep solicitude that the Democratic party counts, as its chief hope of success, upon the electoral vote of a united South, secured through the efforts of those who were recently arrayed against the nation; and we invoke the earnest attention of the country to the grave truth that a success thus achieved would reopen sectional strife and imperil national honor and human rights." At no other time in American history had an entire party threatened civil war in the event of its defeat at the polls.

The first candidate placed in nomination was Marshall Jewell of Connecticut. He was followed by Oliver P. Morton, whose followers were disappointed by the commonplace speech of Richard W. Thompson and an unfortunate and inappropriate allusion to Morton's physical disabilities. In nominating Bristow, John Harlan of Kentucky, said, "His mode has been to execute the law; and if the Republican party contained offenders who betrayed their trust, or who were thieves, he let them be punished as well as anybody else." Unfortunately for Bristow, that was precisely the point. The party leaders were hardly eager to nominate a man who might be prosecuting them next.

The next nomination was the most memorable event of the entire convention. Rising to nominate James G. Blaine was Robert G. Ingersoll of Illinois. The climax of his speech roused the audience to the wildest excitement and provided a sobriquet for Blaine that he would carry for the rest of his life. "Like an armed warrior, like a plumed knight, James G. Blaine marched down the halls of the American congress and threw his shining lance full and fair against the brazen forehead of every traitor to his country and every maligner of his fair reputation." It was a classic of political oratory that a generation of schoolboys would memorize and declaim, and it is still remembered as the most stirring speech ever heard in a Republican convention.

After the brilliance of Ingersoll's speech, there seemed little hope that Blaine could be defeated. Even his enemies were swept away in the enthusiasm. But the time for balloting had not yet come. As Conkling and then Hayes were placed in nomination, the excitement gradually abated. By the time Hartranft had been presented, it was evening, and the anti-Blaine managers had their forces under control.

Confident that their "plumed knight" would be swept to victory on the wings of Ingersoll's oratory, the Blaine managers wished to proceed immediately to the first ballot. But it was discovered that the gas lights were not in working order, and darkness was approaching. There was no alternative but to put the balloting off until morning. It has been frequently asserted that the gas had been deliberately cut off. Various Hayes supporters took credit for this disruption. Whether it was deliberate or accidental, there was no light, and the plumed knight's hopes were gone.

It is doubtful if any man in Cincinnati with an interest in the outcome slept that frantic, hectic night. A decisive meeting took place between the managers of Bristow, Morton, and Hayes. Morton was clearly out of the running, and, among the Bristow men, Stanley Matthews was inclined to Hayes. If the Liberals could be brought over to Hayes, he would have the nomination. Edward Noyes and Stanley Matthews argued, cajoled, and, in all probability, lied manfully through the night to bring the Bristow forces into line. Finally, John Harlan, chairman of the Bristow Kentucky delegation, was offered a place on the Supreme Court if he would take his state into the Hayes column. The deal was made. Well after midnight, the managers agreed to give each of their candidates a chance. They knew they had enough votes to keep Blaine from nomination for a few ballots, and they decided that, if, after a few trials of strength, neither Morton nor Bristow could win, their votes would go to the Ohio Governor. Pennsylvania and New York were left out of this deal; it was assumed they would fall into line once the switch was made.

On Friday, June 16, the delegates met to settle the nomination. On the first roll call, Blaine led with 285 votes, with 378 necessary for victory. Morton was second with 124, Bristow third with 113. The others were Conkling 99, Hayes 61, Hartranft 58, Jewell 11, with 3 votes for William Wheeler of New York.

Before the results of the second ballot could be announced, a Pennsylvania delegate challenged the vote of that state. It had been cast unanimously for Hartranft, but the delegate wished to contest the use of the unit rule and be recorded for Blaine. In spite of the previous agreement with Cameron, three other delegates joined in the request. The chairman ruled that delegates were free to vote as they wished, and, after heated debate, the ruling was sustained by the convention. It was an historic decision, for the unit rule was never again used in a Republican convention.

On the second ballot, Blaine gained 11 votes for a total of 296, Morton dropped to 120, Bristow gained 1 vote for a total of 114, Conkling lost 6, Hayes rose to 64, Hartranft, as arranged, gained 5 Morton votes for a total of 63, while Wheeler still had 3 and Elihu Washburne received 1. Jewell dropped out, with most of his vote going to Bristow.

Blaine lost ground on the third ballot, to stand at 293. Bristow took over second place with 121 votes, and Morton followed with 113. Conkling had 90, Hartranft 68, Hayes, 67, Wheeler 2, Washburne 1. The fourth ballot did nothing to change the essential stalemate.

The first break in the deadlock came on the fifth ballot. The Michigan delegation had come to the convention badly divided. Of its three leaders, Senator Chandler supported Blaine, Governor Bagley stood behind Hayes, and William A. Howard, chairman of the delegation, preferred Morton. As a result of this division, the delegation had, by the fourth ballot, voted 11 for Bristow, 6 for Blaine, and 5 for Hayes. Hayes was the preferred second choice of the entire delegation. Upon hearing that Connecticut planned to lead a switch to Hayes on the sixth ballot, Michigan decided to switch a ballot earlier.

When the clerk called Michigan, William Howard rose, his voice tremulous with emotion, to announce: "There is a man in this section of the country who has beaten in succession three Democratic candidates for President in his own state, and we want to give him a chance to beat another Democratic candidate for the Presidency in the broader field of the United States. Michigan therefore casts her twenty-two votes for Rutherford B. Hayes of Ohio."

As the first anti-Blaine blow, the Michigan switch stirred a tremendous reaction. The Blaine men sat grimly silent, while the other delegates were on their feet cheering wildly. After three long salvos of applause and cheers, order was restored, and the vote continued. Beside Michigan's 22 votes, Hayes picked up an additional 14, to stand third with 104. Blaine lost 6 votes for a total of

286, and Bristow slipped to 114. Following were Morton 95, Conkling 82, Hartranft 69, Washburne 3, Wheeler 2.

Between the fifth and sixth ballots, Don Cameron changed his plans. Hartranft had lost two votes on the last ballot, which technically was enough to release those delegates still abiding by their agreement. Cameron had been left out of the midnight conference between the Morton, Bristow, and Hayes managers, and he therefore took the Michigan switch to presage the collapse of the Bristow movement. Fearing that he would lose control of his delegation if he continued his opposition to Blaine, he sent a proposal to Blaine's manager, Eugene Hale. If a pledge would be given that Pennsylvania would be represented in the cabinet, he would swing to Blaine and nominate him.

Blaine's manager also misread the significance of the Michigan switch. He foresaw the collapse of the favorite sons on the next ballot and an inevitable flocking to Blaine. He therefore refused to consider Cameron's offer.

It looked, on the sixth ballot, as if Hale had been right. Blaine gained an additional 22 votes, 9 coming from Pennsylvania. The rebuffed Cameron was able to hold 44 badly needed votes behind Hartranft. Blaine's total was 308, 70 short of nomination. Hayes gained 9 for a vote of 113. The others were Bristow 111, Morton 85, Conkling 81, Hartranft 50, Washburne 4, Wheeler 2.

Blaine's sudden increase of strength made the other managers realize that the next ballot would be decisive. Delay was imperative.

The chairman's gavel was raised to call for the seventh ballot. The vote was about to begin when a New York delegate called for a ten-minute recess. Blaine's fate hung on that moment. For one disastrous instant, the chairman hesitated, then declared the motion out of order. At that point, he lost control of the convention. Confusion broke out on the floor as delegates cried protest to the chairman's ruling. During the pandemonium, New York and Pennsylvania had time to confer and read the signs. Blaine must be stopped. Who could stop him but Hayes? By the time the chairman regained control of the convention, it was too late. The decisions had been made.

When Indiana was called on the seventh ballot, Morton's name was withdrawn and 25 votes cast for Hayes. The speech withdrawing Morton was a dramatic moment; it made certain the nominee of the convention, but it also marked the end of a great career. Morton had made his last appearance on the national scene. "It was like the folding of a battle flag preparatory to putting it out of sight forever."

Kentucky quickly followed Indiana. John Harlan, with an inner vision of the portals of the Supreme Court opening wide to receive him, withdrew Bristow and cast the unanimous vote of Kentucky for Hayes. The other states fell into line. The Conkling managers, Arthur, Cornell, and Thomas Platt—not yet Boss Platt—agreed to climb on the bandwagon with as much grace as the need for haste would permit. Sixty-one New York votes went to Hayes, but 9 were cast for Blaine. Pennsylvania almost missed the bandwagon, but Cameron threw Hartranft's votes to the winner. At the end of the ballot, Hayes had received 384 votes, to 351 for Blaine. Bristow held 21 votes to the last.

The presidential nomination having been settled, the leaders of the convention decided that New York, which would be of the utmost importance in the election, should be allowed to name the vice-presidential candidate. Webb Hayes, the Ohio governor's son, later reported that the decision was bandied about in a caucus. " 'Take it, Chet,' said one to Chester A. Arthur. 'You take it, Cornell,' another said to A. B. Cornell. Finally someone proposed 'Let's give it to Wheeler.' So William A. Wheeler, a second-rate politician was nominated." This story, demonstrating the sometimes lamentably casual manner in which great questions are settled in political conventions is, alas, apocryphal. Actually Wheeler was not a member of the Conkling machine and was, in fact, hostile to the New York boss. The organization's official choice was General Stewart Woodford, but Wheeler was proposed by other delegations, and his strength was such that New York had little choice but to withdraw Woodford and go along with the majority.

George F. Hoar of Massachusetts spent a busy day urging Wheeler's candidacy. When he approached James Russell Lowell of the Massachusetts delegation, the distinguished author said he was unwilling to vote for a person of whom he knew so little. Hoar said, "Mr. Lowell, Mr. Wheeler is a very sensible man. He knows the Bigelow Papers by heart." Lowell made no reply but was later heard to say to another delegate, "I understand that Mr. Wheeler is a very sensible man." What author could reject a man who had committed his works to memory!

Marshall Jewell, General Woodford, Joseph R. Hawley of Connecticut, and Frederick T. Frelinghuysen of New Jersey were, along with Wheeler, placed in nomination. Woodford withdrew his name, and the balloting began.

When South Carolina cast its vote, Wheeler already had 366 votes. It was moved to suspend the rules, and Wheeler was nominated by acclamation. Hayes's plaintive question as to Wheeler's identity had been answered. He was his running mate.

It is a curious footnote to this convention that Blaine was actually the preference of a majority of the delegates—but never on the same ballot. At one time or another, more than half the delegates cast their votes for the Plumed Knight, but the other managers prevented the united voting that would have nominated him. As one historian explained it, "The hounds pulled down the stag."

"I'd get good and drunk too!"

THE TWELFTH DEMOCRATIC NATIONAL CONVENTION
St. Louis, June 27, 1876

The Democratic outlook in 1876 had changed completely from the previous election year. Then a discouraged and divided party had met disconsolately to ratify the choice of the Liberal Republicans. In the resulting coalition, the Democrats were in the humiliating position of junior partners. This year was different. Victory was in the air, and a resurgent Democracy prepared, for the first time in twenty years, to nominate a candidate who could confidently expect to be the next president.

The leading candidate was that most astute of politicians, the reform Governor of New York, Samuel J. Tilden. A curious figure for a presidential aspirant, Tilden was, at sixty-two, a spare, withdrawn man of poor health, few emotions, and almost pure intellect. He had no close friends and lived a solitary life. Women did not interest him—he never married—and his sole physical pleasures came from wine and food. His greatest joys were his law practice, his books, and dinner-table discussions of economics and politics. A millionaire in his thirties, he entered politics as a writer, speaker, and backstage manager. He had no desire for public office, preferring to guide others.

Tilden might have remained behind the scenes had he not become a national hero through his crusade for reform government.

IIis great fight smashed the Tweed Ring in New York State, sent Boss Tweed to prison, and won his own election to the governorship of New York by a landslide.

As governor, Tilden reorganized the state finances, effected substantial savings in expenditures, and lowered taxes. His greatest triumph was destruction of the Canal Ring, which had for years milked the funds provided for repairing and extending the state canal system. With his two great victories over the Tweed and Canal Rings, Tilden became the obvious candidate for the Democrats in 1876. Tilden was, however, never satisfied to take the obvious at face value.

Tilden conducted the first "modern" campaign for a presidential nomination. He first set up a Newspaper Popularity Bureau, which placed advertisements in over 1200 newspapers throughout the country and supplied them with a steady stream of interesting and well written stories about himself. The number of these stories dealing in "human interest" was, perhaps, the first widespread effort to create that public "image" so dear to the hearts of all modern politicians. A Literary Bureau was established to write news articles, pamphlets, and speeches advocating his candidacy. These efforts went considerably beyond the usual run of campaign literature. They dealt with governmental expenditure, reform of the civil service, the tax structure, means of eradicating patronage and graft, and Tilden's ideas for sound administration. It was his hope to educate while gaining support.

Tilden also went further than any candidate ever had in keeping himself informed of public sentiment. Polls were not then a part of daily life as they are today, but Tilden carefully surveyed attitudes throughout the country. He took a census of college commencement addresses and found the greater number were devoted to himself and reform. He also studied local Fourth of July orations and again found reform the keynote. Primitive as these polling methods may have been, they, along with the steady flow of pro-Tilden literature, gave him an enormous advantage over his opponents for the nomination. By the time the convention met, it was an all but foregone conclusion that he would be the nominee.

His race for the nomination was not without opposition, nevertheless. Naturally, the Tammany and former Tweed forces in New

York were bitterly opposed to him, but his control of the state was strong enough to make their hostility of little consequence. More important was the opposition of some western Democrats. The depression had revived greenback sentiment in the West, and there was strong agitation throughout that region for an abandonment of the hard-money policies that prevailed. The westerners demanded an immediate issue of paper money in sufficient quantity to ease the financial difficulties of the nation and to stimulate the economy. Tilden was, in financial matters, a conservative, unalterably opposed to the greenback program.

Senator Thomas A. Hendricks came forward as the greenback candidate. George H. Pendleton had retired from politics, and Hendricks, a hard-money man in 1868, sought to assume Pendleton's mantle and rally his former supporters.

Other figures from 1868 came forward. Winfield Scott Hancock had the support of Pennsylvania, former Governor Joel Parker was New Jersey's favorite son, and William Allen, although recently defeated by Hayes for re-election to the governorship, was the favorite son of Ohio. Senator Thomas F. Bayard, Democratic leader of the Senate, had the support of his home state of Delaware and a majority of the Georgia delegation. Hendricks was Tilden's only serious rival. With the exception of Allen, these men were in agreement with the New Yorker on financial issues and, unlike Hendricks, represented no particular opposition faction.

The convention met in St. Louis, Missouri, on June 27. It was the first time any major political party had held its national convention west of the Mississippi. The choice of Missouri was a gracious gesture on the part of the Democrats toward the founders of the reform movement, which had begun there six years before.

The meeting hall of the convention, the Merchants' Exchange, was an imposing, four-story structure, of somewhat more tasteful design than was usual in the florid architecture of the period. The main hall seated 6000 people, with room for an additional 2000 in the galleries. Its seventy windows were hung with crimson drapes, and the aisles were richly carpeted. The platform was banked with masses of shrubs and flowers. Beneath the frescoed ceiling, the emblems of the states were hung, encircled with laurel-leaves and budding cereals.

The convention, having been entertained by Postlewaite's band, was brought to order by the chairman of the Democratic National Committee, Augustus Schell of New York. In his opening speech, he threw down the gauntlet to the Hendricks forces: "The Democratic party has, from its origin and through all the time of its existence, and is now, the hard-money party of the country." He then turned the chair over to the temporary chairman, Henry Watterson. "Marse Henry" had been Tilden's choice for this position. When he protested that he knew nothing of parliamentary procedure and that his eyesight was such that he would not be able to see the delegates to recognize them, he was assured that an experienced parliamentarian would be at his side at all times. All he had to do was preside; his aides would make the rulings and do the seeing for him.

At the evening session, General John A. McClernand of Illinois was elected permanent chairman. His speech was a rousing indictment of Republican rule, which concluded with a mythological flourish as he predicted victory in November. Referring to those states already in Democratic hands, he said, "These States, with their thronging populations, like the woods and winds that rose and followed the fluting Orpheus, will rise and follow you to final triumph."

The night proved a hectic one for the resolutions committee. Tilden, leaving nothing to chance, had had the editor of the New York *World,* Manton Marble, write a platform to present to the committee for ratification. He arranged for his lieutenant governor, William Dorsheimer, to be chairman of the committee, in order to insure adoption of his platform. The western greenback men fought the financial plank bitterly, but, after a continuous session of thirty-six hours, Dorsheimer triumphed and brought out of the committee the same platform he had taken in. Due to the strain of the session and the extreme heat, Dorsheimer fainted as he left the committee room. When word reached "Blue Jeans" Williams, Governor of Indiana, and a soft-money advocate, he drawled, "Well, if I had had the triumph that man has had, I'd get good and drunk, too!"

The triumph, however, was by no means assured as yet. General Thomas Ewing led the westerners in preparing a minority report to present to the convention. The problem was that, while a majority

of the delegates favored Tilden, a majority also favored a greenback plank. Tilden had made it very plain that the delegates would
have to choose between him and soft money. If they should decide
to vote for their financial convictions, Tilden's carefully laid plans
could still be upset.

A tense and unruly convention gathered on the second day. The
struggle over the greenback plank was beginning to tell on the
nerves of the delegates. The floor and the galleries were in an
almost continuous uproar. In the midst of the parliamentary skir-
mishing, John Kelly, now Tammany grand sachem, arose and asked
to read a list of New Yorkers opposed to Tilden's nomination. Ruled
out of order, he had at least recorded his opposition to the man
who had broken the back of Tammany.

In the afternoon, William Dorsheimer read the platform to the
convention and offered an amendment that would strike out all
reference to the financial question. The westerners promptly offered a pro-greenback plank. The point of controversy centered on
the Resumption Act of 1875, which would have retired paper currency. The westerners demanded its repeal; the Tilden forces denounced it for not fixing a definite time for the resumption of
specie payments. The majority plank was a compromise intended
to keep the party on the side of hard money, while still making a
gesture toward the greenbackers by denouncing the Resumption
Act in what amounted to meaningless terms. It would seem that
Dorsheimer offered his amendment to strike out even this feeble
concession to the West, in the hope of frightening the greenbackers
into accepting half a loaf.

The debate on the western resolution was carried on amid an
uproar from the shouting delegates. Dorsheimer made the issue
clear when he flatly stated that it was "a straight issue between
soft money and hard money. By that we stand or we fall." As the
chairman threatened to clear the almost riotous galleries, Dorsheimer warned that the Democrats could not win without New
York and that New York—and by implication, Tilden—would
never accept the western proposal. The convention was in bedlam,
but the Tilden steamroller moved on. The western resolution was
pushed to a vote and defeated, 515 to 219. The eastern amendment
was then voted down, 550 to 219, and the platform as originally

presented was adopted, 651 to 83. It was a clear triumph for Tilden, and his nomination could not now be prevented.

The platform as adopted was, as political platforms go, a reasoned, extremely well written, and, on the whole, moderate document. It called for reform in taxation, administration, tariffs, public land policy, financial policy, and the civil service. Its most blatant appeal to any special interest was its plank on immigration. While the Republicans had bowed to western demands and suggested reappraisal of Oriental immigration, the Democrats flatly placed themselves in opposition to "further importation or immigration of the Mongolian race." Apart from this lapse, however, the general tone of the platform was reasonable.

The contestants, in order of nomination, were Senator Bayard, Thomas A. Hendricks, Joel Parker, Governor Tilden, William Allen, and General Hancock. The only excitement came when Francis Kernan placed Tilden in nomination.

John Kelly came forward to speak. Technically the next speaker should have been there to second Tilden's nomination, but the chairman, at something of a loss, permitted him to speak. As Kelly began, he was shouted down. Attempting several times to be heard, Kelly was shouted down each time. Finally, Senator Kernan begged the delegates to allow his opponent to be heard, and the convention quieted enough for the Tammany boss to shout over the uproar. Constantly interrupted, he doggedly warned the delegates that Tilden could not win and that they should choose Hendricks. Many of his words were lost, and his warning had no effect but to push an unruly convention to the point of chaos.

On the first ballot, Tilden received 401½ votes, with 492 necessary for nomination; Hendricks was second with 140½; Hancock had 75; Allen 54; Bayard 33; Parker 18; and 3 Nevada votes went to Allen G. Thurman. Missouri had cast 14 votes for Hendricks and 16 for James O. Brodhead, but, at the end of the roll call, the chairman of the delegation switched the Brodhead votes to Tilden, giving him an unofficial total of 417½.

On the second and final ballot, a few states refused to join the rush to Tilden. Pennsylvania held out for Hancock, as did Ohio for Allen. Indiana and Tennessee cast solid votes for Hendricks, as did scattered delegates from Illinois, Kansas, Maryland, Michigan, Virginia, and Wisconsin. But it was a futile gesture. Hard money and superior organization had carried the day. The final vote stood: Tilden 535, Hendricks 85, Hancock 58, Allen 54, Bayard 4, Thurman 2. The nomination was then made unanimous.

With victory a real possibility in November, the Tilden forces realized that they needed a solidly united party. It was obvious that the best way to placate the soft-money men would be to offer the second place as a consolation prize to Hendricks. His was the only name placed in nomination when the convention met on the third day.

An odd circumstance developed on the roll call for nominations. The clerk had read the roll as far as Indiana without response. When Indiana was called, Joseph McDonald declared that the delegation had come to St. Louis to work for Hendricks's nomination for president and could not take the responsibility of offering him the vice-presidential nomination. It was left to Missouri to place the Indianian in nomination. He received the total vote of the convention.

With the ticket completed, only one task remained to effect harmony in the party. In response to insistent calls and cheers from the delegates, John Kelly took the platform and made a gracious speech of surrender. He admitted that no one in the convention had worked harder to defeat Tilden but pledged that no one would work harder to secure his election.

Samuel J. Tilden and Thomas A. Hendricks, hard money and soft money, joined hands in St. Louis to wage their battle for reform. The Democrats surged forward toward victory at the polls. Tilden and Hendricks were cheered as the winning combination—but the era of Reconstruction was not quite over. Republican politicians and carpetbag governments stole the victory away, and the Democrats never reached the White House. Victory with the voters was one thing, victory with the Electoral Commission quite another. As a united party left St. Louis in June, 1876, it could see ahead only the coming victory at the polls—not the defeat beyond.

CHAPTER 4

"I congratulate you as being the 'dark horse'"

THE SEVENTH REPUBLICAN NATIONAL CONVENTION
Chicago, June 2, 1880

Whatever the validity of his title to the Presidency, Rutherford B. Hayes was peacefully inaugurated on March 5, 1877, and promptly set a course that ensured his serving but one term. He offended Conkling, Blaine, and Cameron by ignoring their cabinet ambitions and outraged most Republicans by removing the last federal troops from the South and allowing the remaining carpetbag governments to fall. He infuriated the party leaders by taking seriously the demands for reform and allowing his Secretary of the Interior, Carl Schurz, and his Secretary of the Treasury, John Sherman, to sweep the thieves out of the Bureau of Indian Affairs and the customs service. The President took a personal hand in attacking the Conkling machine in New York by removing Collector of Customs Chester A. Arthur and naval officer Alonzo B. Cornell, both Conkling Stalwarts, on grounds of incompetence and corruption. "His Fraudlency," as Conkling gleefully dubbed Hayes, found himself a president without a party.

The Hayes administration was unpopular with the country. A serious depression alienated the voters, and the Democrats won both houses of Congress in the mid-term elections. The brilliant fiscal policies of Secretary Sherman and a bumper agricultural crop for export improved the economy in the last year of Hayes's term, but renewed prosperity was not enough to make the President's prospects for re-election very encouraging. The enmity of the party leaders was an insurmountable obstacle to renomination, and Hayes wisely decided to retire.

The President's withdrawal left a wide field of candidates. Blaine, naturally, was in the field again. John Sherman, George F. Edmunds of Vermont, Elihu Washburne of Illinois, and Senator William Windom of Minnesota were active candidates. Congressman James A. Garfield was frequently mentioned as a possible candidate. This year Conkling preferred to act as king-maker. His choice, Ulysses S. Grant, ready and willing to break the third-term taboo, was the most formidable candidate.

After leaving the White House, Grant had embarked on an extensive tour around the world. He was enthusiastically greeted wherever he went, and the tour developed into something of a royal progress. Thorough newspaper coverage kept the General's triumphs before the public, and while his genial remark that Venice would be a pretty city if only it were drained was perhaps his most memorable statement during the years he was abroad, his political prospects were carefully kept alive. The nation's pride in its hero's reception by the monarchs of the Old World did much to erase the memories of eight years of corruption and incompetence. In fact, many suggested, apparently with a straight face, that now that Grant had seen the world and conferred with the rulers of other nations, he was at last equipped to be president.

When the General landed in San Francisco in September, 1879, after an absence of twenty-six months, he received an unprecedented welcome. Wildly cheered by huge crowds on his triumphal progress across the country, his political stock skyrocketed. Conkling, Cameron, and John Logan of Illinois prepared for their own return to national power through support of the compliant General. They argued that the country needed a strong man to lead it and warned that the Democrats who controlled Congress would seek to avenge Tilden's defeat and "would by fair means or foul 'count in' their candidate unless they had for their opponent the resolute and warlike Grant." As for the third-term tradition, it was carefully explained that it applied only to consecutive terms and

should in no way affect Grant, who had been out of office for a full
term.

Grant himself wanted to return to office. In the first place, he
needed a job. He was not a wealthy man, and if he were to continue
the enjoyments of city life and the company of the rich and powerful, as he ardently wished to do, it would be necessary to supple-
ment his private means. In the second place, Grant believed that
his election to a third term would be a vindication of the first two.
He had been stung by the attacks made upon him and his administration and saw re-election as a means of wiping the record clean.

Blaine was the strongest anti-Grant candidate. The Man from
Maine—still inspiring a fanatical loyalty among his supporters—
had weathered the storm of the Mulligan letters. As the leader of
the Half-Breeds, Blaine was expected to make the convention a
contest between himself and Grant.

John Sherman, the administration candidate, hoped to benefit
from a deadlock between the two giants. If he could remain in
the race, he could reasonably expect to be the second choice of the
party. Sherman, because of his successful execution of the Resumption Act of 1875, received the support of the business community, who gave him full credit for the renewal of prosperity in
1878. But however diligent, astute, and dedicated a public servant
Sherman might be, he was colorless. The public considered him
competent but dull. Competing for favor among the hero worshippers of Blaine and Grant would prove a formidable task.

Senator Edmunds of Vermont, generally acknowledged as the
New England candidate, was supported by the liberal and reform
groups. Famed for his contrariness—it was said that if George
Edmunds were the only man in the world, George would object to
everything Edmunds proposed—he admitted he had little interest
in the presidency but thought the vetoing of bills would be good
fun. His candidacy was mainly a holding operation for the Massachusetts and Vermont delegations, who favored neither Grant nor
Blaine.

Congressman James A. Garfield was pledged to John Sherman
and denied having any interest in receiving the nomination for
himself. But he was not unaware that there was a movement to

make him the candidate. Hayes himself favored Garfield, notwith-standing that Sherman was the administration candidate, and so did Carl Schurz. Late in 1879 Wharton Barker, Philadelphia banker, and Henry C. Lea, a noted medieval historian turned amateur politician, set up a committee to further the Garfield candidacy.

Talk of Garfield's candidacy worried John Sherman. It was basic to Sherman's strategy that he must be the only possible compromise candidate. As early as May, 1879, Sherman tried to prevent Garfield from becoming a rival. Through a friend, he asked Garfield not to contest the Ohio delegation. If Sherman had a solid delegation, Garfield was told, it could be swung to him if Sherman failed, but if they divided the delegation, neither would have a chance. Garfield was noncommittal.

Garfield finally gave in to Sherman's pressure and agreed, in exchange for Sherman's promise to give him his support in the event of his own failure, to attend the convention as a delegate-at-large in the Sherman delegation and to act as Sherman's cam-paign manager. It was an act of the greatest political naïveté on Sherman's part to believe he could best silence talk of Garfield's availability by sending him into the midst of the battle where he could hardly help but attract attention. It would have been better for John Sherman if Garfield had been kept as obscure as possible.

Garfield's attitude, as expressed in his journal, was clear. He would not seek the nomination, nor did he expect it. If it were offered to him without any effort on his part and after it had been demonstrated that Sherman had no chance for nomination, he might in good conscience accept.

On April 24, Wharton Barker came to Washington to report to Garfield and the President on the situation in Pennsylvania. Al-though Don Cameron expected a solid delegation for Grant, Barker knew of nineteen delegates who would vote for Blaine first and later for Garfield. Before breakfast the next morning, Garfield called on Barker to announce that he must find another candidate. Garfield told him that he had agreed to place John Sherman in nomination. Barker blandly replied, "I shall go ahead as if nothing had hap-pened. So far as you are concerned, do as you have promised to do. Be loyal to Sherman before and in the convention, and your friends will do far more for you than you could do for yourself."

They agreed to leave it at that. Garfield would work for Sherman, Barker would work for Garfield, and between them they would, if possible, defeat Grant with one or the other.

Sherman needed a solid Ohio delegation as a base from which to work, but the Blaine forces made a raid on the state convention and won nine delegates. This hurt Sherman's candidacy, but as it turned out Blaine was hurt even more. A majority of the Ohio delegation friendly to Blaine—there had been talk of supporting him if Sherman dropped out of the race—was so angered at the raid that it and Sherman decided not to support Blaine under any circumstances. When the convention deadlocked, Blaine's sacrifice of 35 potential Ohio votes in exchange for 9 immediate ones was of crucial importance.

Meanwhile the triumvirate of Conkling, Cameron, and Logan began its drive on behalf of Grant. Calling a state convention in New York for February 25, 1880, Conkling used his Stalwart majority to whip the minority into line. Under ordinary circumstances, the local district conventions issued instructions to the delegates they selected, but Conkling intended the state convention to assume superior authority over the district conventions. The instructions that Lord Roscoe dictated to the state gathering were phrased not only for the delegates-at-large, as was customary, but for all those chosen in separate districts "to use their most earnest and united efforts to secure the nomination of Ulysses S. Grant." The convention adopted these instructions by a vote of 216 to 183 and required each delegate to pledge himself to Grant. The sizable minority protested at being thus bludgeoned into line, but they accepted the instructions.

In May, William H. Robertson, delegate from Westchester County, announced that he was not bound by the pledge to support Grant because he had not attended the state convention—and that he would vote for Blaine until he was nominated. This rebellion provided a rallying point for other dissidents. One delegate announced that, rather than attend the national convention and vote his instructions for Grant, he would send his unbound alternate to vote for Blaine. By June, the insurgents numbered nineteen, two of whom were for Sherman.

In Pennsylvania, Don Cameron secured an ostensibly pro-Grant delegation, but he was aware of an undercurrent of revolt, involving an undetermined number of delegates. General Logan, seeing the difficulties encountered by Conkling and Cameron, decided to make sure that Illinois, at least, would offer no trouble. It was customary for the delegates to the state convention from each congressional district to choose the delegates to the national convention. Several districts showed hostility to Grant and threatened to break away. The state convention therefore changed the rules for selecting delegates and ordered that they be named by a committee appointed by the chairman of the convention. Logan, with a workable majority, was able to dominate both the convention and the committee. Grant delegates were selected to represent anti-Grant districts. The angry Blaine forces threatened to send their own delegates and let the national convention decide who should be seated for Illinois.

Conkling, Cameron, and Logan worked out a plan to hamstring the rebellious minorities in their delegations: the unit rule. It had not been used in the convention of 1876, but the triumvirate decided to re-impose it. Their strategy was simple. Cameron, as chairman of the Republican National Committee, would call the convention to order and preside over the selection of a temporary chairman. If the National Committee proposed an anti-Grant man as temporary chairman, a pro-Grant nominee would be named from the floor. In the contest between the two candidates, Cameron would rule that the unit rule would apply. The anti-Grant minorities would thus be forced to vote for a pro-Grant temporary chairman, who would, in all probability, be elected. This temporary chairman would, in turn, invoke the unit rule in the roll calls relating to credentials and the adoption of permanent rules, assuring the adoption of the unit rule for the presidential balloting.

The National Committee met in Chicago on Tuesday June 1— the day before the opening of the convention—to select a temporary chairman. The Sherman and Blaine forces agreed that William E. Chandler, representing Blaine, would lead the fight against the triumvirate's strategy within the National Committee, while Garfield would lead the forces outside.

The anti-Grant men on the National Committee outnumbered the Grant committeemen twenty-nine to eighteen. A motion was introduced against the unit rule, but Cameron refused to entertain it, maintaining that such action was outside the province of the committee. An angry, all-day wrangle ensued while Cameron sat in stony silence, refusing to listen or even to speak to the anti-Grant men.

While Chandler argued with Cameron, Garfield called on Conkling to suggest a compromise. He proposed that Senator George F. Hoar be named temporary chairman, since he was an Edmunds delegate favoring neither Grant nor Blaine. Conkling declined to take any responsibility for settling the contest. Later in the day, the Grant men rejected the compromise offer.

As frayed tempers grew increasingly shorter, the anti-Grant committeemen threatened to depose the silent Cameron and replace him with Chandler. Were Cameron not to follow the wishes of the majority, they would get a chairman who would. The argument was going further than the Grant men had anticipated. The success of their strategy depended upon Cameron's position as chairman. To gain time to cope with this unexpected development, Cameron adjourned the meeting until the following day.

After adjournment, the Grant managers approached the sergeant-at-arms to find out if he would recognize a new chairman if Cameron were deposed. The unhappy sergeant-at-arms advised them that it would be his duty to recognize the new chairman and obey his lawful orders. That was the end of the plan to dominate the convention through the National Committee.

Cameron submitted with singular ill grace, and, when former Vice-President Hannibal Hamlin proposed Senator Hoar, the triumvirate had to accept him. The next morning, with Cameron sitting "silent and gloomy," the compromise was settled. The question of the unit rule would be left to the full convention, and, with Hoar as temporary chairman, it was probable that the rule would not govern the convention when voting on the question of the rule itself. It was further agreed that, to prevent an untimely contest, Senator Hoar would also serve as permanent chairman.

On the first day of the convention, the two most conspicuous figures were, as they were to be throughout the convention, Conkling and Garfield. Conkling would attract attention in any gathering at any time, and Garfield's role as Sherman's manager, while he was himself a potential candidate, made him especially conspicuous. Garfield was faced with a particularly embarrassing dilemma. If, on the one hand, he made himself at all prominent, which, as Sherman's manager he could hardly keep from doing, he would be suspected of advertising himself at Sherman's expense. On the other hand, if he remained in the background, he would be accused of half-heartedness in his support of Sherman. Either way he would be misjudged.

The second day began the bitter struggle between the Grant and anti-Grant forces. This fight—there was a conflict over every technicality, over every point, major and minor, that came before the convention—was the most acrimonious in the history of national conventions. A fight to the death between Conkling and the rival managers, it was waged with acid sarcasm, thinly veiled insults, and wrangling that was at best undignified and at worst idiotic.

Only the committee on permanent organization reported during the morning session. It being obvious that there was no business before the convention, Conkling sensibly suggested that they adjourn until evening. It was then 11:30 in the morning, and already the temperature outside and more than 10,000 people jammed inside had made the hall unbearable—but any proposal from Conkling, however sensible, was not to go unchallenged. Blaine's manager opposed the motion, asserting that the convention was ready to go to work. Conkling ironically pointed out that the only work that could be done would be to sit "idle on uncushioned seats —fortunately with backs." The anti-Grant men defeated the motion, and the Stalwarts had to sit, steaming and fuming, under the hot roof until 7:30 that evening. The convention, having accomplished nothing, then adjourned.

At the morning session on Friday, Conkling made a critical mistake. The Rev. Mr. Little had hardly had time to finish the opening prayer before Conkling was on his feet with a resolution, "As the sense of this Convention, that every member of it is bound in honor to support its nominee, whoever that nominee may be; and that no man should hold a seat here who is not ready to so agree." On a voice vote, the resolution was overwhelmingly carried, with a few audible voices in the negative. Conkling demanded a roll call, "that we may know who it is in a Republican convention that votes 'No' on such a pledge." On the roll, every delegate supported the pledge or abstained, except three delegates from West Virginia. Conkling thereupon demanded that those delegates should forfeit their right to participate in the convention. Garfield took the floor to plead that the trio from West Virginia be allowed to vote as they wished. "We come here as Republicans, and we are entitled to take part in the proceeding of this Convention, and as one of our rights, we can vote on every resolution 'aye' or 'no.' We are responsible for those votes to our constituents, and to them alone. There never was a Convention, there never can be a Convention, of which I am one delegate, equal in rights to every other delegate, that shall bind my vote against my will on any question whatever." The popular response to Garfield's speech was so great that Conkling had to withdraw his resolution. But even when checked Conkling kept his wits and humor. He sent Garfield a note scribbled on a piece of newspaper, "I congratulate you as being the 'dark horse.'"

The report of the rules committee effectively abolished the unit rule and left the vote in the hands of each individual delegate. If the report were adopted, Grant would be defeated. A minority report was submitted, demanding that the unit rule be adopted. The battle lines were drawn.

Before voting on the rules, however, it was necessary to consider the report of the committee on credentials. The issue was whether delegates should be chosen by district or state conventions. There were more than fifty cases to be considered, but the Illinois contest was the key. The majority report boldly asserted that precedent upheld the system of congressional district representation and therefore recommended seating the dissident anti Grant delegates from Illinois.

A minority report presented the case for the overriding of district by state conventions. The arguments pro and con went on far into the night. For every Stalwart argument, there was a Half-Breed rebuttal. The exhausted delegates agreed finally to file the reports and vote on eleven test cases. The majority report on the first test case was adopted by a vote of 384 to 356. On each subsequent test case the majority report was sustained, and the anti-Grant delegates seated.

Friday, June 4, had been the crucial day in the convention. A majority of the delegates, although not agreed on a candidate, had united in opposition to a third term for Grant. Amid an almost continuous uproar from the floor and galleries, the convention had sat for sixteen hours, checked Conkling, buried the unit rule, seated anti-Grant delegates from Illinois, and seen Garfield emerge to a prominence that effectively removed him from the dark-horse category.

The convention met on Saturday to complete the debate on the contested seats and to consider the rules. Even though the outcome was inevitable, the Stalwarts bitterly contested the majority credentials report on each case. As the day dragged on, it was suspected that Logan and Conkling were deliberately trying to prolong the convention into another week. Logan believed many delegates, especially from the South, could not sustain the expense of a protracted stay in Chicago and would be in a mood to stampede for Grant before their railroad tickets expired. So fearful were some about having to leave that an Alabama delegate begged the convention to ask the railroads to extend the validity of their tickets for at least three days beyond the end of the convention. The railroads graciously obliged, and the delegates were able to carry on their deliberations free from the fear of being stranded in Chicago.

The platform was the usual catalogue of Republican virtues and Democratic failings, but it was silent on the civil service. An amendment offered from the floor asking that reform of the civil service "be thorough, radical and complete," inspired the most refreshingly honest declaration of this or any other convention. Lip service to reform was all very well and was the stock in trade of every politician, but one delegate from Texas had had enough. Webster Flanagan, who should be gratefully remembered as a man who knew his mind and spoke it, said, "Texas has had quite enough of the civil service. During the last four years, Sir, out of 1,400 officers appointed by the President of the United States, 140 represented the Republican party. We are not here, Sir, for the purpose of providing officers for the Democracy. There is one plank in the

Democratic party that I have ever admired, and that is, 'to the victors belong the spoils.' After we have won the race, as we will, we will give those who are entitled to positions offices. What are we up here for? I mean that members of the Republican party are entitled to office, and if we are victorious we will have office." Alas, an honest statement was met with good natured laughter, the civil service amendment was adopted, and Mr. Flanagan returned to Texas a sadder, but, one hopes, not an unemployed man.

It was now ten o'clock in the evening, but the weary convention, which was dogged if nothing else, proceeded to the nominations. The first to be presented was James G. Blaine. The crowd, remembering Ingersoll's stirring oratory four years earlier, eagerly awaited the speech that would once again place the Plumed Knight in competition. It is possible that another such speech would, in view of Grant's declining hopes, have stampeded the convention for Blaine. In a disastrous miscalculation, William E. Chandler decided that Ingersoll's avowed atheism would more than offset any favorable effect his oratory might produce. The great orator was relegated to the role of a supernumerary, waving a red shawl from the platform, while the honor of presenting the candidate went to an obscure Detroit millionaire, James F. Joy.

With an understanding greater than he knew, Joy began by regretting that he had been chosen, since he feared his words would "benefit the candidate but little." He went on to say, among other things, that Michigan was a safe state and would go Republican whether Blaine were nominated or not. This asininity was capped when the hapless titan of business presented to the convention the name of James S. Blaine. It was too much for the disgusted Half-Breeds. In chorus, they shouted: "G., you fool, G.!"

Senator William Windom of Minnesota was perfunctorily presented, and it was the turn of the Stalwarts. General Logan took the platform. "In the name of our loyal citizens, soldiers and sailors —in the name of loyalty, of liberty, of humanity and justice I nominate Ulysses S. Grant for President." The vast cheer that followed these words gave Conkling time to prepare. As the cheers died down, he was seen standing on a reporters' table in the middle of the hall. With consummate dramatic instinct, he waited for absolute silence before beginning the greatest speech of his career. While his audience waited with drawn breath, he intoned the opening lines of a verse by Miles O'Reilly:

> And when asked what State he hails from,
> Our sole reply shall be,
> He hails from Appomattox,
> And its famous apple tree.

That these few lines of sorry doggerel could bring forth an explosion of enthusiasm from the crowd and provoke a near bedlam of noise is, perhaps, the greatest tribute that could be paid to Conkling's oratorical skill.

Conkling delivered a speech magnificent in its tributes to Grant and slashing in its scorn for his opponents. With jibes and sneers, he ticked off one by one all the other contenders and moved the crowd to deliriums of joy and excitement. Nonetheless, the speech did much to destroy Grant. Where a moderate speech of conciliation might have softened some of the hostility of the Blaine and Sherman forces and raised the chances of Grant's being the eventual winner in a deadlock, Conkling's scathing wit solidified the resentment of the Half-Breeds to the point where they would have taken the devil himself before Grant.

After the tumultuous reception of Conkling's speech, any man would have had a difficult time in impressing the convention with the merits of another candidate. As it was now Garfield's turn to nominate Sherman, the task was doubly hard since he was, in effect, also placing himself in nomination, whether he intended to do so or not. Beside he had to place the colorless Sherman in contrast to the hero Grant. It was not an easy task.

He began well enough. He quieted the crowd and prepared them for a sober appraisal of the sober talents of the Secretary of the Treasury. But when, at the end of his opening remarks, he asked the rhetorical question—"What do we want?"—a voice from the audience, with suspicious swiftness, replied, "We want Garfield."

The main body of the speech was a sensible, conciliatory plea for party unity, and it healed some of the angry wounds opened by Conkling. But as Garfield spoke, Sherman's friends became uneasy. When would he mention Sherman? His plea for a winning candidate who could heal the breaches in the party applied as well to himself as to the man he was supposed to be nominating. Garfield's speech ran to seventeen paragraphs. In the sixteenth, he hinted that he intended to nominate someone. At the end of the speech, in the last sentence of the last paragraph, he mentioned Sherman. "I do not present him as a better Republican or a better man than thousands of others that we honor; but I present him for your deliberate and favorable consideration. I nominate John Sherman of Ohio." Garfield had done his duty, as he was honor bound to do. He had placed John Sherman in nomination—but just barely.

George Edmunds's name was placed before the convention against his wishes. He had declared himself for Grant, but Massachusetts wanted a candidate regardless of the candidate's desires in the matter. The final candidate was Elihu Washburne, and the final speech seconding his nomination significantly placed the basic objection to Grant's candidacy squarely before the convention.

As August Brandegee of Connecticut declared that Washburne could carry four-fifths of the German vote in the United States, Conkling was observed to shake his head vigorously, perhaps in denial, perhaps in irritation. Brandegee continued, "The gentleman from New York shakes his head. He shakes his head magnificently. No man can shake it like him, nor shake such rhetoric and wisdom out of it. But let me tell the gentleman from New York he cannot sit down at the ear of every voter and give the argument that he has given tonight against the tradition of our fathers. He may, by the magic of his eloquence, take this Convention and the galleries off their feet, in his fervor; but even his great abilities, even his unmatched eloquence cannot go down to the fireside of every voter and persuade them that all the traditions of the fathers with reference to a third term are but humbug and masquerade. Does he not know that his candidate would be on the defensive, that even the magic name of Grant can hardly carry him in the Convention. Does he not know—no one knows as well as he—that the

name of Grant would carry this Convention through by storm if
there were not an invincible argument against his nomination?"
It was the final speech of the evening and, as the delegates left the
hall, it was Brandegee's warning, not Conkling's oratory, that they
remembered.

Sunday was not a day of rest for the Republicans in Chicago.
The day was spent in gathering last-minute support and exploring
the possibility of a compromise if Grant and Blaine should deadlock. The compromise candidate uppermost in many minds was
James A. Garfield. The Blaine boom appeared to be faltering.
Several of his supporters, including Henry Cabot Lodge, called
on Garfield to ask him to permit the use of his name if Grant and
Blaine eliminated each other. Garfield refused. William Grosvenor
later asked him if he had any ambition to be president. Garfield
replied that he had, but not at that time. In ten years, he would
be glad to accept the nomination, but his time had not yet come.

Although Garfield refused to become an active candidate,
Wharton Barker had gone ahead with his plans to nominate him.
Barker believed that, while Garfield had forbidden his own name
being placed in formal nomination, he would overlook a few scattered votes in his behalf. Barker therefore arranged with a Pennsylvania delegate to cast his vote for Garfield on each ballot to
keep his name before the convention.

Barker also made arrangements with Wisconsin and Indiana.
When the decisive moment arrived—Barker never doubted that
there would be a deadlock—Governor Pound of Wisconsin would
switch that state to Garfield. On the following ballot, as if inspired
by Wisconsin, Indiana would switch. Barker expected the two
switches to provide the impetus for a stampede. Garfield must
have known of these arrangements; he certainly made no effort to
prevent their being carried out.

Garfield was not the only compromise candidate considered
that day. Many of the Stalwarts feared Grant might not be able
to win. Where, then, could they go? A Half-Breed candidate was
out of the question, which eliminated Sherman, Blaine, and Garfield. Washburne was looked upon as a traitor for opposing his
chief, and Edmunds aroused little interest. A group of delegates

decided they had found a solution and called on Conkling to
offer him the nomination. They assured him that, if Grant were
withdrawn, he would meet with little opposition. But the Senator
refused. "Gentlemen, I appreciate your kind proposition. . . . I am
here as the agent of New York to support General Grant to the
end. Any man who would forsake him under such conditions does
not deserve to be elected, and could not be elected." And that was
that. Unlike Garfield, when Conkling said "No" he was believed.

On Monday morning, the day of the balloting, it was learned
that a storm had struck down telegraph wires throughout the
North and East. The candidates were cut off from their forces, and
the managers in Chicago were on their own. The first ballot was
a trial of strength, and a demonstration of the weakness of Grant
without the unit rule.

Illinois gave Grant 24 votes, but the minority gave 10 to Blaine
and 8 to Washburne. In New York, each delegate cast his vote
individually under the cold and hostile eye of Conkling; 17 went
to Blaine and 2 to Sherman. In Pennsylvania, Grant lost 23 votes
to Blaine and 3 to Sherman. The plans of the triumvirate had been
smashed. If the unit rule had been in effect, Grant would have
gained 53 additional votes, which would have placed him only 21
short of nomination. Sufficient changes would probably have been
made to give Grant the nomination on the first ballot. The final
count on the first ballot stood: Grant 304, Blaine 284, Sherman 93,
Edmunds 34, Washburne 30, and Windom 10.

On the second ballot, Grant received 305, Blaine 282, Sherman
94, Edmunds 32, Washburne 31, Windom 10, and Garfield 1. In
announcing the vote of New York, Conkling adopted the attitude
he was to maintain throughout the long sessions of balloting. His
plans thwarted, defeat only a matter of time, Conkling was as
proud as ever. In a studied drawl he announced each vote: "Two
delegates are said to be for Sherman, seventeen are said to be for
Blaine, and fifty-one are for Grant." The West Virginia chairman
in mockery announced the vote of his delegation: "One delegate
is said to be for Grant and eight are known to be for Blaine." For
thirty-three ballots, the enmity of the opposing forces was thus
spitefully displayed before the convention.

Twenty-eight ballots were taken on that Monday, with little change in the relative standing of the candidates. Benjamin Harrison received 1 vote on the third ballot; Hayes had 1 vote on the eleventh and held it for two ballots. On the final ballot of the day, the count was Grant 307, Blaine 279, Sherman 91, Washburne 35, Edmunds 31, Windom 10, Garfield 2.

Grant's case was hopeless. The only possible source of strength lay with the Washburne delegates, who might be persuaded to swing to the former President. But Grant would still lack 33 votes for nomination. Conkling's attitude made it impossible to obtain any of the needed votes from the Half-Breeds.

Grant's forces could be held firm, and that meant that virtually all the delegates not pledged to Grant would have to settle on a single candidate. Blaine was 100 votes short of victory. The obvious source of strength lay in the Sherman vote, but the Secretary would not release his delegates to Blaine. No one wanted Washburne, and Edmunds had declared he did not want the nomination. That left Garfield or Windom. The Wisconsin delegation met in caucus to decide between them and, thanks to the careful work of Barker and Governor Pound, voted by a narrow margin to support Garfield. If the vote had gone the other way, a relieved convention might have turned to Windom, as they were to turn to Garfield.

On the twenty-ninth ballot, the first of Tuesday morning, it looked as if Sherman would, as he had always hoped, actually break the deadlock. The Massachusetts delegation abandoned Edmunds and voted for Sherman. In addition to the 19 Massachusetts votes, Sherman picked up 6 other scattered votes. The results stood: Grant 305, Blaine 278, Sherman 116, Washburne 35, Edmunds 12, Windom 7, Garfield 2.

Sherman gained 4 more votes on the thirtieth ballot, for a total of 120. These votes, however, were coming from the minor candidates, not from the Blaine forces and certainly not from Grant. Unless Sherman could make an impression on the Blaine strength on the next ballot, the flurry in his favor would be a false alarm. Instead, on the thirty-first ballot, Sherman lost 2 votes and, by the thirty-third, had lost 8 more.

After the thirty-third ballot, Sherman, communication having been restored between Chicago and Washington, telegraphed the Ohio delegation: "Whenever the vote of Ohio will be likely to assure the nomination of Garfield I appeal to every delegate to vote for him. Let Ohio be solid."

Wharton Barker put his plan into action on the thirty-fourth ballot. Wisconsin, which had voted 9 Washburne, 7 Blaine, 3 Sherman, and 1 Grant, now voted 16 for Garfield, 2 for Grant, and 1 each for Blaine and Washburne. The count on this ballot was Grant 312, Blaine 275, Sherman 107, Washburne 30, Garfield 17, Edmunds 11, and Windom 4.

When the official tally was announced, Garfield rose to state, "I challenge the correctness of the announcement. The announcement contains votes for me. No man has a right, without the consent of the person voted for, to announce that person's name, and vote for him, in this Convention. Such consent I have not given." The chairman ruled him out of order. According to George F. Hoar, Garfield had not finished speaking. "I recollect the incident perfectly. I interrupted him in the middle of a sentence. I was terribly afraid that he would say something that would make his nomination impossible, or his acceptance impossible, if it were made. I do not believe that it ever happened before that anybody who attempted to decline the Presidency of the United States was to be prevented by a point of order. . . ." Interrupted or not, Garfield, when ruled out of order, quietly resumed his seat and did not attempt to say anything more.

The thirty-fifth ballot was decisive. The swing for Garfield had begun, but it remained to be seen if the plan could be kept moving. Indiana swung 27 of its Blaine, Sherman, and Washburne votes to Garfield, and he gained 4 from Maryland and one 1 each from Mississippi, North Carolina, and Pennsylvania. The count stood: Grant 313, Blaine 257, Sherman 99, Garfield 50, Washburne 23, Edmunds 11, and Windom 3. The tide had turned, and the stampede began on the thirty-sixth and final ballot.

Perhaps from genuine enthusiasm or perhaps from relief that they could now use their railroad tickets, the delegates flocked to the Garfield banner. Not everyone was swept along in the rush. Senator Jones of Nevada hurried to Conkling, begging him to bury

past differences and give New York to Blaine. It was asking too
much of the unforgiving Conkling to help nominate his greatest
enemy. New York defiantly voted for Grant, and nothing could stop
Garfield.

Garfield's own actions during the stampede have been much
disputed. Some observers claimed that he was completely overcome
with emotion and appeared to lose control of himself, but it seems
unlikely. He must have known of Barker's plan, and the stampede
could hardly have come as a complete surprise. A more reasonable
account of Garfield's behavior was reported in the Chicago *Inter
Ocean:* Garfield "insisted that the vote of the delegation should
be cast for Sherman as it had been done. 'You must not desert
Sherman,' he said. 'If this convention nominates me it should be
done without the vote of Ohio.' At this moment Sherman's telegram arrived and was read. 'That settles it,' exclaimed [Benjamin]
Butterworth. 'Cast my vote for Sherman,' said Garfield, but Ohio
was announced and Butterworth, springing upon a chair, announced
forty-three votes for Garfield. Turning to the reporter Garfield
said: 'I wish you would say that this is no act of mine. I wish you
would say that I have done everything and omitted nothing to secure Secretary Sherman's nomination. I want it plainly understood
that I have not sought the nomination and have protested against
the use of my name.'" It was obviously no time for emotional collapse; it was time to set the record as straight as possible under the
circumstances.

Although the convention was successfully stampeded for Garfield, the Grant men refused to give an inch. The winning candidate
received 399 votes on the final ballot, but Grant held at 306. This
Stalwart band, which came to be known as the "306," took pride
as long as they lived that they had gone down to defeat as a solid
bloc, loyal to the end to the hero of Appomattox.

Garfield knew that to ensure victory in November he must
placate the Stalwarts, particularly Conkling. To accomplish this
end, he offered second place on the ticket to Levi P. Morton, a
Conkling supporter. Morton would gladly have accepted, but felt
he must consult with Conkling. The Stalwart leader was not
pleased. "If you think the ticket will be elected," he said coldly,

"if you think you will be happy in the association, accept." Morton replied that he wished Conkling's advice. Conkling refused but suggested he talk with Governor Boutwell of Massachusetts. Boutwell advised against accepting the offer, and Morton rejected the nomination. He would accept the same offer eight years later, but he had missed his chance to be President of the United States.

The other New York Stalwarts were not so sure as Conkling that Garfield would be defeated and, believing that second place was better than none, decided, without consulting Conkling, that they would present Chester A. Arthur as their candidate. Apparently Arthur's recent removal from the collectorship of the Port of New York for corruption in no way disqualified him for the vice-presidency, for Garfield informed the Stalwarts that their selection was acceptable.

It was not, however, acceptable to Conkling. Arthur found Lord Roscoe pacing up and down the press room of the convention hall, deserted of all, save one reporter:

Arthur met Conkling in the middle of the room.

"I have been hunting for you everywhere, Senator," said Mr. Arthur.

"Well, sir," replied Conkling. . . . There was a moment of hesitation under the uncompromising attitude of the Senator. Finally Mr. Arthur said, "The Ohio men have offered me the Vice Presidency."

The Senator's voice rang out in indignant tones: "Well, sir, you should drop it as you would a red-hot shoe from the forge."

There was a flash of resentment in the eyes of Arthur as he replied, "I sought to consult you, not—" Conkling broke in on him: "What is there to consult about? This trickster of Mentor will be defeated before the country."

Arthur hesitated for a moment and said slowly, but with emphasis, "The office of Vice President is a greater honor than I ever dreamed of attaining. A barren nomination would be a great honor. In a calmer moment you will look at this differently."

"If you wish for my favor and my respect you will contemptuously decline it."

Arthur looked Conkling straight in the eye and said, "Senator Conkling, I shall accept the nomination and I shall carry with me the majority of the delegation."

The Senator looked at him for a brief moment, and then in a rage turned and walked away. For another moment Arthur looked after him regretfully and then left the room, unaware that in little more than a year he would obtain an office much higher than that of vice-president.

"We're strong enough to kill if we are not strong enough to win"

THE THIRTEENTH DEMOCRATIC NATIONAL CONVENTION

Cincinnati, June 22, 1880

The race for the Democratic nomination of 1880 began as soon as the Electoral Commission reported the election of Rutherford B. Hayes. The Democrats believed the only way to undo the great fraud of 1876 would be to re-elect Samuel J. Tilden in 1880. Tilden himself was anxious for vindication and held firmly to the claim of being the rightful President of the United States. When, in 1879, he was asked to be a candidate for governor of New York, he refused, giving as his reason that a president-elect could not run for state office. His adherents saw Tilden as a wronged man, deprived of his rightful office, and to them no other candidate was conceivable in the forthcoming election.

Tilden had lost more than the presidency in 1876. He lost what remained of his health as well. Never robust, the strain of the campaign and the long suspense of the electoral dispute shattered the precarious balance of his health. His left hand was paralyzed by arthritis, his walk was a painful shuffle, and his voice was reduced to a hoarse whisper. But his intellect was as brilliant as ever.

The unanimity of the Democrats did not last long. In 1877, Tilden was the only possible candidate; two years later it was doubtful that he would make the race at all or that he could win the nomination if he tried.

87

Two events brought about this reversal of the New Yorker's fortunes. The first was the episode of the Cipher Dispatches. The Tildenites wishes to cloud as much as possible Hayes's title to the presidency. Hayes's claims to the office discredited, nothing could then stop Tilden in the next contest. The Democrat-controlled House set up a committee to re-investigate the charges of fraud in the recent election.

As the Democrats had confidently expected, the Potter Committee uncovered extensive evidence of Republican corruption, which did much to vindicate Tilden in the eyes of the country. But the Republicans were ready with evidence of their own. The Western Union Company had turned over to the House and Senate more than 30,000 telegrams sent during and after the election by Republican and Democratic leaders. The Democrats in the House read the telegrams and returned them to Western Union, but the Republicans in the Senate removed 750 Democratic telegrams and kept them in reserve. The Republican telegrams were then returned and discreetly burned.

When the Potter Committee began its work, these telegrams, soon to be known as the Cipher Dispatches, were passed on to the New York *Tribune,* which deciphered and published them in October, 1878. If the Tildenites wanted sensational disclosures, the Republicans would see that they got them. The dispatches clearly showed that Tilden's nephew, William T. Pelton, assisted by Manton Marble, had attempted to bribe a Republican elector from Oregon and had opened negotiations to purchase electoral votes in Florida and South Carolina. The negotiations had fallen through, but Pelton, though penniless, had expended large sums of money which had come from Tilden's bank of deposit. Everyone asked how Pelton had gotten the money. Was Tilden himself a party to the attempted bribery? On October 12, 1878, Tilden vehemently denied any knowledge of the transactions, and, when rigorously examined by the Republicans on the Potter Committee, managed to survive the two-hour ordeal without making any damaging admissions.

Many of Tilden's friends and all of his enemies were dissatisfied with his testimony, and his presidential stock fell sharply. Abraham S. Hewitt expressed the widely held opinion that Tilden had seen none of the telegrams sent to and from his house in Gramercy Park because he did not wish to see them and that he "could have found out a great deal had he tried."

Despite the Cipher Dispatches, the Tildenites believed they held a trump card. For the first time since the Civil War, the solid South was a reality. If New York's 35 electoral votes were added to the 138 votes of the South, the Democrats would lack only 12 votes for victory. Tilden had, in 1876, carried the Empire State by a plurality of 30,000. This demonstration of strength, alone, might yet make Tilden the candidate—or so it appeared before November, 1879.

Honest John Kelly, Grand Sachem of Tammany Hall, was no admirer of Tilden. In happier days they had worked together to drive the Tweed Ring from power, but both desired to be boss of New York State. Tilden was boss now, but the Tammany chief intended to change that. His chance came with the gubernatorial election of 1879.

The incumbent governor, Lucius "Sore Eyes" Robinson, was a Tilden man, and the Tilden faction was intent on his re-election. When the state convention renominated Robinson, Tammany bolted and offered Kelly himself as a rival candidate. Robinson and Kelly campaigned against one another more than either did against the Republican candidate, Alonzo B. Cornell. Kelly accomplished his purpose. The Republicans swept the field, and Tilden's hold on the state Democracy was broken. It was a crushing defeat for the "old humbug of Cipher alley," as Kelly called him.

The Cipher Dispatches and the struggle with Tammany destroyed Tilden's chances for the nomination, and other candidates came to the fore. The first was Senator Thomas F. Bayard of Delaware, the leader of the Senate Democrats. Bayard was respected and admired by Republicans and Democrats alike, especially in the East. His staunch hard-money stand gave him the support of the eastern business interests, and he had appeal for the same groups who favored Sherman on the Republican side. Bayard also had widespread support among those southerners who remembered his sympathetic attitude during the dark days of Reconstruction.

Bayard had served on the Electoral Commission that gave the election to Hayes, and the Tildenites considered him a traitor who had sold out the victorious candidate to advance his own political fortunes. Henry Watterson and Manton Marble, both liberally subsidized by Tilden, conducted a bitter smear campaign against the Democrats who had served on the Electoral Commission and against Bayard in particular. Bayard refused to respond to the attacks. He took the attitude, "If I really possess the confidence and good will of the American people, such attacks, if unjust, will not weaken me, and if they should show me to be really assailable, then it will be better I should be gotten out of the way. . . ."

Bayard's hard-money policy aroused the opposition of the West, which was again in a ferment of greenback and cheap-silver agitation. The westerners had their own candidates, both soft-money, in Senators Thomas A. Hendricks and Allen G. Thurman. Hendricks was the stronger of the two because he controlled Indiana. Tilden had carried the state by a plurality of 5,000 votes. A combination of the Hoosier State's 15 electoral votes, New York's 35 and the South's 138 would give the Democrats victory by a margin of 3 electoral votes. William H. English, a wealthy banker, former congressman, and Bayard supporter, suggested that Indiana could be won for Bayard if the Senator would agree to co-operate with Hendricks and compromise their differences. A Tilden-Hendricks ticket had worked in 1876; a Bayard-Hendricks combination would be the ideal ticket for 1880.

Bayard rejected the suggestion. "As for the political field," he wrote, "I know not what to say excepting this—that I shall take all my wounds in front (if I am to get any) and not be struck by a stray bullet by dodging." He would fight and win as a straight-out, hard-money man, or he would not win at all.

General Winfield Scott Hancock had been the southern candidate in 1868, with no opinions whatever on financial policy. Because Bayard's inflexible money position made him unacceptable to the West, many Democrats, especially in the South, wondered aloud if it might not be wise to revive their 1868 strategy and unite on the imposing figure of the General.

So strong were the crosscurrents in the Democratic Party early in 1880 that it was impossible to foretell with any confidence who might eventually emerge as the party nominee. None of the leading contenders seemed likely to sweep the convention, and out of the confusion came a host of minor candidates. Samuel J. Randall, Speaker of the House, put himself forward as Tilden's heir, an act many thought inconsiderate, since Tilden was still very much alive politically. Henry B. Payne, congressman from Ohio, was mentioned should Tilden decide to pass his strength on to someone else. Payne was hampered by the fact that his own delegation would be firmly committed to Senator Thurman.

Congressman William R. Morrison of Illinois, best known for his long fight for tariff reduction, was advanced as a favorite son, and Stephen J. Field of California, Associate Justice of the Supreme Court, had appeal for those who believed his position on the bench placed him above factional strife. Another name considered was that most reluctant of candidates, Horatio Seymour. He was deluged with requests to be a candidate, particularly from Democrats who hoped he could heal the wounds caused by the Tilden-Tammany battle. The seventy-year-old Seymour, however, made it perfectly plain that he would, under no circumstances, be a candidate, and his name was soon dropped from speculation.

In the remaining weeks before the Democrats gathered in Cincinnati, the entire situation remained extremely uncertain. No one knew if Tilden was an active candidate or if he wished a courtesy nomination and the right to name his heir. As always, the shrewd invalid played a devious game; neither his supporters nor his enemies were certain of his actual intentions. Bayard, Hancock, Hendricks, and Thurman were active candidates, but no one, including the candidates, had any idea of what their exact strength was.

It was not only a confused convention that gathered in Cincinnati June 22, 1880—it was also close to being an apathetic one. No giants appeared to struggle in mighty battle, as had been the case in Chicago; no great leader dominated the thinking of the delegates. There were no burning issues to inflame the passions; in fact, the only passions apparent were generated by personal vendettas. Soft-money *vs.* hard-money was an old and tired issue in Democratic gatherings, and, while it might cause or prevent a nomination, it no longer aroused the enthusiasm of 1868. Somebody had to be the nominee, but on June 22, no one really seemed to care who it was.

Tilden remained the enigma of the convention. On June 18,

he wrote a letter, which he entrusted to the care of Daniel Manning, hinting that his health might not permit him to accept the nomination. The letter, long and inconclusive, recapitulated Tilden's career and described how he had been deprived of the presidency by the perfidy of the Electoral Commission. He stated that he had worn himself out in the service of his country and desired nothing more than to be allowed to lay down the honors and toils of party leadership. What were his bewildered delegates to make of such a letter? To some it meant that he was refusing the nomination, to others it appeared a subtle bid to force the Convention to right the wrongs of 1876 by demanding his nomination. To Daniel Manning it was clear that Tilden wanted the nomination; to William Whitney it was equally clear that he desired to withdraw and secure the nomination for Henry Payne. Whatever the intent of the letter, the majority of the New York delegation decided to take it as a withdrawal from the race.

William Whitney summarized the muddled situation in a talk with a reporter. He criticized Tilden's ambiguous methods of treating his supposed candidacy and continued, "Well, those methods have lost the game. Mr. Tilden cannot be nominated in this convention. And in the uncertainty and doubt, he cannot name the candidate. It looks to me like Hancock, though Bayard seems to be running up with him. But we will take care that Mr. Bayard, after his course in the Senate four years ago, does not get a two-thirds vote. We're strong enough to kill if we are not strong enough to win." If one of Tilden's chief lieutenants took such a gloomy view of the confusion, what could be expected from the average delegate?

On the second day of the convention, it was necessary to settle the vexing question of the New York delegation. Tammany had bolted the state convention—which had named a Tilden delegation —and had sent its own contesting delegation to the convention. If Tilden were nominated, John Kelly threatened, Tammany would bolt the national convention too. The majority report of the credentials committee recommended that the regular delegation be seated; a minority report asked that the Tildenites be given 50 votes and the Tammany contingent 20. After an acrimonious debate, the convention voted, by 457 to 205½, to seat the Tilden delegation.

The vote was not so much an indication of support for Tilden as a rebuke to the divisive threats of Tammany.

John W. Stevenson, former senator and Governer of Kentucky, was chosen permanent chairman, and the convention proceeded to the nominating speeches while awaiting the platform. The first candidate, Judge Field, was offered as a "child of the Great West" who would "sweep California like the winds that blow through her golden gates."

George Gray of Delaware presented Bayard. In his praise, Mr. Gray asserted, "His name and record are known wherever our flag floats, aye, wherever the English tongue is spoken"—a statement that might have occasioned surprise in some of the more remote outposts of the Empire. The speech impressed the delegates, and Bayard support began to solidify.

In presenting William R. Morrison, the speaker blithely managed to antagonize the southern delegates by glowingly comparing his candidate to Lincoln—a tactless comparison, at best, in a Democratic convention. Thomas A. Hendricks and Allen G. Thurman were then placed in nomination. When New York was called, there was a moment of drama, as many cries for Tilden came from the crowd, but the chairman of the delegation announced that he had no nomination to make. For the first time, it was certain that Tilden was, after all, out of the race.

When the clerk reached Pennsylvania, the chairman announced that the delegation had no candidate to offer, but an individual delegate wished to make a nomination. Daniel Dougherty took the platform to offer "the name of one who, on the field of battle, was styled 'the superb,'" Winfield Scott Hancock. He concluded by saying, "If elected he will take his seat." Hancock's nomination stirred the crowd to the first real enthusiasm of the convention. A great shout greeted Dougherty's last remark, and the galleries were especially noisy in their acclaim for the soldier candidate.

After the clamor subsided, Wade Hampton took the platform to second Bayard's nomination. "We know that if elected, he too would take his place, for he is as brave as Hancock." It was a final effort to stem the inroads Hancock was making on Bayard's southern support.

A motion to adjourn was defeated 395½ to 317½, and the roll

was called for the first ballot. Votes were cast for nineteen individuals: Hancock 171, Bayard 153½, Henry D. Payne 81, Thurman 68½, Field 65, Morrison 62, Hendricks 49½, Tilden 38, Thomas Ewing of Ohio 10, Seymour 8, Randall 6, William Loveland of Colorado 5, Senator Joseph McDonald of Indiana 3, General George McClellan 2, and 1 each for Joel Parker, Jeremiah S. Black, Hugh Jewett, and James E. English. With 492 votes needed for nomination, it was anybody's race, and the convention adjourned for the night.

During the inevitable strategy sessions during the night of June 23, the New York delegation, which had cast its vote for the Ohio millionaire, Henry B. Payne—as William Whitney had insisted Tilden wanted them to do—decided to switch to Speaker Randall. It was hoped that the confusion caused by Tilden's apparent withdrawal could be overcome by a dramatic move to the Speaker of the House, rallying the disorganized Tilden forces to his standard.

Before the balloting began the next morning, Tilden's ambiguous letter was read to the convention, and it was announced that, since its "honored leader" had renounced any claim to the nomination, New York was for Randall. The mention of Tilden's name brought a storm of cheers and applause from the assembled delegates and spectators, but if Tilden had hoped his letter would stampede the convention, it failed in its purpose. The cheers were a valediction to the candidate of 1876, not a vindication.

At the conclusion of the second roll call, the unofficial vote stood: Hancock 310, Randall 128½, Bayard 112, Field 66½, Thurman 50, Hendricks 31, English 19, Tilden 6, Parker 2, and Jewett 1. Randall's surprisingly strong showing indicated that, if the Speaker had had Tilden's official backing earlier, the convention might have united behind him. But the attempt to name an heir came much too late.

As soon as the states had reported their votes, Wisconsin changed its vote to lead a stampede for Hancock—exactly as it had done in Chicago for Garfield. New Jersey and Pennsylvania thereupon switched to Hancock the Superb. "Every delegate was on his feet, and the roar of ten thousand voices completely drowned the full military band in the gallery." The official tally on the second ballot read: Hancock 705, Hendricks 30, Bayard 2, Tilden 1.

It was assumed that New York, having accepted Hancock's

nomination with good grace, could be considered safe for November. It remained to ensure the support of Indiana. Consequently, William H. English, the banker whose qualifications were entirely geographic, was unanimously named the vice-presidential candidate.

The final comment on the convention and on Tilden's enigmatic role came from William Whitney. "Yes," he told a reporter, "it has gone as I foresaw, but not as I hoped. . . . Tilden wasn't out even when he wrote that letter. No, that letter was written to be read to the convention, and Tilden believed that if it had been, the convention would have been swept into a stampede for him. It was a cunning thing. If the convention was determined to nominate someone else, as appeared to be the case, then the result would go down in history as the consequence of Tilden's withdrawal. If in the reading of the letter in the convention it had had the effect intended, then history would say that the party refused to let him withdraw." For once the Sage of Gramercy Park had proved too clever by half, and by his very cunning he lost his last chance to vindicate the fraud of 1876.

CHAPTER 5

"His turn has come"

THE EIGHTH REPUBLICAN NATIONAL CONVENTION
Chicago, June 3, 1884

On July 2, 1881 Charles J. Guiteau, a disappointed and mentally unbalanced office-seeker, shot and mortally wounded President Garfield. The assassin exclaimed, "I am a Stalwart and Arthur is President now." Garfield died on September 19, and Arthur was, indeed, President.

Arthur was expected to be nothing more than a tool for the Stalwarts, his chief claim to fame that he was undoubtedly the best dressed president in history. But the stout *bon vivant* surprised his party and the nation. During Garfield's brief administration, Senator Conkling had entered into a patronage battle with the President and, to strengthen his hold on the New York machine, had dramatically resigned to be re-elected, he thought, by the state legislature. But Lord Roscoe had overextended himself. Even the Stalwarts were weary of Conkling's high-handed methods, and the New York legislature rejected his bid for re-election. Conkling was dead on the field of battle, and Chester Allen Arthur was the leader, not the tool, of the Stalwarts.

Arthur put his new power to good use. He proved an able, decisive president, devoted to, of all things, civil-service reform. He refused to bow to partisan pressure and resisted demands that he replace Garfield-appointed Half-Breeds with Stalwarts. He encouraged reform legislation, filled his office with dignity, and conducted an efficient, scandal-free administration.

The President, wanting to serve a term in his own right, made himself available for the nomination in 1884. But his devotion to civil-service reform had alienated the Stalwarts without winning Half-Breed support. Arthur had made enemies of his friends without changing his enemies into friends. The sweeping Democratic victories in the mid-term elections of 1882 were taken by the party leaders as a repudiation of the administration and proof that Arthur could not be elected to a full term in his own right.

With the Stalwarts disgusted and the Half-Breeds in open opposition, Arthur might have sought support from the third force in the party: the Independents. But the reformers, always quick to condemn in the name of virtue, could not forget that Arthur had been a machine politician. They suspected that his good reform record was the result of making a virtue of necessity, and they expected at any moment to see the spots reappear on the leopard. The Independents turned to Edmunds, and Arthur was left with only scattered support, principally among federal office-holders.

Once again, James G. Blaine was the leading candidate for the nomination. He had resigned as Secretary of State after Garfield's death but had remained in Washington and in the public eye. Blaine took the stance of a reluctant candidate. He appeared not to be greatly interested in the nomination and suggested as possible candidates such men as Senator Allison of Iowa, Benjamin Harrison of Indiana, and Shelby Cullom of Illinois. It was noted that he only suggested candidates whose prospects were absolutely hopeless. In the preconvention period, Blaine humorously remarked that, while he did not expect to be nominated, "I am disturbing the calculation of others at an astonishing rate."

The chief opposition to Blaine came from the reformers. The dislike was mutual. The Plumed Knight detested and mistrusted the Independents. In 1880, he had described them as "noisy but not numerous, pharisaical but not practical, ambitious but not wise, pretentious but not powerful." The Independents vowed to do everything possible to prevent Blaine's nomination, and some even threatened to back Arthur as the lesser of two evils.

None of the other candidates could seriously hope to compete

against Blaine and Arthur. The choice of the Independents, Senator
Edmunds, came from a small state and was neither widely known
nor popular. The same held true for Senator Joseph Hawley, Connecticut's favorite son. John Sherman was willing, but his defeat
in 1880 had eliminated him from consideration. General Logan of
Illinois and Postmaster General Walter Gresham of Indiana were
unable to draw support from any states but their own. The one
potential candidate who might have shown real strength was General Sherman. In spite of his wife's Catholicism, his war record
made him a popular choice as a compromise candidate, but the
victor of Atlanta was more than content to leave presidential ambitions to his brother. In his famous refusal to run if nominated or
to serve if elected, he effectively removed his name from the list
of candidates.

The convention met in Chicago on Tuesday, June 3, and Blaine
suffered a setback at the outset. The Republican National Committee had proposed a Blaine man for temporary chairman, but the
anti-Blaine forces, led by Henry Cabot Lodge, offered the Negro
statesman John R. Lynch. Backed by the Arthur, Edmunds, and
Logan forces, Lynch was elected temporary chairman, 424 to 384.
The anti-Blaine forces were jubilant, but they overestimated the
importance of the vote. Many delegates who supported Lynch were
not necessarily anti-Blaine. The Logan forces, for instance, voted
for Lynch to conciliate the Negro vote and to convince Blaine's
managers of their importance for future ballots.

The convention was, after this opening skirmish, a remarkably
tame and harmonious affair. The permanent chairman, John B.
Henderson of Missouri, was chosen without contest, and the platform, presented by William McKinley of Ohio, was adopted without
discussion and without a roll-call.

Six men were placed in nomination: Joseph Hawley, John
Sherman, John A. Logan, Chester A. Arthur, James G. Blaine, and
George Edmunds. The prevailing sentiment of the convention was
expressed by Tom Platt, who buried the hatchet of the Stalwart-
Half-Breed feud by seconding Blaine's nomination. "I second this
nomination, believing as I do, that his turn has come; believing
as I do, that expediency and justice demand it; believing as I do,

that the Republican people of the Republican states that must give the Republican majorities want him." The juxtaposition of expediency and justice should have satisfied the most discriminating politician. Blaine's turn had come, and not even the Stalwarts were seriously prepared to challenge him.

There were some in the convention who hoped to find a combination that would disprove Platt's statement. Unfortunately, no compromise candidate could be agreed upon. Mark Hanna and the young Theodore Roosevelt, both getting their first taste of national-convention politics, tried without success to start a boom for John Sherman. The Arthur men refused to consider any other candidate, and the Edmunds forces, although inclined to Arthur as a means of stopping Blaine, were too independent to be transferred as a bloc to any candidate. Senator Hoar and George William Curtis tried to stir up enthusiasm for General Sherman but without success.

The first ballot for the nomination ran much as had been expected. With 411 necessary for nomination, the results were Blaine 334½, Arthur 278, Edmunds 93, Logan 63½, Sherman 30, Hawley 13, Robert T. Lincoln 4, and General Sherman 2. One hundred ninety-six of Arthur's votes came from the South, a region the Republicans could not hope to carry in November. He received 31 votes from New York, 11 from Pennsylvania, and 40 from scattered sources. Blaine's vote included only his own state of Maine and 1 Massachusetts vote among the New England delegations, but he received votes from every other delegation except Georgia.

On the second ballot, Blaine gained slightly to a total of 349. Arthur had 276, Edmunds 85, Logan 61, Sherman 28, Hawley 13, Lincoln 4, General Sherman 3.

On the third ballot, Blaine rose to 375, while Arthur had 274. At the end of the ballot, Joseph B. Foraker of Ohio, Sherman's manager, moved adjournment, but the Blaine forces voted him down.

When Illinois was called on the fourth ballot, Shelby Cullom attempted to read a telegram from Logan withdrawing in favor of Blaine. He was ruled out of order but cast the Illinois vote: Blaine 34, Logan 6, Arthur 3. Foraker, "in the interest of the party," withdrew John Sherman and cast Ohio's 46 votes for the Plumed Knight. The final count read: Blaine 541, Arthur 207, Edmunds 41, Hawley 15, Logan 7, Lincoln 2.

At the evening session, General Logan, having given victory to Blaine, was rewarded with the vice-presidential nomination. The ticket was balanced betwen Half-Breed and Stalwart, and the party, with the exception of the Independents, seemed satisfied with its choice.

"They love him most of all for the enemies he has made"

THE FOURTEENTH DEMOCRATIC NATIONAL CONVENTION
Chicago, July 8, 1884

The rise of Grover Cleveland in national politics was the most rapid ascent of any political career in the history of the nation. He emerged from the obscurity of private life to become President of the United States in only four years. In 1880, Cleveland was a prosperous lawyer in Buffalo, New York, who had served as sheriff and been defeated for district attorney. Nominated as a reform candidate for mayor of Buffalo in that year, he was, with independent help, elected by a substantial margin. His record as mayor so impressed the leaders of the state Democracy that they gave him the nomination for governor in 1882.

Alonzo Cornell was standing for re-election, but the collapse of the Conkling machine, as well as a widespread desire for reform, elected Cleveland by a landslide. He proved himself as impressive in Albany as he had been in Buffalo. He secured passage of and firmly administered civil-service laws, a bill creating a bureau of labor, and the Theodore Roosevelt reform bills reorganizing the government of the City of New York. He made free use of the veto power, demonstrating a disregard for political advantage and a high sense of the duty and obligations of the state and its officials.

Cleveland's impressive record as governor was due more to an enormous capacity for hard work and common sense than to any

101

special intellectual brilliance. A contemporary described him: "He represented the practical, everyday, usual citizen of moderate means and no very marked ambitions, a combination of the business man and the unimportant professional person, blunt, hard-headed, brusque, and unimaginative." But his blunt desire to serve the people made a greater impression than the smoother manners and intellectual superiority of many of his more flexible political colleagues. His honesty was as imposing as his bulk, and his energy and determination as bristling as his walrus moustache.

Cleveland might have remained Governor of New York, noted only for his industrious, somewhat stolid administration, had he not crossed swords with the rambunctious, ever-quarrelsome John Kelly of Tammany. The clash came when Cleveland prevented the re-election to the state Senate of Thomas Grady, one of Kelly's chief lieutenants. Honest John bitterly accused Cleveland of being the sole cause of Democratic dissatisfaction in New York County and of attempting to purge the inoffensive Grady from mean motives of spite and personal revenge. The Grand Sachem was on the warpath and intended to add Cleveland's scalp to his collection.

The break with Tammany became a national story and catapulted Cleveland into the front rank of Democratic aspirants for the nomination. The Tilden-Kelly fight had seemed nothing more than the battle of two wily politicians for power, but honest, deliberate Grover Cleveland appeared a stout knight doing fearless battle against machine politics. This picture caught the imagination of Democrats throughout the country and made Cleveland, only three years out of obscurity, the moral hero of reform.

There were, of course, other candidates. Senator Bayard was once again in the race, and Senator Hendricks, as always, was more than available should anyone ask. Indiana had a second candidate in Joseph E. MacDonald, who had lost his Senate seat to Benjamin Harrison. A working man who had risen in politics, he was popular with labor but suspected of leanings toward free trade. His candidacy was actually a blind for Hendricks, who would then be brought forward at the appropriate moment.

Ohio had three candidates: Allen G. Thurman, Henry Payne, and Governor George Hoadly. Thurman and Payne were not taken seriously, Thurman because of his age and Payne because of his connections with the Standard Oil Company and his lack of political experience. Governor Hoadly, however, was a stronger possibility. Originally a Republican, he had joined the Liberal Republicans in 1872 and then the Democrats. He had defeated Joseph B. Foraker for the governorship in 1883. All of the Ohio candidates were doubtful prospects, however, because their state could not be counted safe for the Democrats. Ohio held its congressional elections in October, and the party feared the possible psychological effects of failing to carry their candidate's home state a month before the presidential election.

Rosewell P. Flower of New York also fancied himself as presidential timber, but few agreed with him. A wealthy man, noted for his contributions to charity, he was thought to be a rich man amusing himself in politics. His only support came from Tammany, which hoped to embarrass Cleveland and split the delegation.

The oddest candidate to volunteer—no one had asked him—was Benjamin F. Butler of Massachusetts. The cock-eyed General, still known to many as "Beast" Butler in memory of his occupation of New Orleans during the war, had become a Democrat when Radical Republicanism ceased to offer a means of advancement. Throughout his stormy career, he had appeared in many roles, few of them completely reputable. He was an impudent opportunist willing to win a vote or make a dollar by any means he could get away with. Slipping into the Democratic Party by way of the Greenbackers, he had, thanks to the Democratic "tidal wave" of 1882, finagled his way into the governorship of Massachusetts. He hoped to promote something to his advantage by swaggering his way into the ranks of Democratic aspirants to the presidency.

In spite of the large field of active candidates, there were many Democrats who still hoped to see Samuel J. Tilden in the White House. In the Spring of 1884, Tilden received many letters asking him to make the race. "The people of every part of our broad country are of one voice and opinion," wrote Samuel J. Randall, "that you must be our candidate. You will have to yield, and I know you ought to do so." But Tilden was wracked by illness and could not possibly survive the ordeal of a campaign. When a young reporter called upon him, he was shocked to see Tilden, one eyelid drooping, one arm useless from a stroke, moving painfully with the aid of a cane. To the reporter's remark that he hoped he would be nominated, Tilden, his voice barely audible, replied, "My boy, don't you see it is impossible?" He added that he understood Hendricks wanted the old ticket of Tilden and Hendricks—"and I do not wonder, considering my weakness!"

Because Tilden was unable to enter the contest, Daniel Manning and William Whitney, his ablest lieutenants, prepared to move his machine over to Cleveland. To their embarrassment, Tilden refused to silence those who urged his candidacy. When the New York State Democratic Committee met in May to set the date for the state convention, Manning, as chairman, had no choice but to adjourn the committee subject to the call of the chair. Until Tilden made his decision nothing could be done.

Manning finally decided to hold the state convention at Saratoga on June 18. He journeyed to Graystone, Tilden's country home, to persuade the old leader to give way to a new. Manning informed Tilden that Cleveland had authorized him to give Tilden "any assurances he required in regard to the naming of Mr. Cleveland's cabinet should he be elected, and in regard to the conduct of his administration upon the lines of reform which had been traced by Mr. Tilden during and since his election as governor." After such assurances, which virtually ransomed a future Cleveland administration to the wily old politician of Graystone, Tilden, with a show of reluctance, agreed to publish a letter withdrawing from the contest, without actually declaring his support for Cleveland. But Manning arranged that the timing of the letter, which came just before the state convention would be interpreted as a tacit support of Cleveland's candidacy.

Manning wisely refrained from forcing a solid Cleveland delegation on the state convention. Because of Tammany's opposition, Flower's comic candidacy, and some delegates' hope that Tilden could still be induced to run, the state convention was far from unanimous in its choice of Cleveland. Manning conceded one delegate-at-large to the Flower group and half the delegates from New York County to Tammany. He was playing a ticklish game. Of the seventy-two delegates, twenty were in open opposition to Cleveland, and at least nine were doubtful. If John Kelly could make inroads on the remaining forty-three delegates, the unit rule might boomerang and be used against Cleveland.

To woo away some of the Cleveland reform delegates, John Kelly decided to back Senator Bayard. This support was less than welcome to some of Bayard's other adherents. For one thing, the Republican reformers bolted from Blaine, as they had threatened. At meetings in Boston and New York, the reformers, led by Carl Schurz, Charles Francis Adams, Leverett Saltonstall, and George William Curtis, denounced Blaine and called upon the Democrats to make a nomination they could support. The Mugwumps, as they were called, did not at first declare for any particular candidate, but it was understood that Bayard and Cleveland were acceptable, in that order. It was Carl Schurz who was most unhappy about Tammany's support of Bayard. "It would not be a good thing," he wrote the Delaware Senator, "for you to appear as the club with which Tammany killed Cleveland."

A week or so before the opening of the convention, John Kelly and Republican candidate Blaine sent representatives to Chicago to stir up opposition to Cleveland. Aware that the attitude of the press in a convention city could have an important influence on the delegates, Kelly dispatched Tom Grady to arouse prejudice in the Chicago press against his enemy. He had considerable success, and Manning was hard put to present the Cleveland side of the story.

Blaine, having decided that Cleveland would be his most formidable opponent, hatched an intrigue to kill him off in the convention. Working through Alexander Sullivan, President of the Irish National League, agents were sent to stir up Irish prejudice against Cleveland as an enemy of the race. He was represented as "a Presbyterian bigot" who bitterly opposed anything related to Catholicism. The untrue charges were a sinister portent of the scurrilous campaign to come. Manning countered this intrigue by sending two Irish Cleveland appointees and ex-Senator Francis Kernan to Chicago to put down the rumors that the Governor was anti-Catholic.

The Cleveland-Tammany feud was dramatized by the piecemeal arrival in Chicago of the New York delegation. At dawn on Sunday,

July 6, the New York County Democrats arrived with three brass
bands, their silver and gold Cleveland banners catching the first
morning light. Several hours later, two long trains steamed into the
city bearing Kelly and 700 white-hatted Tammany braves. The
third arrival brought the Tilden Democrats of Irving Hall and
their supporters. Manning arrived early and took charge of three
huge parlors in the Palmer House for headquarters. Over the
entrance hung a life-sized portrait of Cleveland in all his portly
glory.

The first order of business for Manning was to nail down a
majority of the New York delegation. His confident manner belied
the fact that he was 2 votes short. The two doubtful delegates were
alternately cajoled and pressured to commit themselves to Cleveland. On the morning of the caucus to determine how New York
would vote, the two delegates disappeared. Scouting parties were
hastily organized, the two fugitives located and hurried into conference. One was promised the nomination of a state office, and
both delegates emerged from the conference solid Cleveland men.
What methods of persuasion were used on the other delegate has
never been reported. One assumes it was commensurate with the
importance of his ballot.

When Manning clinched control of New York for Cleveland,
"Fire and smoke burst from the nostrils of Tammany." Grady and
Bourke Cockran paced the lobby of their hotel raging like lions,
and Kelly was almost maniacal. He swore that the Knights of
Labor controlled 700,000 votes, all hostile to Cleveland, and that
New York was surely lost to the Democrats. Rage as they might,
the Tammany braves had been outflanked, and New York was safe
for Cleveland.

Bayard's candidacy still posed a possible threat to Cleveland.
Bayard men thronged the lobby of the Palmer House wearing
white hats decorated with tiny blue feathers and badges decorated
with blue hens. When a furious argument broke out between a
Tammany brave and a Cleveland delegate, the delighted Bayard
men interrupted with happy shouts of "Bayard! Bayard! Harmonize
on Bayard!"

The Bayard movement gained momentum when Senator Beck
announced the support of Kentucky once the delegation voted, on

its first ballot instructions, for Speaker of the House John Carlisle. Ex-Senator Henry Davis of West Virginia, Senator McPherson of New Jersey, and Perry Belmont, New York congressman and son of the powerful August Belmont, also announced their support of Bayard.

But the same reasons that had prevented his nomination in 1880 continued to work against him. Many delegates feared that Blaine and Logan would wave the bloody shirt and exploit the Dover speech to good effect. Colonel Morrison of Illinois remarked, "There's a heap more Bayard men among the delegates than will ever vote for him." Congressman Stevens summed up the situation. "No man has a higher admiration for Bayard than I. I believe if he were President his Administration would be one in which every American citizen would take pride. I believe he is a patriot, but it would be a suicidal attempt to nominate him. His Dover speech would be sent into every household in the North." Bayard is a classic example from that long list of distinguished statesmen who, eminently fitted for the highest office, are forever kept from the winners' circle by the necessities of practical politics—at least the necessities as interpreted by practical politicians.

Bayard also had problems with the Mugwumps. When Schurz sent Bayard yet another warning that the Mugwumps would not support a candidate whose nomination represented a victory for Tammany, his long patience snapped. With some asperity, he noted, "The logical result of Schurz' statement is to destroy the independence of any Candidate who does not submit to the Independents. If by advocating me, Tammany can drive the Independents from my support, the latter had better change their name as they will have wholly abandoned their public professions." The Mugwump refusal to combine with Tammany for a common goal made it practically impossible to nominate Bayard.

Of the other candidates, Edmunds had only minor Independent support and could hope only for a prolonged deadlock. Randall's protectionist sentiments were unacceptable to the West, and John G. Carlisle's low-tariff views were anathema to the East. Thurman was approaching senility, MacDonald had no support outside of Indiana, and Hendricks had presented himself as a candidate too many times to be much thought of. Ben Butler was completely unacceptable to the South. To make himself as conspicuous as possible, Butler delivered a rabble-rousing speech from a window of the Palmer House, prompting one disgusted Georgia delegate to exclaim, "We may be willing to eat crow, but we'll be damned if we'll eat turkey buzzard."

The convention was called to order at noon on July 8, and Governor Richard B. Hubbard of Texas took the rostrum as temporary chairman. He had hardly finished the customary plea for reform and harmony when a conflict erupted on the floor. It would not have been a true Democratic convention if Tammany had not made trouble. The braves lived up to expectations.

When the rules were proposed, Tammany offered an amendment that would, in effect, have abolished the unit rule. It was no coincidence that New York was the only delegation so bound. If the amendment were accepted, Tammany would be freed from the necessity of voting for Cleveland.

The battle, as would be expected with Tammany leading it, was long, loud, and bitter. The galleries shouted encouragement, and orators poured forth a torrent of words defending majority rights, minority rights, the rights of state conventions, district conventions, precedent, innovation, and anything else they could think of. Out of the flood of verbiage, the most startling statement from Tammany went unnoticed. Bourke Cockran pointed out that the unit rule "has always been a potent device by which political managers and political engineers have sought to give a false expression to the opinion of the voters of the State and pervert rather than express their voice upon the floor of a deliberative body." It was surprising to hear Tammany admit it, but, after all, who should know better?

The amendment was defeated by a vote of 463 to 332. The majority consisted of nearly all the Cleveland strength plus substantial Bayard support from Maryland, Missouri, Kentucky, and other southern states. Ironically, Tammany, bound by the very rule it was trying to abolish, was recorded as a unit with the New York delegation against the amendment. Bayard's home state of Delaware voted solidly for Tammany's amendment, as did Hendricks's Indiana and the Thurman supporters from Nevada. This first test of strength showed the anti-Cleveland forces to be in a very poor condition to combine against him.

On the second day—the platform not being ready—the convention installed William F. Vilas of Wisconsin as permanent chairman and proceeded to the nominating speeches. Bayard was first to be nominated. Thomas A. Hendricks then nominated MacDonald with a speech designed to place the speaker, not the candidate, in the most favorable light. Everything Hendricks said in behalf of MacDonald could equally be applied to himself. The seconding speeches needed only a change of names to be seconding speeches for Hendricks.

After Thurman and Carlisle were nominated, Mayor Carter H. Harrison of Chicago moved, "on behalf of ten thousand hungry and five thousand thirsty people," that the convention recess until evening. The chairman, apparently neither hungry nor thirsty, ruled the motion out of order, and the speeches went on.

The speeches so far had met with little more than perfunctory enthusiasm. Everyone was waiting for the major nomination. Daniel N. Lockwood of New York mounted the platform to present the name of Grover Cleveland. The speech was brief and disappointingly undramatic. It presented the New York governor's qualifications and made no reference to the split in his delegation. This intentional oversight was immediately corrected. After the first seconding speech, Tom Grady arose to denounce Cleveland and, through a mounting uproar from the floor and galleries, gave his reasons why Cleveland could not carry New York. He had a difficult time finishing his speech and was followed by Bourke Cockran, who had to shout his denunciations over the continuous protests of the audience. He said his feeling toward Cleveland was that of "too warm a friend of his to desire his promotion to an office for which I do not believe he has the mental qualifications." Neither Grady nor Cockran actually suggested another candidate, so their speeches were recorded as seconding speeches for Cleveland, albeit rather odd ones. The convention, disgusted with the Tammany attacks, voted to suspend the roll-call and adjourn for the night.

On the third day, Governor George Hoadly of Ohio and Samuel

J. Randall were nominated. The events of the previous night still rankled in the minds of many delegates, and the answer to Tammany was given by Edward S. Bragg of Wisconsin as he seconded Cleveland. Speaking for the young men of Wisconsin, Bragg, referring to Cleveland, turned his wrath on Tammany. "They love him gentlemen, and they respect him, not only for himself, for his character, for his integrity and judgement and iron will, but they love him most of all for the enemies he has made." The galleries exploded, and Grady's face was contorted with rage. Kelly rushed to the foot of the platform, bawling, "Mr. Chairman, on behalf of his enemies I reciprocate that sentiment, and we are proud of the compliment." As Bragg continued his attack, a voice shouted, "Give them a little more grape, Capt. Bragg." Observers later commented that, if the galleries had been turned loose at that moment, the lives of Kelly and the other braves would have been in danger.

Before presenting the platform at the evening session, the platform committee offered a very significant resolution dealing with the national chairman. Customarily, the national chairman was selected from the ranks of the Democratic National Committee, usually with an eye to his wealth and the wealth of his friends. His chief function was fund raising. But political parties were becoming more complex, and campaigns needed more than money from the national chairman. It was upon the knowledge, prudence, and skill of the chairman that the success of a campaign depended. The platform committee proposed "that the National Democratic Committee be not restricted in its selection of a Chairman to the members of the Committee." The resolution was significant because it took the power out of the hands of the wealthy patron and put it in the hands of professional politicians.

The first ballot for the presidential nomination gave Cleveland 392 votes, with 547 necessary to nominate. Bayard had 170 votes, Thurman 88, Randall 78, MacDonald 56, Carlisle 27, Flower 4, Hoadly 3, and Hendricks and Tilden 1 each. The Cleveland men were jubilant. Believing they could win easily, they clamored for an immediate second ballot. Daniel Manning, however, was not to be rushed. He observed that many of the older delegates, due to the lateness of the hour, had left the hall. He was afraid that their absence would reduce Cleveland's total on the second ballot. He therefore decided to press for adjournment. "We'll have a full house and an increased vote tomorrow morning."

After adjournment, Manning moved to ensure that increase in the morning. Pennsylvania had cast 55 votes for Randall and 5 for Cleveland. Manning met Randall in Alexander P. McClure's hotel room at an early morning hour. He promised the former Speaker the control of patronage in his state in return for his votes. The bargain was made, and Pennsylvania was pledged to Cleveland.

Ben Butler, John Kelly, and Thomas A. Hendricks met that night to plan their own strategy. They sent for Dick Bright of Indiana, the sergeant-at-arms, and instructed him to pack the galleries at the morning session with men who, either from conviction or for cash, would be willing to cheer for Hendricks. Bright withdrew all the tickets that had been issued for the galleries and instructed the door-keepers to recognize only bearers of new tickets, which he had hurriedly printed and placed in the hands of Hendricks men.

The plan was that, when Illinois was called on the roll and the delegate who had cast the lone Hendricks vote did so again, the Indiana Senator would enter the hall by a door beside the speakers' platform. He would thus come face to face with the convention at the precise moment that his name was called. His entrance would be the signal for the galleries to begin a demonstration, which, it was hoped, would stampede the delegates for the old veteran.

Unfortunately for the conspirators, Manning got wind of the plot and spent the rest of the night sending messengers to every member of the convention apprising them of what was planned and warning them not to be taken in by the spurious demonstration. The demonstration occurred as planned, but the cheers were confined to the gallery. On the floor, only Tammany joined the cries of "Hendricks! Hendricks!" Although warned, Governor Waller of Connecticut responded to the cry and jumped to his feet shouting wildly for recognition. Before the chair noticed him, Senator Barnum and another delegate leaped over a row of startled delegates and pulled the excited Governor to his chair. He quietly subsided along with the demonstration.

At the end of the manufactured demonstration, Indiana withdrew MacDonald and cast its vote for Hendricks. Illinois, however, gave an additional 10 votes to Cleveland, and a genuine ovation erased any possible effects the Hendricks demonstration might have had. At the end of the second ballot, the vote stood: Cleveland 475, Bayard 151½, Hendricks 123½, Thurman 60, Randall 5, MacDonald and Tilden 2 each.

As had happened when a winner was in sight in 1880, the South abandoned Bayard. North Carolina was the first to switch, followed rapidly by Virginia and Georgia. Florida, Maryland, and Texas climbed aboard the bandwagon, and the switch of Missouri clinched the nomination.

A large floral anchor surmounted by an eagle with Cleveland's name on the base appeared on the platform, the cannons were fired on the lake front, and, as usual, the convention went wild with enthusiasm. The results were hardly surprising, but the delegates cheered anyway. The final results of the ballot were Cleveland 683, Bayard 81½, Hendricks 45½, Thurman 4, Randall 4, MacDonald 2.

The convention adjourned briefly and then selected the vice-presidential candidate. Pennsylvania, over Indiana's protests, offered Hendricks, who became the unanimous choice of the convention. A perennial candidate since 1868, once deprived of the vice-presidency in 1876, Hendricks was finally to win that office. Within a year of his election he was dead.

CHAPTER 6

"You have nominated a pocket handkerchief"

THE FIFTEENTH DEMOCRATIC NATIONAL CONVENTION
St. Louis, June 5, 1888

The election of Grover Cleveland to the presidency marked the transition from one political era to another. The struggle for reform, which had so long dominated American politics, was won. Since 1872, the reformers had been intent on purifying the processes of government and improving its traditional functions. Honesty and efficiency, rather than innovation, were the aims of the reformers. Cleveland was the ideal reform president. Of limited imagination but great earnestness and industry, he was perfectly suited to bring to fruition the aims of reform and to establish a solid base for the innovations of the future.

Of all the Cleveland reforms, the most important was the decision to revise the tariff—a decision that would become the overriding issue in 1888. The protective tariff was the government's most important source of revenue, and, by 1886, the Treasury had a surplus of nearly $94,000,000, with every prospect of an increased surplus each year. The government and the business community became seriously worried over so much money being kept out of circulation, and because the concept of governmental expansion into welfare fields had not yet been introduced, all plans concerning the surplus involved reducing the revenue, rather than increasing expenditures. Consequently, the President made up his mind that the only way to deal with the surplus was to reduce the tariff by an average of 7%, with several items, most importantly wool and woolen goods, being placed on the free list. The greatest burden of tariff reduction fell on the industrial North, and Congress leaped to defend the protected interests when the Mills Tariff Bill was presented.

The debate in Congress began on April 17, 1888, and continued well into the summer, after both parties had held their conventions. The issue having thus been left open was to influence the selection of candidates and become the central issue of the election.

The Democratic Party that prepared to renominate Grover Cleveland was a different party from the one that had first tendered him the nomination. Most of the old leaders were gone. Tilden, Seymour, Vice-President Hendricks, and the rambunctious John Kelly of Tammany were dead. Thurman was in doddering retirement, and Bayard, as Secretary of State had been removed from active politics. Only William Whitney, Secretary of the Navy, was still active. Among the new leaders, of whom Secretary of the Interior William F. Vilas and Senator Gorman of Maryland were especially prominent, only Governor David Hill of New York was not firmly committed to the renomination of the President.

From a practical point of view, opposition to Cleveland in the convention was unthinkable. To substitute any other candidate would be a repudiation of the first Democratic administration in nearly a quarter of a century. In spite of this political reality, for a time the protectionists and the, as usual, disgruntled Tammany men hoped to find another candidate. The skillful, if slightly sinister, governor of New York, David B. Hill, had been Cleveland's lieutenant-governor and had succeeded to the governorship upon Cleveland's election to the presidency. He became the leader of the New York Democracy by winning a term in his own right in 1885. Never scrupulous about methods when an advantage was to be gained, Hill ruled New York by adroitness and intellectual force. He was a practical, cold, brilliant, domineering man who dearly wanted to be President of the United States. As soon as he had taken his oath as governor, he began wooing the protectionists and dissident Tammany elements in the party.

Hill's plans to challenge Cleveland were quickly forestalled by

William Whitney and his assistant, Daniel Lamont. The pro-Cleveland newspapers launched such an attack on Hill's ambitions that his re-election as governor became doubtful. Whitney and Lamont worked so efficiently that, when the New York delegation was chosen, it was not only solidly pledged to Cleveland, but Governor Hill was pointedly omitted from the delegation. Hill's brief rebellion was over, and the convention prepared to tender the nomination to Cleveland by acclamation.

The convention met on June 5, 1888, in St. Louis, Missouri. It was, for the Democrats, a most unusual gathering. As the official proceedings reported, "Entire harmony prevailed throughout the sessions of the Convention."

The only disruption to the "entire harmony" came over the platform, which was to be presented on the third day. Cleveland, not wanting to be left open to Republican charges of favoring free trade, prepared a tariff plank which endorsed his proposed tariff revisions in moderate language. The plank was entrusted to Senator Gorman. That shrewd gentlemen felt it would be bad politics to force the plank upon the resolutions committee as the President's will, so he casually showed it to Robert Randall, the boss of Pennsylvania, implying that it represented only Gorman's views. Randall agreed to the plank but warned "the Cleveland crowd will kick."

It was not for the Cleveland crowd to kick. A group of low-tariff enthusiasts, led by Henry Watterson, put up a fight for a stronger plank. Gathered in a hot, airless room at the Southern Hotel, the committee battled all night. Reporters crowding around the closed door of the committee room heard Watterson talking on and on, pleading against the sacrifice of principle for expediency. At last the committee agreed to compromise, and the compromises were all in Watterson's favor.

The platform reaffirmed the tariff plank of 1884, which had pledged revision, approved as correct Democratic doctrine Cleveland's proposals, and, by special resolution, endorsed the Mills Bill then being debated in Congress. A somewhat stronger plank than Cleveland had wanted, it was nevertheless mild enough to take the sting out of any free-trade charges. Referring to the enormous surplus lying idle in the Treasury, the platform contrasted, in charges amusing to modern ears, the difference between the Democratic and Republican approaches to federal spending. "The remedy of the Republican party is to meet and exhaust by extravagant appropriations and expenditures, whether constitutional or not, the accumulations of extravagant taxation. The Democratic remedy is to enforce frugality in public expense and abolish needless taxation."

Three names were placed in nomination for the vice-presidency: Governor Isaac Gray of Indiana, Commissioner of Pensions John C. Black of Illinois, and the "Knight of the Red Bandanna," Allen G. Thurman of Ohio. Cleveland acquiesced in Thurman's candidacy, and he was nominated with 684 votes. Gray received 101 votes and Black 36. Thurman's nomination was a serious mistake. He was a greatly loved, almost revered figure in the party, but a tribute based on ancient victories would be of little help to the Democrats in the current battle. One delegate, when asked what he thought of the "bandanna" nomination, snorted, "I think you have nominated a pocket handkerchief!"

"I am a living and rejuvenated Republican"

THE NINTH REPUBLICAN NATIONAL CONVENTION
Chicago, June 19, 1888

James G. Blaine was, despite his defeat by Grover Cleveland, the leading candidate for the Republican nomination in 1888. The closeness of the popular vote in 1884—Cleveland had a margin of only 62,683 out of 10 million votes cast—and substantial Republican gains in the mid-term elections gave the Republicans every expectation of recapturing the White House. The party, considerably sobered by finding itself out of power for the first time in twenty-four years, turned almost defensively to the greatest name in the party.

Blaine's prospects were greatly increased when Cleveland sent his tariff message to Congress. Blaine was in Paris when he learned of the tariff proposals. He immediately issued a statement, which appeared in the newspapers the day following the accounts of the presidential message. Blaine declared himself in favor of high protection and, to deal with the Treasury surplus, suggested that the revenue tax on tobacco be repealed at once, before Christmas, as a present from the government to the smokers of America. He borrowed a Tilden proposal by advocating that the whiskey tax be used to fortify the Atlantic seaboard. The statement was a political masterpiece, offering as it did, in twenty lines, something for high protectionists, lovers of cheap tobacco, temperance advocates, supporters of coastal defense, and those who thought Cleveland a poor Democrat compared to Tilden.

Blaine's tariff stand delighted the Republicans. He had given them the issue with which they could follow him to victory. Then suddenly, Republican confidence turned to dismay. On February 12, 1888, Blaine, writing from Florence to the chairman of the Republican National Committee, declared that his name would not be presented to the convention.

The public letter of withdrawal was brief and offered no real explanation of Blaine's actions. In a private letter to a friend, Blaine had, a few days before his public announcement, given the reasons for his decision. He would not, he wrote, run "if a contest were required to secure my nomination. . . . I thought unanimity was required to give me the prestige and power for a successful canvass. I cannot say that I ever expected unanimity, and therefore it is that I withdraw without surprise, and certainly without regret. . . ." He went on to say that both John Sherman and Benjamin Harrison would be determined candidates and, "having once been nominated and defeated I cannot consent to be a 'claimant,' appealing to the party to 'try me again.'"

Once recovered from the initial shock of his withdrawal, Blaine's supporters refused to believe he was serious. He would, they said, not campaign actively, but he would accept a draft. In May, Blaine tried to discourage such thinking. "I could not accept it," he wrote Whitelaw Reid, "without leaving in the minds of thousands . . . the impression that I had not been free from indirection, and therefore I could not accept it at all."

Final as this closing of the door on any draft was, his supporters ignored it. Maine instructed its delegation to vote for Blaine. Others followed. By early June, 377 Blaine delegates, many under positive instructions, had been selected to the National Convention. Blaine might decline to run; his supporters intended to nominate him anyway.

The best known candidate actively to seek the nomination was the old perennial, John Sherman of Ohio, and in 1888 he had a real chance of winning. Many Republicans felt that, as Blaine's turn had come in 1884, it was now time to give Sherman the chance for which he had been waiting so long. Among other candidates,

Senator William B. Allison of Iowa had the support of the farm bloc, Judge Walter Gresham of Indiana was the Mugwump and liberal favorite, and Chauncy M. Depew, raconteur, attorney, and railroad president, was the choice of New York and the eastern financial interests. General and former Senator Benjamin Harrison of Indiana was a possible compromise choice, and General Russell A. Alger of Michigan, Senator Joseph R. Hawley of Connecticut, and William Walter Phelps of New Jersey were the leading favorite sons. Dark horses, but occasionally mentioned, were Congressman William McKinley of Ohio, ex-Governor Albert G. Porter of Indiana, and Governor Joseph Foraker of Ohio.

Foraker's dark-horse status posed a threat to Sherman's control of the Ohio delegation. In 1880, Sherman had attempted to remove a threat to his candidacy by forcing his potential rival, James A. Garfield, to head the Sherman delegation. The results were, of course, disastrous, and one would have thought that Sherman had learned his lesson. He had not. The strategy that had failed him in 1880 was to be used again in 1888 with equally damaging results.

The young, ambitious Governor Foraker was in his second term. Forty-one years old and a veteran of the war, he was a man with an enormous appreciation of his own talents. He was a controversial but popular executive who had gained national fame in 1887 when President Cleveland ordered that captured Confederate battle flags be returned to their respective states. The Governor bombastically proclaimed, "No rebel flags will be surrendered while I am governor." Promptly dubbed "Bloody Shirt" Foraker by his enemies, the Governor took full advantage of the publicity.

Foraker's rising popularity caused a serious rift between his supporters and the Sherman men in Ohio. Sherman decided the best way to control the Governor, whom he mistrusted, and at the same time turn Foraker's popularity to his own use, was to make him chairman of an Ohio delegation pledged to Sherman.

The Ohio state convention named a pro-Sherman delegation headed by Foraker with the industrialist Marcus A. Hanna as campaign manager. Foraker promised to support Sherman "as long as he had a button on his coat," but the Sherman men were convinced that he would try to steal the Senator's coat, buttons and all. Accordingly, they deliberately excluded him from all policy sessions. The Governor was furious at being reduced to the role of figurehead, and the Sherman-Foraker rift widened.

Benjamin Harrison, the Indiana candidate, was the grandson of the ninth President of the United States. Recently defeated for re-election to the Senate, the fifty-four year old Harrison was practicing law in Indianapolis. His chief presidential assets were his distinguished name, his residence in a doubtful state, and a personality so colorless he would be difficult to attack. Benjamin Harrison was not an ingratiating person. A puritanical austerity of manner discouraged any attempts at familiarity, and, although he was genial to his friends, his formal dignity gave the impression of cold indifference. In the Senate, he had cultivated few friendships and seldom spoke. Most of his senatorial colleagues were opposed to his nomination.

Unknown to Harrison, there were powerful influences working in his behalf. Blaine privately informed his former manager, Stephen Elkins, that he considered Harrison the most eligible candidate, and a Washington diplomat reported that Blaine "intends to be Secretary of State and to run Harrison for President." Elkins met Harrison while vacationing at Deer Park, Maryland, told him that he was presidential timber, and assured him that only Blaine's candidacy stood between him and the White House. After Blaine's withdrawal, Elkins wrote Harrison that he, rather than Sherman, could inherit the Blaine strength. Harrison replied that he was "not fired up much" over Elkins's suggestion. "My ambition is not very inflammable." He added that he still expected Blaine to be the candidate.

Harrison might not be "fired up," but Louis T. Michener, Indiana State Attorney General, was. He formed a Committee of Six to work for Harrison's nomination. Between February and May, 1888, the sextet collected funds, secured favorable editorials in newspapers throughout the country, obtained testimonials from business and labor, mailed thousands of Indiana newspapers into pivotal states, and organized clubs to promote the Harrison-for-President boom.

Harrison decided to lend a hand in publicizing his campaign by accepting an invitation to address the Michigan Club at its annual banquet. It was Harrison's first political speech in nearly a year. "I feel that I am at some disadvantage here tonight by reason of the fact that I did not approach Detroit from the direction of Washington City. I am a dead statesman; but I am a living and rejuvenated Republican." The press responded favorably, and the phrase "rejuvenated Republicanism" received national attention and became a popular slogan for the Harrison campaign.

Encouraged by the response to his Detroit speech, Harrison agreed to speak in Chicago on March 20. Careful to woo the Blaine following, he handsomely referred to the Plumed Knight as the "matchless statesman" of 1884, and vigorously espoused the cause of high tariffs. His protectionist sympathies won him great praise, and such independent Republicans as Theodore Roosevelt and Henry Cabot Lodge beamed affectionately upon the Indiana General. One paper went so far as to hail him all-inclusively as the party's hope "against the Democracy, the flesh, and the devil."

The Indiana state delegation was pledged to Harrison, but another Hoosier candidate entered the race. Judge Walter Q. Gresham was fifty-six years old and had an impressive record as a jurist. He had been a major-general in the war, a judge of the district court of Indiana, and postmaster general in Arthur's Cabinet. He was, in 1884, secretary of the treasury for a month until his elevation to the 7th judicial district as a circuit judge. One of his court decisions—he had removed a friend of Jay Gould's from the receivership of the Wabash Railroad—would have important consequences in the convention.

Gresham was considered a more "progressive" candidate than Harrison. He believed in civil-service reform and moderate tariff reduction, and he had the support of most of the old Arthur faction, the independent press, and many Mugwumps. Joseph Medill of the Chicago *Tribune,* John Wanamaker, the merchant prince, the Chicago *Inter-Ocean,* the Philadelphia *Daily News,* and the Philadelphia *Leader* all supported his candidacy.

In Indiana, ex-Governor Albert G. Porter, a delegate-at-large nominally pledged to Harrison, Charles W. Fairbanks, later Vice-President, and Kenesaw M. Landis led the pro-Gresham forces. There was, as the worried Harrison managers realized, a distinct possibility that, in case of a prolonged deadlock, Gresham might wrest the Indiana delegation from his enemy Harrison.

The bosses, too, were interested in Gresham. The Pennsylvania boss, Matt Quay, sent word he might be willing to support the Judge if certain understandings could be reached. Tom Platt informed him that Gresham was his personal choice, and the Judge should beware of Quay. Judge Gresham was wary of both bosses and spurned all offers of a deal.

New York had a candidate in Chauncey Depew, the urbane and witty president of the New York Central Railroad. Depew had been active in Republican politics since before the Civil War. In 1866 he had been appointed the first United States Minister to Japan, but, before he could depart, he had received an offer from Commodore Vanderbilt to become attorney for his railroads. When Depew hesitated between law and diplomacy, Vanderbilt snapped, "Don't be a damned fool." Depew embarked on a lifetime career as railroad attorney. His candidacy was primarily a holding operation for the New York delegation, because his railroad connections made him completely unacceptable to the Middle West and West. Depew himself took the whole matter with the best good humor and was the first to admit the hopelessness of his candidacy.

Two other candidates whose prospects seemed equally hopeless but who were considerably less good natured about them were Senator William B. Allison of Iowa and Governor Russell A. Alger of Michigan. Senator Allison, a moderate in all things, wielded major power in the upper house as chairman of the Appropriations Committee. His chief assets were his vast knowledge of financial and tariff matters, his moderation, and his reputation as a party wheel horse. The only delegations in his column were his home state and Rhode Island, where Senator Nelson W. Aldrich favored his candidacy.

William B. Allison was a statesman, admired by Republicans and Democrats alike; Russell A. Alger was something else again. Having amassed a large fortune in the lumber business, he entered politics and was elected governor of Michigan in 1884. His popularity as governor gave him greater ambitions, and he set out to buy the nomination through the rotten boroughs of the South, which turned most of the northern delegates against him.

Beside the active candidates, one other man received consideration in the spring of 1888. What, reasoned some of the party leaders, were the most distinguished names in the party? Lincoln and Grant, of course. Then why not a "father's son" ticket of Robert T. Lincoln and Frederick D. Grant? If there was anything in a name, certainly, these two should ensure victory. But while the party leaders speculated, Fred Grant was defeated for election as secretary of state in New York. There was, to answer their question, not enough in a name, and the scheme was shelved.

The convention prepared to open in Chicago on June 19. Blaine was still in Europe and avowedly out of the running, but "Blaine or Bust" flags and banners appeared everywhere. In the Leland Hotel, the California delegation established an unofficial Blaine headquarters. The members had brought with them a carload of California champagne and "not a drop was wasted."

The Alger headquarters were at first the most lavish until the Allison men decided to go one better. Their headquarters blossomed forth with hundreds of roses, lavish banners, and "Allison" emblazoned over the entrance in Edison electric lights. "Verily shekels play a big part in these things," Harrison's son-in-law commented.

The Harrison headquarters, while less lavish, were among the busiest in Chicago. Working from the Grand Pacific Hotel, the Committee of Six concocted the Harrison strategy. The basic plan was to refrain from antagonizing any of the candidates by going for many first-ballot votes. Rather, the diligent managers worked for second-choice ballots that would accrue to Harrison as the other candidates dropped out of the race. It was the same strategy that had won for Hayes in 1876. Michener put together a masterpiece of co-ordinated organization and, by keeping in constant touch with all of the delegates, was able by midnight of each day to tell where Harrison would stand on the following day.

Things were not running so smoothly in the Sherman camp. Governor Foraker arrived in Chicago expecting to be admitted, at last, into the Sherman inner circle. Upon arriving at headquarters in the Grand Pacific, he found to his indignation that he had been assigned rooms not adjoining the Ohio delegation but on the floor above. Furious at what he considered a snub from Hanna, who had booked the rooms, he dispatched a bitter letter of protest and retired to his rooms to sulk. Sherman was informed that Foraker had set up his own headquarters and refused to co-operate. Foraker's temper was not improved when he met Hanna. The Governor was proud of his battle-flag statement, but Hanna tactlessly told him that he considered the gesture "stale" and potentially damaging to Sherman's candidacy. The Governor withdrew in a rage. It was the beginning of an antagonism between Foraker and Hanna that would affect the outcome of the convention and Ohio politics for many years to come.

The breach was widened over the question of the southern delegates. The entire problem of the Negro delegates to the convention of 1888 is a tangled and shady one, and the exact truth will never be known. It involved three of the candidates and was overlaid with charges and counter charges, denials and counter denials.

Both the Sherman and Alger managers had transported Negroes to southern state conventions for election as delegates and then had paid their expenses to Chicago. Once in Chicago, however, these delegates became a doubtful quantity, and there was considerable concern as to whether or not they would stay bought. All the delegates had received extra tickets to the convention for their private use, and the Alger managers and Mark Hanna began buying up tickets held by southern delegates. "They brought their tickets to our rooms at the hotel," wrote Governor Foraker, "and Mr. Hanna, in the presence of us all, bought them." Considering the enmity between Foraker and Hanna, this statement might be open to question had not other members of the delegation attested that Hanna had in his trunk more tickets than he could have acquired by any other means than purchasing them.

Oddly enough, although Hanna's purchasing of southern tickets is much better documented than the same activities among the Alger managers, it was the latter who got all the publicity. On June 19, the Chicago *Tribune* made a typical comment: "There have been many rumors that Alger's friends were making a number of converts among the negro delegates from the South. Only the first ballot will show how much basis there is for these rumors. General Alger is personally conceded to be an estimable man, but the methods of his managers have destroyed whatever chance he may have had for the nomination." There were also rumors that a friend of Harrison's had bought up a hundred Negro delegates at $50 a head, but the charge was never authenticated and appears unlikely.

The southerners were not the only men who had their prices. Tom Platt arrived from New York to take up residence at the Grand Pacific Hotel. Although pledged to Depew, he lost no time in letting it be known that he could be had for the right price. The price was the secretaryship of the treasury. This was the first convention in which Platt—no longer "Me-too" Platt, the Conkling lieutenant—played a decisive role, and he obviously believed in starting at the top.

Platt was still interested in the Gresham candidacy, if terms could be arranged. Gresham refused to make any deals. "If I ever happen to be elected President," he replied, "I will be as free as I was the day I stepped on the bench." Platt tried again by offering to support a Gresham-Depew ticket. Again, Gresham failed to assent, and Platt was still peddling his delegation when the convention opened.

Matthew Quay was also in the market for a candidate and called on Judge Gresham the day after arriving in Chicago. They agreed that Blaine must not be nominated, and Quay offered no objection to Gresham's tariff views but could not accept the Judge's expressed intent to be absolutely free when it came to "dispensing the loaves and the fishes." Although Gresham also rejected the offer of Pennsylvania, the two men parted amiably.

Quay then offered his support to Harrison in return for a promise to include Pennsylvania in the cabinet. Harrison had instructed Michener to make no promises to anyone. Michener, however, sent a letter to Harrison hoping he would sign it and return it to the Pennsylvania delegation. "I write this," read the letter, "to assure . . . Senator Quay that in the event of my nomination and election to the Presidency, I shall regard the State of Pennsylvania as entitled to representation in my Cabinet and shall freely confer with Senator Quay and his confreres in making such selection." Harrison scrawled "I said 'No'" on the letter and returned it unsigned to Michener.

As Temporary Chairman John Thurston of Nebraska brought

down the opening gavel on June 19, the man who was most in the minds of all the delegates was James G. Blaine. He was at the time visiting Andrew Carnegie at the steel baron's Castle Cluny in Scotland, and the band in the convention hall played "My Heart's in the Highlands, My Heart Is Not Here" to the great discomfort of the rival candidates who feared a stampede for Blaine. His portrait had been carried in procession the evening before, and, as the delegates filed into the auditorium, a large crowd outside chanted, "Blaine, Blaine, James G. Blaine,/We've had him once,/We'll have him again."

Blaine had sent his sons Walker and Emmons Blaine to Chicago to discourage a possible move in his direction, but they disregarded their father's instructions and joined with Temporary Chairman Thurston, Stephen B. Elkins, Michel H. DeYoung of California, and Blaine's former managers, Joseph H. Manley and Charles A. Boutelle, to work actively for his nomination. Elkins reflected a popular sentiment when he said to Blaine's sons, "Boys, it *must* come. It's no matter whether Blaine wants the nomination or not; we want him."

The report of the credentials committee on the second day touched off a clash between the Blaine and Sherman forces. The Virginia delegation led by General William Mahone was pledged to Sherman. It was contested by a pro-Blaine delegation under H. A. Wise. The debate over the rival factions was long and confusing, and even Permanent Chairman Morris M. Estee lost track of the proceedings. The delegates finally voted 514 to 249½ to seat the pro-Sherman delegation. Despite his pledge, Governor Foraker and eighteen other Ohio delegates voted against the Sherman Virginians.

The platform was reported on the third day. It had been drawn up, especially the tariff plank, under the supervision of William McKinley, Jr., and reflected the conservative interests of the party. "We are uncompromisingly in favor of the American system of protection," the platform declared. "We protest against its destruction as proposed by the President and his party. They serve the interests of Europe; we will support the interests of America. . . . We denounce the Mills bill as destructive to the general business, the labor, and the farming interests of the country. . . ." To deal with the Treasury surplus, the platform proposed to repeal the taxes upon tobacco and spirits "used in the arts and for mechanical purposes." If the surplus should continue after such repeal, "we favor the entire repeal of internal taxes rather than the surrender of any part of our protective system."

This was a repudiation of the platform of 1884, which had favored a slight downward revision. So extreme was the Republican position that the *Nation* wrote: "It is so at variance with all former deliverances of the party, with scores of resolutions of State Legislatures under Republican control, with hundreds of speeches and votes of Republican statesmen now living, with the report of the Republican tariff commission only five years ago, and with the recommendations of successive Republican Presidents and Secretaries of the Treasury, that the party can be likened only to the man who made a monster of which he became the unhappy victim. Protection is the Frankenstein of the Republican party."

As soon as Walter Gresham read the tariff plank, he wrote a letter to Senator Farwell of Illinois asking that his name not go before the convention. Joseph Medill begged him to reconsider, saying that his withdrawal would embarrass his friends who had worked so long for his nomination. Gresham relented, and the letter was destroyed.

The platform was acceptable to the other candidates. One reaction was expressed by "Pig-Iron" Kelly, a congressman from protectionist Pennsylvania, who was so gratified that he exclaimed, "Lord, now lettest thou thy servant depart in peace, for mine eyes have seen the glory of the Republican party."

The platform adopted, the roll was called for the nominations. Joseph R. Hawley of Connecticut was the first name to go before the convention, followed by that of Judge Gresham. Gresham was nominated by Leonard Swett, one of the Lincoln campaign managers in 1860.

Former Governor Albert Porter of Indiana placed Benjamin Harrison in nomination with a speech designed to help Porter's own dark-horse ambitions more than to aid Harrison. After praising himself by implication, Porter devoted the last third of his speech, not to praise of the candidate, but to praise of his distinguished

ancestors, which gave unfortunate support to the charge that
Harrison was a little man wearing his "Grandfather's Hat."

Senator Allison, Russell A. Alger, and Chauncey Depew were
nominated before it was Sherman's turn. The speech for Sherman
unconsciously pointed up the principal flaw in a Sherman candidacy. "He whom I shall nominate to you needs no introduction.
His career, his character, his manhood, and his illustrious achievements are a part of the Nation's history. The people know him by
heart." That was just the trouble. He had been too long before
the public, and, try as one might, it was impossible to get very
excited over John Sherman of Ohio.

The first seconding speech was delivered by Governor Foraker.
As he approached the speakers' stand, a huge floral piece several
feet high and one-half foot thick was placed at the rostrum. In red
flowers upon a white background blazed forth the battle flag dispatch, "No rebel flag will be returned while I am governor." The
floral offering created a small riot in the hall. It was the gift of two
Chicago women whose brother had been pardoned from prison by
Foraker the year before. Their gratitude was exceeded only by
their political ineptitude. Foraker, visibly embarrassed, motioned
angrily for the display to be cleared away.

Foraker's speech was a triumph—for Joseph Foraker. He paid
full and glowing tribute to Sherman but recognized that someone
other then the Senator from Ohio was needed to electrify the
audience. Referring to Allen Thurman's political emblem, Foraker
declared that, if the Democrats had chosen for their banner the
red bandanna, the Republicans would carry the American flag.
Thousands of American flags were thrown into the air, delegates
jumped upon their chairs and cheered lustily. Who, after all, could
refrain from cheering for Old Glory and the man who had made
such a dramatic gesture? John Sherman was, for the moment, forgotten. The Sherman managers were, of course, furious. They were
convinced that the floral display and the speech were designed to
launch a Foraker boom, and, in reporting the incident to Sherman,
they described Foraker as a man "wild with ambition."

The next two nominations were a surprise. For no apparent
reason, Mayor Edwin H. Fitler of Philadelphia was placed in

nomination. Quay was apparently up to something, but no one could figure out what. Wisconsin offered as its favorite son Governor Jeremiah Rusk, and the convention adjourned for the night.

Before the first ballot on Friday morning, the Massachusetts delegation offered to back Senator Hoar for the nomination. It was estimated that, with scattered support from other states, he would have 70 votes on the first ballot. But Hoar was firm for Sherman and declined the offer.

The first ballot proved a great disappointment to the Sherman forces. Hanna had confidently predicted 300 votes. Foraker had estimated Sherman's strength at 360. He actually received 229 votes, of which 104 were from the South and 35 from the border states. The only large blocs of northern votes were Ohio's 46 and 29 from Pennsylvania. Quay could probably deliver more Pennsylvania votes on later ballots, but Sherman had no other major sources of future strength.

Fourteen men received votes on the first ballot: Sherman 229, Gresham 107, Depew 99, Harrison 85, Alger 84, Allison 72, Blaine 35, Senator John J. Ingalls of Kansas 28, William W. Phelps of New Jersey 25, Rusk 25, Fitler 24, Hawley 13, Robert T. Lincoln 3, William McKinley 2. Four hundred sixteen were necessary for nomination. Only nine delegations voted solidly for their candidates. The others scattered widely. The Territory of Dakota reflected the divisions in most of the delegations when it cast its 10 votes: Allison 1, Rusk 1, Gresham 1, Sherman 1, Alger 1, Fitler 1, Depew 2, Phelps 1.

On the second ballot, Senator Hawley and Mayor Fitler dropped out of the race. Alger showed the biggest gains with 32 new votes, Sherman picked up an additional 24 from Pennsylvania, and Harrison made a net gain of 6. The second ballot stood: Sherman 249, Alger 116, Gresham 108, Depew 99, Harrison 91, Allison 75, Blaine 33, Rusk 20, Phelps 18, Ingalls 16, McKinley 3, Lincoln 2.

Senator Ingalls dropped off the third ballot, and Gresham, Allison, Alger, and Harrison made slight gains. A new name appeared when 2 Kansas votes went to Supreme Court Justice Samuel F. Miller. The third ballot read: Sherman 244, Gresham 123, Alger 122, Harrison 94, Depew 91, Allison 88, Blaine 35, Rusk 16, McKinley 8,

Phelps 5, Lincoln 2, Miller 2. The convention then adjourned until evening.

Immediately after adjournment, a group of party leaders met to agree on a candidate to forestall a prolonged deadlock. Among those present were Senator Hoar for Massachusetts; Tom Platt, Senator Hiscock, and Warner Miller for New York; Senator Quay for Pennsylvania; Senator Spooner for Wisconsin; Senator Farwell for Illinois; James S. Clarkson for Iowa; Chauncey Filley for Missouri; and, although he was not formally authorized to speak for his delegation, Michel H. DeYoung of California. The leaders discussed the candidates, their strength, and their prospects for election should they be nominated. They agreed to support Senator Allison and to nominate him that evening. There would be a short meeting immediately before the evening session to confirm the decision, although no one expected any trouble.

Unfortunately for Senator Allison, Chauncey Depew refused to go along with the plan. He blamed the western agrarians for his lack of success in the convention and decided to withdraw. He absolutely refused to give his support to an agrarian candidate. He urged, instead, that Platt swing New York to Harrison. Platt, Hiscock, and Miller were unenthusiastic; for the moment, they agreed only not to enter the combination for Allison and to decide later on a candidate.

When the leaders reassembled just before seven o'clock on Friday evening, they were greatly disconcerted to hear that New York was withdrawing Depew and refusing to back Allison. With the 72 votes of New York up for grabs, the other managers lost interest in compromising on Allison; they decided to gain time by adjourning the evening session as soon as Depew made his speech of withdrawal. George Hoar later wrote of the break-up of the Allison plan, "If it had gone on, New York, Illinois, Wisconsin, Pennsylvania, Massachusetts, Iowa, California, and perhaps Missouri, would have cast their votes unanimously for Allison, and his nomination would have been sure. I think no other person ever came so near the Presidency of the United States, and missed it."

The situation after Friday's adjournment was as confused as ever. The great question of Blaine's intentions was now revived.

Would Blaine, despite his statements, accept the nomination? Blaine himself had remained silent during the convention. Not so Andrew Carnegie. He was anxious to see Blaine nominated and was following the convention closely. On Wednesday, the second day of the convention, the millionaire industrialist was interviewed in Bellingham, England, and was quoted as saying, "If Mr. Blaine is nominated he will not refuse." Blaine, he said, would feel duty-bound to accept the nomination if it were offered.

After one o'clock Saturday morning, a caucus gathered in the Gresham headquarters in the Grand Pacific Hotel and decided to put off the nomination until Monday, which would allow more time to hear from Blaine and to formulate plans if he remained unavailable.

Immediately after this caucus, a smaller gathering considered possible candidates. Senator Quay proposed nominating McKinley, a proposal that was favorably received by everyone except Boss Platt. Platt had never forgiven Garfield for the Conkling-Garfield feud and, as a consequence, swore that he would never trust an Ohio man's pledge in a national convention.

McKinley took steps to silence the rumors that he might become the compromise candidate. On the fourth roll call, a Connecticut vote was cast for him. Although he had received from 3 to 8 votes on previous ballots, McKinley had not taken them seriously. But he now climbed upon a chair and, in a moving speech, said, "I cannot consistently, with honorable fidelity to John Sherman, who has trusted me in his cause and with his confidence; and above all, I cannot with my sense of personal integrity, permit my name to be used in this convention." His statement was so honest, his delivery so intense, that he was given a great ovation, and his name was whispered excitedly as a coming man.

The fourth ballot proved a real surprise. Depew led 58 New York votes into the Harrison camp, Rusk switched his Wisconsin votes, and a scattering of Gresham votes swelled Harrison's gain to 122 votes. Senator Spooner had tried vainly to prevent Wisconsin's going to Harrison. He gave an interesting reason for his opposition. "Why," he said, "only a few months ago we waited and waited to get a bill from him for some law work he had done for us down in

Indianapolis. Finally we sent him a check for $1,000. His bill crossed our check in the mails. When we opened his letter we found he had charged only $400. No man who under-estimates the value of his services is a big man."

Harrison's increase placed him second with 216 votes, close behind Sherman who had 235. The others were Alger 135, Gresham 98, Allison 88, Blaine 42, McKinley, in spite of his speech, 11, Lincoln 1, Foraker 1, and 1 vote for the Negro orator Frederick Douglass.

Before the fifth ballot, a revolt broke out in the Ohio delegation. A sizable portion of the delegation expressed a desire to bolt Sherman for Blaine. Foraker sanctioned the decision and said that he, too, would go for Blaine, but he took pains to protect himself. It would not do for Ohio to lead the break. It would be better to wait until word came from Blaine that he would accept the nomination and then switch.

On the fifth ballot, what might have been a swing to Harrison faltered when his vote declined by 4. Sherman lost 11 votes, and Alger gained 8. The results were Sherman 224, Harrison 212, Alger 143, Allison 99, Gresham 87, Blaine 48, McKinley 14. As had been arranged the night before, the convention adjourned until Monday morning.

Governor Foraker changed his mind about waiting to hear from Blaine. Shortly after Saturday's adjournment, he announced that he had done everything he could for Sherman's candidacy and on Monday would vote for Blaine. "I do not believe there is any chance for Sherman's nomination. The fact is patent to everyone, and therefore I look for the next man to win, and I believe Mr. Blaine is the only man left to us." Sherman's friends furiously cried treachery. Since Blaine had already twice declined to be a candidate, they charged, Foraker was only making his own bid for the presidential or vice-presidential nomination by attempting to ingratiate himself with Blaine's friends.

The charge that Foraker was aiming for the vice-presidency was untrue. He had already turned down an offer from the Blaine managers to take second place on a Blaine ticket, but he had a grudge against Hanna and was jealous of the interest in McKinley.

His ambition was fired by a poll of the Ohio delegation, which showed that, if both Sherman and Blaine were out of the race, the delegation would vote 38 for Foraker to 8 for McKinley. If his knifing of Sherman should force his withdrawal and if Blaine refused for the third time to be a candidate, a Foraker nomination might materialize. If not, he would at least be able to take credit for having swung the nomination to Blaine.

Sherman's friends thought they could forestall both Foraker and Blaine. They agreed that Sherman was finished but believed McKinley could be nominated. Mark Hanna, Murat Halstead, and Senator Hoar wired Sherman begging him to withdraw in favor of McKinley. Sherman replied with dignity, "let my name stand, I prefer defeat to retreat. . . . Stand to our position and fall, if need be, with honor."

Tom Platt made one last effort to reach an understanding with Judge Gresham. He told the Judge on Saturday afternoon that he was still uncommitted to a candidate. Gresham repeated his stand on tariff reduction and his opposition to the platform. Platt waited politely for an offer on the cabinet, and Gresham as politely avoided the subject. Platt finally left, and the two men did not see each other again during the convention. He did say, however, later in the day that "Gresham will be the easiest of all to elect," and Joseph Medill told the Judge, "We can nominate you now if you will only let me say you will stand as the platform is written." Gresham was firm. "Not for the Presidency, Mr. Medill, with my consent can you make such a statement about me."

Gresham's wife wrote that Platt's overtures on Saturday were only a feint. He perfectly understood Gresham's attitude on the platform and the cabinet, but, by seeming to negotiate, he was able to throw consternation into the Harrison camp. If Platt were to make a deal at all, it would have to be with Harrison. He knew his bargaining position would be stronger if Harrison's backers feared a deal with Gresham.

Later in the evening, several Harrison supporters gathered in the Grand Pacific Hotel to consider his prospects. Among those present were the uncommitted Nicholas Murray Butler and Senator Nelson Aldrich. The uncommitted delegations were wavering in favor of Harrison, but they wanted specific answers to specific questions before they would vote for him. An emissary was dispatched to Indianapolis for a personal interview. Unfortunately, no record exists of what Harrison was asked and what he replied, but the men involved were practical politicians with definite needs to be satisfied, and it is not too difficult to imagine the general tenor of the interview. Whatever was said, the replies were received with favor in Chicago, and Senator Aldrich entered the Harrison ranks.

Sunday, June 24, was the decisive day of the convention. On Saturday, Blaine had wired his friends asking them to respect his wishes not to be a candidate, and Andrew Carnegie wired Stephen B. Elkins on Sunday that there was no way to persuade Blaine to change his mind. Blaine's orders, according to Carnegie, were, "Take Harrison and Phelps."

Elkins immediately contacted Tom Platt. They went for a long carriage ride, and, when they returned, New York was solidly for Harrison. There are conflicting reports about how this change was accomplished. It is possible that Platt agreed to act on Blaine's advice and that no bargain was made. Senator Sherman thought otherwise. "I believed then, as I believe now," he wrote in his memoirs, ". . . that a corrupt bargain was made on Sunday which transferred the great body of the vote of New York to Harrison, and thus led to his nomination. It is to the credit of General Harrison to say that if the reputed bargain was made it was without his consent at the time, nor did he carry it into execution." Platt himself left an account of the Sunday meeting, which was published after his death. Platt claimed Elkins "stated he was authorized to say that if the New York delegation would give General Harrison their support, the latter would appoint Mr. Platt secretary of the treasury in case of his election and allow him to control the federal patronage in the state of New York." He did concede that the pledge was not made in those exact words but was understood by everyone present. A Platt lieutenant who was present said that the story was "substantially correct." Harrison, Elkins, and Michener all denied that any bargain had ever been made. The probable truth is that Platt believed assurances were being given, and that Elkins encouraged him in that belief. The one certainty is that

Harrison had not authorized Elkins to make any promises. Whatever was actually said, New York was firmly for Harrison, and Platt never did get to be secretary of the treasury.

Additional support came to Harrison when Allison's manager, James B. Clarkson, approached Michener to say that Allison would withdraw on Monday. Allison would advise his delegates to swing to Sherman, but Clarkson would do what he could to switch them to Harrison.

Events were moving so swiftly that Governor Foraker found himself in an exceedingly awkward position. His announced plan to switch to Blaine had stirred a far greater storm of protest than the slippery Ohioan had expected. Sherman refused to give up, and then on Sunday Blaine took himself out of the race absolutely. The Governor could hardly follow the Blaine men into the Harrison camp—two turnings of the coat were at least one too many—so the Governor denied that he had ever made the Saturday statement for Blaine and declared that he would stand by Sherman to the end. He was wearing his buttons on the outside again.

There was a final episode to the shabby story of Joseph Benson Foraker. According to his own account, at two a.m. Monday morning, he was awakened by his secretary, who announced a Blaine delegation. While Mrs. Foraker modestly scurried into the bathroom, Stephen B. Elkins, Samuel Fessenden of Connecticut, and others were ushered in. Seated on the side of the bed, they told Foraker that the entire Blaine strength, including New York, would be thrown to him if he would accept the nomination. Foraker thanked them but said he could not accept unless Sherman withdrew and then specifically asked him to become a candidate. The story, although both Governor and Mrs. Foraker report it in their memoirs, is unlikely. Elkins had already received his instructions from Blaine to go to Harrison, and Platt had reached what he believed to be a mutually advantageous arrangement with Harrison's managers. Beside, so many delegates had been angered at Foraker's desertion of Sherman that they would not have voted for him no matter what their leaders ordered. Doubtful as the story is, it enabled Foraker to present himself in his memoirs as a man who had refused the nomination out of loyalty to Sherman.

By the time the convention met on Monday, June 25, the arrangements had been made. They were not, however, immediately evident. On the sixth ballot, both Sherman and Harrison made minor gains: Sherman 244, Harrison 231, Alger 137, Gresham 91, Allison 73, Blaine 40, McKinley 12, Frederick Grant 1, Foraker 1.

The seventh ballot began the swing to Harrison, who picked up 46 new votes. The results were Harrison 279, Sherman 230, Alger 120, Gresham 91, Allison 76, McKinley 16, Blaine 15, Lincoln 2, Foraker 1, and 1 Texas vote for Creed Haymond.

Senator Hoar approached James Clarkson and said, "I think it is time some one gave way for the good of the party." Clarkson agreed and told Hoar he would withdraw Allison on the next ballot. Hoar wanted the Allison men to go to Sherman, but Clarkson declared that they would go to Harrison. Clarkson mentioned how his father had gone to the Harrisburg convention in 1840 to help nominate William Henry Harrison. Hoar exclaimed, "Why, my father was a member of that Convention too, and if the Harrisons were good enough for the elder Clarksons and Hoars they were certainly good enough for the later ones." It was agreed that the votes would go to Harrison. After a quick poll of various delegations, Clarkson started back to the Iowa delegation. Senator Quay stopped him to ask, "What are you and old man Hoar up to?" Lining up votes for Harrison on the next ballot, he was told. Quay didn't believe there had been time to get enough pledges. Clarkson smilingly told Quay that they had even gotten 18 Pennsylvania votes and that Quay "had better get on the wagon."

Allison's name was withdrawn just before the eighth ballot, and Benjamin Harrison was nominated. One by one Harrison had gathered the leaders to his cause. First Depew, then Aldrich, Platt, Clarkson, and finally Hoar. Patient waiting and the all-important blessing of James G. Blaine brought victory. The final ballot read: Harrison 544, Sherman 118, Alger 100, Gresham 59, Blaine 5, McKinley 4.

At the evening session, the convention selected a running mate. Blaine's injunction had been to take William Walter Phelps of New Jersey, but the convention ignored his advice. Henry Stoddard offered an amusing reason for Phelps's failure. "Phelps parted his hair in the middle and wore a bang down his forehead. Had Phelps not been present personally at the convention, the question of his bang might never have come up; but with Phelps and his bang day after day in plain sight of the Western delegates there was no hope that he would win their favor."

Whether it was Phelps's hair style or the rumor that the choice of a candidate had been given to New York, the wealthy merchant-banker Levi P. Morton, who had declined to run with Garfield in 1880, was named the vice-presidential candidate, by 592 votes to 119 for Phelps and 115 votes for three other candidates.

CHAPTER 7

"Who . . . has been President . . .
any how?"

THE TENTH REPUBLICAN NATIONAL CONVENTION
Minneapolis, June 7, 1892

Benjamin Harrison, upon being elected President of the United
States, gave thanks to providence. Boss Platt snorted, "Providence
hadn't a damn thing to do with it." Harrison, he added, would
never know how many men "were compelled to approach the gates
of the penitentiary to make him President." Grover Cleveland had
had a popular plurality of 100,000 votes, but a deal between Platt
and Governor Hill in New York and wholesale voting corruption
in Indiana had given the Republicans a majority in the electoral
college.

For the first time since 1874, both houses of Congress and the
White House were in the hands of a single party, making it possible
for the Republicans to implement their program. First, they passed
the McKinley tariff, raising duty levels 12%, then they embarked on
a spending spree that caused it to be called the first "billion dollar
Congress." A thorough raid on the treasury in the form of bloated
veterans' pensions and bonuses soon wiped out the surplus and
put the government firmly in the red.

Hard-money policies and the elimination of the treasury surplus
placed an enormous burden on the western agrarians, while high
tariff rates drove the cost of consumer goods steadily upward. The
voters registered their protest in the 1890 mid-term elections, in

which the Republicans lost eighty-five seats in the House and had their margin in the Senate cut from ten to six.

The mid-term elections were a crushing repudiation of Republican policies, but they were not an endorsement of the Democratic Party. The appearance of the Populists posed a threat to both major parties. There had been agrarian revolts in the past, none of which had had any lasting influence on national politics, but economic conditions in the West were now so serious that the farmers were driven to concerted action. A series of dry years substantially reduced the grain crops, and this reduction, combined with low cotton prices in the South, placed an intolerable burden of mortgage and debt upon the farmers, who were ripe for revolt.

The discontented farmers banded together into two organizations—the Southern Alliance and the Northwestern Alliance—to work for currency expansion, governmental control of railroads, and other economic and political reforms that would improve their position. In the mid-term elections, the Alliance elected fourteen Congressmen on the Populist ticket and could count on forty-four sympathetic Democrats in the House.

While the Populist revolt threatened their power in the West and South, the major parties prepared to select their candidates. Benjamin Harrison was the logical Republican choice, but he was the most unpopular man in the party. His administration, a lackluster affair, had antagonized most of the party leaders. Tom Platt believed he had been betrayed over appointment to the Treasury Department. Senator Quay and James Clarkson were both in opposition over patronage. Mark Hanna and Joseph Foraker agreed on only one thing: their dislike of Harrison. Speaker of the House Thomas Reed was scathing in his private denunciations of the President. When asked about a renomination for Harrison, he replied that the Republican Party could not be asked to "live four more years in a dripping cave."

Boss Platt, Matt Quay, and James Clarkson hoped to prevent Harrison's renomination by once again bringing forward James G. Blaine, then Secretary of State. But it was too late for Blaine. His health was poor, and his time had passed. He refused to give the bosses any encouragement, and they had a difficult time securing delegates without Blaine's blessing. Louis A. Michener steadily lined up support for the President and, by convention time, had pledges from nearly half the delegates.

At the last minute, Blaine provided a flurry of excitement. Three days before the convention, he abruptly and without explanation resigned from the cabinet. He and Harrison had been on bad terms for some time, but the timing of his resignation appeared to be a bid for the nomination. If so, it came too late. The administration was in firm control.

The tenth Republican National Convention met in Minneapolis, Minnesota, on June 7, 1892. The undisputed star of the occasion was the Governor of Ohio, William McKinley, the permanent chairman. McKinley's selection was considered a coup for Harrison. He was a potential threat to Harrison's candidacy, and the President's managers thought themselves very clever to place the Ohio Governor in a position where he could not work among the delegates to advance his own candidacy. In fact, such a move was unnecessary, for McKinley was not interested in the nomination. Mark Hanna correctly judged that 1892 would not be a Republican year and preferred to have McKinley prominent, powerful, and recognized as a leading candidate for 1896. Ohio was pledged to its favorite son, but the strategy was to bring him to the attention of the party for future honors, not to challenge Harrison.

McKinley in his address as permanent chairman, vigorously defended the protective tariff. In a singularly sticky bit of rhetoric, he said, "We stand for a protective tariff because it represents the American home, the American fireside, the American family, the American girl and the American boy, and the highest possibilities of American citizenship."

On the fourth day, the nominating speeches began. Senator Walcott of Colorado presented Blaine, while Richard Thompson of Indiana, one day past his eighty-third birthday, nominated Harrison. The main speech for Harrison was a seconding speech by Chauncey Depew. He began by warning that the election would be fought on the record of the Harrison administration and that victory could hardly be assured by repudiating the President. He enumerated the accomplishments of the past four years and jabbed at those who praised Blaine's foreign policy, the policies of the Secretary of the Treasury, the policies of the Secretary of the Navy, the tariff policies of McKinley, and so forth, but still damned the administration of Harrison: "Who, during the last four years, has been President of the United States, any how?"

Depew's question was answered in a single ballot. When Texas cast its 22 votes for Harrison, the President had a majority. McKinley thereupon left the chair and, in the role of a private delegate, moved the suspension of the rules and Harrison's nomination by acclamation. A Blaine delegate objected, and McKinley, having made his point of personal loyalty and party regularity, withdrew the motion. The results of the ballot were Harrison 535-1/6, Blaine 182-1/6, McKinley 182, Speaker Reed 4, and Robert T. Lincoln 1, with 2/3 of a vote not cast.

The McKinley vote was a surprise. It was much larger than had been anticipated and came from twenty-five states. He had the majority vote of four delegations, including Matt Quay's Pennsylvania, and substantial minority support from Massachusetts and New York.

Having settled the presidential contest with little difficulty, the convention met in the evening to select a running mate. Vice-President Morton had made little effort to secure renomination, and no one wanted to draft him. At the suggestion of New York, the delegates turned to Whitelaw Reid, editor of the New York *Tribune* and Minister to France. Reid was nominated by acclamation, the first time a Republican candidate had been tendered a nomination without the formality of a roll call.

After adjournment, McKinley retired to the room of a friend in the West House and, stripping to his underwear, lay down on the bed to recover from the oppressive heat. He was soon joined by Mark Hanna who, undressing, reclined on the sofa. For a time, neither of the unclad, portly gentlemen spoke. Finally Hanna said, "My God, William, that was a damned close squeak." They then relaxed to dream of 1896 while Harrison and Reid were led out to slaughter.

"The plain, blunt, honest citizen"

THE SIXTEENTH DEMOCRATIC NATIONAL CONVENTION
Chicago, June 21, 1892

Grover Cleveland, after four years of political retirement, was still the head of the Democratic Party. His wife, whom he had married in a White House ceremony in 1886, in her farewell to the White House staff, had turned to one of the servants to say, "Now, Jerry, I want you to take good care of all the furniture and ornaments in the house, for I want to find everything just as it is now when we come back again." She added, "We are coming back just four years from today." Because of his plurality in the popular vote and his stature as the first Democratic president since the Civil War, the Democratic Party agreed that Cleveland would indeed be coming back. The former President was himself not so sure. He was weary of public office, disgusted at the campaign that had been waged against him, and he looked forward to the ease of distinguished retirement. The resurgence of the party in 1890, with its implied vindication of his tariff policy, changed his mind.

Immediately after the mid-term elections, Cleveland began speaking out on public issues. Then an issue arose to threaten his future. One of the results of the Populist revolt was a revival of free-silver demands. The question had arisen in 1885 but had disappeared in a wave of general prosperity. In 1890, it returned in greater strength. The Republican-inspired Sherman Silver-Purchase

Act provided that the government buy up most of the silver then being produced, but the westerners, particularly among the Democrats, demanded the free and unlimited coinage of silver. A free-silver bill passed the Senate in January, 1891, with strong Democratic support, and many party leaders were inclined to bow before the pressure from the West and accept free silver as a principle. But not Cleveland. He warned in February against the "dangerous and reckless experiment of free, unlimited, and independent silver coinage." His friends were aghast. The West and South denounced him. It was believed that, by taking this stand, he had thrown away his chances for the nomination. But Cleveland stood firm, and in time the situation changed. It was realized that the East, which was delighted by Cleveland's position, was more important in the coming election than the West; the South could be depended upon, no matter how discontented it became. Then there came a lull in the free-silver movement. The Sherman Silver-Purchase Act satisfied the silver men for a time, and the unlimited coinage bill failed in the House. Free silver receded into the background. It would re-emerge in full fury in 1896, but Cleveland had weathered his storm.

During that storm, David B. Hill thought he saw his own opportunity. The slippery Governor had been re-elected in 1888 through a deal that gave New York to Harrison while returning Hill to the governorship. A third term in Albany was an unlikely prospect, so Hill got himself elected to the Senate in January, 1891. He held on to the governorship until he could place the mediocre Rosewell P. Flower, erstwhile presidential candidate, in office in November, then took his seat. With a hand-picked successor in the State House and the state under firm control, Hill was ready to campaign for the Democratic presidential nomination.

Hill made a speaking tour through the South, lining up delegates, and gently placed himself on the side of free silver, while at the same time trying to convince the East that he would be a moderate—safer than a determined western free-silver candidate. For campaign manager, he had the able former Tildenite, Manton Marble. In the South, Speaker of the House Crisp, Senator Colquitt of Georgia, and General Longstreet marshalled his forces.

Hill's prospects were bright during January and February, 1892.

Cleveland was being counted out of the race, and the other possible candidates—Senator Gorman of Maryland, Governor Boies of Iowa, and Governor Gray of Indiana—lacked the stature for national support. Hill then made a fatal blunder.

The Democratic National Committee, late in January, announced that the National Convention would meet in Chicago on June 21. The Hill-controlled New York State Committee immediately called the state convention for February 22. Not in twenty years had a New York convention been held before April, and this "snap convention" aroused a storm of protest. This blatant attempt to bind the New York delegation before any opposition could be organized disgusted Democrats throughout the country and irreparably damaged Hill's candidacy. The state convention met as planned and chose a Hill delegation bound by the unit rule. The aroused Cleveland men cried "steal" and called an "anti-snap" convention, which elected a rival delegation. It had no hope of being seated in Chicago but demonstrated dramatically that New York was for Cleveland. The loyalty to Cleveland shown in the "anti-snap" convention impressed Democrats everywhere and pointed up the fact that Hill's candidacy was the result of clever manipulation, rather than popular support.

By May, the Hill boom—begun so dramatically—had collapsed. Rhode Island, which Hill had hoped to carry, declared for Cleveland, and other states followed suit. The final blow fell in Georgia. That state had been touted as the strongest Hill state in the South, but in the state convention the Cleveland forces, led by General John B. Gordon, routed Speaker Crisp and Senator Colquitt and elected a Cleveland delegation.

The only other candidate to make any impression upon the delegates was Governor Horace Boies of Iowa. He had been, until after the election of 1884, a Blaine Republican, but the Populist revolt carried him into the Democratic Party. Populist support had elected him governor in 1889, and he was re-elected in 1891 thanks to his denunciations of the protective tariff. His Populist leanings made him unacceptable to the East, and he had the solid support only of Iowa, Idaho, and Montana. His candidacy divided the western and southern delegations, which might otherwise have gone to Hill. The other hopefuls had little support. Senator Gorman could not even count on the solid support of Maryland, and Congressman Adlai E. Stevenson of Illinois had only North Carolina pledged to him. His home state was solid for Cleveland, as was Governor Gray's Indiana.

The convention, as far as its main business was concerned, ran smoothly. From his spacious headquarters in the Palmer House, William Whitney, with efficiency and dispatch, gathered up the remaining uncommitted delegates who would give Cleveland his necessary two-thirds vote. In the convention hall, a temporary structure both uncomfortable and inconvenient, things ran far from smoothly. Hundreds of Tammany braves had come from New York to shout their opposition to Cleveland, while thunderstorms roared outside the hall. William Wilson of West Virginia was an ineffectual permanent chairman, unable to cope with unruly galleries and a convention made restless by heat, thunder, and rain that poured through holes in the roof onto the uncomfortable delegates. Most of the proceedings were conducted in a steady uproar of sound. Frequently the gallery mobs, rather than the chairman, controlled the convention.

A sharp contest developed over the platform. The resolutions committee reported a tariff plank embodying recognition of the principle of protection for industry, restricted to "the difference between the cost of labor here and labor abroad." It was a weak plank, far from Cleveland's principles. A substitute plank declared that the federal government had no power to impose and collect tariff duties, except for purposes of revenue, and that revenue should be collected only when necessary. The vote, taken amid the utmost confusion and disorder, adopted the substitute plank 564 to 342. New York, although opposed to Cleveland, supported the substitute.

The platform was ambiguous on the silver question. It denounced the Sherman Silver-Purchase Act as a "cowardly makeshift" and said, "We hold to the use of both gold and silver as the standard money of the country, and to the coinage of both gold and silver without discriminating against either metal or charge for mintage; but the dollar unit of coinage of both metals must be of intrinsic and exchangeable value." It appeared at first to be a plank on the side of the western advocates—but actually it could be interpreted almost any way.

Governor Leon Abbett of New Jersey placed Cleveland in nomination. His speech played on the twin themes of Cleveland's popularity and the principle of tariff reduction. In enumerating the victories won by the party on Cleveland's principles, Abbett called the roll of recent Democratic victors. When he reached the name of David Hill, a great Tammany demonstration broke out, interrupting the speech. The speaker waited patiently for some minutes while the Hill demonstration went on and then presented "the nominee of the people, the plain, blunt, honest citizen, the idol of the Democratic masses, Grover Cleveland."

William C. DeWitt of New York arose to place Hill in nomination but was forced to wait for fifteen minutes until the violent storm outside subsided sufficiently for him to be heard. Early in his speech, he described Hill as "the Blucher who can drive the Republican chieftain to St. Helena in November." Few people would think of Benjamin Harrison as Napoleonic. Rising to florid oratorical heights, DeWitt concluded, "It took just three hundred brave men to stop the Persians at the Pass of Thermopylae and rescue the immortal plains of Greece. If we have three hundred votes upon this floor, give Providence a chance to make a President of the United States, right here and now; and if we have three hundred votes, like the Greeks, let us stand as a wall of living and impenetrable fire." Rarely had so much been said for so little.

John F. Duncombe put Horace Boies in nomination, and there followed numerous seconding speeches for the candidates. At one point during a seconding speech for Hill, his name was greeted with such cat-calls from the galleries that New York threatened to leave the hall.

The session had begun at five that afternoon; it was now past two in the morning. The weary delegates were eager for a vote, but there was one speech yet to be heard. As the thunder rolled outside, Bourke Cockran launched Tammany's attack on Cleveland. He held his exhausted audience rapt for forty-five minutes. It was a brilliant speech, but all the thunderbolts were outside the hall. In spite of Cockran's warning that Cleveland could not carry his own state, the convention was unmoved. After his speech, Tammany attempted to adjourn until the next day, but Whitney had decreed that the balloting would take place that night. It was after three in the morning when the clerk began to call the roll.

With 607 votes necessary for nomination, it was soon over. As state after state fell into line for Cleveland, a Hill supporter gloomily exclaimed, "It's a funeral." The results of the ballot gave Cleveland 617-1/3 to 114 for Hill. The complete ballot included Boies 103, Senator Gorman 36½, Adlai E. Stevenson 16-2/3, William R. Morrison 3, James E. Campbell of Ohio 2, and 1 each for William Whitney, Governor Russell of Massachusetts, and Governor Pattison of Pennsylvania—with ½ vote not cast.

The vice-presidential candidate was selected on June 23, the third and final day of the convention. The race was chiefly between former Governor Isaac Gray of Indiana and Adlai E. Stevenson of Illinois. Stevenson, a native of Kentucky, had served as Illinois state's attorney and two nonconsecutive terms in Congress. As Cleveland's First Assistant Postmaster General, it had been his pleasant task to replace some 40,000 Republican postmasters with Democrats. A mild, gracious man, Stevenson did such a thorough job that he endeared himself to the entire hungry party. He was placed on the ticket as a "soft-money" man whose candidacy would appeal to those opposed to Cleveland's hard-money policies. Stevenson led the first ballot: Stevenson 402, Gray 343, Allen B. Morse of Michigan 86, John L. Mitchell of Wisconsin 45, Henry Watterson 26, 8 votes scattered. Iowa immediately switched to Stevenson, and, after other changes, he was nominated with 652 votes to 185 for Gray, with the rest scattered.

CHAPTER 8

"An American of Americans"

THE ELEVENTH REPUBLICAN NATIONAL CONVENTION
St. Louis, June 16, 1896

A young Kansas editor, William Allen White, viewing the second Cleveland administration, summed it up as representing "protection and conservation of property and privileges of capital." But the privileges of property and capital no longer seemed sacrosanct, and the masses of the people were demanding their own privileges. The years of Cleveland's second term were a time of violence, upheaval, and disaster. The Panic of 1893 brought the country to the brink of financial collapse, the Populist revolt emerged in full fury, and the cry of "Free Silver" raged out of the West with hurricane force.

Labor began major assaults upon the citadels of wealth. In the steel industry, the Homestead strike shook the nation. The heavy, arrogant hand of Henry Clay Frick smashed the strike, but not before an anarchist's bullet had struck him down in his own office. It was something new in America. It was one thing for Pinkerton men to shoot strikers; when a captain of industry became the target, firm action was required. The titans of wealth howled that the anarchists were abroad in the land, and, when the Pullman strike erupted into violence and murder, Grover Cleveland sent in federal troops to protect the "privileges of capital." It was an act that made him bitterly unpopular among the populists, the workers, and the western Democrats.

148

Even more serious than labor unrest was the financial crisis. Cleveland had left office in 1889 with a substantial treasury surplus and a sound currency to his credit. When he returned four years later, the surplus was gone, and $500 million in paper money was in circulation, backed by only $100 million in gold. In prosperous times, this discrepancy was no problem—people preferred the convenience of paper money—but in times of depression, they wanted their money in metal. Although silver money was plentiful, holders of paper money wanted gold instead. Soon there would be nothing but silver left in the government's treasury.

Cleveland, to relieve the situation, asked the repeal of the Sherman Silver-Purchase Act. A Silver Democrat from Missouri, Richard P. Bland, offered in the House a counter bill calling for the unlimited coinage of silver. The demand for free silver, like the greenback movement, was intended to provide cheap, plentiful money. Bland could not prevent the repeal of the Sherman Silver-Purchase Act, but he did become the leader of the Free Silverites, who split the Democratic Party wide open. The Free-Silver Democrats, the Populists, and the Republicans from the western mining states formed one faction, the hard-money Democrats and the eastern Republicans another.

The depression grew steadily worse. While Little Egypt did her belly dance at the World Columbian Exposition in Chicago, financiers read the market quotations and went home and shot themselves. By December, 1893, the Panic had taken a staggering toll. One hundred fifty-eight national banks, 172 State banks, 177 private banks, forty-seven savings banks, thirteen trust companies, and six mortgage companies had failed. The value of stocks on the exchange dropped 50%; business and factories ground to a halt throughout the country. In the South and West, money, even paper money, was so scarce that barter took the place of cash transactions.

The voters blamed the Democrats. In the 1894 mid-term elections, six Democratic senators and 116 congressmen were unseated; the party lost control of both houses of Congress. Cleveland was blamed for the debacle, and he was, by 1896, a man without a party.

With the Democrats in a hopelessly chaotic state, blamed for the hard times and fighting bitterly over the silver question, the

Republicans were jubilantly confident that their presidential nominee would be the next President of the United States. Thanks to the dexterous planning of Mark Hanna, it was virtually certain that the nominee would be William McKinley, Jr., of Ohio.

The McKinley-Hanna friendship was one of the most successful combinations in the history of American politics. The two men complemented each other perfectly. Hanna, the successful Cleveland industrialist, was an unabashed hero-worshipper of the handsome, dignified Governor of Ohio. Hanna himself was bluff, unpolished, cynical, energetic, and hot of temper. McKinley was gentle, kindly, deeply religious, and devoted to a code of ethics more rigid than is customary among politicians. That he was pompous and not especially bright when it came to business or public affairs did not obscure the basic humanity of the man. His hold on his friends was extraordinary, and Hanna was attracted to him "like the hardened man of the world who becomes infatuated with virgin innocence."

Together McKinley and Hanna made the perfect politician: the public McKinley, dignified, diplomatic, a polished speaker who could make platitudes sound like great moral and political truths; the private Hanna, shrewd, indifferent to ideals, a wheeler and dealer clever in organizing and raising money, vicious and hard-hitting in infighting. McKinley found in Hanna an alter ego, a financial angel, a press agent, and a devoted personal manager. It was an unbeatable combination.

From the moment the Republican convention of 1892 adjourned, Hanna worked to capitalize on the reputation McKinley had made in that convention and to assure his nomination at the next. He wrote hundreds of letters, sent a steady stream of callers to McKinley, and spent money prodigiously. His publicity campaign succeeded so well that Theodore Roosevelt exclaimed testily, "He has advertised McKinley as if he were a patent medicine." The comparison was apt. Both the medicine and the candidate were advertised for their ability to sooth and cure, and the candidate was presented as "the advance agent for prosperity."

Hanna retired from business in 1895 to devote himself full time to the campaign. He moved into the South, and, as Boss Platt acknowledged, "He had the South practically solid before some of us waked up." Hanna contacted the now awakened bosses to find out what price they placed on their support. As would be expected, Platt still wanted the treasury, and Matt Quay wanted at least one cabinet post at Pennsylvania's disposal. McKinley responded, "There are some things in this world that come too high. If I cannot be President without promising to make Tom Platt Secretary of the Treasury, I will never be President."

The rebuffed bosses decided to stop the bandwagon while there was still time. It was agreed that the best way to defeat McKinley would be to encourage as many favorite sons as possible. If the delegates were widely scattered, the bosses would be in a good position for some practical horse-trading and could come up with an amenable candidate.

Speaker of the House Thomas Reed of Maine became the favorite son of New England, while ex-President Benjamin Harrison was a "waiting candidate" in Indiana. Senator Shelby Cullom, a party hack whose chief asset was a slight and carefully cultivated resemblance to Abraham Lincoln, was the choice of Illinois, and Senator Allison was again supported by Iowa. New York brought forth ex-Vice-President Morton; Minnesota offered Senator Cushman Davis. Pennsylvania had difficulty finding a candidate, so Matt Quay modestly offered himself.

Speaker Reed, a gargantuan man standing six feet three and weighing nearly 300 pounds, was the only possible threat among the favorite sons. His wit was famous; his sarcasm devastating. As Speaker, he ruled with absolute despotism—earning the nickname "Czar" Reed. He drew support from Theodore Roosevelt, in spite of having once remarked, "Theodore, if there is one thing for which I admire you, it is your original discovery of the ten commandments," and Senator Henry Cabot Lodge, but he was handicapped by being a sectional candidate and a strong gold man. His attempts to equivocate on the money issue did nothing to attract the West and embarrassed his admirers.

Mark Hanna's response to the sudden proliferation of favorite sons was to claim loudly that the campaign represented McKinley against the bosses and to present his candidate as a valiant opponent of boss rule. On the major issue—silver—McKinley played down his friendliness to the western advocates of free silver. He was not a convinced free silverite, but he had voted for the Sherman Silver-Purchase Act, and his stand caused some uneasiness in the East. In trying to placate the gold interests, McKinley was accused by Speaker Reed—hardly in a position to attack anyone else's equivocations—of trying to stand between the "gold bugs" and the "silver bugs" as a "straddle bug."

Straddle bug or not, McKinley soon had the western states behind him. Following Ohio's lead, Wisconsin, Nebraska, South Dakota, and Oregon endorsed him, and when ex-President Harrison took himself out of the race, Indiana joined them. The states without favorite sons were falling into line, but Hanna wanted a victory over a rival. He selected Illinois as his test case.

Senator Cullom was outraged at the invasion of his private preserve and fought back as hard as he could. The McKinley forces, under the leadership of young Charles G. Dawes, spent more than $100,000, and Illinois fell to McKinley. The contest was all but over. Vermont defected from Reed, and, to the Speaker's immeasurable rage, his own campaign manager, Joseph Manley, predicted a McKinley victory on the first ballot.

The nomination sewn up for McKinley, the only problem for Hanna was the platform plank on money. As the delegates gathered in St. Louis, Platt and Cabot Lodge arrived to fight for a gold plank. The austere Massachusetts Senator pressured Hanna to accept a strong gold stand, only to be told to "go plumb to hell." Hanna was, however, prepared to go along with the East on the question. He had prepared a plank that omitted reference to gold but was fully prepared to "capitulate." Before the convention met, it was agreed to include an endorsement of the gold standard, and Platt, Lodge, Joseph Foraker, and Henry C. Payne all claimed credit for having forced a seemingly reluctant Hanna to come to terms. The actual writer of the plank was Melville E. Stone, head of the Associated Press, because he was the only man present in the committee who could spell "inviolable."

The eleventh Republican National Convention opened in St. Louis on June 16, 1896. Charles W. Fairbanks of Indiana served as temporary chairman and Senator John M. Thurston of Nebraska as permanent chairman. The only real trouble in the convention developed on the third day. The first two sessions concerned with routine business and the settling of a few contested delegations, had gone off smoothly. On the third day, the platform was presented, and the free-silverites put up a battle. The platform was "opposed to every measure calculated to debase our currency or impair the credit of our country" and was clearly against free silver.

Senator Teller of Colorado offered a free-silver substitute from the floor. He made a moving speech, warning that he could not accept the gold plank and would be forced to leave the party if it were adopted. There were tears in his eyes as he closed, saying that he would perhaps never again address a Republican convention, and, by the time he took his seat, he was sobbing.

The free-silver substitute was tabled by a vote of 818½ to 105½, and the gold plank was adopted 812½ to 110½. Senator Cannon of Utah then took the platform to announce sadly that he was forced to withdraw from the convention. Through the boos and hisses, Mark Hanna could be heard shouting in fury, "Go, Go!" Senator Cannon was followed by Senators Mantle of Montana and Brown of Utah. The entire convention had picked up Hanna's cry and was shouting "Go to Chicago. Take the Democratic train." Slowly Senator Teller walked up the aisle, leaving the party he had helped to found, and with him went the delegations of Colorado and Idaho and individual delegates from Utah, Montana, and South Dakota— twenty-four in all. As the bolters left the hall, perhaps the happiest, and certainly the most interested, man there was the editor of the Omaha *World-Herald*, a young politician named William Jennings Bryan.

Senator Allison, Speaker Reed, Levi P. Morton, McKinley, and Matt Quay were placed in nomination. McKinley's name was greeted by a twenty-five minute ovation. Joseph Foraker, in nominating him, said, "The American people know him, trust him, believe in him, love him and they will not allow him to be unjustly disparaged in their estimation. They know he is patriotic; they know he is an American of Americans; they know he is wise and experienced; that he is able and just, and they want him for President of the United States"—as handsome a tribute as anyone could ask.

The balloting was little more than a formality. McKinley won against the bosses in a walk. The results were McKinley 661½, Reed 84½, Quay 61½, Morton 58, Allison 35½, and Donald Cameron of Pennsylvania 1.

The two principal candidates for the vice-presidency were Garret A. Hobart of New Jersey and Henry Clay Evans of Tennessee. Hobart was a wealthy lawyer and a loyal member of the McKinley organization. He won the nomination on the first ballot with 535½ votes to 277½ for Evans. The remaining votes were scattered among eight men.

Despite the defection of a handful of delegates, it had been a triumphant convention for McKinley, and Hanna was well satisfied with his work. McKinley was confident that the vexing problem of silver could be overcome. Protection, he believed, would be the main issue, and he predicted that the silver question would drop out of sight within thirty days. He had not, of course, heard of William Jennings Bryan.

"Clad in armor of a righteous cause"

THE SEVENTEENTH DEMOCRATIC NATIONAL CONVENTION
Chicago, July 7, 1896

Free silver was the over-riding issue before the Democratic Party in 1896. It tore the party apart, politically destroyed a president, swept away the old leaders, changed the course of the Democratic Party, created, in effect, a new party, and brought a young messiah onto the national scene. The battle for the presidential nomination in 1896 was more than a struggle between gold bugs and silver bugs. It was a struggle for control of the party and the power to direct its future course.

The Silver Democrats, united in common cause, realized that their strength lay, not with the single issue, but with the great surge of hope and aspiration embodied in the Populist movement. Using free silver as their cornerstone, the silverites intended to build a party that would unite the Democrats with the Populists. The Industrial East could be left to the Republicans, and the new Democratic-Populist Party would sweep the rest of the nation.

The appeal of free silver went far beyond the complicated financial aspects of the question. Actually, apart from the leaders of the movement, few men understood it. It was not fiscal policy that rallied the western Democrats and Populists, but the desire of the have-nots to strike at the classes of wealth and power represented as much by Cleveland and the eastern Democrats as by the Republicans. A Gold Democrat from West Virginia wrote, "I have never seen the masses of the people so wild over a question they know little or nothing about. To reason with them is as impossible as to talk down an angry cyclone, and they turn away from all those whom they have been wont to follow in public matters with contempt." Convinced that they were the victims of a gigantic conspiracy perpetrated by the bloated moneyholders of Wall Street, the silverites believed that only by sweeping away the gold standard could their exploitation be ended.

To the orthodox eastern leaders—Cleveland, Secretary of the Treasury Carlisle, William Whitney, and ex-Governor William Russell of Massachusetts—the free-silver–Populist movement was more than revolt; it was revolution and madness. To their dismay, they saw the Democratic state conventions fall, one after the other, to the free-silver men. In April, 1896, the Missouri convention, after riotous proceedings, led off the parade by declaring for free coinage at a ratio of sixteen to one. Mississippi followed, and, in May, Tennessee, Iowa, South Carolina, Wyoming, and Oklahoma Territory went overwhelmingly into the silver camp. In Nebraska, there were two conventions—one silver and one gold—which named rival delegations, but the silverites had the greater support. The gold bugs took some consolation when Pennsylvania, Massachusetts, Rhode Island, and Michigan declared for gold, but the voices crying for sound money were drowned by a free-silver roar from Virginia and Kentucky. And still the avalanche swept on. Kansas, North Dakota, Utah, Ohio, California, Texas, Georgia, North Carolina, and Indiana swelled the silverite ranks.

The Cleveland forces, almost in despair, hoped to reverse the silver sweep in Illinois and save that state for the gold standard. But Illinois was firmly under the control of Governor Altgeld, and Altgeld was for silver. When the state delegates gathered in Peoria, the gold bugs were routed, and forty-eight delegates, with Altgeld at their head, were pledged to silver.

By July 1, thirty-three of the fifty state and territorial Democratic conventions had declared for free silver. But neither they, nor the gold bugs, had a candidate. As the New York *World* put it, "The Silverites will be invincible if united and harmonious; but they have neither machine nor boss. The opportunity is here; the man is lacking." Chief among the silver candidates were Congressman Richard Bland of Missouri, Governor Horace Boies of Iowa, the Republican bolter Senator Henry Teller of Colorado, William Jennings Bryan of Nebraska, and Senator Benjamin Tillman of South Carolina.

Richard Bland was the leading candidate. At sixty, the veteran legislator proudly wore the nickname "Silver Dick," bestowed on him for his long fight for silver. He had co-authored the Bland-Allison Act of 1878, remonitizing silver and providing for limited coinage; bitterly opposed the Sherman Silver-Purchase Act as a travesty on bimetalism; and vainly fought to substitute a free-coinage act. Defeated for re-election to Congress in 1894 by a declared Populist, he was still the undisputed elder statesman of free silver and the logical candidate for a silver convention. His championship of silver, however, was a weakness, as well as a strength. It caused him to be called a man of one idea, too narrow and old fashioned for the agrarian reformers who wanted to revolutionize the party along many lines beside silver.

Republican Senator Teller was offered by the Silver Republican Party, which had been formed by the bolters from the Republican national convention. Upon Teller, it was argued, Populists, Silver Republicans, and Democrats could unite to place the issue above party. Teller's most important supporter was Governor Altgeld, but most Democrats were skeptical of nominating a Republican. The southerners feared that a Teller candidacy would strengthen the Populists at the expense of local Democratic organizations, and the northerners remembered what had happened when the party backed a bolting Republican in 1872. Teller's best hope of success arose from the possibility of a deadlock in the convention, when his Populist support might tip the balance in his favor.

"Pitchfork" Ben Tillman was certainly the most colorful candidate among the silver bugs. A bitter partisan and supreme demagogue, the South Carolinian had achieved national notoriety as an extreme champion of southern agrarianism. His wrinkled clothes, battered hat, atrocious manners, and free-wheeling denunciations of his enemies made him appear to shuddering eastern Democrats the incarnation of a mob run wild. He earned his nickname by attacking Cleveland and promising to "stick my pitchfork into his old ribs," and, on his way to the convention, he shouted, "If the Democratic party doesn't adopt free silver, it ought to die, and I have a knife with which I'll cut its throat." Such utterances, repeated a hundred times, did little to inspire confidence in his candidacy. The silverites in Congress were unimpressed by his financial views, suspecting that he was merely exploiting a popular issue, and only his home state was instructed for him. Tillman, however, hoped to stampede the convention by the rabble-rousing denunciations of Cleveland and defense of free silver that he intended to hurl at the delegates.

Finally, there was William Jennings Bryan of Nebraska. It is one of the great political myths that the "accident" of one magnificent speech catapulted the young orator to the leadership of his party and that an unknown, unthought of dark horse swept to victory to the utter astonishment of himself, the party, and the nation. Such "accidents" do not happen. Bryan was far from unknown, and his nomination was the result of careful, painstaking, and thorough groundwork. Bryan wanted the nomination, he worked for the nomination, and, even before the convention opened, he was convinced that he would get the nomination. That any Democratic leaders were surprised when he was nominated only indicated that they were not paying attention.

Bryan was thirty-six years old. A friendly magazine described him as "a strong-limbed, strong-lunged athlete, stalwart, confident, and bold, with the rude force and enthusiasm of youth—with something too, of its crudeness and immaturity,—but buoyant, assertive, 'magnetic,' with a power of homely and forceful eloquence that takes popular audiences by storm, a 'man of the people,' a 'commoner,' a radical and an optimist, with unbounded faith in Providence, in the Republic and in himself." Even his enemies, who sneered at him as "the boy orator of the Platte," admitted his strength of personality and physical beauty. Never noted for originality of thought or sophistication, Bryan to the end of his life remained what he had been as a youth—honest, limited in his horizons, holding a child-like and literal faith in the Bible, and dedicated to what a more worldly generation would consider the cliches of patriotism, fundamentalism, romantic agrarianism, and burning conviction that "right" must always triumph over "wrong." To the simple, unimaginative, but sturdy farmers and shopkeepers of the "Bible belt," it was no insult to call him the "Great Commoner," for that is exactly what he was. More than any other figure of his age he embodied to the highest degree the virtues and faults of the Protestant, agrarian West.

Bryan served in Congress from 1890 to 1894. His two terms were not distinguished, and his utterances on the floor were "more notable for fluency of expression than for grasp of his subject." Throughout his career, concrete ideas were difficult for Bryan. He saw issues in terms of emotion and drama and saw himself rather romantically as a crusader for whatever righteous cause engaged his attention.

Silver gave Bryan the great issue for a crusade. He threw himself vigorously into the free-silver fight, and his magnificent voice, perhaps the finest oratorical instrument ever heard in American politics, quickly made him the most popular free-silver speaker in the West. His schedule was crowded with chautauqua lectures, in which he brought the word to the multitudes.

By the time Bryan entered the campaign of 1896, he was well known throughout the West and had a good deal more strength than the older politicians gave him credit for. He and his wife, a remarkable woman lawyer as devoted to Bryan's future as he was himself, worked indefatigably throughout the spring, writing letters by the hundreds. Before each state convention, Bryan wrote to the chairman, bringing his name to his attention; and afterward, he requested the name and address of each delegate to the national convention, many of whom received letters from Bryan. To all state chairmen, he sent a copy of the Nebraska silver delegates' platform, asking that it be adopted by their own conventions. Not only was Bryan calling attention to himself as a potential leader, he was providing a platform on which to run.

All this work did not go unnoticed. In April, Richard Bland wrote Bryan that he regarded him as a possible candidate. Josephus Daniels, editor of the Raleigh, North Carolina, *News and Observer* announced his support of Bryan and became, in Chicago, one of his most active supporters. The Populists inclined favorably to the Nebraskan. One of them wrote to General Weaver, the Populist candidate in 1892, "Mr. Bryan has the courage of his convictions. He is brave to a degree—the very man we want for president in the present crisis." Weaver, while remaining uncommitted, cautiously agreed.

Bryan's confidence was expressed as early as the Republican convention, which he covered as a newspaper man. In speaking to a Minnesota delegate who was bolting, Bryan asked what the bolters were going to do. "We are going to Chicago to nominate Senator Teller," was the reply, "you had better come and help us." "I can't do it," Bryan answered, "I am going to be nominated at Chicago myself." He also told Champ Clark that he would be the Democratic nominee, but Clark refused to take him seriously.

For all the growing interest in Bryan's candidacy, there were some who refused to succumb to the young man's charm. The dominant figure in the silver ranks was Governor John P. Altgeld of Illinois. The first Democratic governor of his state since the Civil War, Altgeld had had a career of violent ups and downs. After he had pardoned certain anarchists imprisoned for alleged involvement in the Haymarket Riots of 1886, he was branded an anarchist and defender of crime. Hooted and vilified throughout his state and the nation, he seemed consigned to political oblivion. Yet, such was the moral and intellectual force of the man, so evident was his genius for politics and his nobility in upholding causes in which he believed, that when he joined the silverites he became the pre-eminent leader of the movement. But for an accident of birth —he had been born in Germany forty-eight years before—he would have undoubtedly been the Democratic nominee in 1896. As it was, he was in a position to determine who would be the candidate. As "Silver Dick" Bland's manager put it, "Altgeld holds the key."

To secure Altgeld's backing would be a tremendous leg up for Bryan, but the Governor inclined to Bland. He told a friend of Bryan's, "Tell Bryan that he's young enough to wait a few years. Dick Bland has earned this nomination and shall have it, if I can influence this convention." Altgeld did casually suggest the possibility of a Bland-Bryan ticket, but Bryan intended to go for first place with or without Altgeld's support.

Shortly before the convention, William Whitney decided to enter the battle in defense of gold. He had planned to sail for Europe on June 17, but, at the urging of Senators Hill and Gorman, he canceled his passage. His decision was made at such a late moment that his luggage sailed without him. The New York leader announced that he would go to Chicago to attempt to insert a gold plank in the platform. He would not, he said, be a candidate but would simply use his personal influence in an unofficial capacity.

Whitney, although he realized the tremendous odds, also had some intention of trying to nominate an eastern candidate. He invited ex-Governor Russell to accompany him to Chicago. Russell agreed to go only if it were clearly understood that he would not be a candidate. Whitney objected that it might be necessary for the gold men to center their fight on Russell. He was, he told Russell, planning a rally in Chicago on Saturday before the convention met and urged him to prepare a sound-money speech with the utmost care. "It will be the opportunity of your life. . . . You have beyond any man in the country the ability to utilize this great occasion."

Whitney left for Chicago in a special train of three handsomely appointed parlor cars, well stocked with food and liquor. It was an oddly assorted group that accompanied him. Senator Hill, for the first time in years, was fraternizing with Cleveland's friends, and Tammany leader Hugh Grant and the editor of the New York *Times* were almost cordial.

On the afternoon of July 2, their palatial train rolled into the Chicago station under the hostile gaze of a silver crowd that had arrived in somewhat less comfortable circumstances. From his suite in the Auditorium Hotel, Whitney dispatched his associates to test the sentiments of the arriving delegations. Within half an hour, the gold men knew that their cause was hopeless. Every hour saw more silverites swarm into the city mad with zeal for their crusade. "Men bitter with a sense of injustice and burning with a desire for redress—not all politicians, but in part plain farmers, storekeepers, and labor representatives"—were preparing to sweep Whitney and the eastern Democracy from the scene. One of the gold bugs fearfully commented, "For the first time I can understand the scenes of the French Revolution!"

William Whitney was not going to ride in a tumbril if he could help it. The elegantly attired New Yorker, hat rakishly tilted over his left eye, intended to exercise all his power and considerable charm in a last-ditch battle. At a secret meeting of gold men in a caucus room of the Chicago Auditorium, he plotted his strategy. His plan was to prevent the silverites from obtaining a two-thirds majority of the convention and then, if possible, to back William Russell for the nomination. To secure his first objective, Whitney would have the gold-dominated National Committee name David Hill temporary chairman. Hill would then rule to seat the contesting gold delegations from Florida, Nebraska, South Dakota, and Texas.

While Whitney planned his strategy, the silverites poured into the city. The Texas delegation, "very cocky, all smoking red hot for free silver, and as dirty as if they had been traveling in a cattle train," whooped it up for Bland, while the contesting Texas gold delegation took one look around the lobbies and decided to return home without even presenting their credentials.

Governor Altgeld arrived to assume the leadership of the silver bugs. The ostensible leaders of the silverites were the "senatorial clique"—Tillman of South Carolina, Jones of Arkansas, George Vest of Missouri, and John W. Daniel of Virginia—but it was to Altgeld's rooms at the Sherman House that they went before making any vital decision. "Altgeld was the ruling power in this seething mass."

The first move in the gold *vs.* silver battle came on Saturday, July 3. Whitney held his sound-money rally in the auditorium theater and lost the first skirmish. Russell spoke with fluency and irresistible personal charm, but he won no converts. Delegates remarked, "We'd like to vote for you, Governor, but not this year!" The meeting was a total failure.

On Sunday, the Fourth of July, as fireworks roared and popped outside, the opposing forces came to grips. Whitney called a conference with the silver men. Senator Hill told them that the National Committee would name the temporary chairman. The committee, chosen four years earlier, was dominated by gold men, who no longer represented the sentiment of their own states. Precedent was on the side of the gold men who wanted the National Committee's choice to be accepted by the convention, but the silverites were through with precedent and tradition.

Late Sunday night, Altgeld coldly informed Whitney that precedent would be thrown overboard and that silver would rule from the beginning. The silver choice for temporary chairman was Senator Daniel of Virginia, who would oppose Hill's selection from the floor. Tillman told the gold men that, if they did not like it, they could bolt and added that he hoped they would. Whitney announced that he would attend the opening session in the place of another delegate to lead the fight for Hill.

During the weekend, Senator Teller made great strides toward the nomination, until he appeared nearly as strong as Silver Dick Bland. The Populists gave the major impetus to Teller's growing stature, and with most of the delegates badly divided among several candidates, the existence of a solid, cohesive bloc of Populist votes was a great advantage. The Populists demanded that the Democrats nominate a man who had thrown off his old ties, and they issued an ultimatum. "We cannot be induced to endorse any candidate for President who has not severed his affiliations with the old political parties."

Bland and Horace Boies, working in the hay fields of their farms, waited "with patriotic resignation to hear their country call," and Teller in the mountains of Colorado trusted to "discretion and patriotism." William Jennings Bryan left his fate to no such noble sentiments. In his memoirs, he wrote that a few days before the convention Bland and Boies seemed the outstanding candidates "and as I looked over the situation, I did not think that the outlook for my candidacy was encouraging." Yet, he could also write, "The possibility of my nomination led me to urge Mrs. Bryan to attend the Convention." Arriving in Chicago, the Bryans went to the Palmer House, only to find it the headquarters of the rival Nebraska gold delegation, so they took rooms at the less fashionable Clifton House. The Great Commoner later noted somewhat smugly, "as the rates were lower at the Clifton House, I can point to a less pretentious hotel bill than I would have had at the Palmer House. I took $100 with me and after paying the hotel bill

of Mrs. Bryan and myself during the Convention week I had about
$40 left, a sum probably as small as anyone has spent in securing
a presidential nomination."

As soon as he had settled at his hotel, Bryan made the rounds of
the delegations. He invaded a caucus of the Illinois delegation at
the Sherman House and button-holed as many of the delegates as
possible. The disgusted Governor Altgeld snapped, "He stands no
more chance of being nominated for President than I, and I was
born in Germany!"

Bryan had more success with North Carolina. Josephus Daniels
arranged for about a dozen delegates to meet Bryan. He later
related that "Bryan captivated them," and they pledged a majority
of the delegation to him. Bryan asked them not to make their
support public at that time. His seat in the convention was contested, he explained, and it might militate against him if he were
contesting for a seat in the convention and the nomination at the
same time. He also thought it would be best "to let the older
candidates measure their strength and for us to be ready to come
to him at the time when it would be more valuable than to bring
him out early as a candidate." The delegates agreed to await his
call.

Rumors, carefully encouraged by Bryan, began to circulate that
he would be the candidate. Congressman George B. McClellan,
Jr., of New York met a congressional colleague and asked who was
to be the candidate. "Mac," was the reply, "I am afraid that it is
going to be that little whelp, Bill Bryan of Nebraska." When
McClellan expressed surprise, his informant continued, "There is
something going on here that I can't get the hang of. There are a
lot of men here who are going to try to slip him over, but how they
are going to do it I can't find out."

One way it was going to be done, although no one knew it but
Bryan, was by a speech. After his preliminary campaigning in
Chicago, Bryan went to Crete, Nebraska, where he was scheduled
for a chautauqua debate on free silver. "In the debate . . . I used
the sentence with which I closed the Chicago Speech—the sentence
which refers to 'the cross of gold and the crown of thorns.' I had
used it a few times before that time, recognizing its fitness for the

conclusion of a climax, and had laid it away for the proper occasion."

While Bryan was, as it were, testing his great climax in an out-of-town tryout, there was some talk in Chicago of making him temporary chairman. Senator Chilton suggested that the Texas delegation back him for the post, but a slashing attack by Joe Bailey, who denounced Bryan as "unsound in Democratic principles," carried the delegation. They dropped any idea of backing Bryan for temporary chairman.

Bryan himself was relieved. He returned to Chicago in time to fight the National Committee's decision to seat the Nebraska gold delegation. He later confided to a friend, "I had, of course, to make the fight, but it is very fortunate for me that the 'gold standard' delegates were seated. The Committee has unconsciously contributed very generously to our plans. As it is, I will not be a member of the Convention tomorrow. If I were, I might be made temporary chairman, which would necessitate my making the keynote speech of the Convention and being deprived of a place when the platform to be adopted is under debate."

The convention gathered in the great Chicago Auditorium on Tuesday, July 7, at twelve noon. The huge structure had been readied at the last moment. In the last four days, the floor had been laid, and 960 chairs had had to be replaced because the chief architect "claimed they would not support a typically-built politician, particularly if he got excited."

Senator Hill was proposed for temporary chairman by the National Committee, and a minority report moved to substitute Senator John Daniel. The debate of the silver delegates set the tone of almost religious fervor that characterized the convention. There would be times in the next four days when it would be difficult to tell whether the gathering was a political convocation or a revival meeting.

On a roll call vote, the convention went for the silver chairman 566 to 349, and the gold bugs had lost their only hope of influencing the convention. Voting solidly for gold were Connecticut, Delaware, Massachusetts, Michigan, Vermont, Wisconsin, and Alaska Territory. Divided on the issue were Florida, Maine, Minnesota,

Virginia, Washington, and West Virginia. The rest were solidly for free silver.

The jubilant silverites gave Senator Daniel a twenty-minute ovation. The lean, clean-shaven "Lame Lion of Lynchburg," Confederate veteran and author of several standard works on the law, looked the perfect Roman senator as he prepared to deliver the keynote address. The most polished speaker in the Senate, Daniels was expected to make the great speech of the convention. With great flourish he paid tribute to the silver movement. "It begins with the sunrise in Maryland, and spreads into a sunburst in Louisiana and Texas. It stretches in unbroken line across the continent from Virginia and Georgia to California. It sends forth its pioneers from Plymouth Rock and waves over the wheat fields of Dakota. It has its strongholds in Alabama and Mississippi and its outposts in Minnesota, Florida and Oregon. It sticks like a tar-heel in the old North State, and writes sixteen-to-one on the saddlebags of the Arkansas traveler. It pours down its rivulets from the mountains of West Virginia and makes a great lake in New Mexico, Arizona, Wyoming, and Idaho, Nevada, Montana and Colorado. It stands guard around the National Capitol, in the District of Columbia, and camps on the frontiers of Oklahoma. It sweeps like a prairie fire over Iowa and Kansas, and lights up the horizon in Nebraska. It marshals its massive battalions in Ohio, Indiana, Illinois, and Missouri." It was a rousing speech, but it had one drawback: No one could hear it. A voice perfect for the Senate or a small gathering could not be heard in a buzzing audience of thousands. The speech was, despite its comprehensive Baedeker quality, a failure. Someone else would have to move the convention to the heights.

After adjournment, the gold men met to decide their future action. Some advised bolting, while others maintained that party loyalty demanded they remain. William Whitney settled the question by advising that, if the platform declared for free silver, the gold men should remain in the convention but take no part and should submit the question to their state organizations when they returned home.

One happy silverite was enjoying his dinner that evening. In company with his wife and Dr. Charles Rosser, William Jennings Bryan partook of a late meal at the Saratoga Restaurant on Dearborn Street. As the bands and crowds outside the restaurant marched up and down for Bland and Boies, Mrs. Bryan wondered aloud if her husband could be nominated. Bryan interrupted genially, "So that you both may sleep well tonight, I am going to tell you something. I am the only man who can be nominated, I am what you call the 'logic of the situation.' "

Bryan had reason for confidence. The Teller boom, so promising the day before, was suddenly disintegrating. The natural hostility of rank-and-file Democrats to a bolting Republican was taking effect, and Governor Altgeld, at one time friendly, declared that he did not think Teller could carry Illinois.

The collapse of Teller's prospects created a difficult situation for the Populists and Silver Republicans. They had declared that they would support neither Bland nor Boies. To whom could they turn? The possibility of supporting Bryan was put to them, and, while the Silver Republicans refused, it was with less conviction than they had expressed on the previous day. Bryan was, for the Populists, a possible way out of their quandary. He had advocated bolting the Democratic Party if it failed to declare for free silver and had thus, to the Populists, identified himself as putting issues above party loyalty. Furthermore, the Populists had never stated that they would not support him. Reluctantly, some of the Populist leaders had to agree that they would not oppose Bryan should he be nominated.

This was Bryan's "logic of the situation." He was the one lifelong Democrat who could unite all the silverites of whatever party behind him.

The immediate problem before the silverites on the second day was to establish a firm two-thirds majority in the convention. The Hill-Daniel vote had shown the silver forces to be 48 votes short of that majority. The silver-dominated committee on credentials took steps to remedy the situation. By a vote of 27 to 16, it increased the delegations from all the territories, unseated four gold men from Michigan—thereby giving that delegation to free silver under the unit rule—and unseated the entire Nebraska gold delegation. The committee decisions were upheld by the convention, and, to great cheering, William Jennings Bryan marched down the aisle with his delegation to take his seat.

Later, A. B. MacDonald of Texas was wandering about the floor and stopped to chat with Bryan, who was eating a sandwich. Hoping to gather material for his newspaper, MacDonald leaned over the Nebraskan to ask, "Who will be nominated?" Bryan smiled. "Strictly confidential," he replied, "not to be quoted for publication, I will be." The reporter laughed and bantered back, "I believe I'll take it myself." MacDonald later wrote of the incident, "I thought so little of Bryan's chances that I did not even mention him in the story I sent in that day for the evening paper, and I am quite sure that no other correspondent thought of him as a candidate. The majority of newspaper correspondents there had never even heard his name to remember it."

Bryan retired to his rooms after the evening session to prepare the speech he would deliver the following day in defense of the platform. It would not be a new speech but would be composed of elements, including the "cross of gold," from previous speeches, rearranged and polished for the occasion.

While mulling the speech over in his mind, he was interrupted by a visit from Senator Towne, Congressman Hartman, and Senator Patterson, who had come to ask him to support Senator Teller. Bryan replied that he did not believe Teller could be nominated. When asked who he thought could be, he replied that he had as good a chance as anybody. Senator Patterson, asking what strength he had, was told Nebraska and half the Oklahoma Territory on the second ballot. North Carolina was not mentioned. The gentlemen were amused but unimpressed and took their leave.

The third day of the convention saw all of Bryan's predictions come true. It was the day of the "cross of gold."

Fortune had favored Bryan to a remarkable degree. He had avoided being named temporary chairman, which would have forced him to speak before the right moment. The platform debate had been postponed for a day, giving him additional time to work on his speech, and through a rather complicated series of circumstances, he had been given the closing spot in the debate. Soon after the permanent chairman, Senator Stephen M. White of California, called the convention to order, a page summoned Bryan to the seat of Senator Jones, chairman of the committee on resolutions. Jones asked Bryan to take charge of the debate, and Bryan agreed. Jones had also asked Senator Tillman to speak, and when Tillman demanded an hour's time, it was agreed that Tillman should open the debate and allow Bryan to close.

Tillman's speech was a disaster. His face flushed, his hair unkempt, his one eye gleaming malevolently, he hurled at the opponents of free silver a stump speech of the worst demagogic kind. His greatest blunder was to revive the spirit of secession. He cried that silver was a sectional issue and that South Carolina had disrupted the Union once and would be willing to do so again to accomplish its purpose. Most of his speech was bellowed above an uproar of hisses and jeers. When it appeared that Tillman would not be allowed to continue, he defied the convention. "The audience might just as well understand that I am going to have my say if I stand here until sundown." He finally roared his way through to conclusion and sat down to repeated howls of rage and denunciation. His repeated use of such words as "secession," "disruption," and "sectional" was too much for silverites and gold men alike.

The rabble-rousing Senator from South Carolina was followed in the debate by Senator Hill. In view of his past record, there was some fear among the gold men, especially William Russell, that Hill would make some compromise statement, desert sound money, and stampede the convention for himself. It was known that Hill still nurtured faint hopes for the nomination and that he had avoided the Whitney party—even staying at another hotel—ever since arriving in Chicago.

Hill's appearance on the platform was greeted by a twenty-minute ovation, which reduced Russell to a state of near nervous exhaustion. Fearing the worst, Russell sat on the edge of his chair and, as Hill spoke, kept mumbling, "It's coming now, it's coming now, it's coming now!" But Hill kept faith. He delivered a sound argument for gold and brilliantly defended the administration. Unfortunately, Hill's voice was not very powerful and could barely be heard in the vast auditorium. Because of this weakness, his speech had to be considered a failure, although his honesty in defending the gold standard did much to rehabilitate a character never noted for straightforwardness. This speech marked Hill's last important appearance in politics, and there is a kind of ironic justice that it should be in defense of his old enemy, Grover Cleveland.

The next speaker, Senator William Vilas of Wisconsin, also defended the gold standard. He seemed to be running over his time, and Russell, who wanted very much to make a strong impression with his own speech, complained to Hill that Vilas was using up all the time. As Bryan described the incident, "My seat was so near Senator Hill's that I could hear the conversation. I immediately stepped across the aisle to Senator Hill and suggested that I was willing to have the time extended to give Governor Russell the time he wanted, the same period to be added to my time. Governor Russell was very appreciative of the suggestion and Senator Hill at once agreed to it. I cannot say that it was entirely unselfish on my side, and I think I would have made the suggestion if the extension of time had fallen to someone else, but as it was, it added about ten minutes to my time and I needed it for the speech I was to make. This was another unexpected bit of good fortune. I had never had such an opportunity before in my life and never expected to have again."

With the extension of time, ex-Governor Russell arose to make the finest speech of his career. His voice lacked the melodious quality of Bryan's, but as the young man—he was only thirty-nine— spoke, in a voice choked with emotion, his handsome face pale and worn, the audience was captivated. "His every sentence was chiselled and he spoke with a sincerity and earnestness that captivated those who heard him."

Russell knew that no man could stem the silver tide in 1896, but he was looking to the future. He was young and the most promising man among the eastern Democrats. Eventually, he knew, the silver movement would end, and the party would turn to new and, as he thought, sounder leaders. His speech therefore offered him a great opportunity to win good will for the future. The speech, although it changed no minds, was well received but would never be used to recommend Russell to the party in the future. Within a few days, he was dead of a sudden heart attack, and the eastern Democracy had lost its most promising leader.

As William Russell finished the last speech of his life, the moment arrived that would ensure William Jennings Bryan's leadership of the party in the years to come. Bryan had been nervous but confident while waiting his turn. He admitted to a feeling of weakness at the pit of his stomach and a slight feeling of faintness. Being unable to lie down, he got a sandwich and cup of coffee, which he consumed while the speeches went on. A friend scribbled, "This is a great opportunity," on an envelope and sent it to him. He wrote in reply, "You will not be disappointed."

At last, the moment had come. Bryan hurried down the aisle and mounted the steps to the platform two at a time. As he stood at the rostrum, looking out over the vast throng, his nervousness left him. After a moment's pause he began. "I would be presumptuous, indeed, to present myself against the distinguished gentlemen to whom you have listened if this were but a measuring of ability; but this is not a contest among persons. The humblest citizen in all the land, when clad in armor of a righteous cause, is stronger than all the hosts of error that they can bring. I come to speak to you in defense of a cause as holy as the cause of liberty— the cause of humanity." From the very first words, the audience reacted as one. "At the close of a sentence, the room was as still as a church. . . . I thought of a choir as I noted how instantaneously and in unison they responded to each point I made."

The rapt convention had found its voice. "When you come before us and tell us that we shall disturb your business interests, we reply that you have disturbed our business interests by your action. We say to you that you have made too limited in its application the definition of a business man. The man who is employed for wages is as much a business man as his employer. The attorney in a country town is as much a business man as the corporation counsel in a great metropolis. The merchant at the crossroads store is as much a business man as the merchant of New York. The farmer who goes forth in the morning and toils all day, begins in the spring and toils all summer, and by the application of brain and muscle to the natural resources of this country creates wealth, is as much a business man as the man who goes upon the Board of Trade and bets upon the price of grain. The miners who go a thousand feet into the earth or climb 2,000 feet upon the cliffs and bring forth from their hiding places the precious metals to be poured in the channels of trade are as much business men as the few financial magnates who in a back room corner the money of the world."

As Bryan spoke, he became aware of two faces in the auditorium. On his left stood ex-Governor Hogg of Texas, his broad, round face beaming with delight. On the right stood Ollie James of Kentucky. "As I turned from one side of the hall to the other, these two faces impressed me, for like the rest of the audience, they were in full sympathy with the sentiments to which I gave expression. They could not have responded to the expressions of my own face more perfectly if I had been speaking a speech that they had prepared."

And still the phrases rolled on. "We do not come as aggressors. Our war is not a war of conquest. We are fighting in defense of our homes, our families and posterity. We have petitioned, and our petitions have been scorned. We have entreated and our entreaties have been disregarded. We have begged, and they have mocked when our calamity came.

"We beg no longer; we entreat no more; we petition no more. We defy them! . . .

"If they ask us here why it is we say more on the money question than we say upon the tariff question, I reply that if protection has slain its thousands the gold standard has slain its tens of thousands. . . . You come to us and tell us that the great cities are in favor of the gold standard. I tell you that the great cities rest upon these broad and fertile prairies. Burn down your cities and leave our farms, and your cities will spring up again as if by magic. But destroy our farms and the grass will grow in the streets of every city in this country. . . . If they dare to come out and in the open defend the gold standard as a good thing, we shall fight them to the uttermost, having behind us the producing masses of the Nation and the world. Having behind us the commercial interests and the laboring interests and all the toiling masses, we shall answer their demands for a gold standard by saying to them, you shall not press down upon the brow of labor this crown of thorns. You shall not crucify mankind upon a cross of gold."

As this great phrase rang through the auditorium, the audience went berserk. Dr. E. B. Bush of Georgia, "bewhiskered and strong of lung," raced down the aisle toward the Nebraska delegation, waving the Georgia banner. A wild yell split the air from the Indian Territory corner as Joe Lacy, a Cherokee delegate, brandishing his standard like a tomahawk, leaped across the disconcerted gold bugs in the New York delegation, trampling their dignity and their feet, in a race to beat Georgia to Bryan. Illinois, South Dakota, Missouri, Virginia, Alabama, Kentucky, Ohio, Iowa, Tennessee, Mississippi, Michigan, Utah, Nevada, and Colorado jammed the aisles around the Great Commoner, crying and shouting at the same time.

As the Chicago *Times-Herald* saw it, "Bryan was carried off his feet in the rush. The air in his vicinity was a kaleidoscope of big hands, all eager to congratulate him. Some felt honored to touch the hem of his alpaca coat. They surged and jostled him into the North Dakota delegation, three rows from his seat. Eight brawny men . . . grasped him and lifted him upon their shoulders. Bryan was physically a heavy load. It was like lifting an ice wagon, or a Graeco-Roman wrestling match with an upright piano in a moving van."

The New York delegation, nursing bruised toes, remained silent. Hill, Russell, and the rest sat like men of stone. Altgeld did not applaud but turned to his neighbor, Judge McConnell, and said, "Judge, I had rather be able to make a speech like that than be president of the United States." But the next day, away from the emotionalism of the scene, he remarked to Clarence Darrow, "It takes more than speeches to win real victories. . . . I have been thinking over Bryan's speech. What did he say anyhow?"

Delegates crowded around the great orator. One man told Bryan he had been accused of drunkenness. Bryan managed to assure him that he was a life-long teetotaler. Other delegates, including Arthur Sewall of Maine, told Bryan he could be nominated that night if the convention could be kept in session. Bryan discouraged them.

"Should I want to be nominated tonight if they would be sorry for it tomorrow? . . . If the people want me nominated and that feeling could not endure overnight, it would perish before the campaign was a week old."

As an anticlimax, the convention returned to the business that had inspired Bryan's speech. Beating down the minority gold plank, the convention accepted the platform 628 to 301. The Democratic Party was officially on the side of free silver.

The nominating speeches at the evening session were, after the events of the afternoon, even more mechanical than usual. No one could have competed with the Bryan speech, and no one tried. Six names were placed in nomination: Governor Boies, Richard Bland, William Jennings Bryan, Governor Claude Matthews of Indiana, Senator Blackburn of Kentucky, John R. McLean of Ohio. William Russell had instructed that his name not go before the convention, and the Teller boom had collapsed so completely that his name was also omitted.

A group of Bryan's friends, including Dr. Rosser and E. J. Dockery of Wisconsin, approached the Ohio delegation with the view of making a deal that would give Ohio to Bryan in return for his support of McLean for vice-president. As Rosser told it, he and Dockery met with an Ohio leader. "The three of us had refreshments as we conferred. Dockery paid for a bottle of champagne, and being myself a teetotaler and Dockery a man of much moderation, it devolved upon the big Ohioan to drink most of it; after which he took our suggestion to his fellow delegates with his cordial endorsement." Ohio reported it was willing to accept the deal and go for Bryan on the second ballot.

Rosser explained the arrangement to Bryan, who rejected it because he did not trust McLean and because he could not afford to sully his nomination with any deals. Then, the practical politician broke through the candidate's idealism. "Besides it is not necessary. There are not enough politicians in the world to defeat me. Let's go to bed now and have some rest; we will have a hard day tomorrow."

On July 10, the Democratic National Convention cast its first ballot for the presidential nomination. Before the roll was called,

Illinois held a caucus. A sizable minority of the delegation wanted to abandon Bland for Bryan on the first ballot. Altgeld held them in check. "We are not political coquettes," he said. "We are here for business and not political play. We are Democrats and we are for Bland and free silver."

The results of the first ballot showed Bland leading with 235, but Bryan was second with 137. The other candidates were Robert E. Pattison of Pennsylvania 97, Blackburn 82, Boies 67, McLean 54, Matthews 37, Tillman 17, Sylvester Pennoyer of Oregon and Senator Teller with 8 each, Vice-President Stevenson 6, William E. Russell 2, and James E. Campbell of Ohio and Senator Hill with 1 each. Not voting on this or any subsequent ballot were the gold men, including all of New York—178 on the first ballot.

Bland gained 46 votes on the second ballot; Bryan gained 60. The totals were Bland 281, Bryan 197, Pattison 100, McLean 53, Blackburn 41, Boies 37, Matthews 34, Stevenson 10, Pennoyer and Teller 8 each, and Hill 1, with 160 not voting. Bland had picked up Alabama from Boies and Virginia from Blackburn. Bryan received Tillman's South Carolina vote and California and Wyoming from Blackburn.

On the third ballot, Bland gained 10. Bryan gained 22. Colorado's Teller votes and 5 of Pennoyer's Oregon votes went to Bryan. The totals were Bland 291, Bryan 219, Pattison 97, McLean 54, Boies 36, Matthews 34, Blackburn 27, Stevenson 9, Hill 1, with 162 not voting.

The break came on the fourth ballot. Alabama, Idaho, and Kansas abandoned Bland, and Nevada switched from McLean to join the Bryan column. Bryan gained 61 votes to take the lead. The results were Bryan 280, Bland 241, Pattison 97, McLean 46, Matthews 36, Boies 33, Blackburn 27, Stevenson 8, Hill 1, with 161 not voting. While the vote was being tabulated, Pennsylvania and Illinois withdrew for consultation.

During the fourth ballot, Altgeld had been subjected to almost inhuman pressures. Excited Bryan delegates had pulled him from his chair shouting, "Vote for Bryan! No Crown of Thorns. No Cross of Gold!" An attempt was made to tear the Illinois banner from his grasp, but the Governor held fast. Now, as Illinois moved from the hall, every eye was on him. "For God's sake, stand by Mr. Bland!" cried an Arkansas delegate, clutching Altgeld's arm as he walked by.

As the clerk called the roll for the fifth ballot, the tension was unbearable. Kentucky switched its 26 votes from Blackburn to Bryan, and Illinois and West Virginia were passed. At the conclusion of the roll call, Bryan had 398 votes with 103 for Bland, 95 for Pattison, 46 for McLean, 30 for Matthews, 26 for Boies, 8 for Stevenson and 1 each for Hill and David Turpie. Two hundred twenty-two votes had not been cast.

The clerk returned to Illinois. Twenty-two thousand people watched, scarcely daring to breathe, as the pale, stocky Governor of Illinois rose slowly to his feet. The hall was absolutely silent. Tensely the convention waited as Altgeld drew a breath and announced, "Illinois casts its forty-eight votes for William Jennings Bryan of Nebraska!" The tension was broken by a roar of sound as delegates and spectators cheered or wept, danced in the aisles, or cursed with clenched fists. Governor Hogg of Texas lumbered down upon the New York delegation and tried to wrest the state standard away from the gold men, roaring "Bryan, Bryan, Bryan!" all the while. Congressman McClellan hit him squarely on the jaw, and the enormously fat Texan collapsed in a heap. "He picked himself up apparently quite unaware that he had been knocked down and went on his way shouting, 'Bryan, Bryan,' just as though nothing had happened."

State after state followed Illinois. Among the stampeding states, Utah, according to its chairman, cast its vote for Willington J. Bryan! The official results of the ballot were Bryan 652, Pattison 95, Bland 11, Stevenson 8, Hill and Turpie 1 each. One hundred sixty-two die-hard gold men refused to vote, and the nomination was made unanimous only among those voting.

Bryan, hearing the news, realized that soon the delegates would be pouring in upon him and calmly went to the barber shop for a shave. He reported that he was not excited, but the barber was so agitated he could hardly handle his razor.

While the delegates were still cheering hysterically, the party leaders gathered to select a vice-presidential candidate. Senator

Jones called to the meeting a representative of each state that had voted for silver. Bryan arrived after the meeting had begun and sat quietly listening to the discussion. Both Bland and Boies were considered, but their friends said that they would refuse. Several senators argued that John R. McLean would be the strongest candidate. "We are going to need money," said a McLean supporter. "You cannot run a campaign or win an election without organization, and you cannot secure an organization without money. . . . John McLean has the money and he will let us have all that is necessary. Nominate him and we need not worry about the finances." Someone suggested that Arthur Sewall of Maine was also a rich man and had the added advantage of being a New England silver man, a fairly rare species.

Bryan was asked for his views. He said that he had had little time to consider and had no wish to dictate to the convention. He reviewed the names mentioned and then said, in substance, "If the Convention should nominate John R. McLean, I would decline the nomination for the presidency. I would not run on a ticket with that man. He is an immoral man. He preaches free silver but all his connections and all his interests are with those who exploit the public for their private benefit. His nomination would . . . be selling the Party's birthright for his campaign money. . . . There are too many clean and honest men who believe in the new doctrine we shall preach in this campaign for the Party to tie to a man of McLean's standards."

In the stunned silence that followed, Senator Blackburn whispered to Josephus Daniels, "Josephus, this is magnificent, but it is not war. You cannot win victory by driving off everybody who isn't 100 per cent virtuous."

The convention balloted on the fifth day for a vice-presidential candidate. Sixteen men received votes on the first ballot. The leaders were Joseph C. Sibley of Pennsylvania 163, John R. McLean 111, Arthur Sewall 100, George F. Williams of Massachusetts 76, Richard Bland 62, Walter A. Clark of North Carolina 50, John R. Williams of Illinois 22, and Senator Blackburn and Governor Boies 20 each. The rest were scattered. Not voting were 260 delegates, including those from Nebraska, who said, "Nebraska, grateful of the very high honor that has been conferred upon it, is prepared to accept the result of the combined wisdom of this Convention, and it is not willing to take any part in this contest."

Before the second roll call, Iowa withdrew Boies. Missouri withdrew Bland, in spite of which he took over first place with 294 votes. McLean had 158, Sibley 113, Sewall 37, with the rest scattered and 255 not voting.

Sibley, before the third ballot, asked that he not be considered. McLean made major gains for a total of 210 votes—only 45 behind Bland. Sewall had 97, and 50 went to Sibley.

After the third ballot, a telegram from Bland was read urging the convention not to "nominate both candidates from the west side of the Mississippi river" and asking that he not be voted for. With Bland out of the race, the fourth ballot gave McLean 298 to 261 for Sewall.

At the conclusion of the ballot, McLean announced by telegram that any votes cast for him were "against my expressed wish and without my authority." The convention then turned to Sewall and nominated him.

Sewall had been in the auditorium through the first few ballots but then left to take a train downtown. As the train waited, a by-passer was asked by a passenger, "Who will be nominated?" Sewall was interested to hear the reply, "It looks like Sewall." As the train began to move, a latecomer raced to catch the last platform. As he swung aboard, he announced, "Sewall is the man," and the wealthy shipbuilder from Maine learned that he would share the ticket with Bryan.

The nomination of Bryan placed the Populists in a difficult position. It was argued that the People's Party should select its own candidate to preserve its identity, but the over-riding question of silver made expediency more important than party identity. The Populists endorsed the Democratic nominee. In a show of independence, they rejected Arthur Sewall at their convention in St. Louis, July 22, in favor of Thomas E. Watson of Georgia.

The eastern Gold Democrats were also in a difficult situation. Bryan and free silver were anathema, but McKinley's high protectionism was no more acceptable. The solution, albeit an unsatisfactory one, was a rump convention and a splinter party. A National Democratic Convention met in Indianapolis, Indiana, on September 2, under the chairmanship of Rosewell P. Flower, with delegates from all the states and territories except Idaho, Nevada, Utah, and Wyoming. John M. Palmer of Illinois and Simon Bolivar Buckner of Kentucky—one a Union general, the other a Confederate—were nominated as the standard bearers of the Gold Democrats. The platform was uncompromisingly for gold and praised the Cleveland administration. The President and Secretary of the Treasury Carlisle endorsed the ticket, as did most of the eastern leaders. An exception was Senator Hill. He stuck to the party, but just barely. "I am still a Democrat," he commented wryly, "very still."

CHAPTER 9

"To see Theodore Roosevelt take the veil"

THE TWELFTH REPUBLICAN NATIONAL CONVENTION
Philadelphia, June 19, 1900

For most men, defeat for the presidency is the end of a political career. For William Jennings Bryan, it was the beginning. The margin of McKinley's victory should have buried Bryan for all time, but the election of 1900 would, with one notable exception, be staged with the same cast.

The new high-tariff policies protected business, the Alaska gold rush stimulated the economy without a resort to silver, a bumper farm crop calmed the West, and the Populist storm melted away under the warm glow of prosperity. Excesses of national energy and pride were satisfied by the jingoistic war with Spain.

Having given America renewed prosperity and an empire, William McKinley would unquestionably be the Republican candidate in 1900. There was a brief flurry in the spring, when Admiral George Dewey, the hero of Manila Bay, announced that he too would be a candidate. The office, he felt, was not too arduous, and he coyly hinted that he was willing to accept nomination from either party. The recent cheers for the naval hero changed to hoots of laughter for the political aspirant. It took only a few days to laugh the Admiral out of politics.

The nomination of McKinley was a certainty, and there would be no problems about the platform, which would be of the "pointing with pride" variety, but there was one minor detail that the Republicans would have to settle when they met in Philadelphia. Vice-President Hobart had died the year before, and a new running mate would have to be found.

The President took the public position that he would not influence the delegates' choice and declared an open race. Privately, he urged Senator Allison to be a candidate. Allison, proud of his position as dean of the Senate, refused. The Republican National Committee wanted Elihu Root, but McKinley refused to part with his excellent Secretary of War. Mark Hanna intended to select a safe candidate, one who could be trusted to support the administration and stay quietly in his place out of the sun that was reserved for McKinley. He considered either Representative Jonathan P. Dolliver of Iowa or the recently resigned Secretary of the Interior Cornelius Bliss of New York as suitable.

Others mentioned as possibilities included Secretary of the Navy John D. Long, Senator Fairbanks, and Senator Spooner. For a time, Secretary Long appeared the favorite, but McKinley's refusal to support him or any other candidate prevented his gaining any support outside his native Massachusetts. The Lieutenant-Governor of New York, Timothy L. Woodruff, was an active candidate, but he could not get anyone to take him seriously.

The foremost candidate for the vice-presidency, although he had repeatedly said he did not want it, was the young Governor of New York, Theodore Roosevelt. The charge up San Juan Hill had carried the flamboyant Roosevelt into the executive mansion at Albany, where he had made a good record. This exuberant, dynamic, rather tiresome exponent of the strenuous life approached the world as if it were an eternal sporting event, but he was an able, dedicated politician. Noted as a naturalist, historian, and war hero, Theodore Roosevelt exemplified the hearty, supremely self-confident, and somewhat naive American spirit. With an absolute faith in American destiny, Roosevelt appealed especially to westerners and to the younger generation of voters, who believed him clearly destined for the White House.

Roosevelt desperately wanted to be president; the problem in 1900 was how to get there. There were three paths open to him. He could run for re-election as governor, or he could get himself appointed secretary of war; either office would place him in a good position for the presidential nomination in 1904. Or he could run for vice-president.

McKinley showed no inclination to offer Roosevelt a cabinet post. Re-election as governor seemed the best course to follow. He was convinced that the vice-presidency would put him on the shelf and be a sidetrack to oblivion. Most of his friends and all of his enemies agreed. The one exception among his friends was Henry Cabot Lodge, who thought he could use the vice-presidency as a stepping stone. No vice-president since Martin Van Buren had been elected president, but, Lodge pointed out, the best way to break a precedent was to make one.

Some of Roosevelt's enemies also wanted him to be vice-president. Senator Platt had given the Rough Rider the governorship in 1898 and bitterly repented of it. Although Roosevelt had made considerable concessions to Platt, he had acted too independently on occasion to suit the boss of New York. Platt could refuse to allow Roosevelt's renomination for governor, but that would be a dangerous course and would lead, in all probability, to defeat in November. A much better course would be to kick the protesting governor upstairs to the oblivion of the vice-presidency —anything to get him out of New York. Accordingly, Boss Platt and Boss Quay put their venerable, disreputable heads together and launched a Roosevelt-for-vice-president boom.

The boom got off to a rousing start. Western leaders announced themselves delighted at Roosevelt's candidacy, and Lodge worked tirelessly in his behalf. But the candidate refused to run. On February 6, he announced, "It is proper for me to state definitely that under no circumstances could I or would I accept the nomination for the Vice Presidency."

As the convention approached, Roosevelt wavered in his resolve. He certainly did not want the nomination, but he slowly came to realize that renomination for governor might not be his for the asking. Next to being vice-president, the worst thing Roosevelt could imagine was having no office at all. Platt implied that that was exactly what would happen.

Roosevelt finally decided to attend the convention as a delegate. Lodge warned that if he went he would be nominated, but Roose-

velt replied, "I would be looked upon as a coward if I didn't go."
He added on April 23, "By the way, I did *not* say that I would not
under any circumstances accept the vice-presidency."

In an agony of indecision, Roosevelt went to Washington in
early June to assure the administration that he was not a candidate.
With a murderous smile, Elihu Root told him, "Of course not—
you're not fit for it." The President remarkedly mildly that he
would be much more valuable in New York. Hanna was horrified
at the very suggestion.

The twelfth Republican National Convention met in Philadelphia on June 19, 1900. It was a staid, conservative gathering, but
one delegate stood out conspicuously from the rest. Roosevelt, in
spite of his denials, in spite of Lodge's warning, arrived in company
with Boss Platt and acted very much the candidate. Amid the straw-
hatted delegates his Rough-Rider black felt, worn at a rakish angle,
reminded everyone of San Juan Hill. "Gentlemen," commented one
delegate, "that's an acceptance hat."

On Sunday morning, June 17, Senator Boies Penrose, Quay's
man from Pennsylvania, called on Roosevelt at the Walton Hotel
to assure him that he had the solid support of Pennsylvania. Hanna
had prevented Quay from taking his seat in the Senate, and Quay
was avenging himself by promoting the Roosevelt candidacy. Penrose was followed by the chairman of the California delegation, and
soon the Governor's rooms were filled with enthusiastic delegates,
crowding around offering support. Roosevelt flashed his prominent,
dazzling teeth and expressed regret that he had been forced into
the field.

Mark Hanna was furious. He begged McKinley to declare for
Cornelius Bliss to stop the Roosevelt movement. The President
replied, "The President has no choice for Vice President . . . The
choice of the convention will be his choice; he has no advice to
give."

Hanna took up his command post on Monday morning, ready
to do murder if need be to prevent Roosevelt's nomination. But
the strain was beginning to tell. He was in poor health, and he
feared he had lost McKinley's confidence. His nerves finally
snapped. When the national committeeman from Wisconsin stopped
by for instructions, Hanna raged, "Do whatever you damn please!

I'm through! I won't have anything more to do with the convention!" His passion increasing, Hanna finally shouted, "Don't any of you realize that there's only one life between that madman and the Presidency?"

After this tirade, Hanna pulled himself together and went to see Roosevelt. He accused the Governor of bad faith in allowing himself to be a candidate and got him to agree to a statement disavowing his candidacy. The statement was issued on Monday afternoon. Roosevelt said he could best help the ticket by running again for governor and asked his friends to respect his judgment. It was an open invitation to have his judgment ignored.

The statement resulted in Platt's decisively increasing his pressure. He was tired of Roosevelt's shilly-shallying. He had made it quite clear that Roosevelt could not have another term as governor. Now he blandly indicated that he had no wish to push the Governor against his will and said that another candidate might be given the vice-presidency. That settled Roosevelt. "Buttons Bim" Bimberg flooded the streets with "McKinley-Roosevelt" buttons and souvenirs, declaring, "If it isn't Roosevelt there will be a dent in the Delaware River caused by Bim committing suicide."

Eager as the delegates were for Roosevelt, they were disturbed by the charges that his candidacy was the doing of the bosses. Much as they wanted the New Yorker, they were reluctant to be the tools of Platt and Quay. Accordingly, Roosevelt, in a well publicized manner, denounced Platt to a New York caucus and repudiated his support. Platt, quite unperturbed, announced that New York would support Lieutenant-Governor Timothy Woodruff for vice-president. This move was Platt's finishing touch. He had first forced Roosevelt into the race and now made it appear that the bosses were trying to force him out. As soon as the convention began whooping it up for the man who had defied the bosses, the wily old New York boss knew he had won. Lieutenant-Governor Woodruff was never mentioned again, and the delegates honestly believed that they had put Platt in his place.

Mark Hanna was crushed on the second day of the convention. His one hope of stopping Roosevelt lay in holding the southern delegates in line. Matt Quay rose in the convention to dash that last hope. He proposed an amendment to the rules that would base representation in national conventions on the size of the Republican vote in the last elections. This move would strip the South of virtually all its strength in Republican conventions. Having frightened the southerners out of their wits, Quay suavely suggested that discussion of the proposal be delayed for a day or two.

Frantic southerners flocked to Hanna to report that Quay had offered to withdraw his motion if they would support Roosevelt. The battle was over. After Secretary Long and Representative Dolliver announced their withdrawal from the race, Hanna surrendered. At one in the morning, he called in the reporters to announce that it was his decision that "Roosevelt should be nominated with the same unanimity as the President."

On Thursday, June 21, Joseph B. Foraker placed McKinley in nomination, and his speech was seconded by Theodore Roosevelt. The nomination was unanimous. Roosevelt was then nominated and received every vote in the convention except his own.

Tom Platt had not stayed to see his victory. Well satisfied that he had settled the problem of Theodore Roosevelt, he had returned to New York before the balloting. After the election, when asked if he would attend the inauguration, he gleefully replied, "Yes, I am going down to see Theodore Roosevelt take the veil." In his self-satisfaction, he did not foresee the act of a madman in Buffalo, but at least he had gotten Roosevelt out of New York State.

"A compact and undismayed army"

THE EIGHTEENTH DEMOCRATIC NATIONAL CONVENTION
Kansas City, July 4, 1900

There was no question in the minds of any of the delegates who gathered in Kansas City, Missouri, for the July 4th opening of the Democratic National Convention that William Jennings Bryan would again be the candidate. For a defeated candidate, Bryan had a remarkable hold on the party. As he himself put it, the six and a half million voters who had supported him "came out of the campaign of 1896 a compact and undismayed army."

The Democrats had two questions to settle in Kansas City: preparation of the money plank and selection of a vice-presidential candidate. All the party leaders, with one exception, were resolved to keep free silver out of the 1900 platform. With the country on a gold standard and prosperity achieved without free silver, they believed that the issue was dead. Any attempt to exhume it would only lose votes. Bryan was the one exception. He was a free-silver man first and last, and he would run, if he ran at all, on a silver plank. The question was, Would Bryan accept a compromise on the platform?

The eastern delegates were willing to go so far as to reaffirm the 1896 platform without a specific reference to free silver, but Bryan, who remained at his home in Lincoln, Nebraska, informed the party leaders that he would not run unless free silver were

186

specifically endorsed. He also sent word that, if the resolutions committee rejected the silver plank, he would come to Kansas City and lead a floor fight for it. By a margin of 1 vote, the committee accepted the platform Bryan wanted. It was an irony that Republicans were quick to point out that Bryan, the enemy of expansion, had had his plank saved by the vote of the delegate from Hawaii. David Hill wished to submit a minority report, but Richard Croker informed him that Tammany and New York would vote for the majority report, and Hill dropped his opposition.

Bryan was placed in nomination by William D. Oldham of Nebraska. His speech did not fire the imagination, but it served its purpose. Bryan received a unanimous nomination.

There were no outstanding candidates for the vice-presidential nomination. No one seemed very interested in the office except William Sulzer of New York, who was an active candidate. Richard Croker ruined his chances when he sneered, "Bryan and Sulzer! How long before everybody would be saying 'Brandy and Selzer?' "

Former Vice-President Adlai E. Stevenson and Charles A. Towne of Minnesota, chairman of the national committee of the Silver Republican party, were the chief candidates. Bryan's personal choice, although he made no effort to impose it on the convention, was Towne, but the delegates had no intention of nominating a Silver Republican. Stevenson, the sixty-five-year-old wheel horse, was considered a safe, competent, and tested campaigner who had the prestige of having formerly held the office.

On the first ballot, Stevenson led Towne 559½ to 89½. Two hundred eastern votes went as a protest to David Hill, who had refused to be a candidate. Before the results were announced, there were enough switches to give Stevenson the nomination, which was made unanimous.

CHAPTER 10

"The nominee of the American fireside"

THE THIRTEENTH REPUBLICAN NATIONAL CONVENTION
Chicago, June 21, 1904

The bullet fired by a demented, self-styled anarchist on September 6, 1901, ended the Golden Age of William McKinley and put "that damned cowboy" in the White House. The "square deal" of trust-busting and big-stick foreign policy brought dismay, anguish, and, finally, hatred to the hearts of the conservatives who had basked so contentedly in the soothing McKinley sun. Roosevelt honestly abhorred the misuses of wealth and power that had flourished under McKinley, but he was, at best, a moderate reformer. If his opponents, especially in the Senate, had not been so reactionary, it is doubtful that Roosevelt would ever have won the reputation for progressivism that he did. He could be called a radical only when compared to Mark Hanna or Senator Aldrich.

Opposition to Roosevelt's nomination to a term in his own right centered on the stout, reluctant figure of Mark Hanna. For all his misgivings about Roosevelt, Hanna conducted himself in a loyal and honest manner. He supported the leading policies of the Square Deal and kept on good terms with the new President. But, as the leading figure in the conservative wing of the party, it was inevitable that he would be pressured by his reactionary colleagues to oppose Roosevelt's nomination.

Although Hanna maintained, quite sincerely, that neither his health nor his inclinations would permit his being a candidate, he refrained from giving public support to Roosevelt's nomination. The possibility of a Hanna candidacy had Roosevelt seriously worried. It would be well financed and could quite likely buy up the southern delegates. Platt could swing New York, Penrose would control Pennsylvania, and Hanna himself could bring Ohio into line. With these three pivotal states and possibly other machine-dominated states and the southerners, Hanna would stand an excellent chance of winning the nomination. But Hanna was stricken with typhoid fever and died on February 15, 1904. His death removed any possibility of a reactionary coalition against Roosevelt and made his nomination a certainty.

The Republican National Convention of 1904 met in Chicago in the Coliseum, which could comfortably seat 10,000 and was suitable for roller skating, balls, and circuses. Palms and potted plants were set around the walls, and the girders beneath the saffron-colored roof were festooned with fresh oak boughs. A huge portrait, twenty by seventeen feet, of the late Mark Hanna was hung above the rostrum as a wistful reminder to the conservatives of a past age, and engravings of Roosevelt, bunting, and baskets of ferns completed the decor. The total effect was heavy, opulent, and undeniably hideous.

During the keynote address of Temporary Chairman Elihu Root, there was an odd occurrence. Root was paying tribute to Hanna and indicating the portrait above his head, when the sun came out from behind the clouds and the hall "was filled with a golden radiance. So peculiar was the coincidence that there was a buzz of surprised comment on every side." The surprise was probably due to the fact that no one, during Mark Hanna's lifetime, had ever expected him to be illuminated by heavenly light.

The permanent chairman was Speaker of the House Joseph Cannon. His despotic rule in the House had made him a legendary figure, and, in a convention without excitement, he was the most entertaining thing that happened. He delivered a rambling, humorous address, partly prepared, partly extemporaneous. He admitted that he had written a speech but was incapable of committing it to memory. Cannon likened Bryan, without mentioning him by name, to the river Platte—"fourteen miles wide and four inches deep."

On the third day, Roosevelt was placed in nomination by former Governor Frank Black of New York, and the nomination was seconded by Senator Beveridge of Indiana. Beveridge defined the difference between the Democrats and the Republicans: "They select their candidate for the people, and the people select our candidate for us. . . . Theodore Roosevelt, like William McKinley, is the nominee of the American fireside." Roosevelt received the unanimous vote of the convention.

The vice-presidential nomination, too, had been settled in advance. The conservatives, unable to present a candidate for president, wanted, at least, to name the running mate. Their choice was the wealthy Senator Charles Warren Fairbanks of Indiana. He had been Mark Hanna's second in command in the Senate and stood solidly for the principles of the conservative wing of the party. Roosevelt, having no desire to antagonize the old guard, meekly acquiesced in the choice, and Fairbanks was nominated without opposition.

"Into a cloudless atmosphere
of party peace"

THE NINETEENTH DEMOCRATIC NATIONAL CONVENTION
St. Louis, July 6, 1904

After his second defeat for the presidency, William Jennings Bryan announced that he would not be a candidate in 1904. For the first time in twenty years, the Democrats were without a national leader. They were, in fact, virtually without a candidate. The party held only six nonsouthern seats in the Senate—all from the West—and the only state houses outside the South held by Democrats were those of Montana, Nevada, Oregon, and Rhode Island—all quite hopeless for a national candidate.

Only two figures in national politics were given consideration for the nomination and then only briefly. After two "radical" campaigns led by free silver, the eastern leaders intended to name a conservative candidate in 1904, and Senator Arthur P. Gorman of Maryland, Senate minority leader, was soundly conservative. He received favorable press mention and the support of Senator Jones of Arkansas, one of Bryan's closest friends, Daniel Lamont and William Whitney of New York, and former Vice-President Morton. But on February 23, 1904, the Senate ratified the treaty with Panama. Gorman, who had marshalled all his forces to defeat the treaty, saw half the Senate Democrats desert him to vote for rati-

fication. Having received a stunning defeat from the senators under
his leadership, Gorman quietly took himself out of the race and devoted himself to securing the nomination of a conservative candidate who, even if defeated, would return control of the party to
eastern hands.

Grover Cleveland was also briefly considered. The bitter repudiation handed him by his party in 1896 had been forgotten, and
the former President was now a much-beloved elder statesman.
As the most distinguished exponent of Democratic conservatism,
he would have been a logical choice to lead the resurgent eastern
conservatives. But Cleveland was enjoying his retirement and had
no desire to risk his present esteem by a return to active politics.

With the only well-known leaders—Bryan, Gorman and Cleveland—out of the race, it was a year for dark horses, especially dark
horses from fields not usually associated with presidential candidacies. In New York, David B. Hill and Charles Murphy of Tammany turned to the judiciary and backed the distinguished, but
little known, fifty-one-year-old Alton B. Parker, Chief Judge of the
New York Court of Appeals. Parker was a conservative who had
supported Bryan in 1896. He had no desire to be president; his
only ambition was a place on the Supreme Court, and he refused
to speak out on political issues that might compromise his position
as a judge.

The bench provided a second candidate in former Senator
George Gray of Delaware, a federal circuit judge. The sixty-four-
year-old jurist had left the Senate in 1899 and had made a distinguished record for himself on the bench. He was popular with
Republicans as well as Democrats, admired for his integrity and
open-mindedness, and well thought of by labor. But Delaware was
not a sufficiently important state from which to draw a candidate,
and Gray had been a Gold Democrat in 1896, which made him
unacceptable to the Bryan wing.

The only other important candidate represented the "radical"
wing of the party. The publisher William Randolph Hearst decided
he wanted to be president, and, when Hearst wanted something,
he wanted it very badly indeed. To the dismay of the conservatives, the powerful Hearst press, with all the enthusiasm and dis-

regard for truth with which it had campaigned for war with Spain, launched a drive to put its publisher in the White House. Hearst was, perhaps, the most controversial figure of his time. Certainly he was the least understood. The son of a semiliterate mining multi-millionaire who had bought a seat in the Senate before the turn of the century, Hearst used his father's and later his mother's fortune to build a chain of newspapers as vulgar, as dishonest, and as entertaining as anything the nation had ever seen. The man himself was a mass of contradictions that defied analysis. He made his own rules, his own reality, and his own power—to serve his own ends and his own ambitions.

The reactionary and "crackpot" aspects of Hearst's career were in the future, and he entered the presidential race of 1904 as a liberal. He favored control of the trusts, an ending of secret railroad rebates, an eight-hour work day, and government ownership of railroads, telegraphs, and possibly mines. He fought for the graduated income tax and the direct election of senators. He carried his campaign for better schools nearly to the point of fanaticism. He had always been a regular Democrat, had supported Bryan in both campaigns, and hoped to inherit Bryan's western strength. With a liberal program, a powerful chain of newspapers to publicize him, unlimited funds with which to buy delegates, and popular western support, Hearst was a formidable candidate, and he frightened the eastern leaders half to death.

The conservative Democrats had a threefold goal as the campaign for the presidential nomination opened in early 1904: to discredit Hearst and prevent his nomination; to remove Bryan from party power and eradicate all traces of Bryanism from the party image; and, finally, to nominate a conservative who would embody the new "safe and sane" Democratic Party. Whether or not a conservative could be elected was of little concern to the party leaders. The outlook for winning the White House was not encouraging, and the eastern Democracy considered the final defeat of Bryanism more important than the defeat of Theodore Roosevelt.

To weaken Hearst, the conservatives brought as many candidates as possible into the field, hoping to dissipate his strength among the favorite sons. Cleveland was prevailed upon to "stop declining," Richard Olney took control of the Massachusetts delegation, Judge Gray accounted for Delaware, Senator Cockrell for Missouri, and John Sharp Williams, House minority leader, tied up North Dakota. Olney considered any competition with Hearst "demeaning of itself," but swallowed his pride for the good of the party.

Senator Gorman, although not a candidate, tied up Maryland with an uncommitted delegation that would do his bidding, and ancient, canny Henry Davis swung the West Virginia state convention away from Hearst. The delegation pledged twelve for Gorman, two for Hearst.

The Hearst papers stepped up their praise of the "Chief," and Hearst, who had secured a seat in Congress two years earlier to bolster his role of statesman, was frequently seen in Washington. On February 28, the Hearst press blazoned in headlines the names of the first two instructed delegates chosen in any state. Not surprisingly they were for Hearst.

California, South Dakota, Wyoming, and Arizona Territory swung into line for Hearst but not, it was rumored, without the expenditure of considerable sums from open-handed Hearst lieutenants. Iowa also declared for the congressman-publisher, but Indiana provided fireworks. As the Indiana state convention met, John W. Kern let loose a blast: "We are menaced for the first time in the history of the Republic by the open and unblushing effort of a multi-millionaire to purchase the Presidential nomination. Our state has been overrun with a gang of paid agents and retainers. . . . The Hearst dollar mark is all over them." If the allegation was true, it was money ill-spent. Indiana instructed for Parker.

Parker lost the fight for Nebraska. Bryan, outraged that a Parker Club had been set up in his private preserve, announced that he would be a delegate to the convention. He swept the state convention, which named an uninstructed delegation submissive to Bryan's wishes.

Parker was beginning to roll up an impressive array of support. Connecticut declared for him, and Cleveland announced, "I do not see how anyone professing to be a real intelligent Democrat can hesitate to accept Mr. Parker." David Hill routed Tammany in the state convention, and New York selected a Parker delegation. When Indiana declared for the Judge, *The Nation* editorialized that, because no Democrat could be elected without New York, New Jersey, and Connecticut, three of which had already declared for Parker, he was the only reasonable candidate.

The eastern leaders had succeeded in rallying the conservatives around the colorless Parker, but the liberals were flocking to Hearst. Westerners who remembered his loyalty to Bryan and labor leaders who approved of his progressive program generally moved into the Hearst column. By convention time, it was estimated that Hearst would have 215 delegates, Parker 302.

The uncommitted delegations and the favorite sons provided the key to the nomination. Olney and Gray could be expected to go to Parker in a showdown, but this switch could be offset if Bryan would give Hearst his outspoken support. Senator Gorman conferred with the Parker leaders in early June, and it was rumored that a deal had been made. In return for Gorman's support of Parker, he or a man of his choosing would be made chairman of the National Committee and, in the event of Parker's election, be given a free hand with patronage.

The Democratic National Convention met in St. Louis, Missouri, July 6, 1904. The conservatives, in complete control, had come to bury William Jennings Bryan once and for all. The National Committee had selected in advance John Sharp Williams of Mississippi for temporary chairman and Senator Joseph Bailey of Texas for permanent chairman. Bailey had been chosen over Congressman Champ Clark of Missouri by two votes. Clark was seated after dinner in the parlor of the Laclede Hotel, preparing his nominating speech for Senator Cockrell when a shadow fell across his writing paper. It was Senator Bailey, who asked what he was doing. When told, Bailey surprised Clark by saying, "Quit that; you can make an adequate speech for Cockrell without preparation; go to writing your speech as permanent chairman!" He went on to tell Clark that he did not want to be permanent chairman and was on his way to the National Committee to make them accept Clark.

Hill was furious, argued bitterly that Clark did "not train with their crowd" and might ruin their plans to nominate Parker. Bailey retorted that if Clark wanted to oppose their plans he could do it less effectively as chairman than he could from the floor. Finally, Hill, "swearing he would ne'er consent, consented."

At the second day's afternoon session, the conservatives who had been congratulating themselves on the political demise of Bryan received a rude shock. As the Great Commoner entered the hall, a great ovation rose from the delegates and spectators. Bryan ignored the cheering, but for eighteen minutes delegates carrying the standards of Kentucky, Nebraska, North Dakota, Iowa, Missouri, Montana, and Michigan marched around the hall. The conservatives nervously wondered if Bryan's burial had not been a bit premature.

For the moment it seemed not. The credentials committee reported a conflict over the Illinois delegation. The majority had voted to seat the delegation led by the Chicago boss, Roger Sullivan. A minority report recommended seating a delegation loyal to Bryan. Both delegations favored Hearst, so it was a question of whether or not Bryan would control the delegation. After a long debate led by Bryan in favor of the minority report, the convention voted 647 to 299 to seat the anti-Bryan delegation.

The real drama of the convention of 1904 would not be played out on the convention floor. It would, instead, be enacted in the room where the resolutions committee was in session through the night of July 7-8. The vote on the Illinois contest demonstrated that the Bryan-Hearst forces could not command even a one-third veto power. But if the battle was lost for the nomination, there could still be a victory on the platform.

David Hill entered the resolutions committee as the spokesman for the conservative majority; Bryan represented the minority. It was a long, exhausting fight, but Bryan mopped the floor with Hill and tore the platform to shreds. For sixteen hours—from eight in the evening to noon the following day—Bryan took up the platform plank by plank, moving to strike out phrases and planks and substitute his own. Surprisingly, for a man who was supposed to be dead and buried, he carried a majority of the committee with him on each point. Sweat streaming down his face, his clothes in disarray, his voice hoarse with arguing, William Jennings Bryan won, in the face of what should have been overwhelming opposition, one of his greatest victories.

Hill demanded a strong gold plank, although he admitted that he had no idea what Parker's money views were. When over half the committee claimed a gold plank would weaken the party in their states, it was decided to omit from the platform any reference to money.

When the exhausted committeemen finally emerged into the light of day, reporters rushed up to congratulate Hill upon his victory in preparing a platform that would be offered without minority reports. With a sad smile, Hill turned wearily to Bryan and said, "I am afraid you will have to give this man credit for the victory rather than me." Bryan himself later wrote, "I did not get into the platform all that I wanted, but . . . I kept out of the platform everything to which I objected."

The platform was accepted by the convention on a voice vote, and the roll was called for the nomination of candidates. In nominating Parker, Martin W. Littlejohn of New York described him as a man who would "lead us up toward the future into a cloudless atmosphere of party peace" and concluded with a plea for unity and an end to factional strife. Nowhere did he emphasize the fact that Parker might be able to win the election. Hearst, General Nelson A. Miles of Massachusetts, who had made his name in the Spanish American War, Senator Cockrell, Richard Olney, Edward C. Wall of Wisconsin, and John Sharp Williams were also nominated. Williams asked that his name be withdrawn and that his votes go to Parker.

The great fear harbored by the conservatives that Bryan would come out for Hearst was dispelled when he arose to second Senator Cockrell's nomination. The speech was not intended so much to support Cockrell as it was to vindicate Bryan. He announced before he began that he would require more time than the four minutes allotted for seconding speeches—Bryan could hardly get warmed up in that space of time—and asked for a suspension of the rules to give him all the time he wanted. If the convention should refuse, he warned, he would not second Cockrell but make a nominating speech, which would have no time limit, for someone else—perhaps former Governor Pattison of Pennsylvania. Even though it was now four o'clock in the morning, he was given unlimited time, a tribute either to Bryan or to the stoicism of the audience.

The main point of Bryan's long speech came when he said, "Eight years ago a Democratic National Convention placed in my hands the standard of the party and commissioned me as its candidate. Four years later that commission was renewed. I came tonight to this Democratic National Convention to return the commission. You may dispute whether I have fought a good fight, you may dispute whether I have finished my course, but you cannot deny that I have kept the faith." The convention agreed and gave him a great ovation.

It took only one ballot for the conservatives to take over the commission Bryan had just resigned. The results of the roll call were Parker 658, Hearst 200, Cockrell 42, Olney 38, Wall 27, Gray 12, Williams 8, Pattison 4, McClellan and Miles 3 each, Senator Gorman and Charles A. Towne of New York 2 each, and Bird S. Coler 1. Parker was only 9 votes short of nomination.

Senator Dubois of Idaho changed his 6 Hearst votes to Parker; 2 Nevada votes switched, and 3 West Virginia votes—1 Hearst and 2 Gorman—put Parker over. Washington switched its 10 Hearst votes, and the official results showed Parker with 679 to 181 for Hearst. At five minutes before six in the morning, with the sun streaming through the windows of the hall, the nomination was made unanimous.

Ordinarily the nomination of a vice-presidential candidate is an anticlimax at any political convention. The Democratic National Convention of 1904 had its anticlimax in the nomination of Alton B. Parker, so it can be imagined how much interest there was in the second place on a doomed ticket. Delegates began leaving St. Louis even before the vice-presidential nomination, and William Randolph Hearst gloomily boarded his private train to return to New York.

There were few candidates for the vice-presidency. William Harris of Kansas, George Turner of Washington, and Robert Williams of Delaware had their advocates, but David Hill and the other Parker men in consultation decided to give the nomination to eighty-one-year-old Henry Gassaway Davis of West Vir-

ginia. Their reasons for giving their blessings to this most ancient
of party leaders was simple. He was a conservative, which would
appeal to the East, but he had also advocated free silver, which
would sweeten the ticket for Bryan. He had no known enemies—
probably because he had outlived anyone who might have been—
and, most important, he was the richest man in West Virginia.

The delegates were gathered on the afternoon of the fourth
day to ratify Hill's choice when a bombshell rocked the convention.
Reports had circulated through the city that William Sheehan of
New York had received a telegram from Parker demanding that
the convention endorse the gold standard. Sheehan did not produce
the telegram when questioned, and the convention buzzed with
speculation. Finally, some newspapermen, bored with the vice-
presidential nominating speeches, decided to stir things up. A message to Senator Carmack was concocted, and the papers reported
it as saying, "The Gold Standard is established by law, and I
cannot accept the nomination unless that plank is contained in the
platform." The alleged telegram was signed "Alton B. Parker." The
convention was thrown into an uproar. Many delegates who still
had a sentimental attachment to bimetalism had voted for Parker
with the understanding that money would not enter the campaign.
Had not Hill, after all, stated that he knew nothing of Parker's
fiscal views, implying thereby that he had none? The party leaders
hastily conferred, and the convention was recessed. The vice-
presidential nomination was completely forgotten in the scramble
to ascertain Parker's views on gold.

The western delegates were near hysteria. Missouri demanded
that Parker's nomination be withdrawn. Champ Clark was summoned to a conference at the Southern Hotel. He "found the
rotunda seething with angry, swearing, perspiring men from west
of the Alleghenies. They were demoralized and frenzied. . . . My
fellow delegates were wild." Acting on the supposition that the
telegram was genuine, Missouri concocted a strategy to withdraw
Parker's nomination. It hinged on Clark's ruling that a simple majority vote would rescind the two-thirds rule. They believed that
a majority of the convention would vote to abolish the two-thirds
rule and then vote to withdraw Parker's nomination.

Bryan had taken to his bed to nurse a severe cold, which was threatening to turn into pneumonia. When several delegates came to report the Parker-Carmack telegram and vow that they "had been bunkoed," he responded to the challenge. Eluding his doctor, Bryan dressed and hurried to the convention hall to lead the battle against Parker and the gold standard.

When the convention reconvened, a major effort was begun to repudiate Parker. As the orators roared, Ben Tillman turned to David Hill and commented wryly, "The Democratic party can always be relied on to make a damn fool of itself at the critical time." Tillman was, for once, absolutely right. Before Missouri could put its plan into action, the truth came out.

Senator Carmack denied that he had ever received any sort of telegram from Parker in his entire life, and William Sheehan read the real telegram to the convention. In it, Parker said, "I regard the gold standard as firmly and irrevocably established. . . . As the platform is silent on the subject, my views should be made known to the Convention, and if they are proved to be unsatisfactory to the majority, I request you to decline the nomination for me at once. . . ." Suddenly a great many angry people felt rather foolish. As Champ Clark put it, the real telegram "reduced the excitement several degrees and knocked the parliamentary program of the Missourians and their allies into a cocked hat."

The convention decided to send the following reply to Judge Parker: "The platform adopted by this Convention is silent on the question of the monetary standard, because it is not regarded by us as a possible issue in this campaign, and only campaign issues were mentioned in the platform. Therefore, there is nothing in the views expressed by you in the telegram just received which would preclude a man entertaining them from accepting a nomination on said platform." It was a fine piece of hair-splitting, but it served its purpose.

With the tea-pot tempest of the Parker telegram settled, the convention belatedly remembered that it was in the midst of selecting a running mate. It took only one ballot to nominate wealthy and, it was to be hoped, generous Henry G. Davis, who thus received the dubious honor of being the oldest man ever nominated on the national ticket by either major party. Oddly enough, although he was attacked during the campaign as being too old for the office, he survived for another twelve years. At one-twenty in the morning, the convention made the Davis nomination unanimous, and Davis, who had left the convention after Parker's nomination, was reached by telegram at Greenville, Ohio, and notified of his place on the ticket.

CHAPTER 11

"Make it the presidency"

THE FOURTEENTH REPUBLICAN NATIONAL CONVENTION
Chicago, June 16, 1908

The Democratic Party, on Election Day, 1904, received from Theodore Roosevelt its soundest drubbing since Grant had overwhelmed Seymour. Exhilarated by his triumph, Roosevelt uttered the famous words that he would never cease to regret. He would not, he said, under any circumstances depart from the two-term tradition to seek re-election in 1908. Roosevelt had good reason to wish he had never made such a statement. His popularity remained as great as ever, and it was evident that he could have had another nomination for the asking. Since he had removed himself from consideration, however, there was nothing he could do except select his successor.

Secretary of State Elihu Root was Roosevelt's first choice for the 1908 candidate, but his age and Wall Street connections made his candidacy impractical. Roosevelt, looking over the field of potential candidates, decided to swing the administration behind the Secretary of War, William Howard Taft. The fifty-year-old Taft had served in a number of appointive offices, including those of solicitor general and governor of the Philippines. Although Taft had never held elective office, Roosevelt did not think that would be a problem. Taft, however, wanted to be Chief Justice of the Supreme Court, rather than president. Mrs. Taft, on the other hand, wanted to see her husband in the White House. One evening several months before the convention, the President, who was dining with the Tafts, said in a playful mood that he was given to visions. He saw, he said, a man weighing 350 pounds with something hanging over his head. He could not tell whether it was the presidency or the chief justiceship. "Make it the presidency," cried the eager Mrs. Taft. "Make it the chief justiceship," begged her husband. Taft's plea was ignored. Under pressure from the President, from his wife, and from his brother Charles, he finally agreed to be a candidate.

As soon as Taft agreed, Roosevelt gave him the full support of the administration. Assistant Postmaster General Frank H. Hitchcock and William Loeb, the President's private secretary, were put in charge of rounding up delegates. Of 194 southern delegates, 128 were secured. Of 125 delegates who were federal office-holders, ninety-seven were for Taft. By the end of May, Hitchcock was able to report that 563 delegates were firmly committed to Taft— seventy-two more than were needed for nomination.

Taft's claim as heir apparent was challenged by a group of candidates known as the "Allies." The anti-Taft group included Governor Charles Evans Hughes of New York, Senator Philander Knox of Pennsylvania, Vice-President Fairbanks, Speaker of the House Cannon of Illinois, and Senator LaFollette of Wisconsin. Senator Foraker tried, with old-guard support, to challenge Taft in Ohio, but he was easily routed.

None of the Allies had the slightest chance of nomination. There was no consensus on who might have the best chance to take the nomination away from Taft. The old guard, led by Senator Murray Crane of Massachusetts and Uncle Joe Cannon, refused to consider either Hughes or Knox, and none of the other candidates had more than the most minor favorite-son support.

When the Republican National Convention opened in Chicago on June 16, the conservatives scored a minor victory. Roosevelt had wanted the historian Senator Albert Beveridge of Indiana chosen as temporary chairman, but the old guard argued that, because Indiana had a candidate in Vice-President Fairbanks, it would be unsuitable to select an Indianian as temporary chairman. The administration forces were not enough concerned to contest the issue, and conservative Senator Julius C. Burrows of Michigan was given the honor of the keynote address. He delivered one of the longest, dullest keynote speeches on record and choked badly when he had to mention Roosevelt's name. Taft he mentioned not at all.

After pausing to pay tribute to three spectators who had been delegates to the first Republican National Convention in 1856, the convention took up the credentials-committee report. There were 223 contested seats, mostly southern, and the convention seated, in each contest, the pro-Taft delegates, who generally represented the regular organization.

Senator Henry Cabot Lodge, in his address as permanent chairman, provoked the greatest demonstration of the convention. When he pointed with pride to the accomplishments of the Roosevelt administration, the floor exploded in a roaring forty-nine minute demonstration. To the intense relief of Mrs. Taft, the ovation was a tribute, not a stampede to the Rough Rider.

Seven candidates were placed in nomination on the third day: Speaker Cannon, Vice-President Fairbanks, Governor Hughes, Taft, Senator Foraker, Senator Knox, and Senator LaFollette. Before the balloting, a group of spectators in the gallery made an unexpected attempt to stampede the convention for Roosevelt. Chanting "Four-years-more" and displaying a portrait of the President, the galleries and then the delegates took up the demonstration. In Washington, the Tafts, listening on a long-distance telephone, sat nervously while the demonstration went on. Mrs. Taft was tight lipped and white faced. Her husband tried to look unconcerned, secretly hoping, perhaps, that he might yet be spared the nomination he did not want.

Chairman Lodge, to prevent the ovation from leading to a stampede, ordered the roll to be called even though no one could hear the voting. It was not until Massachusetts had voted that most of the delegates realized the ballot was in progress. Mrs. Taft could relax at last when the results were announced: Taft 702, Knox 68, Hughes 67, Cannon 58, Fairbanks 40, LaFollette 25, Foraker 16, and Theodore Roosevelt 3.

The administration lost out on the vice-presidency. Taft, who wanted a liberal middle-westerner on the ticket, favored Senator

Johnathan Dolliver of Iowa. But Dolliver refused to be a candidate, as did Governor Hughes. The Taft forces next asked Vice-President Fairbanks to run again and, upon his refusal, approached Senator Long of Kansas, who also declined.

While the Taft forces were searching unsuccessfully for a candidate, Speaker Cannon lined up support for "Sunny Jim" Sherman, a portly, rubicund congressional hack from New York. Sherman and former Governor Franklin Murphy of New Jersey were placed in nomination. Senator Lodge paid off a political obligation by nominating Governor Curtis Guild of Massachusetts. The Taft forces had no official candidate. The delegates, willing to follow Speaker Cannon's powerful advice, nominated Sherman with 816 votes to 77 for Murphy, 75 for Guild, and 11 scattered.

"Their accustomed occupation of electing a Republican President"

THE TWENTIETH DEMOCRATIC NATIONAL CONVENTION
Denver, July 7, 1908

The Democratic National Convention of 1908 was William Jennings Bryan's all the way. His hold on the party was remarkable. *The Wall Street Journal* wrote, "He has built up a personal following unparalleled for one with a record of nothing but defeat, and with no patronage to strengthen his control." Parker's crushing defeat had so demoralized the conservatives that there was no hope of effective opposition to the Great Commoner's bid for a third nomination. Minor candidates appeared in Judge Gray of Delaware and Governor John A. Johnson of Minnesota. Neither had any prospect of nomination. Judge Gray was sixty-eight, and Governor Johnson —young, vigorous, and engaging—intended only to bring his name before the public in order to be well known the next time around.

The twentieth Democratic National Convention met in Denver, Colorado, on July 7, 1908. Denver welcomed the delegates with open-handed western hospitality, including free shows and cowboys and Indians for the goggle-eyed pleasure of the eastern tenderfeet, but all the excitement attendant on the gathering took place outside the convention hall. Bryan had remained at home in Lincoln, Nebraska. His absence made for a colorless convention.

The Bryan demonstration broke out early in the proceedings. In addressing the delegates, blind Senator Gore of Oklahoma mentioned Bryan's name. In the ensuing uproar, a new record for convention demonstrations was set when the cheering dragged on for one hour and twenty-seven minutes.

After accepting the platform, which read like a Bryan campaign speech and which had been prepared by the candidate himself, the convention cast the one ballot necessary for the nomination. Bryan received 892½ votes to 50½ for Judge Gray and 46 for Governor Johnson.

Bryan dictated the choice for vice-president with as firm a control as he had used to secure his own nomination. His choice was a fifty-eight-year-old Indiana lawyer and long-time personal friend John W. Kern. New York offered Charles A. Towne, who had been a senator from Minnesota and later a congressman from New York. Connecticut and Georgia also presented candidates. Bryan wanted Kern, and the convention made him the vice-presidential candidate by acclamation.

The Democrats had once again turned to Bryan, but there was little hope of his being elected president. George Harvey, one of the disgruntled but impotent conservatives in the party, spitefully but correctly remarked, "The Democrats will now resume their accustomed occupation of electing a Republican President."

CHAPTER 12

"Toot! Toot!"

THE FIFTEENTH REPUBLICAN NATIONAL CONVENTION
Chicago, June 18, 1912

Theodore Roosevelt, having seen his hand-picked successor inaugurated as president, departed for big-game hunting in Africa. Wall Street, breathing a sigh of relief, expected "every lion to do his duty." While the former President, once again Colonel Roosevelt, reduced the animal population of Africa, his heir moved to the right. Taft, the President created by Roosevelt to carry on his policies, was deprived, at the outset of his administration, of Roosevelt's counsel and support. Politically maladroit, conservative by nature, unaware of and indifferent to the value of public relations, the new President was described as "a large body surrounded by men who knew exactly what they wanted." Taft turned to these men—Aldrich, Penrose, Joe Cannon, and the rest of the Old Guard for guidance. Although never so conservative as the progressives made him out to be, Taft appeared to have turned his back on Roosevelt and his policies.

Taft's alleged conservatism and his alleged betrayal of the Roosevelt policies were sufficient reason for the estrangement between the two men. But the real reason was much more simple. Theodore Roosevelt wanted to be president again, and, when Roosevelt wanted something, he could always justify his desire somehow.

Roosevelt returned from abroad in 1910 to find that a powerful

Repuplican minority had been waging the progressive fight against the administration. The Colonel decided to turn the growing power of the "insurgents" to his own purpose. The Old Guard, the "stand-patters," were for Taft. The insurgents must be for Roosevelt. He joined the progressives on August 31, 1910, while dedicating a monument to John Brown at Osawatomie, Kansas. Roosevelt enunciated his program of "The New Nationalism," calling for control of corporations and the prohibition of the use of corporate funds for political purposes, tariff revision, a graduated income tax, direct primaries, the initative, referendum and recall, workmen's compensation, and other points in the insurgent program.

Until the early months of 1912, Roosevelt denied that he had any presidential ambitions, and progressive support centered on Senator Robert M. LaFollette of Wisconsin, the Insurgents' leader and, in many ways, the father of the progressive movement. If any man deserved the support of the progressives, LaFollette did. His candidacy, launched in 1911, drew enthusiastic support throughout the country, and it appeared that the Wisconsin Senator would have an excellent chance of defeating Taft in the convention. Even Roosevelt gave tacit support to the LaFollette cause, although he never actually gave him his endorsement.

When Roosevelt realized that the Insurgents might defeat Taft for the nomination, he began seriously to think of becoming a candidate himself. To this end, he decided to arrange a draft. On January 18, 1912, he sent letters to Governors Osborn of Michigan, Glasscock of West Virginia, and Hadley of Missouri suggesting that "a group of governors write him . . . asking him to respond to the popular demand" that he become a candidate.

On February 9, seven governors signed a letter asking Roosevelt to enter the race. They were Hadley, Glasscock, Osborn, Stubbs of Kansas, Bass of New Hampshire, Carey of Wyoming, and Aldrich of Nebraska. They were joined the following day by Governor Vessey of South Dakota. The eight governors, together with delegates from twenty-eight states, met in Chicago to organize a draft-Roosevelt movement, to endorse his candidacy, and to endorse the direct primary.

Senator LaFollette realized that his strength was melting away, and he himself delivered the fatal blow to his own candidacy on

February 2. With Governor Woodrow Wilson of New Jersey, he had been invited to address the annual banquet of the Periodical Publishers Association in Philadelphia. The Senator arrived at the banquet exhausted from work and an all-night vigil at the bedside of his daughter, who was seriously ill. LaFollette was unaware that many newspapermen and publishers were present as guests of the magazine publishers, and he launched a violent attack upon the newspapers, which was coupled with almost fawning praise of the periodicals. The audience reaction was immediately hostile. Greatly disturbed when some of the audience left the room, LaFollette lost his head. For two tragic hours, he harangued his audience, repeating whole sections of his speech and frequently lapsing into incoherence. Those who did not leave sat embarrassed as the Senator rambled on and on. Reports began to circulate immediately after the speech that he had suffered a nervous breakdown and would withdraw from the race for the nomination.

LaFollette was in perfectly good health, suffering only from fatigue, but his momentary mental collapse at the publishers' banquet gave his erstwhile supporters the excuse they needed. Within the next two weeks, Gifford and Amos Pinchot, James Garfield, George Norris, and Governor Hiram Johnson, along with numerous lesser supporters, defected to Roosevelt. So hasty was the scramble away from LaFollette that the New York *Tribune* was prompted to express its sympathy. "The haste with which most of the insurgent leaders are seeking to clamp the lid down on Senator LaFollette's candidacy must excite the compassion of those who believe that there should be at least some moderate standard of honor among politicians. . . . He is being hustled ruthlessly inside the hearse, although he still insists that he is strong enough to occupy a seat alongside the driver."

Along with the Insurgents, financial leaders were enlisting in the Roosevelt cause. George W. Perkins, a Morgan partner, and publisher Frank A. Munsey became principal financial backers. Thomas W. Lawson contributed $100,000, and the president of the Crucible Steel Company helped to swell the war chest.

With Insurgent backing and a war chest that would eventually total more than a half-million dollars, Colonel Roosevelt needed no further reasons for entering the contest, but Taft provided him one anyway. Taft had viewed the forthcoming battle with misgivings. He had no real desire for a second nomination, but he resented being shoved out of office. He decided to make the race and opened his attack against the progressives in an address to the New York Republican Club on Lincoln's Birthday. The progressives, he said, "Would hurry us into a condition which would find no parallel except in the French Revolution." Then, in one of those unfortunate remarks that plagued him throughout his political career, Taft said, "Such extremists are not Progressives, they are political emotionalists or neurotics." Although Taft later said that he had had someone else in mind, the highly emotional Roosevelt took great offense at the remark and decided to make the race a personal contest between Taft and himself.

The Colonel, while passing through Cleveland, Ohio, on February 21, coined a political phrase. In reply to a reporter's question about his intentions, he said, "My hat is in the ring," then threw everything else in after it. "The fight is on and I am stripped to the buff."

The contest would be a straight-out battle between the progressives and the conservatives, but there were some who questioned the sincerity of Roosevelt's progressive spirit. LaFollette, of course, bitterly obsessed with the idea that Roosevelt had betrayed him, challenged his right to wear the progressive badge, and his old friend Elihu Root, firmly committed to Taft, took a shrewdly appraising view of Roosevelt's progressive principles. "He is essentially a fighter," Root wrote, "and when he gets into a fight he is completely dominated by the desire to destroy his adversary. He instinctively lays hold of every weapon which can be used for that end. Accordingly he is saying a lot of things and taking a lot of positions which are inspired by the desire to win. I have no doubt he thinks he believes what he says, but he doesn't. He has merely picked up certain popular ideas which were at hand as one might pick up a poker or chair with which to strike."

But most of the progressives had no doubts about Roosevelt's sincerity, and thousands of eager volunteers set up Roosevelt clubs throughout the nation. Pledges of support poured in to Oyster Bay. The famous diva, Mme. Schumann-Heink trilled, "I love Teddy Roosevelt. I could eat him; and I wish he would be President all the time." More restrained was Skookum Wallikee, a Klickitat Indian chief who urged all Indians with the vote to cast it for Roosevelt. "He heap big man, all same chief," he said, perhaps with the assistance of an imaginative reporter.

One problem that had to be settled before the campaign could get underway was Roosevelt's unfortunate statement in 1904 that he would not be a candidate for the third term. The Colonel smoothly explained: "My position on the third term is perfectly simple. I said I would not accept a nomination for a third term under any circumstances, meaning of course a third consecutive term. . . ." The *Outlook*, for which Roosevelt was a contributing editor, offered a cozy, if specious, argument. "When a man says at breakfast in the morning 'No, thank you, I will not take any more coffee,' it does not mean that he will not take any more coffee to-morrow morning, or next week, or next month, or next year." Throughout the spring, any vaudeville comedian could always get a laugh by asking his audience, "Have another cup of coffee?" The third term issue, however, was completely overshadowed by other questions and played no significant part in the campaign for the nomination.

The Roosevelt forces decided that, if they were seriously to challenge Taft, it would be necessary to win in the state primaries, which would be in use for the first time on a wide scale. The direct primary to select convention delegates had been initiated in Wisconsin in 1905 and, by early 1912, was operating in South Dakota, Oregon, Nebraska, New Jersey, North Dakota, and California as well. Pennsylvania and Ohio had provision for the election of district delegates, and, in New York, district delegates could be elected at the option of the state committees. Roosevelt entered all the existing primaries and made plans to add other states to the primary system. Roosevelt supporters were successful in passing primary laws in Illinois, Maryland, and Massachusetts.

The first primary was held in North Dakota on March 19 and was a substantial victory for LaFollette. The Senator had campaigned vigorously to belie the rumors that he had suffered a nervous breakdown, and he swept the primary with 34,123 votes to 23,669 for Roosevelt and 1,876 for Taft.

The next test went to Taft. During the last week in March, the vote in New York gave Taft eighty-three of the ninety district delegates who would attend the convention. Roosevelt cried that the vote was "a wicked and howling farce." He had, he charged, been stabbed in the back by the bosses. Roosevelt had not entered the Wisconsin primary against LaFollette and, on April 5, the Senator overwhelmed Taft. It was LaFollette's last primary victory.

The remainder of the primaries were a clear victory for Roosevelt. He swept Illinois on April 9, won sixty-four delegates to Taft's twelve in Pennsylvania, and added Nebraska to his total later in the month. At the beginning of April, Taft had 265 pledged delegates to Roosevelt's thirty-five and LaFollette's ten. By the end of the month, Taft had increased to 383, while Roosevelt had jumped to 209. LaFollette had thirty-six, and favorite son Senator Cummins of Iowa had ten.

The primary contests brought forth the most remarkable and, in some respects, the most degrading exhibition ever staged by a President and a former President of the United States. Roosevelt charged the President with attempting to steal the nomination, with being a tool of the bosses, with being a traitor to progressivism and to Roosevelt himself. At first, Taft refused to answer in kind. In March, he plaintively used one of Roosevelt's own catchphrases when he said that all his administration wanted from the Colonel and the voters was a "square deal," but by April he had been goaded beyond his endurance. Campaigning in Boston, Taft began, "I am here to reply to an old and true friend. I do not want to fight Theodore Roosevelt, but sometimes a man in a corner fights. I am going to fight." For two hours, he refuted, point by point, the Roosevelt accusations and branded the former President a false friend and a poor loser. After the speech, he retired to his private car. There, when a friend found him, he said brokenly, "Roosevelt was my closest friend," and began to weep. Taft was not the man to compete in gutter tactics with the rough-riding Teddy Roosevelt. As William Allen White put it, "Roosevelt was not the weeping sort. When he decided to cut a throat, he generally justified it and rarely regretted it." The Colonel replied to the Taft attack by shouting in his high, piping voice that Taft had been "disloyal to our past friendship . . . disloyal to every canon of ordinary decency."

The relationship between the two Presidents was brought into sharp focus the night before the Massachusetts primary, when the protégé cried out in anguish and rage, "I was a man of straw, but I have been a man of straw long enough." In spite of this unfortunate, if accurate, phrase, the "man of straw" won eighteen of the thirty-six Massachusetts delegates. Ten went to Roosevelt, and eight were uninstructed.

As Roosevelt stepped up his personal attacks on Taft, the President blurted to a Maryland audience, "I am a man of peace and I don't want to fight. But when I do fight I want to hit hard. Even a rat in a corner will fight." Roosevelt had another addition for his arsenal of personal abuse against the luckless "cornered rat."

Sometimes the Colonel, bringing the progressive message to the people, let his evangelistic fervor play havoc with his syntax. He tried, in Louisville, Kentucky, to define progressivism. "The essential difference between men who . . . stand for the forward movement, the men who stand for the uplift and betterment of mankind, and who have faith in the people—on the one hand, and on the other, the men of narrow vision and small sympathy, who are not stirred by the wrongs of others, and with these men stand those other men who distrust the people, but wish to keep them helpless so as to exploit them for their own benefit." The next day he was somewhat more coherent when he declared that the fundamental issue of the campaign was that the country "must be a pretty good place for all of us if it is to be a good place for any of us."

The people were for Roosevelt, coherent or not. He swept the remaining primaries: Maryland, Oregon, California, New Jersey. Even Taft's own home state of Ohio gave him 34 of its 48 votes. By the first of June, Taft had collected 472 pledged delegates, Roosevelt 439, LaFollette thirty-six, and Cummins ten, with seventy-five uninstructed. Five hundred forty were necessary to nominate. Of 388 delegates elected in the primaries, Roosevelt won 281, Taft 71, and LaFollette 36. But Roosevelt, clearly the popular choice of Republicans, was far short of the necessary votes for victory. Consequently, the Roosevelt forces hatched a strategy to gain the needed votes.

The strategy was to challenge as many Taft delegates as possible—especially among the southern delegates, who had been selected before Roosevelt's entry into the contest—in order to make the public believe that Taft and Roosevelt were evenly matched in uncontested delegates and that the settlement of the contests would decide the outcome of the convention. If the pro-Taft National Committee should rule in Roosevelt's favor—an unlikely event as the Colonel knew—he would have made a successful raid on the Taft strength. If, as was more likely, the National Committee ruled in Taft's favor, then Roosevelt could claim that the Old Guard, the standpatters, and the bosses had stolen the nomination away from him. In all, Roosevelt challenged 248 delegates. Most of the challenges were based on the flimsiest of evidence, and it was necessary to shout "thief" loudly and often to confuse and cloud the issue.

That the famous charge of a "stolen nomination" was the result of a cynically calculated power play was perfectly revealed by a dispatch in the Washington *Times*, one of Frank Munsey's pro-Roosevelt newspapers. Published on June 9, while the National Committee was ruling in favor of Taft, the dispatch admitted: "For psychological effect, as a move in practical politics, it was necessary for the Roosevelt people to start contests on these early Taft selections in order that a tabulation of delegate strength could be put out that would show Roosevelt holding a good hand. In the game a table showing Taft 150, Roosevelt 18, contested none, would not be very much calculated to inspire confidence, whereas one showing Taft 23, Roosevelt 19, contested 127, looked very different. That was the whole story of the larger number of southern contests that were started early in the game. It was never expected that they would be taken very seriously. They served a useful purpose, and now the National Committee is deciding them in favor of Taft in most cases without real division."

Throughout the preconvention campaign, Roosevelt stormed about the country crying "theft," and Dixon, Pinchot, and the other leaders chimed in with "stolen goods." So extreme did the Roosevelt charges become that the New York *Sun*, admittedly an unfriendly paper, satirized the whole affair. They had the Colonel crying, "The bestial nature of the indecent hordes of pirates, second story men, porch climbers, gun men and short card dealers who oppose me is now perfectly manifest. . . . This strikes at the

very foundation-stone of pure democracy, for it misrepresents me.
. . . This despicable effort to confuse and obscure the public mind
I denounce as a machination of the special interests in their loath-
some campaign for the submergence of innocence, childhood,
motherhood, womanhood, and Abraham Lincoln." After hearing
the Roosevelt charges, the *Sun* satire of which was not too far from
reality, Mr. Dooley remarked, "Yes, sir; th' republic is doomed to
desthruction again."

The Republican National Committee met in Chicago on June 7
to consider the cases of the challenged delegates and to prepare a
temporary roll to be used in organizing the convention. The fifty-
three-man National Committee had been chosen in 1908 to serve
until the adjournment of the 1912 convention. Over a dozen committeemen, including the acting chairman Victor Rosewater were
lame ducks who had been defeated in the recent state conventions.
The Roosevelt forces demanded that they be replaced immediately
by the newly elected committeemen, but this suggestion, against all
precedent, was ignored. Two members of the committee favored
LaFollette, and eleven, including William E. Borah of Idaho, T.
Coleman Du Pont of Delaware, and Frank Kellogg of Minnesota,
were pro-Roosevelt. The other forty, led by Senators Penrose and
Crane, were for Taft.

The National Committee met, appropriately enough, in a large
room in the Chicago Auditorium recently occupied by the me-
nagerie of the Ringling Circus, to begin by what Roosevelt called
"steamroller tactics" to seat the Taft delegates. On June 7, sixteen
Alabama and eight Arkansas contests were settled in Taft's favor.
The next day gave forty-eight more Taft claimants seats in the
convention, and, on Monday, June 10, ten Indiana contests went to
Taft. By June 11, Taft had been awarded 101 delegates, Roosevelt
one, and there were 152 yet to be considered.

The Colonel breathed fire. "Again and again," he shrilled from
Oyster Bay, "we have sent to the penitentiary election officials for
deeds not one whit worse than what was done by the National
Committee at Chicago yesterday." He called the seating of the Taft
Indiana delegates "a fraud as vulgar, as brazen, and as cynically
open as any ever committed by the Tweed regime. . . ." Loudly
he proclaimed the issue to be "simply whether or not we shall

permit a system of naked fraud, of naked theft from the people to triumph."

For all his charges of "steamroller" and "theft," Roosevelt had a very flimsy case. Senator Borah, staunchly for Roosevelt, admitted as much. After the first seventy-two contests had been settled, the Senator stated that only two contests heard thus far had, in his opinion, any merit, and, on June 10, he said, "There have been many frauds at the primaries, I don't say there were not. But there is no evidence of that fact presented. . . . Under the circumstances, I could not vote to sustain the Roosevelt delegates."

Of the 248 challenged seats, thirty-six were settled for Taft by unanimous consent on a roll call. Twenty-six were given to the President on a voice vote announced as unanimous, and eighty-eight were seated by voice vote unchallenged by the pro-Roosevelt committeemen. The Roosevelt supporters thus admitted that 150 Roosevelt challengers had no case. Of the remaining cases, fourteen Roosevelt challengers withdrew before being acted upon, and nineteen contests were decided in Roosevelt's favor. That left sixty-five contests given to Taft over the protests of the Roosevelt committeemen. An analysis of the evidence indicated that, of these sixty-five contests, forty-nine could fairly be said to have shown evidence favoring the Roosevelt delegates. True, the Taft majority would have seated the Taft delegates, regardless of the validity of their claims, in exactly the same manner that the National Committee had, at Roosevelt's insistence, seated the pro-Taft delegates to the 1908 Convention. The methods were identical. It was only when the Colonel was on the losing end that he shouted "thief." It is likely that forty-nine delegates were indeed stolen by the Taft forces, but, even if they had not been, Roosevelt would have been far short of a controlling majority of the convention.

Realizing that he was in danger of losing the nomination, Roosevelt decided that his campaign needed his own dramatic presence. He announced on Friday, June 14, that he would go to Chicago, an unprecedented step for an active candidate. A huge crowd greeted him at the Chicago station when his train pulled in on Saturday morning. Synthetic rough riders on rented horses, blaring bands, and thousands of cheering, perspiring admirers screamed their adulation. The crowds broke through the police lines to surround the beaming, waving Colonel, who, when asked how he felt, repeated a happy phrase he had used in an interview two weeks earlier. He felt fine, he said, "just like a bull moose," and a political symbol was born.

Roosevelt was escorted through the Chicago streets to the Congress Hotel, while the bands played "There'll Be a Hot Time in the Old Town Tonight." Traffic came to a standstill as the Roosevelt supporters milled about outside the hotel until the Colonel appeared on a balcony to address the multitude. "It is a naked fight against theft," he cried, "and the thieves will not win." While the crowd roared, "Soak 'em, Teddy," he charged, "the politicians will be made to understand that they are the servants and not the masters of the plain citizens of the Republican party."

Mr. Dooley reflected the attitude of the thousands who poured into the city, eagerly anticipating the brawling battle to come. "Am I goin' to th' convention?" he said. "What a question to ask a spoortin' charakter! If a fellow was to come to ye an' say: 'Here's a free ticket f'r a combynation iv th' Chicago fire, Saint Bartholomew's massacree, the battle iv th' Boyne, th' life iv Jesse James, an th' night iv th' big wind,' wud ye take it or wud ye not? . . . Iv coorse I'm goin'!"

On the evening he arrived, Roosevelt met with his leaders to plan his strategy. Prominent among the Roosevelt leaders were his manager, Senator Dixon; Governor Hadley, who was named floor leader; William Flynn, boss of Pittsburgh, who was supporting the Colonel as a power play against the pro-Taft Penrose machine; Gifford Pinchot; James R. Garfield; and William Allen White and Henry Allen of Kansas. They knew that the Taft forces would present Elihu Root for temporary chairman and that, if he were elected, the Roosevelt forces would have no hope of controlling the convention or winning the nomination. At first, they intended to offer Senator Borah as their candidate against Root, but the Colonel decided it would be wiser to woo the LaFollette delegates by making Governor McGovern of Wisconsin their candidate for temporary chairman. Senator LaFollette was bitterly opposed to McGovern's candidacy, but the Governor expressed his willingness to go along with the Roosevelt strategy.

To improve McGovern's chances of winning, Roosevelt decided

that, as soon as the convention convened, Governor Hadley would move to amend the temporary roll to substitute seventy-two Roosevelt men for the Taft delegates accepted by the National Committee. How Roosevelt arrived at the figure of seventy-two is an interesting story.

After the National Committee had completed its deliberations, Hadley, Borah, and Frank Kellogg decided that twenty-eight seats clearly should have gone to Roosevelt and that they would fight for them on the floor of the convention. When Hadley told Roosevelt, the Colonel exploded. "Twenty-eight?" he roared. "Twenty-eight! Why if you got the whole lot, it wouldn't change the result or give you control of the convention. You must make it at least a hundred. Contest at least a hundred seats!" Hadley protested that it was impossible to find a hundred dubious Taft delegates, so the compromise figure of seventy-two was arrived at.

Roosevelt held a mass meeting at the Auditorium Theatre on Monday evening, June 17. Twenty thousand people tried to gain admission, but the theater could accommodate only 5000. For more than an hour, Roosevelt exhorted them in the greatest speech of his life. Victory would be theirs; the theft would not be allowed. William Jennings Bryan, covering the convention as a reporter, commented on the Colonel's reiterated charges of thievery, "The Arabs are said to have seven hundred words which mean 'camel'; Mr. Roosevelt has nearly as many synonyms for theft, and he used them all tonight." But Bryan could not jibe at the climax of the speech, when Roosevelt, with a religious fervor worthy of Bryan himself, hurled forth his great battle cry: "We fight in honorable fashion for the good of mankind; fearless of the future; unheeding of our individual fates; with unflinching hearts and undimmed eyes; we stand at Armageddon, and we battle for the Lord."

The fifteenth Republican National Convention met at twelve noon on Tuesday, June 18, 1912. Ominously, the date marked the 100th anniversary of the battle of Waterloo. The coincidence was carried further by the fact that, opposite the elevator in the corridor leading to the Roosevelt headquarters in the Congress Hotel, was a large painting of Napoleon's retreat from Moscow, which the Roosevelt forces eyed ruefully every time they went to see the Colonel.

The air was heavy with barely suppressed violence as Victor Rosewater called the delegates to order. The Roosevelt charges of theft and steamroller and his call to Armageddon had whipped his partisans to fighting pitch. The hall was patrolled by more than 1000 police gripping their nightsticks and grimly prepared for a fight, and, unbeknownst to the delegates, the railings approaching the rostrum were wound with concealed barbed wire. The Taft forces were in a virtual state of siege.

Little Victor Rosewater, small of stature and weak of voice, was in an unenviable position. Ordinarily the chairman of the National Committee plays a brief, unimportant role in a national convention, but this time he would preside for seven grueling hours over the most important contest of the entire convention. His mind could hardly have been eased when Senator Watson advised him to finish his business quickly and leave the platform before someone took a shot at him, but he presided with firmness and considerable courage.

Immediately after the opening preliminaries, Governor Hadley offered a motion to remove the seventy-two contested delegates from the roll. He was opposed by Senator Watson, who argued that the only business before the convention was the selection of a temporary chairman. The battle raged for hours until Rosewater finally ruled Hadley out of order and Elihu Root and Governor McGovern were nominated for temporary chairman. During the nominating and seconding speeches, the galleries screamed insults and curses at the Taft men, most of whom screamed right back. The aisles were jammed with shouting, struggling delegates, and the cry of "steamroller" echoed through the auditorium. At the height of the turmoil, "when some of the Pennsylvania delegates were acting like madmen, dancing, shouting, and screaming," Nicholas Murray Butler, sitting on the platform, turned in disgust to Senator Penrose to ask how such men got elected as delegates. The Pennsylvania boss replied, "Oh, those are the corks, bottles and banana peels washed up by the Roosevelt tide!"

Each time a contested delegate cast his ballot, he was challenged by Roosevelt's managers, and Rosewater ruled the challenge out of order each time. These rulings infuriated the Colonel's supporters, and the gathering ceased to be a national convention and became a howling mob. The vote was, however, inexorably pushed through to a conclusion. Root won the ballot with 558 votes to 501 for McGovern, with 19 votes scattered or uncast. It was a narrow victory for the Taft forces, but the steamroller, if such it was, had triumphed, and there was no hope that Roosevelt could be nominated.

Although the Taft forces had won the battle, they were depressed at the prospects ahead. Rumors were gaining strength that the Roosevelt men would bolt the convention, and everyone knew that Taft was virtually certain of defeat in November. The depressed Taft leaders gathered in Senator Root's rooms after the first day's session to appraise the situation. They knew the President was in the race to prevent Roosevelt's nomination. Privately he had expressed a willingness to withdraw in favor of Justice Charles Evans Hughes, once Roosevelt had been eliminated, but Hughes refused to consider being a candidate. Senator Watson suggested that Governor Hadley was popular with the convention and could become a compromise candidate. If both Taft and Roosevelt withdrew, Hadley could hold the party together and possibly win the election. But Senator Penrose took a pessimistic view. "Jim, you are mistaken," he said to Watson. "The Republican party is in for a lickin'. The people are tired of it, they are tired of the tariff, they are tired of prosperity, they are tired of you, they are damned tired of me, and they get awfully weary whenever they think of any of the gang in this room." Penrose thought Republican defeat would be all for the best. Senator Crane agreed that what they were there for was to defeat Roosevelt "regardless of what happens anywhere or to anybody or to the party itself" in the campaign.

But Senator Watson, believing that there was a possibility of nominating Hadley, privately worked out a stratagem to stampede the convention. As the debate over the contested delegates dragged on through the Wednesday session, Watson deliberately made a statement in reference to Hadley, which was challenged by the Roosevelt forces, who set up a cry for Hadley to come forward. As Watson later recalled the incident, "As soon as they did this, I walked back the whole length of the stage extension and up to where Hadley was sitting, took him by the hand and raised him up, put my arm around him, and walked back to the very front of the stage." As the delegates began cheering, a shout of "Three cheers for Governor Hadley, the next President," was heard. Watson whispered to him, "This is your reception, and I am going to give you the full benefit of it," and withdrew to the back of the platform. While the slim, youthful looking Governor of Missouri stood patiently accepting the growing demonstration, the other Roosevelt leaders decided to act before a stampede developed. Plans had been made for a Roosevelt demonstration to take place whenever a propitious moment should arise. Cheer leaders "fully equipped with the needed paraphernalia" had been strategically spotted around the hall, and now Senator Dixon gave the signal. Led by Dixon, Governor Johnson, and Medill McCormick, the Roosevelt men began to cheer for Teddy. A "woman in white" by prearrangement unfurled a large portrait of the Colonel, rushed to the edge of the balcony, and began waving it before the shouting delegates. Hadley was forgotten, and the demonstration became a swelling chorus for Roosevelt. Bryan reported that the Taft delegates "preserved a proper decorum during the entire performance, their faces wearing an expression suited to the occasion."

Immediately after the demonstration, Watson went to Frank Kellogg to ask to see Roosevelt and to suggest that the Colonel withdraw in favor of Hadley. Senator Borah had the same idea. When Kellogg saw Roosevelt the Colonel seemed receptive to the idea, but Borah had a different experience. Borah told the former President that he had an offer from the Taft forces. "The roll will be purged of the 72 delegates we claim are tainted, a progressive platform acceptable to us will be adopted, Taft and Roosevelt will withdraw from the race, and we will name Hadley by acclamation." Roosevelt sprang to his feet and, raising his arm, smashed his fist into the glass chandelier over his head. Then he whacked the table with his hand and shouted, "By God, I will never do it. Let them purge the roll and then come to me and I'll tell them what I will do." There was a moment's silence, then Borah, angry but controlled, said, "Well, Colonel, in the future you and your friends can do as you please, but you can't make a jackass out of me any longer," and left the room.

Hadley was then brought to see Roosevelt. The Colonel told

him that his supporters were so bent on his nomination that they
would follow no one else. Hadley then assured the Colonel that
he would not think of opposing him for the nomination. To make
sure that he did not and to undermine the effect of Hadley's
prominence as floor leader, Roosevelt replaced him with Henry
Allen, and the Missouri Governor was relegated to obscurity for
the rest of the convention.

On Wednesday afternoon, a handbill appeared, which commented acidly on the exaggerated fervor of the Roosevelt supporters. The public, it read, was invited to gather at the lakeside
before the Congress Hotel at six o'clock that evening, when Colonel
Theodore Roosevelt "will walk upon the water of Lake Michigan."
Roosevelt roared with laughter when he saw it but did not make
his scheduled appearance.

More serious was the decision to bolt. Many of the Colonel's
friends, including Borah and former Senator Beveridge, alarmed at
rumors that he would form a third party, had for weeks been warning him against such action. But Wednesday night the Roosevelt
men on the credentials committee, unable to prevent the pro-Taft
majority from accepting the contested Taft delegates, walked out
and, at two in the morning, held a protest meeting in the Florentine
Room of the Congress Hotel. The room was jammed with sympathetic rebels. Roosevelt told them, "So far as I am concerned, I am
through. If you are voted down I hope you, the real and lawful
majority of the convention, will organize as such. . . . I hope you
will refuse any longer to recognize a majority thus composed as
having any title in law or morals to be called a Republican Convention." Plans were made for a rump convention to be held in
Orchestra Hall.

The battle continued inside the convention. When the credentials were considered on June 21, the Taft majority sustained
the Taft delegates in each contest. The galleries shouted "Toot!
Toot!" and mockingly imitated the whistle of a steam roller on each
vote, but, now that the battle was lost, they were in a somewhat
better humor than before. Even Root relaxed. As he kept steadily
over-ruling the insurgent motions, a delegate called out, "I make
the point that the steamroller is exceeding the speed limit!" Amuse-

ment flickered on Root's face as he replied, "The Chairman rules that the gentleman's point of order is well taken," but he did not reduce speed.

On Friday, Roosevelt gave up the battle. In a statement read by Henry Allen, the Colonel said that, because the convention had refused to purge the roll of what he considered fraudulent delegates, he hoped "the men elected as Roosevelt delegates will now decline to vote on any matter before the Convention. I do not release any delegate from his honorable obligation to vote for me if he votes at all, but under the actual conditions I hope that he will not vote at all." Allen was careful to avoid the suggestion of bolting. "We do not bolt. We merely insist that you, not we, are making the record. And we refuse to be bound by it. . . . We fight no more, we plead no longer. We shall sit here in protest, and the people who sent us here shall judge us."

The nomination itself was quickly disposed of. A handsome Ohio politician, Warren C. Harding, placed Taft in nomination. LaFollette was also presented to the convention; Roosevelt was not. On the single roll call, the results were Taft 561, Roosevelt 107, LaFollette 41, Cummins 17, Charles Evans Hughes 2, 7 absent, 348 present and not voting. Immediately after the results were announced, Vice-President Sherman was renominated with 595 votes to 58 scattered, 72 absent, and 352 present and not voting.

As the delegates left the hall for the last time, jaunty old Chauncey Depew quipped, "The only question now is which corpse gets the most flowers."

"We stand for a nobler America"

THE FIRST PROGRESSIVE CONVENTION
Chicago, August 6, 1912

A few hours after the convention adjourned, the Roosevelt forces jammed into Orchestra Hall and nominated Roosevelt as an independent candidate. The Colonel accepted conditionally until a formal convention could be called. On July 7, the formal call went out for a national convention to be held in Chicago on August 6.

Two thousand delegates and alternates met in the auditorium where they had so recently done "battle for the Lord." The gathering resembled a religious meeting more than a political convention. The New York delegation marched down the aisle the first day singing "Onward Christian Soldiers" to set the tone of the meeting. Among the delegates were Senator Dixon, William Allen White, George Perkins, Jane Addams, Hiram Johnson, Albert J. Beveridge, and Gifford Pinchot. Significantly, neither Borah nor Hadley joined the new party.

There was a nasty episode early in the convention, which cast some doubt on how "progressive" the new party might be. The call for delegates from Mississippi had specifically excluded Negroes, and a contesting Negro delegation was sent to Chicago. Although this was a gathering of insurgent Republicans who sang "The Battle Hymn of the Republic" at every opportunity and who promised a braver, brighter tomorrow for all Americans, they decided to keep the convention lily white. Roosevelt advised "that the Negro delegates ought to be approved by the White Progressives in their several districts. In other words, the Progressive party in the South should be a white party with such colored members as the whites found acceptable."

Apart from this ugly beginning, the Bull Moose convention was conducted on the loftiest plane. In his keynote address, Senator Beveridge began his one-and-one-half-hour speech by saying, "We stand for a nobler America; we stand for an undivided nation; we stand for a broader liberty, a fuller justice; we stand for social brotherhood as against savage individualism; . . . we stand for equal rights as a fact of life instead of a catch-word of politics; . . . we battle for the actual rights of man." The speech made interesting reading for those Negro delegates not allowed inside the auditorium to hear it.

Roosevelt and Governor Hiram Johnson were nominated for president and vice-president, and the convention then adopted a platform. It was an impressive, ambitious and, for its time, radical document. It was the platform, rather than the shallow, self-seeking theatrics of Theodore Roosevelt, that truly represented the Progressive Party of 1912. The platform called for direct election of senators, recall of judicial decisions, woman suffrage, minimum wages for women, a graduated inheritance and income tax, prohibition of child labor, direct primaries, the initiative, referendum and recall, the exclusion of federal officeholders from party conventions, an anti-trust plank, and a tariff commission. Theodore Roosevelt would be the candidate, but the platform was a monument to Robert M. LaFollette.

"The Princeton schoolmaster"

THE TWENTY-FIRST DEMOCRATIC NATIONAL CONVENTION
Baltimore, June 25, 1912

Woodrow Wilson, the reform Governor of New Jersey, was, when the campaign year of 1912 opened, the leading candidate for the Democratic presidential nomination. A Virginian by birth, Wilson had attracted wide attention as president of Princeton University and had been picked by Senator James Smith, Democratic boss of New Jersey, as the party's candidate for governor in 1910—to give a cloak of respectability to the New Jersey machine and to head off the growing progressive movement in the state. Once elected, Wilson broke with Smith and his machine, blocked his re-election to the Senate, and embarked on a reform program that made him one of the nation's leading progressive governors.

Wilson had originally been a protégé of Colonel George Harvey, conservative publisher of *Harper's Weekly*, but his progressive record alienated many of the more conservative Democrats and the bosses, who were unenthusiastic about a candidate who had smashed the machine of one of their own number. Colonel Harvey was given his walking papers early in 1912, and the conservatives began to look for another candidate.

The Wilson campaign was launched in May, 1911, when the Governor made a speaking tour through the West. In three weeks, he covered seven states, drew large and enthusiastic crowds, and

227

gave his candidacy such a boost that he immediately became the front-runner for the nomination. For the rest of the year, Wilson made frequent speeches, met with party leaders, and gathered an impressive array of magazines and newspapers to his support. Even William Randolph Hearst indicated that he was willing to support the New Jersey Governor, but Wilson would have no Hearst support. "Tell Mr. Hearst to go to hell," he curtly remarked.

Mr. Hearst, far from going to hell, went instead to Wilson's most formidable rival, Champ Clark, the Speaker of the House. The sixty-two-year-old Missourian had, except for one two-year period, served in the House for the past nineteen years and had built a progressive record to rival that of Wilson or any other Democratic candidate. Clark was a regular party man, something of a hack, who appealed to the organization Democrats and those who sought a middle-of-the-road candidate. He was more than liberal enough to appeal to progressives, but his party regularity and his record for conciliation attracted moderates. Even the conservatives were not so opposed to Clark as they were to Wilson.

For the first time since 1860, a resident southerner became an active candidate in the person of Congressman Oscar W. Underwood of Alabama. At fifty, he was the House majority leader and, as chairman of the Ways and Means Committee, which passed all legislation to the floor, he wielded even greater power over the House than did the Speaker. An expert on the tariff, Underwood was a conservative, but a conservative who was prepared to accept change as necessary in the modern world. He was respected by his colleagues and popular on both sides of the aisle. He was primarily a regional candidate, drawing nearly all his strength from the South.

Governor Judson Harmon of Ohio was widely considered to be the leading conservative candidate. Murphy of Tammany was for him, which assured his control of New York's ninety votes. Governor Thomas Marshall of Indiana was backed by his state boss, Tom Taggart, but was relegated to the dark-horse category. Marshall, whose sense of humor tended to confuse most party leaders, took his status philosophically. He wrote to a friend, ". . . bitterness may induce the Democrats to nominate a dark horse and my enemies will tell you I am the blackest one you ever saw."

Among the favorite sons were Governor John Burke of North Dakota, Governor Simeon Baldwin of Connecticut, and, for a time, Mayor Gaynor of New York City.

Finally, there was the question of William Jennings Bryan. Upon his return from Europe in June, 1910, reporters had asked if he would be a candidate in 1912. "How do I know?" he replied. "Much depends." Bryan later announced and frequently repeated that he would not be a candidate and that he thought either Clark or Wilson would make a satisfactory nominee. He would, he said, remain neutral between the two progressives, but he was absolutely opposed to the nomination of either Underwood or Harmon. Despite his frequent denials, many believed that Bryan would like to have a fourth nomination. During the primary period and throughout the convention, it was an open question whether or not Bryan would be a candidate. He was probably sincere in saying that he was not after the nomination, but he was an important factor to be reckoned with by every candidate.

Only Woodrow Wilson, of all the candidates, decided to make a national primary campaign. Clark, Underwood, and Harmon apparently entered into an understanding to combine against Wilson. The Deep South, with the exception of Louisiana, was left to Underwood; Clark did not contest Harmon for Ohio; and Underwood and Harmon left the Far West, except for Oregon, to Clark. Wilson entered primaries throughout the country and campaigned in Michigan, New Hampshire, Virginia, Kentucky, Illinois, Iowa, Pennsylvania, Kansas, Tennessee, Georgia, and Maryland.

The first important test for Wilson and Clark came in Wisconsin in the April 2 primary. In many states, the Wilson forces were composed of amateurs contending against the local machines backing Clark, but in Wisconsin there was a smoothly running organization headed by the national committeeman, Joseph E. Davies. The effectiveness of the organization was demonstrated when Wilson won the primary and took twenty delegates to four for Clark.

Elation over Wilson's Wisconsin victory was short lived. The

Democrats in Illinois were hopelessly split between a progressive faction led by Mayor Carter H. Harrison of Chicago and the machine of boss Roger Sullivan. Harrison and the Hearst press were backing Clark, and Sullivan was too preoccupied with local contests to take much interest in the presidential primary. The results on April 9 were a smashing victory for Clark, who defeated Wilson 218,483 to 75,527. The lopsided results were especially significant because only six states had selected their delegations before the Illinois primary. Many state leaders had been waiting to see an indication of popular sentiment in the Illinois vote and, when the returns were in, decided to back Clark, who became the front-runner almost overnight.

Two days after the Illinois debacle, the Wilson forces suffered another setback but an expected one. New York picked an uninstructed delegation that would take its instructions from Boss Murphy. The Tammany chief detested Wilson, and there was no hope of gaining the ninety votes, even though a minority of the delegates, including William Gibbs McAdoo and Senator O'Gorman, were Wilson men.

Wilson scored a much-needed victory in the Pennsylvania primary on April 13, winning seventy-four delegates to two for Clark. Oregon went for Wilson and Nebraska for Clark on April 19, while on April 30 Massachusetts and Maryland went to Clark and Delaware to Wilson. It had been a bad month for the New Jersey Governor. True, he had added 110 votes to his total, but Clark led in pledged delegates—151 to 125—and Wilson had been soundly beaten in Illinois, Nebraska, and Massachusetts.

Wilson needed victories, but they were not forthcoming. Georgia, where he had many personal ties, went to Underwood on May 1, and in the next two weeks Washington, Wyoming, Nevada, New Mexico, and New Hampshire moved into the Clark column. A heavy blow fell on May 14, when Clark, assisted by the regular organization and the Hearst press, swamped Wilson in the California primary. By the middle of May, Clark had won sixty-eight more delegates, Wilson none. Their totals stood 219 delegates pledged to Clark, 125 to Wilson.

Things began looking up for Wilson during the last two weeks of May. He took nineteen delegates away from Harmon in Ohio, won South Carolina and Texas, and turned back a challenge from the Smith machine to win twenty-four of New Jersey's twenty-eight delegates. The four delegates controlled by Smith came from his home bailiwick, and the Wilson forces were relieved that he had not won more.

A major ally was enlisted in the Wilson cause on May 30, when the New York *World*, the leading Democratic newspaper in the nation, declared for him, and a week later Minnesota gave him its 24 votes. By June 20, with all the delegates selected, the totals of pledged delegates were Clark 413, Wilson 274, Underwood 91, Harmon 57, Marshall 30, Baldwin 14, and Burke 10, with 205 uninstructed. Seven hundred twenty-six votes were required for nomination. Wilson had made a poor showing and was convinced by early June that he would not receive the nomination. Clark, thanks to better organization and a greater appeal to party professionals, was now the man to beat.

The Democratic National Convention was scheduled to open in Baltimore on Tuesday, June 25. Wilson headquarters were opened in the Emerson Hotel, but it was the Clark men who attracted most of the attention. Clark's campaign symbol was a "hound dog," and his supporters, wearing huge buttons reading, "You've got to quit kickin' my dawg around," loudly sang the hound-dog song in the streets and lobbies of the city. So pervasive was the "Houn' Dawg" that William Gibbs McAdoo was later to write, "The whole place was in such a turmoil over the sanctity of hound dogs that I would have let one bite me without the least resistance, for fear of reprisals." One nettled Wilson supporter threatened to take a dog out into the street and kick it just to see what would happen, but he was quickly dissuaded by the prudent Wilson managers.

None of the leading candidates was present in Baltimore. Clark and Underwood were in nearby Washington, and Harmon was at home in Ohio. Wilson and his family were at the Governor's summer home at Sea Girt, New Jersey, where tents had been erected on the broad lawns for the newspapermen and telegraphers. A private telephone connected Sea Girt with the office of Wilson's manager, William F. McCombs, in the Emerson Hotel.

A major battle developed before the convention opened. William Jennings Bryan had been offered the temporary chairmanship but, fearing that he would be accused of trying to stampede the convention, had refused. A subcommittee of sixteen was selected by the National Committee to recommend a temporary chairman. The subcommittee first asked Bryan to reconsider and, upon his refusal, offered the post to Senator Kern of Indiana, who also refused. Both Bryan and Kern suggested that the post go to a thoroughly progressive Democrat like Congressman Ollie James, the Clark candidate, or Congressman Robert L. Henry of Texas, the Wilson candidate.

When the subcommittee met on June 21, eight members voted for former candidate Alton B. Parker, three for James, three for Henry, one for Kern, and one for Senator O'Gorman. The Wilson forces agreed to back James to prevent Parker's selection, but the Clark forces, hoping to win New York on the presidential balloting, switched to Parker. The National Committee selected Parker for temporary chairman by a vote of 32 to 20 for James and 2 for O'Gorman.

Bryan was furious. It was, he believed, outrageous to give the keynote address and control of the opening days of the convention to a conservative, Tammany-backed New Yorker. He decided to make a fight of it and wired all the candidates to put them on record. Would they stand with him and the progressives, or would they stand with the reactionaries? Harmon and Underwood replied that they would support Parker, and Clark straddled the issue with a vague plea for party harmony. Governor Burke came out strongly on Bryan's side.

Before receiving the Bryan telegram, Wilson had been asked by the Baltimore *Sun* for his views on the selection of Parker. He had replied, "My friends in Baltimore, who are on the ground, will know how to act in the interest of the people's cause in everything that affects the organization of the convention. . . . I have neither the right nor the desire to direct the organization of a convention of which I am not even a member." McCombs was delighted. He had been furiously angling for the New York delegation and feared anything that would further antagonize Boss

Murphy. But after receiving Bryan's telegram, Wilson reconsidered. Joseph Tumulty and Mrs. Wilson argued that Bryan was not asking Wilson to interfere but only to declare where he stood. The Governor thereupon wired Bryan, "You are quite right. . . . The Baltimore convention is to be a convention of progressives—of men who are progressives on principle and by conviction." The Bryan telegram and Wilson's unequivocal stand against Parker were a masterstroke. While McCombs disconsolately argued that by opposing Parker New York would be lost and that without New York the nomination would be lost, the effect of the Bryan-Wilson stand was to unite the progressives upon a clear-cut, simple issue. If the conservatives tried to take over the Democratic convention as they had the Republican, Bryan and Wilson would lead the progressive fight against them.

Bryan had difficulty in finding a candidate to oppose Parker. His old friend Ollie James had to decline because the Clark forces were supporting Parker, and Senator O'Gorman, although a Wilson man, was bound by New York's unit rule to support Parker also. Senator Kern embarrassedly pointed out that he was pledged to Marshall and that Marshall was for Parker. Bryan himself should be the candidate, Kern suggested. Bryan remonstrated that it was his intention to present an argument against Parker's candidacy, which he could not do if he were a candidate himself. Kern did not positively decline to be a candidate, and Bryan therefore went ahead with his plan to support him.

At twelve noon, June 25, the venerable cardinal of Baltimore, scarlet robed with a skullcap covering his silver hair, raised his hand in benediction and prayed for peace and concord in the deliberations to come.

Cardinal Gibbons had barely had time to finish before the fight was on. William Jennings Bryan was on his feet once again to do battle against the forces of evil as he saw them. The New York *World* described the aging Commoner, as he stood accepting the cheers of the crowd. "His heavy black brows were contracted over his piercing eyes. His hawk nose had an extra downward twist. His lipless mouth was like a thin dagger-slit across his broad face. . . ." He motioned for quiet, but the cheering kept up. Bryan sat down,

placidly fanning himself with a big palm leaf until the noise subsided. Then he launched his attack on Parker. He accused him of
being the representative of Tammany and Wall Street and asked
the delegates to reject the reactionaries. "I appeal to you: Let the
commencement of this convention be such a commencement that
the Democrats of this country may raise their heads among their
fellows and say, 'The Democratic party is true to the people. You
cannot frighten it with your Ryans nor buy it with your Belmonts.' "
This cry, hurled at August Belmont, delegate from New York,
and Thomas Fortune Ryan, delegate from Virginia, electrified the
audience. All over the hall, men leaped to their feet cheering for
Bryan. It was a fine climax to a fighting speech. Unfortunately, the
great orator kept right on talking and talking and talking. As
the New York *World* sadly commented, ". . . poor Bryan who had
begun as a prophet, concluded as a bore and sat down amid a roar
one-quarter of enthusiasm, three-quarters of relief."

But if Bryan had weakened the drama of his speech, he had
also placed the issue squarely before the convention. "This one
thing I know," said one delegate, "the fight is on and Bryan is on
one side and Wall Street is on the other." To the progressives it
was clear that Champ Clark was on the other side with Wall Street
and Tammany Hall.

Senator Kern, having been nominated by Bryan, arose to plead
for harmony and, facing the New York delegation, asked Parker
to withdraw. Parker sat in silence while Kern awaited his reply.
Kern then asked Murphy to use his influence to induce Parker to
withdraw. Still silence. Receiving no reply to his appeal for harmony, Kern turned to the convention and cried that, if there must
be a contest, Bryan was the only man to lead the fight. He thereupon withdrew and nominated William Jennings Bryan for temporary chairman. The convention exploded. The Wilson forces
cheered wildly for Bryan, while the conservatives vented their
bitterness in hoots and curses. Cardinal Gibbons, appalled at the
uproar and perhaps dismayed at the ineffectiveness of his prayer
for concord, gathered his scarlet cloak about him and left the hall.

When the convention finally came to a vote, Parker was elected
temporary chairman with 579 votes to 508 for Bryan. The Wilson

men and much of Clark's western support went to Bryan, but 288 Clark delegates combined with the Harmon, Baldwin, and Underwood strength for Parker. The conservatives had won the first skirmish, but popular sentiment was with Bryan. When Parker began his keynote speech, "the galleries rose . . . a brutal, noisy crowd and left a rather dazed old gentleman reading a long manuscript, nervously looking over his glasses occasionally at the vanishing crowd."

The battle for temporary chairman had vital effects on the outcome of the convention. Clark had been identified with the conservatives, and the progressives were aroused. Telegrams demanding a progressive candidate began pouring into Baltimore and reached avalanche proportions by the end of the convention. It was estimated that more than 100,000 telegrams were sent; Bryan himself received 1182, each with an average of three names.

Another significant result was to alienate Bryan from Clark. Before the convention, Bryan had maintained that he would consider either Clark or Wilson an acceptable nominee, and, indeed, he was pledged to Clark. But the deal between the Clark forces and Tammany convinced Bryan that the Speaker had been captured by the conservatives. When Senator Martine urged Bryan to recognize that Clark was against him and to declare openly for Wilson, Bryan replied, "I know what has happened. I am with you."

The Clark and Tammany forces wanted to avoid another battle, and they therefore offered the permanent chairmanship to Bryan. He declined, caustically pointing out that "those who owned the ship should furnish the crew." It was agreed to compromise on Bryan's friend Ollie James, who was selected permanent chairman without opposition.

Wilson's prospects markedly improved on the second day. The rules committee had declared that nineteen Wilson delegates from Ohio were bound to vote for Harmon because the state convention had so instructed them. The issue was whether or not a state convention could instruct district delegates elected by primary vote. The Wilson forces fought the ruling on the floor and, brilliantly led by Mayor Newton D. Baker of Cleveland, attacked the whole unit-rule system. The Underwood and some Clark men agreed with the Wilson position, and, by a vote of 565½ to 492⅓, the Wilson delegates were freed of their Harmon instructions. The decision did not affect the unit rule in other delegations, but it gave Wilson 10 more first-ballot votes.

On Thursday, Wilson picked up additional strength. He had won the South Dakota primary with a plurality. The two defeated slates had been for Clark, and their combined vote was greater than that for Wilson. The Clark forces, therefore, contested the seating of the ten South Dakota Wilson delegates. The credentials committee met on Wednesday, June 26, to consider South Dakota and two contesting delegations from Cook County, Illinois, of which one set was controlled by Roger Sullivan and the other by the Hearst-Harrison faction. Whoever gained control of the contested delegates would, under the unit rule, be able to control the entire Illinois delegation.

Joseph E. Davies had offered Mayor Harrison Wilson support for his faction if the Mayor, in turn, would swing Illinois to Wilson. When Harrison refused, Luke Lea, Wilson's leader in the credentials committee, made a deal with Roger Sullivan. The Wilson forces would support the Sullivan men, even though, on the evidence, they had no legitimate claim to their seats, if Illinois would support the Wilson delegation from South Dakota. Sullivan agreed, and his men were seated by the credentials committee, which also voted to seat Clark's South Dakota delegation. When the full convention considered the contest on Thursday, Roger Sullivan threw Illinois behind the Wilson delegation, the Clark men were ousted, and 10 more votes were added to Wilson's total.

The convention gathered on Thursday evening to hear the nominating speeches—or so its members thought. Instead, it witnessed the noisiest battle of the convention. Bryan, hoping to thwart a New York-Clark combination, arose to introduce a resolution. "As proof of our fidelity to the people, we hereby declare ourselves opposed to the nomination of any candidate for president who is the representative of or under obligation to J. Pierpont Morgan, Thomas Fortune Ryan, August Belmont, or any other member of the privilege-hunting and favor-seeking class." The second part of the resolution read, "we demand the withdrawal from this convention of any delegate or delegates constituting or representing the above-named interests." The sound of the resulting explosion must have carried nearly to Wall Street itself. Shouting, angry delegates cried out that Bryan be lynched, and one of them was heard to offer $25,000 to anyone who would kill him. A Virginia delegate leaped onto the platform and shook his fist in Bryan's face but became completely hysterical and was led away by his friends before he could do physical damage. Bryan was unmoved by the storm. When he could be heard he thundered, " 'If thy right hand offend thee, cut it off.' The party needs to cut off those corrupting influences to save itself." Bryan knew perfectly well that the resolution to expel Ryan and Belmont was illegal and could not possibly be adopted by the convention. Just before the vote was taken, he craftily withdrew it, leaving many delegates ready to accept the pious generality of opposition to Wall Street. Even New York went along with the amended resolution. As Boss Murphy prepared to cast the vote of New York, he turned to Belmont and laughed, "August, listen and hear yourself vote yourself out of the convention." The resolution passed by 889 to 196.

Oscar W. Underwood was the first candidate nominated in a speech by Senator John H. Bankhead. After a twenty-six-minute demonstration, Senator James A. Reed of Missouri named Champ Clark, calling him the man "whose breast is covered with the scars of honor; who leads today and who should lead tomorrow—the Lion of Democracy. . . ." Reed finished his speech at 12:25 Friday morning, and the Clark demonstration went on for one hour and five minutes.

Connecticut nominated Governor Simeon Baldwin, and then at 2:08 a.m. Judge John W. Westcott came to the platform to nominate Woodrow Wilson. The Wilson demonstration broke out before Westcott could begin—perhaps his supporters feared that they would fall asleep if they waited any longer—and it continued for one hour and fifteen minutes. Westcott then nominated "the seer and philosopher of Princeton, the Princeton schoolmaster, Woodrow Wilson."

Dawn had broken by the time Governors Marshall and Harmon were placed in nomination. Governor Burke withdrew his nomination in favor of Wilson, and the weary convention, yawning and bleary-eyed from an all-night session, cast the first ballot for the presidency.

The results of the first ballot were Clark 440½ Wilson 324, Harmon 148, Underwood 117½, Marshall 31, Baldwin 22, Representative William Sulzer of New York 2, and Bryan 1. Clark had the solid support of twenty-one delegations and at least half of four others. Wilson had seven solid delegations and nearly all of New Jersey and Pennsylvania, as well as majorities in six other delegations. Clark received votes from a total of thirty-four delegations, Wilson from twenty-one. It was obviously going to be a long struggle, and at 7:36 Friday morning the convention adjourned until afternoon.

The second ballot, the first of Friday afternoon, showed little change. Vermont switched its 8 votes from Baldwin to Wilson, who made a net gain of 15¾. Clark gained 6. By the ninth ballot, Clark had gained only 11½ votes, Wilson 28½. Baldwin had dropped out, his vote scattering; Underwood had a net gain of 5, Harmon a loss of 21.

The first break came on the tenth ballot. New York had been casting its 90 votes for Harmon, but on this ballot it substantiated the suspicions of a deal between Tammany and Clark by casting its entire vote for the Speaker. This gave Clark a majority of the convention, and, not in sixty-eight years, had a candidate won a majority and failed to go on to the required two-thirds. "The fight is over," shouted the Clark men as they poured into the aisles for a victory celebration that went on for an hour. In Washington, Clark prepared his telegram of acceptance and told George W. Norris that he would be nominated on the next ballot.

The victory celebration was a fatal blunder. The badly shaken Wilson managers quickly gathered on the platform for consultation. Agreeing on a plan of action, A. Mitchell Palmer, the floor leader, McAdoo, Willard Saulsbury of Delaware, Henry Morgenthau, Senator Gore, A. S. Burlson and Thomas B. Love of Texas, and the other Wilson leaders scurried about the hall. Ignoring the tumultuous demonstration blaring in their ears, they persuaded the Underwood leaders, who were considering giving up, to stand fast.

If they would hold their lines, they were told, and Wilson later failed of nomination, his votes would go to Underwood. The Marshall and the remaining Harmon forces also agreed to stick with their candidates.

When the roll call resumed, Oklahoma struck the keynote of the anti-Clark forces. A Clark delegate demanded a poll, hoping to break the Wilson strength in the delegation. Up rose "Alfalfa Bill" Murray, who announced with waving arms that Oklahoma had no objection to a poll but roared, ". . . we do insist we shall not join Tammany in making the nomination." The Wilson men went wild and roared their approval back.

Wilson's managers had done their work well during the Clark demonstration. If the roll had not been interrupted for an hour, it is quite likely that New York's switch would have started a landslide for the Speaker. But when the results of the ballot were announced, although Clark had 556 votes, 11 more than a majority, Wilson had lost only 2 votes for a total of 350½, Underwood had lost 5 for 117½. Harmon and Marshall held 31 apiece.

On the eleventh ballot, Clark actually lost 2 votes, while Wilson gained 4. There would be no stampede. On the final ballot of the night, the twelfth, the results were Clark 547½, Wilson 354, Underwood 123, Marshall 30, Harmon 29, Bryan and Kern 1 each.

The Wilson managers had stopped Clark for the moment, but at Sea Girt Wilson lost his nerve. Exactly what happened in the early morning of Saturday, June 29, is difficult to ascertain, because of conflicting testimony. Apparently, after Wilson heard that Clark had a majority and before he could have learned that his and the Underwood forces were holding fast, he sent a telegram to McCombs authorizing him to release his delegates. According to Mrs. Wilson, "Mr. Wilson thought that it was all over, and we tried to pretend to think we were glad it was over." McCombs later claimed that he had received the telegram but had refused to make use of it.

McCombs may have had confidence then, but, within a few hours, he went completely to pieces. He had been without sleep for two days, his health was poor, his nerves were never good at the best of times, and finally he lost his head. Utterly discouraged, he called Wilson to ask for authorization to release his delegates. He seemed to have forgotten that he already had a telegram of release in his pocket. Wilson agreed to send another telegram but refused McCombs's suggestion that he release his delegates to Underwood.

A short time later, McAdoo visited McCombs and was dumb-founded to learn that Wilson was giving up. After a bitter exchange, McAdoo called Wilson to convince him that Clark could never win two-thirds of the convention and that he should not for a moment think of withdrawing. Wilson, greatly heartened, told him to tell McCombs not to release the delegates.

In Baltimore, a few hours' reflection did much to restore McCombs's shattered nerves, and he went back to work. He met with Tom Taggart, boss of Indiana, and promised the vice-presidential nomination to Marshall if his votes would swing to Wilson. Taggart agreed that, if Wilson could hold his position until Monday, Indiana would be his.

While the first ballot on Saturday afternoon, the thirteenth, was in progress, Wilson called McCombs and gave him a message to deliver to Bryan. "It has become evident that the present deadlock is being maintained for the purpose of enabling New York, a delegation controlled by a single group of men, to control the nomination and tie the candidate to itself. In these circumstances it is the imperative duty of each candidate for the nomination to see to it that his own independence is beyond question. I can see no other way to do this than to declare that he will not accept a nomination if it cannot be secured without the aid of that delegation. For myself I have no hesitation in making that declaration. . . ."

It is not known whether or not McCombs delivered the message, but Bryan had already made up his mind. On the thirteenth ballot, Nebraska had voted 13 for Clark, 3 for Wilson. When Nebraska was called on the fourteenth roll call, Bryan arose to explain his vote. Speaking for himself and the Clark delegates, he stated, "these delegates will not participate in the nomination of any man whose nomination depends upon the vote of the New York delegation. Speaking for myself and those who join me, we, therefore, withhold our vote from Mr. Clark as long as New York's vote is recorded for him. . . ." Nine Clark Nebraska votes were then cast for Wilson. The Wilson forces were so elated that they overlooked the fact that Bryan had not endorsed their candidate. He had merely stated that he was withholding his support from Clark as long as New York voted for him. The implication was that he would switch back if New York abandoned Clark.

When Champ Clark heard of Bryan's action, he exploded in anger. His progressive record was as good as anyone's, and he was furious at Bryan's imputation that he was a tool of Tammany and Wall Street. In a rage, he boarded a train for Baltimore to settle accounts with William Jennings Bryan.

If Bryan or the Wilson managers thought that the Great Commoner could start a stampede for Wilson, they were wrong. Wilson gained only 1½ votes on the next ballot. But Clark's strength was slowly being eroded. He had started the day with 554½ votes. By the eighteenth ballot, he had fallen to 535—10 less than a majority. Most of the Clark losses went to Underwood, who reached his highest vote on the nineteenth ballot, with 130 votes.

On the twentieth ballot, Kansas, which had been voting for Clark, gave its vote to Wilson, but still the deadlock could not be broken. Wilson kept creeping up—388½, 395½, 396½, 399, until, on the twenty-fourth ballot, he went over the 400 mark. In Sea Girt, Wilson remarked, "We have been figuring that at the present rate of gain I will be nominated in 175 more ballots."

Clark continued to lose ground. After the Kansas switch, the next major loss came on the twenty-second ballot, when Massachusetts abandoned him to vote for its governor, Eugene N. Foss. On the last ballot of the day, the twenty-sixth, the results were Clark 463½ Wilson 407½, Underwood 112½, Foss 43, Marshall 30, Harmon 29, Bryan 1, ½ not voting.

On Sunday, William Jennings Bryan, whose switch had so gladdened the Wilson managers the day before, issued a statement that infuriated them and again raised the speculation that he was after the nomination for himself. There was no reason, he announced, why the party could not finish its business on Monday. If Clark and Wilson were deadlocked, the progressives should find Senator Kern, Ollie James, Senator O'Gorman, Senator Culberson of Texas, or Senator Rayner of Maryland acceptable as the nominee. None of course had the slightest chance of nomination, and the inference was unavoidable that Bryan was tacitly including his own name on the list.

McCombs was so angry at Bryan's statement that he called Wilson and told him that Bryan's unpopularity with the delegates was so great that Wilson could not be nominated unless he gave assurances that he would not, if elected, appoint Bryan secretary of state. McCombs hoped such a statement would help placate Murphy of Tammany, to whom he had been making overtures. Wilson, of course, refused to make any such commitment. He did, however, later in the day, issue a statement to counteract rumors of deals being made. "There cannot be any possibility of any trading done in my name; not a single vote can or will be obtained by means of any promise." He was blissfully unaware of the arrangements to give the vice-presidency to Marshall, and none of his managers was willing to bring him up to date.

Wilson won an important new source of strength on Sunday afternoon. Willard Saulsbury had been negotiating with the Clark forces in Maryland, West Virginia, Kentucky, and Virginia. He and McCombs met with leaders of the first three delegations, and Virginia sent word that it would go along with whatever was decided. They concluded that Clark probably could not be nominated and agreed to go to Wilson when a favorable moment arose. Senator Clarence Watson of West Virginia, a particularly bitter foe of Wilson, agreed to support him if the Baltimore *Sun* would give him credit for the action. Charles H. Grasty of the *Sun* was delighted to give the Senator whatever publicity he wished.

The Clark men spent Sunday trying to break up the Wilson forces. The bosses—Murphy, Taggart, and Sullivan—approached A. Mitchell Palmer to persuade him to withdraw Wilson's name. If he would do so, Murphy promised, they would give Palmer the nomination. Palmer refused.

After failing with Palmer, Tammany approached the Texas delegation and offered to nominate Senator Culberson if Texas would desert Wilson. Culberson and Texas angrily rejected the deal and remained loyal. Having failed to break the solid Wilson front,

Sullivan told McCombs, after a Sunday night caucus, that, while he could not promise support on any specific ballot, Illinois would swing to Wilson as soon as possible.

Clark made a slight recovery on the twenty-seventh ballot on Monday morning, gaining 5 votes, but, on the next ballot Tom Taggart fulfilled his promise, and 29 Indiana votes went to Wilson, who then had 437½ to Clark's 468½.

Wilson passed Clark on the thirtieth ballot. When reporters at Sea Girt rushed to tell Wilson, the Governor replied, "You might say that Governor Wilson received the news that Champ Clark had dropped to second place in a riot of silence."

First place was still a long way from nomination. Midnight came, and the perspiring, bone-weary delegates saw no end to the deadlock. On the final ballot of the night, the forty-second, the count stood: Wilson 494, Clark 430, Underwood 104, Foss 28, Harmon 27, James, Kern, Mayor Gaynor, and James Hamilton Lewis of Illinois 1 each, and Bryan ½.

It was time for Roger Sullivan to do some hard thinking. He had told McCombs that he would come to Wilson's support when his nomination seemed probable, but, as things stood, only Illinois could make it probable. Otherwise, the deadlock might go on forever. Sullivan realized that, if Clark were nominated and elected, the Harrison-Hearst faction would have first call on favors from the White House. Also, he owed Wilson a favor over the contested Illinois delegates, and his wife and son, ardent for Wilson, had for days been urging him to switch. Finally, the fear that Bryan was angling for the nomination tipped the scales in Wilson's favor. After adjournment, Sullivan called a caucus and, with his blessing, Illinois voted 45 to 13 to swing to Wilson.

As the forty-third ballot got underway on Tuesday, McCombs came over to Sullivan to say, "Roger, we've got to have Illinois, or I'll withdraw." Sullivan calmly replied, "Sit steady, boy," and cast 58 votes for Woodrow Wilson. "What did you get for it, Roger?" the Clark men shouted angrily. "The choice of this convention, that's all!" Sullivan shot back.

Illinois' switch was all Virginia and West Virginia had been waiting for. Twenty-four Virginia votes, including, ironically, the vote of Thomas Fortune Ryan, went to Wilson, followed by West Virginia's 16. At the end of the ballot, Wilson had 602 votes to Clark's 329, but he was still 120 votes short of nomination.

Champ Clark, who had been in and out of Baltimore for the last few days, desperately wanted to appear before the convention in a last effort to prevent defeat. His managers talked him out of it, and, for a time, kept him locked in a room at the Baltimore Club. There was a story, reported long after the event by Senator Gore, to the effect that Clark went as far as the outside of the convention hall, where, seated in a taxi, he conferred with Roger Sullivan. If he did meet with Sullivan, Clark no doubt gave assurance that he would recognize his position in Illinois, and Sullivan was reported to have told Clark that he would switch back on the forty-sixth or forty-seventh ballot.

Sullivan had also told the Underwood forces that he would swing to their candidate sometime during the day. Underwood's managers waited through the forty-fourth and forty-fifth ballots and saw Wilson rise to 633 votes, with no sign from Sullivan. They were under intense pressure from the Wilson men to give up the fight, and after the forty-fifth ballot Senator Bankhead and several others went to find out what Sullivan intended to do. He informed them that he would take Illinois back to Clark on the forty-sixth ballot.

It was obviously hopeless for Underwood, and Bankhead mounted the platform to withdraw his name. Mayor "Honey Fitz" Fitzgerald of Boston then released the Foss delegates, and Harmon was also withdrawn. Senator Stone acknowledged defeat by releasing the Clark delegates but declared that Missouri would give its last vote to its native son. When John J. Fitzgerald of Tammany moved the nomination be made by acclamation, Senator Reed protested. It was nothing personal against Wilson, he stated, but Missouri must vote for Champ Clark. A roll call was taken, and, at 3:30 in the afternoon of Tuesday, July 2, Woodrow Wilson was declared the Democratic nominee for president, with 990 votes to 84 for Clark and 12 for Harmon, with two delegates not voting.

Wilson's personal preference for a running mate was Underwood, but he refused to accept. Albert Burlson telephoned Wilson to tell him that the convention was inclined to Marshall. "But

Burlson," the Governor protested, "he is a small-calibre man." Burlson argued that Marshall was an excellent politician and well located geographically. Wilson finally agreed to accept him. He still had not been told that the Marshall nomination had been arranged days before.

In all, nine men received votes in the first roll call. Marshall led with 389 votes to 304⅗ for Governor John Burke of North Dakota. On the second ballot, Marshall climbed to 644½, and New Jersey pointedly moved that the nomination be made unanimous. Marshall was Wilson's choice, and the convention immediately went along.

CHAPTER 13

"The tongue and brain behind the door"

THE SIXTEENTH REPUBLICAN NATIONAL CONVENTION
Chicago, June 7, 1916

The contest—it was too apathetic to be called a battle—for the Republican presidential nomination of 1916 was waged—and often drowned out—amid the thunder of guns in Europe. As the pre-convention campaign began, the Germans launched the senseless slaughter of Verdun, and the battleships had barely ceased to roar off Jutland when the Republicans gathered in Chicago. The New Freedom of Woodrow Wilson and the New Nationalism of Theodore Roosevelt were alike victims of the war in Europe, and it seemed only a matter of time until the United States was involved. The question of preparedness and whether or not to enter the war dominated the preconvention period, with Pancho Villa's raids on Texas providing a bellicose theme right at home.

Although the war was the dominant event of 1916, the Republican leaders had more immediate problems, especially the question of the Progressive Party. Under Roosevelt's leadership, the new party had polled more than four million votes and had won 88 electoral votes, compared to slightly less than three and one-half million popular and 8 electoral votes for Taft. But in the mid-term elections of 1914, the Progressives had lost eleven of their eighteen house seats, and their popular vote had been cut in half. The new party was in a bad way, but, if Roosevelt should choose to lead it again, there would be serious difficulties ahead for the Republicans in 1916.

But Colonel Roosevelt was not interested in lost causes. His defeat in 1912 had convinced him that the road back to the White House did not lead through the Progressive Party, and he was quite willing to be a candidate for the Republican nomination. The Republicans, while they very much wanted the Progressives to return to the fold, would not for a moment consider Roosevelt for the nomination. The party therefore had the twofold problem of finding a candidate and of winning back the Progressives without taking Roosevelt.

There was a plethora of candidates for the nomination, but none of them looked very promising. Roosevelt was willing to receive the nomination if he did not have to enter the field to fight for it. He refused to allow his name to be entered in any primaries and contented himself with speaking tours in which he attacked the Wilson administration.

The most distinguished of the announced candidates was the seventy-one-year-old Elihu Root. He had repeatedly said that he did not want the nomination, but, on April 7, seventy-four prominent New Yorkers, including nineteen who would be delegates to the convention, issued a statement in support of Root's candidacy, and he reluctantly agreed to go before the convention.

Most of the candidates were members of the conservative wing of the party, and most represented holding operations for their state organizations. Former Vice-President Fairbanks, Senator John Weeks of Massachusetts, former Senator Theodore Burton of Ohio, and Senators Albert B. Cummins of Iowa, Lawrence Y. Sherman of Illinois, and Robert M. LaFollette of Wisconsin were candidates, as were Philander C. Knox and Governor Martin G. Brumbaugh of Pennsylvania. In the strictly favorite-son category were auto manufacturer Henry Ford of Michigan, Coleman Du Pont of Delaware, Governor McCall of Massachusetts, and Senator Borah. Fairbanks, Weeks, Burton, and Cummins were the most important of the minor candidates, and all, with the exception of Cummins, were acceptable to the conservatives.

The leading contender for the nomination, however, was not a candidate and gave no indication that he would accept the nomination were it offered him. Associate Justice of the Supreme Court Charles Evans Hughes, whose position on the bench had kept him from involvement in the Progressive schism, appealed to Progressives because of his record as a reform governor of New York, while he appealed to conservatives for his able record as a jurist. Conservatives also liked him because Theodore Roosevelt disliked him intensely.

Because the Republicans would not accept Roosevelt, because Root was too old and unacceptable to the Progressives, and because the other candidates were undistinguished, more and more Republicans inclined favorably to the notion of a Hughes candidacy. Hughes, however, refused to be a candidate. In May, 1915, he had asked that no steps be taken to bring his name before the convention and, in November, had threatened court action to remove his name from the ballot of the Nebraska primary. But several New York leaders, including Governor Whitman, declared for him in January, 1916, and the drive to secure his nomination was organized by Frank Hitchcock, who had done the same job for Taft in 1908. Colonel George Harvey announced that the people wanted Hughes, and several opinion polls seemed to bear him out. In the two primaries from which Hughes could not remove his name— Vermont and Oregon—he won the delegations by a landslide, and Senator Borah believed that Hughes would have carried every primary in the country had his name been on the ballot.

Hughes genuinely did not want the nomination. He was happy as a justice, and he saw quite clearly the problems ahead. "I do not want the work that is before the next president," he told Henry L. Stoddard, editor of the New York *Evening Mail*. "He may wear a crown, but it will be a crown of thorns." At one time, when his wife urged him to enter the race, he replied, "When you see me in my coffin, remember that I did not want to take this burden on myself."

Even though he did not want to be a candidate, Hughes maintained a judicious silence, rather than flatly refusing to run. He had made such a refusal in 1912, but at that time there was no crisis facing either his party or his country. This time, Hughes knew, the Republican Party must be reunited, or it would die, and he feared, because of Wilson's policies, that the nation was not prepared for its own defense. If he were, as his friends kept telling him, the one man who could reunite his party and be elected, then he did not believe he had the right to refuse. But the nomination, if it were coming, would have to seek him out—he would not encourage it.

That Hughes was, despite his silence, the leading candidate and that he would be a formidable opponent in the election were not lost on Wilson. A short time before the convention, Chief Justice White called on Hughes to tell him, "Before you decide what course you will take I feel that you should know that I am going to retire and that if you do not resign you will succeed me." The incredulous Hughes protested that Wilson would never appoint him chief justice, to which White answered, "Well, he wouldn't appoint anyone else, as I happen to know." Hughes realized that the President was offering him a handsome prize to stay out of the presidential race, but such deals were alien to Hughes's nature. He told the Chief Justice that he would follow his own conscience and that the offer would not influence his decision.

When the delegates gathered in Chicago for the opening of the convention on Wednesday, June 6, 1916, Hughes was far short of a majority. The New York *Times* estimated on the day before the first session that no fewer than fifteen men would have votes on the first ballot and that perhaps nine of them could be considered serious candidates. Hughes was estimated to have 224 first-ballot votes, followed by Cummins, Root, Fairbanks, and Weeks, with 80 or more votes each. The Fairbanks men were claiming up to 160 first-ballot votes, while Burton's managers were claiming 130. All claims were, however, vague, and no one really knew what the situation was.

Contributing greatly to the confusion and the lack of any clear trend were divisions among many of the larger delegations. In Massachusetts, for instance, the delegation was headed by four men, of whom former Senator Murray Crane was for Hughes, Senator Lodge was for Roosevelt, and Governor McCall and Senator Weeks were for themselves. The only certainty was that, even though the delegation was pledged to Weeks, it was expected to scatter in all directions after the first-ballot courtesy vote. But, on the Sunday before the convention, it was announced that Weeks's delegates would stick for the second ballot also.

New York was also hopelessly split. The state Republicans were engaging in bitter factional strife and were considerably more interested in who would be the next state chairman and who the next national committeeman than they were in who would be the candidate. The delegation was expected to divide between the Hughes men, led by Governor Whitman, and the Root men, led by Senator Wadsworth, but it was not expected that the Empire State, so often a dominating force in convention politics, would have much influence in the present convention.

The most important delegation after New York was Pennsylvania, and Pennsylvania meant Boies Penrose. Senator Penrose, "silent as the sphynx and watchful as a lynx," controlled at least 50 votes, and he intended to use those votes "in such a way as to extract the last possible ounce of credit for Penrose." But the boss of Pennsylvania did not know in which direction his best interests lay. His position was complicated by several factors. He was feuding with Congressman William S. Vare and his brother Edwin Vare of Philadelphia, and the Vares, with some 20 votes under their control, were backing Governor Brumbaugh. Penrose, to defend himself against the Vares, had been forced in the spring to enter into negotiations with the Roosevelt forces.

Murray Crane, violently anti-Roosevelt, had become alarmed at the Penrose-Roosevelt flirtation and had sent Nicholas Murray Butler to see Penrose a few days before the May 16 Pennsylvania primary. Penrose was able to reassure Butler. "My dear boy," he told the dignified president of Columbia University, "you people must remember that the Progressives carried Pennsylvania in 1912, and that they are very strong there now. I am going to have a hard fight in the primaries next Tuesday, so I have entered into partnership with the Roosevelt men, which partnership will be dissolved on Tuesday afternoon at six o'clock. I shall have all the assets and they will get all the liabilities."

Gaining those assets in no way solved Penrose's problem. His personal inclination was toward Fairbanks, but not even he could get his delegates to go along, and he therefore declared his support for the aging former Secretary of State Philander C. Knox. When asked on Sunday, June 4, when he and the other leaders would select a serious candidate, Penrose candidly admitted his uncertainty. "You might just as well ask me when the grass there will spring up and the flowers begin to bloom," he said, waving toward a lake-front park below the window of his hotel room. "The situation," he added darkly, "is in the hands of somebody else." The problem, he should have said, was that the situation was in the hands of everybody else.

The final complication adding to Republican confusion was the question of the Progressives, who would be meeting in their own convention in the Congress Auditorium, while the Republicans were meeting a few blocks away in the Coliseum. The Progressives had come to Chicago for one specific reason. One columnist neatly summed it up: "the progressive party advertised that it would be on a certain corner at a certain time, wearing a red carnation, and that its intentions were matrimonial." George Perkins, chairman of the Progressive National Committee, was the most matrimonially inclined of the Progressive leaders. He hoped to see the Republicans take Roosevelt as their candidate, which would be fine for the Colonel but would mean extinction for the Progressive Party. One wing of the Progressives, including the Pinchots, Bainbridge Colby, and William Allen White, was determined to keep the party alive. While Perkins was opening negotiations with Crane and the other Republican leaders, these men decided the best plan would be to go ahead and nominate Roosevelt on a Progressive ticket before the Republicans could act on their own nomination.

As if disarray among the Republicans and confusion about the future reunion of the two parties were not enough to plague the delegates, even the weather turned against them. Chicago was cold and stormy, with a driving rain turning to sleet. White-suited, straw-hatted delegates huddled miserably in the lobbies and corridors of hotels, attempting to whoop up a brave show for their candidates amid the rain and confusion. The Roosevelt Republican headquarters were the most ardent, the Fairbanks the noisiest, but the Cummins headquarters were the most popular. It was the only one with "alcoholic beverages constantly and publicly on tap" to ward off the effects of rain and cold winds blowing in off the lake. There were no Hughes headquarters and no formal organization, although blue tickets labeled "Put on your overcoat and hustle for Hughes" began appearing in the pockets of the delegates. Despite the uncertainty among the leaders, Frank Hitchcock kept predicting a third-ballot victory for the Justice.

Sunday, June 4, gave the first indications of the intentions of some of the uncommitted delegations. In an unofficial poll, the New York delegation favored Hughes by 43 votes to 38 for Root, 2 for Roosevelt, 1 for Major General Leonard Wood, and 3 uncommitted. Illinois, pledged to Senator Sherman, estimated 30 to 35 of its 58 votes to Hughes as a second choice; eight said that they would vote for Roosevelt when released, and a few were expected to go to Weeks. In Missouri, a Weeks supporter defeated former Governor Hadley, a Hughes delegate, for the chairmanship of the delegation, and the state voted to go 15 for Weeks, 9 for Fairbanks, 6 for Hughes, and 3 for Root; three others had yet to make up their minds. Weeks also led the poll of the Oklahoma delegation.

Both Hughes and Root gained strength on Monday. Senator Borah released his fourteen Idaho and Wyoming delegates, and they were expected to go to Hughes. At the same time, Kansas caucused and decided to give 18 of its 20 votes to Root.

The Republicans who gathered in the Coliseum on Wednesday, June 7, were for the most part conservative in outlook. National Chairman Hilles had worked for months, passing judgment on prospective delegates to make sure that no one with the faintest resemblance to an insurgent was selected. It was a gathering of loyal, tried-and-true Republicans, who had not been lured by the siren song of the Bull Moose. But loyal, conservative Republicans did not mean boss-controlled Republicans. One reason for the absence of boss control was the fact that there were fewer pliable southern delegates. The South had given Taft control of the convention of 1912 and, in consequence, had split the party. After the election, the National Committee had reorganized the apportionment of seats, with the result that there were seventy-eight fewer southern votes in the convention.

Although most observers believed that Hughes could not be stopped, there was the customary talk of possible dark horses. Prominently mentioned as a compromise candidate should one be needed was the handsome freshman senator from Ohio, Warren G. Harding.

Harding was to be temporary chairman and pinned great hopes on the effect of his keynote address. Perhaps, after all, someone could stampede the convention. As the editor-politician arose to make his speech, the delegates seemed more interested in the afternoon papers with their headlines—"Kitchener and His Staff Perish at Sea"—than they were in the speaker. Harding talked for an hour and fifty minutes and failed utterly even to interest the delegates, let alone to stampede them. The *Times* sniffed, "Harding could not stampede any convention. . . . His full name is Warren G. Harding and he is Senator in Congress from Ohio; but it is not necessary to burden one's memory with these statistics if one is merely trying to remember the names of persons likely to be nominated for President."

As the convention droned through its first sessions, reporters scratched their heads trying to remember a duller convention. They failed. Such descriptions went out over the wires: "Somewhere between 12,000 and 14,000 graven images gathered together in the Coliseum at 11 o'clock this morning and viewed each other with cold unwinking eyes and chilled steel faces for something like three hours, then dispersed." Calling it "the most lifeless convention that ever convened," the *Times* explained, "The reason is that mixed and dubious as the situation is, it is not being fought out, it is being settled. It is a convention of the tongue and brain behind the door, not of the fist and club in the ring."

On Thursday afternoon, some of the backstairs conferences came out into the open. Senator Harding, now permanent chairman, announced that he had received a letter from O. K. Davis, Secretary of the Progressive convention, asking that a joint committee on conference be set up to find a mutually satisfactory candidate. The Republicans promptly selected Senators Reed, Smoot, and William E. Borah, former Senator Murray Crane, Nicholas Murray Butler, and Congressman A. R. Johnson of Ohio. The Progressives named George W. Perkins, former Attorney General Charles Bonaparte, Governor Hiram Johnson, former Governor John M. Parker of Louisiana, and Horace S. Wilkinson of New York.

Before the conference committee held its first meeting, new

events strengthened the belief that Hughes would be the Republican nominee with or without Progressive acceptance. Michigan, instructed for Henry Ford, decided, after a courtesy vote for Ford, to cast its 30 votes for Hughes at the end of the first ballot. Missouri, despite the Weeks sentiment in the delegation, voted in caucus to give its entire 36 votes to Hughes on the second ballot.

The Republican members of the conference committee met for dinner at the Chicago Club and were joined later by the Progressives. Charles Bonaparte led off the discussion by declaring that it was the Progressives' conviction that Roosevelt should be nominated by both conventions. For two hours the other Progressives expanded this theme. Then, at midnight, Nicholas Murray Butler declared that the Republicans would never accept Roosevelt and that they should agree on a second choice. The Progressives had no second choice, Perkins declared, but would like to know who the Republicans had in mind. The Republicans refused to say. At 3:30 a.m., the conference adjourned with an agreement to meet the next evening.

The Republican convention heard the nominating speeches Friday afternoon and evening. Charles Evans Hughes was nominated by Governor Whitman, who called the Justice, among other things, "the American spirit incarnate." Next, Elihu Root was presented by Nicholas Murray Butler, and then Senator Burton, Senator Weeks, Coleman Du Pont, Senator Sherman, former Vice-President Fairbanks, and Senator Cummins were named. Senator Albert Fall of New Mexico placed Theodore Roosevelt in nomination with the rather odd promise that "Starving mothers in Mexico . . . will put their hope in one great American and one alone—and that one is Theodore Roosevelt." The Colonel was accorded a thirty-six-minute ovation, mostly from the galleries. After Roosevelt's nomination came those of Senator LaFollette and Governor Brumbaugh, bringing the total of nominees to eleven.

The first ballot gave Hughes 253½ votes, 29½ more than had been predicted earlier, with Weeks second with 105 and Root third with 103. The others were Cummins 85, Burton 77½, Fairbanks 74½, Sherman 66, Roosevelt 65, Knox 36, Ford 32, Brumbaugh 29, LaFollette 25, former President Taft 14, Du Pont 12, Frank B. Willis 4, Borah 2, Governor McCall 1; 2½ were absent. Four hundred ninety-four were necessary for nomination. Following the first ballot, Governor Brumbaugh withdrew and asked the convention to vote for Theodore Roosevelt.

On the second ballot, Hughes gained 75 votes for a total of 328½. The official results were Hughes 328½, Root 98½, Fairbanks 88½, Cummins 85, Roosevelt 81, Weeks 79, Burton 76½, Sherman 65, Knox 36, LaFollette 25, Du Pont 13, John Wanamaker 5, and McCall, Willis, Leonard Wood, and Warren G. Harding 1 each. The convention then voted to adjourn.

The Progressives had been marking time all day, awaiting further action from the conference committee. But the western Progressives, including Harold Ickes, the Pinchots, James Garfield, Hiram Johnson, and William Allen White, decided to go ahead and push for Roosevelt's nomination. Gifford Pinchot was on his feet seeking recognition from Chairman Raymond Robins when Perkins realized what was about to happen. He quickly signaled for adjournment, and the motion was passed before Pinchot could place Roosevelt before the Progressive convention.

Having prevented the Progressives from taking any action, Perkins hurried off to the second meeting of the conference committee. Again, the Progressives refused to consider a compromise candidate, and the Republicans restated their opposition to Roosevelt but would name no alternate candidate. The meeting broke up at 3 o'clock Saturday morning with an agreement to meet again at 9:00 a.m.

At 4:00 a.m., Nicholas Murray Butler, with the approval of the Republican leaders, called Roosevelt over a private wire from George Perkins's suite. Unless the Colonel agreed to back Root, Knox, or Fairbanks, Hughes would be nominated, Butler told him. Roosevelt refused to discuss Root and indicated that he found neither Knox nor Fairbanks satisfactory. Why not, he asked, nominate either Leonard Wood or Senator Lodge? Perkins was greatly discouraged because neither party would take either Wood or Lodge. The Republicans agreed that Hughes would be nominated on the next ballot.

Even if Roosevelt had agreed to back Root, Knox, or Fairbanks at such a late date, the events of Friday night would have made it virtually impossible to prevent Hughes's nomination. After adjournment, Cummins's delegates, who were eager to switch to Hughes, convinced him that his case was hopeless. Cummins agreed to withdraw. Senator LaFollette also decided to release his delegates and, although he did not feel he could instruct them, told them that he personally favored Hughes.

With Cummins and LaFollette out of the race, 110 delegates were free to vote for Hughes, and the other candidacies began to collapse. At 2:30 Saturday morning, Senator Sherman withdrew. Frank Hitchcock convinced the Vare brothers that Hughes could win, and they in turn convinced Pennsylvania to unite behind the Justice. Senator Penrose had been outflanked, and there was nothing he could do but follow the delegation into the Hughes camp.

The conference committee held a final meeting on Saturday morning. Hiram Johnson and John Parker were so disgusted at Roosevelt's suggestion of Lodge that they refused to attend the meeting. The Republicans at last announced that Hughes was their candidate. Perkins said he would confer with the other Progressive leaders and let the Republicans know if they would go along.

The Progressives would not. Perkins's announcement that Roosevelt had proposed Lodge and that the conference committee proposed Hughes was shouted down. The convention was in pandemonium. Perkins begged them to wait for the outcome of the third Republican ballot, but Governor Parker shouted that Roosevelt should be nominated. When word was received that the Republican ballot was underway, Chairman Robins recognized Bainbridge Colby, who placed Roosevelt's name before the convention. Perkins leaped to the rostrum and began to shout. He knew that Roosevelt would not accept the nomination, but he could not make himself heard over the uproar. The Progressives nominated Roosevelt by acclamation.

Meanwhile, in the Republican convention, Senator Weeks withdrew just before the beginning of the ballot, and Burton, Fairbanks, and Root withdrew while it was in progress. The results of the third ballot gave Hughes the nomination with 949½ votes to 18½ for Roosevelt, 7 for Lodge, 5 for Du Pont, and 3 each for LaFollette and Weeks.

In Washington, Justice Hughes was at lunch with his family when word came that he had been nominated. With tears in his eyes, he went downstairs to exchange a few words with reporters and then retired to his study to write out his letter of resignation from the Court, which was sent to the President, and his letter of acceptance, which would go to the convention. Until he actually began to write, neither his family nor his secretary had known whether or not he would accept the nomination.

The vice-presidential nomination was a contest between former Vice-President Fairbanks and former Senator Elmer E. Burkett of Nebraska. Because Indiana was considered more important in the coming election than Nebraska, Fairbanks, as bewhiskered as Hughes, received the nomination with 863 votes to 108 for Burkett, with 12 votes scattered.

The Progressives, having nominated Roosevelt, gave the second place to John Parker and sat back to await word from Oyster Bay that the Bull Moose would fight again. Roosevelt's message to the convention, in which he conditionally refused the nomination until he determined what Hughes's policies would be, "fell upon them like a curse." William Allen White wrote, "For a moment there was silence. Then there was a roar of rage. It was the cry of a broken heart such as no convention ever had uttered in this land before. . . . I saw hundreds of men tear the Roosevelt picture or the Roosevelt badge from their coats, and throw it on the floor. They stalked out buzzing like angry bees and I followed them."

On June 26, Roosevelt informed the Progressive National Committee that he would support Hughes, and, by a vote of 32 to 6 with 9 silent, the committee endorsed Hughes. Roosevelt had no further use for the Progressives, and the Bull Moose party was dead.

"He kept us out of war"

THE TWENTY-SECOND DEMOCRATIC
NATIONAL CONVENTION
St. Louis, June 14, 1916

The Democrats gathered in St. Louis, Missouri, on June 14, 1916, to ratify the foregone nomination of Woodrow Wilson for his second term. The convention orators bore down heavily on Wilson's policies of neutrality, and the keynote speaker, Martin H. Glynn of New York, developed the "He kept us out of war" theme that would become the major Democratic cry of the campaign.

Wilson's was the only name presented to the convention, but a delegate from Illinois objected to the motion that the nomination be made by acclamation, and the official results declared that Wilson had been nominated by 1092 to 1. Vice-President Marshall was chosen for a second time by acclamation.

CHAPTER 14

"Ohio's second McKinley"

THE SEVENTEENTH REPUBLICAN NATIONAL CONVENTION
Chicago, June 8, 1920

Two years before the national conventions, most political observers believed that the race for the presidency in 1920 would be between two previous presidents of the United States—each seeking a third term. Theodore Roosevelt was expected to be the Republican nominee, and Woodrow Wilson gave every indication of desiring reelection to ensure success for his vision of the peace. Each could have had his party's nomination for the asking, but death and illness intervened. Theodore Roosevelt died suddenly in January, 1919, and, nine months later, Wilson was struck down by a stroke in the midst of his battle for the League of Nations. At the beginning of 1920, both political parties were leaderless.

The American people were, however, little concerned with the absence of national leadership. The war was over; it was time to relax. Walter Lippmann caught the mood of the nation when he wrote, "The people are tired, tired of noise, tired of politics, tired of inconvenience, tired of greatness, and longing for a place where the world is quiet and where all trouble seems dead leaves. . . ." "Tired of greatness" could be the epigraph of both presidential conventions in 1920.

The nation might be tired of politics, but the politicians were not. If anything, they were exhilarated at the thought that, for once, they could settle matters without interference from the voters. The Democrats would be somewhat inhibited by the palsied hand of Woodrow Wilson, but, for the Republicans, it was open season. In a party without a leader, every man could hope to lead.

As the Republican Party split into its component parts to groom several factional candidates, the Roosevelt wing of the party found its leader first. Two weeks before his death, Roosevelt told friends that, if he were unable to be a candidate, he wanted them to support General Leonard Wood, and, shortly after the former President's death, his family asked Wood to assume command of the Roosevelt forces. "It would seem as if the funeral baked meats had furnished forth the feast for the heir," dryly commented William Howard Taft.

Roosevelt's heir had much to recommend him. A physical giant at fifty-nine, General Wood still had the driving energy he had displayed as commander of Roosevelt's roughriders in the Spanish-American War. Like the former President, General Wood had been prevented by the Wilson administration from participating in the fighting in World War I and was therefore regarded by many admirers as a military martyr.

It was the military aspect of the Wood candidacy that gave him his greatest strength. The war had, surprisingly, produced no military heroes whose popularity could be transferred to the political sphere. General Wood, many thought, could have been that hero had he not been thwarted by Wilson. As a result, he attracted many super-patriots who thrilled to the sight of a uniform. The General campaigned in uniform, surrounded by military aides, and advocated military preparedness while attacking "reds" and the League as it was advocated by Wilson. To believe that the League would prevent war was "idle twaddle and a dream of mollycoddles," the General cried, but he did advocate ratification of the Versailles Treaty with the Lodge reservations. He was, he said, for the "Americanization" of the League.

In his emphasis on the military and "Americanization," Wood was the heir to the "big stick" side of the Roosevelt legacy. On matters of economics and social liberalism, he declined the legacy. When progressives asked for his views on economics and welfare, the General at first declared there was little point in going into matters that could only be decided after long consultation with the "best brains," but he finally stated that he favored the repeal of the excess profits tax, a protective tariff, and economy in government. This stand brought him the support of eastern conservatives, Elihu Root and most of Taft's cabinet, and certain business interests, who, according to Harry Daugherty, believed "that he would use the military arm of the government to break up strikes and destroy the unions." Walter Lippmann, in somewhat exaggerated alarm, said of Wood's supporters, "They have the mood, if not the courage of the coup d'etat."

The strong militaristic aspect of the Wood candidacy eventually became a liability. Remembering that all those mothers who had tearfully sung "I Didn't Raise My Boy to Be a Soldier" would be voting for the first time, many of Wood's backers urged him to resign from the army and tone down the more blatant "man on horseback" aspect of his campaign. Unfortunately, the General knew little of politics or national problems outside the army and continued of necessity to be a military candidate.

What would ultimately be an even greater liability to the Wood candidacy in a year when the party "pros" would reign supreme was his lack of political experience and his unfortunate choice of a campaign manager. Wood had originally asked Roosevelt's former campaign manager, John King, Connecticut national committeeman, to manage his campaign. King was a skilled professional, who advised Wood to negotiate with local party leaders, spend whatever money was necessary, and line up delegates quietly and unobtrusively.

King soon clashed with Colonel William Procter of Ohio, a millionaire soap manufacturer, who headed the amateur "Leonard Wood League." When Procter demanded authority to direct the entire campaign and not merely the popular, amateur effort, Wood approved, and King indignantly resigned. The Wood forces, in effect, had broken with the regular organization.

Procter knew far more about soap than he did about politics. Arrogant, ruthless, and intolerant, he poured great sums of money into a nation-wide Wood campaign that threatened or insulted the regular organizations in most of the states. Expressing his contempt for "bartering and manipulation," the autocratic Procter advised

Wood to wage a "clean-cut fight out in the open," regardless of
how many state bosses and favorite sons had their toes trampled
in the process. The enormous amount of ill-will stirred up by Procter's tactics would prove fatal to the General when the time for
bargaining came in the convention.

Next to Wood, the leading candidate was fifty-nine-year-old
Frank Lowden, Governor of Illinois. Lowden's career had embodied all the classic elements of the success story. Born in a log
cabin, the son of a blacksmith, he had worked his way through law
school, set up in Chicago as a successful corporation lawyer, and
married an heiress to the Pullman fortune. He had become a gentleman farmer presiding over a great estate in northern Illinois
and had served two undistinguished terms in Congress. Elected
governor in 1916, he had proved, to the astonishment of everyone,
to be a brilliant executive. He reorganized the state government,
worked efficiently and harmoniously with party leaders, business
and labor, and made no enemies. His record appealed to conservatives without alienating liberals. He approved the League with
reservations and avoided most of the red hysteria currently sweeping the country. He did offend big-city bosses by being "dry" but
aroused no strong opposition from any quarter. When he formally
entered the race in November, 1919, he was expected to overcome
Wood's initial lead and emerge as the Republican nominee.

Following third, after Wood and Lowden, was the only genuinely progressive candidate, Senator Hiram Johnson of California.
Johnson could be expected to attract the majority of the liberals in
the party, but his position as the leading irreconcilable eventually
lost him their support. Johnson was absolutely opposed to the
League of Nations, with or without reservations. This stand attracted many conservatives, many hyphenated Americans, and
William Randolph Hearst, whose own liberal banner had for some
years been trailing in the dust. As Johnson lost liberal support, his
candidacy became increasingly nationalistic. This brought him
close to the Wood forces, who, however, would never accept him
as one of their own because of his progressivism in domestic affairs.

There are many myths connected with the Republican convention of 1920, and, like most myths, although they may contain elements of truth, their total effect is false. The first of the myths is

that Senator Warren G. Harding, the handsome, somewhat simple-minded newspaper editor from Ohio, was a dark horse sprung unexpectedly upon a surprised convention. No one, according to this myth, gave the slightest consideration to the Harding candidacy until it was born, like Athena, full-grown from the collective brow of the senatorial cabal on the sixth day of the convention. A romantic and dramatic story—but one that is, for the most part, quite false.

At fifty-four, Warren G. Harding was completing his first term as a senator. Publicly, Harding was a spectacularly handsome man, a loyal party follower, an impressive orator, and an undistinguished but dignified senator. Privately, he was an amiable, weak philanderer, naïvely trusting of unworthy friends, easily influenced, and at heart insecure—even at times aware of his own mediocrity. He was happy as a senator. His duties were light, and his position impressive. All he really wanted out of life was to go on looking impressive and not to have anything to worry about.

Harding might have served out his time as an obscure, but well-liked member of the Senate, had he not been closely allied, personally and politically, with an unsavory Ohio politician, Harry M. Daugherty. It was Daugherty who pushed Harding into the successful race for the Senate in 1914 and who took control, through Harding, of the Ohio Republican organization. Daugherty himself had served two terms in the Ohio legislature and had run unsuccessfully for attorney general, governor, congressman, and senator. Frequently charged with unethical law practice, the bribing of legislators, and extortion, he took pride in the fact that none of the charges had ever been proved in a court of law. Such was his reputation, however, that he could only achieve political power through a front man, and in Harding he had the perfect front.

Harding would be up for re-election in 1920, which posed a problem for Daugherty. Enemies of the two men were hatching a scheme to pledge Ohio's votes to Wood, which would, by undermining Daugherty's control of the state delegation, seriously threaten Harding's chances for re-election. If Daugherty were not to lose control of the state organization, Harding would have to tie up the Ohio delegation as a favorite son.

The Senator was not enthusiastic. He protested that he was unfit to be president, but Daugherty assured him that greatness in presidents was "largely an illusion of the people" and that true greatness lay in being kind. Harding was unconvinced but allowed himself to be persuaded. As Daugherty smugly told it years later, "I found him sunning himself, like a turtle on a log, and I pushed him into the water."

Harding announced his candidacy in November, 1919. To counteract the charge that he was not a serious candidate, he filed in the Indiana as well as in the Ohio primary, and Daugherty announced that they would fight for delegates in the Kentucky and West Virginia state conventions. Harding embarked on an extensive speaking tour, preaching "America first" and displaying his profile to admiring crowds.

Initial response to Harding's candidacy among the party professionals was encouraging. Boies Penrose was favorable, at least to using Harding as a means of stopping Wood and Lowden, Senators Watson and New of Indiana announced their support, and Daugherty informed Harding that he had considerable second-choice sentiment in several delegations. The press rated Harding's chances fourth behind Wood, Lowden, and Johnson.

Although Harding's support was never of major proportions, everyone was aware of his candidacy, and all considered him an outside possibility. Daugherty outlined the Harding strategy in a frank talk with the reporter Mark Sullivan. "All I'm doing is getting in touch with the leaders and delegates who are for Wood and Lowden, being friendly with them. When the convention comes, those two armies will battle each other to a standstill. When both realize they can't win, when they're tired and hot and sweaty and discouraged, both the armies will remember me and this little headquarters. They'll be like soldiers after the battle, who recall a shady spring along a country road, where they got a drink as they marched to the front. When they remember me that way, maybe both sides will turn to Harding—I don't know—it's just a chance." He predicted that Wood's militarism, Lowden's wealth, and Johnson's record as a bolter would eliminate them from the race, leaving the way clear for Harding.

Daugherty was also reported to have made another prediction of Harding's victory, which gave rise to the second great myth of the convention. In February, 1920, the New York *Times* reported Daugherty to have told a reporter, "I don't expect Senator Harding to be nominated on the first, second, or third ballots, but I think we can afford to take chances that at about eleven minutes after two, Friday morning of the convention, when fifteen or twenty weary men are sitting around a table, someone will say, 'Who will we nominate?' At that decisive time, the friends of Harding will suggest him and we can well afford to abide by the result." This was the origin of the famous "smoke-filled room." What actually happened was somewhat less dramatic.

According to an eyewitness, Daugherty was packing his bags in a New York hotel when the *Times* reporter called. Daugherty regretted that he did not have time to grant an interview, but the reporter followed him into the corridor to the elevators asking questions. Nettled by Daugherty's laconic replies, the reporter said that since Harding had so few pledged delegates he supposed Daugherty expected to win the election by manipulation. Would he be correct in presuming that the weary leaders gathered in a smoke-filled hotel room at two in the morning would turn to Harding? Unruffled by the sarcasm, Daugherty shot back, "Make it 2:11," and stepped into an elevator. The reporter wrote up his own prediction, made the time 2:11, and a legend was born. When the article appeared, Daugherty accepted it because it gave major publicity to his candidate, and, after events proved the prediction remarkably correct, took full credit for having made it. He had not, but the effect was the same.

Beside the four serious candidates, there were several favorite sons and true dark horses. The taciturn Governor of Massachusetts, Calvin Coolidge, who had won national fame for his role in breaking up the Boston police strike, had the support of his home delegation. William Allen White launched a small boom for Henry Allen, Governor of Kansas, who, it was hoped, would be the second choice of the Wood delegates and, as an original Progressive, the Johnson delegates. Boies Penrose again announced his support for his aged senatorial colleague Philander C. Knox, while the rest of the Pennsylvania delegation favored Governor William C. Sproul. The New York favorite son was Dr. Nicholas Murray Butler, and Senators Coleman Du Pont of Delaware, Robert M. LaFollette,

Howard Sutherland of West Virginia, and Miles Poindexter of Washington had favorite-son status with their home delegations.

One dark-horse candidate was the former United States food administrator, Herbert Hoover of California. No one was quite sure of Hoover's party affiliation. He had supported the Progressives in 1912 and held high office in the Wilson administration. Hoover himself said that he had been a progressive Republican before the war, nonpartisan during the war, and an independent progressive since. He was as frequently mentioned for the Democratic nomination as for the Republican, but, not being a regular member of either party, he was a very dark horse indeed.

Hoover finally announced his Republican affiliation in April, 1920, when he entered the California primary, but his defeat by Hiram Johnson removed him from any consideration in the Republican convention. The only other dark horse was General John Pershing, who was entered in the Indiana primary in an effort to embarrass Wood. His candidacy, in which he was not personally interested, came and went without notice.

General Wood was the most active campaigner in the primaries, entering eleven primaries and spending more than a million and a half dollars in his quest for delegates. Lowden entered few primaries, preferring to work with local leaders in state conventions. He spent more than $400,000 on his campaign, nearly all of which came out of his own pocket. Most of the Lowden money went for campaign literature, none of it for paid advertising, which Lowden expressly forbade. "I would rather lose any primary state, including my own," he wrote, "than to put the Presidency on the plane of a patent medicine."

When the state primaries were completed, Wood had won 124 instructed delegates, Johnson 112, Lowden seventy-two, and Harding thirty-nine. The total of the popular vote was more revealing. Johnson was clearly the popular choice with 965,651 votes from all the primaries he entered to 710,863 votes for Wood. Lowden's vote of 389,127 was less significant because he entered so few primaries. Harding trailed badly with only 144,762 votes. According to the newspapers, Harding's poor showing "practically eliminated" him from contention.

Shortly before the convention met, Lowden was almost eliminated from the race, as were Wood and Johnson. Senator Johnson, incensed at the enormous amounts of money spent by the Wood forces, demanded, through Senator Borah, that the Senate investigate campaign expenditures. The resulting explosion not only blighted the prospects of Wood and Lowden but also ruined Johnson's own hopes.

A Senate subcommittee uncovered Wood expenditures of $1,-500,000. There was nothing illegal in spending such a large sum, but disgusted Republicans were willing to believe that Wood was attempting to buy the nomination.

Lowden had spent only $414,150 but, unbeknownst to the candidate, $5,000 had gone into the private bank accounts of two St. Louis men who had become Lowden delegates. Despite Lowden's repudiation of the two delegates, the apparent attempt at bribery smashed his candidacy. The old guard, who might be expected to take a tolerant view of such matters, was convinced that it was "impossible for him to go out and get the votes," even though everyone realized that Lowden himself had had nothing to do with the bribe.

The third victim of the Senate investigation was Hiram Johnson. Party regulars were furious that two leading candidates had been discredited at his instigation, and they were determined that Johnson would never receive the nomination. With Wood, Lowden, and Johnson discredited, the party leaders would have to turn to a minor candidate, and they played right into the slippery hands of Harry Daugherty. The only beneficiary of the investigation was Warren G. Harding.

The Republican National Convention opened in Chicago on June 28, 1920. Virtually all the party leaders were in attendance, with the exception of Boies Penrose, who was critically ill and thought to be dying. Closely involved in the convention were the representatives of business, industry, and finance. Harry F. Sinclair, Edward L. Doheny, and Jake Hamon spoke for oil, Elbert M. Gary for steel, and Cornelius Vanderbilt for himself. Four Morgan partners worked closely with publisher George Harvey, who still fancied himself a kingmaker. Never, wrote William Allen White, had he seen a convention "so completely dominated by sinister predatory economic forces."

From the outset, it was clear that the senatorial leaders were in full control. Henry Cabot Lodge, his patrician beard still stained with the blood of the Versailles Treaty, was named temporary chairman and keynoter and then kept on as permanent chairman. In his keynote address Lodge spewed forth an astonishing stream of venom for one hour and twenty minutes. It was, said one newspaper, "a hymn of hate," in which Lodge tried to make the League the key issue of the campaign, with personal hatred of Woodrow Wilson as the supplementary theme.

The convention marked time for two days while awaiting the platform. While the delegates happily defied the Volstead Act by crowding the hotel bars for $1.10 highballs and 25¢ beer to alleviate the near 100-degree temperatures, the platform committee wrestled with the problem of the League. It was the original intent of the committee to present a pro-League plank endorsing the senatorial reservations. The plank had the backing of the party elder statesmen William Howard Taft, Charles Evans Hughes, and Elihu Root and reflected the opinion of most of the convention. Senator Lodge wanted a plank endorsing the Senate's rejection of the Versailles Treaty and making no promises for the future, while the irreconcilables, led by Senators Borah and McCormick, threatened to denounce the platform and the party unless the League were rejected. After much wrangling between the pro- and anti-League representatives, Elihu Root offered a compromise, which the committee adopted. Wilson's League was condemned, but one plank called vaguely for an "international association" based on "international justice," which was not defined. The plank was a meaningless mishmash upon which any candidate, pro-League or outright irreconcilable, could run. The rest of the platform offered no problems and no ideas and was acceptable to everyone.

While the convention moved sluggishly toward the nominating speeches, the candidates operated in an atmosphere of uncertainty and waning confidence. Harding was particularly dejected. He had never shared Daugherty's confidence and was appalled at the expenditure of $750 a day for his headquarters. Meeting Nicholas Murray Butler one day, he said he was giving up his rooms because he would never be nominated and had decided to quit politics. Most of the time he sat with a young friend in his hotel room, reminiscing about his youth in rural Ohio and expressing the hope that he would not be nominated.

The convention got down to business on Friday morning with the inevitable, interminable ritual of nominating speeches. Governor Allen, still considered a possible dark horse, placed General Wood in nomination. The speech did neither man much good. Wood's managers, fearing that a good speech would enhance Allen's prospects, edited it to make sure that it would not unduly impress the convention. At its conclusion, the Wood forces put on a forty-two minute demonstration.

Frank Lowden was next in nomination and was accorded a forty-five minute demonstration, marked by a huge banner carried by the Kentucky delegation and reading, "Every traveling man wants a businessman for President—Lowden." What the farmers' daughters wanted was unspecified.

The nominating speech by Charles Stetson Wheeler of California for Hiram Johnson was a disaster. Originally Borah was to have made the speech, but Johnson was fearful that Borah's eloquence might set off a stampede for himself, and he decided to choose a less persuasive speaker. It was an unfortunate decision. Wheeler bitterly attacked the bosses and called on southern "hand-picked delegates" and northern "political slaves" to revolt against boss rule. He managed to reopen almost every old wound in the party and fully demonstrated what most delegates feared: that Johnson was a divisive influence in the party. The thirty-seven-minute demonstration did nothing to soothe the ire of the "political slaves."

Calvin Coolidge and Judge Jeter Pritchard of North Carolina were nominated next, followed by Nicholas Murray Butler and Herbert Hoover. Then Frank B. Willis of Ohio placed Warren G. Harding before the convention. In keeping with the Harding strategy of conciliation and good will to all candidates, Willis gave an old-fashioned, friendly speech. As Mark Sullivan commented, "To hear Willis was to get the combined enjoyments of oratory, grand opera, and hog-calling." He evoked the greatest laughter of the convention when, leaning chummily over the speakers' railing and referring to the twenty-six women delegates, he remarked, "Say, boys—and girls, too—why not name as the party's candidate," which was as far as he got, while delegates called out, "That's right; we are all boys and girls" and "The girls are in politics now as well as the boys." Willis also paid Harding the dubious compliment, "he is Ohio's second McKinley." The ten-minute ovation was as friendly as the speech.

Governor Sproul of Pennsylvania, Senator Poindexter of Washington, and Senator Sutherland of West Virginia completed the roster of candidates.

The first ballot for the nomination only proved what everyone had expected all along—none of the candidates looked like a winner. The first ballot vote, with 493 necessary for nomination, was Wood 287½, Lowden 211½, Johnson 133½, Sproul 84, Butler 69½, Harding 65½, Coolidge 34, LaFollette 24, Pritchard 21, Poindexter 20, Sutherland 17, Coleman Du Pont 7, Hoover 5½, Borah 2, Charles B. Warren 1, with one delegate not voting.

During the roll call, the chairman of the Missouri delegation answered "Not ready" when his state was called, prompting a wag in the gallery to call out, "Still counting the cash?" The crowd roared derisively, but the Lowden forces were not amused.

Both the Harding and Lowden votes were deceptive. Before the balloting, Daugherty arranged with Lowden's manager to give some Harding votes to Lowden to help stop Wood, but he warned, "the minute you pass Wood, the minute Wood is out of the race, all friendship between us on the floor of this convention ceases."

The problem facing the senatorial leaders, who were determined to have a candidate of their own choosing, was to stop Wood by building up Lowden, then to eliminate Lowden. But how? There were few sources of new strength for Lowden. The largest bloc of votes, Sproul's, could not be released because 25 or 30 Pennsylvania votes were waiting to go to Wood. Michigan and Massachusetts posed a similar threat. New York seemed the safest source of new Lowden strength. Dr. Butler agreed to release 14 New York votes to Lowden on the second ballot. Daugherty also provided 3½ more Harding votes but could not prevent 3 Harding votes in Wyoming from switching to Wood.

The results of the second ballot were Wood 289½, a gain of only 2 votes; Lowden 259½, a gain of 48; Johnson 146, a gain of 12½; Sproul 78½, Harding 59, Butler 41, Coolidge 32, LaFollette 24, Poindexter and Sutherland 15 each, Pritchard 10, Du Pont 7, Hoover

5½, and Borah and Senator Knox 1 each. A motion to adjourn after the second ballot was overwhelmingly defeated on a voice vote.

Wood gained 13½ votes on the third ballot for a total of 303, while Lowden gained 23 for a total of 282½. The others were Johnson 148, Sproul 79½, Harding 58½, Coolidge 27, Butler 25, LaFollette 24, Poindexter 15, Sutherland 9, Hoover 5½, DuPont 2, Knox 2, Senator Watson 2, Borah 1. Again, the motion to adjourn was made, and a roll call was demanded. The Convention voted 701½ to 275½ against adjournment.

The fourth ballot showed Wood still creeping up. He gained 11½ votes while Lowden gained only 6½. Clearly the strategy to have Lowden overtake Wood was in danger of collapse. The fourth ballot totals were Wood 314½, Lowden 289, Johnson 140½, Sproul 79½, Harding 61½, Coolidge 25, LaFollette 22, Butler 20, Poindexter 15, Hoover 5, Watson 4, Sutherland 3, Du Pont and Knox 2 each, and Borah 1.

During the roll call, Senators Lodge, Smoot, McCormick, Warren, and Borah and Mr. Alvin Hert of Kentucky, decided to adjourn the convention to work out a plan for stopping Wood. Accordingly, after the results of the fourth ballot were announced, Reed Smoot moved adjournment. In response to the question, there was a scattering of ayes and a thunderous roar of noes, but Lodge declared the motion carried, banged down his gavel, and turned away from the rostrum before the surprised Wood forces could demand a roll call. When Smoot was asked why the old guard had forced adjournment clearly against the wishes of the convention, he candidly replied, "Oh, there's going to be a deadlock, and we'll have to work out some solution; and we wanted the night to think it over."

The night of June 11-12 was a night for little men involved in great schemes. Offers and counter-offers filled the air, and the "smoke-filled room" myth was born. "Nineteen hundred twelve was a Sunday-school convention compared with this," snorted Hiram Johnson.

Johnson spent most of Friday night avoiding the vice-presidency. The Wood and Lowden forces approached him and were rebuffed. Harding came personally to offer Johnson second place on the ticket with no success. Some of the eastern leaders suggested a

Philander Knox-Johnson ticket, hinting that Knox's poor health might make the vice-presidency more important than usual. Again, Johnson refused. If he could not run for the presidency, he said, he preferred to remain a senator.

General Wood was also the recipient of offers on Friday night. Boies Penrose, who had been in a coma most of the day, roused himself about 10:00 p.m. to offer Pennsylvania to Wood in exchange for three cabinet posts. Wood refused. Then Jake Hamon offered the General the Oklahoma delegation, which had been voting for Lowden. All he wanted in return was the right to name the secretary of the interior and the ambassador to Mexico. Turning purple with rage, Wood roared, "I am an American soldier. I'll be damned if I betray my country. Get the hell out of here!" Hamon went.

Oklahoma went eventually to Harding, which was a mistake for Jake Hamon. He would have been better off to have avoided politics. A few months later, having helped to nominate Harding, he prepared to attend the inauguration. He decided to take Mrs. Hamon with him, a decision that so enraged his mistress that she shot him dead. It was left to others to name the secretary of the interior.

Harding was completely discouraged. William Allen White saw him on Friday afternoon, disheveled, unshaven, with bloodshot eyes, and obviously drunk. He was so convinced that he would not be nominated that he wired an assistant standing by in Ohio to make the midnight deadline to file for the Senate race.

Harding need not have worried. George Harvey dined with Senator Brandegee in the suite on the thirteenth floor of the Blackstone Hotel that Harvey shared with Will Hays. After dinner, Senator Lodge joined them, and the smoke began to rise. Harvey was a curious sort. "He affected formally statesmanlike attire, great, horn-rimmed spectacles, a pontifical carriage, and a weighty quietude of confidential speech." He was so impressive, it was said, that he impressed himself.

In the course of the evening, most of the senatorial leaders drifted in and out of Harvey's rooms. "Here is the Senate in epitome," said one. Among the conferees were, beside Harvey, Brandegee, and Lodge, Senators Watson of Indiana, Smoot of Utah,

McCormick of Illinois, Wadsworth and Calder of New York, Curtis of Kansas, Phipps of Colorado, Frelinghuysen of New Jersey, Borah, and Spencer of Missouri as well as former Senators Crane and Weeks of Massachusetts and Mr. Joseph Grundy of Pennsylvania. Alvin Hert, Lowden's floor manager, also attended. Noticeably absent was Harry Daugherty.

It was a gathering noted for its negativism. With the exception of Borah, these senators were small men whose careers had been "against" rather than "for." They had recently emerged from their greatest collective triumph in smashing Wilson's dream of a League of Nations and, puffed with their own importance, wanted to guarantee the power of the Senate, which they controlled. The deadlock in the convention provided them with the opportunity to select a president. What they wanted, of course, was a president who would sign bills sent up from the Senate and who would not presume to send bills down to the Capitol. The man who would "go along" was the man they were looking for. Also, they wanted a man smaller than themselves, which proved difficult.

Wood, of course, was out. He was too independent. Lowden, too, showed signs of thinking for himself. From 8:00 p.m. until 2:00 a.m., the cabal in the "smoke-filled room" discussed the situation. "All was confusion, puzzlement, and divided counsels," Senator Watson later described the meeting. One by one the possible candidates were considered. Sproul was from a solidly Republican state and was not therefore needed. Coolidge was from Republican New England and was opposed by Lodge. Johnson was impossible. Hughes was opposed by the New York organization, and Allen had a poor labor record. Knox had voted against the Eighteenth and Nineteenth Amendments and would lose the women and the drys. Will Hays was known only as a politician. Someone suggested Lodge, who "shook his head, half ruefully, and said, 'Seventy, a month ago!' "

One potential candidate had not been eliminated—Harding. He was weak; he could be managed. He was from the swing state of Ohio; he certainly looked like a president. Everyone liked him. Why not? As one senator put it, "We have got a lot of second-raters. This man Harding is no world beater, but we think he is the best of the bunch." Senators Curtis, Lodge, Smoot, Brandegee, and

McCormick were the most active in supporting Harding. The rest decided to go along.

At no time was there an over-all plan, a clear-cut decision to force Harding on the convention. The "smoke-filled room" was not a collection of master politicians working out a campaign to dictate a nomination. Rather, as Wadsworth said, "The alleged influential senators were as futile as chickens with their heads cut off. If they came to any decision at all it was a decision to let the Harding suggestion go through, the fact being that they did not have anyone else to propose."

Actually, Harvey, Lodge, Brandegee, and Smoot did have someone else to propose, but they were keeping their plans quiet. It was George Harvey's scheme, with the three senators going along, to back Harding only until he had eliminated Wood and Lowden. Then they planned to switch to Will Hays and swing the convention to the National Chairman. Hays was not, so far as is known, a party to this scheme.

For the time being, Harding was the man. About 1:00 a.m., George Harvey called in two newsmen of the Kansas City *Star* and told them it had been decided to nominate Harding. To avoid the appearance of manipulation, Wood and Lowden would be allowed to run for about four ballots, then Harding would be nominated.

All that remained was to tell the candidate. Harding was summoned to Harvey's suite. Was there, he was asked, any disability that might disqualify him or jeopardize the campaign? Harding asked for ten minutes alone. Did he think of his mistress? Did he think of his appalling lack of ability and his oft-repeated statement that he was unfit for the presidency? Did he think at all? He returned to the room to tell Harvey that there was no impediment to his nomination.

The senators went to work. The national committeemen from Connecticut and Indiana were in control of about 200 floating, uncommitted delegates. Alvin Hert and the two committeemen arranged to feed votes from Missouri, West Virginia, Indiana, Wyoming, and Kansas to Harding, building his strength to appear as a gradual swing to the Ohio Senator.

The convention reassembled for the fifth ballot on Saturday

morning. The air was filled with rumors that Harding had been chosen, but the results of the fifth ballot hardly bore the rumors out. For the first time, Lowden passed Wood for a total of 303. Wood had 299 and Johnson 133½. The others were Sproul 82½, Harding 78, Coolidge 29, LaFollette 24, Poindexter 15, Du Pont and Hoover 6 each, Butler 4, and Sutherland, Frank Kellogg, W. L. Ward, and Knox 1 each.

Ohio had been voting 39 for Harding and 9 for Wood, but four Harding delegates planned to switch to Wood on the sixth ballot. Harry Daugherty passed the word to "watch now for the attempted betrayal," and, when the defection occurred, the deserters were hissed and booed. The results of the sixth ballot were Wood 311½, Lowden 311½, Johnson 110, Harding 89, Sproul 77, Coolidge 28, LaFollette 24, Poindexter 15, Hoover 5, Du Pont and Butler 4 each, W. L. Ward 2, and Knox, Kellogg, and Senator Watson 1 each.

Harding continued to gain on the seventh ballot, while Wood and Lowden remained virtually tied: Wood 312, Lowden 311½, Harding 105, Johnson 99½, Sproul 76, Coolidge 28, LaFollette 24, Poindexter 15, Hoover 4, Du Pont 3, Butler 2, and W. L. Ward, Knox, Kellogg, and Lenroot 1 each.

The eighth ballot spelled the end for Wood, who lost 13 votes, and Lowden, who lost 4½. The losses themselves were minor, but any decrease of strength at such a crucial time was fatal. Harding, meanwhile, had gained another 28½ votes.

The break in the Wood and Lowden strength meant that they had been stopped. Now it was time to arrange for the nomination of Will Hays. Alvin Hert moved a recess until 4:00 p.m. Frank Willis, who had nominated Harding, roared for a roll call, but it was explained to him privately that there was no question of stopping Harding. The leaders merely wanted a recess to avoid the appearance of steamrolling. Accordingly, the convention recessed, although Daugherty, who had not had anything explained to him, rushed to the front of the platform shouting, "You cannot defeat this man this way."

During the recess, Wood and Lowden made a last effort to stave off defeat. Lowden called Wood asking for a meeting. The General drove to the Congress Hotel to pick up Lowden. As the two candidates drove through the streets of Chicago, Lowden appeared badly shaken. His own delegates were being used against him, he told Wood. They agreed that, with the help of Johnson and the favorite sons, they could muster enough strength to stop Harding and force a recess over the weekend. This recess would give them time to work out a coalition.

Wood dropped Lowden at his hotel and went to see Johnson, who agreed to the plan. But Lowden balked at taking second place on a Wood ticket. The negotiations were on the verge of collapse when Will Hays arrived to smooth things over, and all agreed to a recess until Monday.

The flaw in the plan was the reliance placed on Alvin Hert. It was arranged that Lodge would delay the opening of the afternoon session until the Wood-Lowden-Johnson combination had lined up enough support, and then Hert would move for adjournment. As they were leaving the room, however, Hert dropped behind with Procter and said, "Wood and Lowden are out of it, and we will have a chance by Monday to make our arrangement." Procter refused to stab his candidate in the back, and Hert looked to make arrangements elsewhere.

Kansas decided in caucus to go over to Harding, despite the violent protests of William Allen White. Governor Allen told the delegation that he had been promised the vice-presidency in exchange for the swing to Harding. White agreed to follow the delegation on the condition that, if Harding did not make it after two more ballots, Kansas would follow White's suggestion to back Herbert Hoover. The delegation agreed.

A second "smoke-filled room" conference was in session that Saturday afternoon. Senator Brandegee called the chairman of the Connecticut delegation to Harvey's rooms and told him to switch Connecticut to Hays on the next ballot. The chairman protested that the delegation had already decided to vote for Harding. That would be foolish, Harvey and Brandegee told him, because they had lined up 600 votes for Hays, who was going to be the nominee. Looking into the adjoining room, the Connecticut chairman saw Smoot and a man he thought to be Lodge, but he refused to be pressured. As Dr. Butler later wrote, "the stubborn independence of the Connecticut delegation" foiled the plans to nominate Hays. Brandegee's bluff of 600 votes had not worked, and the senatorial cabal was no longer in control of the convention.

In the convention hall, four o'clock came and went. Lodge warned the proponents of delay that he could not wait much longer. But Hert was nowhere to be found. Someone said that Hert was on his way, and Lodge agreed to wait ten minutes more. Hert did not appear. Down came the gavel, and the ninth ballot began.

When Lowden reached the auditorium, he was stunned to find the balloting underway. What had happened to the plan for a weekend recess? In despair, Lowden decided that the game was lost. Finding the elusive Hert, who had finally arrived, Lowden told him that he was withdrawing. He then joined Harding in a little alcove under the speakers' platform.

The decisive moment came when Kansas was called. Kansas had voted 10 Wood, 6 Lowden, and 4 Harding, but it now cast all 20 votes for Harding. The convention exploded into a frenzied twenty-minute demonstration. William Allen White presented a touching, comic portrait of a man of conscience faced with a singularly unpleasant decision. "I was torn, as I often am in politics, between the desire to jump in the fiery furnace as a martyr, and the instinct to save my hide and go along on the broad way that leadeth to destruction. In the end I toddled along, followed the Kansas banner in the parade, ashamed, disheveled in body and spirit, making a sad, fat figure while the bands played, the trumpets brayed, and the crowd howled for Harding; . . . A sad spectacle I made, and time has not softened the shabby outlines of the picture in all these long years."

Hert was on the bandwagon next, throwing Kentucky to Harding. The results of the ninth ballot were Harding 374½, Wood 249, Lowden 121½, Johnson 82, Sproul 78, Coolidge 28, LaFollette 24, Poindexter 14, Hoover 6, Butler 2, and Knox, Hays, Lenroot, and H. F. McGregor 1 each.

On the tenth ballot, Harding swept to victory. He was waiting nervously in a small room off the auditorium with Lowden and Butler. When Pennsylvania cast its vote for him, one of Lowden's managers burst into the room shouting that Harding was nominated. Harding took Lowden's and Butler's hands, saying in a choked voice, "I shall need all the help that you two friends can give me." Daugherty hurried him away before he could say more.

During the tenth ballot, the leaders met in an open space beneath the platform to select the vice-presidential candidate. Hert, Daugherty, McCormick, Weeks, and Borah agreed that Harding needed a liberal running mate. McCormick suggested Senator Lenroot of Wisconsin. He had been a Progressive in 1912, was acceptable to Johnson even though he supported the League with reservations, and would placate the LaFollette Wisconsin followers. Plans were quickly improvised, and Senator McCormick mounted the rostrum to present Lenroot's name to the convention.

Lenroot, after consulting with his wife, decided he did not want the nomination, but, before he could inform the leaders, the convention acted on its own. The delegates had gone along with what they believed to be the wishes of the senatorial leaders in nominating Harding, but another senator was one too many. In a rare burst of independence, Calvin Coolidge was nominated from the floor and won the nomination in a landslide.

Coolidge had been following the convention from the Adams House in Boston. He and his wife were preparing to go to dinner when the phone rang. Coolidge listened, then turned to his wife and said, "Nominated." The Coolidges then went to dinner.

"We either have an ace in the hole or we haven't"

THE TWENTY-THIRD DEMOCRATIC NATIONAL CONVENTION
San Francisco, June 28, 1920

The preconvention campaign for the Democratic nomination of 1920 was complicated by the silence and ambiguity of Woodrow Wilson. Would he seek a third term? If not, who was his choice for the nomination? Most reporters and politicians believed—until his physical collapse in September, 1919—that Wilson would seek a third term. When the state of his health became a matter of acute concern, they were convinced that he was too ill to run again, but the President himself gave no indication of his plans.

Democratic aspirants hoped that the President's letter addressed to the Jackson Day Dinners of January 8, 1920, would indicate a willingness to compromise on the League of Nations and would announce his withdrawal from the race. Instead, the letter called for a campaign based solely on the issue of the League and was silent concerning the nomination. Republicans declared that the letter was an announcement of Wilson's candidacy.

The candidate to suffer most from Wilson's flirtation with a third term was William Gibbs McAdoo, recently resigned as secretary of the treasury. McAdoo very much wanted the nomination, but it would be disloyal, he thought, to seek it if his father-in-law, the President, wanted to run again. McAdoo had the backing of the administration liberals, the Anti-Saloon League, and organized labor. Active in his campaign were Commissioner of Internal Revenue Daniel C. Roper, Bernard Baruch, George Creel, and Thomas B. Love, national committeeman from Texas.

Throughout the preconvention period, McAdoo remained agonizingly indecisive. He told his supporters that he could not seek the nomination but would accept it if it were offered by the convention. On the other hand, he said, he would not try to stop his friends from doing whatever they felt they ought to do in his support.

While McAdoo tried to avoid a conflict with Wilson's ambitions, Attorney General A. Mitchell Palmer suffered from no such delicacy of feeling. Named to the Justice Department in 1919, Palmer had embarked on a vigorous "red hunt" and succeeded in whipping the country into a state of acute hysteria. Bolsheviks were seen to be hiding under every bed, arrests and deportations were wholesale, and a bomb demolished Palmer's Washington home.

Palmer hoped to ride the wave of his popularity as a hunter of subversives into the nomination and announced that he would enter the Georgia primary. He offered to resign from the cabinet if his candidacy should prove embarrassing to Wilson, but the President replied that the convention should be entirely free to make a choice and that he would not interfere with Palmer's campaign.

The Attorney General was the favorite candidate of the National Committee, of which he was a member, but he fared poorly at the polls. The red hysteria reached its climax in the New Year's Day arrests and then died down. Palmer's exaggeration of the menace made him appear by spring slightly ridiculous. In the Michigan primary, Palmer was the only active candidate and had the backing of the state organization, but he lost out to Herbert Hoover, who was not even a Democrat. William Jennings Bryan, McAdoo, and Governor Edwards of New Jersey all polled more votes than Palmer.

The Georgia primary was nearly as discouraging. Although Palmer won the state delegation by winning a plurality of county units, he received only 47,000 votes to 54,000 for former Populist Tom Watson and 46,000 for Senator Hoke Smith. When the convention opened, only Palmer's home state of Pennsylvania and

Georgia were pledged to him, although these 104 votes made him
the front-runner in pledged strength.

The third candidate to enter the race was three-time Governor
of Ohio James M. Cox. A newspaper publisher and self-made millionaire, Cox at fifty had an effective, progressive record as governor. A friend described his character, "When he goes fishing he
wants to catch all the fish in the creek; when he goes hunting he
never quits until he has the legal limit; when he starts to make
money he wants to make every nickel the enterprise affords." He
was popular with labor and had softened his early progressivism
enough to appeal strongly to the moderates in the party.

Cox announced his candidacy on February 1 but made an open
fight only in Kentucky, where he won twenty of twenty-six delegates. He waged a modest campaign, spent only $22,000, and
summed up his strategy shortly before the convention: "My friends
are urging me to open up a vigorous campaign. But I prefer to
wait. If, when the convention opens, they finally turn to Ohio, all
right. We either have an ace in the hole or we haven't. If we have
an ace concealed, we win; if we haven't, no amount of bluffing and
advertisement can do much good."

Cox based his hope for an ace on three factors. First, Harding's
nomination would enhance the availability of an Ohio Democrat.
Second, Cox favored liberalizing the Volstead Act, which made
him attractive to the big-city bosses. Third, unlike Palmer and
McAdoo, he had no ties with the administration and was completely
removed from the League fight. He endorsed, in a general way,
the party's position but did not support Wilson's uncompromising
attitude. Cox would not offend the League's supporters, but neither
would he alienate its opponents.

There were only two dark horses in the Democratic convention
—John W. Davis of West Virginia, who was supported by Under
Secretary of the Navy Franklin D. Roosevelt, and Secretary of the
Treasury Carter Glass of Virginia. Both Davis and Glass were seri-
ously handicapped because they did not come from pivotal states
and had no real organization. Among the favorite sons, Secretary
of Agriculture Edwin T. Meredith of Iowa, Governor Al Smith of
New York, and National Committee Chairman Homer Cummings

of Connecticut were the most prominent. Vice-President Thomas R. Marshall also had his adherents, and, while neither a dark horse nor a favorite son, William Jennings Bryan was, as always, available for the asking.

As the convention neared, the question of Wilson became more pressing. It was reported that more than one-third of the delegates were absolutely opposed to Wilson's candidacy and many more believed that he was too ill to run. To disprove such reports, Wilson made a bold move on June 15, 1920. He held a three-hour interview with a reporter from the New York *World,* allowed the reporter to watch him signing bills and conducting business, and then accompanied him to a showing of a William S. Hart western, which the President vastly enjoyed. The interview, published on June 18, was a sensation. It presented Wilson as healthy, active, and decisive in manner. It was, everyone believed, expressly designed to show that the President was fit to serve another term.

It may have been a coincidence, but McAdoo announced, on the same day that the interview was published, his "irrevocable" decision not to allow his name to go before the convention. He denied that he was withdrawing in favor of Wilson, but he was not believed. Daniel Roper and Bernard Baruch took McAdoo at his word and canceled plans to attend the convention, but others thought that McAdoo would be back in the race as soon as it was shown that Wilson could not win the nomination. As the Chicago *Tribune* waspishly put it: "Mr. McAdoo wishes us all distinctly to understand that if the San Francisco convention does not offer him the nomination he will not accept it."

A few days later, McAdoo was again a candidate. National Committeeman Love told the press that Texas's 40 votes were for McAdoo, and McAdoo assured the North Carolina delegation by telegram that he would make no more withdrawal statements.

No one knew what the convention, which met in San Francisco on June 28, would do. Of the 1092 delegates present, only 336 were instructed, and many of them had only token pledges to favorite sons. The situation promised a prolonged deadlock, and the location did nothing to help matters. This convention was the first held on the Pacific Coast. When the party gathered in the steaming heat of Chicago or Philadelphia, there was always a desire to get things over with as quickly as possible. But the cool ocean breezes and physical beauty of the Golden Gate city, the excellent restaurants, and the comfortable Civic Auditorium made the prospect of deadlock a positive pleasure to everyone but the actual candidates.

There were, as the convention met for the first time, three factions fighting for control—the Wilsonites representing the administration; the Bryanites representing the Drys, the isolationists, and the remnants of the agrarians; and the bosses of the big cities—Charles Murphy of Tammany, Thomas Taggart of Indiana, and George Brennan of Illinois—representing themselves. The three Irish bosses were perfectly frank about what they were after. They had had enough of Wilson and idealism; they wanted a man in the Harding image who would "go along." Second, they wanted "booze" and as wet a candidate as would float. Finally, as the icing on the shamrock, they wanted a platform plank declaring in favor of Irish independence.

The first excitement of the convention came with the keynote address of the temporary chairman, Homer Cummings. In a strong speech, Cummings placed the convention firmly behind the League of Nations and touched off a roaring demonstration. Immediately a Cummings boom got under way with the slogan, "A Great Moment Has Produced a Great Man."

On the second day, Wilson suffered a setback but later won a triumph. The setback came over the selection of the permanent chairman. Wilson wanted Secretary of State Bainbridge Colby for the post, but Bryan objected and proposed Senator Thomas J. Walsh of Montana. Cummings wired Wilson that it would be better to avoid a fight and suggested putting Colby on the platform committee where he could defend the administration from the expected attacks of the Bryanites. Wilson reluctantly agreed, and both sides settled on Senator Joseph T. Robinson of Arkansas as a compromise.

The triumph came when the band struck up "Hail to the Chief" and a huge oil painting of Wilson was lowered from the ceiling. With a great roar, the delegates leaped to their feet and began parading around the auditorium in a demonstration for Wilson. State after state fell into line, standards waving, but Tammany-controlled New York remained firmly seated. Suddenly Franklin

D. Roosevelt leaped for the standard and, after a brisk struggle, bore it off while the crowd cheered. Within minutes the story was circulating that there had been a fist fight. No blows were actually struck, but Roosevelt was, for the moment, the hero of the convention, which would stand him in good stead a few days later.

Because the platform committee had run into major difficulties, it was decided to make the nominating speeches on Wednesday. The flood of oratory took up the entire day and the first session on Thursday. Senator Robert L. Owen of Oklahoma was first before the convention, followed by former Ambassador to Germany James W. Gerard of New York. Homer S. Cummings of Connecticut and Senator Gilbert M. Hitchcock of Nebraska were then nominated, followed by A. Mitchell Palmer, Edwin T. Meredith, James M. Cox, Al Smith, William Gibbs McAdoo, Governor Edward I. Edwards of New Jersey, Senator Furnifold Simmons of North Carolina, Carter Glass, John W. Davis, and Francis B. Harrison, Governor General of the Philippines. Of all the nominations and their attendant demonstrations, only the forty-three-minute demonstration for McAdoo seemed really convincing.

The platform was not presented to the convention until Friday morning. The difficulties had arisen over the prohibition, Irish independence, and League of Nations planks. Wilson had sent a plank to the committee advocating a liberalization of the Volstead Act, but the Dry Carter Glass, chairman of the committee, did not produce it. Consequently, he managed to get through a plank that sidestepped the question of liberalization. Ireland was disposed of innocuously, but the League gave the committee real trouble.

After an all night session, the committee agreed on the general formula approved by Wilson—"We advocate the immediate ratification of the treaty without reservations which would impair its essential integrity"—but accepted the qualification offered by Senator Walsh of Massachusett—"But we do not oppose the acceptance of any reservations making clearer or more specific the obligations of the United States to the League associates." It was a compromise by which the Wilsonites and the reservationists could both claim essential victory. The entire platform of thirty-eight planks and 8000 words was the longest ever presented to a Democratic convention and took the exhausted Glass more than two hours to read.

William Jennings Bryan offered a minority report. He asked for complete endorsement of prohibition and a constitutional amendment providing that treaties be ratified by a majority, rather than two-thirds, of the Senate. He also expressed his opposition to universal compulsory military training in peace time.

Bryan spoke in favor of his amendments and received the greatest personal ovation of the convention. "A great shout went surging up into the vaulted dome of the roof in an endless sea of sound," and for twenty-three minutes the Great Commoner acknowledged the tribute, tears streaming down his cheeks. For a moment it appeared that the convention might be stampeded, but 1920 was a long way from 1896. Microphones allowed other orators to compete on equal terms with Bryan, and urbane Bainbridge Colby calmly and wittily demolished his arguments. The delegates would cheer for Bryan, but they would not follow him. His amendments were defeated by roll-call vote, and the platform was adopted without change.

Late Friday night, the convention cast its first ballot for president. The results proved only that no candidate was the popular choice of the delegates. With 729 votes necessary to nominate, McAdoo led with 266, followed by Palmer with 256. The others were Cox 134, Smith 109, Edwards 42, Marshall 37, Owen 33, Davis 32, Meredith 27, Glass 26½, Cummings 25, Simmons 24, Gerard 21, Senator Williams of Mississippi 20, Hitchcock 18, Champ Clark 9, Harrison 6, Wood 4, Bryan, Colby, William Randolph Hearst, and Josephus Daniels 1 each, and Oscar W. Underwood ½.

McAdoo's managers, seriously handicapped by the absence of Roper and Baruch, had agreed to show the full McAdoo strength on the early ballots in hopes of starting a bandwagon. It was a dangerous strategy because, if the bandwagon did not develop, McAdoo had few reserves of strength to show gains on later ballots.

McAdoo did gain on the second ballot, increasing to 289. Palmer picked up only 6 votes for a total of 264, while Cox gained 25— mostly from Mississippi—for a total of 159. Smith slipped to 101, and the others trailed far behind. At the conclusion of the ballot, the convention having been in session for thirteen hours, it was agreed to adjourn until Saturday morning.

President Wilson had not received even a token vote on the first two ballots, a fact that did nothing to dampen the enthusiasm of Bainbridge Colby. Secretaries of state do not ordinarily attend conventions, especially as last-minute additions to District of Columbia delegations, but Colby had done precisely that. It is more than probable that Colby had been sent to San Francisco by the President to organize a drive for a third term.

On Friday night, Colby decided to act. He believed that a motion to suspend the rules and nominate Wilson by acclamation could be carried at any time, and he wired Wilson that he intended "to take advantage of the first opportune moment to move suspension of the rules and place your name in nomination." When Wilson's friends heard of the proposal, they were aghast. Postmaster General Burlson and Carter Glass were both convinced that Wilson wanted the nomination but were equally convinced that he could not get it. The President's physician had warned that another campaign would kill him. Early Saturday morning, Burlson, Glass, Cummings, Senator Robinson, and Josephus Daniels met in Colby's room to oppose his plan. "I never saw more indignation and resentment in any small gathering," wrote Daniels. Cummings bluntly told Colby that to nominate Wilson would be to sign his death warrant, and Colby plaintively protested that they were making him feel like a criminal, but he finally gave way, and the scheme was dropped. There would be no effort to stampede the convention for Wilson.

The Palmer and Cox managers met at 2:00 a.m. Saturday morning to discuss the situation. It was agreed that McAdoo's nomination should be prevented, but no other agreement could be reached. Palmer doubted, because of the Dryness of many of his delegates, if he could deliver his strength to the Wet Cox, and Cox was not interested in withdrawing in favor of Palmer.

McAdoo gained 34½ votes for a total of 323½ on the third ballot, while Palmer slipped to 251½—a loss of 12½. McAdoo's gains were a matter of 1 to 3 votes scattered through ten delegations and did not represent any strong sentiment for a swing in his favor. Cox gained 18 for a total of 177. By the sixth ballot, McAdoo had risen to 368½, and Palmer had 265½. Cox had gained to 195.

There was a dramatic break on the seventh ballot. The 90 New York votes that had been going to Al Smith were now switched—

68 to Cox, 16 to McAdoo, and 2 to Palmer. Tammany had swung behind Cox, while the McAdoo votes were led by Franklin Roosevelt.

McAdoo held onto his lead on the seventh ballot with 384 votes, but Cox had now taken over second place with 295½, a gain of 100½ votes. New Jersey had followed Tammany's lead to give Cox 25 of Edwards's 28 votes. Palmer held his own with a total of 267½. Cox continued to gain on the next four ballots until he had a total of 332 votes, with 380 for McAdoo and 255 for Palmer.

Then, on the twelfth ballot, Cox surged dramatically into the lead with a gain of 72 votes, mostly from Palmer. Cox now had 404 votes to 375½ for McAdoo and 201 for Palmer. But still the deadlock was not broken. The frustrated and weary convention cast four more ballots before agreeing to a three-hour recess. By the sixteenth ballot, Cox had gained 50½ more votes, but he was still 272½ votes away from the nomination. The totals on the sixteenth ballot were Cox 454½, McAdoo 337, Palmer 164½, Davis 52, Owen 34, Glass 25, Cummings 20, and Clark 4.

Cox's lead came mainly from the gradual collapse of the Palmer vote and the disappearance of favorite sons. McAdoo, although he had lost 49 votes from his peak on the ninth ballot, was actually 13½ votes ahead of his total when the balloting had begun that morning. Palmer was out of the race, but McAdoo was not. Also worrisome to the Cox forces was the dark-horse threat of Davis, who had gained 23½ votes in the last thirteen ballots.

During the recess, Jouett Shouse and other McAdoo supporters met with Palmer and his manager. Having no power to bargain in McAdoo's name, all Shouse could suggest was that Palmer withdraw in McAdoo's favor to unite the administration forces against Cox. Palmer angrily stalked out of the conference vowing, "If I am not nominated you can be assured that the nominee for President will be someone other than McAdoo or Cox." The convention wearily went back to the deadlock.

Five ballots were cast Saturday night. Cox's vote fluctuated between a high of 468 and a low of 426½, and he ended the day with 430 votes. The results of the twenty-second and final ballot on Saturday were Cox 430, McAdoo 372½, Palmer 166½, Davis 52, Owen 35, Glass 25, Cummings 6, and Clark and Wilson 2 each. The two

Wilson votes represented the first appearance of the President's name in the balloting, but the convention took little notice.

On Sunday, July 4, the McAdoo managers met to consider a line of action in case it should prove impossible to nominate McAdoo. They agreed that they could not accept Palmer or any of the dark horses. Most of the McAdoo delegates questioned re-vealed that Cox was their second choice, and the leaders decided to swing the McAdoo votes to Cox if it became necessary. Unaware of this decision, Boss Murphy offered McAdoo the vice-presidency on a Cox ticket, but McAdoo refused. He might help to nominate Cox if he had to, but he would not work with Tammany in doing so.

The first ballot taken on Monday morning showed little change. The big-city bosses were determined to push ahead with Cox but had yet to prove that they could do it, while McAdoo and Palmer remained firmly, if hopelessly, in the race. On the twenty-third ballot, Cox lost 5 votes for a total of 425, McAdoo lost 8 for 364½, and Palmer gained 15 for 181½. As a reflection of the disgruntled attitude of the rank-and-file delegates, 1½ votes were cast for Irvin S. Cobb and ½ vote for Ring Lardner.

On the twenty-ninth ballot, Indiana switched 19 Cox votes to McAdoo, who rose to 394½, while Cox slipped to 404½. The thirtieth ballot was tensely watched by both sides. To the wild excitement of the McAdoo forces, it was evident that their candidate was overtaking the Ohio Governor. While the opposition derisively sang, "Every Vote Is on the Pay Roll," referring to the enormous patronage McAdoo had controlled in the Treasury Department, McAdoo regained first place, with 403½ votes to 400½ for Cox and 165 for Palmer. Davis had 58 votes.

Although McAdoo was gaining, Palmer came back into the race when the Davis votes switched on the thirty-fifth ballot to give him 222 votes, his best showing since the eleventh ballot. He con-tinued to gain on the next ballot and reached 241 votes, against 399 for McAdoo and 377 for Cox. The McAdoo and Cox forces realized that it was necessary to stop the Palmer drive and moved a recess until evening.

During the recess, the Davis delegates decided that Palmer could not win the nomination, and they therefore deserted him on the first ballot taken Monday evening. The Davis defection doomed

Palmer, who gave up on the thirty-ninth ballot. His campaign collapsed, and eighty-five of his delegates switched to Cox, with fifty-two going to McAdoo and Davis. The results of the thirty-ninth ballot were Cox 468½, McAdoo 440, Palmer 74, Davis 71½, Owen 32, Cummings and Clark 2 each, and Colby 1.

The Palmer switch to Cox marked the beginning of the end, but the McAdoo forces refused to give up. Cox continued to gain strength but had a narrow escape on the forty-third ballot. Forty-seven New York delegates had left the convention to return home, leaving their proxies with Boss Murphy. Although the permanent chairman had earlier ruled that proxies could not be voted, Murphy had secured the promise from the McAdoo leaders, Roosevelt and Mayor Lunn of Schenectady, that they would not challenge the New York vote. Just before the forty-third ballot, Lunn announced his intention to challenge the vote. Cox would have lost more than 40 votes, and his drive would probably have been stalled with fatal results.

Immediately, a violent argument broke out among the New Yorkers, and one Tammany stalwart shouted at Lunn, "You withdraw that motion now. If you don't, when you wake up in the hospital you will hear that Cox has been nominated." Lunn withdrew his motion.

The forty-fourth ballot brought an end to the weary proceedings. It was obvious to the McAdoo forces that they could not possibly win. They decided to climb on the bandwagon while they could. At the end of the forty-fourth roll call, Cox had 699½ votes— 26½ short of nomination. McAdoo polled 240 to 52 for Davis, 34 for Owen, 1½ for Glass, and 1 each for Palmer and Colby. The McAdoo managers then moved that the nomination be made unanimous. Like the Republicans, the Democrats preferred, in the end, a safe candidate. They had nominated an intelligent Harding.

Six men were placed in nomination for the vice-presidency on Tuesday: General Lawrence D. Tyson of Tennessee, Governor Sam V. Stewart of Montana, oilman Edward L. Doheny of California, Franklin D. Roosevelt of New York, former Governor James H. Hawley of Idaho, and W. T. Vaughan of Oregon. Senator Lewis of Illinois was offered and withdrawn at his own request, as was Governor Francis of Missouri.

Cox had decided the night before that Roosevelt would make the best running mate. New York support was necessary for his election, and Roosevelt was a magic name. But he told his manager that, if Boss Murphy strongly objected to Roosevelt, he would take Secretary of Agriculture Meredith.

During the nominating speeches, the leaders gathered beneath the platform. Murphy was opposed to Roosevelt's nomination. He preferred, he said, Bainbridge Colby. But Brennan of Illinois and Senator Pat Harrison led the argument for Roosevelt, insisting that his name would be much stronger on the ticket than Colby's. Finally, Murphy agreed to go along. The decision was passed on to the delegates, the other candidates withdrew, and Roosevelt was nominated by acclamation.

CHAPTER 15

"The blood of a death struggle"

THE TWENTY-FOURTH DEMOCRATIC
NATIONAL CONVENTION
New York, June 24, 1924

The old Democratic Party committed suicide in 1924. The rural Protestant party of Bryan met the urban Catholic party of the city bosses in Madison Square Garden, and, in sixteen days of the bloodiest, most bigoted convention in American political history, the party of Cleveland, Bryan, and Wilson died. A new party would be born under Franklin D. Roosevelt eight years later, but, by the time the Democratic convention of 1924 had adjourned, the old party was nothing but a mangled corpse.

At the beginning of 1924, there was no hint of the disaster to come. Democrats were jubilant at the malodorous scandals of the Harding administration, and, as Senator Walsh of Montana ferreted out the details of corruption to rival even that golden age of civic malfeasance under the Grant administration, the party saw good reason to expect victory in November. A film of oil covered the entire Republican Party and gave promise of a Democratic return to the White House.

Which Democrat would go to the White House was an open question. As in 1920, the party was without a leader. Cox's smashing defeat in 1920 made his role as titular leader even more hollow than that unenviable position usually is and left the way open to a host of potential candidates. During the spring, however, the contest was considered to have settled down to a race between William Gibbs McAdoo, now of California, and the Governor of New York, Alfred E. Smith. The candidacies of these two men brought into sharp focus the divisions that would split and then destroy the party.

McAdoo, the small-town Georgia boy who had made good, the go-getter and promoter *par excellence,* was the Horatio Alger ideal of rural and small-town Protestant America. No longer the heir apparent of the Wilson era, McAdoo became in 1924 the heir of the Bryan tradition. A bone-Dry, native American of Anglo-Saxon stock, McAdoo drew to his standard western and southern Democrats who saw in liquor and the urban masses the source of all evil.

On the other side was Al Smith, cigar-chewing, derby-hatted product of the sidewalks of New York and Tammany Hall. Wet, Irish, and Catholic, Smith was, to the rural wing of the party, symbolic of the sophisticated city slicker it feared and hated. East *vs.* West, Protestant *vs.* Catholic, big city *vs.* small town, Wet *vs.* Dry: Such were the lines upon which the battle would be drawn. Racial, social, and religious fears and hatreds would torment the delegates to the 1924 convention to a degree never before seen in a presidential convention.

The differences between the two wings of the party were personified in the sinister, bed-sheeted form of the Ku Klux Klan. The old Klan of Reconstruction days had been revived in recent years and had drawn into its ranks the racial and religious bigots who feared change, who feared anyone different from themselves, and who most of all feared a world that they no longer understood. Throughout the South and Middle West the Klansmen exerted tremendous and often decisive influence on the elections of local and state officials and were, by 1924, a force to be reckoned with on the national scene.

Naturally, the Wet, urban, Catholic Smith was anathema to the Klan. At all cost, Smith must be defeated. But with whom? It was the tragedy of McAdoo's long and otherwise distinguished life that he became the candidate of the Ku Klux Klan. He was not the Klan's man. There was nothing in his past record, and there would be nothing in his future record to suggest the slightest sympathy with the bigotry of the Klan. But he wanted very much to be President of the United States. The Klan represented a major source of strength to a candidate who knew that the East would be for Smith and the other large states for favorite sons. The Klan itself might have preferred a more sympathetic candidate—Henry Ford, for instance, who was occasionally mentioned for the nomination— but McAdoo offered their best bet. He was Dry and Protestant, and, unlike other candidates who denounced the Klan, he was available. While other men, like Senator Oscar W. Underwood of Alabama, risked their chances for the nomination by repudiating the Klan, McAdoo took refuge in dignified silence. He never spoke in favor of the Klan; he never spoke against it.

At the opening of the race, McAdoo was the odds-on favorite to take the nomination, but the ubiquitous oil of Teapot Dome dealt his candidacy a serious blow. Ironically, it was the day after Woodrow Wilson was laid to rest in Washington Cathedral that Senator Walsh's investigating committee brought McAdoo into the oil scandals.

Testifying before the Walsh Committee, Edward L. Doheny, one of the chief figures in the Teapot Dome scandals, testified that McAdoo, after leaving government service, had been employed by Doheny as legal counsel for five years with a $25,000 yearly retaining fee. The Democratic Party, which so far had been untouched by oil, was stunned. McAdoo denied to the committee any knowledge of wrongdoing. Actually, Doheny was but one of McAdoo's many clients, and the candidate was not even remotely connected with the oil scandals. But such was the climate of the time that any connection, however innocent, with any of the oil thieves was considered damning in itself. The Smith forces happily chanted, "There ain't no oil on Al" for the rest of the campaign.

Despite the damaging connection with Doheny, McAdoo did well in the primaries. He captured North Dakota unopposed and soundly defeated Senator Underwood in Georgia and Florida. Beer-loving Milwaukee helped Al Smith defeat McAdoo in the Wisconsin primary, but it was not considered a serious setback. By convention time, McAdoo's manager, Judge David Ladd Rockwell, was claiming up to 500 first-ballot votes, and the New York *Times* estimated his committed strength at 450 delegates. McAdoo was the front-runner, but he needed 731 votes to win.

The Smith campaign received a temporary setback in the spring, when Boss Murphy of Tammany died suddenly. The key to the nomination was supposed to be held by the city bosses, Murphy, Taggart, and Brennan. Murphy was Smith's chief contact with the other bosses. His death raised the possibility that Taggart and Brennan would try to become kingmakers with candidates of their own—especially Senator Ralston of Indiana—rather than go along with Smith.

Boss Murphy's death turned out to Smith's advantage, however, by weakening Tammany's influence in the convention and giving Smith the opportunity to avoid the label of Tammany's candidate. To underscore his independence from Tammany, Smith chose Franklin D. Roosevelt for his campaign manager. Roosevelt, recovering from his polio attack, was anti-Tammany, Dry, and a Protestant from rural up-state New York. These qualities made him the perfect emissary to the anti-Smith, pro-McAdoo wing of the party.

Roosevelt put to good use the many contacts he had made as a vice-presidential candidate and, working with Louis Howe, was in constant correspondence with most of the party leaders. His greatest success of the preconvention period was swinging Joseph Guffey and a majority of the Pennsylvania delegation behind Smith.

The fact that McAdoo and Smith represented opposing extremes in the party made a long deadlock likely. Smith, it was feared, would control the vital one-third of the convention that could veto McAdoo, who, in turn, could veto Smith. When Roosevelt's old chief in the Navy Department, Josephus Daniels, who was a McAdoo delegate, jokingly suggested a Daniels-Roosevelt ticket, Roosevelt replied that, around the 255th ballot, they could put their respective candidates in a room "armed with a complete Navy outfit ranging from bean soup to 16″ guns with orders that only one man come out alive. Probably neither will come out alive and a grateful Convention will give us the nomination by acclamation."

If some party leaders worried over the possibility of a long deadlock, many anticipated it. As the list of dark horses and favorite sons grew, it seemed that nearly every registered Democrat was a candidate. Chief among the dark horses was John W. Davis of

West Virginia and New York. The former Ambassador to London was perhaps the greatest constitutional lawyer in the country and had a long record of service to the Democratic Party. His father had helped to nominate Horatio Seymour in 1868, and Davis himself had been active in nominating Alton B. Parker in 1904. He was conservative, wealthy, staunchly pro-League and had almost as much appeal for Republicans as he did for conservative Democrats.

Although an economic conservative, Davis had an excellent labor record. He had served as counsel for unions on several occasions, had helped to draft antitrust legislation while in Congress, and had fought for labor and liberal causes while serving as solicitor general. But for the past three years he had been a Wall Street lawyer, representing the interests of J. P. Morgan and Co. This association was enough to earn the implacable opposition of liberals and the thundering denunciations of William Jennings Bryan. His only immediate source of strength lay in the West Virginia delegation, but he was considered a likely compromise choice.

Senator Ralston of Indiana, Senator Carter Glass of Virginia, Governor George S. Silzer of New Jersey, and Senator Oscar W. Underwood of Alabama were also dark horses. Underwood, even though a southerner, might inherit Smith strength because of his strong anti-Klan stand, while Glass appealed to the McAdoo Drys. Silzer was also closely allied with the Smith forces, while Ralston, who was backed by Brennan, might become the bosses' candidate.

In the favorite-son ranks were Senator Joe Robinson of Arkansas, Governor Jonathan Davis of Kansas, Governor Albert C. Ritchie of Maryland, former candidate James M. Cox of Ohio, Governor Charles W. Bryan of Nebraska (William Jennings Bryan's younger brother), Senator Pat Harrison of Mississippi, Governor Fred Brown of Kansas, and Senator Woodbridge N. Ferris of Michigan. Finally, William Jennings Bryan was, as usual, available. Most of the favorite sons were entered only to keep their delegations uncommitted.

The Democratic National Convention of 1924 opened in the old Madison Square Garden in New York City on June 24. New York had been chosen by the National Committee in January before the Smith candidacy had assumed major proportions. New York had outbid San Francisco with an offer of $205,000 toward the convention expenses, and "it was a case of Party finances first, candidates afterward." The old Garden was decorated with over 3500 flags and bunting until it looked to one observer like the inside of a cheap candy box. The ventilators of the tin-roofed building were covered with decorations "so the delegates could stew in their own juice," and provision was made for 15,000 spectators in the galleries. The building was scheduled for demolition at the conclusion of the convention, and, in the next fifteen days, the Democrats nearly saved the wreckers a job.

A major innovation at this convention was its full coverage by radio. For the first time in history, millions of people could listen in on the process of selecting a candidate. William Allen White wrote, "It is the new order. The convention is no longer held within four walls, but is out in the broad universe. In another dozen years arrangements will be made by which the voice of the people will get into the convention and sass back," a prediction, alas, yet to be realized.

William Gibbs McAdoo arrived shortly before the opening of the convention to be awarded a hero's welcome by his western supporters. Many were facing the perils of what to them was a modern Sodom for the first time, and the welcoming cheers of 2500 people sounded brave but thin in a city of more than six million people. But undaunted by the enemy surrounding them on the sidewalks of New York, McAdoo's supporters escorted him, accompanied by two bands, to his headquarters in the Vanderbilt Hotel.

Al Smith was, of course, on home ground. Every motion-picture theater in greater New York showed films of the Governor, and one offered the novelty of "phonofilm or talking movies" of Smith. Theater orchestras played "East Side, West Side," and everywhere the delegates turned there were Smith banners, Smith buttons, and Smith posters. Cab drivers harangued visitors to vote for Al, and Babe Ruth announced that Al was his candidate.

Most of the New York papers were for Smith, with the exception of the *American*. Arriving delegates were greeted by that paper with a signed Hearst editorial stating that the Hearst papers would oppose "any candidate representing 'booze and boodle.'"

Smith had blocked Hearst's senatorial ambitions the year before, and the publisher was now paying him back.

Hearst further wooed the anti-Smith forces with a Lucullan party for more than 600 delegates and their wives. The entire first floor of the Ritz-Carlton was taken over, and McAdoo and Bryan were the most honored guests. The highlight of the evening for the dazzled delegates was an entertainment starring Will Rogers, Clifton Webb, Jimmy Savo, and Mistinguett, with dancing afterward to the Paul Whiteman orchestra. Sauk Center had never been like that.

On the first day of the convention, it was plain that there would be a deadlock. The McAdoo forces flooded the Garden and the hotels with anti-Catholic literature, which hardened the lines between the opposing forces, while the Smith and Underwood followers stepped up their attacks on the Ku Klux Klan. William Allen White said, "A Democratic convention has to smell the blood of a death struggle before it can decide whom it will honor." As the delegates met the first day to hear Senator Pat Harrison's keynote address, the steamy air in the Garden was already heavy with the promise of blood.

Harrison's attack on the Republicans and the oil scandals was largely wasted on a gathering more interested in fighting each other than fighting Republicans, but it was marked by one amusing misunderstanding. In a rolling oratorical flourish, the Senator cried in his rich Mississippi accent, "What this country needs is a Paul Revere," and was greeted with prolonged cheers. It was later learned that the audience had thought Harrison had said, "What this country needs is real beer."

McAdoo received two setbacks the first day. Iowa, which had been expected to support him, announced that it was offering former Secretary of Agriculture E. T. Meredith as a favorite son, and six North Dakota delegates pledged to McAdoo announced their defection to Smith because McAdoo had refused to explain his position on the Klan.

After the installation of Senator Walsh of Montana as permanent chairman on the second day, the roll was called for the nominating speeches. In the next two and a half days, forty-three speeches were made for sixteen candidates. Underwood and Senator Robinson of Arkansas led the list. Senator Phelan, in nominating McAdoo, gave a "long speech (which) would have stopped the nomination in a Democratic convention of Thomas Jefferson running on a ticket with Andrew Jackson," but the McAdoo men gave him a demonstration for an hour and seventeen minutes, accompanied by the hoots and jeers of the rowdy, pro-Smith galleries.

One of the most dramatic moments of the convention came when Franklin D. Roosevelt placed Al Smith in nomination. For once, there was complete silence as the crippled Roosevelt moved slowly on crutches down a ramp from the back of the platform to the speakers' stand. Even the anti-Smith forces gave a great ovation for this triumph over physical disability. The speech was as effective as the speaker's appearance was moving. It was near the end that Roosevelt gave Smith the name of the "Happy Warrior," which would be his sobriquet for the rest of his life. Will Rogers wrote that when Roosevelt finished, "you would have thought somebody had thrown a wildcat in your face. The galleries went wild and about ten State delegations marched and hollered for an hour." Most of the demonstration was for Smith, but a good deal was for Roosevelt too. Aware of the impending deadlock, delegates throughout the hall turned to each other wistfully, remarking, "If only he hadn't had polio."

A long procession of minor candidates followed the Smith nomination. "Speeches nominating the little fellows filled the dull afternoon," wrote William Allen White. "The delegates began to vanish. Empty benches began to shine out. At four o'clock the orators were talking to the radio receivers and to such ox-eyed delegates as sat gaping at the speaker's stand, not realizing that nothing would happen. An interminable procession of nobodies followed, nominating anybody they could think of. Glass, a couple of Davises, Barney Google, Doctor Copeland, Meredith, Santa Claus, Ritchie, the Smith and Brooks Brothers, Walsh, Ibid and Anon, were passed before the gaping, upturned faces of the delegates as presidential possibilities, before the cataract of oratory was dammed." Dammed it was at last, and the bemused delegates had sixteen candidates from which to choose, including six present or former senators, six governors, two former secretaries of the Treasury, one former ambassador, and one former presidential candidate.

At the afternoon session on the fifth day, June 28, the hatreds and bigotry that were to disgrace the convention exploded in full fury. When Homer Cummings offered the platform, a minority plank involving the Ku Klux Klan was submitted. The majority plank spoke out in general terms for religious freedom and deplored any efforts to create religious or racial dissension. The minority plank, for which Senator Underwood had fought in the resolutions committee, denounced, in the strongest terms and by name, the Ku Klux Klan. The next few hours were worthy of the *Inferno*. Delegates and spectators howled and cursed, screamed and roared as speakers attempted to be heard above the din. No one actually favored the Klan in specific words, and no one admitted actual membership in that organization, although one speaker ominously referred to "343 members of the Klan who are members of this Convention."

Perhaps the saddest of all the speeches was that of William Jennings Bryan. Old and tired, bewildered and out of step in a world that had passed him by, the Great Commoner arose to use his magnificent voice in defense of the Klan. To William Allen White, the burden of his speech was "that the members of the Ku Klux Klan are poor misguided creatures, but none the less fellow followers of the Christian faith who should be treated as honest men and taught their error. Also they should not be rebuked by the Democratic convention because the Ku Klux Klan has more than a million votes!" Wryly, White continued, "His speech was an apology for expediency in the name of party solidarity; a rather damp theme with which to fire one's blood." Bryan finished his speech with difficulty as the galleries attempted to boo him from the stage.

If Bryan's speech enraged the opponents of the Klan, the band infuriated its supporters. When an Underwood supporter from Georgia spoke in favor of the minority plank, the band played "Marching Through Georgia" to the bellowing outrage of that delegation.

While the delegates from Georgia, Missouri, Kansas, and the other strong Klan states "pulled the pillow slips over their eyes and, blinding their minds to reason, began parading spiritually in their

nighties," the issue was finally brought to a vote. The tensions that
accompanied the roll call were nearly unbearable. The threat of
physical violence was strong; a thousand blue-coated policemen
roamed the floor, and every delegate was within reach of a night-
stick. By the narrowest vote in any convention, the anti-Klan plank
was defeated 543-3/20 to 542-7/20. By less than one full vote, the
Klan, Bryan, and expediency had won a bitter, hollow victory.

The platform was adopted by the convention at 2:00 a.m. Sunday morning, and the first ballot for the nomination was put off
until Monday. The day of recess was one of sullen quiet. In contrast to most conventions, there was little last-minute scurrying
to win new support or arrange winning combinations. The McAdoo
and Smith forces waited in mutual hostility for Monday, while the
favorite sons and city bosses sat tight.

Nineteen men received votes on the first ballot. McAdoo led
with 431½, 116½ short of a majority, 299½ short of nomination. Smith
was second with 241 and Cox third with 59. McAdoo received
votes from thirty-four of the fifty-four delegations. He had the
solid support of twenty-one delegations and a majority of two
others. Only 30 of his votes came from the East—25½ from Pennsylvania. The rest were from the West and South.

Smith had the solid support of only two delegations—New York
and Rhode Island—with majorities in Massachusetts, Vermont, and
Wisconsin. He received votes from fourteen delegations, including
35½ from Pennsylvania. Only 41 of his votes came from outside the
East—he had won 23 in the Wisconsin primary—and he received
no votes from the South.

The results of the first ballot were McAdoo 431½, Smith 241,
Cox 59, Senator Pat Harrison 43½, Underwood 42½, Governor Silzer
38, John W. Davis 31, Senator Ferris and Senator Ralston 30 each,
Senator Glass 25, Governor Ritchie 22½, Senator Robinson 21, Gov-
ernor Davis 20, Governor Bryan 18, Governor Brown 17, William
E. Sweet of Colorado 12, former Senator Willard Saulsbury of New
York 7, John B. Kendrick of Wyoming 6, and Houston Thompson 1.

The third ballot held an unpleasant surprise for the Underwood
forces. Louisiana had originally intended to vote for Harrison on
the first ballot and Robinson on the second and then to settle per-

manently on Underwood. But former Governor Jared L. Saunders was John W. Davis's floor leader, and he convinced the delegation to go to Davis rather than to the Alabama Senator. For the time being, Louisiana decided to stick with Robinson and then to give courtesy votes to Glass and Ritchie. The delegation finally settled on Davis on the sixth ballot, giving him a total of 55½ votes.

The tenth ballot saw the first break. Governor Davis of Kansas gave up and threw his 20 votes to McAdoo. But the McAdoo forces had hardly finished cheering when Governor Silzer switched New Jersey's 28 votes to Smith. In ten ballots, McAdoo had gained 40.1 votes for a total of 471.6. Smith had picked up 58½ votes for 299½. By the fifteenth ballot, the last of the day, McAdoo had a net gain over the first ballot of 47½ votes. Smith had gained 64½, and John W. Davis had gained 30. The totals of the fifteenth ballot were McAdoo 479, Smith 305½, John W. Davis 61, Cox 60, Underwood 39½, Ralston 31, Glass 25, Harrison 20½, Robinson 20, Ritchie 17½, Governors Bryan and Davis 11 each, Brown 9, Saulsbury 6, and Senator Walsh and Newton D. Baker 1 each.

On the sixteenth ballot, Senator Pat Harrison withdrew, throwing his votes to Senator Robinson, while Governor Brown's New Hampshire votes went 3 for McAdoo and 1 for Smith.

There were two events on the eighteenth ballot. Mississippi, which had gone from Robinson to Glass on the seventeenth, introduced the name of Cordell Hull and gave him 20 votes. Al Smith received his first, and only, southern vote from a Florida delegate. As Smith later related, when the delegate returned to his seat, "the Florida delegation pushed him off his chair and would not let him sit with them until he returned to the McAdoo camp."

Mississippi, having wandered among four candidates on as many ballots, decided to swing on the nineteenth to John W. Davis. Bryan, horrified, rushed over to the delegation. Sweat pouring off his bald dome, he argued, "This convention must not nominate a Wall Street man. Mr. Davis is the lawyer for J. P. Morgan." "And who is Mr. McAdoo the lawyer for?" snapped a young woman in the delegation.

The switch of Mississippi to Davis was followed on the next ballot by McAdoo's 36 Missouri votes. A strong minority of the delegation had opposed McAdoo all along. They were friends of Champ Clark, whom McAdoo had helped to defeat in 1912. Crowing that the day they had been waiting for since 1912 had arrived, the late Speaker's son, Bennett Clark, said, "I don't care whom they nominate so long as they defeat McAdoo."

The thirtieth ballot was the last of the day. In the fifteen ballots taken on July 1, McAdoo showed a net loss of 62½ votes. Smith had a net gain of 18. John W. Davis had doubled his vote with a gain of 63½, mostly from McAdoo. The chief McAdoo losses had been the defection of Missouri to Davis and the switch of Oklahoma to favorite son Robert L. Owen.

The results of the thirtieth ballot were McAdoo 415½, Smith 323½, Davis 126½, Cox 57, Underwood 39½, Ralston 33, Owen 25, Glass 24, Robinson 23, Ritchie 17½, Saulsbury and Governor Davis 6 each, and Walsh 1½.

The deadlock could not be broken, and Smith, speaking through Roosevelt, offered to withdraw if McAdoo would. McAdoo angrily refused, and the convention wearily prepared for the third day of deadlock.

The first 2 ballots of July 2 were uneventful, but, on the thirty-third, Michigan, which had been scattered among McAdoo, Smith, and Davis, gathered itself together and gave its 30 votes to Senator Ferris, who had not appeared since the ninth ballot. If, however, Michigan hoped to break the deadlock by introducing its seventy-one-year-old favorite son, the move failed. McAdoo won back Oklahoma on the next ballot and picked up enough additional strength to make a net gain of 43½ votes. But on the next ballot Oklahoma again switched back to Senator Owen.

During the thirty-eighth roll call, William Jennings Bryan rose to explain his vote. It was Bryan's last attempt to sway a convention with the power of his great voice. If the Great Commoner was by then an anachronism, neither he nor his enemies realized it. William Allen White wrote a penetrating comment on the power of Bryan's personality. "It is odd about Bryan. For three years and fifty-one weeks of every quadrennium Bryan holds a commission as the 'national old dear.' Everybody loves him, pokes fun at him, ignores him, pretends he is dead and laments the neglect of the undertaker. Then, during the week of the national Democratic convention, Bryan suddenly appears in shining armor, a plumed knight of the prevalent righteousness, and becomes a force in American politics."

Bryan began with a plea for unity and a break in the deadlock. At first, he was heckled rather good-naturedly as he pointed out seven Democrats whom he believed the convention could nominate: Dr. A. A. Murphee, president of Florida State University, Josephus Daniels, Senator Robinson, Senator Ralston, E. T. Meredith, his brother Charles Bryan, and Senator Walsh of Montana. But when he reached the real point of his speech, a plea to nominate McAdoo, the galleries howled with rage. A delegate shouted, "Tell us about Doheny and McAdoo and oil." The chairman ordered the galleries cleared, but they quieted down enough to hear Bryan say, "If any oil has ever touched William G. McAdoo, the intense, persistent, virulent opposition of Wall Street washes all the oil away." Continuing with difficulty over the outcry that this statement brought forth, Bryan went on, "No man who allows Wall Street to influence his action has any right to criticize McAdoo, who cannot be controlled by Wall Street." At this juncture, the Davis men joined the Smith forces in trying to shout Bryan down.

The convention had gone berserk. Not only the galleries but the delegates too screamed curses at Bryan, hissed and booed his every word, drowning his speech in a torrent of sound. If the old leader was dismayed, he showed no sign. When he said that this convention would be his last and his enemies cheered, he shot back, "Don't applaud, I may change my mind." At last, he finished. If his enemies had not feared his influence, they would not have treated him so harshly, but his influence was a thing of the past.

For a moment though, it seemed that Bryan might be able to swing the convention to McAdoo. On the thirty-ninth ballot, Missouri abandoned Davis, and Oklahoma gave up Owen to return to McAdoo. But the two delegations had agreed to return to McAdoo for only five ballots. If he did not have a majority vote by then, they would swing away again.

By the end of the day, the forty-second ballot had given McAdoo 503.4 votes, a net loss for the day of 12.1 votes. Smith had 318.6, which was a net loss of 3.9. The Davis drive had apparently collapsed, his vote having fallen from 127½ to 67 in the course of the day.

That evening McAdoo tried vainly to break the ranks of the favorite sons. He was visited in his suite at the Madison Square Hotel first by Senator Robinson and later by Claude Swanson, representing Carter Glass. To both, McAdoo pleaded that they swing their strength to him. The 23 Robinson votes and the 28½ Glass votes would give McAdoo a majority of the convention and keep Oklahoma's vote in his column. But Robinson was expecting Oklahoma's vote himself and refused to withdraw. Swanson was noncommittal. The deadlock would continue.

As expected, Oklahoma switched to Robinson on the forty-third ballot on Thursday morning, while Mississippi switched to Ralston on the forty-ninth. July 3 was Ralston's day. While Tom Taggart strolled about the floor, one pocket full of cigars for the gentlemen and another pocket full of chewing gum for the ladies, his candidate began a slow rise. Ralston began the day with 31 votes. Twelve ballots later he had 97. Taggart had begun the slow push that, he hoped, would capture the imagination of the convention and swing the nomination to the Indiana senator.

While Ralston began to climb, Smith decided that it was time to face the fact that he could not win. His one remaining concern was to keep the nomination from McAdoo. Contacting Senator Underwood, who, like Smith, was Wet and anti-Klan, the New Yorker offered to withdraw in his favor if Underwood could secure the support of two southern delegations. The Senator asked for twenty-four hours. But the South was for McAdoo, the Klan, and Prohibition. Underwood could win no southern support apart from his home state, and Smith stayed in the race.

The fifty-eighth ballot provided some excitement. Ralston's drive suddenly collapsed, Louisiana deserted Davis for Mayor Behrman of New Orleans, and McAdoo jumped 65 votes. But on the next ballot, erratic Oklahoma, which had gone from Robinson to Mc-Adoo, skipped back to Senator Owen, and McAdoo suffered a net loss of 21½ votes. And so it went. Ralston had pushed and failed. McAdoo had made a big step forward, followed by a series of half steps backward. On the sixty-first ballot, the last of the day, McAdoo had 469½ votes—a net loss for the day of 13.9 and a loss of 33.9 from the last ballot on Wednesday. Smith showed a gain of 16.4 for a total of 335½.

Friday, July 4, was no day of patriotic celebration in the Democratic convention. The deadlock ground on. Elmer Davis, in despair, wrote: "Time disappears and eternity steals in as this interminable convention keeps on balloting. The Judgement Day will come with Tom Walsh still pounding his gavel in the Garden, crowds still booing Georgia and cheering Massachusetts, and earnest delegates from Oklahoma or the Canal Zone challenging the report of the vote and demanding a poll of their delegations."

Before the sixty-fourth ballot, Senator Ralston decided that he had had enough. Tom Taggart read the Senator's withdrawal to the convention. It was received with cheers of relief. "Ralston got more applause from the convention by withdrawing than he ever did by running," wrote Elmer Davis. "Many a man has died for his country, but few have withdrawn for the party. If all the candidates would withdraw this convention might get somewhere." Most of the Ralston votes went to McAdoo, although 10 Indiana votes went to Smith.

Another candidate dropped out after the sixty-fifth ballot. James M. Cox, convinced that McAdoo was stopped, withdrew and threw his support to Newton D. Baker. No longer a candidate, Cox immediately boarded a train for New York to see what he could do to bring sanity back to the party.

After the sixty-sixth ballot, a Massachusetts delegate moved that the rules be amended and that the convention meet that evening as an executive session without spectators. It was further requested that all the candidates be invited to address the convention. The motion was defeated. The Massachusetts delegation had good reason for wanting to settle the issue—it was running short of money. The chairman had told the delegates, "Gentlemen, we are faced with a choice—either we have to move to a more modest hotel or to a more liberal candidate."

On the sixty-eighth ballot, an Arizona delegate had the very sensible idea of casting a vote for Will Rogers, but unfortunately the idea did not catch on. The next ballot saw McAdoo reach his peak with 530 votes, only 20 short of a simple majority. The bulk of McAdoo's gain came from the peripatetic Oklahoma delegation.

The seventieth ballot was the last of the day. The band, with weary humor, played "What Shall I Do?"—but the delegates could not tell. McAdoo had 528½ votes—a gain of 59½. Smith closed with 334—a loss of 4½.

At the morning session on Saturday, it was proposed that the low man on each ballot be withdrawn until only two candidates remained; the suggestion was defeated and followed by a proposal to adopt it for the current day only until five candidates remained. The second suggestion was also defeated; it was then proposed that the convention forget the whole thing, adjourn, and reassemble in Kansas City on the 21st. That, too, was voted down.

Seven ballots were taken on Saturday. At the end of the day, McAdoo had 513—a loss of 15½—and Smith had 367—a gain of 32½. Tom Taggart proposed that the candidates or their representatives meet during the weekend recess "for the purpose of reaching an understanding so as to hasten the conclusion of this Convention." The motion was unanimously accepted.

The candidates' conference met in National Chairman Cordell Hull's room in the Waldorf-Astoria that night. There were forty party leaders in attendance, including Tom Brennan and Roosevelt for Smith; Daniel Roper, Homer Cummings, and Arthur Mullen for McAdoo; Senator Caraway for Robinson; Taggart for Ralston; Harry S. Byrd and Claude Swanson for Glass; and Frank Hague and Bryan.

The meeting failed to arrive at a solution to the deadlock. The McAdoo men were only interested in changing the rules to permit McAdoo's nomination, while the Smith forces refused to withdraw unless McAdoo did. It was suggested that all the candidates announce that they would release their delegates from their instructions. Everyone agreed but McAdoo. Since he clearly wanted all compromises to be in his favor, the meeting broke up.

On Monday, July 7, McAdoo and Smith met face to face. Smith admitted that he could not win and suggested that they both withdraw. McAdoo indicated that he would if Smith would agree on

E. T. Meredith as a compromise choice. Smith maintained that he could only release his delegates and could not tell them how to vote. This meeting, too, broke up with neither candidate agreeing to withdraw.

When the convention met on Monday, the candidates' conference submitted a proposal signed by everyone but McAdoo offering to release his delegates. McAdoo offered to join the proposal if the rules were changed to abolish the unit rule and the two-thirds rule. Naturally, both offers were rejected, although later in the day the delegates voted to free themselves of any pledged commitments. By this time, such a move could have little effect.

Throughout Monday, McAdoo's strength crumbled away. On the seventy-eighth ballot, he had 511 votes. On the eighty-seventh, he had slipped to 336½. Smith passed McAdoo on the eighty-sixth ballot but showed a net loss for the day of 2 votes. All that the weakening of McAdoo did was to increase the number of favorite sons. Glass was given a run early in the day, beginning with 21 votes on the seventy-eighth ballot and rising to 78 on the eighty-second. But his drive aroused little interest, and he had slipped back to 71 votes by the end of the day.

Ralston, who had reappeared on the seventy-fourth ballot with a handful of votes, suddenly spurted forward on the eighty-second with McAdoo votes and then received most of Robinson's vote on the eighty-fourth ballot. His total was still climbing on the day's final ballot, when he received 93 votes. Owen was back in the running, and Iowa abandoned McAdoo on the eighty-sixth ballot to reintroduce Meredith as a candidate. On the last ballot, Kansas brought Governor Davis back into the running. The balloting might have gone on all night, but word was received after the eighty-seventh ballot of the death of the President's son, Calvin Coolidge, Jr., and the convention adjourned out of respect.

The eighty-eighth ballot on July 8 proved that McAdoo was finished. He lost 21 more votes, while Smith gained only ½ vote. The field was enlarged, when North Carolina gathered up its votes, scattered among five candidates, and gave 23 to Josephus Daniels.

Ralston continued to climb through the afternoon. By the ninety-third ballot, a stampede seemed to be in the making, when he

reached 196¼ votes—compared to 355½ for Smith and 314 for
McAdoo. To give Smith time to decide what to do, Tom Brennan
moved a recess until evening. The die-hard McAdoo forces were
willing to have additional time in the hopes of effecting a miracle,
and the favorite sons were eager to stop Ralston's drive—the motion
therefore carried easily.

During the recess, Smith wrestled with the question of withdrawal. Clearly, neither he nor McAdoo could win. To prolong the
convention would be to compound the folly that had already kept
the Democrats in session for two weeks. Unfortunately, the Governor's bitterness toward McAdoo was such that he decided not to
withdraw unless McAdoo did. McAdoo was equally stubborn,
and, like two schoolboys—to use the phrase of a later era—they
stood eyeball to eyeball, determined to stare each other down,
regardless of the consequences.

When the convention reassembled, it was surprised to hear the
secretary read a telegram from Ralston withdrawing from the
contest for the second time. The sixty-six-year-old Senator had
thought it over and had decided that he did not want the
nomination.

After Ralston's withdrawal, Roosevelt announced that, for the
good of the party, Al Smith would withdraw if McAdoo would, but
"until such withdrawal has been made by Mr. McAdoo, I can say
that Governor Smith's supporters will continue to vote for Governor
Smith." Roosevelt's blunt statement, unbeknownst to himself, lost
him votes. Florida and North Carolina were in caucus at the time
that Roosevelt made his statement trying to decide whether or not
to give up on McAdoo and throw their strength to Roosevelt. His
speech demanding McAdoo's withdrawal so angered them that
they decided to stick with their candidate.

Ralston's withdrawal sent eighty-one delegates back into the
McAdoo camp, while Kansas returned to Governor Davis and
17 votes went to Senator Royal S. Copeland of New York. On the
ninety-fourth ballot, third place went to John W. Davis, with 81¾
votes.

Davis's managers had played a quiet, waiting game. They reasoned that the deadlock would produce so much animosity among

the active candidates that ultimately the convention would have to turn to a man like Davis who was not closely connected with either wing of the party. Davis was best known as an ambassador and lawyer, not as a politician. As Cox put it when he decided to back him, "Davis could lift the campaign above the level of the convention."

The delegates agreed. On the next six ballots, Davis gained 128¼ votes for a total of 210, compared to 362 for Smith and 315½ for McAdoo.

During the ninety-sixth ballot, McAdoo finally listened to reason. Bernard Baruch and other McAdoo leaders saw him in his room at the Madison Square Hotel. He was trembling with fatigue and disappointment. He must, Baruch said, quit for the good of the party. Sagging with weariness, McAdoo agreed. His floor leaders were summoned, and he began to draft a message to the convention. But for two hours he fumbled with pen and paper. He couldn't bring himself to write the death sentence to all his hopes. Finally, he finished the message, in which he did not actually withdraw but released his delegates. It was all over. The message was read to the convention at 3:00 a.m. following the ninety-ninth ballot.

On the 100th ballot, 163½ McAdoo votes scattered to seven candidates, including Senator Walsh, Meredith, Senator Owen, and Josephus Daniels. The results of the 100th ballot were Smith 351½, Davis 203½, McAdoo 190, Meredith 75½, Walsh 52½, Robinson 46, Underwood 41½, Glass 35, Daniels 24, Owen 20, Ritchie 17½, James W. Gerard 10, David W. Houston 9, Saulsbury 6, Newton D. Baker 4, Charles W. Bryan 2, and George L. Berry 1. At the conclusion of the ballot, the convention adjourned until the next day.

Smith had decided during the overnight recess to swing to Underwood, a decision that frightened the Dry McAdoo forces into the Davis column. It took only three ballots to settle the issue. On ballot 101, Davis had 316 votes to 229½ for Underwood. On the 102nd ballot, the count was Davis 415½, Underwood 317. Before the results of the 103rd ballot were announced, the vote was Davis 575½, Underwood 250½, Walsh 84½, Glass 79, Meredith 42½, Robinson 21, McAdoo 14½, Smith 10½, Gerard 8, three scattered. Iowa led off the changes, switching from Meredith to Davis, and, when the uproar of relief at having found a candidate was over, the official tally was Davis 844, Underwood 102½, Walsh 58, Glass 23, Robinson 20, Meredith 15½, McAdoo 11½, Smith 7½, Gerard 7, and Hull 1, with 8 not voting. The nomination was then made unanimous, and John W. Davis of West Virginia had received what was undoubtedly the most worthless nomination any party ever bestowed on a candidate.

The convention had no more finished cheering Davis when the cry "We want Walsh!" for the vice-presidential nomination rang through the Garden. Walsh would have been a popular candidate and was obviously the choice of the convention, but he wanted no part of it. Quickly entertaining a motion to adjourn, Walsh rammed it through and left the platform while the delegates continued to cheer him.

A conference of party leaders met in the dining room of the Manhattan Club across the street from the Garden. Tom Taggart suggested that the party nominate former Vice-President Marshall, and Al Smith proposed Governor Silzer of New Jersey. When it was pointed out that Davis's residence was now New York City, it was decided that the running mate should come from the Middle West. Charles W. Bryan was mentioned. His candidacy would have the advantage of tying his brother to the "Wall Street" candidate he had so violently opposed. Smith was against choosing Bryan, but he agreed to leave the decision to Davis, who chose Bryan.

Senator Walsh, to avoid a stampede in his direction, turned the chair at the evening session over to Alben W. Barkley of Kentucky and sent a letter to the convention requesting the delegates not to consider him. Twelve men and one woman were placed in nomination: John C. Greenway of Arizona; Commander of the American Legion Alvin Owsley of Texas; labor union executive George L. Berry of Tennessee; Governor Silzer; Mrs. Leroy Springs of South Carolina; Governor Davis of Kansas; Bennett Champ Clark of Missouri; William A. Gaston of Massachusetts; Mayor John F. Hylan of New York City; Edwin T. Meredith; William Smith Flynn of Rhode Island; James W. Gerard of New York; and Charles W. Bryan. At the conclusion of the nominations, the Gaston candidacy was withdrawn.

On the roll call, Berry led with 263½, with Bryan second at 238. Owsley was third with 152, followed by Hylan with 110. The others had minor support. The swing to Bryan was led by Brennan of Illinois, who changed 29 Hylan votes to give Bryan the entire delegation. New York immediately swung 80 votes behind Bryan, and the rush was on. Alben Barkley later described the confusion: "There were at least eighteen delegations on their feet, all waving their standards in my face and clamoring for recognition. Losing my patience and forgetting for the moment that this new contraption, radio, was carrying our proceedings to the nation, I snapped, 'Dammit, can't you wait!' " On that slightly profane note, Charles W. Bryan became the running mate by a vote of 740—8 more than needed—to 208 votes for Berry and scattered votes for others.

"I hereby decline the nomination
for Vice President"

THE EIGHTEENTH REPUBLICAN NATIONAL CONVENTION
Cleveland, June 10, 1924

Two weeks before the Democratic convention, the Republicans had met, on June 10, in Cleveland to "Keep Cool With Coolidge." Even the weather was cool and rainy to match the President's wintry personality. To the keen disappointment of Cleveland businessmen, the convention was quiet and perfunctory. There were no bustling campaign headquarters, hotel rooms were plentiful, and, at the insistence of the administration, the town was bone dry.

The senatorial clique that had dominated the 1920 convention was conspicuously without power in 1924. Henry Cabot Lodge was denied the chairmanship of the Massachusetts delegation and wandered about the convention a pathetic old man shorn of all power and influence. Coolidge was the boss of the party now, and the public humiliation of Lodge underscored the point.

The President was the only candidate placed in nomination, and he received a four-minute ovation—hardly an overwhelming demonstration of popular affection. The single ballot gave Coolidge 1065 votes to 34 for Senator LaFollette and 10 for Hiram Johnson.

The only business of the convention was the selection of a vice-presidential candidate. Coolidge refused to exert any direct pressure but privately favored Senator Borah, who refused to be a candidate. The Senate group and many party leaders supported Governor Frank Lowden, but he announced that he was not interested. Charles G. Dawes, retired general, banker, and former director of the budget, had the support of Nebraska and New Jersey, as well as substantial strength in several other delegations.

Sixteen men received votes for vice-president on the first ballot. Lowden led with 222, followed by former Senator William S. Kenyon of Iowa with 172 and General Dawes with 149. The keynote speaker, Representative Theodore E. Burton of Ohio was fourth with 139.

On the second ballot, Lowden received 413 votes to 288 for Burton and 111 for Dawes. Kenyon dropped to 95 votes. Immediately there was a rush to Lowden, who was given the nomination 766 to 94 for Burton, 68 for Kenyon, and 49 for Dawes, with the rest scattered. The nomination was being made unanimous when the permanent chairman, Rep. Frank W. Mondell of Wyoming, read a letter from Lowden to the convention. It was terse and to the point. "Though greatly appreciating the honor I hereby decline the nomination for Vice President which is tendered me." The flabbergasted convention thereupon took a recess to decide what to do.

During the recess, the congressional leaders decided to give the nomination to Senator Charles Curtis of Kansas, while the administration representatives decided to work for Herbert Hoover. The convention, however, had other ideas. Most of the delegates were bored with the cut-and-dried nature of the proceedings and resented having their decisions made for them. General Dawes was a colorful, profane, rambunctious figure whose independence and outspokenness appealed to the delegates. Beside, they reasoned, the convention had gone along with the party leaders and nominated Lowden, only to have him refuse. It was time for a little independent thinking.

On the third ballot, the congressional group could muster only 75 votes for Kenyon, while the administration rounded up 234½ votes for Hoover. But General Dawes received the nomination with 682½ votes.

After the matter-of-fact Republican convention and during the Democratic convention, a third party entered the scene. Gathering in Cleveland on July 4, liberals, dissatisfied with both major parties, launched a farm-labor movement, the Progressive Party of 1924. There was no question of who their candidate would be. As progressivism's most distinguished leader, Senator LaFollette was the unanimous choice of the new party. Senator Burton K. Wheeler of Montana, a Democrat, was chosen as his running mate. The Progressive convention adopted a platform in sharp contrast to the flabby, conventional documents offered by the major parties. Declaring that domination by monopolies was the great issue, it called for public ownership of railroads, natural resources, and water power; a popular referendum on declarations of war; arms reduction, direct nomination of presidential candidates, popular election of federal judges; and the abolition of injunctions in labor disputes. The new party knew its nominees could not win the election but, in view of the apathy toward Coolidge and the suicide of the Democrats, hoped to muster enough electoral votes to throw the election into the House of Representatives. Considering the candidates offered to the American people by the Republican and Democratic National Conventions of 1924, it was not such a bad idea.

CHAPTER 16

"His age will be the reflection of himself"

THE NINETEENTH REPUBLICAN NATIONAL CONVENTION
Kansas City, June 12, 1928

The presidential conventions of 1928 were a rarity in American politics, for both parties selected their candidates on the first ballot, virtually without contest. Remembering the Republican deadlock of 1920 and the Democratic massacre of 1924, the two parties turned to their strongest candidates and, for once, gave them the nominations.

The Republican presidential race began abruptly on August 3, 1927, when President Coolidge, vacationing in the Black Hills of South Dakota, made his surprise announcement, "I do not choose to run for President in 1928." The deliberately enigmatic use of the word "choose" created uncertainty within the party right up to the opening of the convention ten months later. Would the President accept a draft? The taciturn Coolidge refused to amplify his statement.

Herbert Hoover, Secretary of Commerce, and Republicans in the Senate of the United States both decided that Coolidge was out of the race and began making their own plans. Hoover launched an all-out drive for the nomination, spent more than $400,000, and tried to ascertain Coolidge's attitude with little success. Relations between the two men were formal to the point of coldness. When the Secretary of Agriculture once mentioned Hoover, the President

315

snapped, "That man has offered me unsolicited advice for the past six years, all of it bad." Knowing the President's lack of affection for him, Hoover called at the White House in February, 1928, to see if Coolidge would oppose his candidacy or, perhaps, run himself. Hoover explained that he had been asked to run against the favorite-son candidacy of Senator Willis in Ohio. The President said he would not enter the primary, and, when Hoover asked if he should, Coolidge laconically replied, "Why not?" That was all Herbert Hoover ever received in the way of a blessing from Calvin Coolidge.

By May, 1928, Hoover had won most of the state primaries and lined up 400 delegates. He went again to the White House to make the gesture of offering them to Coolidge should he wish to seek renomination. Said Silent Cal, "If you have 400 delegates, you better keep them."

Although Coolidge refused to commit himself for or against the Hoover candidacy, the attitudes of the Senate group and the White House circle were another matter. Both factions flatly opposed Hoover. The Senate group encouraged favorite sons to tie up the convention and prevent Hoover's nomination. Chief among this group were Vice-President Dawes and Senators Curtis of Kansas, Watson of Indiana, Goff of West Virginia, Steiwer of Oregon, and Willis of Ohio. Senator Willis's death gave Ohio to Hoover, but the others secured the support of their home state delegations. Curtis was the chief senatorial candidate. The great grandson of an Osage Indian chief, the sixty-eight-year-old Curtis was Republican leader in the Senate, successor to the deceased Lodge of Massachusetts, and the last of the old Old Guard. He had entered Congress in 1893 and was the lone survivor of the Hanna-Aldrich-Penrose days. Curtis and the others had visions of another deadlock and another senatorial "smoke-filled" room.

Also hoping for a deadlock—although not a smoke-filled room— were Andrew Mellon, who controlled, he thought, the Pennsylvania delegation, and National Committeeman Charles D. Hilles, who controlled the New York delegation. It was their intention to await deadlock and then stampede the convention for Coolidge.

One problem among the anti-Hoover forces was their attempt to use the same means to different ends. The White House circle wanted to draft Coolidge; the senators wanted to nominate one of their own. Eighteen Republican senators joined with thirty-seven Democrats to pass a resolution condemning any departure from the no-third-term tradition as "unwise, unpatriotic and fraught with peril to our free institutions." The fact that the senators were opposed to both Hoover and Coolidge made an anti-Hoover coalition difficult.

Most of the delegates realized this difficulty and were eager to back a winner. Hoover was popular and greatly admired as the ablest man in the administration. By convention time, genuine admiration or the desire to get on the bandwagon had given Hoover 450 pledged delegates.

Right up to the opening of the convention in Kansas City on Tuesday, June 12, Secretary Mellon held frequent meetings with Charles D. Hilles and Henry Roraback, boss of Connecticut, to lay plans for a swing to Coolidge. Whether or not the President knew or approved of these plans has never been discovered. He steadfastly refused to give any hint that might encourage a draft movement, but Senator Butler, a close friend and political advisor, was convinced that Coolidge hoped for a deadlock that could be resolved in his favor.

The campaign for Coolidge came to an end on Monday, June 11. William Vare, boss of Philadelphia, decided to undercut Mellon and put Pennsylvania on the bandwagon. There was considerable pro-Hoover sentiment in the delegation, and on Monday afternoon Vare announced that Pennsylvania would support the Secretary of Commerce. "Mellon was left suspended on a limb, his political feet dangling in the air." A coalition could not succeed without Pennsylvania, and Mellon made the best of failure by joining the rush to Hoover.

It is not known what went on in Coolidge's mind when he heard of Pennsylvania's defection. Ike Hoover, long-time White House usher, later reported that the President was crushed by the news. Monday night, looking visibly strained, Coolidge abruptly left Washington for his summer camp in Wisconsin—still silent.

The nominations were made on Thursday, June 14. John L. McNab led off with Hoover's nomination. He had hardly begun to speak when his mention of Hoover's name set off a twenty-four-minute demonstration. It proved the candidate's popularity but ruined Mr. McNab's speech. He called Hoover a great engineer and a great humanitarian and continued, "He may be called the creature of his age. In many respects his age will be the reflection of himself," which considering what was coming in October, 1929, now seems an unfortunate way of putting it.

Senator James E. Watson was next to be nominated, followed by Senator Curtis, who received a great spontaneous demonstration as a personal tribute to the last of the old guard. Senator Goff and Senator George Norris were presented to the convention, and then, in a surprise move, a delegate from Ohio placed Calvin Coolidge in nomination.

The convention needed only one ballot. When the roll was completed, the results were Hoover 837, Frank Lowden 74, Curtis 64, Watson 45, Norris 34, Goff 18, Coolidge 17, Vice-President Dawes 4, Charles Evans Hughes 1.

Before the party leaders could make up their minds who should be the vice-presidential candidate, Senator Borah made up their minds for them. He loudly demanded the nomination of Senator Curtis, who, considering his active opposition to Hoover, did not appeal very strongly to the candidate's supporters. But Borah threatened to make a floor fight for Curtis, and the Hoover forces, not wanting to disrupt the harmony of the convention, agreed to let Borah have his way. Curtis received the nomination by a vote of 1052 out of 1089.

"Victory is his habit"

THE TWENTY-FIFTH DEMOCRATIC NATIONAL CONVENTION
Houston, June 26, 1928

The Democratic nomination was even more matter-of-fact than the Republican. At least there had been a feeble "Stop Hoover" movement. There was no "Stop Smith" movement among the Democrats. It was obvious even to the rural Dry Democrats who hated him that Smith was the strongest candidate. He had been re-elected Governor of New York in 1926 by the largest margin in the state's history. He had the solid support of every northern state east of the Mississippi and, for lack of candidates to oppose him, had major support in the West. William Gibbs McAdoo, not wishing to repeat the experience of Madison Square Garden, refused to be a candidate, and only a few nominal favorite sons appeared.

To conciliate the anti-Smith Democrats, the convention was held in Houston, Texas, the first southern city to entertain a Democratic convention since the Baltimore convention of 1860.

The keynote address of the diplomat and historian Claude Bowers was one of the most distinguished ever heard in a national convention and set a high tone, which contrasted sharply with the convention of four years before. Even that traditional battleground of Democratic conventions—the platform committee—was pervaded by sweetness and light. Carter Glass wrote a plank pledging an honest attempt to enforce prohibition, and the platform as a whole

319

was conciliatory, uncontroversial, and bland. Newton D. Baker exclaimed unhappily, "McKinley could have run on the tariff plank and Lodge on the one on international relations."

At the second session on June 24, Franklin D. Roosevelt once again nominated Al Smith. Walking now with canes, Roosevelt impressed the convention with his physical appearance nearly as much as he did with his oratory. The conclusion of his speech was a ringing call to victory. "To stand upon the ramparts and die for our principles is heroic. To sally forth to battle and win for our principles is something more than heroic. We offer one who has the will to win—who not only deserves success but commands it. Victory is his habit—the happy warrior, Alfred E. Smith."

On the only ballot taken, Smith received 724⅔ votes—10 short of nomination. Immediately, Atlee Pomerene gave Ohio's 47 votes and victory to the Happy Warrior. After changes, the official results of the ballot were Smith 849⅗, Senator Walter George 52¼, Senator Reed of Missouri 52, Cordell Hull 50 5/6, Jesse Jones of Texas 43, and 49½ votes scattered among nine other men.

To make the nomination of a Wet Catholic more palatable to the South, the Smith forces decided to give second place to a southerner. Senator Joseph T. Robinson of Arkansas and Senator Alben W. Barkley of Kentucky were the leading contenders, although General Henry T. Allen of Kentucky, former Governor of Wyoming Mrs. Nellie Tayloe Ross, and Senator Duncan U. Fletcher of Florida were also placed in nomination. Senator Robinson was nominated on the first ballot—the first southerner to be named to a presidential ticket since the Civil War.

CHAPTER 17

"He knows that rewards come to
those who bear the burden"

THE TWENTIETH REPUBLICAN NATIONAL CONVENTION
Chicago, June 14, 1932

Basking in the warm glow of popularity engendered by his land-slide victory, Herbert Hoover, on his inauguration day, confidently stated that the future of America was "bright with hope." That bright hope—and the President's popularity—lasted about seven months. The harvest of economic irresponsibility sowed by Harding, Coolidge, Andrew Mellon, and the tycoons of finance and industry was reaped by Herbert Hoover on that day in October, 1929, when the stock market collapsed and brought down with it the economies of the world, the hopes and fortunes of many individuals, and, incidentally, the immediate future of the Republican Party.

The Republicans were faced with a dispiriting task in their national convention of 1932. Defeat in November was virtually assured, but it would become an absolute certainty should the party repudiate its leader. There was nothing for it but to give the nomination once again to Herbert Hoover and to hope that the Democratic Party's penchant for committing suicide in its conventions might make a miracle possible for the Republicans.

There was, before the convention, some half-hearted activity among the Republicans to find another candidate. Hoover had never been popular among the regulars of the party, and a few of them began talking wistfully of bringing Calvin Coolidge out of retirement. But Coolidge remained as silent as ever, and the notion soon faded. Former Senator Joseph I. France of Maryland entered several primaries and won a number of them. Only in Oregon, however, was the primary binding on the delegates. France was not a serious candidate. He wished to call attention to the sizable opposition to Hoover within the party with a view to making a Coolidge draft possible.

France demonstrated that, when it came to popularity contests, almost anybody could win over Hoover, but his demonstration did nothing to alter the fact that the President had to be given an opportunity to defend his record. Most of the party leaders either backed Hoover or, like Senators Borah, Johnson, and Norris and LaFollette, Jr., and Frank Lowden, remained silent.

Although Hoover's renomination was assured, the questions of prohibition and the vice-presidency had to be settled by the convention that opened in Chicago on June 14, 1932. The party was badly split over repeal of the Eighteenth Amendment, and the only excitement of the convention was promised by a battle between the Wets and the Drys. For showmanship, the Wets clearly had the edge. A six-mile-long antiprohibition parade, a yacht show, and an aerial circus all proclaimed the national desire for a drink without the danger of going blind in the process. As for the vice-presidency, no one really had anything against Vice-President Curtis, but many leaders believed a new face on the ticket might help the party image. Among the prospective candidates hoping to bring a touch of freshness to the ticket were former Deputy Chief of Staff Major General James A. Harbord of New York; Hanford MacNider of Iowa, national commander of the American Legion; and Alvin T. Fuller of Massachusetts.

Unlike most national conventions, this one had nothing of the circus about it. Reporters noted that there were few portraits of Hoover in evidence, and the bands were generally silent. About the only thing the delegates could enjoy was the air conditioning in the Chicago Stadium, which permitted them to lay the Republican Party to rest in comfort.

The platform was presented on the second day by James R. Garfield. Although it was obvious that most of the delegates were ready for a drink, Hoover straddled the issue. The plank as presented had as its main statement: "We therefore believe that the people should have an opportunity to pass upon a proposed amendment the provision of which, while retaining in the Federal Government power to preserve the gains already made in dealing with the evils inherent in the liquor traffic, shall allow States to deal with the problem as their citizens may determine, but subject always to the power of the Federal government to protect those States where prohibition may exist and safeguard our citizens everywhere from the return of the saloon and attendant abuses." Senator Hiram Bingham of Connecticut offered a minority report calling for outright repeal, but Hoover had more than enough votes to have his way. While the galleries shouted "We Want Beer," the convention adopted the Hoover plank 690 19/36 to 420 2/9.

On the third day, Herbert Hoover was placed in nomination by Joseph Scott of California. As soon as possible, the sacred spirit of Lincoln was invoked. "I want you to think of him (Hoover) as I think of him in his study in the White House, in the room where Lincoln signed the Emancipation Proclamation, working through ceaseless hours over the problems that are your problems, seeking solutions that will aid mankind." He also cited Edmund Burke, the California pioneers, Valley Forge, Jesus Christ, and the San Francisco earthquake in the defense of the man he described as a past master of "human engineering." After comparing the spirit of Hoover's life to the Sermon on the Mount, he presented him as a man who "has taught us to strain our individual selves to the limit rather than cowardly to lie down under a paternal government because he knows that rewards come to those who bear the burden of the heat of the day."

The beauty of the occasion was marred by the next speech. An Oregon delegate with a name worthy of W. C. Fields—L. B. Sandblast—arose to nominate Joseph I. France and to take a few jabs at the living embodiment of the Sermon on the Mount. The speaker referred to France as a man, by implication unlike certain other candidates, who put devotion to principle before personal advantage and "whose ambition was not for office, but to serve his country." After the speech, France himself appeared upon the platform, although he was not a delegate. It was assumed that his purpose was to withdraw his name in favor of Calvin Coolidge in the hope of starting a stampede, but the Hoover men hustled him out of the hall before he could speak. Hoover was then nominated with 1126½ votes to 23½ votes for five other men.

The vice-presidency was settled even more calmly than the question of repeal. Thirteen candidates received votes on the single ballot, but Vice-President Curtis was renominated. The same ticket that had so confidently prepared for victory four years before now prepared for slaughter.

"A pleasant man who . . . would like
very much to be President"

THE TWENTY-SIXTH DEMOCRATIC NATIONAL CONVENTION
Chicago, June 27, 1932

If the Republicans approached the presidential election of 1932
with all the enthusiasm of condemned men on the way to the
gallows, the Democrats, believing that victory was as certain as
anything in politics can ever be, looked forward eagerly to selecting
the next President of the United States from a wide range of
candidates.

The leading contender was the Governor of New York, Franklin
Delano Roosevelt. His election to the governorship in 1928, while
Al Smith was losing the state to Hoover, marked him as the coming
man. When he was re-elected in 1930 by an unprecedented majority
of 725,000 votes—even carrying the Republican areas upstate—he
became the man to beat for the presidential nomination. The
Roosevelt majority in 1930 was so large that even Democrats were
stunned, and James Farley, Chairman of the Democratic State Committee, declared, "I do not see how Mr. Roosevelt can escape becoming the next presidential nominee of his party, even if no one
should raise a finger to bring it about." Roosevelt's private reaction
to this comment was to tell Farley, "Whatever you said, Jim, is all
right with me."

Farley's statement was the beginning of the Roosevelt-for-Presi-
dent drive, but a good many fingers were raised before the nomina-

tion was secure. Over the next few months, Roosevelt put together his organization. The nerve center would be Louis McHenry Howe, long-time advisor to Roosevelt, who drove his asthma-wracked, gnome-like body with a furious energy to make Roosevelt president. Next in the organization was the tough, shrewd boss of the Bronx, Ed Flynn. Flynn was not gregarious and preferred to work in the background. He therefore proposed Jim Farley as the perfect contact man to deal with leaders in other parts of the country. Bluff, of breezy manner and good humor, and gifted with a phenomenal memory for names, faces, and personal details, the State Chairman was ideally suited to weld Roosevelt's friends into an effective national organization. He was at this time the Exalted Ruler of the Elks, which gave him an excellent reason for traveling about the country without drawing too much attention to his political activities. The job of fund-raising was given to Frank Walker, a New York businessman formerly of Montana.

In late June, 1931, Jim Farley set off on a trip around the country. Ostensibly he was going to the national Elks convention in Seattle, but he managed to cover eighteen states in nineteen days and to meet more than a thousand key figures in the party. Everywhere he went he found such enthusiasm for Roosevelt that he wrote from Seattle that if the rest of the trip were as successful, "My statement upon reaching New York will be so enthusiastic that those who read it will think I am a fit candidate for an insane asylum."

Although Franklin Roosevelt was the first candidate off and running, he was not the only aspirant for the nomination. The first to be formally entered in the race was Speaker of the House John Nance Garner of Texas. The crusty, sixty-one-year-old Speaker was launched on his campaign on New Year's Day, 1932, by William Randolph Hearst, still hoping to be kingmaker. Hearst took to the radio and, in his soft, high-pitched voice, delivered a furious tirade against the "internationalists" in the party—meaning Roosevelt, Smith, Newton D. Baker, and Owen D. Young. What America needed, Hearst said, was a president whose motto would be "America First," and, for the California publisher, Cactus Jack Garner was such a man. The next day Garner's name was splashed across the front page of every Hearst paper in an editorial, "Who Will Be the Next President?"

Garner himself was unimpressed. "There are no presidential bees buzzing around my office," he wrote, and he told a delegation of Texans that, while he appreciated the honor, he was not a damned fool. He knew his limitations, he said, and in the speaker-ship he had achieved all the honors he wanted. He really did not want to be president. "I always thought of the White House as a prison," he once remarked, "but I never noticed until today how much the shiny latch on the Executive office door looks like the handle on a casket."

Garner, despite his reluctance, soon had a considerable follow-ing. His western background and outspoken advocacy of strong measures to fight the Depression made him popular throughout the West, and, oddly for a man with a well known fondness for good bourbon, he became a rallying point for the Drys. Before long a Garner boom was in full swing, with Representative Sam Rayburn and Senator Tom Connally organizing Texas and William Gibbs McAdoo lining up California.

Texas's neighboring state of Oklahoma also had a candidate in its eccentric Governor Alfalfa Bill Murray. An unkempt, elderly man who disguised a tough political sense in a professional hay-seed appearance, Murray was the darling of the poverty-stricken western farmers and gained much publicity with his slogan "Bread, Butter, Bacon and Beans."

Senator J. Hamilton Lewis, the favorite son of Illinois, was another eccentric candidate. An able lawyer, persuasive orator, and brilliant politician, Ham Lewis had many excellent qualities that should have recommended him as a presidential candidate. Unfortunately, his personal characteristics made it impossible to take him seriously. His rather startling taste in clothes—he was credited with introducing spats to America—made him a figure of dazzling splendor and once prompted Speaker Reed to refer to him as "that garrulous rainbow." He also affected pink whiskers and a wig that fooled nobody. His appearance could always be counted on for a laugh, and it was his misfortune that political parties rarely select laughable candidates intentionally. Lewis's only strong points were that he had been elected to the Senate in 1930 from normally Republican Illinois by a majority of 700,000 and that he was one of the nation's leading Wets.

A more serious favorite son was Governor Ritchie of Maryland. Four times elected to the governorship, he was noted for his uncompromising wetness and conservative economic views. He appealed to the East as a possible compromise candidate but was hampered by his single-minded championing of the old Jeffersonian doctrine that the country is best governed when least governed. The depths of the Depression was no time for a return to Jeffersonian democracy, and Ritchie remained in the favorite-son class largely because of this attitude.

Newton D. Baker was a reluctant and undeclared candidate, but he remained in the background as a potential threat to the active candidates. He was supported by a number of influential newspapers, and Robert Woodruff, the Coca-Cola tycoon, tried to organize a Baker delegation in Georgia. Senator Carter Glass, the dramatist Robert Sherwood, Adolph Berle, and newspaperman Mark Sullivan were all Baker supporters, while Walter Lippmann believed that he was the inevitable candidate.

The last candidate to enter the field was Al Smith. Retired from active politics after his defeat in 1928, he had kept in touch with party affairs through National Chairman John Raskob, and he maintained his position as titular head of the party. His bitterness over his defeat and especially his resentment of Roosevelt, who he felt was ignoring him, eventually led him to make another try for the nomination.

Roosevelt formally announced his candidacy on January 23, 1932, but remained for the next two months as silent as possible on the issues. He maintained that, as governor of New York, he was not in a position to comment on national affairs. Not until the first week of April did he make a positive declaration of his views. In a nation-wide radio speech on April 7, he laid down the outlines of a progressive program.

Roosevelt asserted that the Depression was a graver emergency than the World War and that, in this emergency, the Hoover administration had forgotten "the infantry of our economic army."

Economic assistance at the top would not solve the nation's problems; it was upon the "forgotten men" that a program must be built. "No nation can long endure half bankrupt. Main Street, Broadway, the mills, the mines will close if half the buyers are broke." It was to the half of the nation that was broke, to the "forgotten man" that Roosevelt made his appeal, and it was an enormous success. Mild though the speech actually was, it was received as a bold challenge to the conservatives. Western and southern Democrats were delighted at the attack on the Republican theory that assistance at the top would trickle down to the masses.

To the conservatives, the speech was nothing less than demagoguery. The New York *Times* blushed that its candidate should indulge in what would be considered, had it come from anyone else, demagogic claptrap. Walter Lippmann sniffed, quite correctly, that Roosevelt had misrepresented the Reconstruction Finance Corporation and had offered no explanation of how he would increase the "forgotten man's" purchasing power.

Al Smith seized upon the speech to deliver a blistering attack on Roosevelt. "I will take off my coat and vest and fight to the end against any candidate who persists in any demagogic appeal to the masses of the working people of this country to destroy themselves by setting class against class and rich against poor." Republicans cheered and urged, "Hit him again, Al!," but Democrats were disquieted and began wondering if perhaps there was some truth after all to the reports that Al had traded in his derby for a high silk hat. Seeing the Republican press embrace Al Smith as one of its own profoundly shook many Democrats. Roosevelt's own reaction was to joke, "Wasn't that a terrible attack Al made on Alfalfa Bill Murray?"

Smith's attack made him Roosevelt's leading rival. He would be a formidable contender, having, as he did, the support of most of the big-city machines. Tammany and Boss Hague of New Jersey were for him, and the Kelly-Nash machine in Chicago and the Pendergast machine in Kansas City would probably be friendly once their favorite sons were eliminated.

With Smith's entry into the race, the next few months were taken up with the battle for delegates. In state primaries and conventions, the opposing candidates finagled, plotted, wheedled, threatened, and occasionally stole in their efforts to reach the magic number of 770 votes. The Roosevelt strategy was to avoid offending the favorite sons. His managers carefully refrained from entering him in the home state of any candidate, with, of course, the exception of New York, but they were ready to fight it out with Smith, Murray, and Garner anywhere in neutral territory. Actually, Roosevelt was the only candidate with enough support to make a nation-wide campaign. The others concentrated on the areas of their greatest personal strength. Smith was most active in Massachusetts, New Jersey, Pennsylvania, Rhode Island, and New York. Garner concentrated on Texas and on California, where Hearst's support would be helpful. Murray limited himself to Oklahoma and North Dakota, where his extreme views on agriculture had wide appeal.

The first primary clash came on March 6 in New Hampshire. Smith was considered the preprimary favorite, but Roosevelt had the backing of the state organization and swept to a 7-to-4 victory in the statewide vote. In North Dakota, Roosevelt won handily over Murray to prove that he could draw support from the prairie states.

Roosevelt defeated Garner in the Georgia primary and then met Smith again in Wisconsin on April 5. The state organization was for Roosevelt, but Smith's ardent Catholic support made it likely that he would capture five of the twenty-six delegates. Jim Farley assured Milwaukee voters that Roosevelt was for repeal, and the Progressives swung behind Roosevelt, with the result that he won more easily than had been expected and took the entire delegation.

New York picked its delegation on the same day, and, despite heroic work by Flynn and the Roosevelt organization, the contest had to be considered a draw. The delegation was uninstructed. Boss Curry of Tammany, who headed the delegation strongly favored Smith, but an undetermined minority of the delegates could be considered for Roosevelt. Both Smith and Roosevelt would have to wait until the convention to see who would win their home state.

So far Roosevelt had had an easy time of it. The only setback had been in New York, but even there the failure to secure a pledged delegation was not without its compensations. At least

Smith had not taken the delegation, and, in view of the Mayor Walker and Tammany scandals, it was an advantage to have the solid opposition of Tammany. But the Roosevelt forces were in for a rude jolt in the Massachusetts primary.

Roosevelt should have avoided the Massachusetts contest, for the state organization, led by Governor Ely and Senator Walsh, was solidly for Smith, and the large Irish Catholic population of Boston made his victory a virtual certainty. But the Roosevelt forces allowed themselves to be persuaded by Mayor Curley of Boston to enter the primary, and they were soon embroiled in a fight between local factions. Curley was at odds with the Ely-Walsh organization and hoped to use Roosevelt to gain a victory over them. The vote was a smashing victory for Smith, who carried the state 3 to 1 and won all thirty-six delegates.

The jubilant Smith forces predicted that the Roosevelt band-wagon had been stopped, and the results of the Pennsylvania primary two days later on April 26 gave little comfort to the Roosevelt men. The New York Governor won the preference vote and the delegates-at-large, but Smith ran much stronger than had been expected and claimed thirty-four of the sixty delegates.

The faltering Roosevelt drive received a stunning blow in California on May 3. The state had seemed safe for Roosevelt since he had the backing of the state organization, but then Al Smith filed in the primary, followed by Speaker Garner. The Wet forces, particularly in San Francisco, were enthusiastic for Smith, and the Drys, led by William Gibbs McAdoo, supported Garner. The Speaker also had the backing of the Hearst press and the 100,000 members of the Texas Society of California. Roosevelt found himself squeezed between the Los Angeles Drys and the San Francisco Wets. Still, no one really expected the outcome. Either Roosevelt or Smith, it was believed, would eke out a narrow victory. The results were a sensational upset: Garner carried the state with 216,000 votes against 170,000 for Roosevelt and 138,000 for Smith. It was freely predicted that the loss of California's 44 votes was the death blow to Roosevelt's candidacy.

Roosevelt began to recover from the California defeat with a series of quick victories. Alabama, Arizona, and Wyoming declared for him, and, on May 10, he easily defeated Murray in the

West Virginia primary. By the middle of June, he had picked up an additional 150 votes.

The last slate of delegates to be chosen for the convention was that of Louisiana. There was some question of when the delegation had actually been chosen since Huey Long put it together when and how he saw fit. But on June 25, the Long delegation, already in Chicago, was instructed by the Kingfish to back Roosevelt. Whether or not the instructions would stick was something else again. Long had already made and unmade pledges of support to Pat Harrison and Al Smith. It was the influence of Republican Senator George Norris that finally brought Long into the Roosevelt camp. Norris had told Long that he would not support Hoover and that Roosevelt was the only hope of the country. Long had an additional reason for going with Roosevelt, since his enemies in Louisiana had sent a contesting delegation and Long would need the Roosevelt majority to get his own delegation seated. In typical Long fashion, the Kingfish had further complicated the issue by putting together a mock delegation to challenge both the contesting delegations.

When all the delegates had been chosen, Roosevelt had won thirty-four states and three territories for a total of 417 votes. He also claimed 129 votes from Indiana, New York, and Pennsylvania. Smith had 94 votes pledged, with 111 votes claimed from New York, Pennsylvania, and three territories. Garner had the 90 votes of Texas and California, and favorite sons controlled the 208 votes of Illinois, Ohio, Missouri, Oklahoma, Virginia, and Maryland. In Roosevelt's New York headquarters, there was a large map of the United States, and, as each state pledged for Roosevelt, the area was filled in with pink. What came to be known derisively to the opposition as "Field Marshal Farley's Map" had an impressive spread of pink, but votes rather than area counted, and the Roosevelt forces were far short of the necessary 770 votes.

While Roosevelt and Smith fought for delegates, their lieutenants fought for control of the convention machinery. National Chairman John Raskob wanted to name the pro-Smith Jouett Shouse temporary chairman and keynoter. Not only could Shouse set a pro-Smith tone at the outset of the convention with his keynote speech, but he could also select a pro-Smith committee on permanent organization, which would, in turn, select a Smith man for permanent chairman.

The committee on arrangements, which, because the National Committee reflected the party of 1928 rather than the party of 1932, had a pro-Smith majority, met in Chicago on April 4. Ed Flynn objected to Shouse as temporary chairman, and Harry Byrd of Virginia offered a compromise by which Senator Barkley would be named temporary chairman and Shouse would be permanent chairman. Shouse agreed, provided that Roosevelt give his personal approval. Farley immediately telephoned Roosevelt, who said he had no objection if the committee on arrangements wished to "commend" Shouse to the convention, which formula the Smith forces accepted.

Later, when the Roosevelt forces decided to make Senator Walsh of Montana permanent chairman, Shouse cried that he had been betrayed, but Roosevelt's managers blandly asserted that a "commendation" could not be considered a commitment. By this time, Roosevelt had enough pledged delegates to make this particular bit of political sleight-of-hand stick, and Shouse, "commended" or not, was out. The Smith forces, with a majority of the arrangements committee, had been neatly outfoxed and could do nothing but try to claim Shouse as a martyr—at which they singularly failed.

On June 5, the Roosevelt leaders gathered at Hyde Park for a final strategy session. It was decided to back Senator Walsh for permanent chairman, and, at Farley's insistence, Arthur Mullen of Nebraska was chosen floor leader. Farley would be Roosevelt's direct representative at the convention.

Those at the meeting discussed the question of the two-thirds rule. Roosevelt had a clear majority of the delegates, and it would be to his advantage to do away with the necessity for a two-thirds vote. Unfortunately, 218 of the pledged Roosevelt delegates were from the South and border states, and it was doubtful that they could be induced to go along with such a move. It was finally decided to let the matter hang fire until the convention met and to decide what to do then.

After the discussion, Roosevelt revealed for the first time that, if he received the nomination, he intended to fly to Chicago to accept in person. A final note was provided by the Governor's mother, who remarked firmly that she did not want to see her son nominated if he had to be elected on a liquor ticket.

In the remaining days before the convention, Louis Howe continued to plan for every contingency. For example, he sent Fred Roper, the young son of Daniel C. Roper, to see the producer of the musical hit *Of Thee I Sing* to ask if he would be willing to change the lyrics of "Wintergreen for President" to "Roosevelt for President." The producer, firmly believing in a nonpartisan box office, refused. Howe grinned, "I thought he would, but it was worth a try, anyway."

Howe also used Fred Roper on a rather more important mission. He knew that Jouett Shouse had taken over almost every room in the Chicago Stadium in the name of the National Committee, and it was apparent that there would be no rooms for the Roosevelt managers. Howe sent the twenty-three-year-old Roper to Chicago to obtain two or three conference rooms for Jim Farley. The discouraged Roper called Howe in New York to report that there were no rooms available and that he did not see how they could get any short of bribery. Howe replied sweetly, "I told you to get those rooms. I didn't tell you *how* did I? That's up to you, my boy." So Roper bribed the caretaker to appropriate three rooms and lock them for the Roosevelt managers. Fearing that the opposition might slip in during the night, remove the locks, and regain the rooms, Roper, on Howe's orders, put up a cot and slept there until the opening of the convention.

Meanwhile, Arthur Mullen and J. Bruce Kremer of Montana were working out the seating arrangements. As Mullen related it, "Remembering the old adage of the one bad apple in the barrel, we put California behind New York, and both of them a half-mile away from Texas. We left New York and New Jersey together, but took Illinois away from both of them. . . . Texas, with its four delegates to every vote, we put in splendid isolation."

With the seating arrangements completed, young Roper holding down the meeting rooms under siege, and the final strategy sessions held, the Roosevelt managers prepared to move their operations to

Chicago. Farley and Flynn traveled together and admitted their nervousness at embarking on the national political scene. Astute politicians though they were, neither they nor most of the other leaders in the Roosevelt organization had had much experience in politics beyond the state level. Ed Flynn later estimated that, when it came to national convention politics, about 90% of their organization was made up of newcomers and amateurs.

Newcomers the Roosevelt managers might have been, but they began with all the confidence of veterans. Farley established the main campaign headquarters in room 1102 of the Congress Hotel. Ed Flynn had rooms nearby, and Louis Howe's were on an upper floor. The main feature of the "reception center" presided over by Farley was a huge version of "Field Marshal Farley's Map," designed to overawe visiting delegates with the widespread popularity of Roosevelt. Al Smith snorted that it showed Roosevelt to have "lots of area" but not "lots of delegates."

Howe had brought his own telephone operators from New York, and he set up a special switchboard to insure against leaks of confidential information. The special switchboard also provided a unique method of contacting delegates. Howe had a direct line from his suite 1702 to Albany and had arranged to hook it to a loudspeaker. When a group of delegates assembled in Howe's rooms, Roosevelt would be called on the telephone to address the delegates. Not only was it psychologically effective, but it gave many delegates an opportunity to make their first personal contact with the Governor of New York. In recalling the constant flow of delegates in and out of Howe's rooms, one of his secretaries remarked, "We never knew when we went into Louis' room whether we'd trip over a Senator, a Governor, a farm delegation, a labor group or a bunch of coils and wires."

The delegates could meet Roosevelt only over the telephone, but most of the other candidates attended in person. Al Smith, James Reed, Governor Ritchie, Harry Byrd, and Alfalfa Bill Murray set up their headquarters and searched relentlessly for delegates. Upon arriving in Chicago, Smith held a press conference and denied that he was there solely to stop Roosevelt. He had come, he said, to fight a stop-Smith movement and expected to be nominated. The belief that Smith was a candidate only to stop Roosevelt was a

serious miscalculation on the part of the anti-Roosevelt forces.
They had sufficient votes to prevent Roosevelt's nomination—but
only if they stuck together. If they could have united on a single
candidate, they might very well have stopped Roosevelt's drive.
But the rival candidates did not believe Smith was in the race to
win the nomination for himself. Each expected to be the beneficiary of the Smith strength and influence and refused to give up
his own chances to a rival.

One candidate who was not in Chicago was John Nance Garner.
The Speaker remained in Washington but was represented by Sam
Rayburn. The day before Rayburn left for Chicago, Garner gave
him his instructions. He wanted, he said, his name to remain before
the convention as long as there was any reasonable expectation of
his nomination. But, remembering the Madison Square Garden
convention, he emphasized that the interests of the party were to
be considered above his personal interests. He said much the same
thing to Bascom Timmons, an old friend from Texas. "I am not
going to deadlock the convention against the leader. Roosevelt is the
leader in delegates. He will have a majority, but not two-thirds. . . .
Roosevelt is both strong and weak. He seems to have practically no
second-choice delegates. . . . The stop Roosevelt men could, with a
little help, deadlock the convention." Timmons left for Chicago
with the distinct impression that the help would not come from
Garner.

The undeclared candidate, Newton D. Baker, remained away
from Chicago. He stayed in his office in Cleveland and spent the
evenings attending the summer opera at the Cleveland Stadium,
but the Baker men were active in his behalf. Ralph Hayes, Baker's
manager, opened campaign headquarters in the Congress Hotel
and had the active support of John W. Davis, Judge Samuel Seabury, John Stewart Bryan, editor of the Richmond News-Leader,
and a young lawyer from Indiana named Wendell Willkie. It was
the strategy of these men to keep Baker's name circulating among
the delegates to prepare the ground for Baker's sweeping the convention as everyone's second-choice candidate in the event of a
deadlock. When William Randolph Hearst became aware of the
compromise sentiment building up in Baker's favor, he thundered

editorially, "Ladies and gentlemen of the Democratic Convention: There are in the United States of America approximately 125,000,-000 persons and among the least desirable of these as a candidate for President is Newton D. Baker of Ohio."

The Roosevelt leaders seemed safely launched in convention politics when their fears of inexperience came back to them with a vengeance. The two-thirds rule suddenly became an issue, and Jim Farley, to his intense discomfort, found that he still had much to learn in leading a campaign for a presidential nomination. On the evening of June 24, the first Roosevelt organization meeting was attended by sixty-five delegates, representing every delegation. The meeting was progressing smoothly under Farley's chairmanship when Huey Long took the floor to propose a resolution pledging the friends of Governor Roosevelt to do all in their power to abolish the two-thirds rule in favor of majority rule. Farley pointed out that the meeting had no power to decide such a question and that it would be unfair to take such a stand without consulting Roosevelt. It was decided to defer the resolution, but various individuals began speaking against the manifest unfairness of the two-thirds rule. The alarmed and perspiring Farley heard Senators Dill, Hull, and Wheeler speak out against the rule, along with Governor Woodring, J. Bruce Kremer, Arthur Mullen, Homer Cummings, and Josephus Daniels. Long asked to be allowed to second his own motion and, with coat unbuttoned, tie askew, and arms flailing, delivered a rousing stemwinder of a speech that stampeded his listeners into adopting a resolution pledging the Roosevelt forces to a fight to abolish the two-thirds rule. Farley had lost control of the meeting and suddenly found himself in the middle of a storm that threatened to wreck the whole Roosevelt campaign.

Naturally the rival candidates set up a howl of opposition. Al Smith charged that the resolution was an attempt to change the rules in the middle of the game. The former nominees, James M. Cox and John W. Davis, went on record against the change, and Newton D. Baker declared that any nomination won by changing the rules would have a "moral flaw" in its title. The greatest opposition, however, came from the southern delegates, most of whom were for Roosevelt. They would not give up their cherished veto

power without an all-out fight, and Senator Josiah Bailey of North
Carolina raged that, if the Roosevelt managers went ahead with
the proposal, they would lose nearly every southern vote. As Ed
Flynn remarked, "Farley and I took a lesson in national politics
then and there." It was obvious that, with the South against the
proposal, it would be impossible to achieve its passage, and the
only course was to retreat as quickly and as gracefully as possible.
Accordingly, Roosevelt issued a statement in which he said that,
although he opposed the two-thirds rule on principle, he would not
"permit either myself or my friends to be open to the accusation of
poor sportsmanship or to the use of methods which could be called,
even falsely, those of a steamroller." The statement quieted the
southerners, and the whole episode was quickly forgotten in the increasing frenzy that always accompanies nominating conventions.

Jim Farley had hardly recovered from the effects of his first
blunder when he committed another. On Saturday, June 25, Senator
Ham Lewis withdrew as a favorite son and released the Illinois
delegation. Farley exclaimed jubilantly, "This is the beginning of
the end. Roosevelt will be nominated on the first ballot." He called
a news conference and released the text of the Lewis telegram, fully
confident that the rush to the Roosevelt bandwagon was on. But,
as he himself later admitted, "we muffed the ball badly." By releasing the Lewis statement nearly a week before the actual balloting, Farley gave the opposition forces plenty of time to regroup.
Mayor Cermak was fully aware of Lewis's intentions before Farley
obtained a copy of the withdrawal telegram, but he was in no
hurry to make it public. Cermak intended to keep control of the
delegation with or without Lewis. There was considerable Roosevelt sentiment in the Illinois delegation, but it was too early to
build that sentiment into a majority opinion. If the Lewis telegram
had been released later after greater pressure for Roosevelt had
been built up, Illinois might have been won. As it was, Mayor
Cermak, having lost one favorite son, simply found another in the
person of Melvin A. Traylor, a Chicago banker. The delegation was
duly pledged to Traylor's sudden candidacy, and 40 first-ballot
Illinois votes were lost to Roosevelt.

The preconvention activities were finally transferred to the
Chicago Stadium at 12:50 p.m. on June 27. After the opening prayer

by Commander Evangeline Booth of the Salvation Army, John J. Raskob delivered a short address. With a view to the forthcoming struggle for the permanent chairmanship, he began his speech with a warm tribute to Jouett Shouse and, although he admitted that as chairman of the National Committee he could not recommend a platform to the convention, concluded with a strong appeal for a repeal plank. Such an appeal could only bring to mind, as it was meant to do, that wettest of all candidates, Al Smith. Raskob also attacked the Republicans with good humor. "Religion teaches us that the three great virtues are faith, hope and charity. Under the Republican administration faith has been so far destroyed that people have little hope left and if a change is not quickly secured we shall all be subjects of charity."

After a reading of Jefferson's first inaugural address, the temporary chairman, Senator Barkley, delivered a lengthy keynote address. The two-hour speech caused some grumbling among the delegates, but, as Will Rogers pointed out, "It had to be a long speech, for when you start enumerating the things that the Republicans have got away with in the last twelve years you have cut yourself out a job."

The first order of business on the second day was the seating of the contested delegations, chief of which was Louisiana's. Huey Long's delegation was seriously opposed by a delegation led by former Governor Jared Saunders and comically opposed by a rag-tag group of clowns specially selected by Long himself to make a mockery of the whole contest. Long's antics offended many delegates, and Arthur Mullen warned him to stop clowning when the contest went before the convention. The majority report of the committee on credentials recommended seating the Long delegation, while a minority report backed the Saunders group. To the surprise of most of the delegates, who were only familiar with the more flamboyant aspects of Long's career, the Kingfish made a sober and reasoned speech in defense of his delegation. The speech did much to dissipate the ill feeling generated by his earlier farcical behavior, and the Roosevelt forces had little difficulty in voting down the minority report by 638¾ to 514¼. With the 20 Long votes seated in the convention, the contest over the Minnesota delegation was settled 658¼ to 492¾ in favor of the Roosevelt delegation. Since everyone knew that Roosevelt had a majority of the convention, the votes offered no surprises, but the 44 votes of Louisiana and Minnesota were welcome additions to the Roosevelt column.

The permanent roll of delegates was studded with distinguished names, but by all odds the most surprising delegate was Alcalde Jaime Miguel Curleo, delegate from Puerto Rico. Startled onlookers recognized him as Mayor James Michael Curley of Boston. He had, it was reported, with the help of several martinis, persuaded a delegate to turn his credentials over to him, and the Mayor of Boston became a Roosevelt delegate after all. The total convention consisted of 1736 delegates with 1154 votes.

The Roosevelt-Smith rivalry came into the open over the permanent chairmanship. Both Senator Walsh of Montana and Jouett Shouse were brought forward for the post. The debate centered on the actions of the National Committee meeting of April 4, and the subtle distinctions between "commend" and "recommend." The Shouse forces, believing that they had been double-crossed, charged Roosevelt with bad faith in offering Walsh. Senator James F. Byrnes denied any imputation of bad faith and maintained that the two-thirds vote for Walsh in the committee on permanent organization entitled him to the chairmanship. The plain fact was that the Roosevelt forces had implied in April that they would go along with Shouse because they did not at that time have enough strength to fight him openly. As soon as they controlled a majority of the delegates, however, they were ready to dump him. It may have been bad faith, but it was good politics, and, however much they might protest, the Smith men knew it. Walsh was elected 626 to 528.

The significance of the vote was not that it placed Walsh in the chair, but that it showed Roosevelt to be 144 votes short of a two-thirds majority. The three delegations most in doubt—Indiana, New York, and Pennsylvania—were being claimed, at least in part, by both Roosevelt and Smith. The vote on the permanent chairmanship showed Roosevelt's claims to be doubtful. Indiana voted solidly for Shouse; 67 of New York's 94 votes also went for Shouse. Pennsylvania was more encouraging, as 48½ Walsh votes were cast, with only 27½ going to Shouse. Still, Roosevelt was a long way from the nomination, and the vote for permanent chairman indicated that the anti-Roosevelt forces had every intention of standing firm.

The platform was submitted to the convention at the third day's evening session. The original draft had been prepared by Cordell Hull and former Attorney General A. Mitchell Palmer during several conferences in Washington that spring. Palmer was suffering from a serious heart condition and wanted to perform one last service for his party by helping to draft the platform. The Hull-Palmer draft was substantially accepted by the resolutions committee.

There were, however, exceptions. Hull and Palmer had prepared a prohibition plank recommending that the question of repeal be referred to the states. Al Smith demanded total repeal and threatened a floor fight. Roosevelt withdrew his objections to the repeal plank, and it was accepted by the committee in place of the Hull proposal.

One plank, favored by the committee but not included in the platform, would have guaranteed bank deposits in member banks of the Federal Reserve system. Roosevelt called Arthur Mullen to say, "These bankers here in New York think that I'm a Communist now, so let's leave that plank out of the platform. I'll take care of it later." The plank was removed, but William Gibbs McAdoo announced that he would submit a minority report from the floor.

The bank-deposit guarantee plank was offered by McAdoo and a minority prohibition plank by Hull. Alfalfa Bill Murray offered his own program as a minority report to be incorporated in the platform. Murray advocated an immediate payment of the soldiers' bonus and legislation to give the states clearly defined powers to levy taxes on interstate commerce. He proposed that, since Congress could coin money, "it is the duty of the Government to coin both gold and silver in sufficient quantities to meet the requirements of the normal demands of business." Murray called for the conscription of men and property in time of war and said in one plank, "We declare for an act by Congress providing for a moratorium throughout the United States against the foreclosure of mortgages on the homes of the people. We favor legislation, state and national, which will discourage and prevent our farm lands from becoming permanently owned or controlled by corporations, with additional provision to aid the actual home owners to acquire homes for themselves and their families. We hold that every law—state and national—should have for its ultimate purpose the fortification of the American home, the preservation of the family, and the security of the wife and mother."

Wives and mothers notwithstanding, Murray's platform was not acceptable to the convention. Hull's prohibition plank was rejected 934¾ to 213¾, and the other minority planks were turned down on a voice vote.

Despite a bold call at the beginning of the platform for a "drastic change in economic governmental policies," it was a far from revolutionary document. It promised to reduce government expeditures by at least 25% and, like the Republican platform, favored a balanced budget. It called for a sound currency and opposed the cancellation of debts owed the government by foreign nations. There were some planks that did set the platform apart from that adopted by the Republicans. It called for a competitive tariff for revenue only—not for protection—and advocated unemployment and old-age insurance under state laws. It also proposed price supports for farm commodities, but there was little hint in the platform of the changes that would actually occur once the Democrats came to power. The very fact that immediate repeal was the most enthusiastically received plank suggested that the Democrats had, at that time, as few ideas for coping with the Depression as had the Republicans.

As the roll was called for the presidential nominations on June 30, the candidates took stock of their positions. Al Smith could count on perhaps 200 votes on the first ballot, but that was his peak strength. He was confident that the convention would deadlock and that he would be the eventual choice; the other candidates did not agree. Baker, Ritchie, and Byrd were counting on a deadlock, but each hoped that he, rather than Al Smith, would be the ultimate choice of the convention. Garner had no intention of letting the convention deadlock. It was a serious mistake on the part of the other candidates not to have ascertained the Speaker's attitude on this matter. Their strength so obviously lay in standing firm that Smith, Ritchie, and the others took it for granted that Garner would do the same.

Garner had, however, by no means given up the race. Several states that were pledged to Roosevelt—especially Alabama, Mississippi, Arizona, and Arkansas—were voting under the unit rule and had considerable second-choice sentiment for Garner. Representative John McDuffie of Alabama hoped to swing his state to Garner on the fifth or sixth ballot and believed that Arkansas and possibly Arizona could be taken along. If these states at the top of the roll call swung away from Roosevelt, a deadlocked convention might be stampeded to the Speaker of the House.

Baker's managers were also depending on second-choice support in a deadlock. No delegates were pledged to Baker, but publisher Roy Howard promised Paul V. McNutt the support of the Scripps-Howard papers in Indiana for his campaign for the governorship if Indiana would give Baker a minimum of 8 votes on the first three ballots to keep his name before the convention. Eventually Baker could expect to receive the vote of Ohio. Governor White, the favorite son, announced that he would not release his 58 votes because doing so would violate his understanding with Baker and James M. Cox. It was assumed that the "understanding" was that White would hold the votes for Baker.

Before the balloting, Baker was seen by Walter Lippmann as the acceptable second choice of nearly everyone. "Although there is not a single delegate instructed to vote for him, he is the man who, once preconvention pledges have been fulfilled, could most easily be nominated." Mr. Lippmann may have been influenced in his judgment because he preferred Baker to Roosevelt. "Franklin D. Roosevelt is no crusader," he wrote. "He is no tribune of the people. He is no enemy of entrenched privilege. He is a pleasant man who, without any important qualifications for the office, would like very much to be President."

While the anti-Roosevelt candidates sat waiting for a deadlock, the Roosevelt managers worked feverishly to break the favorite-son front. Huey Long labored indefatigably on the edges of the Roosevelt inner circle, scurrying among the delegates, keeping the southerners in line, and attempting to win over the Murray forces.

He charged into Alfalfa Bill's hotel room early one morning shouting, "This is a hell of a time for the farmer's candidate to be asleep." While the rudely awakened Governor of Oklahoma shaved and dressed, the Kingfish sat down, ate the Governor's breakfast, and tried to make a deal for Oklahoma's votes. Not surprisingly, the sleepy and probably hungry Murray was not interested.

Jim Farley used the vice-presidency as bait for several candidates. He offered the nomination to Governor Ritchie, who turned it down on June 29, and, through Admiral Richard E. Byrd, to Virginia's Harry Byrd, who was more interested in his own dark-horse chances than he was in the vice-presidency and who refused to consider it. Farley also worked with no success on Mayor Cermak, hoping to secure Illinois in exchange for second place on the ticket for an Illinois man. Cermak preferred to wait and see what would happen when the balloting began.

More promising negotiations were opened with the Garner forces. On Monday evening, June 27, Senator Harry Hawes of Missouri and Senator Key Pittman of Nevada were discussing Roosevelt's prospects in Hawes's office in Washington. Like all the Roosevelt men, they feared a deadlock and decided it could be avoided if Garner would accept the vice-presidency. They called Roosevelt in Albany to ask if Garner would be a satisfactory running mate. Roosevelt replied, according to Senator Hawes, "Senator, that would be fine; the Governor from New York and the Speaker of the House from Texas—clear across the country." He then told Hawes to get in touch with Farley. Hawes wired Farley, "Group believe winning ticket would be Roosevelt and Garner stop ninety votes of California and Texas would eliminate dispute stop am advised would be satisactory to party here stop see Sam Rayburn Tom Connally and check my own impressions stop best wishes." Farley called Hawes and Pittman back, thanked them for the suggestion, and went to find Sam Rayburn.

That same night, Hawes sent hundreds of telegrams to Democratic leaders urging a Roosevelt-Garner ticket. Word of this move soon reached the Speaker. Senator Hawes was awakened at 7:30 in the morning to hear over the telephone the Speaker's high-pitched voice, soundly thrashing him for suggesting that he would be willing to accept the vice-presidency. Garner was in a rage and declared that he had not authorized anyone to consider such an offer.

Farley, meanwhile, had arranged through Silliman Evans to meet Sam Rayburn in Farley's apartment in the Congress Hotel at eleven o'clock Tuesday night. Evans and Rayburn arrived and joined Farley in his bedroom. The New Yorker turned on all his considerable charm and salesmanship to plead the Roosevelt cause. He argued that having a majority of the delegates entitled Roosevelt to the nomination. He concluded by saying that he would do everything in his power to secure the vice-presidential nomination for Garner if Texas would switch.

Sam Rayburn considered his answer, then said carefully, "We have come to Chicago to nominate Speaker Jack Garner for the Presidency if we can. We are not against any other candidate and we are not for any other candidate. Governor Roosevelt is the leading candidate and naturally he must be headed off if we are to win. But we don't intend to make it another Madison Square Garden." Farley was satisfied. Rayburn had promised nothing but had indicated his willingness to listen to reason. They agreed to keep this first meeting secret and to meet again.

The second meeting took place during the evening recess on Thursday, June 30. Roosevelt had been placed in nomination with an unimpressive speech by John E. Mack of New York. Senator Connally presented Speaker Garner in a spread-eagled, rousing tribute to the State of Texas as well as to Texas's favorite son. Governor Ely of Massachusetts delivered the best nominating speech of the convention when he placed Al Smith in nomination, and then, with the tumultuous ovation for the Happy Warrior still ringing in their ears, Farley and Rayburn moved a step closer to an arrangement that would render Ely's stirring speech useless.

Meeting at Garner headquarters, Farley promised to secure the vice-presidency for the Speaker and proposed that Texas record its first ballot for Garner and then switch to Roosevelt at the end of the roll call. Rayburn commented rather dryly that he had 360 Texas delegates and alternates who had come to Chicago to back Garner and that it would be unfair to them and to Texas to agree

to such an arrangement. Texas would vote for Garner for two or
three ballots until it was demonstrated whether or not he could be
nominated. How long, Rayburn asked, could Farley hold the Roosevelt forces in line? Farley replied cautiously, "Three ballots, four
ballots, and maybe five."

"Well," replied Rayburn, "we just must let the convention go
for a while, even if we are interested in the Vice-Presidency, and
I'm not saying that we are."

The convention reconvened at 9:15 p.m., and the nominating
speeches droned on. With what Jim Farley called "a merciless
and unholy flood of oratory," Harry Byrd, Melvin Traylor, Governor
Ritchie, James A. Reed, Governor White, and Alfalfa Bill Murray
were placed in nomination, and the party faithful trooped to the
microphones to second one nomination or another. Not only were
the orators apparently without number, but the band and the pipe
organ contributed to prolonging the night. Over and over, as they
had all week, the wearying delegates heard "Happy Days," "The
Sidewalks of New York," "Maryland, My Maryland," and "How
Dry I Am," until Farley was driven to record that most of the
listeners "wished they had the power to throw both the organ and
the bands into near-by Lake Michigan."

Around midnight, the exhausted Farley called a strategy meeting. Lying on a cot, too weary to get up, he discussed the situation
with the leaders. The question of whether they should force an
immediate ballot after the oratory finally wore itself out or adjourn
for the night was considered. It was decided that delay would be
dangerous. Alabama, Mississippi, Maine, Michigan, and Iowa
were wavering, and an adjournment would only give the opposition time to apply more pressure. After getting Roosevelt's approval, Farley called in the chairmen of the Roosevelt delegations,
asked them to stand fast, and explained that they should be prepared to ballot no matter how late the hour.

Having decided to ballot, Farley now attempted to shut off the
seconding speeches for Roosevelt. He sent messengers with the
suggestion that several speeches could, considering the lateness of
the hour, be dispensed with. What happened is best told by
Farley himself. "I learned something on that occasion that perhaps we should have learned before: a thorough-going Democrat

will give you his support, his loyalty, his vote, and his money—but never his radio time. When a Democratic orator has his throat cleared and ready, holds his manuscript in his hand, and knows the folk back home are there at the radio, it's too much to expect him to give way. Our appeal was in vain." At 4:28 a.m., Chairman Walsh banged down the gavel on the last bedraggled demonstration and announced, "The clerk will call the roll." By this time the convention was a shambles. The kleig lights still burned brightly as they swept back and forth across the hall, although the dawn was beginning to dim their brightness. The galleries, which had favored Smith over Roosevelt, were nearly empty at that hour. Amid the clutter of abandoned banners, old newspapers, crumpled coffee cartons, and stale, half-eaten sandwiches and hot dogs, the weary, rumpled delegates sat slumped in their seats or stretched out asleep on the chairs. Some had to be awakened to cast their votes.

In the Executive Mansion in Albany, Governor Roosevelt, his wife, his mother, and Sam Rosenman sat waiting expectantly for the roll call to begin. Roosevelt smoked steadily and used the telephone frequently to keep in touch with Chicago. As the balloting went on and on, Sara Roosevelt decided to leave. She was upset at hearing some of her friends in the New York delegation voting for Smith, and she grimly announced during the second ballot that it was more than she could stand. She was thoroughly disgusted with the entire proceeding and returned to Hyde Park. The Governor and his wife stuck it out, although Mrs. Roosevelt, perhaps to relax the tension, went to the kitchen to make scrambled eggs for the sleepy reporters who had set up their press headquarters in the garage.

The first ballot took nearly two hours to complete. Most of the delay was caused by polling in various delegations. The rival forces called for a poll whenever it would show a strong minority for a candidate other than the one being supported under the unit rule.

Tammany boss Curry wanted to put his delegation on record for Smith and demanded a poll. The actual effect was to demonstrate the unpopular Tammany's hostility to Roosevelt, which helped him considerably in other delegations. The poll also provided the most dramatic event of the ballot. There had been a great deal of speculation whether Mayor Walker, facing trial before Roosevelt because of the Seabury investigations, would attempt to curry favor with the Governor by voting for him. When Walker's name was called, a hush fell over the auditorium, and a spotlight picked out the slight, dapper figure as he defiantly announced, "I vote for Alfred E. Smith." The cheer that followed was as much for Beau James as it was for the Happy Warrior.

The first ballot did not provide many surprises. Roosevelt led with 666¼ votes—104 short of nomination. He had the total vote of forty of the thirty-five delegations, 44½ of the 76 Pennsylvania votes, 28½ of New York's 94, and 15¼ of Illinois' 58. Illinois and Indiana were the most badly split of all the delegations. Illinois divided its vote among Roosevelt, Smith, Garner, and Traylor, while Indiana gave votes to Roosevelt, Smith, Garner, Byrd, Ritchie, and Baker.

The vote for the other candidates was Smith 201¾, Garner 90¼, White 52, Traylor 42¼, Byrd 25, Reed 24, Murray 23, Ritchie 21, and Baker 8½. The Smith vote came from Connecticut, Massachusetts, New Jersey, Rhode Island, and the Philippines, with 65½ from New York and 30 from Pennsylvania, as well as scattered votes from Illinois, Indiana, and Wisconsin. The largely regional nature of the vote showed that he had virtually no hope of the nomination for himself.

Between the first and second ballots, Dan Roper contacted William Gibbs McAdoo and urged California to switch on the next ballot, but McAdoo said he could do nothing without a caucus, and there was no time to call one. Actually, McAdoo had little enthusiasm for Roosevelt, although he had even less for Al Smith. He was committed to Garner and was not interested in changing as long as the Speaker had any chance.

Farley went out on the floor to plead with Mayor Cermak, knowing that Indiana would follow the lead of Illinois. Cermak was friendly but unco-operative. Like McAdoo, he insisted that he could do nothing without a caucus. In McAdoo's case, the excuse was true, but Cermak could do whatever he wished whenever he wished with the 40 Traylor votes. He was not counting out the possibility of a deal, but it was much too early to consider it.

Arthur Mullen reported a curious offer from New York. John J. Curtin, Jimmy Walker's attorney, approached Mullen after the first ballot with the proposition that, if Governor Roosevelt would take care of Walker, the Tammany votes in New York would swing to Roosevelt. Whether Walker could actually have delivered any votes was doubtful, and Mullen did not think they were necessary. He felt that Walker would be too much of a liability in a national campaign and rejected the offer without consulting any other Roosevelt leaders.

During the second ballot, which began at 5:15 a.m., the Roosevelt managers increased their pressure on the Garner forces. Joseph P. Kennedy called William Randolph Hearst in California at 5:00 a.m. to warn that, unless Garner switched to Roosevelt, "the fat was going to be in the fire." Kennedy insisted that, if Roosevelt were stopped, the nomination would go to Baker, a prospect sure to horrify the isolationist publisher. A few hours after the conversation, Hearst called his editor George Rothwell Brown in Washington and ordered him to ascertain from Garner whether or not the Speaker would throw his strength to Roosevelt to save the party from Baker.

Arthur Mullen sought out Tom Connally on the floor and offered to make Garner the vice-presidential candidate—the same offer that Farley had previously made to Sam Rayburn. Connally replied, "There are, I hear, a half dozen men whom you've promised the vice-presidential nomination." Ignoring Farley's offers to Byrd and Ritchie, Mullen denied that any such offers had been made by himself "or by any one else who has any authority to speak for Roosevelt in this convention." Connally was not convinced but agreed to an adjournment after the second ballot to see how Garner felt about the offer.

While Mullen negotiated with Connally, Dan Roper and Senator Cordell Hull again approached McAdoo. Roper asked the California chairman if he would consider accepting appointment as secretary of state. McAdoo flatly refused, saying that, whatever happened in the convention, no personal advantage must accrue to him. He said that he would consider the offer to Garner but gave no assurances, although some years later Roper implied that McAdoo had agreed to a switch at that time.

The results of the second ballot were announced at 8:05 a.m.

Roosevelt had gained 11½ votes. Two votes came from Indiana and 6 from Missouri, where Tom Pendergast, having given Reed his complimentary vote, was ready to swing to Roosevelt. It was expected that, except for Mrs. Nell Donnelly, the entire Missouri delegation would follow Pendergast. Mrs. Donnelly was engaged to marry Senator Reed and would vote for him even if no one else did, which, according to Arthur Mullen, "was true love, but bad politics." The other Roosevelt gains were 1 New York vote, 1 from North Dakota, 1 from Alaska, and ½ from Ohio. It was not a very impressive showing, but at least the Roosevelt delegations were holding the line. Smith dropped to 194¼, and the other votes were Garner 90¼, White 50½, Traylor 40¼, Byrd 24, Ritchie 23½, Reed 18, and Baker 8. Murray's 22 Oklahoma votes went to Will Rogers. Six and one-half votes were not cast: The delegates were probably asleep.

If the Roosevelt managers had hoped to create a bandwagon atmosphere on the second ballot, they had plainly failed. It was time for negotiations, which could be better carried on during an adjournment. Accordingly, Arthur Mullen moved for adjournment. But the anti-Roosevelt forces, believing that he had been stopped, were anxious for a third ballot. On a voice vote, Chairman Walsh was unable to tell whether or not the motion to adjourn had carried. A New York delegate immediately demanded a roll call. Walsh told Mullen that the motion would probably lose, and it was withdrawn. The third ballot began a few minutes after eight o'clock.

The Roosevelt forces nearly lost Mississippi on the third ballot. Senator Pat Harrison, knowing of the plan to adjourn, left the Stadium and returned to his hotel. As he was undressing to go to bed, he happened to turn on the radio and heard to his horror that the third ballot was about to begin. Mississippi was held for Roosevelt under the unit rule by 10½ to 9½ votes. Without Harrison, the delegation would bolt. Not bothering to dress, the partially clad Senator rushed into a taxi and arrived at the Stadium just in time to save the delegation.

North Carolina was also wavering, but there was some doubt whether, in the event of a break, it would go to Garner or Ritchie. Eighteen delegates favored Garner, eleven Ritchie—and for a rather odd reason. Dr. Hugh Young, a famous surgeon at Johns Hopkins Hospital, had successfully performed serious operations on each of the eleven delegates. As one explained, "I think Garner would make a great President, but I may have to go back to Johns Hopkins and if I did Doc Young might not admit me. He's that strong for Ritchie." Medical pressure notwithstanding, Josephus Daniels and the other Roosevelt men held the delegation in line for the third ballot.

While the ballot was in progress, Arthur Mullen again talked with Tom Connally. Munching hot dogs at a stand near the entrance to the Stadium, they discussed the situation, and Connally finally agreed that, if the vice-presidency were acceptable to Garner, he would go along. On the way back to the platform, Mullen stopped by the California delegation to ask McAdoo if he would make a motion to adjourn after the third ballot. McAdoo replied that he would second the motion if Mullen made it.

When North Carolina was called on the roll, a confusing bit of mathematics came up. Senator Barkley was presiding as acting chairman. The North Carolina vote was announced as 25.04 for Roosevelt and .96 for Byrd. Looking at the delegation, the mystified Barkley exclaimed, "It is impossible for the Chair to make any such division," and asked for an explanation. The chairman of the delegation said, "Three of the delegates vote two votes, or .67 of one vote. In one district there are seven delegates elected to vote two votes and one delegate there has one-seventh of two votes, or .29 of one vote." Barkley replied, "It is easier to count it as it has been reported than to understand how you arrived at it, so it will be recorded as reported."

The results of the third ballot were Roosevelt 682.79, Smith 190¼, Garner 101¼, White 52½, Traylor 40¼, Reed 27½, Byrd 24.96, Ritchie 23¼, and Baker 8½. The Garner increase came from Oklahoma.

McAdoo decided, after speaking with Mullen, that he would make the motion to adjourn and sent a note to that effect to Mullen on the platform. Mullen passed the note on to the Chairman. After the results of the ballot were announced, Barkley looked toward the California delegation and saw McAdoo deep in conversation. The Chairman waited expectantly, but McAdoo did not see him. Finally, Barkley asked pointedly, "For what purpose does the delegate from California rose?" McAdoo leaped to his feet and moved adjournment, which was carried by voice vote. At 9:15 a.m., exactly twelve hours after the session began, the convention adjourned until 8:30 that night.

Jim Farley and Mrs. Farley took a cab back to the Congress Hotel. There they found Senator Harrison nervously pacing the lobby, chewing on a frayed cigar. Harrison warned Farley that Mississippi was in grave danger and could not be counted on much longer. Farley asked Harrison to locate Sam Rayburn and hurried upstairs to confer with Louis Howe.

Several Roosevelt leaders, including Joe Guffey, Frank Walker, Ed Flynn, and Vincent Dailey, gathered in Howe's suite. Louis Howe was lying on the floor, his collar unbuttoned, his head resting on a pillow. Two electric fans blew on him to give relief from the oppressive heat, and a radio was close to his ear. He had been in that position all night listening to the balloting and was exhausted almost beyond endurance. Joe Guffey, seeing his drawn and haggard face, thought that Howe looked as if he would not live through the day. Farley stretched his long frame on the floor beside Howe and reviewed the situation. It was agreed that success depended on Texas and that everything should be staked on securing the Garner votes.

While Farley and Howe plotted their strategy, Pat Harrison located Rayburn, who agreed to meet Farley shortly after 10:00 a.m. in the hotel suite shared by Harrison and George Allen, at that time a commissioner for the District of Columbia. Farley arrived first and, at Allen's suggestion, lay down on his bed and promptly fell asleep. Rayburn and Silliman Evans arrived a few minutes later and listened quietly while Farley and Harrison pleaded with them to swing Texas to Roosevelt. The conference lasted only a few minutes, and neither Texan said anything about the vice-presidency or made any promises, but as they were leaving Sam Rayburn said, "We'll see what can be done." Farley was convinced that they had been won over and that Garner would release his delegates. He rushed back to tell Howe the good news and then collapsed into bed.

What happened next is open to considerable dispute. George Rothwell Brown, as instructed by Hearst, saw Speaker Garner at 11:00 a.m. According to Brown, Garner decided at that time to release his delegates. Arthur Mullen also claimed that he had contacted Garner through a friend, Representative Edgar Howard of Nebraska. According to Mullen's account, Howard called him from Washington at 11:15 a.m. to say that Garner had agreed to accept the vice-presidential nomination. Mullen thereupon communicated this information to Senator Connally. There are several doubtful elements in the Mullen account. If Garner had actually made up his mind as early as eleven o'clock in the morning and if Mullen knew about it, it seems odd, to say the least, that neither Sam Rayburn, Louis Howe, nor Jim Farley had been informed. Senator Connally, in his account of the convention, gave no indication that he knew of any such decision until Sam Rayburn talked to Garner in mid-afternoon. It is possible that Howard saw Garner, who may have indicated an open mind concerning the release of his delegates, but Mullen was undoubtedly mistaken in claiming that any final decision was reached before noon on Friday. As for Brown's story, it is possible that he wished to enhance the prestige of his chief by lending credence to a myth popular at the time that William Randolph Hearst was responsible for Roosevelt's nomination.

Whenever Garner decided to withdraw from the race, he had made up his mind by three o'clock that afternoon. He called Sam Rayburn and informed him that he thought it was "time to break that thing up." Garner believed a decision should be reached on the next ballot and wanted Rayburn to release his delegates to Roosevelt. Rayburn asked Garner to be patient while he tried to work it out and then called a caucus of the Texas delegation for early evening.

Having gotten some rest, Jim Farley was prepared to enter the struggle once more. At 4:00 p.m., he met with Thomas Storke and Hamilton Cotton of the California delegation in the bedroom of his suite. With a fine sense of drama, Farley pounded on a chair and, with tears in his eyes, said, "Boys, Roosevelt is lost unless California comes over to us on the next ballot. I am 87 votes short, and I cannot hope to get them unless you switch to Roosevelt on the fourth ballot." Either Farley was a first-rate actor, or he was not so confident that Rayburn had been won over as he later claimed. Probably at that moment Farley really did not know whether Texas was won or not. Rayburn was playing a very cautious and close-mouthed game, and it is likely that Farley intended to force his hand by getting California away from Garner.

Thomas Storke was receptive to the idea of California's eventually going to Roosevelt but felt that the delegation owed it to Garner to stay with him for one or two more ballots. Farley said that in that case Baker would win. He explained that Minnesota, Iowa, the two Dakotas, and Mississippi, all held under the unit rule, would break on the fourth ballot unless California led the bandwagon to Roosevelt.

The two Californians still hesitated, and Farley asked them what McAdoo wanted. When told "nothing for himself," Farley asked if he would consider the vice-presidency. Told "no" again, Farley suggested the Court of St. James's or the Treasury Department. When finally convinced that McAdoo was not interested in the vice-presidential nomination, he asked, "Who *will* he agree to, then?" Storke and Cotton did not know, and Farley innocently inquired, "Well, do you think he might be agreeable to John Nance Garner?" Being told that he would, Farley generously said, "All right, then, let's make it Roosevelt and Garner." The Californians, convinced that something must be done immediately, agreed to see McAdoo to advise him that it was "now or never" so far as Roosevelt was concerned and to try to persuade him to switch California at the earliest possible moment. Farley had been very clever in bringing up the subject of Garner for vice-president without revealing the negotiations with Rayburn, but it is interesting to speculate about his position had he miscalculated and McAdoo had showed interest in the nomination for himself.

Storke and Cotton went to McAdoo's suite in the Sherman House and caught him emerging from the shower. As he dressed, they reported the conversation with Farley and expressed their opinion that, unless Roosevelt won on the next ballot, Baker would win the nomination. McAdoo told them that he had received a call from Garner at 6:00 p.m., in which the Speaker had said that he did not think he had any chance for the nomination and that whatever the California delegation wanted to do would be agreeable to him. He had also heard from Hearst that the publisher had given up on Garner and had no further interest in the nomination. McAdoo agreed to call a caucus for seven o'clock, and, as it was then six-thirty, Storke and Cotton rushed off to round up delegates.

The caucuses of the Texas and California delegations were to be the deciding factor in the convention, but throughout the day other negotiations were attempted. While Farley was dealing with the Garner leaders, Louis Howe, according to Lela Stiles, one of his secretaries, held a conference with Harry Byrd of Virginia. According to Miss Stiles's account, Howe asked Byrd what would induce him to switch his 24 votes to Roosevelt. Byrd replied that he wanted to be a United States senator. Howe thought it over, then offered to put either Carter Glass or Claude Swanson in the cabinet, opening a vacancy for Byrd. Senator Byrd, who was later appointed to fill the seat left vacant when Senator Swanson resigned to take the post of Secretary of the Navy, has categorically denied that any such deal was made. Virginia did, however, go to Roosevelt on the fourth ballot, along with the other favorite-son delegations.

The anti-Roosevelt forces, unaware of the Texas-California situation, were feeling extremely confident on the afternoon of July 1. The betting odds in Chicago were five to one against Roosevelt and several party leaders were quoted in the afternoon papers as saying, "We have Roosevelt licked." To make sure of the Garner strength, Al Smith tried all afternoon to reach the Speaker by telephone, but Garner, having made up his mind, refused to take the call. Smith, having given up all hope of winning the nomination for himself, was now leading the stop-Roosevelt forces to Garner. It was hinted to the Garner managers that the various candidates might unite on Garner on the fourth ballot, and Frank Hague offered to swing the 36 New Jersey votes to the Texan.

The anti-Roosevelt men were uncertain of what headway they had made to keep Garner in the race, but they had what appeared to be one solid victory for the day. The Mississippi delegation had finally cracked and agreed to abandon Roosevelt. It was not clear who would get the 20 votes, but there were reports that they would go to Baker. When the Roosevelt leaders heard of this break, they feared that Arkansas would follow the lead of Mississippi and sent Huey Long to rescue the two states if he could. Long threatened to break Pat Harrison if he allowed Mississippi to bolt, but Harrison was powerless, and the opposition was jubilant.

Meanwhile, Texas and California were preparing to caucus. California met in the Sherman House, and McAdoo opened the caucus by explaining that, if either Smith or Roosevelt showed signs of collapse or made significant gains, California would have to decide what to do. He did not indicate any course of action, and the suggestion to abandon Garner precipitated a near brawl. The delegates were trying to outshout each other, some for Garner, some for Smith, and at least one for Baker. Grace Bryan Hargreaves, the Great Commoner's daughter, kept shouting, "We came here to nominate JOHN NANCE GARNER and no one else! I am ready to stay right here in Chicago until we nominate JOHN NANCE GARNER!" It was finally agreed that a steering committee of three and McAdoo would be empowered "to determine when, and to whom, the vote of California should go in the event of a switch from John Nance Garner." The steering committee, without polling the delegation, instructed McAdoo to vote for Roosevelt on the next ballot.

Before the Texas caucus met, also at 7:00 p.m., Sam Rayburn called Garner. "Do you authorize me to release the Texas delegation voting for you for the presidential nomination?" asked Rayburn. "Yes," was the reply. "Do you release the Texas delegation from voting for you for the presidential nomination?" Again the reply was "Yes."

Many of the delegates had not been able to reach the caucus, but those who did attend were bitterly divided. It took all of Rayburn's skill to overcome the violent opposition of a die-hard group led by Amon Carter, who wanted to stick to Garner no matter what happened. Matters were not improved by two Illinois delegates who had slipped by the guards at the door and went around the room telling the delegates that Garner would get 30 Illinois votes on the fourth ballot. Finally Rayburn succeeded in getting the delegation, by a narrow vote of 54 to 51 to agree to swing to

Roosevelt. If all the delegates had attended the caucus, Farley's plans might have been completely upset, even though California was ready to switch.

The deal had been consummated, but the opposition did not yet know it. Just before leaving for the Stadium, Chairman Walsh was approached at dinner by a New York delegate who asked to be allowed to present his name to the convention as a compromise candidate. Senator Walsh, having just heard of the arrangement with the Garner forces, was rather startled but replied dryly that he had no presidential ambitions.

Jim Farley, now that the nomination was secure, could not resist the impulse to drop in at New York headquarters. He saw Tammany chief John Curry, who informed him that he was sure Roosevelt was stopped. Farley had planned to tell him of the Garner switch but, on hearing this comment, decided to let Tammany find out the hard way. Too nervous to eat dinner, he went on to the Stadium in a taxi with two Smith men who spent the whole trip trying to convince him to desert Roosevelt for Smith.

New York did not learn of the switch, but Mississippi did. Pat Harrison met Silliman Evans in front of the platform in the auditorium, and Evans told him that everything was set for California and Texas to go to Roosevelt. Harrison started to move away, then turned back and raced to Evans. "Are you sure?" he shouted. Assured that it was true, Harrison began to run for his delegation to stop them from jumping off the winning bandwagon.

It had been agreed among the Garner managers that, since California came early in the roll call, McAdoo would make the announcement withdrawing Garner in favor of Roosevelt. But when the roll call began, McAdoo was nowhere to be seen. Arkansas was casting its vote when the Californian came rushing down the aisle. His car had run out of gas on the way to the Stadium. He had leaped from the car and climbed behind a policeman on a motorcycle, but his long legs kept scruping the pavement, and he had had to dismount after going a few yards. The almost frantic McAdoo was bundled into a passing taxi and, with the motorcyclist as screaming escort, arrived at the convention in the nick of time.

As the flushed and breathless McAdoo mounted the platform,

a great cheer broke from the Smith forces. Somehow they had gotten the idea that California was going to switch to the Happy Warrior. Smith himself had not heard of this hope. When asked before the balloting began how he felt, he snapped, "Not so hot!"

McAdoo, a lone figure in the spotlight, waited for the cheering to die down. He could afford to wait. He had waited eight years for his chance to settle the Madison Square Garden score with Al Smith. When there was quiet, he said, "California came here to nominate a President of the United States. She did not come here to deadlock this convention or to engage in another disastrous contest like that of 1924," a reference that should have sent shivers of apprehension down the spines of the Smith men. As he spoke, McAdoo said that he believed California should support the candidate who had almost 700 votes behind him. Before he could utter Roosevelt's name, the pro-Smith packed galleries broke out in a torrent of abuse. The booing went on for several minutes, and no one heard Walsh's gavel or the band playing "California Here I Come." McAdoo relished the outburst. Standing slim and erect, he waited patiently. A sly smile crossed his face, and Thomas Storke thought of "a cat advancing craftily upon its prey." Finally, at the request of Mayor Cermak, the galleries subsided, and McAdoo cast 44 votes for Franklin Delano Roosevelt.

It was all over. Illinois, Maryland, Texas, and the others trooped into line. But the Smith supporters did not accept defeat gracefully. Only 4 Smith votes switched to Roosevelt, and, on the final ballot, the embittered Smith received 190½ votes. Roosevelt received 945, with 5½ for Baker, 3½ for Ritchie, 3 for White, and 1 for James M. Cox. The Smith delegates refused to make the nomination unanimous. A wry comment came from Will Rogers, who had supported Garner. "Here I have been neutral all my life until now, and the first time I come out for a man he throws his strength to a fellow with a Harvard accent. No good can come to a Texan who does a thing like that."

The final business of the convention was to formalize the deal with Garner. Unaware of the agreement, several delegations urged candidates upon the triumphant Farley. Governor Dern of Utah, Senator Dill of Washington, and Senator Wheeler of Montana were suggested, and Bernard Baruch called to ask if it were too late to consider Governor Ritchie. Farley gently replied that it was. Ed Flynn, even though he knew of the agreement with the Garner forces, was opposed to naming the Speaker as running mate. He argued that, because Texas had gone Republican in 1928, many Catholics, disappointed that Smith had lost the nomination, would use that fact as an excuse for opposing the ticket. He wanted to see a westerner like Senator Wheeler nominated. But a bargain had been made and would be carried out. At the afternoon session on July 2, Garner was placed on the ticket without opposition.

That night Governor Roosevelt flew in from Albany to address the convention. It was a dramatic moment, which highlighted the sense of urgency felt throughout the country. "I have started out on the tasks that lie ahead by breaking the absurd traditions that the candidate should remain in professed ignorance of what has happened for weeks until he is formally notified of that event many weeks later.

"My friends, may this be the symbol of my intentions to be honest and to avoid all hypocrisy or sham, to avoid all silly shutting of the eyes to the truth in this campaign." He covered recent events and outlined the problems that lay ahead. He closed his speech with a phrase that served as the slogan for his campaign and, indeed, for the entire Roosevelt era.

"I pledge you—I pledge myself to a new deal for the American people. Let us all here assembled constitute ourselves prophets of a new order of competence and of courage. This is more than a political campaign; it is a call to arms. Give me your help, not to win votes alone, but to win in this crusade to restore America to its own people." As the magnificent voice rolled through the Stadium and by radio across the country, pledging a new deal for the American people, the charisma of Roosevelt began to take hold, and the outcome of the election could hardly be in doubt.

If the Chicago convention of 1932 was the triumph of Roosevelt, it was the tragedy of Al Smith. The once Happy Warrior was now a jealous, bitter man. He had failed to stop Roosevelt and, in his bitterness, had destroyed himself politically. H. L. Mencken wrote his political epitaph. "The failure of the opposition was the failure of Al Smith. From the moment he arrived on the ground it was apparent that he had no plan, and was animated only by his fierce hatred of Roosevelt, the cuckoo who had seized his nest. . . . Perhaps the Al of eight or ten years ago, or even of four years ago, might have achieved the miracle that the crisis called for, but it was far beyond the technique of the golf-playing Al of today. He has ceased to be the wonder and glory of the East Side and becomes simply a minor figure of Park Avenue."

CHAPTER 18

"Here is a homely record"

THE TWENTY-FIRST REPUBLICAN NATIONAL CONVENTION
Cleveland, June 9, 1936

The Republican Party had expected defeat for Herbert Hoover in 1932; it had not expected near annihilation. Hoover carried only six states, the new Congress was heavily Democratic, and only ten state houses remained in Republican hands. Worse was yet to come. In 1934, reversing the tradition of mid-term losses, the Democrats picked up another eleven seats in the Senate, leaving only sixteen Republicans; there were only ninety Republicans in the House and only seven Republican governors. At no time in its history had the Republican Party been so nearly moribund. The old guard was dead, its successors apparently stillborn, and from the Atlantic Coast to Kansas nothing could be seen but Democrats.

The one ray of hope for Republicans came from Kansas. A millionaire, independent oilman Alfred E. Landon, had been elected governor in the face of the Roosevelt sweep and had been re-elected in 1934 by an increased plurality. When the Republicans began to look over the decimated field for a presidential candidate in 1936, Alf Landon was one of the few survivors.

In his terms as governor, Landon had a solid record of achievement. He had run the state efficiently, effected economies, and maintained a soundly balanced budget. He was popular and mildly progressive, and careful publicity could give him the simple, folksy

public speaker and, for all his admirable qualities as an administrator, a bit dull, endeared him even more to a party seeking the
antithesis of the sophisticated, colorful incumbent of the White
House. Reckless spending could be countered with Kansas thrift,
a mellifluous, almost hypnotic orator offset by a halting, labored
midwestern twang, and eastern worldliness contrasted to homespun
simplicity.

Politically, Landon stood halfway between old-guard Republicanism and the New Deal. He had been a Bull Moose Republican
in 1912 and had voted for LaFollette in 1924. He favored balanced
budgets and the gold standard, preferred states' rights to federal
control, and feared inflation. But he generally approved of the administration's activities in regulation of business, social welfare, and
conservation. He objected to the execution rather than the objec-
tives of the New Deal policies. "We have had too much of the
slap-dash, jazzy method" in the approach to national problems, he
said, but he warned, "four more years of the same policies that we
have had will wreck our parliamentary government, and four years
of the old policies will do the job also." If he was not so conservative as the image the Republicans wished to present, neither was
he so folksy. He was appalled to hear himself rapturously described
as a "Kansas Coolidge," and, despite Landon's friendly, off-hand
openness and casual manner, William Allen White commented that
"nothing in Alfred Landon's life has ever been casual." White continued that Landon's chief faults were "a mulish stubbornness and
a Napoleonic selfishness."

Landon was not the only Republican candidate. Herbert Hoover
traveled about the country denouncing Roosevelt and advocating
the gold standard, retrenchment, high tariffs, and the return of
relief to the states. The ex-President was eager to return to power,
but his party, remembering 1932, stayed as far away from him as
possible.

Another candidate who believed denunciation of the New Deal
to be the road to nomination was Colonel Frank Knox, publisher
of the Chicago *Daily News*. The publisher patterned himself on
his hero, Theodore Roosevelt, and cried of the other Roosevelt,
"What madness has seized him? Does he not see how dangerously
close this comes to conspiracy to break down our institutions of

quality for which the Republicans yearned. That he was a wretched government?" The Hoover-Knox denunciations prompted a news-paperman to ask Roosevelt if they were being paid by the Democrats to discredit the Republican Party. "Strictly off the record," came the reply, "it is a question of how much longer we can afford to pay them. They have been so successful that they are raising their prices."

A different caliber of candidate was that irascible old liberal, Senator Borah of Idaho. His vigor at seventy was undiminished, and he seemed to take his candidacy with the utmost seriousness. Senator Arthur Vandenberg of Michigan, not yet transformed into the mellow internationalist of his last years, was beating the drums of reaction and isolation and preparing for what would be a virtual lifetime career as hopeful dark horse. His prospects in 1936 were no better than they would be in future years.

The Landon campaign, managed by Kansas National Committeeman John D. M. Hamilton and Roy Roberts of the Kansas City *Star,* was officially launched at the American Legion Convention in the fall of 1935. The enthusiasm shown for Landon by the Legionnaires gave his candidacy national prominence and attracted the attention of William Randolph Hearst.

Hearst, traveling to California with Arthur Brisbane, Cissy Patterson, and Marion Davies, stopped off in Topeka to meet the Governor and decided, despite Landon's having supported the League of Nations and the World Court, that he was the man to receive the somewhat dubious blessings of the Hearst press. "I think he is marvelous!" Hearst beamed, and Mrs. Patterson reverently murmured, "I thought of Lincoln." Miss Davies's opinion was not recorded.

Announcing that Landon was "a man of destiny," Hearst ordered his publishing empire to back him to the limit. Damon Runyon, no doubt feeling rather uncomfortable so far from Broadway, visited Landon in Topeka and published the "Horse and Buggy Governor" in *Cosmopolitan.* The veteran sob sister, Adela Rogers St. John, abandoned ax murders and vivisection and undertook to make the Landons "the best-loved family in America." The country was flooded with pictures of Landon at home, Landon with his dog, Landon in the oilfields, Landon at his desk, the Landons in the nursery, in the kitchen, and in every possible situation except, as one observer acidly remarked, "skinning the cat atop the state building."

Landon, to avoid creating factional bitterness and making commitments to local leaders, planned not to enter the primaries. He was, however, entered in several without his consent. He easily won in Massachusetts and overwhelmed Borah in New Jersey. Borah took Wisconsin, defeated Knox in Illinois, and was himself defeated in Ohio by favorite son Robert A. Taft. By convention time, Landon had an estimated 400 delegates and, even though New York and Pennsylvania were uncommitted, was expected to win on the first ballot.

The Republicans gathered in Cleveland for their convention on June 9. It was a very different meeting from the dispirited convention of four years earlier. The band played "Oh, Susanna," the Landon song, and "Onward Christian Soldiers" over and over. The latter perhaps summed up the mood of most of the delegates. Most of the country might be for the New Deal, but the Republicans had met to save the nation from the horrors of socialism by nominating a man of whom it was said by one delegate, "God has His hand on Alf Landon's shoulder."

Senator Frederick Steiwer of Oregon, as temporary chairman, reflected the Republican mood in his keynote address. "The chief reason for the present unemployment in this Country is the blocking of the progress of the American system by trying out plans and ideas borrowed from the poverty economies of Europe. . . . Not content to employ professors and theorists as economic advisors the New Deal has placed the affairs of government in their hands. It depends on bookworms for practical experience and on bookworms for energy. . . . This is the only administration in our history which has deliberately impaired private credit, destroyed confidence and intimidated capital. . . ." He bravely concluded, "We will again force recognition of the one great fact: that the most precious privilege of citizenship under the American flag is the right to seek and obtain merited reward, unhampered, unrestrained and unafraid."

Herbert Hoover addressed the convention on the second day. He received a great ovation, now that the party was free of the embarrassing necessity of having him for a candidate. Hoover denounced Roosevelt as a dictator and exhorted his listeners to lead a holy crusade for freedom that would recapture the citadels of liberty. After the backward-looking former President left the hall, Mrs. Benjamin Harrison was introduced to the delegates.

The nomination was easily settled. John D. M. Hamilton presented Landon's name, praising him as a self-made man, a friend of the farmer, and one who "met his payrolls." Of his record, Hamilton said, "Here is a record of a modern American—unpretentious, unassuming, willing to serve—but not eager to dictate. Here is a homely record, if you will, and here are homely virtues and common-sense answers."

Any question of opposition to Landon was settled when Vandenberg, Frank Knox, and Robert A. Taft arose to second the nomination. A single ballot saw Landon nominated with 984 votes to 19 for Borah.

The vice-presidency was settled almost as easily. The first potential candidate eliminated was the conservative Governor of New Hampshire, Styles Bridges. In a discussion of his availability, someone remarked, "Landon-Bridges falling down," and that settled that. The Landon forces agreed on Senator Vandenberg, who reluctantly agreed to accept if the nomination were offered by acclamation. As soon as he heard that Pennsylvania was going to offer Frank Knox, Vandenberg withdrew with relief, and Knox was nominated without opposition.

Herbert Hoover expressed the party's hopes when he was asked to comment on the ticket. "For a year and a half I have been conducting a crusade vital to the American people to regenerate real, individual freedom in the United States. The election of Governor Landon is the next step to the attainment of the purpose." It was such attitudes that would sweep Maine and Vermont into the Republican column in November.

"A son of all the 48 states"

THE TWENTY-SEVENTH DEMOCRATIC
NATIONAL CONVENTION
Philadelphia, June 23, 1936

The Democratic National Convention of 1936, beginning in Philadelphia on June 23, was, without question, the most unlikely convention of Democrats ever assembled. There were no suicidal quarrels, no debates, no roll calls, and no question about the ticket. All the delegates were for Roosevelt and the New Deal—any Democrats who were not were either joining the Republican Party or fuming privately at home.

The one major event of the convention occurred during the evening session on the third day. The rules committee offered as one of the rules, "That all questions, including the question of nominations of candidates for President and Vice President of the United States, shall be determined by a majority vote of the delegates of the convention, and the rule heretofore existing in Democratic conventions requiring a two thirds vote in such cases is hereby specifically abrogated." There was a kind of justice in the presentation of this rule to the convention by Senator Clark, whose father had, in 1912, been denied the nomination by that very two-thirds rule. To reward the South for finally giving up its cherished veto power, the rules recommended a bonus system of choosing delegates, which would, in future conventions, give the southerners more votes than they had previously had.

On the fourth day, after a nominating speech that described him as "no longer a citizen merely of one state, but a son of all the 48 states" and fifty-eight seconding speeches, Roosevelt was renominated by acclamation. Garner, befitting his secondary position, was allowed only seventeen seconding speeches but was also nominated by acclamation.

CHAPTER 19

"Guests, hell! We're the People!"

THE TWENTY-SECOND REPUBLICAN
NATIONAL CONVENTION
Philadelphia, June 24, 1940

The election of 1936 was a triumph of unprecedented proportions for Franklin D. Roosevelt and the Democratic Party, but the almost monolithic power and popularity of the administration lasted only from the election until the opening of Congress. The coalition of western Democrats and southerners that had made possible much of the legislation of the preceding four years began to break up, and the Republocrat coalition—of Republicans and southern Democrats—improved the Republican position in Congress beyond what would be expected from their low numbers. The obstructionist faction in Congress, coupled with outrage at the plan to reorganize the Supreme Court, the recession in 1937, and severe labor troubles, all combined to increase Republican strength in the 1938 mid-term elections. The party gained six Senate seats, eighty-one House seats, and eleven governorships. The powerful states of Massachusetts, Ohio, and Pennsylvania returned to the Republican ranks.

The revival of Republican strength, an unsatisfactory recovery from the 1937 recession, the outbreak of war in Europe, and a widespread sentiment against breaking the third-term tradition gave the Republicans real hope for the presidential election of 1940. Nevertheless, the party had been so decimated of its old leaders that there were few men of national experience and reputation among the Republican aspirants.

The "big three" were Senator Arthur Vandenberg, Robert A. Taft, newly elected senator from Ohio, and the gangbusting District Attorney of New York, Thomas E. Dewey. Other Republicans mentioned a year before the convention included Governors Arthur James of Pennsylvania and John Bricker of Ohio, Congressman Joseph W. Martin, Jr., of Massachusetts, New York publisher Frank Gannett, and, as a very dark horse, the public-utility magnate, Wendell Willkie.

The young gangbuster, thirty-seven-year-old Thomas E. Dewey, was the early front-runner. His sensational activities as a special prosecutor investigating crime in New York had made him a national figure, and, while serving as district attorney, he had run for governor in 1938 against the incumbent Herbert Lehman. Dewey lost the race but came close enough to victory to become immediately a presidential prospect. His campaign for the nomination was officially opened on December 1, 1939, when J. Russell Sprague, Nassau County leader, announced that Dewey was the candidate of the state Republican organization. The young District Attorney declared that he would be glad to make the fight, prompting Harold Ickes to observe that Dewey had "thrown his diaper in the ring."

Lacking Taft's and Vandenberg's advantages of national offices from which to speak, Dewey took his campaign for delegates to the country. Guided by Sprague and Ruth Hanna McCormick Sims —Mark Hanna's astute daughter, who was as much the politician as her father had ever been—Dewey stumped the country, challenging his rivals in the primaries and traveling more than 25,000 miles. It is perhaps difficult, after more than twenty years, to think of Thomas E. Dewey as an exciting or romantic figure, but in 1940 the little man with the hairbrush mustache had all the glamour and popularity inspired by his crusade against crime and was, to thousands of voters, a composite of the Lone Ranger and Dick Tracy come to life.

In April, Dewey was catapulted to first place in the race when, to everyone's surprise including his own, he won a smashing victory over Vandenberg in the Wisconsin primary. He repeated his triumph in Nebraska, and his stock rose rapidly as Vandenberg's fell.

By June, his supporters were claiming 400-450 votes, while the Taft forces conceded him 279.

Senator Taft preferred to take his campaign to the politicians rather than to the voters. Although not yet "Mr. Republican," Taft already embodied many of the qualities and principles that endeared him to the Republican Party in every year that was not a convention year. His keen mind, frank conservatism, distinguished name, and record of party regularity made him popular among the older party leaders, especially in the South. His liabilities were his colorless personality, his poor speaking style, and the appearance of aiming for the White House before he had proved himself in the Senate. He left the rough and tumble of the primaries to others and showed his strength wherever delegates were chosen by state conventions. By convention time, he was claiming 328 delegates and was conceded 200 by the Dewey forces. Taft was confident that his loyalty to Republican principles would turn the convention to him after the first ballot.

The other candidates had little strength. Senator Vandenberg had only his own state delegation and a scattering elsewhere. He asserted he would win if his supporters held for five or six ballots— that is, if there were a deadlock. Frank Gannett took his own candidacy very seriously indeed. The sixty-three-year-old publisher was a bitter critic of the New Deal and gloried in his position as chairman of the National Committee to Uphold Constitutional Government. Backed by unlimited funds and his nineteen newspapers scattered throughout New York, New Jersey, Connecticut, and Illinois, he hoped to rally the more conservative elements of the party to his banner. His only real source of strength lay in the New York delegation. Led by Representative James W. Wadsworth and several upstate leaders opposed to Dewey, the Gannett forces managed to win 17 of the state's 92 votes. It was, however, too small a minority of the delegation to do Gannett much good, although it was enough to inconvenience Dewey.

In the spring of 1940, the race for the nomination seemed to be proceeding according to form. Dewey was conceded the greatest number of pledged delegates, Taft was second, and Vandenberg was rated an excellent prospect in case of a deadlock. But 1940 was not a typical convention year because of Wendell L. Willkie of Indiana and New York.

Willkie, born in 1892, was a large, rumpled man of expansive nature, ready wit, and boundless energy and drive. A career in corporation law had led him into the public-utility business, and in 1929 he became counsel for the Commonwealth and Southern, a newly formed giant holding company that controlled power companies from Michigan to Alabama. In four years, Willkie had moved up to the presidency of the corporation.

A Democrat, he had supported Roosevelt in 1932 but soon moved into opposition. He strenuously objected to what he considered the dominance of big government and believed that the New Deal was destroying initiative. His philosophy was best expressed in his argument that, "In the prewar years we fought against the domination of the people by Big Business. Now we face the domination of the people by Big Government. The liberal who fought against one kind of domination thirty-five years ago should find himself fighting against this new kind of domination today."

Willkie found his opportunity to fight big government when the newly formed Tennessee Valley Authority came into direct conflict with Commonwealth and Southern. Incisive and articulate, Willkie appeared before congressional committees to hit hard at the government's entry into the power business. At the height of his fight against T.V.A., *Fortune* magazine described Willkie in words that would, three years later, be used as the basis for a carefully worked-out image of a presidential candidate. "Wendell Willkie is the Mississippi Yankee, the clever bumpkin, the homespun, rail-splitting, cracker-barrel simplifier of national issues. He feels a dedication to the cause of private ownership; he knows all the arguments; they are persuasive on his tongue not because they are new but because he frames them intelligently and hence makes them sound new." Or as Willkie himself said, with what from anyone less candid would have sounded like cynicism, "It's an asset to my business to look like an Indiana farmer." Harold Ickes was perhaps closer to the truth when he cracked that Willkie was "just a simple barefoot Wall Street lawyer."

Through 1938 and 1939, Willkie made speaking engagements

and wrote a number of articles for national magazines—articles with such old-fashioned but effective titles as "Brace Up, America!," "The Faith That Is America," and "The New Fear." The enunciation of his philosophy made Willkie an exciting new figure to those Republicans who opposed the New Deal and who believed such statements, apparently written with absolute sincerity, as "No duty has ever come to me in my life, even that in the service of my country, which has so appealed to my sense of social obligation, patriotism, and love of mankind as this, my obligation to say and do what I can for the preservation of public utilities privately owned." He was a far cry from the man who had, as recently as 1929, called himself a LaFollette Republican and who had only changed his registration from Democratic to Republican in 1938, but it struck a responsive chord in many members of the Grand Old Party.

The first public mention of Willkie as a presidential candidate came from Arthur Krock, who wrote, on February 23, 1939, that his nomination would be a "highly improbable event." General Hugh S. Johnson wrote in his column that Willkie would make a powerful candidate if nominated and, if elected, a great president. Willkie replied, "If the government keeps on taking my business away at its present rate, I'll soon be out of work and looking for a job. Johnson's offer is the best I've had yet."

As 1940 opened, Willkie's candidacy was a matter of mere speculation. He told the press in January, "I am not running for President. Of course, it is not going to happen, but if the nomination were given to me without strings, I would have to accept it. But I couldn't go out and seek delegates and make two-sided statements. I value my independence."

Some Republicans were not so sure as Willkie that it was not going to happen. A businessman with an articulate philosophy and no connections with politics appealed to many people, and *Fortune* and the *Saturday Evening Post* began building the image of the newcomer, the fresh face, the man who did not want to be president but who would accept as a public duty.

A Willkie group began to form. Russell Davenport, managing editor of *Fortune*, took a leave of absence to devote his full time to managing the campaign. He was joined by financier Harold E.

Talbott, industrialist Charlton MacVeagh, and banker Frank Altschul, a former chairman of the Republican finance committee. MacVeagh scored a major coup by recruiting National Chairman John D. M. Hamilton to the Willkie cause, although, as national chairman, Hamilton had to remain ostensibly neutral for the time being.

Equally important recruits to the Willkie campaign came from a group not previously closely identified with presidential campaigns—the public-relations experts. The voluntary enlistment of the advertising men represented the first deliberate effort to manufacture, through modern advertising techniques, an artificial image for a candidate and opened the era of "instant images and packaged nominees." Working individually and in concert, they launched a massive campaign to sell Wendell Willkie to the people. Their job was to play down the corporation-lawyer and utilities-tycoon aspects of their product. Taking their cue from the *Fortune* article of 1937, they offered "a fascinating picture of a homespun, hardworking Indiana small-town boy; a carelessly dressed, friendly, Horatio Alger type, opposed in a mighty crusade to the Country Squire in the White House." To avoid the impression that any large sums of money were being spent in the campaign, newspapers were asked to reject several full-page advertisements offered by enthusiastic supporters. It was feared that the delegates would connect full-page ads with Wall Street and utility money, and the banker Frank Altschul, when he appeared at the convention, was asked to return to New York. Right up to the time of the nomination Willkie was presented as "just folks."

While money interests and public-relations experts formed one pillar of the Willkie campaign, another equally important source of strength came from the amateur volunteers. Wall Street could provide the money, Madison Avenue the image, but it remained for a twenty-nine-year-old lawyer to arouse the popular support.

In April, 1940, Oren Root, Jr., a nephew of the great Secretary of State, read "We, the People," a declaration of Willkie's principles. Impressed, he spent $40 to have copies printed with petitions endorsing Willkie's candidacy, which he sent to associates and friends. The response was spectacular. Root organized the first "Willkie for President" club and guided the establishment of similar

clubs throughout the country. Eager amateurs from what Tom
Dewey called the "station wagon set" flocked to the call, and thousands of young, middle-class Republicans, whose previous experience with grass roots had been limited to crab grass, found themselves in the vanguard of a great, spontaneous movement.

The Willkie campaign had, until May, 1940, been largely a
matter of publicity and volunteer activities. He had made no bid
for delegates, believing his wisest course to be to wait for a deadlock. But a speech in early May changed his thinking. He had been
invited to address a Republican dinner in St. Paul, Minnesota,
where he read a mediocre prepared speech that left the 700 attending Minnesota Republicans completely unmoved. Willkie, disgusted,
threw the speech into the air and, as the pages fluttered to the ballroom floor, said, "Some damn fool told me I had to read a speech
to you. Now let me tell you what I really think." He caught fire with
a free-swinging, rousing speech that had his listeners on their feet
cheering and shouting for more. He repeated the speech in Des
Moines with equally enthusiastic results and decided to change his
whole strategy. From early May until the convention, he made
speeches to political gatherings and was determined to meet every
delegate to the convention. He could, he was convinced, take the
nomination without a deadlock.

His campaign began to move with greater and greater speed.
There were nearly 500 Willkie clubs in existence, and requests for
Willkie buttons were running to 50,000 a day. Over 150,000 copies
of "Willkie's principles" were distributed, and Lewis Douglas,
former Director of the Budget, established a Democrats-for-Willkie
organization, stressing the fact that Willkie was a Democrat whom
the party had left. By the end of May, although he still had no
pledged delegates, Willkie was claiming the support of Governor
Vanderbilt and the Rhode Island delegation, as well as Connecticut's 16 votes. He had, he declared, made inroads in New Jersey,
Iowa, Indiana, Minnesota, and Missouri, as well as in New York,
where National Committeeman Kenneth F. Simpson was active in
his behalf.

The public-opinion polls showed an astonishing gain for the
man who had just begun to campaign. The poll of the American

Institute of Public Opinion, taken on May 8, showed Dewey leading with 67%, followed by Vandenberg with 14%, Taft with 12%, and Willkie with a mere 3%. By May 31, Willkie had 10% of expressed preferences, and on June 21, only three days before the opening of the convention, the poll showed Willkie with 29%—compared to 47% for Dewey and 8% each for Vandenberg and Taft. The businessman without political experience, the newcomer to the Republican Party, had gained 26% in only six weeks, with the major effort yet to come.

The twenty-second Republican National Convention was scheduled to open in Philadelphia on Monday, June 23, 1940. The German armies had swept through Norway and Denmark, Belgium, Luxembourg, and the Netherlands, and, on the day, before the convention opened, France had surrendered. The issue of aid to the allies, which so deeply divided the Republican Party, was overshadowed by the very real fear that in a short time there might be no allies to aid.

One aspect of the war and American defense that caused great discomfort to the Republicans was a spectacular defection within their own ranks. Only a few days before, President Roosevelt, in a master stroke to align the Grand Old Party with the administration's policies toward the war, had raided its ranks of elder statesmen and had named Henry L. Stimson as secretary of war and Frank Knox as secretary of the navy. Understandably, those who wished to see the GOP identified as the "peace party" were apoplectic with rage. Stimson and Knox were angrily read out of the party, and the isolationists determined to make a platform fight to condemn their apostasy.

Of more immediate concern was the final push by the candidates for the nomination. Taft's headquarters occupied 102 rooms in the Benjamin Franklin Hotel, and the Vandenberg managers had forty-eight rooms at the Adelphia. Frank Gannett occupied the Harvard Club and spilled over into forty-eight rooms in the Benjamin Franklin. Seventy-eight rooms at the Walton were deemed sufficient to house the Dewey forces, and outside the hotel stood a huge auto trailer, with kitchen, bath, and a bedroom of seven beds for the convenience of "Guests of the Thomas E. Dewey committee." The

National Committee luxuriated in the entire fifth floor of the Bellevue-Stratford. Wendell Willkie occupied a two-room suite at the Benjamin Franklin.

But Willkie's ostentatious lack of ostentation did not leave him without facilities for campaign headquarters. The candidate's "poor boy from Indiana" image was satisfied with two rooms, while the Willkie clubs had spacious headquarters in an office building and an entire store a block from Willkie's hotel. The money was being spent but not on the candidate himself.

Willkie arrived in Philadelphia on Saturday, June 22. When reporters asked where his entourage was, he replied, "I haven't any," and declared that his headquarters were "under my hat." Asked if he would consider the vice-presidency, he drawled, "Politics isn't a career with me, and if I can't win the presidential nomination I would just as soon go back to my old job."

Leaving the station, Willkie went to the Willkie clubs' headquarters and then led a large, cheering crowd down Broad Street toward his hotel. Swinging along with an easy stride, forelock disarranged, grinning and waving to the crowds, Wendell Willkie set off the excitement that would build steadily into an avalanche of enthusiasm as the week progressed. His natural friendliness and good nature and his high spirits infected everyone he met. As he passed the Union League Club, members "of this staid institution pressed to the open windows and gave the marchers a sedate cheer." Arriving at the Bellevue-Stratford Hotel, he headed straight for the bar. Candidate for the presidency or not, Willkie had no inhibitions about drinking, and he happily downed two whiskies and soda while wisecracking with the delighted crowd. He then went out onto the street again and walked up and down shaking hands. It was a performance that must have made stiffer men—like Taft and Dewey—sick with envy.

For all the triumph of his impromptu parade up and down Broad Street, Willkie was not universally accepted. Older Republicans resented the intrusion of the newcomer whose unorthodox methods threatened to take the prize from life-long servers of the party. Cranky old Senator Jim Watson bluntly expressed the feelings that Willkie would have to overcome. Meeting him in the lobby of the Bellevue-Stratford, Willkie asked the former Senator why he would not support him. Watson looked him straight in the eye and said, "You have been a Democrat all your life. I don't mind the church converting a whore, but I don't like her to lead the choir the first night!"

The isolationists began to organize against Willkie. On Sunday, June 23, Ezra Whitla, a Dewey supporter and national committeeman from Idaho, called a meeting of delegates from thirteen western states and Alaska. Resolutions were adopted denouncing reciprocal tariffs and opposing American intervention in any European or Asiatic war. The next day, forty-five members of the House and Senate held a meeting to oppose Willkie's nomination. After the meeting, eight congressmen, including Harold Knutson of Minnesota and Karl Mundt of South Dakota, signed a resolution urging the delegates to "nominate a candidate for President whose personal views will present an opportunity for a clear-cut vote on foreign and domestic issues in harmony with the Republican record in Congress."

The opposition to Willkie was formidable but shortsighted; it carried within it the seeds of defeat. Despite the great popular upsurge of support, the professionals and the pundits refused to take the Willkie threat as seriously as they should have. That a candidate without any apparent organization, without experience, and, most important, without any pledged delegates could pose a serious threat seemed a violation of all the rules of politics. It was the misfortune of the other candidates that they did not realize until too late that the rules had been changed.

When Dewey and Taft were asked to join forces for a stop-Willkie movement, both refused. Together they had better than 500 votes—enough to prevent Willkie's nomination—but Dewey would not accept second place on the ticket, and Taft believed that he would eventually be nominated.

Similarly, Vandenberg believed that the contest would be between Willkie and himself and would result in his own eventual victory. When Dewey offered him the vice-presidency, Vandenberg refused. Through Styles Bridges, he offered the vice-presidency to Dewey with a pledge to serve but one term, giving Dewey the inside track for 1944. He then said, "if this is too much for him to swallow all at once, I'll make him a sporting proposition. I'll meet him at eleven o'clock and flip a coin to see which end of the ticket we each take." Vandenberg heard no more from Dewey.

Willkie, meanwhile, received his first pledged delegates. Governor Baldwin, in return for a promise of the vice-presidential nomination, agreed to withdraw as Connecticut's favorite son and to deliver his 16 votes to Willkie.

Harold Stassen delivered the keynote address at the convention's first evening session on Monday, June 24, and then, freed from the necessity for neutrality, called on Willkie at 1:00 a.m. Tuesday morning. For an hour they discussed Willkie's state-by-state support, and Stassen agreed to support him on the condition that he be made the floor manager. On Wednesday, Stassen announced to the press, "After weighing all the factors and in view of the critical situation facing this country, . . . I have decided to cast my vote on the first ballot for Willkie because I believe him best fitted for leadership in utilizing our mass-production system and preparing to make this country safe for any eventuality." He then selected his floor organization. Among the twelve floor leaders chosen were Charles Halleck, Sinclair Weeks, Walter Hallanan, and Governors Baldwin, Vanderbilt, and Carr of Colorado.

Much was made at the time and later of the fact that Willkie had no organization until the day of the nominating speeches. In fact, Arthur Krock, writing after Willkie's death, told how he had had to explain, two days before the convention opened, why Willkie would need a floor leader. The candidate seemed, to Krock, to be completely innocent of the workings of the convention. Willkie had, however, attended other conventions and had worked actively for Baker at the Democratic convention of 1932. His wide-eyed innocence was obviously his little joke for Krock's benefit. In fact, he remarked after Krock left him, "Someday they will write about how naive I was, but I didn't want to spoil their illusions." Actually, even though the formal Willkie organization was not given final shape until Wednesday, the members of the floor organization had, with the exception of Stassen, been active in the Willkie cause for some time. The impression that the Willkie organization sprang up almost overnight was simply another element in the carefully created amateur, nonpolitical image of the candidate.

Once the convention opened, the Willkie drive was characterized by an unprecedented outpouring of popular support. From the first gavel stroke, the chant of "We Want Willkie," which would grow in intensity through the following days, roared from the galleries, and the barrage of telegrams increased until the delegates were, at times, literally knee-deep in demands for Willkie's nomination. Between Saturday and Tuesday nights, nearly one million messages were delivered, and Kenneth Simpson alone received more than 100,000 telegrams, letters, and cards supporting Willkie. Lawyers received telegrams from their clients, and businessmen were pressured by their customers and creditors. The volume became so enormous that it overwhelmed the opposition's charge that the messages were prepared and directed from a central source. As Oren Root said, "There was absolutely no one directing it. There couldn't have been, it was too colossal!"

Everywhere the delegates went they were confronted with "We Want Willkie." Not even their clothes were safe. Suits returned by the hotel valet had campaign literature in every pocket; laundry packages came back with "Vote for Willkie" emblazoned in stickers; and one delegate found a Willkie pamphlet in his pajama pocket.

The "We Want Willkie" chant from the galleries became increasingly maddening to the opposition. When it was discovered that Samuel Pryor, chairman of the committee on arrangements, had packed the galleries by issuing thousands of tickets to the Willkie supporters, there were angry demands that new doormen be put in the galleries to prevent the use of the unauthorized tickets. Pryor piously replied to the charges by maintaining that he had merely issued standing-room tickets to anyone who wanted them. "Those tickets went to the average people on the street who, I knew, were ardent supporters of Wendell Willkie. . . . A political party belongs to the people; it is not a country club not a private organization. The people had every right to be there."

While the galleries chanted inside the convention, Alf Landon and the platform committee wrestled with the foreign-policy plank. The Republicans were united in their desire to fight the New Deal and the third term. They were far from united in a desire to fight a war in Europe. Willkie was uncompromisingly in favor of all possible aid to the Allies. Dewey and Taft, while not insisting on an isolationist platform, had so vacillated in their statements on foreign policy that the delegates were unsure of what sort of platform they wanted.

Before the convention, a majority of the platform committee, speaking in preliminary hearings, seemed to favor unlimited aid to the Allies "short of war." Pro-Ally Alf Landon was named to head a subcommittee on national defense and foreign policy. In the uproar over Roosevelt's appointment of Stimson and Knox to the Cabinet, Landon's progress toward a pro-aid plank was seriously threatened. National Chairman Hamilton, when he read the two new cabinet members out of the party, shrilly cried, "the Democratic party has become the war party," which of necessity forced the Republicans to become the "peace party."

Landon and his subcommittee labored grimly to write a keep-out-of-war plank that would be acceptable to those who favored intervention. In despair, the subcommittee proposed to leave the whole question up to the nominee, but the isolationists defeated the proposal. C. Wayland Brooks of Illinois and Senator Henry Cabot Lodge, Jr., of Massachusetts argued against any plank endorsing aid to the Allies, and the harried Landon finally offered a compromise. Shortly before midnight on Wednesday, June 26, the subcommittee agreed that the Roosevelt administration was responsible for unpreparedness in defense and that "we shall support all necessary and proper defense measures proposed by the Administration in its belated effort to make up for lost time." At Landon's insistence, the plank also stated, "We favor the extension to the Allies . . . of such aid as shall not be in violation of international law or inconsistent with the requirements of our own national defense." The isolationists argued that Britain was the only nation still at war with Germany and that we were not her ally. The statement was therefore amended to read, "We favor the extension to all peoples fighting for liberty, or whose liberty is threatened, of such aid . . ." etc. It was a plank that, as H. L. Mencken snorted, "is so written that it will fit both the triumph of democracy and the collapse of democracy, and approve both sending arms to England or sending only flowers."

The platform, as presented to the convention on June 26, included the conglomeration of generalities, fatuous platitudes, and denunciations that is characteristic of any political document designed to offend no one within the party and to concede no virtues to the opposition. It was scathingly inaccurate in its attacks on the administration, pious in its declarations of good will and promises of future glories under the Republican banner, and forthright in its conviction that only the Republican Party could save the nation. It was, in short, very much like the Democratic platform with the labels reversed.

After adopting the platform, the convention began the roll call for the nominations. Dewey led off the list of candidates in a speech by John Lord O'Brian of New York, who promised that Dewey "can be trusted to keep us out of war." The speaker neatly sidestepped the fact that Dewey had been defeated for the governorship in 1938 by claiming that of five million votes he had lacked only 65,000 of winning, "and 100,000 of those who voted against him were Communists." In conclusion, O'Brian spoke of this thirty-eight-year-old candidate, who had never held elective office, in terms that indicated previously unsuspected possibilities in the role of "gangbuster." "He is known the world over as one of the great outstanding Americans of his time because his candor and courage have brought to him the confidence and the faith of his fellow-men. His election will bring fresh hope to a world distraught. His high-minded and able service as President will renew the spirit of America as a beaconlight for the guidance of free men everywhere."

Frank Gannett was nominated in a speech by Representative Wadsworth, who praised the publisher's business background, sense of thrift, and steadfast opposition to the New Deal. At the conclusion, he received a two-minute round of applause, which must have been small recompense for the half-million dollars Gannett had poured into his candidacy.

Grove Patterson, editor of the Toledo *Blade*, presented Taft. He took a subtle swipe at Willkie by complimenting Taft: "His record is irreproachable. He is the candidate invulnerable. He has always been a Republican," which was boisterously received by the delegates, and he constantly reiterated, "He is an amazing vote getter." But the strength and weakness of the Taft candidacy, now and in the future, was summed up early in the speech. Taft, said Patterson, had a program. "That program is built to turn back a tragic march

382 "Guests, hell! We're the People!"

toward an 'equalitarian destitution'—this barefoot crusade in which
the New Deal is attempting to lead us all to a secure poverty." It
was the phrase "turn back" that unfortunately came to characterize
the Taft philosophy.

Finally came the moment the galleries had been waiting for.
They had, for the most part, held off their chanting during the
speeches for the other candidates, but, as the moment drew near
for Willkie's nomination, "We Want Willkie" began once again to
shake the hall. The politicians on the floor must have experienced
involuntary shudders when, after Joe Martin demanded that, as
guests of the convention, the galleries mind their manners, a voice
shot back, "Guests, hell! We're the People!" The people they were,
and it was enough to frighten the wheelhorses of any party.

Willkie did not depend on the nominating speech of Charlie
Halleck to stampede the convention. In view of the thundering
galleries, the speech delivered by the brash, cocky Halleck was very
nearly superfluous. As soon as Halleck had finished, pandemonium
swept the galleries. In louder and louder waves, "We Want Willkie"
crashed down upon the delegates. But on the floor no one moved.
Even Indiana remained in its place. Then a Willkie delegate
grabbed the New York standard and began to march around the
hall, and other delegates fell into line. The twenty-minute demonstration, which had not been planned, was more impressive to radio
listeners, who could hear the frenzied roar of the galleries, than it
was to the delegates on the floor.

The chanting continued with hypnotic insistence through the
seconding speeches for Willkie, and, after adjournment, the delegates left the chanting of the galleries to enter streets and hotels
jammed with fervent, shouting Willkie partisans, to put on pajamas
stuffed with Willkie literature, to brush the flood of Willkie telegrams off the beds, and to collapse and dream, no doubt, of being
pursued by raging, insistent Willkie volunteers.

One delegate who did not go immediately to bed was Alf
Landon. The Kansas delegation was pledged to Arthur Capper as
a favorite son and had agreed to vote for him on the first two
ballots. After that, it would be time to select another candidate.
Landon did not favor Willkie but had not made up his mind whom
to support. Before leaving for Philadelphia, he had talked by phone

to at least two-thirds of the Kansas county leaders, who told him "Anyone but Taft." Whether it would be Dewey, Vandenberg, Willkie, or a dark horse was left up to Landon.

Wednesday night Arthur Krock came to Landon's room to suggest that he meet Willkie. "A situation might arise tomorrow where you would want to act quickly and you ought to make sure that there will be nothing that would develop in the campaign that would embarrass your party." Landon agreed and asked Roy Roberts to bring the candidate to see him.

There had been rumors that Willkie, while a utilities lawyer in Ohio, had exerted undue pressure on the state legislature and had carried "a black satchel to the Ohio legislature." Landon thoroughly cross-examined Willkie about this story and was satisfied with his categorical denial. But Dewey was his first choice, and he saw no reason for switching to Willkie.

The climactic day of the convention—Thursday, June 27—began with an anticlimax. After the thunderous demonstration for Willkie the night before, the convention continued with the nomination of more candidates. Hanford MacNider of Iowa, Senator Vandenberg, Senator Styles Bridges, Senator McNary of Oregon, Governor James of Pennsylvania, and Governor Harlan J. Bushfield of South Dakota were placed in nomination. The convention then recessed.

The results of the first ballot bore out the belief that it was anybody's convention. Neither Taft nor Dewey did so well as they had expected, and Willkie did much better than had been predicted. The first ballot was Dewey 360, Taft 189, Willkie 105, Vandenberg 76, James 74, Joe Martin 44, McNider 34, Gannett 33, Bridges 28, Capper 18, Hoover 17, McNary 13, and Bushfield 9.

Dewey received votes from thirty-seven of the fifty-three delegations, with majorities in seventeen. Taft had support in thirty-two delegations but majorities in only five. Willkie was represented in twenty-five delegations, with only Connecticut solid, but significantly he had twelve votes from New Jersey, 0 from Indiana, and 7 from California.

Willkie's position improved dramatically on the second ballot. He gained 66 votes for a total of 171, while Dewey lost 22 for 338. The results of the second ballot were Dewey 338, Taft 203, Willkie 171, Vandenberg 73, MacNider 34, Gannett 30, James 66, Martin

26, Hoover 21, Capper 18, McNary 10, Bridges 9, and Fiorello LaGuardia 1. Although Willkie had made substantial gains and Dewey was fading, there was no clear indication of a trend to a single candidate. It was time for taking stock and, if possible, swinging a few deals, and the convention recessed until evening.

The Kansas delegation immediately went into caucus. Landon told the delegates that he could recall no instance in which a man who led on the first ballot and then lost on the second had been nominated. Personally, however, he intended to vote for Dewey. The delegation decided to scatter for a ballot or two, although ten delegates indicated a willingness to follow Landon to Dewey. The rest decided to go four for Wilkie, two for Taft, and one for Hoover.

Harold Stassen and Raymond Clapper, the newspaperman, were waiting for Landon outside the caucus room. Landon refused to tell Stassen anything except that he was voting for Dewey. Clapper asked if he thought Dewey would be nominated. When Landon replied, "No," Clapper exclaimed, "Well, I'll say that's going into a ditch for your man."

The Willkie forces exerted pressure during the recess, principally on New York, Pennsylvania, and Massachusetts. Joe Martin agreed to release his delegates but refused to release them specifically to Willkie. In spite of this refusal, the Willkie managers managed to swing twenty of the twenty-one delegates. The Gannett forces in New York were beginning to crack, and Kenneth Simpson was confident of picking up some of these votes.

Stassen was convinced that Joe Pew of Pennsylvania was ready to reach an accommodation over Governor James's 72 votes. Stassen told Willkie, "You are gambling with the biggest thing you've ever gambled with . . . Shall I have a talk with Joe Pew?" Willkie thought for a moment and then said, "No." He wanted no deals with the boss of Pennsylvania and believed he could win without the Keystone State.

The convention reconvened at 8:30 p.m. to take the third ballot. Willkie jumped into second place with a gain of 88 votes for a total of 259. Taft gained 9 votes, and Dewey lost 23. The results were Dewey 315, Willkie 259, Taft 212, Vandenberg 72, James 59, Hoover 32, MacNider 28, Gannett 11, McNary 10, and Bridges 1.

Willkie's largest gains came from Massachusetts (20), New York (14), and Pennsylvania (10). The 10 Pennsylvania votes gave rise to hopes that Joe Pew would be willing to swing the entire delegation. Accordingly, Governor Baldwin tried to convince Pew to switch. He refused, and Willkie, when informed, succinctly dismissed Pennsylvania by saying, "Pew be damned!"

Willkie had reason for confidence. On the fourth ballot, he gained 47 votes to take the lead at 306. Taft followed with 254, a gain of 42, and Dewey slipped to third place with 250. The others were Vandenberg 61, James 56, Hoover 31, MacNider 26, McNary 8, Gannett 4, and Bridges 1.

Before the fifth ballot, Landon went up to the platform to speak to Joe Martin. "If this convention doesn't recess," Landon said, "Willkie will be nominated." "Alf," replied Martin, "we agreed before the convention that for the sake of the party we ought to make a nomination from the floor. I think we should stick to it." "All right, Joe," said Landon, "that means that Willkie will be nominated."

Unwilling to support Taft and realizing that both Dewey and Vandenberg were out of the running, Landon decided to swing to Willkie. The alternative, he knew, would be a "smoke filled room nomination," which he did not want. The Kansas delegation agreed to follow Landon. Although this decision meant only 13 more votes, it had an importance beyond the delegate strength. That the 1936 standard-bearer would come out for the man so recently a Democrat was of psychological importance and gave Willkie, as it were, his official membership card in the Republican Party.

The fifth ballot began under tremendous tension, which built steadily as it became apparent that Willkie and Taft were entering the final phase of a neck-and-neck race. Dewey had collapsed completely, and his votes began going to the two leaders. The Kansas switch brought a great cheer from the galleries, and then Willkie received a tremendous boost when the Dewey New York votes split 40 for Willkie, 5 for Taft.

As the delegations continued to split between the Senator and the utility tycoon, the tension became unbearable. Joe Martin saw a welcome excuse to relieve it when the chairman of the North Dakota delegation announced, "North Dakota casts four votes for

Senator Taft and four votes for Vendell Villkie." "For who?"
Martin innocently inquired. "For Vendell Villkie," came the reply.
"Spell it," requested the Permanent Chairman. The tension-breaking
laugh that swept the auditorium was, as Martin said, "the most
welcome laughter I have ever heard."

The results of the fifth ballot showed Willkie gaining 123 votes
for a total of 429—71 short of nomination—while Taft gained exactly the same number for 377. The others were James 59, Dewey
57, Vandenberg 42, Hoover 20, McNary 9, MacNider 4, and Gannett
1. When the results were announced, the galleries, now joined by
many delegates, redoubled their cries of "We Want Willkie!" Joe
Martin shouted back, "Well, if you'll be quiet long enough maybe
you'll get him."

John Bricker, Taft's manager, rushed to the platform to beg
Martin to entertain a motion to adjourn. It was his last frantic hope
that an overnight recess would give the Taft men time to arrange a
coalition to stop Willkie. Martin protested that he had already
asked the convention to prepare for the next ballot and that such
a motion would be out of order.

Landon emerged from the milling mass of men on the platform
to tell Martin that, if the convention were recessed, Martin might
have a chance of emerging as the candidate of a deadlocked convention. In such an event, Landon said, he would support him. "But
the rules are clear," Martin replied. "We have to go on. Anyway
I don't know whether the nomination would do me any good, because under the circumstances I would be the choice of smoke filled
rooms. It would take me two months to get over that stigma. By
that time the campaign would be lost."

As the sixth ballot began, events backstage were rapidly moving
to a climax. Vandenberg, learning that he could no longer keep
Michigan in line, decided to withdraw. Frank McKay, national committeeman from Michigan, and two local bosses met John D. M.
Hamilton on the platform. Would Willkie, they wanted to know,
give the state organization the right to name federal judges if
Michigan swung to him, or would that patronage be given to the
Willkie clubs? Hamilton told them that only Willkie could answer
such a question. McKay went to Samuel Pryor's desk and asked
him to call Willkie. To Hamilton's suprise, Willkie readily agreed

that McKay, along with the state leaders, could choose the judges.

When Michigan was called, Vandenberg's manager withdrew his name and voted Willkie 35, Taft 2, Hoover 1. The roar of triumph from the galleries set off a landslide for Willkie. From all over the auditorium, votes were changed as quickly as the Permanent Chairman could recognize the waving, shouting delegates. The results of the sixth ballot as officially announced were Willkie 998, 2 votes absent. The convert was going to lead the choir after all.

All that remained was the selection of a running mate. Governor Baldwin had been promised the vice-presidential nomination, but the party leaders decided that the ticket needed a better geographical balance. Bowing to the age-old cry of "for the good of the party," Governor Baldwin stepped aside. In the early-morning hours after the nomination, Willkie, Samuel Pryor, Styles Bridges, and other members of the Willkie high command gathered to balance the ticket. Their choice of Senator McNary of Oregon made for a very odd balance indeed.

Willkie was an internationalist pledged to the cause of all possible aid to the Allies; McNary was a leading isolationist who had even voted against repeal of the arms embargo. Willkie endorsed reciprocal trade agreements and lower tariffs; McNary was a high-tariff man. Willkie came to national fame fighting public ownership of utilities and T.V.A.; McNary favored the New Deal power program. Willkie was supremely confident of his ability to win the election; McNary was on record as predicting certain defeat if Willkie were the nominee. McNary, as a life-long Republican and party leader in the Senate, did, at least, help to offset Willkie's johnny-come-lately Republicanism.

On the final day of the convention, the die-hard conservatives, who believed that McNary's support of several New Deal policies made him too liberal, placed Dewey Short of Missouri in nomination. It was impossible, however, to overcome Willkie's endorsement, and McNary was nominated with 890 votes to 108 for Short and 2 for Styles Bridges.

"I could not in these times refuse"

THE TWENTY-EIGHTH DEMOCRATIC
NATIONAL CONVENTION
Chicago, July 15, 1940

At the annual Gridiron Club dinner, the newspapermen acknowledged the great question facing the Democratic Party in 1940 by unveiling a large pâpier-maché sphinx, which sported a jaunty cigarette holder. The riddle of the Democratic sphinx dominated all party thinking. Would he or wouldn't he? Would Roosevelt, even with his enormous popularity, dare to challenge the third-term tradition? Grant had tried and failed. Another Roosevelt had tried and failed. What would the Democratic Roosevelt do?

The President himself did nothing to throw light on the question. He evaded it in news conferences and talked wistfully in private of his desire to retire. Actually, Roosevelt had still not made up his mind well into the spring of 1940. He wanted a third term; he also wanted to retire. Until he made his decision, he followed two courses of action. One was to allow the party leaders to form a draft movement that would dominate the convention if he should decide to run. The second course was to encourage other candidacies, especially that of Cordell Hull, so as to leave open a line of retreat if he should decide not to run.

Hull's candidacy was especially useful. The Secretary of State was, Roosevelt intimated to nearly everyone but Hull himself, his choice for the nomination. Hull was not particularly anxious for the nomination and, believing that if it came to him it would come through the President, made no effort to enlist support. His possible candidacy depended entirely upon Roosevelt, which would make him no candidate at all if Roosevelt chose to run.

Two men who decided to be candidates were Vice-President Garner and Postmaster General Jim Farley. They refused to wait, as did Hull, for a presidential laying on of hands and determined to seek delegates to the convention. Garner filed in the primaries in Wisconsin, Illinois, California, and Oregon and contested for the New York State convention endorsement. Farley, after obtaining Roosevelt's permission, filed for the Massachusetts primary. He had been careful not to ask the President for an endorsement of his candidacy but merely asked if Roosevelt had any objection to his bidding for the Massachusetts delegation.

Roosevelt, although he gave permission for Farley to file in Massachusetts, was opposed to his candidacy, even if he himself should decide to retire. Ernest K. Lindley published an article purporting to set forth the President's attitude toward the third term and the various candidates. Roosevelt, the article said, would not run again unless Britain fell to the Nazis, and Hull was his choice to succeed him. Senator Wheeler, Paul McNutt, and Attorney General Robert Jackson would be the chief contenders for the vice-presidency. Farley, the President had said, according to Lindley, was not a sound candidate because of his Catholicism.

The bluff Postmaster General was deeply hurt by this statement, and it marked the real beginning of the deep estrangement that would embitter his relations with Roosevelt in the future. The President, when questioned, at first said he had not read the article and later denied the entire story, but the damage had been done.

Even though the President was enigmatic about his plans, he had no difficulty in winning the primaries in which Garner challenged him. In Wisconsin, Garner won two delegates, but Roosevelt beat him 3 to 1 in the popular vote. Illinois went for Roosevelt by more than a million votes to less than 200,000 for Garner, while in California the President defeated the Vice-President 6 to 1. It was the same story in Oregon, where the primary voters favored Roosevelt 7 to 1. The only sure support pledged to Garner came from Texas, but even there Sam Rayburn had to arrange a compromise between the Garner and Roosevelt forces. To stave off the possibility that Roosevelt's supporters would push through an uninstructed delegation, Rayburn had to agree to Garner's being presented as a favorite son—a considerable come-down for a serious candidate.

Farley had little better luck. Massachusetts was instructed for him but by no means solidly, and he had considerable minority support in New York, which had ignored Garner's bid for support. South Dakota picked a slate favorable to Farley but unpledged. In the event of Roosevelt's announcing his candidacy, most of this strength could be expected to evaporate.

In a last-minute effort to patch up their differences and, if possible, to prevent Farley from going before the convention, Roosevelt invited him to Hyde Park in early July. Roosevelt told Farley that he did not want to run, and Farley replied that in that case he should issue a "General Sherman statement." Roosevelt, "his right hand clasping the arm of his chair as he leaned back, his left bent at the elbow to hold his cigarette, his face and eyes deadly earnest," said, "Jim, if nominated and elected, I could not in these times refuse to take the inaugural oath, even if I knew I would be dead within thirty days." Farley knew Roosevelt meant it and that he would be the candidate.

The convention that met in Chicago's Stadium on Monday, July 15, was confused and dispirited. Without leadership, the delegates were worried. No delegate really likes an open convention, and a convention without leadership—almost without a candidate—was a nightmare. Unhappily the delegates gathered in little knots in the Stadium, the bars, and the hotel lobbies, waiting to be told what to do. There was no word from Roosevelt; Ickes, Mayor Kelly, even Harry Hopkins, had received no instructions. Hopkins had a direct wire to the White House—the telephone had been installed in his bathroom to ensure privacy—but it was more to keep the President informed than to receive instructions. Roosevelt was insistent on a draft movement in which he would play no part, but he had a little surprise prepared to help the draft along.

On Tuesday night, Senator Barkley delivered the keynote address in his best Kentucky stump style. Then he sprang Roosevelt's surprise. He had, said the Senator, a message from the

President. "I and other close friends of the President have long known that he has no wish to be a candidate again. We know, too, that in no way whatsoever has he exerted any influence in the selection of delegates, or upon the opinion of, delegates to this convention.

"Tonight, at the specific request and authorization of the President, I am making this simple fact clear to this convention.

"The President has never had, and has not today, any desire or purpose to continue in the office of President, to be a candidate for that office, or to be nominated by the convention for that office.

"He wishes in all earnestness and sincerity to make it clear that all of the delegates to this convention are free to vote for any candidate."

The delegates were stunned. Apparently Roosevelt had released his delegates. Had he taken himself out of the race?

Before the uncertainty of the delegates could become panic, a thunderous voice roared from the loudspeakers, "We Want Roosevelt!" A few delegates moved into the aisles, echoing the cry. "Everybody Wants Roosevelt!" thundered the voice. More delegates took up the cry. Soon a full-scale demonstration, dominated by the voices of the loudspeakers, was roaring its way around the hall, banners waving and bands playing. Before a microphone in the basement of the Stadium, Boss Kelly's superintendent of sewers, carefully coached in his role, continued to roar in leather-lunged enthusiasm for Roosevelt. The demonstration set off by Kelly's careful arrangements went on for an hour. It might be assumed the delegates were cheering from relief. They were no longer in any doubt; they knew what was expected of them.

On Wednesday, July 17, Roosevelt was placed in nomination by Senator Lister Hill of Alabama. Aged and ailing Senator Carter Glass, in a rasping voice that could barely be heard by the delegates, placed Jim Farley in nomination, and he was followed by nominations for Vice-President Garner, Cordell Hull, and Senator Millard Tydings. It was a pathetic show of opposition. On the one ballot taken, Roosevelt received 946 13/30 votes to 72 9/10 for Farley, 61 for Garner, 9½ for Tydings, and 5⅚ for Hull.

Roosevelt had his nomination, but the convention was not yet over, and there was trouble ahead. Many party leaders believed

that, since they had gone along with the President and given him
the nomination, they should have a free hand in selecting the vice-
presidential candidate. Garner, because his presidential candidacy
had estranged him from Roosevelt, was clearly eliminated.

Actively seeking the nomination were Secretary of Commerce
Jesse Jones, who had Farley's backing, Secretary of the Interior
Harold Ickes, Senator James F. Byrnes, Paul McNutt, Assistant
Secretary of War Louis Johnson, Senator Scott Lucas, Governor
Culbert Olson of California, and Speaker of the House William
Bankhead of Alabama. The President dropped a bombshell when
he passed the word that his choice was Secretary of Agriculture
Henry A. Wallace.

Upon hearing this news, the convention exploded into angry
revolt. Wallace, whose stauch liberalism appealed to Roosevelt, was
considered by many of the party leaders to be a mystical, impractical dreamer. They were convinced that his nomination would
be a disaster. Their attitude was summed up when the Governor
of Georgia turned to the Governor of Oklahoma to ask what he
thought of Wallace. "Why, Henry's my second choice," the Oklahoma Governor replied. When asked who his first choice might be,
he answered, "Anyone—red, white, black, or yellow—that can get
the nomination."

There was little, however, that the convention could do. All the
aspirants dropped out except McNutt and Bankhead. Still, it was
a near thing. The delegates were angry and rebellious, and Bankhead made a strong showing. What finally turned the tide for
Wallace was Roosevelt's threat not to accept the nomination if
Wallace were not nominated.

On the roll call Bankhead and Wallace ran extremely close
because several large delegations had passed. But these delegations swung to Wallace, who was nominated by 626 11/30 to
329 3/5 for Bankhead. Eleven other men received scattered support, including Paul McNutt, who, although he had withdrawn his
name just before the balloting, received 68 4/5 votes. The revolt
had been put down, and Roosevelt had the running mate of his
choice.

CHAPTER 20

"Calm, neat, painstaking and deadly efficient"

THE TWENTY-THIRD REPUBLICAN NATIONAL CONVENTION
Chicago, June 26, 1944

Dissatisfaction with the course of the war, a growing weariness of the long Democratic tenure in office, and the traditional mid-term gains of the minority party gave the Republicans their greatest strength since 1930. Especially encouraging to Republican prospects was the fact that in the major states, which would be most important in the presidential election—California, Illinois, Massachusetts, Michigan, Minnesota, New York, Ohio and Pennsylvania, totalling 207 electoral votes—were in Republican hands. In all, the Republicans controlled states totalling 279 electoral votes, which, if state control could be translated into electoral votes would give the Republicans 14 more votes than needed to oust the New Deal from power.

For a time after his defeat in 1940, Wendell Willkie was the leading candidate for the 1944 nomination. But his prospects were threatened by the opposition of most of the party's older leaders. Alf Landon, Colonel McCormick, John D. M. Hamilton—who was piqued because Willkie had not kept him on as National Chairman—oilman Joe Pew, Herbert Hoover, Senator Taft, and the conservatives stood between Willkie and the nomination. They had many reasons for opposing him. Some resented having been snubbed in the 1940 campaign; others were opposed to his internationalist ideas; still others distrusted him for personal reasons or because they did not believe he was a true Republican. Beside these men, who were against Willkie rather than for anyone else, were the leaders who preferred Thomas E. Dewey, Governor John W. Bricker, Harold Stassen, or the new war hero, General Douglas MacArthur.

While Willkie's popularity in the party declined, the new Governor of New York, Thomas E. Dewey, gained wide support. Dewey had pledged to serve his full term as governor and therefore could not be an avowed candidate. He refused to comment on rumors that he would make the race and finally began to issue statements, including one in which he said he intended to serve the people of New York for four years. In what capacity he carefully declined to state.

Although Dewey declined to be an active candidate, Edwin F. Jaeckle, the state chairman, and J. Russell Sprague, the boss of Nassau County, worked to create an atmosphere that would make a draft movement possible. Throughout 1943, Dewey was given national publicity and pictured as "calm, neat, painstaking and deadly efficient," which does not, at first glance, seem a very exciting way to describe a presidential candidate. But when one considers the short, dapper, youthful figure of the man described in a much quoted and deadly accurate phrase as "the groom on a wedding cake," it was, perhaps, the best that could be done.

By the end of 1943, Dewey seemed to be the most popular candidate with the party leaders. According to a poll of the 206 members of the House, eighty-nine expressed a preference for Dewey, while thirty were for MacArthur. Only six were for Willkie, and even Governors Bricker and Saltonstall drew more support. Alf Landon predicted in December that Dewey would be nominated not later than the second ballot and that Willkie's name would not even be placed before the convention.

Governor John Bricker became the leading conservative candidate. Senator Taft, having had his chance in 1940, agreed to leave the field to Ohio's other favorite son. The floridly handsome, silver-maned Governor operated on the assumption that Dewey could have the nomination if he wanted it and avoided primary contests. Traveling extensively, he, personally or through fourteen lieutenants, contacted most of the leading machine politicians throughout the country. IIis was a "campaign of friendliness" designed to make him the second-choice candidate should Dewey decline to run. Only Ohio was pledged to him, but he had considerable second-choice support.

General Douglas MacArthur became the favorite of a mixed group of conservatives, ranging from the respectable Senator Vandenberg and Joe Martin to the somewhat less reputable Father Coughlin. Many of the old America-First crowd also enlisted in the MacArthur cause. The General, already suffering from a strong Mount Rushmore complex, which would become more virulent in later years, was delighted to be considered presidential timber. But enthusiasm cooled when the fantastic, but apparently accurate, story began to circulate that the General planned to accept a draft and, if elected, to stay on in his command in the Southwest Pacific while his vice-president—presumably Vandenberg—served as president pro tem.

Representative Everett Dirksen, of ample figure and mellifluous voice, announced in October, 1943, that thirty-six congressional colleagues from thirteen states had presented him with a petition urging him to try for the nomination. The Illinois Congressman was naturally flattered and denied that his candidacy was to be construed as part of the stop-Willkie campaign, even though thirty-five of the thirty-six petitioners were active in opposing Willkie's nomination.

Apart from the usual crop of favorite sons, chief of whom was the newly elected Governor of California, Earl Warren, the only other serious candidate was the young Governor of Minnesota, Harold Stassen. Stassen had won re-election in 1942 and had then resigned to serve as a naval officer in the Pacific. His youth—he was only thirty-six—and his absence from the country made his nomination unlikely. He was also handicapped in appealing most strongly to those elements of the party who were attracted to Willkie. His candidacy, although his few supporters were extremely enthusiastic, was considered to be more of a trial run for 1948 than a serious attempt to be the nominee in 1944.

Wendell Willkie behaved as if his nomination were a foregone conclusion. Never lacking in self-confidence, Willkie, who had become chairman of the Twentieth Century-Fox Film Corp., traveled to Los Angeles in late September, 1943. There he boldly announced to newsmen that he would receive 400 votes on the first ballot and listed his expected strength in each delegation.

Such bravado was too much for John D. M. Hamilton. In November, he set out to visit seventeen states. To each local leader he asked the same question: Had the delegation been pledged to Willkie? Upon denial he would produce from his briefcase the newspaper story assigning the delegation to Willkie. Hamilton put the resentment thus stirred up to good use. He advised the local leaders to encourage as many favorite sons as possible so that the party leaders could name their own candidate out of a deadlock. Hamilton's trip was so successful that he predicted in Denver that the nominee would come from among the twenty-four Republican governors and later stated that he had found Dewey among the candidates to have strength in every community he visited.

In February, the Willkie group, including Sinclair Weeks and Ralph Cake, a Portland banker and Oregon national committeeman, surveyed the situation and decided that Willkie should formally announce his candidacy in spite of a Gallup poll that showed Dewey leading Willkie 42% to 23%. Willkie was confident that he could overcome this apparent lack of popularity by waging whirlwind primary fights.

But the primaries presented certain difficulties. Willkie believed his greatest strength to be on the West Coast, especially in California, where local polls showed him running ahead of Dewey and Warren. But Governor Warren was firm in his intent to head a favorite-son delegation, and the California primary was closed to Willkie. The Pennsylvania primary was also closed. Governor Edward Martin announced that the state organization would oppose any attempt by Willkie or any other candidate to line up votes in the state primary. With more candor than is usual from a state boss who intends to keep his delegation in a good trading position, the Governor said, "We feel it is good, common-sense Americanism for the Pennsylvania delegates to go to the convention uninstructed so they will have an opportunity to talk with delegates from other states and in that way secure the strongest candidate."

With California and Pennsylvania closed to him, Willkie decided to enter four primaries: New Hampshire, Wisconsin, Nebraska, and Oregon. Wisconsin would be the first major test. It was, on the face of it, an unfortunate choice because Wisconsin was staunchly isolationist and had been solid Dewey territory in 1940. But Willkie had little choice. At a meeting of his backers in February, Willkie had been bluntly told that, unless he could prove his strength in the isolationist Midwest, there would be no money forthcoming for his campaign, He could expect financial backing only if—and after—he had carried Wisconsin. Dewey, Stassen, and MacArthur were also entered in Wisconsin, but with Dewey declaring that he was not a candidate and Stassen and MacArthur out of the country, only Willkie would actually have to face the voters.

The New Hampshire primary was held March 14. Willkie won six delegates, Dewey two, and three were unpledged. It was hardly a sweeping victory, but his three-to-one edge over Dewey gave Willkie grounds for optimism.

Four days after the New Hampshire primary, Willkie invaded Wisconsin. He began his campaign on March 18 and concluded on the 30th, having traveled 1500 miles and made forty speeches. He campaigned against his Republican opponents as much as he did against Roosevelt and devoted much of his time to attacking, with increasing bitterness, those of his own party who disagreed with him. He was dynamic, powerful, and scathing, and, unlike the shadow candidates, he made his position on every conceivable subject crystal clear. So clear, in fact, that many party regulars thought he was being disloyal to the party as a whole.

Willkie and his managers made many mistakes. Willkie had always been impatient with local politics and, in his eagerness to wage a national campaign, brushed aside and deeply offended many of the grass-roots politicians who would have to bring out the vote on election day. His manager, Ralph Cake, had little knowledge of Wisconsin politics and aroused antagonism by ignoring the local Willkie supporters and running the campaign out of New York. The Willkie leaders believed the personality of their candidate would be sufficient to swing the vote, and no effort was made to set up local organizations, to ring doorbells, to win over precinct workers, or to talk directly to the individual voters.

Despite the complete ineptness of Willkie's campaign, most political observers conceded that the powerful Willkie personality would win him perhaps half the delegation. But on election day, local politicians stood the legal distance from the polls asking people to vote for anyone but Willkie, and they did. Of the twenty-four delegates, Dewey won fifteen, and two uninstructed delegates favored him. Stassen took four delegates and MacArthur three. Willkie won not a single delegate. The popular vote was equally dismal; the Willkie delegates ran last in every contest.

Willkie learned the results in Wisconsin while campaigning in Nebraska. He refused comment, but the following day in Omaha, after delivering a slashing attack on Roosevelt's foreign policy, he said, "I wish I could speak to you from my heart tonight. I cannot, because there are too many factors that prevent it. If I spoke of what's on my mind, I would make too great a castigation of American politics.

"I had been encouraged to believe that the Republican party could live up to the standards of its founders, but I am discouraged to believe that it may be the party of negation. It is apparent that the average citizen fails to realize the far-reaching effect upon him of what is going on in the rest of the world or to realize that a war anywhere has its effect upon him. . . . Perhaps the conscience of America is dulled. Perhaps the people are not willing to bear the sacrifices, and I feel a sense of sickening because I know how much my party could do to make it worthy of its traditions." He explained that he had entered the Wisconsin primary, "to test whether the Republican voters of that State would support me personally and in the advocacy of every sacrifice and cost necessary to winning and shortening the war and in the advocacy of tangible, effective economic and political cooperation among the nations of the world for the preservation of the peace and the rebuilding of humanity." He concluded, "It is obvious now that I cannot be nominated. Therefore, I am asking my friends to desist from any activity toward that end and not to present my name at the convention. I earnestly hope that the Republicans will nominate a candidate and write a platform which really represents the views which I have advocated and which I believe are shared by millions of Americans. I shall continue to work for these principles and policies for which I have fought during the last five years." Thus, with the arrogance but also with the nobility and the honesty of a Coriolanus, Wendell Willkie ended his political career and rejected the party he had led for such a brief but spectacular time.

Willkie's withdrawal removed the last possible obstacle in the path of the carefully uncommitted Governor of New York. Stassen was too young, MacArthur announced in May that he would not accept the nomination, and Bricker could make no headway. Delegation after delegation fell in behind the banner of "deadly efficient" Thomas E. Dewey. By the time the convention met, the nomination was a foregone conclusion.

Even though the outcome of the convention was decided, the candidates put up a brave front. Dewey's followers had headquarters of 356 rooms in the Hotel Stevens, and Stassen's men occupied 167 rooms and twelve suites at the Sherman House. The Minnesota delegation augmented this space wtih 144 rooms of its own. Governor Bricker went all out. Headquarters in the Hotel Stevens were in the charge of the thirty-four-year-old, go-getting mayor of Columbus, Ohio, James L. Rhodes, who oversaw the distribution of 15,000 blue and white Bricker badges, 10,000 "Bricker for President" pencils, 1000 copies of a campaign biography, and two and a half tons of leaflets, pamphlets, and campaign booklets. Scores of banners around Chicago read "Let's Not Bicker, It's Bricker" and "Get the Boys Home Quicker With Bricker." A final touch was added when the obliging telephone company assigned a telephone to Bricker for his Chicago stay with the number WAbash 1944.

Willkie refused to attend the convention. Many friends urged that he appear in Chicago, believing that his presence would block Dewey's nomination and swing the convention to Bricker. Willkie, however, preferred Dewey over Bricker, although his personal choice was Governor Saltonstall of Massachusetts, who had no chance whatever. So Willkie remained in New York to receive frequent reports by telephone.

The convention opened on Monday, June 26, 1944, in the Chicago Stadium and went off smoothly and uninterestingly. Governor

Earl Warren, who had firmly rejected all Dewey offers of the vice-presidency, delivered the keynote address, and Joseph W. Martin, Jr., took his accustomed place as permanent chairman.

On Tuesday evening Herbert Hoover addressed the convention with his usual warnings of imminent disaster, but the high spot of the evening was reserved for the Connecticut Congresswoman, Claire Boothe Luce. Mrs. Luce's chic and attractive exterior did not conceal a political instinct that would have been appropriate in any jungle. After a glowing tribute to "G.I. Joe," who was fighting to save the world, Mrs. Luce unsheathed her lacquered nails to consider "G.I. Jim." "Who is G.I. Jim? He was Joe's pal, his buddy, his brother. Jim was the fellow who lived next door to you. But 'He shall return no more to his house, neither shall his place know him any more.' Jim was, you see, immobilized by enemy gunfire, immobilized for all eternity." After an ethnic list of Jim's names, which would have done credit to any Hollywood war film, Mrs. Luce asked, "Do we here in this Convention dare ask if Jim's heroic death in battle was historically inevitable? If this war might not have been averted? . . . The last twelve years have not been Republican years. Maybe Republican Presidents during the 20's were overconfident that sanity would prevail abroad. But it was not a Republican President who dealt with the visibly rising menaces of Hitler and Mussolini and Hirohito. Ours was not the Administration that promised young Jim's mother and father and neighbors and friends economic security and peace. Yes, peace. No Republican President gave these promises which were kept to their ears, but broken to their hearts. . . . Jim was the heroic heir of the unheroic Roosevelt decade: a decade of confusion and conflict that ended in war." Questions of taste and morality notwithstanding, laying the war dead at the door of the administration and using corpses to make a political point made for a brilliantly vicious speech, and the audience loved it. Mrs. Luce was undisputedly, in the parlance of her own Broadway *milieu*, the smash hit of an otherwise prosaic convention.

Governor Dewey was placed in nomination by Governor Dwight Griswold of Nebraska on the third day and was followed by John Bricker, who withdrew in favor of Dewey. Senator Ball of Minnesota then withdrew the Stassen candidacy, after which

Everett Dirksen also withdrew and pledged his support to the Governor of New York.

No other names were placed in nomination, but it took a bit of political skulduggery to prevent MacArthur's being presented to the convention. Dr. John Koehler of Wisconsin was adamant in his plans to nominate the General. Joe Martin and Senator Vandenberg did not wish anything to disturb the love feast for Dewey, and they therefore worked out a little scheme. As Dr. Koehler approached the platform, he was waylaid by Vandenberg, who kept him in conversation until Wisconsin was called on the roll. As Joe Martin told it, "He engaged him just long enough for me to give Wisconsin the barest time I decently could on the roll call. By the time Koehler got past Vandenberg, Wyoming had been called, and I ruled him out of order."

This tactic so enraged one MacArthur supporter that he insisted on voting for the General on the one roll call taken. The vote on the only ballot stood: Dewey 1056, MacArthur 1.

Immediately after the Dewey nomination, the convention moved on to the vice-presidential nomination. Warren having refused to be considered, the Dewey forces turned to John Bricker of Ohio. The Governor was delighted to accept, no other candidates were offered, and Bricker received every vote of the convention.

"You are not nominating a
Vice President ... but a President"

THE TWENTY-NINTH DEMOCRATIC NATIONAL CONVENTION
Chicago, July 19, 1944

Franklin D. Roosevelt did not announce his intention of seeking
a fourth term until shortly before the Democratic convention met
in Chicago, but no one ever doubted that he would run again.
This certainty created a macabre problem. The California oil man
and treasurer of the National Committee, Edwin Pauley, cold-
bloodedly summed up the thinking of the party leaders when he
told various local leaders in the spring of 1944, "You are not nominating a Vice-President of the United States, but a President."
There was little doubt in the minds of the party bosses that Roosevelt would not live to complete his fourth term, and a powerful
group led by National Chairman Robert Hannegan, Pauley, Postmaster General Frank Walker, Ed Flynn, and Mayor Ed Kelly of
Chicago was determined that Henry Wallace would never be
President of the United States.

Their first and greatest problem was to convince Roosevelt that
Wallace would make an unsatisfactory running mate. They emphasized that he would be a drag on the ticket and insisted that he
would lose the South. Throughout the late winter and spring, they
kept an unrelenting pressure on Roosevelt until the worried President asked Ed Flynn to survey Wallace's strength in certain key
states. Flynn plainly told him that New York, Pennsylvania, Illinois,

New Jersey, and California would go Republican if Wallace were on the ticket in November. Roosevelt did not indicate that he had decided to abandon the Vice-President, but he fell silent when Wallace was criticized, and the bosses correctly believed that he would accept another running mate.

Hannegan and Pauley favored replacing Wallace with Senator Harry Truman, who had made an impressive record with his investigations of defense contracts, while Roosevelt himself began to think of either Supreme Court Justice William O. Douglas or Director of War Mobilization James F. Byrnes. In June, Roosevelt discussed the situation with Jonathan Daniels and two other administrative assistants. "Of course," the President said, "everybody knows I am for Henry Wallace," but he went on to say that he had come to believe that the opposition to Wallace ran far deeper than he had believed. Even allowing for exaggerated reports, he feared that Wallace's name on the ticket might cost the Democrats a million or two votes in November. He admitted that he did not know Truman well but agreed that he had done a magnificent job in his investigation and had had a good press. He concluded by saying that Ambassador John Winant might make a good candidate and that West-Coast industrialist Henry Kaiser was another possibility, but he didn't know if Kaiser could be trusted politically.

Roosevelt was playing his usual game of refusing to commit himself in advance. He was pleasantly noncommittal on every candidate suggested, refused to name his own choice, and let all candidates think that they had the inside track. It is likely that Roosevelt at that time was not really sure what he wanted to do. With the war reaching a climax in the Normandy invasion, he had more important things on his mind than a candidate for vice-president. Ed Pauley might be convinced that the running mate would become president, but Roosevelt himself thought of him only as someone to preside over the Senate.

The President announced on July 10 that he would run for re-election and held a dinner conference with party leaders. Seated around the table were Roosevelt, Bob Hannegan, Mayor Kelly, Postmaster General Walker, Ed Flynn, Pauley, and George Allen, secretary of the National Committee. The vice-presidency was uppermost in everyone's mind, but Roosevelt amused himself all through dinner by keeping the bosses on tenterhooks. Sensing, perhaps, their morbid interest in his running mate, the President discoursed all through dinner on poisons and various means of assassination, including the attempts on his own life. Finally, seated in his study after dinner, he allowed his guests to bring up the one subject that most interested them.

The group considered the various possibilities. Rayburn had taken himself out of the race. Byrnes was discussed without enthusiasm, and Barkley was dismissed because he was five years older than Roosevelt. The President suggested both Winant and Justice Douglas, but their names were greeted with icy silence. Roosevelt said that he favored Douglas because he would draw the same liberal support that Wallace did, "and, besides, he played an interesting game of poker."

Only Truman's name elicited enthusiasm from the politicians. Ed Flynn stressed his good record in Congress and the fact that labor was friendly. In an oddly negative bit of reasoning, Flynn argued "that Truman was the man who would hurt him least." Roosevelt objected to Truman's age, which he thought was about sixty. Douglas, he pointed out, was under fifty. John Boettiger, the President's son-in-law, was sent for a copy of the *Congressional Directory* to establish Truman's age. Realizing that if the President knew that Truman was sixty, it would eliminate him from consideration, Ed Pauley took the *Directory* from Boettiger when he returned and easily changed the conversation. The distraction made Roosevelt forget all about checking Truman's age, and he eventually said to Hannegan, "Bob, I think you and everyone else here wants Truman." Having accomplished their purpose, the leaders quickly left.

Wallace refused to be counted out. He returned from a trip to China to find his position seriously undermined. At Roosevelt's request, Harold Ickes and Judge Samuel Rosenman lunched with Wallace to tell him that they thought he would split the party if he ran again. Wallace demanded to hear it from Roosevelt himself and saw the President on July 13.

The Vice-President showed Roosevelt a list of 290 delegates pledged to him and an unreleased Gallup poll showing Democratic preferences to be 65% Wallace, 17% Barkley, 5% Rayburn, 4% Byrd,

3% Byrnes, and 2% each for Douglas, Truman, and Secretary of State Stettinius. Roosevelt's reaction was a loud, "Well, I'll be damned!" At Wallace's urging, the President agreed to write a letter, dated July 14, stating that, if he were to be a delegate to the convention, he would personally vote for Wallace. It was something less than an official blessing, but Wallace was satisfied.

The letter, however, was only Roosevelt's way of letting Wallace down easily. He had made up his mind, and he told Mrs. Roosevelt, "Wallace had his chance to make his mark and if he could not convince the party leaders that he was the right person, I cannot dictate to them twice."

If Wallace was out, it was not yet settled who was in. Hannegan had gone to Roosevelt asking for a letter backing Truman. The wily Chief Executive obliged by writing, "Dear Bob: You have written me about Bill Douglas and Harry Truman. I should, of course, be very glad to run with either of them and believe that either of them would bring real strength to the ticket." Hannegan was not pleased. He wanted no mention of Douglas, and he especially did not want Douglas's name first. He decided to bide his time and settle the matter later.

Truman, meanwhile, was having misgivings. He had come to realize that Roosevelt probably would not live out his term and decided that he was satisfied to remain in the Senate. "I've made up my mind," he told a friend. "I'm not going to get into this thing unless the President wants me to." Referring to the possibility of Roosevelt's death, he continued, "Do you remember your American history well enough to recall what happened to most Vice-Presidents who succeeded to the Presidency? Usually they were ridiculed in office, had their hearts broken, lost any vestige of respect they had had before. I don't want that to happen to me." When Jimmy Byrnes asked him to place his, Byrnes's, name in nomination at the convention, Truman agreed.

A week before the convention, there were only three serious candidates, Wallace, Byrnes, and Truman. Truman had decided that he did not want the vice-presidency, and both Byrnes and Wallace believed that they were running with Roosevelt's personal blessing. This misapprehension ultimately defeated both. So sure was each that he was the chosen candidate that neither made so

great an effort to secure support as he might have done. With
Roosevelt's blessing, who needed to scramble for delegates? Meanwhile, the Hannegan-Pauley-Kelly group industriously cut the
ground from under them.

Hannegan, however, had some bad moments. He arrived in
Chicago on July 14 and went to map strategy with Truman in his
suite in the Stevens Hotel. He was stunned when Truman told
him that he was working for Byrnes's nomination. The National
Chairman was so unnerved that he told Ed Flynn, "It's all over!
It's Byrnes!" Hannegan was further upset by rumors that Mayor
Kelly was toying with the idea of backing Byrnes to deadlock the
convention, at which time he might slip Senator Scott Lucas on
the ticket.

Hannegan decided that the only way to avert defeat was to
take the matter up with Roosevelt. The President was on his way
to Hawaii to confer with General MacArthur, but he reluctantly
agreed, at Hannegan's insistence, to stop off in Chicago to confer
with Hannegan.

Mayor Kelly, by now playing his own game, called Byrnes in
Washington on Sunday, July 15, to tell him that he and Hannegan
were seeing the President that afternoon and would give Byrnes
a big build-up. He called back later and told Byrnes that everything was settled and that Byrnes would be the candidate.

Byrnes was delighted. Unfortunately, the story was untrue.
Kelly did not see Roosevelt that day; only Hannegan and Pauley
boarded the President's train. The President refused to give a complete endorsement to Truman but agreed that Byrnes was out. He
had the previous "Bill Douglas and Harry Truman" letter retyped
to read "Harry Truman or Bill Douglas" but would go no further.
Hannegan was satisfied.

Truman spent Monday promoting the cause of Jimmy Byrnes,
but the reaction of Sidney Hillman, boss of the C.I.O.'s political
action committee, was typical. Hillman listened to Truman's booming of Byrnes over the breakfast table, then threw up his hands
in protest. "We're for Wallace," he told Truman. "There is only
one other man we could consider supporting." When asked who,
Hillman replied, "I'm looking at him right now." Other labor
leaders told him the same thing. Phil Murray, Dan Tobin, and the

head of the Railroad Brotherhood all told him that, if Wallace could not be nominated, they would support Truman. William Green bypassed Wallace when he told Truman, "The A. F. of L. is for you and will support no one else."

With labor showing itself friendly to Truman, Hannegan decided to finish off Byrnes. Hannegan told Byrnes that he personally favored his nomination but that Roosevelt had told him to "Clear it with Sidney." Then Hannegan told the unhappy Byrnes that Hillman had not "cleared" his candidacy, and Byrnes realized that his position was much less secure than he had thought.

Hannegan then leaked to the press a story that Roosevelt had chosen Truman. When challenged, he released Roosevelt's letter with Truman's name first, Douglas's second. Over the wire services went the stories that the President preferred Truman or Douglas in that order. Byrnes's candidacy was crumbling away, and the angry South Carolinian could not be sure exactly how it was happening. Meanwhile, Hannegan had finally won over Truman.

Summoned to a meeting in the Blackstone Hotel on Thursday afternoon, Truman was confronted by Hannegan, Walker, Kelly, Ed Flynn, and Frank Hague. "The President wants you to be Vice-President," Walker told him. Truman refused to believe it until the phone rang. It was Roosevelt asking if Truman had agreed. Hannegan said no, and Truman could hear the President's voice booming out of the receiver, "Well, tell him if he wants to break up the Democratic Party in the middle of a war, that's his responsibility." "My God," was Truman's reaction, but he agreed to run.

Truman told Byrnes that he was Roosevelt's choice, and Byrnes, after trying to reach Roosevelt by phone without success, had no choice but to release Truman from his pledge of support and withdraw from the race. He vented his anger when he saw Senator Barkley, who was to place Roosevelt in nomination. "If I were you," snarled the disappointed candidate, "I wouldn't say anything too complimentary about FDR in your nominating speech!"

The Democratic National Convention opened in the Chicago Stadium on Wednesday, July 19. On Thursday, Senator Samuel D. Jackson of Indiana took the chair as permanent chairman and delivered the *coup de grâce* to the Wallace candidacy. Under the dating of July 14, Roosevelt had written his weak letter of endorsement for Wallace and sent it to Senator Jackson, who read it to the convention. In the letter, Roosevelt said he would personally vote for Wallace were he a delegate to the convention, but, the letter continued, "At the same time, I do not wish to appear in any way as dictating to the convention. Obviously the convention must decide. And it should—and I am sure it will—give great consideration to the pros and cons of its choice." If there had been any doubt in anyone's mind before, it was now most clear that Henry Wallace had just been forced to walk the plank—in the nicest sort of way, of course.

Senator Barkley placed Roosevelt in nomination for his fourth term, and Mrs. Fred T. Nooney of Florida, expressing southern dissatisfaction with the administration, nominated Senator Harry Flood Byrd. The only ballot taken nominated Roosevelt with 1086 votes to 89 for Byrd and 1 for James A. Farley.

It had been Hannegan's intention to push on to Truman's nomination immediately after the convention heard Roosevelt's acceptance speech, which had been broadcast to the Stadium from San Diego, but his plans were upset. The Wallace supporters had pushed their way into the Stadium, packed the galleries, and set up a screaming demonstration for their candidate. The organist had been enlisted in the cause and played "Iowa, That's Where the Tall Corn Grows" over and over until an angry Ed Pauley threatened to chop through the cables for the amplifier with an ax unless he switched to nonpartisan songs. Wallace banners appeared on the floor, and a full-scale demonstration threatened to stampede the convention. Mayor Kelly said that he could speak for the fire chief and declare the Stadium so crowded as to constitute a fire hazard. With this excuse, a motion to recess until the following day was rammed through, and the Wallacites were left to cheer to no purpose.

The Wallace demonstrators were kept out of the Stadium on Friday. Beside Truman and Wallace, nine names were placed in nomination: Senator John H. Bankhead of Alabama, Senator Joseph C. O'Mahoney of Wyoming, Senator Scott Lucas of Illinois, Paul V. McNutt, Senator Barkley, Supreme Court Justice Frank Murphy, Governor Joseph M. Broughton of North Carolina, Governer Prentice Cooper of Kentucky, and Senator Elbert D. Thomas of Utah.

Wallace took a strong lead on the first ballot, with 429½ votes; 589 were necessary to nominate. Truman was second with 319½. The other totals were Bankhead 98, Lucas 61, Barkley 49½, Broughton 43, McNutt 31, O'Mahoney 27, Cooper 26, Kerr 23, Governor O'Conor of Maryland 18, Thomas 10, Senator Pepper of Florida 3, Murphy and Sam Rayburn 2 each, and Bascom Timmons of Texas 1.

The delegates had been in session for more than six hours by the time the first ballot was completed, and hunger demanded a recess. But outside the Stadium waited a great crowd of Wallace supporters with tickets for the evening session. Fearing a repetition of the demonstration of the previous night, Hannegan ordered Chairman Jackson to begin the second roll call.

On the second ballot, Wallace was leading Truman 148 to 125, when Maryland was called and Governor O'Conor threw his delegation to Truman. Next came Governor Kerr's turn. As Ed Pauley put it, "At the given signal I pointed my finger at Kerr and gave the signal for Truman, and I must say that Kerr looked a little pale at the moment." But Kerr did as he was told, and "the rest was relatively easy." One by one the delegations fell into line. At the end of the roll call, before any changes, the count stood Truman 447½, Wallace 373, Lucas 58, Barkley 40, Broughton 30, Cooper 26, McNutt 25, Bankhead 23½, O'Mahoney 8, Pepper 3, and Kerr and Justice Douglas 1 each.

Then came the stampede. Mayor Kelly, who in playing his game with Lucas was nearly left behind, was recognized when the Truman vote stood at 586½—2½ votes short of nomination— and threw 55 votes to the winner. The final total was Truman 1031, Wallace 105, Cooper 26, Barkley 6, Douglas 4, and McNutt 1. The nomination was not made unanimous.

Truman then appeared before the convention to express his thanks in a brief speech. As he and his wife left the Stadium, fighting through a crowd of reporters and well-wishers, Mrs. Truman muttered to her husband, "Are we going to have to go through this all the rest of our lives?" In eight months they would have to go through a great deal more.

CHAPTER 21

"Unfettered by a single obligation or promise"

THE TWENTY-FOURTH REPUBLICAN
NATIONAL CONVENTION
Philadelphia, June 21, 1948

Every presidential nominating convention has rung with the proud and sometimes wistful boast that the delegates are gathered to nominate the next President of the United States. Even more than "the man who," "the next President" is the magical phrase in the ritual, which every four years selects one politician to oppose another politician for the highest office in the land. To the Republicans gathered in Philadelphia in June, 1948, the phrase was more than a ritual incantation—it was, they believed, literal truth. There was no doubt in anyone's mind, with the possible exception of the incumbent President, that the man selected by the twenty-fourth Republican National Convention would become the thirty-fourth President of the United States.

Republican expectations had begun to turn to certainty with the mid-term elections of 1946. A nation weary of war and eager to enjoy the relaxations of peace was dismayed to find that peace brought with it its own problems. Consumer goods were in short supply, the spiral of inflation moved steadily upward, labor troubles beset the country, and the hot war had been exchanged for a cold one. The rallying cry of the Republicans in 1920 had been "normalcy." In 1946, it was "Had enough?"

The Democratic defeat was crushing. Twenty-eight of thirty-six states outside the South went Republican, and thirteen new Senate and fifty-six House seats gave the Republicans control of Congress for the first time since 1928.

Because of the bright Republican prospects for the forthcoming presidential election, there was a plethora of candidates for the nomination. Among the active candidates, the leaders were Governor Dewey, Senator Taft, Harold Stassen and Governor Earl Warren. Inactive, but eager, was General Douglas MacArthur, while Senator Vandenberg, inactive and reluctant, was believed by no one when he said that he was not a candidate. Among the second-rank candidates, Speaker Martin was judged to have the best chance should the leaders be eliminated. General Eisenhower was a potential candidate, but his disinterest and uncertain political inclinations made him a shadowy candidate throughout the early preconvention period.

The first candidate off and running was Harold Stassen. Most presidential candidates coyly feign disinterest in their candidacies until a few months before the convention, but Stassen displayed a refreshingly candid eagerness. On December 17, 1946, he announced that he was, indeed, a candidate for the nomination and began running as hard as he could. He opened headquarters in Washington, but few professional politicians took his candidacy very seriously. Most of them believed that he was actually running for the vice-presidency.

The other candidates were still in the speculative stage. Tom Dewey led in the public opinion polls but partly, at least, because his name was better known to the average voter. Dewey's greatest problem was that the Republicans had never renominated a defeated candidate. As Alice Longworth was reputed to have said, "You can't make a *soufflé* rise twice." The *soufflé* principle of politics would dog Dewey right up to the convention, and it accounted for the relative lack of enthusiasm even among his pledged supporters.

An interesting turn of events occurred in October, 1947, when the liberal Stassen and the conservative Taft became surprisingly friendly. They agreed to appear together at an Iowa Republican luncheon in Des Moines on October 8, where they vigorously competed in throwing bouquets at each other. Taft stated that he and

Stassen had differed on issues "but not on the fundamental principles," while Stassen applauded Taft's "integrity, sincerity and
ability." Taft blandly asserted that a coalition to cut Dewey's throat
couldn't be further from his mind, but astute observers could
detect the sound of stropping razors in the background.

After the display of affection between him and Stassen, Taft
formally announced his candidacy and called for a "wide open"
race. He stated that his Senate duties would give him no time to
enter primaries. As in 1940, he would seek his support among the
professionals in state conventions and behind the scenes.

Early in 1948, the line-up of contenders for the nomination
was dramatically changed. At the end of January, General Eisenhower wrote his supporters in New Hampshire asking them not
to enter a slate of delegates in the primary. "I am not available
for and could not accept nomination to high political office. . . . I
could not accept the nomination even under the remote circumstances that it were tendered me. . . . The necessary and wise sub-
ordination of the military to civil power will best be sustained . . .
when lifelong professional soldiers . . . abstain from seeking high
political office."

As one general stalked out of presidential politics, another
jumped in. On March 1, 1948, the Hearst press declared for Mac-
Arthur in page-one editorials, and soon the Hearst papers blazed
like enlistment posters for the hero of the Pacific. In a series, "Why
I'm for MacArthur," the General was hailed as "man of the hour,"
"greatest man since George Washington," and "savior of our
country" by such Hollywood names as Fifi D'Orsay, Claire Windsor,
and Marion Davies, and it was announced with appropriate breath-
lessness that Shirley Temple would, if she were old enough, gladly
vote for MacArthur. A MacArthur-for-President committee was
formed, headed by Wisconsin's Secretary of State Fred Zimmerman
and former Governor Phillip LaFollette. Perhaps because Hearst
was in, Colonel McCormick of the Chicago *Tribune* counted himself
out. An early MacArthur booster, the redoubtable reactionary announced that he would be for MacArthur only in case of a deadlock. Otherwise, he was for Taft. The General himself, speaking as
proconsul of Japan, announced that he would be available for any
public duty to which the American people might call him.

The first five months of 1948 were, as far as the Presidential contest was concerned, an almost unbroken triumph for Harold Stassen. The man who had been considered only a vice-presidential candidate had, by the first of May, eliminated one major contender, nearly eliminated a second, and scared the wits out of every presidential aspirant, active or hopeful, in the Republican Party.

Stassen's rise began unimpressively enough in New Hampshire. He contested Dewey in the March 9 primary and won two of the eight delegates. The Wisconsin primary on April 6 pitted Stassen, Dewey, and MacArthur against each other. MacArthur, of course, could not campaign, and Dewey did not choose to campaign. He was following his 1944 strategy of remaining aloof, devoting himself to his job as Governor of New York, and maintaining an unruffled, statesmanlike pose. Stassen soon changed that strategy.

Visiting Wisconsin ten times in the preprimary period, Stassen barnstormed up and down the state, dazzling the voters with his friendliness and energy and exhausting his associates and the weary reporters who tried to keep pace with him. State boss Thomas E. Coleman, Senator Joe McCarthy, the national committeeman, and the state chairman all backed him. The campaign was run by Victor Johnston, who had managed the Stassen drive in 1944. Assisting Coleman, Johnston put together a grass-roots organization that blanketed the state with direct-mail, newspaper, and radio advertising. Auto caravans headed by Minnesota Governor Luther Youngdahl roamed the rural areas, where the Governor had great appeal among the Scandinavian-Americans.

This impressive support was not all given out of love for Harold Stassen. His appeal was undeniably great, but Tom Coleman had other motives. The Coleman machine feared that the MacArthur candidacy was being used as a stalking horse to return the LaFollettes to power. MacArthur, as a favorite son with Phillip LaFollette's backing, was expected to win a substantial victory, and the only way the Coleman organization could stay in power would be to make an impressive showing for Stassen.

So alarming were the reports coming out of Wisconsin that Dewey hastily abandoned his above-the-battle stance and hurried into the state to campaign personally for his slate of delegates. It did little good.

Before the primary, Dewey had privately predicted, "I will probably be lucky if the result is not worse than this: MacArthur 19, Stassen 6, Dewey 2. In the popular vote, I expect the vote to be much closer and in the following order: MacArthur, Dewey, Stassen." When the votes were counted the night of April 6, Stassen had won nineteen delegates, MacArthur had taken eight, and Dewey had none. Stassen took all the delegate-at-large races and polled 40% of the popular vote to 36% for MacArthur and only 24% for Dewey.

The Wisconsin primary had four immediate results. First, it placed Stassen alongside Taft and Dewey in the inner circle of candidates. Second, it virtually eliminated MacArthur from consideration. Third, it badly damaged Dewey's prospects. And fourth, it made most of the political experts, who had confidently predicted a MacArthur victory, look foolish.

Dewey put as good a face on it as he could. In his statement, he referred to the New York State convention, which had met the same day as the Wisconsin primary. "Now we have lost one primary and won one primary. On the total yesterday was a pretty good day. We gained 90 delegates in New York which was more than four times the number any other candidate acquired." Keeping a stiff upper lip under his moustache, Dewey obviously hoped that no one would be unkind enough to mention that he had, naturally, been unopposed in New York.

General MacArthur also reacted publicly to the Wisconsin vote. Striking a slightly larger than life pose, which is difficult for any man on horseback who has just had the horse shot out from under him, the General intoned, "My statement of March 9, that I was available for any public duty to which I might be called by the American people, was not limited to any particular political test. That was a restatement of the responsibility of citizenship on which I then stood, I now stand, and I shall continue to stand until I die." Henceforth the proconsul of Japan would not figure in the race for the nomination.

The next Stassen victory came a week later, on his forty-first birthday, in the Nebraska primary. The Nebraska state primary law did not require a candidate's permission to enter his name, nor did it allow a candidate to withdraw his name once it was entered.

Accordingly, a young Nebraska editor, Raymond A. McConnell, Jr., with, one suspects, a certain amount of fiendish delight, formed a committee to enter the names of all the candidates. It is one of the most cherished privileges of any presidential candidate to select his primaries with care, making sure that each race will do him the most good and avoiding, as far as is humanly possible, any contest that could conceivably test him on an equal footing with other candidates. The terrors of "sudden death" primaries stalk the dreams of every candidate, so it was with collective dismay that Dewey, Taft, MacArthur, Vandenberg, Warren, and Joe Martin found themselves entered in company with Stassen. What made the primary ironic was that it was strictly a popularity contest— the results would not be binding on the state's fifteen delegates.

Harold Stassen, backed by an effective organization headed by Fred A. Seaton, thirty-eight-year-old state legislator, roared through the state as if he had not even been through the grueling Wisconsin campaign. From neighboring states, "Paul Revere Riders" swarmed across Nebraska beating the drums for Stassen until Senator Hugh Butler, Taft's state manager, roared in angry protest against the "dramatic and extravagant circus tactics of the Minnesota carpetbaggers."

Taft, backed by Butler and the state organizations, spent three days campaigning in the state. Dewey relied on the work of his manager, Herbert Brownell, Jr., and placed his faith in advertisements and recordings of speeches delivered in the resonant Dewey baritone.

On April 13, Nebraskans cast more ballots than had ever been cast in their presidential primary and gave a resounding victory to Stassen. The results, ruefully surveyed by the other candidates, were Stassen 43% of the total vote, Dewey 35%, Taft 11%, Vandenberg 5%, MacArthur 1%, Warren 1%, and Joe Martin ½%. It was beginning to look as if it would be Stassen all the way.

The Pennsylvania primary on April 27 gave no solace to the bruised losers in Nebraska. In the Keystone State, delegates were not entered under the names of particular candidates. If the voter wished to express a preference, he had to write in his favorite's name. More than 74,000 voters wrote in the name of Harold Stassen on their ballots, while 68,161 wrote in Dewey's name. Senator

Edward Martin received 41,764 write-in votes, and MacArthur, Taft, Vandenberg, and Eisenhower trailed far behind.

The write-in vote was another boost for Stassen but would have no binding effect upon the delegation, which was split into several factions. Ancient boss Joseph R. Grundy and oilman Joseph N. Pew, Jr., controlled one faction, which inclined to Taft. Jay Cooke, Philadelphia banker, inclined to Stassen, and Governor James Duff's faction favored Vandenberg. As a result, the only way to avoid immediate bloodshed was to pledge the delegation to Senator Edward Martin as a favorite son.

Ohio spelled the beginning of the end for Stassen's chances. Ordinarily, Ohio would have been sacred territory consecrated to Senator Taft, but Stassen decided to give the Senator a race on his home ground. The GOP state chairman was so shocked at Stassen's audacity that he declared, "Stassen is unsportsmanlike, un-American, and unfair," to which any favorite son, jealously clutching his state delegation, would add a fervent "amen."

Carefully selecting his districts, Stassen entered twenty-two district candidates, mostly in urban areas that should have been liberally inclined, and one delegate-at-large to test his state-wide appeal. Publicly he hoped for twelve winners out of the twenty-three. When the primary was held on May 4, he won nine district delegates, while the delegate-at-large was decisively defeated. It was neither a victory nor a major defeat, but it was the first indication that Stassen could be stopped. By breaking the Stassen winning streak, Ohio gave fresh hope to the other candidates.

The Oregon primary was scheduled for May 21 and would be the last direct contest between Stassen and Dewey. Stassen covered the state with his by-then familiar campaign, and an alarmed Dewey realized that his rival was likely to sweep the primary. If Dewey should lose Oregon, he would be finished.

The New York Governor decided to barnstorm the state and, what was more, to project a new Dewey. Tom Dewey entered Oregon fighting, but astonished observers wondered if it were really Dewey they were seeing. Gone was the cold, precise, immaculate, slightly fussy figure. This man was no groom on a wedding cake but a fighting bantam rooster, rumpled, folksy, and actually human. The new Dewey was an enormous success. He shook hands, kissed beauty queens, paraded with fur-draped cavemen, and beamingly accepted gifts of live salmon and damp boxes of Oregon clams as if he really appreciated the gifts.

There was at least one amusing episode as the rival candidates stumped the state. Stassen was in the tiny town of Cascade Locks, charming a group of school children, when it was announced that the Dewey bus was approaching. The mayor, sporting a Dewey button, and the children rushed to meet the bus as did a grinning Stassen. The bus slowed, the occupants took one look, and with a grinding of gears the bus roared off down the road. The mayor promptly replaced his Dewey button with two for Stassen as the children delightedly yelled, "Phooey on Dewey."

Despite the contretemps at Cascade Locks, Dewey made steady gains. Most effective was a letter writing campaign emanating from New York. "Big shots in New York were persuaded to write to their little-shot associates in Oregon; lawyers to lawyers, doctors to doctors, businessmen to their opposite numbers. The bankers—headed by Winthrop Aldrich—were especially energetic; as one man put it, 'They really put the screws on the boys in Oregon.' "

The screws were effective, but much more so was a Stassen blunder of fatal proportions. Stassen had challenged Dewey to debate with him in the Wisconsin primary, but it had not come off. The challenge was repeated for Oregon, and Dewey replied that he would debate but on his own terms. Stassen agreed without hearing those terms. Dewey made two conditions: The debate was to be by radio from a studio without an audience, and Dewey was to make the closing statement. The topic agreed upon was, Should the Communist Party be outlawed? Stassen took the affirmative, Dewey the negative.

The debate was held four days before the primary. Apart from the disadvantages of competing with the impressive Dewey voice and not having an audience to sweep along by his physical charm, Stassen was ill prepared, tired to the point of exhaustion, and not nearly so equipped for advocacy as Dewey, the experienced lawyer. The New York Governor cut him to ribbons in his closing statement and won support far beyond Oregon by contending that outlawing the party would be un-American. Beside, he argued, it would be futile to try to shoot an idea with a law.

The new Dewey image, the letter-writing campaign, and, above all, the debate, gave Dewey a 9000-vote victory over Stassen. He swept the entire delegation. Stassen was dead, Dewey was once again the front-runner, and the hesitant party leaders knew which way to jump. Only the strongest stop-Dewey coalition could prevent his winning a second nomination.

A move toward such a coalition began two days after the Oregon primary and involved an attempt to revive the blighted romance between Taft and Stassen. Stassen still controlled a sizable bloc of votes, and Taft decided to send word to him that, despite the invasion of Ohio, he was not unfriendly. Stassen flew to Topeka, Kansas, on May 30 to discuss the Taft feeler with Alf Landon. Landon told him bluntly that he could not be nominated but that he had the power to nominate Dewey, Taft, or Joe Martin. Later, Landon and Stassen took the same train from Chicago to Philadelphia, and Landon repeated his arguments, but Stassen could not make up his mind to withdraw in favor of any other candidate. He was still undecided when events at the convention gave him hopes of a deadlock, and he informed Taft that any chance of an alliance was off.

Vandenberg, maintaining his position of not being a candidate, was being subjected to increasing pressure to declare himself. Governor Duff, Michigan National Committeeman Arthur Summerfield, and Arthur Vandenberg, Jr., were unrelenting in their efforts to have the Senator enter the race. Finally, on June 19, the reluctant candidate agreed to accept a draft if it were offered, and Governor Kim Sigler was authorized to announce that the Vandenberg hat was in the ring.

For a moment, the late Vandenberg candidacy seemed to change the preconvention picture completely, but actually it came far too late for success. As it turned out, the chief beneficiary was Tom Dewey. Vandenberg's announcement convinced Stassen that a deadlock was likely and his own chances greatly improved. By calling off the negotiations with Taft, he ruined the best chance the stop-Dewey forces had of an effective coalition.

Just before the opening of the convention, Joe Martin received an offer of support. Texas National Committeeman H. J. Porter, informed the Speaker that oil millionaire H. Roy Cullen wanted to back him for the nomination. It was explained to Porter that Martin was not a candidate. Martin later wrote, "Porter was insistent, however. He not only took an option on a ballroom to be used as a headquarters if I became a serious contender, but as a sort of interim headquarters he also rented the rooms of the Harvard Club in the Bellevue-Stratford Hotel and kept them so full of turkey sandwiches that one could hardly move about."

The convention was called to order at 11:00 a.m. Monday, June 21, and that evening Governor Dwight Green of Illinois delivered a rousing and—if it had been delivered anywhere but at a political convention—libelous keynote address. Describing the New Deal as an alliance of "bosses, boodle, buncombe, and blarney," the Governor attacked "the motley collection of embittered failures, back-alley revolutionaries, and parlor anarchists with which the New Deal has disgraced the party of Jefferson and Jackson." He then tore into what would be a major theme of the campaign. "The cold war we face today is the lusty child of the New Deal's rendezvous with Communism. And I say to you tonight that rendezvous began with recognition of the Soviets in 1933. It continued with the socialistic compromises with Communism preached by Henry Wallace and the vote-catching compromises engineered by Harry Hopkins. It reached its tragic climax in those years when we supinely suffered Communism to master half of Europe." Naturally, he did not neglect to invoke the unholy trinity of the new Republican canon: Teheran, Yalta, and Potsdam.

The next speaker, the Honorable Claire Boothe Luce, expanded the theme. She had no war dead to blame on the Democrats this time, but she still managed to pour a good deal of venom on troubled waters. She described the three wings of the Democratic Party—the Jim Crow wing, the left or Moscow wing—"a motley of labor racketeers, native and imported Communists, and foreign agents of the Kremlin," who, apparently, were neither native nor imported—and the center or Pendergast wing, "run by the wampum and boodle boys."

Having warmed up, Mrs. Luce, who would go on to more distinguished achievements as Ambassadress to Italy and author of *Child of the Morning*, swung into the main body of her speech. "History shows that the New Deal seemed to share the Communist opinion that government of, and *by* the people was outmoded." The people "understand now why the New Dealers were attracted— and are still attracted—by the Communists, and the Communists are even more attracted to the New Dealers."

On Tuesday, the Dewey forces swung into high gear. The original strategy had been to start with about 325 delegates on the first ballot and throw in reserve strength until victory on the fourth. To permit an uninterrupted series of ballots, they favored delaying the roll calls until Thursday morning. But the entry of Vandenberg into the race clouded the picture, and it was decided to switch to Wednesday night balloting and to aim at a second-ballot victory. It was an important change of strategy but was apparently worked out by Herbert Brownell and Russell Sprague without consulting their candidate. At least, by his own admission, Tom Dewey "was not as closely familiar with the mechanics of the Convention" as he might have been and professed ignorance of the strategy change.

In order to put the new strategy into effect, it was necessary to win major new support, and Brownell and Sprague increased their pressure on the Pennsylvania delegation. Senator Martin and the National Committeeman G. Mason Owlett were the active representatives of the faction controlled by eighty-five-year-old Joe Grundy. Grundy had originally favored Taft, but the Dewey forces had been bombarding him with anti-Taft arguments. They succeeded so brilliantly that Grundy was heard to declare a few days before the convention that Taft was a "socialist" because he had favored federal aid to education and housing.

Governor Duff, realizing that Grundy was about to go over to Dewey, entered the Pennsylvania caucus on Sunday, June 20, prepared to prevent any such switch. The best he could do was to fight for time, and he therefore joined in urging that the delegation continue to support Senator Martin as a favorite son, which it did.

On Tuesday, the Dewey managers summoned Martin to a 9:00 a.m. conference with Dewey. That afternoon Martin announced that he was withdrawing as a favorite son and had accepted an invitation to place Dewey's name in nomination. The erstwhile favorite son, more than 40 votes tucked snugly in his pocket, then slipped upstairs to be photographed with the beaming Dewey.

The Martin announcement caused panic in the camps of the

other candidates. Taft immediately called Stassen, Duff, Warren, and Sigler. Within an hour, Duff and Stassen were in conference with Taft. Could they unite to stop Dewey? Taft refused to join with Stassen and Duff in supporting Vandenberg, and Stassen balked at joining Duff in support of Taft. Neither Taft nor Duff was interested in backing Stassen, and the meeting broke up without any progress having been made.

Taft received a further setback on Tuesday. The credentials committee, considering the four contested delegations of Georgia, Mississippi, South Carolina, and Alaska, accepted the pro-Taft delegations from Mississippi and South Carolina but voted to seat the pro-Dewey Georgia and Alaska delegations. Taft had been so confident of picking up all the delegations that he had turned down an offer to split Georgia on an even basis. Four Taft members of the committee defected to give Georgia to Dewey by a 26-24 vote. The Taft forces angrily claimed that the committee defectors had been offered federal judgeships but couldn't make the story stick. An interesting story, probably untrue, had it that one Mississippi delegate, after voting against Taft, ran for a departing train and died of a heart attack after catching it. In his pocket were $1500 in new bills, which the Mississippi delegation is supposed to have claimed should have been divided evenly among them. At any rate, Taft had lost 16 Georgia votes he had been counting on.

Dewey, meanwhile, continued to gain new support. Governor Driscoll announced that he would release his delegation to Dewey after the first ballot, and Senator Saltonstall also climbed on the bandwagon. Senator Kem of Missouri, at the urging of Charlie Halleck, declared for Dewey, which meant at least half the Missouri delegation. Why Charlie Halleck urged Senator Kem to back Dewey provided the most interesting story of the convention.

On Wednesday afternoon in Dewey's suite, Charlie Halleck sat on a bed and listened to Russell Sprague pour honeyed words into his ears. Also present were Brownell, Ed Jaeckle, and Representative Leonard Hall. Tom Dewey was conveniently out of sight in another room. Whether or not he was also out of hearing is still a matter of contention. Sprague told Halleck, "you look to us like the Vice-Presidential nominee"; all he had to do was deliver

Indiana. It was as simple as that. A third of the Indiana delegation favored Taft, but when they caucused and heard that their Charlie could be the next Vice-President of the United States, there was no hesitation. Indiana swung unanimously into the Dewey column.

While Charlie Halleck was being filled with dreams of glory, one Dewey move was spiked that afternoon. Rumor had it that Governor Green had also been wooed with the vice-presidency and was thinking of switching away from Taft. As soon as Colonel McCormick heard of it he exploded. Moustache bristling with anger, he picked up the phone and yelled for Green. He wanted a statement immediately, McCormick told his political protégé, that Green was releasing the Illinois delegation after the first ballot in favor of Taft or else. The docile Governor issued the statement.

Wednesday night seven candidates were placed in nomination: Dewey, Taft, Warren, Stassen, Senator Baldwin of Connecticut, Vandenberg, and General MacArthur. By the time the speeches were concluded it was 4:03 in the morning, and the convention recessed without putting through the Dewey plan for an immediate blitz victory.

During the long night of nominating speeches, another detail had been cleared up. The Pennsylvania delegation had met in caucus and, as Dewey had hoped, voted to split 41 for Dewey, 27 for Taft, and 1 each for Vandenberg and Stassen, with 3 still undecided.

The first ballot for the nomination was cast on the afternoon of Thursday, June 24. Dewey led with 434 votes; 548 were needed for victory. Taft was second with 224 and Stassen third with 157. The rest of the vote was Vandenberg 62, Warren 59, Green 56, Driscoll 35, Baldwin 19, Martin 18, B. Carroll Reece 15, MacArthur 11, and Everett Dirksen 1.

Dewey gained 81 votes on the second ballot for a total of 515— 33 short of nomination. Taft gained 50 for a total of 274. The others were Stassen 149, Vandenberg 62, Warren 57, Baldwin 19, Martin 10, MacArthur 7, and Reece 1.

Dewey's victory seemed inevitable, but his opponents made one last frantic attempt to stop him. Governor Duff moved a recess until 7:30 p.m. and was hastily seconded by Senator Knowland of

California and Representative Brown of Ohio. When the motion was put to a voice vote, Chairman Martin professed to be unable to tell whether or not it had carried. Privately he believed that the "ayes" had it, but he preferred to let a roll call decide. Before a roll call could be taken, the New York delegation announced that it had no objection to a recess. New York, of course, did not want to recess but feared the psychological effects on the Dewey bandwagon should it be carried on a roll call. Also, Russell Sprague could hear the nearby Connecticut delegation arguing with Senator Baldwin to swing to Dewey, and he felt a little time to convince the Senator would do no harm.

There are three reports of what happened among the anti-Dewey forces during the recess. One has it that Taft phoned Stassen to tell him that their only chance would be for Stassen to release his delegates to him. Stassen said that he would not consider it until after another ballot. Because Dewey was only 33 votes short, Taft was appalled at Stassen's stubborn belief that there could possibly be a fourth ballot. He accordingly decided to give up the fight as hopeless.

Another report was that a last conference was held between Stassen, Taft, Warren, and Duff, in which they agreed that they would all withdraw in favor of Vandenberg. Colonel McCormick threatened, "If you vote for Vandenberg, I'll give Illinois to Dewey." That settled that.

Finally, Stassen himself later reported that he, Senator Lodge, and Mrs. Ogden Reid attempted to reach General Eisenhower at Columbia University to see if he could be used to stop Dewey. The General was unavailable, and the plan collapsed.

Whatever actually happened in the two and a half hours between sessions, the candidates had made up their minds. At 7:25 p.m., Taft phoned Convention Hall and dictated his letter of withdrawal for Senator Bricker to present to the convention. As soon as the convention reconvened, Taft, Warren, Stassen, Baldwin, Vandenberg, and MacArthur withdrew. Dewey had won his second chance at the presidency.

Dewey appeared on the platform a short time later and delivered his acceptance speech. In it he set the lofty, statesmanlike tone that would dominate his campaign and help to lose him the election. But he made one statement of more than passing interest. "I am happy to be able to say," intoned the nominee, "that I come to you unfettered by a single obligation or promise to any living person." One can see Charlie Halleck's ears pricking up at that one.

Upon leaving the convention hall, Joe Martin ran into Representative Forest Harness of Indiana, who told him happily that Halleck was going to be number-two man on the ticket. Martin seemed skeptical. "If they don't give it to him," Harness threatened, "there's going to be hell to pay in Indiana." "I'm afraid, Forest," was Martin's gentle rejoinder, "there's going to be hell to pay in Indiana."

At eleven o'clock, various leaders gathered with Dewey in his suite to discuss the vice-presidency. Among those present were Governors Bradford of Massachusetts, Driscoll of New Jersey, and Langlie of Washington; Senators Vandenberg, Saltonstall, and Martin; Ed Jaeckle, Russell Sprague, Herbert Brownell, Leonard Hall, Mason Owlett, John Foster Dulles, and Roy Roberts. After being sworn to secrecy by Dewey, the group began to canvass possible running mates. Governor Green was quickly dismissed and then someone asked, "Well, how about Charlie?" Vandenberg asked, "Charlie who?" When he was told "Charlie Halleck," the Michigan Senator roared a disgusted, "Oh, my God!" Bradford and Saltonstall, who favored Stassen, and Driscoll were also opposed to Halleck. Brownell and Sprague remained discreetly silent, but Leonard Hall argued that they had a commitment that should be honored. Finally, Dewey, no longer needing Indiana's votes to help win the nomination, calmly said, "Halleck won't do." Several hours after his acceptance speech, Tom Dewey was indeed unfettered by promises to anyone.

Having double-crossed Halleck, Dewey went on to consider other names. Stassen, Warren, Knowland, Bricker, Senator Hickenlooper, and Senator Furguson, were all considered, and, little by little, it became evident that the Governor of California was the overwhelming choice of those present. The meeting broke up about three in the morning without a formal decision, and, when the group reassembled six hours later, it was unanimously agreed to offer the nomination to Warren. The Californian had already met with Dewey at 4:30 that morning and had agreed to accept the nomination.

As for Charlie Halleck, Dewey has since stated that he had informed his lieutenants to tell him that Wednesday afternoon that he "looked like *a* Vice-Presidential candidate," not "*the* Vice-Presidential candidate." A smooth but hardly convincing explanation.

"Don't you forget that"

THE THIRTIETH DEMOCRATIC NATIONAL CONVENTION
Philadelphia, July 12, 1948

As far as everyone—Republicans and Democrats alike—was concerned, Harry Truman was doomed to certain defeat if he ran for the presidency in 1948. His popularity rating in the polls sagged to 36% in the spring, and the Republican Congress had made mincemeat of his legislative program. The South was in revolt over the Truman civil-rights program, the liberals represented by the Americans for Democratic Action were disgusted because they thought Truman too conservative, and Henry Wallace announced his intention of forming a third party to battle those Truman policies that Wallace believed were leading the nation into war. With so many elements in the party galloping off in all directions in frantic efforts to repudiate Truman, it appeared that the Democratic Party had collapsed in ruins.

If the Democrats could not possibly win with Truman, who could replace him? The disgruntled, dissident, or plain panic-stricken factions of the party all arrived at the same conclusion. Why not Eisenhower? Hopefully believing that the General's refusal to be a candidate on the Republican ticket meant that he was secretly a Democrat who could be drafted, labor, liberals, die-hard southerners, and northern machine bosses whooped up a draft-Eisenhower campaign.

426

The Democratic efforts to dump Harry Truman brought together under the same motley banner one of the oddest collections of politicians who had ever fought the same cause for a dozen different reasons. The entire political spectrum was represented, from the militant liberalism of Leon Henderson, Mayor Hubert Humphrey of Minneapolis, and Chester Bowles to the benighted white supremacists of the South. Floundering loudly and enthusiastically were three Roosevelt sons—Franklin, Jr., James, and Elliot—along with bosses Jake Arvey of Chicago, Frank Hague of New Jersey, and Mayor William O'Dwyer of New York. If, at any previous time, anyone had predicted that Leon Henderson, Frank Hague, and Strom Thurmond would all be lying in the same political bed, he probably would have been certified as lunatic.

If the Democrats had expected Eisenhower to give aid and comfort to their cause, they were soon disappointed. On March 29, an aide of the General's announced that "under no conceivable circumstances" would Eisenhower accept a Democratic draft. Asked by reporters if he would stand on his January letter taking himself out of the Republican race, Eisenhower replied, "I wrote a letter and meant every word of it. I told my aides they could do the talking from now on. I'm not talking any more. I find it doesn't do any good." Indeed, it did not. The draft-Eisenhower forces ignored his disclaimers of availability. Senator Russell hailed him as a states' rights man acceptable to the South, and a week before the convention Leon Henderson was saying, "Claims that the President's nomination is in the bag are entirely unfounded. The convention is already wide open. President Truman is clearly not the first choice of the delegates."

A call went forth to each delegate urging him to join an insurgent caucus on Saturday, July 10—two days before the opening of the convention. The aim would be "To seek the ablest and strongest man available." Among the signers of the call to caucus were Jimmie Roosevelt; Jake Arvey; Mayors O'Dwyer and Humphrey; Senator Lister Hill; the Governors of Arkansas, South Carolina, Virginia, and Texas; Chester Bowles; the national committeemen from Michigan, Wisconsin, Kansas, and Arkansas; and the state chairmen of Nebraska and Utah. On July 4, Frank Hague swung New Jersey into the draft-Eisenhower movement, and the following day Governor McCord of Tennessee promised the General the 28 votes of his state.

Meanwhile, Harry Truman was calmly riding out the storm. Before Eisenhower's retirement from the army, Truman had called him to his office and asked point-blank if he intended to run for president. Eisenhower assured him that he had no such intention, and Truman believed him. The President's attitude was very shrewd. Absolutely convinced that Eisenhower would not permit a draft, he was perfectly willing to see the insurgents crawl out on a very long limb. When Eisenhower sawed off that limb, the anti-Truman movement, with no alternative candidate, would collapse.

On July 5, Eisenhower again stated that he would not be a candidate, whereupon Senator Pepper of Florida, who had apparently taken leave of his senses, made a fantastic proposal. The Florida liberal proposed that Eisenhower be drafted as a "national" rather than as a "party" candidate. He would be free of all "partisan" obligations and was invited to write his own platform and select his own running mate. The Democratic Party would, under this incredible scheme, confine itself to congressional and state elections.

Eisenhower telegraphed Pepper his reaction on Friday, July 9. "No matter under what terms, conditions, or promises a proposal might be couched, I would refuse to accept the nomination. . . . I (ask) you to accept my refusal as final and complete, which it most emphatically is." Even the wishful thinking, self-deluded insurgents had to face the cold political reality. Humbly, Mayor O'Dwyer and Jake Arvey issued a joint statement. "We are now convinced that General Eisenhower is unavailable. . . . It is in the best interest of our country and party that our democracy unite for President Truman."

A bit of comic relief added a final postscript to the anti-Truman movement. With a perfectly straight face, Senator Pepper announced on Sunday, July 11, that he was yielding to a draft and would be a candidate for the presidency. Two days later, when the laughter had subsided enough for him to be heard, the Senator issued a dignified statement withdrawing his candidacy.

The convention opened to a half-empty hall in Philadelphia on Monday, July 12. Nothing seemed to go right. At a memorial service for the war dead, the bugles playing taps hit a number of sour notes, and, when Lawrence Tibbett sang "The Star Spangled Banner," the organist pitched the accompaniment so high that the famed baritone sounded as if he would strangle. There was, however, one bright spot.

On Monday night, the old war horse Alben Barkley arose to deliver the keynote address. Speaking from memory for sixty-eight minutes, Barkley delivered a rousing speech that belied reports that the Democratic Party was dead. It was exactly what the convention needed to come to life, and the delegates responded with a heart-felt twenty-eight-minute ovation.

The revived spirit continued through the second day, but there was an angry explosion on Wednesday when the platform was presented to the convention. A threatening battle between North and South had been shaping up for several days, and it erupted over the civil-rights plank. The plank, as presented by the platform committee, was couched in general terms designed to placate the South without offending the North. Three southern minority reports were submitted, the Mississippi report being the most outspoken for states' rights.

Beside the majority report and the three southern minority reports, the northern liberals presented their own plank. Having failed to dump Truman, the liberals were now ready to end their cozy alliance with the South and to resume the battle for civil rights. The opening sentence of their report was ironic. "We highly commend President Harry Truman for his courageous stand on the issue of civil rights." Having done their best to ditch Truman for a man Senator Russell believed to be a states' righter, the liberals now saw merit in the President. The rest of the plank read, "We call upon the Congress to support our President in guaranteeing these basic and fundamental American principles: the right of full and equal political participation, the right of equal opportunity of employment, the right of security of persons, and the right of equal treatment in the service and defense of our Nation."

In the explosion that followed, the southerners argued constitutional and states' rights, carefully avoiding the moral and human issues involved. The liberals, led by Hubert Humphrey, Jimmie and Franklin Roosevelt, and G. Mennen Williams, argued the human side of the issue. The most effective statement came from Humphrey. "To those who say that this civil rights program is an infringement on States' Rights, I say this, that the time has arrived in America for the Democratic Party to get out of the shadows of States' Rights and to walk forthrightly into the bright sunshine of human rights."

The convention agreed. The southern minority reports were rejected, and the strong liberal plank was substituted for the original by a vote of 651½ to 582½. To the accompaniment of jeers and the waving of Confederate flags, Mississippi and half the Alabama delegation walked out of the convention, while other southerners threatened to bolt later.

On Wednesday, July 14, the convention nominated Harry Truman for the presidency. The South, in a last-ditch effort, backed Senator Richard B. Russell for the nomination, but on the one roll call taken Truman received 923½ votes to 266 for Russell, with 18½ scattered and 23½ not voting. After changes, the official total was Truman 947½, Russell 263, and Paul V. McNutt ½.

Truman had wanted Justice William O. Douglas for his running mate, but, when Douglas refused to be a candidate, Leslie Biffle, minority secretary of the Senate, decided to secure the nomination for his old friend Barkley. Truman did not particularly favor Barkley as a candidate, fearing that his age would be a liability. But, when on Tuesday, July 13, Barkley and Biffle called Truman at the White House to ask if his candidacy would be all right, Truman replied, "Why didn't you tell me you wanted to be Vice-President, Alben? . . . It's all right with me."

Immediately after their nominations, Truman and Barkley appeared before the convention. As they appeared on the rostrum, a flock of pigeons, supposed to represent victory or some such thing, was released to fly around the hall. One perched for a moment on the glistening bald head of Sam Rayburn, much to the Permanent Chairman's disgust and the President's delight. Another pigeon, blinded by the lights and overcome with heat, fell dead.

Harry Truman quickly dispelled any thoughts of dead pigeons. It was after two in the morning, and the delegates were discouraged and weary. But the President came out fighting. "Senator Barkley and I will win this election and make those Republicans like it. Don't you forget that." The audience rose up cheering the cocky candidate who did not recognize defeat when he saw it. He delivered a slashing attack on the Eightieth Congress and then, in a bold stroke, summoned that Congress into special session to dare the Republicans to enact their program into law. Truman had captured the initiative in the campaign, and the delegates, who thought they were cheering a game loser, had no idea that the spirit they had just seen and heard would carry the party to another victory in November.

CHAPTER 22

"It kills me to have to do this to him"

THE TWENTY-FIFTH REPUBLICAN NATIONAL CONVENTION
Chicago, July 7, 1952

The Republican Party quickly recovered from the shattering upset of Thomas E. Dewey in 1948 and made substantial gains in the mid-term elections of 1950. The party had found a new issue, claiming to have found at least one Communist under every bed in the administration. Senator McCarthy, with the blessing of the Republican leadership, was successfully spewing his poison over the Democratic Party, and, on a slightly less scurrilous level, the junior senator from California, Richard M. Nixon, was belaboring the State Department with more vigor than accuracy. A carefully nurtured atmosphere of fear and witch hunting and a national frustration at the hopelessness of the Korean War, combined to discredit the Fair Deal and to enhance Republican prospects for 1952.

In the three previous presidential contests, the moderate, internationalist eastern wing of the party had captured the Republican nomination and gone on to defeat. The old guard, led by Robert A. Taft, was determined that that would not be the case in 1952. Senator Taft announced on October 16, 1951, that he would enter the Wisconsin primary for his third major effort for the nomination. Arguing that "me-tooism" had led to defeat by failing to offer an alternative to the voters, "Mr. Republican" set out to battle on conservative lines that would firmly establish the differences between the two parties. Taft announced himself in opposition to virtually every major policy of the Truman administration and underscored his own party record and regularity. He was a party man first, last, and always, and he aimed his appeals for delegates at the regular, old-line party leaders. The only way to capture the White House, he argued, was through an aggressive attack against the "compete failure of the Truman, Acheson, and Marshall" foreign policy and the creeping socialism of domestic policies.

Tafts' views found a receptive audience among the old-guard party leaders of the Middle West and South, but the eastern wing of the party had no intention of letting the nomination go by default. They needed a candidate who could offset Taft's "Mr. Republican" label and who could overcome the real admiration felt for him among rank and file Republicans.

The first move toward finding a candidate to oppose Taft came in October, 1950. Appearing on "Meet the Press," Governor Dewey announced that he would not be a candidate in 1952 and suggested that the party draft General Eisenhower. The General immediately issued a statement disclaiming any interest in politics. His popularity was, however, undisputed, and the Dewey faction proceeded to create the climate necessary for a draft. By late 1951, the General, by this time recalled to active duty as NATO commander in Paris, was Taft's leading opponent for the nomination.

The question of Eisenhower's party affiliation, if any, was settled in September, 1951, when an old friend, Roy Roberts, president of the Kansas City *Star*, reported that Eisenhower had told him that he was "a good Kansas Republican." Following this news, Governor Sherman Adams of New Hampshire announced at the governors' conference that the General would be entered in the New Hampshire primary the following March. At the same time, seven Republican governors, including Adams, Dewey, Thornton of Colorado, Langlie of Washington, and Peterson of Nebraska endorsed the General's candidacy.

Eisenhower continued to deny any interest in being a candidate, but each denial was weaker than the last. Finally, in November, 1951, he flew to Washington to confer with President Truman on NATO problems. Asked by reporters if Senator Duff had any authorization for the active work in which he was engaged for a draft-Eisenhower movement, the General replied, in the style that would soon become the despair of reporters, "If I have friends that have been my friends so long they believe they know how I would act and react under given conditions, that's their own business and I have never attempted to interfere with any man exercising his own privileges as an American citizen." The General, it would seem, was willing.

The first draft-Eisenhower strategy meeting was held shortly before Thanksgiving at the Hotel Roosevelt in New York City. Among those attending were the men who would be the leaders of the Eisenhower drive—Senator Henry Cabot Lodge of Massachusetts, Governor Dewey and his political aides, Herbert Brownell and J. Russell Sprague, Senator Duff, Senator Frank Carlson of Kansas, Arthur H. Vandenberg, Jr., and General Lucius D. Clay. At the outset, the strategy board decided to base the entire campaign on the single, effective note, "Taft can't win." Lodge was made campaign manager, while Brownell was charged with rounding up delegates.

Beside the "Taft can't win" theme, the Eisenhower managers emphasized that only Eisenhower could carry a Republican Congress, as well as the White House, and that he was the only candidate with major experience in military and foreign affairs. To counter the Taft brand of Republicanism, they argued, the party should not be merely negative but should adopt a program that would safeguard the social and economic reforms already achieved. The Republican Party, they maintained, should be mildly progressive, not staunchly reactionary. Using these arguments, the Eisenhower supporters set out to package a product under the brand name "Ike," which would appeal to moderates, independents, hero worshippers, and anyone in search of a father surrogate.

On Sunday, January 6, 1952, Senator Lodge formally announced the Eisenhower candidacy by entering his name in the New Hampshire primary and assuring the nation "that General Eisenhower is in to the finish." The next day Eisenhower announced from SHAPE headquarters that he was, indeed, willing to be drafted but would not actively seek the nomination. "Under no circumstances will I ask for relief from this assignment in order to seek nomination to political office and I shall not participate in the pre-convention activities of others who may have such intention with respect to me." At that time, Eisenhower believed that the nomination would come to him as a gift of the Republican Party and that all he had to do was to sit back and wait for it.

Taft and Eisenhower would be the leading contestants, but there were others. Harold Stassen had been reported in the fall of 1951 as seeking an understanding with the Taft forces concerning the Minnesota delegation, which he was expected to control. A short time later, he was reported as favoring Eisenhower, which he denied. Still later, he was apparently negotiating with Taft again and was even supposedly saying kind things about Mac-Arthur. He finally made up his mind and announced in December that he was himself a *bona fide* candidate for the nomination.

Stassen in 1952 was a far cry from the liberal boy wonder of 1940 and the sensational campaigner of the spring of 1948. In announcing his candidacy, he came out foursquare for "old fashioned honesty" and a "solid dollar anchored to a modern gold standard." Even more surprising to his one-time supporters, he pledged, if elected, to solicit the advice of such leaders as General MacArthur, Herbert Hoover, Jim Farley, Ralph Bunche, Bernard Baruch, Harry Byrd, and Eisenhower. The Stassen campaign never got off the ground. Poorly financed and completely overshadowed by the Taft-Eisenhower battle, Stassen's candidacy was taken seriously by no one but the candidate, and there were indications that he was more interested in helping Eisenhower than in winning the nomination.

The only other active candidate was Governor Earl Warren of California, who was now in his third term in Sacramento. Warren represented the most liberal wing of the party and could expect to be popular among those Republicans to whom Taft was too conservative and Eisenhower too new a party member. He planned to enter only the California and Wisconsin primaries and counted on a deadlock between the two leading candidates.

The first contest came in the New Hampshire primary. Eisenhower, Taft, and Stassen all entered. Taft had the strong backing of the vitriolic reactionary William Loeb, publisher of the Manchester *Union Leader,* and Wesley Powell, a former assistant to Senator Bridges, who was feuding with Governor Adams and Senator Tobey, both of whom were backing Eisenhower. Taft campaigned vigorously in the state, making thirty speeches in three days, and was reported to have spent more than $50,000 in his campaign.

The Eisenhower forces, whose candidate was overseas, flooded the state with speakers, including Senator Lodge and his brother the former film actor John Lodge, then Governor of Connecticut; Rep. Christian A. Herter of Massachusetts and Walter Judd of Minnesota; Senators Duff, Saltonstall, and Carlson; and Paul Hoffman, Jinx Falkenburg, and Fred Waring and his "Pennsylvanians." In all, $65,000 was spent.

In spite of heavy, cold rain that turned to snow in some areas, the voters turned out in record numbers on March 11. Eisenhower swept to victory with 46,661 votes to 35,838 for Taft. Stassen trailed far behind with 6574. It was a solid victory for Eisenhower, and his prose met the occasion. "Any American," the General said from Paris, "who would have that many other Americans pay him that compliment would be proud or he would not be an American."

If Taft was discouraged by the New Hampshire results, he had still further bad news to face. Appearing in Albuquerque, New Mexico, a few days later, the Senator submitted to having a blessing bestowed on him by a Navaho medicine man. The medicine man had left his turkey-feather wand at home, and he had to improvise the ceremony with a wand of chicken feathers. When asked what he thought of Taft's chances, the medicine man replied, "Maybe fine before ceremony. But the wand had chicken feathers instead of turkey feathers. So now Taft is finished." Considering the bitter charges made later in the campaign, it is surprising that the Taft forces did not accuse the Eisenhower managers of deliberately hiding the turkey wand.

The Minnesota primary came on March 18 and gave Stassen the scare of his life. It was assumed that Stassen would have a clear field in his home state, and the Eisenhower managers therefore decided not to file a slate of delegates. An independent group filed anyway but were too late to get Eisenhower's name on the ballot. So much popular resentment was aroused by this failure that it was decided to organize a write-in campaign in his behalf. The results were startling.

Only Stassen and a stand-in for MacArthur were on the ballot, and it was a grim day, with sleet and rain; a light turn-out of voters was expected. By noon, however, many polling places had run out of ballots, and plain paper slips had to be substituted to accommodate the long lines of voters. The results gave Stassen 44% of the total vote, but Eisenhower's name was written in by 37% of the voters. Taft received 8% by write-in, and the MacArthur slate received 7%. Stassen led by only 20,000 votes and was eliminated from consideration.

The next contest was in Wisconsin on April 1. Taft, Warren, and Stassen were entered. Eisenhower stayed out. Stassen campaigned ineptly and tried at the last minute to gain support by announcing that he would permit half of the delegates he might win to support Eisenhower at the convention. Taft and Warren campaigned in the state, with the result that the Ohio Senator won twenty-four pledged delegates, while Warren won six. Stassen, despite his rather pathetic offer to split his winnings, won none.

On the same day, Taft won a victory in Nebraska. The presidential primary was not binding on the delegates, and only Stassen entered his name. Taft had planned to keep out of the contest, but a strong write-in campaign for Eisenhower forced him to wage a write-in campaign for himself. He won the primary with 36% of the vote to 30% for Eisenhower and 24% for Stassen. The delegation split fourteen for Taft, two for Eisenhower, and two uncommitted. The jubilant Senator declared that his victory proved that there was "just as much groundswell for Taft as for Eisenhower" in the Middle West. Taft also picked up 20 additional votes the following day when Tennessee declared for him.

It was becoming increasingly clear that Taft would be no easy rival and that the nomination would not come to Eisenhower unless he fought for it. Of the delegates chosen so far, seventy-four were for Taft, and only twenty-seven were for Eisenhower. Following the Taft victories in Wisconsin and Nebraska, Senator

Lodge flew to Paris. Eisenhower wrote the Secretary of Defense asking to be relieved of his command, and, on April 11, the White House announced that the General would be relieved as NATO commander on June 1. The General was coming home to fight.

The Illinois primary on April 8 gave Taft another victory. The Eisenhower forces had attempted to roll up a large write-in vote but received only 147,518 votes to Taft's 935,867. The delegation divided fifty-nine for Taft, one for Eisenhower.

A bitter situation developed in New Jersey. Taft had entered the primary believing that Governor Driscoll would remain neutral. When the Governor announced himself for Eisenhower, Taft angrily declared that he had been "double-crossed" and tried to withdraw. After a complicated legal battle, it was ruled by the courts that Taft could not withdraw his name, but he closed his headquarters and canceled his speaking engagements. Many of his supporters, however, continued to campaign for him, and the Eisenhower forces sneered that the withdrawal was merely a ruse to claim victory if he won and discount defeat if he lost. Eisenhower swept the primary, and at least thirty of the thirty-eight delegates would support him in the convention.

The battle see-sawed during the rest of April, with both candidates gaining new strength, but the seventy-man Pennsylvania delegation was no help to anyone. There was a three-way split among Governor Fine, Senator Duff, and G. Mason Owlett. Senator Duff's faction was for Eisenhower, Owlett's was for Taft, and Governor Fine, controlling an estimated 30 votes, was uncommitted. As nearly as anyone could tell, twenty to twenty-five delegates favored Eisenhower, eighteen favored Taft, and twenty-seven to thirty-two were willing to jump with the Governor. The confused situation would make Governor Fine one of the most sought after men at the convention.

In the next two primaries, Taft won easily in West Virginia, where he had the backing of the state organization, while Eisenhower swept the field in Oregon. California went as expected to Warren, and, in the last popular test before the convention, Taft defeated Eisenhower in the South Dakota primary by about 800 votes. By the time all the delegates had been chosen, the Associated Press reported 458 pledged to Taft, 406 pledged to Eisenhower, and ninety-three contested. There were 115 uncommitted delegates, and 134 were pledged to minor candidates. It had been a close and bitter preconvention race, and the outcome was still very much in doubt. The contested delegations would be of the utmost importance.

Mississippi, Florida, Georgia, and Texas were contested. Mississippi was simple enough. There were two rival factions—the Black and Tans and the Lily Whites. At every Republican convention since 1924, the Black and Tans, led by Washington lawyer Perry Howard, had been contested by the Lily Whites, led by an aged former Governor of Nebraska who had moved to Mississippi in 1909. In every convention, the Black and Tans were seated, and the Eisenhower forces made no effort to prevent their being seated in 1952, even though the delegation was solidly pro-Taft.

Florida also offered little problem. The delegation was originally chosen, as provided by state law, by the state executive committee and divided fifteen for Taft, three for Eisenhower. But a dissident group offered a contesting delegation, also pro-Taft. Again, the Eisenhower forces had no reason to be interested in the contest.

Louisiana was another matter. The contest was based largely on the effort of a pro-Eisenhower group to overthrow the machine of the national committeeman who had rammed through a pro-Taft delegation. The methods of selecting the delegation were high handed, to say the least, and the contesting Eisenhower delegation had an excellent case for its demands for representation.

If Louisiana was a simple case of stolen delegates, Georgia was more complicated. In 1944, a split had occurred in the Republican state party, and the rival groups became known as the Tucker and Foster factions. In 1944, the Tucker faction had been pro-Dewey, the Foster faction uninstructed. The Dewey forces seated the Tucker delegation. In 1948, the question arose, whether or not either delegation was the "legal" Republican Party in Georgia, and the Georgia secretary of state ruled in favor of the Foster delegation, which was pro-Taft. But the National Committee and credentials committee reversed this ruling and seated the pro-Dewey Tucker delegation.

In 1952, the two factions chose their delegations—the Tucker group was for Eisenhower, the Foster group for Taft. Seventeen votes were at stake. Before the convention, the Foster factions filed suit in Superior Court asking that they be declared the legal Republican Party in Georgia, and the court so ruled. By the time of the convention, the pro-Taft Foster faction had the ruling of the Georgia secretary of state in 1948 and the Superior Court ruling in 1952 that it was the legal representative of the Republicans in Georgia. The Tucker faction had on its side the fact that it had been seated in the last two national conventions. There was no question of a "steal" or any more skulduggery than usual. It was simply a matter of a long-standing factional fight that had always been settled in favor of the delegation supporting the candidate who had a majority of the National and credentials committees.

Texas was the most confused of all. The Republican Party in the state was firmly under the control of Henry Zweifel, the national committeeman, who favored Taft. An upsurge of popularity for Eisenhower caused formation of a faction headed by Jack Porter of Houston. Many Democrats wished to see a pro-Eisenhower delegation from Texas and threatened to swamp the regular state Republican Party. To offset the influx of Democrats into local and county conventions, Zweifel ordered that all participants in local conventions sign a statement swearing that they were Republicans and wished to participate. Once the Democrats signed such a pledge—and they did by the hundreds—they were legally Republicans in terms of the party conventions.

The influx of new Republicans dominated most of the precinct and county conventions, but the pro-Taft forces managed to send mostly "regular" Republicans to the state convention. Both factions made a determined fight, and it was later estimated that the pro-Eisenhower forces spent from three to six million dollars in Texas before the state convention.

The state convention met in Mineral Wells on May 27. On the previous day, the state executive committee, dominated by the Zweifel pro-Taft group, sat to consider contested delegations from thirty-one counties. "Regardless of the evidence," they accepted twenty-six Taft delegations, assuring control of the state convention.

The Eisenhower delegations were rejected as not being true Republicans, and Zweifel was quoted as saying that the Republican Party had been saved from "mob rule."

On the 27th, the "regular" convention selected an uninstructed delegation, which gave 30 votes to Taft, with 4 each for Eisenhower and MacArthur. The rejected Eisenhower delegates met across the street in rump session on the same day and picked a delegation instructed 33 for Eisenhower, 5 for Taft. The basic argument, which would be carried to the national convention, was that the Eisenhower delegation did not represent true Republicans, even though they had signed pledges attesting to their Republicanism, no matter how new.

The Eisenhower forces saw in the events in Texas and Georgia a major issue. The General had returned from Europe and made his first political appearance at Abilene, Kansas, on June 4. It was a disaster. Speaking to a national television audience in a rainstorm, Eisenhower appeared old, tired, and hesitant. His speech was trite, platitudinous, and crushingly dull. With Taft leading in pledged delegates and this inauspicious political debut, Eisenhower was plainly in trouble. He needed an issue quickly if the Taft drive were to be stopped.

Texas came as a gift from heaven to the Eisenhower forces. The General might be an unimpressive public speaker, and his knowledge of government and politics might be nil, but he could be counted on to know right from wrong. Turn Eisenhower into a militant crusader doing battle against the greedy politicians who attempted to disenfranchise the voters of Texas, and who could tell what might happen? It should be emphasized that the morality of the Texas case was always secondary to its political usefulness. Virtue may be its own reward in most cases, but in politics it is merely a means to an end. True, there had been dirty work in Texas, but the cry of "steal" went up more to stop Taft than to achieve justice for its own sake.

The righteous cries of "theft" caught on brilliantly. It was a popular issue and served to dramatize the Eisenhower candidacy, as no discussion of his qualifications for office could ever have done. In Dallas on June 21, Eisenhower kicked off his crusade by blasting the Texas Taft men for "deliberately and ruthlessly" disenfranchising the Eisenhower forces and declared, "the rustlers stole the Texas birthright instead of steers."

The Republican National Convention was scheduled to meet in Chicago on July 7. On the 1st, the National Committee met to begin hearings on the contested delegations. At the outset, a bitter clash developed. The Eisenhower forces argued, in order to dramatize their issue as widely as possible, that the hearings should be televised. Taft himself had no objection, but his supporters argued, with some merit, that television was not conducive to a judicial atmosphere. By a vote of 60 to 20 the National Committee barred the television cameras.

The National Committee sat for four days in an atmosphere of acrimonious, often violent, debate. Georgia was heard first. The committee had a strong Taft majority and voted to seat the Foster faction, giving all 17 votes to Taft. The thirteen contested Louisiana delegates were awarded two to Eisenhower, eleven to Taft.

On Friday, July 4, it was the turn of Texas. Chairman of the National Committee Guy Gabrielson opened the hearing with two unexpected proposals. First, he read a telegram from Herbert Hoover, suggesting that both sides select an individual to meet with him and arbitrate the Texas contest. Second, the chairman read a letter from Taft proposing to compromise by giving Eisenhower sixteen delegates, while keeping twenty-two for himself. Obviously the cry of "steal" was beginning to hurt, and Taft was willing to concede part to save all.

The committee adjourned to await the Eisenhower reply, which came quickly. The General liked the Taft proposal and favored accepting it, but Senator Lodge apprised him of the political realities of the situation. They wanted the issue even more than the votes, and Eisenhower changed his mind. Lodge thereupon rejected the Hoover proposal and said loftily of the Taft offer, "General Eisenhower is a no deal man." The National Committee then voted to accept the Taft compromise 60 to 41.

The Taft forces had, as expected, won the first round, but they suffered a stunning blow from another direction. From the governors' conference then meeting in Houston came, on July 2, a manifesto signed by twenty-three of the twenty-five Republican governors. The governors' manifesto urged that, contrary to usual practice, contested delegates not be allowed to vote in the convention until after their contests had been settled. Ordinarily in a national convention, delegates are seated on a temporary roll approved by the National Committee and permitted to vote on all questions except their own contests. If usual procedure were to be followed, the pro-Taft Texas and Louisiana delegations would be allowed to vote to seat the pro-Taft Georgia delegation, which in turn would join with Texas to seat Louisiana, and so forth. If the governors' manifesto were accepted, it would mean the loss of 50 Taft votes on the crucial roll call vote on the credentials committee report.

Chairman Gabrielson replied by arguing that a convention could be rendered helpless if every delegation were contested and commented tartly, "It is difficult for me to understand why some of those who controlled the Republican National Conventions of 1944 and 1948 did not seek such a rule then, but demand it now."

But the Eisenhower forces went right ahead. It was announced that Governor Langlie of Washington would offer a change in the rules to prevent contested delegations from voting until after their contests had been settled. This "Fair Play Amendment," as it was shrewdly called, had been Herbert Brownell's idea, and the details had been worked out by Christian Herter. It was a master stroke to dramatize for the delegates and the nation the Eisenhower fight. As one Taft supporter bitterly asked, "Who can be against fair play?"

During the weekend before the convention, attention shifted to the uncommitted delegations. Governor Fine was thoroughly enjoying his position as potential kingmaker and remarked with obvious delight, "I'm being kinda wooed." Privately, he let it be known that he favored General MacArthur but would listen to blandishments from Taft and Eisenhower. He intended to play his cards very close to the chest until events indicated the best way for an ambitious governor to jump.

Fine kept in constant touch with Arthur Summerfield, whose Michigan delegation was also waiting to see which bandwagon to board. Summerfield set up an organization to keep close contact with the key delegations. Reports were made twice daily to Michigan headquarters, and the reports were plotted on special charts to gauge the sentiments of the convention. Neither Fine nor Summerfield would move until he was absolutely sure, despite the mounting pressure on both delegations to break for either Taft or Eisenhower.

The already committed delegations were being used by Taft to exert part of that pressure. On Sunday, the day before the opening of the convention, the Senator announced that he had pledges from 500 delegates, who had formed a Taft Delegates Club, with the avowed purpose of staying with the Senator until the very end. It was an impressive display of strength but was, unfortunately for Taft, a display of his maximum power. He would have to overcome the constantly repeated "Taft can't win" argument to secure an additional 104 delegates necessary to nomination, and among those 500 pledges were the contested delegates. If he lost them, his Delegates Club would be substantially reduced.

One potential source of additional strength was denied to Taft on that same Sunday. The New York delegation was officially for Eisenhower, thanks to Tom Dewey, but more than 40% of the delegation wished to vote for Taft. Dewey settled that by reminding them in caucus that he would be "Governor for the next two and one-half years" and threatened to wreck the political career of any delegate who dared to abandon Eisenhower. The reminder was brutal but effective. Only four of the ninety-six delegates were willing to risk the Governor's wrath by voting for Taft.

When the convention opened on Monday, it appeared that, for all his troubles with the contested delegations, Taft still had a firm grip on the nomination. The convention organization was stacked solidly in his favor. Walter Hallanan of West Virginia would be temporary chairman and former Speaker Joe Martin permanent chairman. As an added pro-Taft attraction, General Douglas MacArthur was scheduled as keynoter, and, of course, Herbert Hoover would put in his usual appearance. If the Eisenhower managers were to win, they would have to do it outside the regular organization of the convention.

The first Taft-Eisenhower battle came almost immediately. Senator Bricker proposed the adoption of the previous rules, and the

Eisenhower forces countered with the Langlie "Fair Play Amendment." In listing the contested delegates who would be excluded from voting until their cases had been settled, the Langlie Amendment included seven Louisiana delegates whose contests had been settled by the state committee. Congressman Brown of Ohio, Taft's manager, proposed an amendment that would exclude those seven delegates from the Langlie amendment. It was a fatal move. By implication the Taft forces were accepting the Langlie amendment if the convention would include the Brown amendment. It was a serious sign of weakness in the Taft forces.

The debate on the two amendments took up most of the afternoon session and was highly technical, citing precedent and previous rules. Both sides were, they said, for fair play, but the Taft forces argued that changing the rules in the middle of the game was less than fair. In the crucial test—the vote on the Brown amendment—the convention disagreed with the Taft argument and defeated the amendment on a roll call 658 to 548. It was a stunning blow to Taft but not necessarily fatal. While the outcome of the vote was taken as a measure of the strength of the respective candidates, many delegates who were not Eisenhower men voted against the Brown amendment. California, for instance, voted solidly against Taft on the issue, but Eisenhower could not expect to have the state on the presidential roll call. Twenty-four delegates who voted against Taft on the Brown Amendment subsequently voted for him on the presidential ballot. Even though many delegates saw this initial contest as something more than a straight Taft-Eisenhower contest, however, the loss to Taft when the Langlie amendment was adopted by voice vote was considerable. It was evident that the "steal" and "steamroller" charges had taken effect and that the Eisenhower men had the immense advantage of having taken the initiative and having won the first test. A typical reaction to the adoption of the Langlie amendment came from Harry Truman, who remarked, grinning gleefully, "I am afraid that my favorite candidate is going to be beaten."

There was more bad news for Taft that day. The Eisenhower managers had been steadily increasing their pressure on the bloc of votes held by Warren, Stassen, Fine, and Governor McKeldin of Maryland. McKeldin was the first to break. While the Maryland delegation was in caucus deciding to cast its 24 votes on the first ballot for the Governor as a favorite son, McKeldin was called to the telephone. He returned to the caucus room to announce jubilantly, "I'm going to nominate Ike." He released the delegation, which ultimately went 16 for Eisenhower, 8 for Taft.

If the Taft forces hoped to recover something from the defeats of the afternoon through MacArthur's keynote address in the evening, they were sadly mistaken. The old soldier had faded more than he knew. His speech attacked the Democrats on all fronts but sounded more like a presentation of his own availability than an endorsement of Taft. Various MacArthur supporters had hoped that their hero could stampede the convention for himself, but the delegates were unimpressed. The battle was between Taft and Eisenhower, and MacArthur flew back the same night to his Waldorf-Astoria tower, straining to hear the trumpet call that would never be sounded.

Tuesday continued the steady deterioration of the Taft forces. The credentials committee had agreed to television coverage, and the second round of the contested delegations battle was fought out in full view of the convention and the country. Meeting at 10:00 a.m. in a room in the Congress Hotel, the committee took up the case of Georgia. Many weary, argumentative hours later, the committee voted 30 to 21 to sustain the National Committee and seat the Taft delegation. But it was no victory. Senator Lodge immediately announced that the fight would be carried to the floor of the convention, and the minority report favoring the Eisenhower delegation was signed by committeemen from twenty-two delegations with a total vote of 646. The balance of power had clearly shifted to Eisenhower.

By the time the credentials committee had disposed of Georgia, it was 1:30 Wednesday morning. The committee had been in session for more than fifteen hours. Realizing that most of the television audience had long since gone to bed, the Eisenhower men moved to recess until 10:00 a.m. In a moment of carelessness, Representative Brown, speaking for Taft, agreed. As an Eisenhower man said later, "How dumb can a man get? At 1:30, we had practically no audience. At 10:00, we had millions listening to our case." Taft had lost another psychological round.

The main events in the Eisenhower camp on Tuesday consisted of naming Governor Sherman Adams as floor manager and a three-hour conference between Governor Fine and Eisenhower. After the meeting, Fine revealed more of himself than he perhaps intended. Announcing that he still had no preference, he said that the conference had been devoted to "practical politics—I never discuss anything else but." Suddenly remembering that the Eisenhower forces were supposedly engaged in a great moral struggle, he hastily amended his statement to admit they had, indeed, discussed matters of principle. "I am primarily interested in principles," said Fine, adding after a pause, "at this time."

The credentials committee reconvened on Wednesday morning to be met with a surprise offer from Taft. The National Committee had voted to seat eleven Taft delegates and two Eisenhower delegates from Louisiana. The Taft forces now proposed to give all thirteen votes to Eisenhower. It was a desperation move to remove the "steal" stigma that was enveloping the entire Taft campaign, but it was also a sign of weakness. As expected, Senator Lodge had no intention of accepting the delegates as a peace offering. What were eleven delegates compared to the issue that was providing the steam for the Eisenhower roller? With a piety more arrogant than believable, the Senator announced that both the Georgia and Louisiana contests would be fought on the floor because they were "stains on the integrity of our party that we must erase if we are to go to the people with clean hands and ask them to have faith in our party to lead the nation in the years that lie ahead." Having failed to effect a compromise on Louisiana, the committee then voted 27 to 24 to seat the Texas compromise delegation of 22 Taft and 16 Eisenhower delegates. The way was now cleared for the floor fight.

As the final battle approached, both sides became increasingly bitter and vicious. The Eisenhower camp flooded Chicago with extremely effective pamphlets comparing the steamroller that "stole" delegations for William Howard Taft in 1912 to the attempted "steals" in favor of his son forty years later. The Taft forces, in reply, aimed their attack at the supposedly cold-blooded machine of Thomas E. Dewey, who was accused of trying to ram an Eisenhower nomination down the throat of the Republican

party. Under the heading of "SINK DEWEY!!" the Taft managers
circulated a broadside remarkable for its vitriolic abuse of the
Governor of New York. "TOM DEWEY IS THE MOST COLD-
BLOODED, RUTHLESS, SELFISH POLITICAL BOSS IN THE
UNITED STATES TODAY. He stops at nothing to enforce his
will. His promises are worthless. He is the greatest menace that
the Republican party has. Twice he has led us down the road to
defeat, and now he is trying the same trick again hidden behind
the front of another man." The fear of impending defeat was driving the Taft forces to the edge of hysteria.

Amid the welter of broadsides, attacks, and counterattacks and
a violent emotionalism rarely matched in political conventions, the
undecided delegations began slipping one by one into the Eisenhower camp. Wednesday afternoon the Michigan delegation was
visited by several leaders of the automotive industry, including
Henry Ford II and Charles E. Wilson of General Motors, who
were believed to favor Eisenhower. It was widely rumored that
Arthur Summerfield had agreed with Governor Fine to go to Eisenhower. Fine announced that afternoon that he was supporting the
General. The Langlie-amendment victory and the expected victory
in the contested-delegation floor fight had been enough to convince
the Governor that his own best interests lay with the winner,
Eisenhower.

The Taft forces were determined to go down fighting. When
the delegates took their seats for the Wednesday session, which
would settle the contest battle, they found on their chairs a mimeo-
graphed statement from Herbert Hoover favoring Taft for the
nomination. As the arguments over the Georgia delegation raged
through the convention and the tension rose to the breaking point,
Senator Dirksen unleashed a blast at the forces who were depriv-
ing Taft of his life-long ambition. Pointing one of the most eloquent
forefingers in politics at the New York delegation, he roared at
Tom Dewey, "we followed you before and you took us down the
path to defeat." In the pandemonium of boos and catcalls that
followed, it was difficult to tell whether the convention was booing the Governor of New York or the attacks made upon him.
Most observers believed that the uproar was a heartfelt expression
of the opinion most delegates had of Tom Dewey. They were

willing to face up to the political reality and go along with the Eisenhower bandwagon, but they welcomed the opportunity to express themselves on the subject. Having touched off the violent demonstration, Senator Dirksen mildly asserted, "This is no place for Republicans to be booing other Republicans."

The contest was never really in doubt. During the roll call on the Georgia contest, the Puerto Rico delegation won a moment in history by providing a bit of comic relief (some insisted carefully planned) arising out of Chairman Martin's inability to cope with the intricacies of Latin names and accents. The diversion helped to break some of the tension, which threatened to erupt into physical violence, but it could not save the Taft forces. By a vote of 607 to 531, the convention voted to seat the Eisenhower delegation from Georgia. Louisiana and Texas were both debated at length, but the Taft forces were beaten. On a voice vote, the Eisenhower delegations were seated, and "fair play" carried the day.

After the intensive struggle over the contested delegations, the nominations of candidates, which came on Thursday, were an anticlimax. The signs of an Eisenhower victory were clear, and the supporters of the other candidates put up a brave but hopeless show. Taft, Warren, Eisenhower, Stassen, and MacArthur were placed in nomination. The Eisenhower demonstration was the most efficient, the Taft the most fervent, and the MacArthur the oddest. A singularly gamy collection of demonstrators had been gathered for MacArthur, and when, after the demonstration, a delegate complained to the police that his watch was missing, he was told that when demonstrators like that were hired off the streets he had been lucky to lose only his watch.

Bit by bit the forces holding out against Eisenhower crumbled away. A portent of the future came from the Minnesota delegation, which had ordered signs reading "Minnesota Wants Stassen" on slip-over paper that could be torn off to read, "Minnesota Wants Eisenhower." During the Eisenhower demonstration, Michigan had met in caucus and voted to go 34 for Eisenhower, 12 for Taft. Of the major blocs committed neither to Taft nor Eisenhower, only California showed no signs of succumbing to the Eisenhower bandwagon.

The roll call for the presidential nomination was held on Friday morning. The only real question was whether or not Eisenhower could be prevented from winning on the first ballot. Few delegates in the convention really wanted Eisenhower; their hearts were with Taft. He was Mr. Republican, and his services to the party merited the nomination, but could he win? The party loved Taft, but it loved a winner even more. As one delegate who planned to desert Taft for Eisenhower wailed, "My God, I love him. It kills me to have to do this to him."

At first, it seemed as if Taft had been counted out too soon. The first seventeen delegations on the roll call gave Eisenhower 140 votes, but Taft led with 188. Maryland, the first uncommitted state, narrowed Taft's lead by voting 16 Eisenhower, 8 Taft. When the next doubtful delegation, Michigan, cast 35 votes for Eisenhower and only 11 for Taft, the General was leading the Senator 225 to 211. Slowly the lead see-sawed. As thousands of delegates and spectators hung breathlessly over their tally sheets, Eisenhower gradually increased his lead. Then Pennsylvania swung 53 votes to Eisenhower, who at that point led 492 to 365. At the end of the roll call, the unofficial results were Eisenhower 595—9 votes short of nomination—Taft 500, Warren 81, Stassen 20, MacArthur 10.

The stampede came as soon as the Virgin Islands unanimously cast its 1 vote for Eisenhower. All over the auditorium, state banners were being frantically waved to attract the chairman's attention, but Harold Stassen was more agile than the rest. The Minnesota delegation had met in caucus early Friday morning. Several delegates had become nervous at being bound to Stassen, and finally five demanded their release. Senator Thye told Stassen that Eisenhower would have at least 580 votes on the first ballot and recommended that Minnesota be allowed to switch to ensure Eisenhower's nomination. Stassen consented. Later, Stassen said that it had always been part of his plan to wait to see if Minnesota held the balance of power and then to throw his support to Eisenhower as the more liberal of the two leading candidates. He refrained from saying what he had in mind if Minnesota had not held the balance of power. At any rate, Minnesota was recognized by Chairman Martin and gave Eisenhower the nomination.

In the midst of the stampede to be with the winner, the die-hard Taft men held out. As Senator Dirksen told the Illinois delegation, "Bob Taft wouldn't think much of us if we ran for the bandwagon now." Considering how bitter the fight had been, it was not surprising that many Taft delegates would stick to the end. What was surprising was that most of Warren's votes also held out. California, the six Wisconsin delegates, and one North Dakota delegate remained aloof from the scramble to Eisenhower. After all the changes had been made, the official results of the ballot were Eisenhower 845, Taft 280, Warren 77, MacArthur 4. "Taft can't win," fair play, and a war hero with an engaging grin and no discernible political views had carried the day.

As the delegates were streaming out of the auditorium, a florid delegate shouted laughingly to the crowd, "Last one out is Vice President." The selection of the running mate was not so casual as all that but came as something of a surprise to many delegates.

The Eisenhower managers met with the nominee in his suite at the Blackstone Hotel. Present were Governor Dewey, Senators Lodge and Carlson, Herbert Brownell, and Arthur Summerfield. Eisenhower expressed reluctance to dictate the choice of a running mate but offered a list of acceptable candidates: Senator Nixon, Lodge, Governor Thornton of Colorado, Governor Langlie, Governor Driscoll, Senator Knowland, and Harold Stassen. Unlike the others at the meeting, Eisenhower apparently attached no special significance to the order of the names.

Senator Richard Nixon was considered the leading candidate for various reasons. First, his youth would make a good contrast with the sixty-one-year-old General. As a Californian, Nixon would provide a good geographic balance to the ticket and could be expected to help carry an important state. He had made a national reputation for himself in the Hiss case, and, finally he had a reputation for what might politely be called a hard-hitting campaign style.

The Senator himself had not been inactive in his pursuit of the vice-presidential nomination. Before the convention, Paul Hoffman had conferred separately with Senators Knowland and Nixon, holding out the hope of second place on the ticket if California could be swung from Warren to Eisenhower. Senator Know-

land had already turned down such an offer from the Taft camp
and was firm in his resolve to keep the California delegation
committed to Warren.

Nixon was more receptive. He went to Chicago on July 1 to
work on the platform and then flew to Denver on the 4th to board
the train carrying the California delegation to Chicago. Within
minutes, the previously harmonious train was seething with rumors
that California would be "left at the post" unless it abandoned
Warren and switched to Eisenhower. If California climbed on the
bandwagon early enough, so the arguments ran, the state would
be in a position to name Nixon as the vice-presidential candidate.
Ill feeling ran so high at the suggestion of abandoning Warren
that some angry delegates proposed denying Nixon a berth on the
train. He remained, but it was an angry, divided delegation that
arrived in Chicago. Neither then, nor at any time thereafter, did
the California delegation make the slightest effort to promote
Nixon for the nomination.

During the convention, Nixon scurried busily around Chicago
doing what he could to advance the Eisenhower candidacy. His
most valuable contribution came over the Langlie amendment.
Not wishing to help either leading candidate, California had decided to split its vote on the Langlie amendment, half for the
Eisenhower position, half for Taft's. But in caucus Nixon so per-
suasively argued the moral issue that the delegation agreed to vote
as a unit for the Langlie amendment and against the Brown
amendment.

Once the Eisenhower managers had Eisenhower's list of preferences, they held a conference in the Hilton Hotel with some thirty
or forty party leaders. Dewey did not appear, but Brownell, Lodge,
Russell Sprague, Sinclair Weeks, Governor Fine, Senator Duff,
Sherman Adams, Summerfield, Paul Hoffman, and Roy Roberts
were among those present. All were tired to the point of exhaustion, and the discussion was desultory. Their immediate goal had
been Eisenhower's nomination, and now sleep seemed more important than a running mate. The first name suggested was that
of Taft, together with the assurance that he would accept in the
interest of party harmony. There was a heavy silence. Then Russell Sprague said flatly that the Republicans could not carry New

York with Taft on the ticket. Taft himself had by telephone suggested Dirksen, but the Illinois Senator was vetoed by Governor Beardsley of Iowa. Again there was silence. Nixon's name was offered third, and Paul Hoffman spoke well of him and implied that Dewey favored him. No one had any objections. Without debate, the consensus was that Nixon would be satisfactory. The Eisenhower list of seven names was never produced or mentioned. Eisenhower was immediately called and told that the caucus had decided on Nixon, and he replied, "That's fine by me."

Friday afternoon, the convention met to ratify the caucus decision. Senator Knowland, whatever his private feelings, placed Nixon's name in nomination with a short speech that placed most of its emphasis on the junior senator's drive and determination. Nixon was thereupon nominated by acclamation.

At the final session, both candidates addressed the convention. In beginning, Eisenhower paid tribute to his running mate as a man with "a special talent and an ability to ferret out any kind of subversive influence wherever it may be found, and the strength and persistence to get rid of it." He then made graceful obeisance to Taft, Warren, and Stassen and went on to pledge a great crusade for "a more secure, a brighter and an even better future for all our people." Only a cynic would point out that a crusade is something a politician leads when he has no program.

"Times when a man is not permitted to say 'no'"

THE THIRTY-FIRST DEMOCRATIC NATIONAL CONVENTION
Chicago, July 21, 1952

The last strains of "I Like Ike" had hardly faded from the streets and hotel lobbies of Chicago when the Democrats moved in to prepare for their convention. Down came the portraits of Lincoln, the Taft and Eisenhower banners and posters were swept off the streets, and in the lobby of the Hilton Hotel appeared an entire log cabin—a facsimile tribute to the humble beginnings of Oklahoma's favorite Democratic son, Senator Robert S. Kerr. Donkeys replaced elephants, and groggy Chicagoans braced themselves for a week of "Happy Days Are Here Again" and the "Missouri Waltz."

The Democratic National Convention of 1952 was, for the Democrats, that almost forgotten phenomenon—an open convention. Not since Cactus Jack Garner swung to Franklin D. Roosevelt on the fourth ballot in 1932 had there been an open race for the Democratic nomination for president.

Until March 29, 1952, the dominant question among Democrats had been, Will Truman run again? At the Jefferson-Jackson Day dinner in Washington on that date, Harry S. Truman took himself out of the race, and an array of heirs apparent—bewildering in number—leaped eagerly for the nomination. Senator Estes Kefauver of Tennessee; Senator Richard Russell of Georgia; Senator Kerr; Vice-President Alben W. Barkley; and Director of the Mutual

Security Agency W. Averell Harriman were all active campaigners for the nomination. Adlai E. Stevenson, Governor of Illinois and grandson of a vice-president, was, despite his best efforts, also considered a major contender. In the favorite son and dark-horse categories were Senators Brien McMahon of Connecticut and Hubert Humphrey of Minnesota; Governor Paul Dever of Massachusetts; Federal Security Agency Administrator Oscar Ewing; and Speaker of the House Sam Rayburn.

The first to be off and running was the carefully folksy, coonskin-capped hero of the Senate investigations of organized crime, Estes Kefauver. He was a liberal who had made his first reputation in politics as a reformer and opponent of bossism. Through his televised investigations into crime, Kefauver was one of the best known figures in the party. At the beginning of 1952, he was in a difficult position. President Truman had not yet announced whether or not he would seek another term. Those candidates with strong regional or organizational backing could afford to wait on the President's decision; Kefauver could not. He had no backing from the power blocs or party leaders, and his only chance for the nomination was to go directly to the voters. To do so, however, would mean antagonizing the party's leaders, especially Truman.

In an effort to solve this problem, Kefauver called on Truman on January 15 to sound out his plans. The President, however, was noncommittal. Would he attempt to block Kefauver's bid for the nomination? The President indicated that he would not but gave no hint of whether or not he planned to run again. Taking Truman's vague assurances as an indication of neutrality, Kefauver announced on January 23 that he was a candidate for the nomination and would enter several primaries, including New Hampshire, where Truman was already entered.

Many Democrats were aghast at the brashness of a freshman senator's challenging the President in a primary. Truman himself was obviously nettled. Presidential primaries, he snapped, were "eye-wash," and, if he decided to seek renomination, he would not need any primaries to get it. A few days later, at the frantic urging of New Hampshire Democratic leaders, who had entered a slate of delegates in his name, the President reconsidered and permitted his name to remain in the primary. Also, to soften what appeared to be his contempt for the primaries, he asserted that he had merely meant to point out that preference primaries were not binding on the delegates. As for himself, he had "long favored a nation-wide presidential primary, so that the voters could really choose their own candidates."

It was Kefauver's strategy to present himself as a political moderate slightly left of center, and in New Hampshire this moderate stance appealed to the voters. Kefauver waged an intensive campaign, shaking hands up and down every main street in the state—and wandering inadvertently on one occasion over the border into Vermont. The results of his campaigning stunned the Senator as well as the Democratic Party. On March 11, the voters gave him a 19,800-to-15,927 victory over President Truman and all eight delegates. From Key West, Florida, where he was vacationing, Truman announced that the primary outcome would have no influence on his decision whether or not to run for re-election.

The President was speaking the absolute truth when he stated that the New Hampshire primary would not affect his decision. He had long before made up his mind not to be a candidate and had told his staff in November, 1951. The only decision he had to make was whom to back for the nomination. His first choice was Chief Justice Fred Vinson, but Vinson told him that his health would not permit his candidacy.

After looking over the field, the deeply disappointed President decided that the fifty-two-year-old Governor of Illinois, Adlai Stevenson, was the best. Stevenson had had wide public experience in service in the Navy and State Departments, and he had played a leading role in the writing and implementing of the charter of the United Nations. He had been elected governor in 1948 by more than 500,000 votes and had made an impressive record in that office. In all, he had the background, the administrative experience, proven ability as a vote-getter, and style, wit, and intelligence that would make him an impressive campaigner.

Stevenson called on the President on January 22 to discuss, he thought, mine-safety legislation. The Governor arrived at Blair House at 8:30 p.m. and stayed until after eleven. Truman asked him if he would accept the nomination, giving assurances that, if he agreed, he could be nominated. Stevenson was flabbergasted by the offer, but Truman was even more flabbergasted when he refused. Stevenson had, on January 7, announced that he would seek re-election as Governor of Illinois and felt an obligation to make the race. Beside, he didn't want to be president.

Stevenson was eagerly questioned by the press as he left Blair House. He refused to discuss whether or not presidential politics had come up in the conversation but inadvertently gave himself away when a reporter asked if the President had mentioned Stevenson's divorce. "Yes," the Governor replied. "He said it wouldn't matter." But, he insisted, he was not and would not be a candidate.

Even though the Governor maintained that the only office he was interested in was the one he presently held, a group of admirers organized in early February an Illinois Stevenson-for-President Committee. Led by Walter Johnson, Professor of History at the University of Chicago, and Leo Lerner, Chicago newspaper publisher, the committee ran a full page advertisement in the Chicago *Sun-Times* announcing a draft Stevenson movement and asking for support. Reaction was favorable, and, although Stevenson refused to have any dealings with the committee, the draft movement began to pick up support.

Early in March, the White House asked Stevenson to call again upon the President. Traveling under an assumed name to prevent newsmen from finding out that he was going to Washington, Stevenson flew to see the President. Again he was urged to seek the nomination, and again he replied that he could run for only one office—Governor of Illinois. The somewhat exasperated Truman urged him at least to think it over.

Speculation over Stevenson's availability reached major proportions on March 29, 1952. On that night, President Truman announced that he would not be a candidate for re-election. After the President's speech, nearly everyone in the ballroom rushed toward Stevenson. Jacob Arvey said that it was one of the most amazing things ever seen in politics. "Photographers literally knocked each other down to get pictures of him. Reporters crowded around to ask if he would be a candidate. Party leaders from all over the country pumped his hand. The Governor seemed to be enjoying it, but he still refused to change his stand."

Later, having fought his way out of the ballroom, Stevenson

said to Arvey, "Jack, I'm going to take myself out of the race. My God, did you see what happened?" The astute boss of Chicago insisted that Stevenson had no right to say that he would not accept the nomination. Stevenson merely shook his head in bewilderment.

The next day, Stevenson appeared on "Meet the Press." When asked if he would refuse the nomination, he replied, "I will not say that. I will say that that's a bridge that I can't cross until I come to it and I see very little likelihood that I will have to come to it." Later in the program, he sounded the note that he would keep repeating right up to the opening of the convention. "The answer is just what I have said repeatedly and that is that I am pledged to run for Governor. I must run for Governor. I want to run for Governor. I seek no other office. I have no other ambition."

After the Stevenson television appearance, Mayor David Lawrence of Pittsburgh said, "I heard Stevenson on 'Meet the Press.' There's our man." Two days later the Illinois Draft Committee changed its name to the National Committee Stevenson for President and announced that "the wave of Stevenson sentiment in the last forty-eight hours has confirmed the Committee's belief of the popular support for the governor."

At the same time, Harry Truman made one last effort to make Stevenson change his mind. The President sent National Chairman Frank McKinney to see the Governor. McKinney reported back that Stevenson refused, under any circumstances, to make the race. Truman gave up and began to look elsewhere for a candidate.

On April 16, Stevenson issued a statement that, he hoped, would settle the matter once and for all. Having been nominated for another term as governor the week before, Stevenson said, "I have repeatedly said that I was a candidate for governor of Illinois and had no other ambition. To this I must now add that in view of my prior commitment to run for governor and my desire and the desire of many who have given me their help and confidence in our unfinished work in Illinois, I could not accept the nomination for any other office this summer." The Draft Committee immediately seized upon the words "could not" and pointed out that, if he really were completely unavailable, he would have said "would not." Jacob Arvey tended to assume that Stevenson really was out of the race, but the Draft Committee went right on insisting that he was available for a draft.

Two days after issuing the statement, Stevenson appeared as speaker at a dinner in New York honoring Averell Harriman, who was launching his campaign for the nomination. Originally, Stevenson had been reluctant to attend, believing that an appearance would be misinterpreted as trying to further his own candidacy, but, feeling that his statement had at last taken him out of the race, he agreed to appear as a courtesy to Harriman. He should have stayed at home. The dinner was for Harriman, but all the interest centered on Stevenson. The New York *Times* had said on April 17 that Stevenson's statement "seems effectively to have closed the door to his nomination," but on April 19, the New York *Post* wrote, "the man who said he could not accept the presidential nominaiton . . . was the one speaker whose oratory, wit and liberal commentary evoked a spontaneous and prolonged response . . . the dinner for Harriman may come to be remembered as the starting point for a real draft-Stevenson movement."

Stevenson's attitude toward the nomination was expressed at a later time, when he wrote, "It was no longer 'Will you be a candidate for the nomination?,' but 'Will you accept the nomination?' This was more difficult. If I said, 'Yes,' publicly or covertly, it would start the draft movement in earnest. If I said, 'No,' how would it reconcile with all my preaching about public service and politics? How could I foretell then, long before the convention, what manner of deadlock and bitterness might develop to the lasting damage of my party? And, finally, could anyone in good health and already in public life refuse the greatest honor and greatest responsibility in our political system? So I concluded to keep still and say nothing more to anyone, contenting myself with confidence that no one could in fact be drafted by a modern convention against his oft-expressed wish." Student of American history that Stevenson was, he should have paid greater heed to the fate of Horatio Seymour before contenting himself with confidence that it could not happen unless he let it happen.

Between the eager front-running of Estes Kefauver and the reiterated reluctance of Adlai Stevenson, the other candidates took their places in the contest. On February 28, Senator Richard B.

Russell of Georgia announced that he was a candidate, in the belief that President Truman would not seek re-election. But he was explicit that he was in the race, regardless of what the President might ultimately decide. Russell was, of course, the southern candidate and could hope for little, if any, support outside his own region. He was not, however, the Dixiecrat candidate. While campaigning in Florida, he firmly announced that, while he would not accept nomination on a platform that contained a compulsory FEPC plank, he would not bolt the convention or fail to support its nominee. He would be the southern Democratic candidate, not the Dixiecrat candidate for the nomination.

Senator Kerr announced on February 6 that he was entering the April 1 Nebraska preferential primary but would be an active candidate only if President Truman decided not to run. Kerr spent two weeks stumping in Nebraska but was decisively defeated by Kefauver. This defeat reduced his candidacy to little more than that of a favorite son, although he traveled extensively in search of delegates.

Averell Harriman formally entered the contest on April 22 as the avowed liberal candidate. Originally, he became a candidate in order to keep New York out of the Kefauver camp, but he soon went on to be a serious contender. His strategy, supported by Senator Lehman and Congressman Franklin D. Roosevelt, Jr., was to reintegrate the New Deal elements of the party into an effective force. He spoke for social progress and took an especially strong stand on FEPC, but outside of New York and a scattering of liberal support elsewhere, his campaign made little progress.

The final entry in the race was the jovial, much-loved "Veep," Alben W. Barkley. The Vice-President had told Truman late in 1951 that, if the President decided to run for re-election, he would be glad to seek another term as vice-president. He would not, however, run for vice-president with any other candidate and would, if Truman decided to retire, consider seeking the nomination himself. After Truman had announced that he would not run again and Stevenson had apparently taken himself out of the race, many of the party leaders believed that Barkley was the only possible candidate who could unite the party.

With this goal in mind, Barkley, already Kentucky's favorite son, announced on May 29 that he would not actively seek the nomination but, "if the forthcoming Chicago convention should choose me to lead the fight in the approaching campaign, I would accept."

Although Kefauver led the field, Barkley was given the best chance of nomination. Kefauver's front-running position was more impressive on paper than in reality. The Senator from Tennessee had won 174 delegates in eight primaries—New Hampshire, Wisconsin, Maryland, Florida, Ohio, Oregon, California, and South Dakota. But only in New Hampshire and Florida had he run against real opposition, and in Florida Senator Russell took 19 of the votes to Kefauver's 5. In the District of Columbia primary, he was defeated by Averell Harriman, and his victory over Kerr in Nebraska was not binding on the delegates. The coonskin-capped candidate was in a dangerously weak position as far as the party leaders were concerned. Truman opposed him, and the Kefauver strategy of charging the "big city bosses" meeting in "smoke filled rooms" of plotting against him angered many of those bosses, who also resented the implication that Kefauver was fighting the bosses and the underworld crime leaders at the same time and for largely the same reasons. A slashing crusader against crime and political bossism might appeal to the voters, but he did not appeal to the men whose support would be needed to win the nomination.

Barkley, on the other hand, was popular with all elements of the party and, despite his age, seemed the one candidate, except for Stevenson, who could bring a degree of unity to the forthcoming campaign. On July 5, Barkley attended a luncheon in the office of Secretary of the Senate Leslie Biffle. Present were President Truman, Speaker Rayburn, Senator Clements of Kentucky, House Majority Leader John McCormack, and White House Secretary Matthew J. Connelly. These were the "old pros," and they reviewed the situation carefully. Truman had given up on Stevenson and took the occasion to emphasize that he did not and would not oppose Barkley's candidacy. From then until the first day of the convention, Barkley was the administration candidate.

Although the President did not make his backing of Barkley public, word quickly spread that Barkley was the man. Jacob Arvey called Barkley, offering his support and assurances that

Stevenson was definitely out of the race. Arvey even offered to ask Stevenson to place Barkley's name in nomination, but nothing more was heard of the suggestion. Shortly before the convention, Senator Clements, Barkley's manager, claimed that the Vice-President was assured of 225 votes on the first ballot and 360 on the second. After the second ballot, the Kerr and Russell forces could be expected to provide enough additional support to give Barkley the nomination on the third or fourth ballot.

Even though Kefauver had the most pledged delegates and Barkley had the presidential blessing, the situation was still extremely confused. A dark horse who hoped to take advantage of that confusion was Speaker Sam Rayburn. The Speaker had no pledged delegates and had given no public indication that he was interested in the nomination, but his friends, led by Senator Mike Monroney of Oklahoma, hoped to take advantage of a deadlocked convention. Their strategy was to have the Speaker remain aloof from the throat-cutting that would go on among the active candidates and then to advance him as the unifier of the party after the others had exhausted themselves. "Ours is a tenth ballot proposition, not a first ballot one," Monroney explained. The fact that Rayburn would be permanent chairman of the convention would greatly help his strategy. As one supporter expressed it, "He'll be standing there with the klieg lights bouncing off that bald dome looking as solid and substantial and trustworthy as the rock of ages."

The Stevenson Draft Committee intended to open headquarters in the Hilton Hotel on Saturday, July 19. Until that time, they felt that Representative Sidney Yates's office in the Chicago Loop would provide sufficient space for their activities. The Committee ran into immediate difficulty. All available space at the Hilton was controlled by the National Committee, which refused to provide space for an unauthorized movement. But, through personal contacts with the Hilton management, the draft committee managed to obtain three rooms on the fifteenth floor, with the offer of three other rooms held by friendly delegates. The response to the draft movement was so great that the committee found it necessary to open headquarters three days earlier on Wednesday, July

16 and, by Saturday, had expanded to include a total of eight rooms.

In opening headquarters, the Draft-Stevenson leaders had no help from the regular Democratic organization. On Monday, July 14, Walter Johnson and Leo Lerner met Colonel Arvey in the Hilton Hotel. Arvey asked what they were doing there and, when told that they had rented rooms to open a draft-Stevenson headquarters, replied in amazement, "I don't know what you are doing that for; Governor Stevenson is not a candidate." At that point, a reporter came up to ask Arvey some questions about Stevenson. The Chicago boss told him as he walked away, "Ask these two, they seem to know more than I do."

It had been the original intention of the draft committee to use the headquarters as a clearing house for information and as a center to stimulate consideration of Stevenson's candidacy. Almost immediately, Johnson and Lerner realized that they would have to do much more. Each day, more and more delegates poured into Chicago, all of them confused and looking for guidance. The Baltimore *Sun* reported, "Chicago is filling up with a throng of leaderless and bewildered delegates and minor local bosslets looking vainly for someone to tell them which way to go and what to do." It would not be enough to suggest that Stevenson be drafted and then to let spontaneous enthusiasm take its course. If the draft were to be successful, friendly delegates had to be organized, a floor leader selected, a speaker found to make the nominating speech, and an organization set up to bring pressure upon the uncommitted delegations. All this work would have to be done by the draft committee if it were to be done at all.

The first question to be settled was whether or not Stevenson should be placed in nomination. The Governor had stated that he did not want his name to go before the convention, and Jacob Arvey had announced that Illinois would accede to Stevenson's wishes. But the Draft Committee decided on Wednesday that Stevenson should be placed in nomination, and, on Thursday, July 17, Archibald Alexander, former Under-Secretary of the Army and a candidate for the Senate in New Jersey, offered to make the nominating speech if no one better known could be found. Governor Henry Schricker of Indiana had also expressed interest in nominating Stevenson but was not yet ready to commit himself fully.

The committee announced in a press release on Friday that Stevenson's name would go before the convention. It was the first public statement of positive action, and the delegates who inclined to Stevenson now had the assurance that they would have a candidate to vote for.

Stevenson, who was a member of the Illinois delegation, arrived in Chicago on the same afternoon that it was announced that he would be placed in nomination. Met at the airport by reporters and television cameras, the Governor stated, "I shall never be a candidate in the sense that I'll ask anybody to vote for me here. On the contrary, I'll do everything possible to discourage any delegate from putting me in nomination or nominating me." When told that rumor had it that either Governor Schricker or Archibald Alexander might make a nominating speech for him, Stevenson said that he would do everything he possibly could to discourage them. He later called Alexander specifically to request that he not be placed in nomination.

At no time did Governor Stevenson have any contact with the Draft Committee, but the Stevenson family was not unrepresented at the Hilton headquarters. On Saturday, July 19, the Governor's sixteen-year-old son, John Fell Stevenson, arrived at the bustling fifteenth-floor headquarters, saying that he wanted to see the people who were trying to make his father do what he said he did not wish to do. Later in the day, he returned with his older brother Borden and three friends. Walter Johnson explained to them that if the press saw Stevenson's sons at the draft headquarters it might be taken as proof that the Committee was a front organization for their father. They were asked to leave and not come back. When Borden Stevenson asked if they were not to come back to the hotel at all, Johnson patiently explained, "You can visit the Harriman, Kefauver, Russell, and Kerr headquarters as much as you like. But never come back to the fifteenth floor." The Governor's sons were then escorted down the back stairs without being seen by reporters.

Until Saturday, the draft movement had been moving fairly

slowly. More than 300 delegates had visited the headquarters, and various individuals had expressed interest, but so far no major delegation had offered support. On Saturday, July 19, the draft began picking up momentum, and major sources of strength began moving behind the reluctant Governor. Walter Johnson and another member of the Draft Committee met with James A. Finnegan, president of the Philadelphia City Council, and two other Pennsylvania delegates at their Morrison Hotel headquarters. Johnson reviewed the situation and assured the delegates that Stevenson would accept the nomination. Finnegan expressed his interest in advocating Stevenson to the Pennsylvania delegation and asked for some Stevenson buttons. He even offered a check to have them made. The delighted draft men immediately sent seventy buttons to the Pennsylvanians, although some had to be removed from the shirts of Stevenson volunteers to make up the quota.

That same afternoon, Kenneth Anderson, national committeeman from Kansas, indicated that there was strong Stevenson support in his delegation, and Indiana and New Jersey also seemed inclined to support the draft movement. The Draft Committee estimated that the Governor would receive 75 votes on the first ballot, with an additional 60 to 100 votes on the second. These estimates did not include the support Stevenson might expect from Illinois.

On Sunday morning, Finnegan, Mayor David Lawrence, and former Senator Francis J. Myers of Pennsylvania held a meeting in which they decided to support the Stevenson candidacy in the delegation caucus that evening. While the Pennsylvania leaders were swinging to Stevenson, the reluctant candidate attended church. Even there he could not avoid politics. The minister, a personal friend of the Governor's, pointedly used as his text, "If any of you lack wisdom, let him ask of God, that giveth to all men liberally, and upbraideth not; and it shall be given him." The many reporters present, believing that the minister was admonishing Stevenson not to decline the nomination, asked him what he thought of the sermon. "Superb," replied Stevenson with, one might suspect, the merest touch of irony.

On Sunday night, Illinois held its first caucus. It was a closed caucus, but some twenty reporters lying on the floor in the adjoining room could hear what was being said through the folding doors that closed off the caucus room. In the strongest terms he had yet used, Stevenson begged the delegates not to nominate him. He did not, he said, want the nomination. He concluded by telling the story of the man who said he did not want to go to heaven and did not want to go to hell. If you don't want to go to Heaven or Hell, where do you want to go," he was asked. "I want to stay right here," came the reply. After Stevenson's talk, Jacob Arvey announced that, while his personal desire was to follow the Governor's wishes, his duty was such that he reserved the right to vote for Stevenson on the first ballot. The cheering delegation agreed and made it clear that Illinois would do everything it could to promote the Stevenson draft.

After the caucus, Stevenson said to Arvey, "I'm going to issue a statement taking myself out of this damn thing. You're making me look silly. All those statements from Cook County and Illinois people that I'm the only man for the nomination! How can anybody believe I'm sincere?" Arvey argued that he should issue no statements and should let events take their course, and finally Stevenson agreed to keep silent. As he left the caucus room, reporters asked if he would yield to a draft in the event of a deadlock. "Show me the deadlock first," was the reply.

At 11:00 p.m. Sunday, the Draft Committee met to formalize the draft procedure. Among those attending the meeting were Finnegan, Myers, and Mayor Lawrence; Governor Schricker, Paul M. Butler, and Congressman Winfield K. Denton of Indiana; and Leo Lerner, Congressman Yates, Hubert Will, and Walter Johnson of the Draft Committee. Will announced that Stevenson now had a total of 178½ votes, including 35½ from Pennsylvania and 25 from Indiana. The Pennsylvania and Indiana delegates confirmed the figures.

Mayor Lawrence was suggested for floor leader, but he declined, saying, "You need a man with more vitamins than I've got to do floor work," and he suggested former Senator Myers, who was accepted by the committee. Schricker was asked to make the nominating speech. He said that he would talk it over with some of his delegates and give his decision the following day.

While Stevenson was gaining support, Kefauver suffered the

loss of Vermont. The Tennessee Senator had established lavish headquarters, which the Vermonters considered extravagant, and they thought the distribution of orchids to the ladies too costly a bid for votes. Vermont decided to look for a more economical candidate.

The Harriman headquarters also had its more amusing problems. Undoubtedly the most sought after individual attending the convention was Thomas J. Gavin of Missouri, President Truman's alternate. Wherever he went, he found himself treated with the greatest deference. Everyone hoped to learn what his instructions were and whom the President was supporting. When a Mr. Gavin was announced at the Harriman headquarters, he was ushered in, offered a drink, and surrounded by an expectant group who hoped his visit might be the sign they had been waiting for. The gentleman was respectfully asked his opinions on a variety of subjects until, finishing his drink, he explained that he had come to fix the television set. The red-faced politicians never did see the Mr. Gavin who represented Harry Truman.

Vice-President and Mrs. Barkley arrived in Chicago on Saturday. Instead of riding to his headquarters, the Vice-President, to squelch fears that he was too old, led a parade for a half-mile through the sweltering heat. Waving jovially to the crowd, Barkley was the very picture of vigor and confidence.

On Sunday, the Barkley forces played what they expected to be their trump card. National Chairman Frank McKinney told several delegations that the President wished the Vice-President to be nominated, and that evening the Barkley managers made public an announcement that Truman was supporting Barkley. According to the Alsops, this announcement did not have the effect Barkley had hoped. They reported that it caused "a violent countersurge among the delegates. The delegates wished to win, thought the Democratic party could win but did not believe the party could win with a seventy-four-year-old standard bearer."

Labor also did not believe that the party could win with a seventy-four-year-old candidate. A number of labor leaders met in conference on Sunday and announced that labor could not support Barkley. George M. Harrison, an AFL vice-president, said, "We can't sell Barkley to labor, not because of his record but his age." Jack Wroll, director of the CIO's Political Action Committee, expressed the warmest regards for the Vice-President but went on to say, "It is a matter of extreme regret and concern that we are not able to support his candidacy."

Labor's rejection came as a stunning blow to Barkley. He had always had an extremely liberal record on labor legislation and had every reason to expect that labor would support him. He asked sixteen of the labor men to breakfast with him on the morning of Monday, July 21, the opening day of the convention. It was an awkward meal. As the union men, who were personally fond of the Vice-President, tried to choke down their breakfasts, Barkley asked them about their statements as reported in the morning papers. Finally, they told him that the reports were correct and that they could not support him because of his age.

That afternoon Barkley called Truman in Washington to tell him that he was withdrawing from the race. Truman insisted that he stay in, but the dejected Vice-President replied, "It's too late because I've already told the press." The Barkley boom, which had begun so well, was over.

Although labor's rejection of Barkley may have been the decisive factor in the failure of his candidacy, there were other reasons too. His age was a serious obstacle. Barkley had hoped to overcome the problem by putting a young man like Congressman Franklin D. Roosevelt, Jr., who was thirty-eight, or Governor G. Mennen Williams, who was forty-one, on the ticket, but the delegates were not convinced. An unexpected weakness in Barkley's campaign was, paradoxically, its early success. According to Governor Weatherby and Senator Clements, the Barkley managers, some of the party leaders who favored Stevenson had supported Barkley with the intention of deadlocking the convention and forcing Stevenson to accept the nomination. Jacob Arvey, for example, pledged 40 Illinois votes, and Mayor David Lawrence pledged a like number from Pennsylvania. When the Barkley campaign began picking up speed, however, they feared that the Vice-President might run away with the nomination before the draft-Stevenson movement could get off the ground. Accordingly, on Sunday night, Arvey and Lawrence withdrew their 80 votes

from the Barkley camp and joined the first-ballot drive for
Stevenson.

Apart from Barkley's dramatic withdrawal, the outstanding
event of the first day of the convention was the welcoming address
to the delegates by the Governor of the host state of Illinois.
Many delegates had not yet seen Stevenson, and few were prepared for his oratorical style, which was to set a new high standard
in American politics.

Stevenson was introduced to the convention by Chairman
McKinney and received a ten-minute ovation. His fourteen-minute
speech was repeatedly interrupted with applause and cries of "We
Want Stevenson." He began by saying, "I thought I came here
to greet you, not you to greet me." Referring to the recent Republican convention, Stevenson delighted his audience with the wit
that was so much a part of his style. "For almost a week pompous
phrases marched over this landscape in search of an idea, and the
only idea they found was that the two great decades of progress
in peace, victory in war, and bold leadership in this anxious hour
were the misbegotten spawn of bungling, corruption, socialism,
mismanagement, waste and worse. . . . After listening to our mis-
deeds for awhile I was surprised the next morning when the mail
was delivered on time. Our friends were out of patience, out of
sorts and, need I add, out of office."

After the speech, the convention burst into applause, but,
before a demonstration could develop, Stevenson abruptly left the
platform. He took his seat in the Illinois delegation beside Jacob
Arvey, who told him, "You had better get out of here. It doesn't
look good for a candidate to be here." At first, Stevenson was
reluctant to believe that the ovation that had greeted him had
been sincere and spontaneous. When Arvey convinced him that it
was, he remarked it was all "very flattering" and left the hall.

The delegates had seen the reluctant candidate and had been
impressed by what they saw. Many delegates who had been curious about or mildly receptive to the notion of a draft were now
convinced that the Governor of Illinois had the makings, not only
of a winner, but of a statesman as well. The draft boom was well
under way. As Doris Fleeson wrote, "It now looks as though Gov.

Adlai Stevenson will be dragged protesting to the presidential altar by the Democratic party. His shrieks are growing fainter. His suitor more importunate."

Before the morning and evening sessions on Monday, new supporters flocked to the Stevenson banner. Jonathan Daniels of North Carolina announced his support, saying, "I know he'll run. He's running now. The convention is running him." Governor Carvel of Delaware stated that, since Barkley had withdrawn, he and most of the delegation would support Stevenson and added that he would like to make a seconding speech for the Governor. Jim Farley, also left without a candidate by Barkley's withdrawal, swung his massive frame aboard the bandwagon, while Congressman John F. Kennedy of Massachusetts and Michael DiSalle of Ohio volunteered to organize the draft among the Democratic congressional candidates.

The Draft Committee, to avoid the reporters who were swarming over the Hilton Hotel headquarters, met at 4:00 p.m. in Congressman Yates's law office. Governor Schricker agreed to make the nominating speech, and the committee, to dramatize the growing bandwagon, decided to announce that evening Myers's appointment as floor leader and to hold off announcing that Schricker would make the nominating speech until Tuesday.

Monday night's session opened conventionally enough with the keynote address by Temporary Chairman Paul Dever of Massachusetts. The stout Governor, who could emphasize a point with his jowls as other men did with their forefingers, delivered an hour-long stemwinder, the most memorable part of which was the Governor's voice, which cracked near the end. As the temporary chairman, hoarse and wet with perspiration, finished his speech, a major battle broke out between the northern liberals and the southerners.

Averell Harriman's strategy, which was matched in part by the strategy of the Kefauver managers, was to set such a Fair Deal stamp on the convention that it would have to turn to him as the candidate most representative of that imprint. He also hoped to place so strong a civil-rights plank in the platform that the South, the faction most opposed to his nomination, would bolt the convention. But in the platform committee the South accepted a strong plank and showed no desire to bolt. Perhaps part of the South's unexpectedly conciliatory attitude was due to the fact that President Truman, when told by Senator Humphrey that there was a plan afoot to soften the 1948 civil-rights plank, had threatened, "If that convention tries to disavow all I have worked for in the last seven years, I'll come out there and announce I'll run for another term."

Whatever the reason, the South intended to stay in the convention. Realizing that the South would not bolt over the platform, a group of liberals, led by Senator Blair Moody and Governor Williams of Michigan, Senator Humphrey, and Franklin D. Roosevelt, Jr., decided to force the issue with a "loyalty oath." Designed to prevent a recurrence of the events of 1948, when Dixiecrats had run in Alabama, Louisiana, Mississippi, and South Carolina under the official Democratic label, the Moody resolution provided that no delegation should be seated unless its chairman assured the credentials committee that it would exert every honorable means to insure that the nominees of the convention would appear on the ballot under the official Democratic designation. It also provided that, if a delegation refused to take the loyalty oath, individual delegates who accepted it could be seated. Later the resolution was amended to read, "Provided that such assurance shall not be in contravention of existing law of the state or of the instructions of the state's Democratic governing body."

The loyalty-oath resolution was presented by Senator Moody during the contest over seating the Texas and Mississippi delegations. Each state had sent two sets of delegates—one representing the "regular," formerly Dixiecrat state organization, the other representing the "loyalists," who had not bolted the party in 1948. Since the "regular" delegations, whatever their past performances, had been legally selected, the credentials committee accepted them. The Moody resolution was designed to ensure that they would not, having been seated in the convention, repeat the events of 1948.

The Moody resolution was accepted by voice vote on Monday night, and it appeared that even a loyalty oath would not force the South to bolt. But on Tuesday, Louisiana, South Carolina, and Virginia announced that they would not give the required assurances. Governor James F. Byrnes of South Carolina and Senator Harry Byrd of Virginia led the southerners who rejected the loyalty oath, while Senator Russell Long of Louisiana was conspicuously courageous in supporting it. The three delegations were removed from the convention rolls but kept their seats, while the moderates looked for ways to restore them to full voting rights.

The ill temper of the hold-out southerners was demonstrated on Tuesday evening when Mrs. Eleanor Roosevelt addressed the convention. Introduced as the "First Lady of the World," Mrs. Roosevelt received one of the longest demonstrations of the convention. The delegates rose for a standing ovation—all, that is, except the Texas delegation, which remained sullenly seated, and Senator Byrd, who in a rare display of bad manners stalked from the hall.

The Stevenson bandwagon continued to pick up speed on Tuesday. Roscoe Drummond wrote, "There is ascending, almost crescendo determination to nominate the reluctant candidate. Unless Gov. Adlai E. Stevenson hires a B-36 and sky writes a signed affidavit saying more than General Sherman—that he will not accept even if unanimously nominated and will not serve even if unanimously elected, positively—few observers give this convention more than two or three ballots to reach its decision."

The draft committee was so deluged with phone calls and offers of assistance that it was forced to expand its operations to fourteen rooms and to hire a squad of ushers under the direction of R. Sargent Shriver, Jr. The city thoughtfully provided a round-the-clock detective service to keep order among the crowds milling around the fifteenth floor.

Governor Stevenson was, if anything, irritated by the increased activity. Watching the proceedings on television, he saw a long file of delegates moving to the Illinois delegation to talk to Arvey. Finally, in exasperation, he called Arvey on the telephone to ask him to stay off the convention floor. "The cameras keep showing you talking to people. It may leave the impression you are trying to set up a phony draft." From then on, Arvey kept out of sight and worked out of Frank McKinney's backstage office.

While Jacob Arvey was lost to the television cameras on Tuesday, Estes Kefauver was not. Breaking a long-standing tradition that candidates do not appear on the convention floor, Senator Kefauver and his eighty-one-year-old father put in an appearance during the afternoon session. When his presence became known, a twenty-five-minute demonstration broke out. The Senator later said, "My Father and I wanted to sit in and listen to the proceedings. I didn't expect a demonstration. I was pleased, though, that so many people wanted to give me a hand." Ingenuous as the explanation was, critics could not refrain from pointing out that shortly before the Senator arrived his supporters had been seen passing out Kefauver whistles and noise makers among friendly delegations. "Carefully planned spontaneity" was the way some observers saw the demonstration. Spontaneous or not, it did the Senator's candidacy little good.

The final important event of Tuesday was a major blow to the Kefauver and Harriman forces. New Jersey caucused in the evening and voted 23½ for Stevenson and 3 for Kefauver, with 5½ absent or not voting. This vote was the first official commitment to Stevenson from a major state and had considerable influence in making up the minds of wavering delegates who were still skeptical that a draft was possible.

On Wednesday, Vice-President Barkley was suddenly reinjected into the race for the nomination. The disappointed candidate had intended to leave Chicago after withdrawing from the contest. Hearing of this plan, President Truman called Frank McKinney to tell him, "I want you to invite Alben to address the convention. And I want the works. I want him to get the greatest ovation of his life." As it turned out, the President need not have worried. The party and the delegates loved the gallant old Vice-President too much to need any prompting when it came to giving him an ovation. Barkley was cheered for nearly half an hour when he appeared on the platform, and, after he had finished his lengthy but impromptu speech, his ovation went on for another forty-five minutes. It was a touching, heartfelt tribute to an old warrior and perhaps made up in some degree for the disappointment that he had received. So enthusiastic, in fact, was the reception for Barkley that some leaders began speculating on the possibility of reviving his candidacy in an effort to stop Stevenson. The Vice-President, himself, had no such thoughts and gave no encouragement to such a movement.

Even if Barkley had considered lending himself to a stop-Stevenson move, the events of Wednesday indicated that it was too late. Delaware in caucus pledged its votes to Stevenson; Missouri did the same. Senator Brien McMahon informed President Truman and Frank McKinney that he would release Connecticut to Stevenson when the time came and left orders to be notified whenever the votes were needed, even though he was at that time on his death bed. He died two days after the close of the convention.

Maryland indicated that it would be on the bandwagon "when this Stevenson thing really starts," while New Jersey added 4½ more votes to make a Stevenson total of 28. Indiana pledged 25 of its 26 votes to the Illinois Governor.

The position of the Illinois delegation became increasingly embarrassing. As one newspaper observed, "They feel like the kid who owns the baseball but is wearing his Sunday clothes and can't play." Jacob Arvey called Stevenson to beg him to announce that he would accept the nomination, but the Governor refused. He continued to insist that he was a candidate for re-election as governor and nothing more. Despite this, Illinois caucused and pledged him 46 votes. Three votes went to Kefauver, and 11 remained uncommitted but were expected to go to Stevenson. Although the delegation decided to support Stevenson contrary to his wishes, the chairman did say, "We are not going to nominate or second anybody. We're respecting Gov. Stevenson's wishes in that regard."

Illinois may have been determined not to nominate Stevenson, but Jacob Arvey was not going to be left out. His relations with the draft committee had been nonexistent, and he had done what he could to discourage its activity when he believed that Stevenson would not be a candidate. But events were sweeping the convention to the inevitable nomination of the reluctant candidate, and Arvey decided it was time to take control. The Draft Committee had arranged for Governor Schricker to nominate Stevenson, but about one o'clock Thursday morning Paul Butler roused Walter

Johnson out of bed to tell him that Arvey had tried to dissuade Schricker and had then told him that Governor Carvel of Delaware was going to make the nominating speech.

The committee had no personal objection to Governor Carvel but believed that the nominating speech should come from a midwestern, rural state to demonstrate the broad base of Stevenson support. Finally, at 5:30 a.m., Butler called Arvey to tell him that if Schricker did not make the nominating speech he would bring the matter before the National Committee. After fifteen minutes of argument, it was agreed that Schricker would speak first but would share his time equally with Carvel, eliminating any seconding speeches. James Finnegan explained the episode by saying, "It's obvious what has happened. Everybody is on the bandwagon."

In an effort to stop the bandwagon, the Kefauver forces fought back as hard as they could. James Roosevelt charged that the Stevenson draft was a deep-laid plot backed by the big city bosses, to which the Draft Committee replied that the draft was "uncontrolled, unbossed, and unstoppable."

The Kefauver forces hoped to help the Senator's campaign by bringing a minority report on the platform to the floor of the convention. Chief among its planks was a strong anticorruption plank to remind the delegates of Kefauver's crime investigations. The Kefauver men were told to take seats on the rostrum to be available to speak in support of amendments to the platform.

The platform was read to the convention on Wednesday night. It was much like the 1948 platform, pledging to continue the New and Fair Deals, and the civil-rights plank was as strong as it had been in 1948. After the reading of the platform, Permanent Chairman Sam Rayburn put it to an immediate voice vote and declared it carried. When the Kefauver men angrily protested, Rayburn coolly offered them two minutes to "explain" the proposed amendments. Since the platform had already been adopted, there was nothing the Kefauver leaders could do but express their anger and frustration.

Thursday turned out to be a rip-snorter of a day, even for a Democratic convention. It began with the roll call for presidential nominations. Senator Russell was first to be nominated, followed by Senator Kefauver. Senator Kerr came next and was followed by Arkansas' favorite son, Senator William Fulbright, and by Averell Harriman and Oscar Ewing. Senator Benton of Connecticut paid moving tribute to the dying Senator McMahon when he told the convention that he was placing him in nomination as a token of respect and devotion but was not asking the convention to vote for him.

After Benton's speech, Governor Carvel yielded to Governor Schricker. Schricker began by telling the delegates that interest in Stevenson had grown "without the benefit of a candidacy or the stimulus of an organized campaign" and, after describing the candidate's career and intellectual attainments, concluded by saying, "there are times when a man is not permitted to say 'no.' I place before you the man we cannot permit to say 'no,' Adlai E. Stevenson of Illinois."

G. Mennen Williams had just been placed in nomination as Michigan's favorite son when an unscheduled interruption exploded on the convention floor. When called on the roll, Louisiana yielded to Virginia. Governor Battle arose amid a growing uproar to ask for a ruling "as to whether we are entitled to full participation in the deliberations and votes of this Convention." The debate was long, violent, and at times nearly hysterical. It had been a long day in the steaming Chicago heat, and nerves were rubbed raw. As if the debate itself were not sufficiently dramatic, a fire broke out among the piles of discarded newspapers littering the floor. After a few moments of near pandemonium, the fire was brought under control, and Governor Byrnes, who had been speaking, remarked dryly, "Mr. Chairman, I want to announce that I did not set the place on fire." At long last, a motion was made to seat the recalcitrant delegations from Louisiana, South Carolina, and Virginia, and a roll call was requested.

As the roll call progressed, it became clear that the convention was going to unseat the three southern delegations. But during the vote, Rayburn received word from Harry Truman that he wanted the southerners seated, and the chairman began to stall the proceedings while messengers were sent to find Jacob Arvey. Not expecting anything to interrupt the long dreary process of nominating speeches, Arvey had gone to the nearby Stockyard Inn for dinner. Informed of what was happening, he hurried back to the hall.

Arvey realized that, if the southerners were unseated, 64 votes that could be used to stop Harriman and Kefauver would be lost. Illinois had already voted 45 to 15 against seating the southerners, and, at the conclusion of the long and confused roll call it appeared that they would indeed be unseated by a vote of 621 to 473½. Arvey ordered Illinois to change its vote, and the delegation voted 52 to 8 in favor of seating the southerners. The 8 votes opposed included those of Senator Paul Douglas and the other Kefauver men in the delegation. Word quickly spread that "Stevenson wants them seated." Enough votes were changed to seat the three delegations by a vote of 615 yes, 529 no, 86 not voting. It was not accurate to say that Stevenson wanted the delegations seated, for he had not been consulted on the matter, but Harry Truman and Jacob Arvey wanted them seated, and they wanted Stevenson—the results were the same.

In a crashing anticlimax to the long fight over unseating the southerners, the nominating roll call was resumed, and Governor Dever was named as Massachusetts's favorite son, followed by the nominations of Senator Humphrey and Vice-President Barkley.

After a confused roll call to determine whether or not the convention would adjourn for the night—few delegates seemed even to know what they were voting for—the nominating roll was concluded with the placing of Harry Truman in nomination as a tribute. The nomination was immediately withdrawn at the President's request. Finally, the weary delegates staggered out into the humid night.

Events had been moving rapidly outside the convention hall. Governor Stevenson had finally made up his mind. During the afternoon, he placed a call to the President in Washington. "My friends want to nominate me for President," he told Truman. "Would you object if I agreed to run?" As Truman later wrote, "Well, I blew up. I talked to him in language I think he had never heard before." After unburdening himself of some earthy expletives, the exasperated President said, "I have been trying since January to get you to say that. Why would it embarrass me?"

Stevenson was, privately at any rate, at last a candidate, and that evening Truman's alternate, Thomas Gavin, announced that he was instructed to vote for Stevenson on the first ballot. The importance of the announcement that Truman was officially backing Stevenson could not be exaggerated. The Alsops had observed earlier that "by an authoritative estimate, President Truman can swing at least 400 Democratic delegate votes to any candidate the convention likes; and can give at least 200 delegate votes to a candidate the convention does not like."

The hopes of the Kefauver and Harriman camps grew increasingly forlorn. After the adjournment on Thursday night, a much publicized caucus of liberal and labor elements met in the Florentine Room of the Congress Hotel. They discussed the possibility of uniting on one candidate to stop Stevenson, but, for all the brave talk, neither the Kefauver nor the Harriman forces would give way to the other. Senator Humphrey bluntly warned them that they had better give consideration to playing a part in the Stevenson nomination before the conservatives and the South took the credit for putting him over.

A more significant meeting was being held simultaneously in another room of the Congress Hotel. Among those present were Walter Reuther, Senator Douglas, James and Franklin Roosevelt, Congressman Holifield of California, Francis Biddle, and Gael Sullivan, Kefauver's manager. Reuther was firm in stating that Stevenson was acceptable to labor and that he and the CIO would repudiate any stop-Stevenson movement. Gradually, the group came to a reluctant acceptance of the Stevenson nomination.

Early in the afternoon of Friday, July 25, the convention settled down to the first roll call. An hour before the balloting, the draft committee estimated that Stevenson would receive 272 first-ballot votes. The estimate was 1 short of the actual total. The roll call was taken amid much confusion and what seemed to spectators interminable polls of delegations. So great was the tumult at the conclusion of the ballot that Sam Rayburn was moved to chide the convention with gentle sarcasm. "The Convention will be in order. I know there are some people interested in knowing the result of their first roll call." Those results were Kefauver 340, Stevenson 273, Russell 268, Harriman 123½, Kerr 65, Barkley 48½, Dever 37½, Humphrey 26, Fulbright 22, Senator Murray of Montana 12, Truman 6, Ewing 4, Senator Douglas 3, Justice Douglas ½. One thousand two hundred twenty-nine votes were cast, with 616 needed for nomination. A curious aspect of this ballot was that three of the candidates were related. Governor Stevenson, Vice-President Barkley, and Senator Russell were cousins in varying degrees of kinship, having all been descended from a common ancestor who was a Kentucky pioneer. This fact had prompted the Vice-President to remark after his withdrawal that at least the nomination would be kept in the family.

The results of the first ballot indicated that a deadlock might be in the making. In Washington, Harry Truman thought it likely, and he and Mrs. Truman therefore boarded the *Independence* and flew to Chicago. They watched the second ballot on television while *en route*.

After the first ballot, Jacob Arvey put in a call for Stevenson. With him was Governor Dever, who controlled 37½ Massachusetts votes. Arvey asked Stevenson to tell Dever that he would accept the nomination. When Stevenson asked if he were sure that the convention could not agree on another man, Arvey replied, "If anyone else is nominated he'll split the party wide open." Stevenson then told Dever that he would accept the nomination. Dever hurried back to the Massachusetts delegation and asked them to vote for him again on the second ballot while he lined up support for Stevenson on the third. Thirty and one-half votes agreed to this proposal.

There were other switches in the making on the second ballot. Oklahoma hoped for a deadlock that might keep Senator Kerr "available" and decided to swing to Barkley on the second ballot. They reasoned that Barkley would be the best man to stop Stevenson and believed that it would be easier to work out a satisfactory strategy with the Barkley people than with Russell's supporters.

The Russell managers went to work on the Arkansas delegation. The delegation was told that Russell realized he could not be nominated but that he had been promised the selection of the vice-presidential candidate if he gained strength after the first ballot. Arkansas was led to believe that Fulbright would get the nod, and the elated delegates were eager to support Russell on the second ballot.

The results of the second ballot seemed to confirm the fears

that a deadlock was in the making. Kefauver picked up 22½ votes
to keep first place with 362½ votes, but Stevenson gained 51½ votes
for a total of 324½. The other totals were Russell 294, a gain of 26;
Harriman 121, Barkley 78½, Dever 30½, Truman 6, Kerr 5½, and
Ewing and Senator Douglas 3 each. After the second ballot, the
convention recessed for two and one-half hours.

During the recess, the final decisions were made. President
Truman was now in Chicago and met with Averell Harriman. The
President ordered Harriman to throw his support to Stevenson.
This order was not so dictatorial as it might sound. When Harriman had decided to make the race, he had asked Truman if he
had any objections. Truman told him that he did not object but
that "when the time came for the convention to nominate its candidate for President I wanted him to be in line to help nominate
that man, whoever he was. . . . I assured Harriman that, if it came
to a showdown between him and Stevenson, I was committed to
Stevenson because I felt he would be the strongest candidate. . . ."
The time had come, and Harriman agreed to switch to Stevenson.

Later Senator Moody and Governor Williams visited Harriman
at his convention-hall headquarters and were told he was about
to withdraw. Moody and Williams quickly informed Kefauver,
who agreed it was all over and that he should withdraw too. Unfortunately, he insisted on locating Senator Douglas first and arrived at the convention hall just in time for Sam Rayburn to teach
him a painful lesson in party infighting.

The convention reconvened at 8:45 p.m., and Harriman immediately withdrew as did Governor Dever. The third roll call
was then begun. Senator Kefauver, accompanied by Senators
Douglas, Moody, and Humphrey and Governor Williams approached the platform, but Chairman Rayburn refused to recognize
him while the balloting was in progress. Kefauver and his liberals
had given the old professionals nothing but trouble throughout
the convention, and Sam Rayburn was determined to teach them
a lesson. Parliamentary law was on the chairman's side, but a little
charity would have spared Kefauver the humiliation of sitting on
the platform in full view of the delegates and the television audience while waiting to concede defeat. That the Senator took his
punishment patiently was a considerable tribute to his manners

and his courage. At the conclusion of the roll call, Mr. Sam had had his little revenge, and Kefauver was permitted to withdraw.

The results of the final ballot were announced as Stevenson 617½, 1½ more than was necessary for nomination, Kefauver 275½, Russell 261, Barkley 67½, Senator Douglas and Oscar Ewing 3 each, and Governor Dever ½. The nomination was then made unanimous.

After a brief recess, President Truman and nominee Stevenson entered the hall. Many of the delegates had accepted the Stevenson draft as an inevitable movement that could unite the party but were still unfamiliar with the candidate. His acceptance speech brought the delegates to a pitch of fervor approaching adulation. Rarely had a political convention heard as sober, honest, and distinguished a speech as Adlai E. Stevenson's acceptance of his party's nomination in 1952.

"Even more important than winning the election is governing the Nation. That is the test of a political party—the acid, final test. When the tumult and the shouting die, when the bands are gone and the lights are dimmed, there is the stark reality of responsibility in an hour of history haunted with those gaunt, grim specters of strife, dissension and materialism at home; and ruthless, inscrutable and hostile power abroad.

"The ordeal of the 20th Century—the bloodiest, most turbulent age of the Christian era—is far from over. Sacrifice, patience, understanding and implacable purpose may be our lot for years to come.

"Let's face it. Let's talk sense to the American people. Let's tell them the truth, that there are no gains without pains, that this is the eve of great decisions, not easy decisions, like resistance when you're attacked, but a long, patient, costly struggle which alone can assure triumph over the great enemies of man—war and poverty and tyranny—and the assaults upon human dignity which are the most grievous consequences of each." It was strange talk from a presidential candidate, but the audience was entranced, even when it did not know for sure what he was talking about. As one listener explained, "I didn't know what he was saying, but it sure sounded like Franklin D. Roosevelt all over again."

The minor detail of the running mate was settled later that night. Stevenson, Truman, Rayburn, and several others gathered about 1:00 a.m. Saturday morning. Rayburn suggested that Kefauver "could run like a scared wolf," but Truman vetoed the idea. Stevenson said he favored Senator John Sparkman of Alabama, and the President replied, "So it shall be." The convention ratified the choice that afternoon. The second successful genuine draft in the history of the Democratic Party had been accomplished, and Adlai E. Stevenson of Illinois set out to "talk sense to the American people."

CHAPTER 23

"The damnedest fool idea"

THE THIRTY-SECOND DEMOCRATIC NATIONAL CONVENTION
Chicago, August 13, 1956

The race for the Democratic presidential nomination in 1956 was a repeat of that in 1952, with one important difference—this time Adlai E. Stevenson was an active, eager contender. Rather than being crushed by his defeat in 1952, Stevenson, who had acquired a taste for campaigning, was anxious to vindicate his campaign of that year through victory in 1956. Averell Harriman, by then Governor of New York, was once again a candidate, but Stevenson's chief rival was Senator Kefauver, who hoped to repeat his 1952 primary sweep.

Stevenson and Kefauver waged an intensive primary campaign, with the Senator drawing first blood by winning in New Hampshire. Minnesota was expected to go to Stevenson, who campaigned with the blessings of Senator Humphrey, but Kefauver promised more farm-price support, shook more hands, and scored a stunning upset by sweeping the primary. The badly shaken Stevenson forces realized that an all out effort would be needed to head off the Tennessee Senator.

Minnesota was the high-water mark of Kefauver's campaign. Stevenson barnstormed Florida, California, and Oregon in a fight that became increasingly heated. Bitter personal charges were hurled by both candidates, and Stevenson made a clean sweep of all three primaries. Kefauver was finished. Although he had won 165 delegates, Kefauver announced on August 1 that he was withdrawing from the race to prevent a deadlocked convention. "Victory in November is more important than the victor in August. I am anxious that the resources of the party, of myself and of Governor Stevenson not be dissipated by continuing the contest." It appeared that Stevenson had the nomination in the bag.

Once again the Democrats gathered in Chicago to open the convention on August 13. Stevenson was far out in front—reporters estimated that he had 404½ of the needed 686½ votes—and only Averell Harriman, with an estimated 141 votes, threatened any sort of challenge. Senator Lyndon Johnson of Texas had tried to raise himself out of the favorite-son ranks but with little success.

Harriman, whose campaign had languished during the primary battles between Stevenson and Kefauver, received a major boost on the Saturday before the convention, when Harry Truman arrived in town and scrappily announced that Stevenson could not win. He was, said the former President, backing Harriman for the nomination. Harriman, whose fifty-two-room campaign headquarters contrasted unfavorably with Stevenson's seven, announced that the former candidate was stopped and jubilantly predicted victory.

It was a short-lived hope. Times had changed, and Harry Truman, reluctant as he might be to admit it, was no longer a kingmaker. Mrs. Eleanor Roosevelt came out strongly for Stevenson, and Governors Meyner of New Jersey and Williams of Michigan announced that they were releasing their favorite-son delegations to Stevenson. Estes Kefauver spent an hour and a half going over the list of Kefauver delegates with Stevenson and James Finnegan, and he promised to call personally on each delegate to ask him to swing to Stevenson.

While Harry Truman waged his forlorn battle, the convention proceeded without major incident. The young Governor of Tennessee, Frank Clement, delivered an old-fashioned, stemwinding keynote address that seemed oddly anachronistic in the television age, and Sam Rayburn took his accustomed place as permanent chairman.

After the battles of 1948 and 1952, the party was in a mood for harmony, and the South remained quiet. The platform offered a mild civil-rights plank that did not specifically endorse the Supreme Court desegregation decision. The liberals, especially the Harriman forces, wanted a stronger plank, but Sam Rayburn was not going to allow anything to upset the smoothly running convention. Deliberately ignoring the many state standards waving for recognition to demand a roll-call vote on the strong minority civil-rights report, the chairman declared the report defeated by voice vote and rammed through the platform without opposition.

On Thursday, ten candidates were placed in nomination. Senator Magnuson of Washington and House Majority Leader John McCormack withdrew, leaving Stevenson, Lyndon Johnson, Congressman James C. Davis of Georgia, Governors Chandler of Kentucky and Timmerman of South Carolina, Harriman, Senator Stuart Symington of Missouri, and former Governor John S. Battle of Virginia as the contestants.

It took only one roll call to give Stevenson his second nomination. Victory came when Governor Leader threw 67 Pennsylvania votes to Stevenson. A victory demonstration immediately broke out on the floor but was quickly gaveled down by Rayburn. The results of the ballot were Stevenson 905½, Harriman 210, Johnson 80, Symington 45½, Chandler 36½, Davis 33, Battle 32½, Timmerman 23½, and Governor Lausche of Ohio 5½. After the nomination was made unanimous, a short recess was taken during which the nominee prepared a surprise that would provide the greatest excitement of the convention.

The party leaders gathered in Stevenson's suite in the Stockyard Inn to be told that the candidate had decided not to name the vice-presidential candidate. He would, he said, leave the choice entirely in the hands of the delegates. The leaders were stunned. Not since 1896 had there been an open convention for running mates. "It's the damnedest fool idea I ever heard of," snorted Sam Rayburn, but Stevenson was adamant. Actually, the decision to throw the vice-presidential nomination open was shrewd politics. Everyone was aware that Richard Nixon would be the running mate on the Republican ticket and that he would be a major campaign issue in view of Eisenhower's health. What better or more dramatic way to point out the cut-and-dried nature of the forthcoming Republican nomination than an open convention?

When Stevenson announced on Thursday night that he would play no part in the selection of his running mate, he set off one of the wildest scrambles in convention history. Almost before Stevenson had finished speaking, vice-presidential candidates sprang up with bewildering profusion. Senators Kefauver and Gore of Tennessee, Kennedy of Massachusetts, and Humphrey of Minnesota, Governors Collins of Florida and Hodges of North Carolina, and Mayor Robert Wagner of New York City all jumped feet first into the battle.

The contest quickly narrowed to Kefauver and Kennedy. Both had been on the Stevenson bandwagon, and both were acceptable to the nominee. Senator Kennedy had made the nominating speech for Stevenson, an honor that he feared had been offered as a consolation prize while the vice-presidency went to someone else. Labor, the Middle West, and the Far West backed Kefauver. Most of the party professionals, New England, and the South backed Kennedy. The young Senator's Catholicism was, as far as the South was concerned, more acceptable than Kefauver's apostasy on civil rights. Most delegates who gave any consideration to the Catholic issue thought it might strengthen the ticket since the Stevenson divorce had obviously hurt him among Catholic voters in 1952.

Senator Kennedy had been a candidate for the vice-presidency for some weeks before the convention and had an organization in operation when Stevenson threw the race open. For the twelve hours before the balloting, the Kennedy forces worked tirelessly, seeking support. Carmine DeSapio pledged New York after a first ballot compliment to Mayor Wagner, but Eleanor Roosevelt was frosty when approached by the youthful candidate. Because of the ambiguity of his stand on the issue of McCarthy, Kennedy could not, Mrs. Roosevelt led him to understand, expect the support of the liberals in the convention. Several southern delegations, however, indicated that they would support him.

The first ballot for vice-president showed many delegations still confused by the unexpected freedom of choice. Only fourteen delegations cast solid votes—the other thirty-nine delegations scattered their votes among thirteen candidates. The results of the first ballot were Kefauver 483½, Kennedy 304, Gore 178, Wagner 162½, Humphrey 134½, Hodges 40, Pitt Tyson Maner of Alabama 33, Senator Clinton Anderson of New Mexico 16, Clement 13½, Collins 1½, Symington and Attorney General Brown of California 1 each, and Lyndon Johnson ½. There were 3 votes uncast; 687 were needed for nomination.

The second ballot was wildly confused. The huge tally board had been dismantled after the presidential nomination, and candidates and delegates were reduced to frantic attempts at keeping track of the vote on tally sheets. As a result, no one really knew what the score was. But it was apparent to everyone that Kennedy was taking a strong lead. At the end of the roll call, Kennedy had 559 votes to Kefauver's 479½, with 156 votes passed on the roll. When the states that had passed voted, the total gave Kennedy 618, Kefauver 551½. Other totals were Gore 110½, Humphrey 74, Wagner 9½, and Hodges, Clement, and Brown ½ each.

As soon as the roll was completed, Kentucky, which had voted for Gore, switched its 30 votes to Kennedy, giving him 647½—39 short of nomination. But then, in one of the most stunning reversals in convention history, a stampede developed for Kefauver. Senator Gore withdrew and threw Tennessee's 32 votes to Kefauver. Oklahoma followed with 16 more votes. At that point, Kennedy still had 647½, while Kefauver had increased to 527½. Then Minnesota, at the request of Senator Humphrey, gave an additional 16½ votes to Kefauver for a total of 554.

What happened next is open to some dispute. While Sam Rayburn looked out over a hall seething with standards waving for recognition, John McCormack called up to the rostrum for Rayburn to recognize Missouri. McCormack and Kennedy had been involved in a bitter battle for control of the Massachusetts delegation, and there was little love lost between the old Bay State leader and the new. Perhaps, as has been suggested, McCormack believed that Missouri was ready to swing from Humphrey to Kennedy, perhaps not. At any rate, Rayburn heeded McCormack's plea and recognized Missouri, which threw 32 more votes into the Kefauver column. The landslide was on. State after state switched its vote, and, at the end of the changes, the official roll call stood Kefauver 755½, Kennedy 589, Gore 13½, Wagner 6,

Humphrey 2, and Clement ¼. The bandwagon psychology was best expressed when the Virgin Islands, the last delegation to switch, candidly announced, "Mr. Chairman, for the sake of expediency, the Virgin Islands decides to change their vote to Estes Kefauver." Senator Kennedy then appeared on the platform to ask that Kefauver's nomination be made unanimous.

At the evening session, the nominees made their acceptance speeches and appeared with Harry Truman. Stevenson had at first balked at appearing with the former President but was convinced that party unity demanded it. Truman, who a few days earlier had accused Stevenson of being a defeatist, took his own defeat with good humor and told the convention, "Governor Stevenson is a real fighter and I ought to know. He's given some of us here a good licking." Stevenson had the last word when he saluted Truman and remarked, "I am glad to have you on my side again, sir."

"An open convention, secretly arrived at"

THE TWENTY-SIXTH REPUBLICAN NATIONAL CONVENTION
San Francisco, August 20, 1956

The Republican National Convention of 1956, which gathered in San Francisco on August 20, was, as several commentators pointed out, a coronation rather than a convention. Once the party had convinced itself that a man who had suffered a severe heart attack and a major operation within the past year was healthier than ever, there was no question of who the presidential nominee would be. If he could be kept alive, he would run.

The question of a running mate, however, was not quite so simple. Eisenhower appeared to be curiously ambivalent toward the future of Vice-President Richard Nixon, although he did say, after 22,000 voters in the New Hampshire primary wrote in Nixon's name for vice-president, that he "would be very happy to be on any political ticket" with Nixon. Naturally, the choice of a running mate would rest ultimately with the President, and Nixon waited impatiently to be asked. He was stunned when Eisenhower first suggested that Nixon might be better off in the cabinet and then loftily informed him that he would have to make his own decision as to whether or not to seek renomination. The Vice-President searched his conscience, wrestled with the problem, and then shyly informed Eisenhower that he would, indeed, like to stay on in his present job.

489

Not everyone in the party viewed Nixon's decision with complete joy. Harold Stassen was particularly unhappy at the prospect of Nixon's running again and decided to do something about it. Calling on Eisenhower, Stassen broached the subject of replacing Nixon. The President told him that he should feel entirely free to try to line up support for another candidate, so long as he did not purport to speak in Eisenhower's name.

On July 23, Stassen announced that he would propose the name of Governor Christian A. Herter of Massachusetts as a vice-presidential candidate. The response was overwhelmingly negative. The party leaders, with the conspicuous exception of Governor Goodwin Knight of California, rallied to Nixon's support. Stassen was game, but it did no good. He claimed to have a poll showing that 8% of the Republican vote would be lost with Nixon on the ticket, but Senator Styles Bridges countered that he had a poll showing that 54% of the voters favored the Eisenhower-Nixon ticket, while only 25% favored the Eisenhower-Herter ticket. Furthermore, the Bridges poll had been taken by ex-FBI agents, and who could argue with them?

Apparently no one. Stassen was booed wherever he went. National Chairman Leonard Hall announced very firmly that the ticket would be Eisenhower and Nixon, period. Finally, Herter himself announced that he would place Nixon in nomination. The battered Stassen capitulated and, with a trace of whimper, let it be known that he would be happy to second the nomination.

Except for the lonely Stassen crusade, the convention went off without a hitch. It was cynically but accurately described as "an open convention, secretly arrived at." A brief moment of spontaneity occurred when a Nebraska delegate tried to nominate "Joe Smith" for the vice-presidency, but an enraged Chairman Joe Martin ordered the offender and his "Joe Smith" out of the hall. The renominations of Eisenhower and Nixon were unanimous.

CHAPTER 24

"I think you can guess what the answer will be"

THE THIRTY-THIRD DEMOCRATIC NATIONAL CONVENTION
Los Angeles, July 11, 1960

The mid-term elections of 1958 marked the opening of the contest for the Democratic presidential nomination of 1960. The Democrats had won heavily—fourteen new seats in the Senate and fifty-two in the House plus six new governorships—and among the biggest winners were two potential candidates for the nomination. Senators John F. Kennedy of Massachusetts and Stuart Symington of Missouri needed major victories in their re-election bids to launch their presidential campaigns. Both were eminently successful. Symington won in Missouri with 66.4% of the vote, and Kennedy did even better with 73.6% in Massachusetts.

1960 was a year of senatorial candidates. Beside Kennedy and Symington, the other leading candidates were Senators Lyndon B. Johnson and Hubert Humphrey. Outside the Senate, only Adlai Stevenson, who was silent about his plans, was considered a serious contender for the nomination.

Although they were colleagues in the Senate, the four active candidates divided into two major strategies. For Kennedy and Humphrey the path to the nomination lay in the primaries; for Johnson and Symington it lay in negotiations with the state bosses and the power brokers. Senator Kennedy had two major liabilities to overcome in the primaries: his youth, and, more important, his

491

Catholicism. The ghost of Al Smith haunted the early days of the Kennedy campaign, and only sweeping victories in primaries throughout the country would convince his coreligionists who controlled the major delegations—Mayor Daley of Chicago, Tammany boss Carmine DeSapio, and Governors Lawrence of Pennsylvania, DiSalle of Ohio, and Brown of California—that a Catholic could be elected president.

The question was, Which primaries to enter? New Hampshire, as the first in the nation, had to be entered, but, because New England was home ground, a victory there would mean little. Wisconsin would be a good place to challenge Humphrey but would be a dangerous contest. Most of Kennedy's advisors, including his brother Robert Kennedy, opposed entering the Wisconsin primary, but the Senator, supported by his father and the pollster Lou Harris, finally decided to take the risk. West Virginia, a predominantly Protestant state, would be a good place to test the religious issue, and Oregon and Nebraska would give a wider regional basis for the Kennedy candidacy.

Ohio and California, it was decided, should be left to Governors DiSalle and Brown—but not as completely free gifts. The Senator informed DiSalle that, unless Ohio's favorite son pledged himself to the Kennedy cause, he would contest the primary. A private poll convinced the Governor that Kennedy would sweep the primary with disastrous results for DiSalle's future control of the state party, and, early in January, 1960, the Governor, one arm firmly twisted behind his back, announced that he would run as a favorite son who would deliver the entire Ohio delegation to Kennedy on the first ballot. In California, Governor Brown was allowed to run unopposed, with the understanding that California would be delivered to Kennedy when needed.

Hubert Humphrey also recognized that he must contest the primaries. He was not especially well known outside his own state and Washington, D.C., and was known as an extreme liberal. The party leaders, especially in the South, would never of their own free will take a candidate as liberal as Humphrey. He must, therefore, enter the convention with sufficient votes won in the primaries to establish a bargaining position that would command the attention of the eastern leaders. Also, by demonstrating his vote-getting ability, Humphrey could expect to secure the backing of the liberal volunteer-citizen organizations and the Stevenson supporters.

Humphrey did not have the funds or the organization to make the race in many of the sixteen scheduled primaries. Two, the District of Columbia and South Dakota, could be easily won but would prove nothing. Wisconsin and West Virginia, however, would be excellent battlegrounds for Humphrey. Wisconsin was highly diverse in its make up—both industrial and agrarian, populated by a wide range of sizable ethnic minorities, and 31% Catholic. A victory there would prove that Humphrey could appeal to a wide political spectrum. Also, it was conveniently close to Minnesota and could be subjected to intensive week-end campaigning by Humphrey's Minnesota staff and local volunteers. In West Virginia, widespread unemployment and a depressed economy should have made Humphrey's liberalism attractive to the voters, and winning there would add a new regional dimension to his candidacy. Finally, the free-for-all in Oregon would complete Humphrey's primary campaigns.

Stuart Symington's strategy was to offend no one, avoid the blood-letting primaries, and hope for a deadlock. The primaries, he hoped, would be inconclusive and might serve to eliminate both Humphrey and Kennedy—"A good clean fight from which no survivors emerged," in the words of one observer. Symington's assets included an impressive record of success in private business, in the executive branch as Secretary of the Air Force, and as a liberal senator. Coming from an industrial border state, he could appeal to both the northern and southern wings of the party, and he had as his principal backer Harry S. Truman, who, it was hoped, would still wield major influence in the convention. Among Symington's liabilities were the facts that, like Humphrey, he was little known nationally, he had few political contacts on a nation-wide basis, and he was known principally though unfairly as a monomaniac on the subject of defense who had little interest in other areas. His many excellent qualities were, however, well known to the party leaders, who might logically turn to him in the event of a deadlock.

Lyndon Johnson also hoped for a deadlock. In that case, he

and his chief backer, Speaker Rayburn, could draw upon the vast reservoir of congressional debts and obligations they had amassed in their control of Congress to win the congressional leaders and, through them, the state bosses to the Johnson cause. Johnson, a master of manipulating the Senate, believed that the same tactics could be applied to manipulation of the convention. Johnson also had the potential asset of being, more than any other candidate, the heir of the New Deal. The aging apostles of the Roosevelt era, disconcerted by the younger and brasher men who had taken away their power, turned to Johnson, who had been, they remembered with nostalgia, a favored protégé of Roosevelt. Dean Acheson, Oscar Chapman, Justice William O. Douglas, and Tommy "The Cork" Corcoran set up the northern branch of the Johnson campaign but proved to be completely ineffectual.

The former standard-bearer, Adlai Stevenson, refused to take any public position on the nomination. To the great frustration of his supporters, he refused to announce himself as a candidate, and to the irritation of the other candidates, he refused to take himself completely out of the race. His attitude seems to have been that, having twice been nominated, he should make no effort to secure a third nomination, but, on the other hand, if the nomination should be freely offered without any effort on his part, he should not refuse it. Stevenson left the country in January, 1960, for a two-month business trip to South America and remained, until the collapse of American foreign policy in May, a figure of minor importance in convention speculation. His possible candidacy was, however, kept alive by a devoted group led by Senator Mike Monroney, his executive aide Tom Finney, Washington lawyer George Ball, former Wisconsin National Committeeman James Doyle, and movie producer Doré Schary.

The first major clash in the campaign came between Kennedy and Humphrey in Wisconsin on April 5. The Kennedy organization, the Kennedy family, and the candidate himself blanketed the state in an all-out drive for the thirty-one delegates. At least one Kennedy brother, sister, or in-law—and they were legion—appeared at least once in every Wisconsin town with a population over 300. Senator Humphrey, who had good reason to feel himself surrounded, ruefully admitted that he felt like a corner grocery store trying to compete with a chain of supermarkets. So intensive was the Kennedy drive that it was an all but foregone conclusion that he would have a major victory in the primary. The forecasters were mistaken.

Kennedy did win 56% of the popular vote, but the margin came from the four districts that were heavily Catholic. He lost the four predominantly Protestant districts, and he barely carried the one unclassified district. The delegation votes were divided 20½ for Kennedy, 10½ for Humphrey. The results were interpreted as a Protestant-Catholic split, and they left unanswered the question, Could a Catholic win?

When the results were known, Humphrey elatedly claimed a moral victory and announced that he would enter the West Virginia primary. His decision would do more than any other single event to secure the nomination for John F. Kennedy. If Humphrey sincerely wanted to stop Kennedy, he would have been wiser to let Kennedy run unopposed in that primary. Then the religious issue would never have been resolved, and a Kennedy victory would have been meaningless in terms understandable to the party bosses.

Wisconsin had been fought on a fairly high level, but West Virginia, where politics is always sordid at best, degenerated into a vicious, bitter campaign. Both candidates were fighting for their political futures, and the campaign grew progressively rougher and more personal. Much as Humphrey tried, he could not control an undercurrent of religious bigotry that began to creep into the campaign. Kennedy, in a brilliant move, met the issue head on with a forthright statement over television on May 8 and made religious tolerance the major issue from then on. It was an issue Humphrey could not possibly fight.

Immediately after the Wisconsin primary, polls had shown Humphrey leading Kennedy 64% to 36% in West Virginia. Two weeks before the primary, the standings were 55% to 48%, and Kennedy continued to gain ground. To make certain of victory, the Kennedy forces moved against the sources of Humphrey money. Many Stevenson backers, hoping for a deadlock, had been contributing to the Humphrey campaign. In New York, Governor Ribicoff of Connecticut, acting on instructions from Kennedy, informed the Stevenson people that, unless they stopped contributing to Humphrey, Stevenson would not even be considered for secretary of state. Connecticut State Chairman John Bailey bluntly told former Senator William Benton that, if he continued contributing to Humphrey, he would never hold another office in Connecticut so long as Bailey had anything to say about it.

The cutting off of Humphrey campaign funds and the more important religious issue, which implied that a vote for Humphrey would be a vote for religious intolerance, finished Humphrey. A few days before the election, the polls showed Humphrey ahead 45% to 42%, with 13% undecided, but on election day, May 10, Kennedy won the primary and, as far as the convention was concerned, buried the religious question once and for all. He also buried Hubert Humphrey, who announced on the same night that he was withdrawing as a candidate. Stuart Symington too, although he didn't realize it at the time, had lost his best argument—that only he could draw support from all the diverse elements of the party.

From West Virginia on, the primaries were all for Kennedy. Nebraska had gone to him on the same day as West Virginia; Maryland followed on May 15; and, on the 20th, Oregon went to him with a sixty-forty margin over favorite son Wayne Morse. Kennedy clearly looked like a winner, and some of the big states began to fall into line. On June 2, after a conference with Kennedy on Mackinac Island, Governor G. Mennen Williams announced his support, which gave Kennedy most of Michigan's 51 votes.

Kennedy also won an important victory in New York. John Bailey had been quietly working across the border from Connecticut on the upstate counties, while Joseph P. Kennedy worked with Congressmen Buckley of the Bronx and Keogh of Brooklyn on the counties around Manhattan. Before Carmine DeSapio realized what was happening, 80 of New York's 114 votes were firmly tied up for Kennedy. There was nothing for Tammany to do but go along with an accomplished fact, and most of New York would be in the Kennedy column on the first ballot.

Having eliminated Humphrey as a candidate, Kennedy began raids on the Johnson strength. The majority leader was attempting to overcome the stigma of being a southern candidate by winning as much support as possible in the Rocky Mountain states and the Far West. After all, Texas had as many cowboys as Montana, New Mexico, or Arizona—why should not the owner of the LBJ ranch be a *bona fide* western candidate? Johnson was strongly supported in New Mexico by Senators Chavez and Anderson and was expected to take all seventeen delegates, but Kennedy visited the state convention and came away with four delegates. In Arizona, former Governor Ernest McFarland was expected to deliver the state to Johnson, but Congressman Stewart Udall and the Kennedy rustlers took the entire delegation. There was more bad news for Johnson in Colorado. The state leadership was badly divided, with Senator Carroll supporting Stevenson and Governor McNichols and former Senator Edwin C. Johnson supporting the Texas Senator. When the state convention met, the Kennedy posse was led by brother Ted Kennedy and Byron White—and ten more delegates went to Kennedy.

By the end of June, Kennedy could count on at least 550 first-ballot votes: 114 from New England; 265 from Delaware, Indiana, Maryland, Michigan, New York, and Ohio; 36 from the farm states; 31 from the South, which was mostly for Johnson; 61 from the western states; 28 on the Pacific Coast; and another dozen scattered throughout the territories. Symington and Humphrey were eliminated from practical consideration, and Johnson was, despite his best efforts, still the southern candidate.

But there was one man who could still pose a threat to a Kennedy victory: Adlai Stevenson. The former candidate was giving no encouragement to a draft movement, but the foreign policy disasters of May—beginning with the U-2 fiasco and culminating in the collapse of the Paris summit conference—caused many Democrats to turn instinctively to Stevenson as the leader best qualified to deal with foreign affairs. Eleanor Roosevelt and elder statesman Herbert H. Lehman were active in his behalf in New York, and a draft-Stevenson movement was formally launched in Washington, D.C. By the end of June, there were draft-Stevenson clubs in forty-two states, and the first full-page advertisement in the New York papers appealing for money drew $40,000 in contributions.

The Stevenson managers estimated that Kennedy would have 600 votes on the first ballot, with 150 to 200 for Johnson and 100 to 150 for Symington. Stevenson could probably command somewhere between 50 and 80 votes. The decisive factor would be the uncommitted and favorite-son states of Iowa, pledged to Governor Loveless; Kansas, pledged to Governor Docking; Minnesota, pledged to Humphrey; California, pledged to Governor Brown; New Jersey, pledged to Governor Meyner; Illinois, controlled by Mayor Daley; and Pennsylvania, controlled by Governor Lawrence. In all, these states represented a bloc of 350 votes. To ensure that these votes remained frozen but friendly to Stevenson, Senator Monroney and lawyer John Sharon traveled 30,000 miles around the country in May and June urging support for Stevenson. Governors Brown and Lawrence were friendly but cautious because they could get no hint from Stevenson himself of whether or not he would make the race. Without Stevenson's co-operation, the best that Monroney and Sharon could do was to try to convince the favorite sons to stand fast and keep open minds on Stevenson's candidacy.

The thirty-third Democratic National Convention was scheduled to open on Monday, July 11, in the sprawling megalopolis of Los Angeles. Previous conventions had been relatively compact events, with delegates crowded into single down-town areas within easy reach of each other. But the 45,000 delegates, alternates, officials, hangers-on, and spectators who attended the 1960 convention were scattered from down-town Los Angeles to Beverly Hills to Pasadena to Hollywood and other points all around the compass. The average delegate, lonely, lost, and beguiled by offers of tours around the movie studios, the swimming pools, and the ersatz attractions of Disneyland, had little opportunity to feel that he was actually participating in a convention. There were, of course, the official candidates' headquarters in the Biltmore Hotel, and, across Pershing Square with its assortment of oddities, the Paramount Building housed the Stevenson headquarters. But the Biltmore was more than an hour away by peril-fraught freeways for most of the delegates. Those who did make the journey could be regaled by taffy at the Johnson headquarters (a half-ton flown in from Austin, Texas); Pepsi-Cola from Symington; coffee, buns, and motion pictures from Kennedy; and orange juice from favorite-son Senator George Smathers of Florida.

For 3000 party faithful there was somewhat more substantial nourishment at a gala banquet held in the Beverly Hills Hotel on the night before the first session. As they listened to speeches from Senators Kennedy, Johnson, and Symington and from Adlai Stevenson, the Democrats, according to the New York *Times*, which dutifully chronicles such details, consumed along with their steaks, sixty-two cases of scotch, thirty-five of bourbon, twenty-six of vodka, twenty of gin, and 150 of soft drinks—and forty-five gallons of orange juice.

A notable feature of this convention was the passing of the old guard. Such ghosts as Jim Farley, Scott Lucas, and Claude Pepper wandered through the lobbies, and recent leaders like DeSapio, Sam Rayburn, Eleanor Roosevelt, Averell Harriman, and Michael Prendergast were most conspicuous for their lack of power. Their places had been taken by the bright young men of the Kennedy clan and organization, who, to the older leaders, must have seemed little more than boys. Conspicuously absent was Harry Truman, who had announced that the convention was "rigged" to force Kennedy upon a party that did not really want him. Truman was very sensibly avoiding the licking he knew was coming.

If Truman had given up the fight against Kennedy, Johnson had not. He had formally announced his candidacy only five days before the convention and had plunged into a frantic, last-minute stop-Kennedy drive. To strengthen his bargaining position he, along with Speaker Rayburn, had recessed Congress until after the convention—a reminder to those delegates who were also members of Congress "that who supported whom" would be remembered when Congress met again and when pet bills were to be considered. But, although Johnson and Mr. Sam radiated confidence, few were convinced. As one skeptical Texan remarked dryly, "Mr. Sam has thumped and pulled some mighty big watermelons in his day, without even plugging them, but this one looks green to me."

On Sunday, Governor Meyner decided to hold his delegation on the first ballot, which was good news to the stop-Kennedy forces, but this gain was offset by bad news from Illinois. Mayor Daley had been under intense pressure from Joe Kennedy all through the spring, while Senator Monroney had been begging him to keep the delegation uncommitted. Of the 69 Illinois votes, Daley controlled an estimated 55, and he announced after a secret caucus on Sunday afternoon that Illinois would vote on the first ballot 59½ for Kennedy, 6½ for Symington, and 2 for Stevenson, with 1 still uncommitted.

The break for Kennedy led by Illinois was quickly followed up on Monday. New York caucused and announced the official poll of the delegation: 101 for Kennedy, 14 more than had been announced for him at the state convention; 4½ for Johnson; 3½ for Stevenson; 2 for Symington; and 1 for Humphrey, with 1½ votes unrecorded.

Governor David Lawrence of Pennsylvania was in a difficult position. His admiration for Stevenson was close to adoration, but Kennedy looked like the winner. There had been no Kennedy organization in Pennsylvania to challenge the Governor's control, but Congressman William Green, boss of Philadelphia, was strongly in favor of Kennedy and had been lining up support within the delegation. Lawrence was met at the airport by John Bailey when he arrived on Saturday, and Bailey arranged for the Governor to meet with Kennedy on Sunday. He conferred with the Massachusetts Senator for an hour and then, Sunday night, drove to the Beverly Hills Hotel for a two-hour conference with Adlai Stevenson. On Monday, Governor Lawrence announced that Pennsylvania would vote 64 Kennedy, 8 Stevenson, and 9 scattered on the first ballot.

Kennedy was close to victory, but the Stevenson forces were still fighting. The delegates gathered for the first session in the Sports Arena on Monday evening, making their way through the typical crowd attracted to demonstrate at political conventions. In Los Angeles, the crowd was perhaps more typical than ever. Along with the inevitable signs announcing the imminence of God's wrath, were such signs as "Vote for Prohibition" and, of special interest, "Relief for the Isle of Man." Other demonstrators exhorted the delegates to abolish the McCarran-Walters Act, capital punishment, and so forth. But within an hour the crowd changed. The delegates inside the hall, preparing to hear young Senator Frank Church's keynote address became aware of a rumbling noise outside. When the curious investigated, they found the crackpots, the prohibitionists, and the Isle of Man defenders gone. Now the Arena was encircled with a great crowd marching in an endless chain for Adlai Stevenson. "Young and old, boy and girl, husband and wife, some wheeling babies in carriages, some in overalls, others in business suits . . . all of them together were marching, close-locked, chanting 'We Want Stevenson!'" Hundreds demonstrated the first night; by Tuesday there were thousands.

The demonstration had a strong effect on many delegates. Governors Loveless and Docking had pledged their Iowa and Kansas delegations to Kennedy, but now the delegates rebelled and decided to support their favorite sons on the first ballot, regardless of their wishes. If Stevenson could stop Kennedy, they would give what help they could. North Dakota threatened to bolt Kennedy, but Sargent Shriver worked all Tuesday night to keep the delegation in line.

The major break for Stevenson came Tuesday night in California. Governor Brown found himself at the head of an increasingly unruly delegation. It had become apparent that the entire delegation could not be delivered to Kennedy, as Brown had intended. Newspaper accounts at the time and post mortems after the convention describe how the Governor lost control of his delegation. The reports, it seems, while accurate to a point, were greatly exaggerated. The delegation had been elected to vote for Brown. Once released, the pro-Stevenson delegates could never have been delivered no matter how firm the Governor's control. Certainly, by Tuesday the Stevenson delegates were out of anyone's control. In a stormy session that night, the California delegation threw off its cloak of unanimity and split virtually down the middle. Thirty-one and one-half votes would go to Stevenson on the first ballot; 30½ would follow the Governor into the Kennedy camp. The other nineteen delegates expressed a preference for either Symington or Johnson.

Before the California break, the Minnesota delegation had been torn by indecision. Governor Freeman was going to place Kennedy in nomination, Senator Eugene McCarthy would nominate Stevenson, and Hubert Humphrey had also indicated his willingness to support Stevenson. But he would not instruct his released delegation to do so. The uncertain Minnesotans had caucused on Sunday, twice on Monday, and twice on Tuesday and still could not agree on a candidate. Finally, in despair, they decided to vote for Humphrey as instructed, although there was a distinct possibility that the state would go to Stevenson on the second ballot—if there should be a second ballot.

Stevenson himself finally decided to test the sentiment of the convention on Tuesday afternoon by taking his seat with the Illinois delegation. When he appeared on the floor, the galleries and delegates exploded in an affectionate demonstration for their former leader. Despite the efforts of Permanent Chairman Governor LeRoy Collins of Florida, the ovation went on for eighteen minutes, and Stevenson, nearly crushed by the crowd, took refuge on the platform. He thanked the audience for the demonstration and said, "after getting in and out of the Biltmore Hotel and this hall, I know whom you are going to nominate. It will be the last survivor." The question was, Was the ovation merely a gesture of affection, or was it proof of popular support? Many claimed that his appearance implicitly denied his candidacy because of the long-standing tradition that active candidates do not appear before conventions. But Stevenson had decided to make the fight.

At one o'clock Wednesday morning, he met with 250 delegates and alternates in the LaFayette Room of the Sheraton-West Hotel, and it seemed as if a Stevenson bandwagon were about to start. His managers calculated that, beside the announced California vote, there would be 12 more on the second ballot, and the shift of ½ vote could deliver Iowa, North Dakota, and Alaska, while 1 shifted vote could deliver Kansas. There was also the possibility that Minnesota could be induced to switch, and it was hoped that Illinois would rally to him if his drive began to pick up momentum. Stevenson delivered a moving speech to the assembled delegates, and, while he did not actually announce his candidacy, he closed with the Robert Frost lines, later so closely identified with the New Frontier, "The woods are lovely, dark and deep,/ But I have promises to keep/ And miles to go before I sleep,/ And miles to go before I sleep." By Wednesday morning, it was accepted that Stevenson was belatedly in the fight to the finish.

But Stevenson entered very late, and the Kennedy bandwagon continued to roll. Governor Nelson of Wisconsin, neutral until then, announced his support, and on Wednesday morning the Kennedy forces estimated a first-ballot strength of 739½ votes—only 21½ votes short of victory.

The convention adopted the platform before hearing the nominating speeches. It was the most liberal document ever adopted by the party, and the civil-rights plank, although challenged by a southern minority report, was the strongest ever adopted in a national convention in either party. It called for a federal fair employment practices commission and declared, "The time has come to assure equal access for all Americans to all areas of community life, including voting booths, schoolrooms, jobs, housing and public facilities."

The nominating speeches began on Wednesday evening. Speaker Rayburn nominated Johnson, Governor Freeman placed Kennedy before the convention, Governor Blair of Missouri named Symington, and, in the emotional high point of the convention, Senator Eugene McCarthy pleaded Stevenson's cause. "Do not reject this man who has made us all proud to be Democrats," said McCarthy. "Do not leave this prophet without honor in his own party."

The Stevenson managers had taken great care in preparing for the demonstration that they hoped would stampede the convention. Allotted only thirty-five gallery tickets for Wednesday night, they had collected another 1000 tickets from contributors who were not going to use them, had prevailed upon the host California delegation to turn over another 1000, and had then outfitted their supporters with Kennedy buttons, put them in line where 2500 Kennedy tickets were being distributed, and gathered another 1500 tickets. In all, the Stevensonians managed to put nearly 4000 people in the galleries that night to cheer for their man.

Stevenson supporters on the floor exhorted the delegates to join in the demonstration. Mercedes McCambridge, the film star, cajoled and argued with the Illinois delegation to join the clamor for their native son but with no success. As the demonstrators shouted, "We Want Adlai," the Illinois delegates roared back, "We Want Kennedy!"

In the New York delegation, eighty-two-year-old Herbert Lehman struggled with two Tammany stalwarts for the state standard.

They were holding fast, when Mayor Wagner shouted at them, "I told Lehman he could have the standard; give it to him *now!"* The elder statesman bore it off in triumph to join the tumultuous crowd jamming the aisles for Stevenson.

Brave as the show for Stevenson was, the battle was already lost. Most of the demonstrators had come in from outside the hall, and few delegates joined in. They were unaware that the Stevenson movement had collapsed a few hours earlier. When Stevenson finally decided on Wednesday morning to make a fight of it, he had tried without success to reach Mayor Daley. Finally at 4:00 p.m., Jacob Arvey located the Chicago mayor on the convention floor and insisted that he return Stevenson's call as a courtesy. When Stevenson told Daley that he was willing to fight, he was told that he had no support. Did he have no support, period, or was it because the delegates thought that he was not a candidate? He had no support, period, Daley replied. That ended the Stevenson candidacy.

There were, however, still dangers to Kennedy. If he did not win on the first ballot, he might not win at all. Kansas, Iowa, and Minnesota could not be relied upon, and he might lose California votes on the second ballot. There is reason to believe that some 45 Pennsylvania votes would have switched to Stevenson on the second ballot, with the prospect of 20 more on the third. Indiana was also eager to break away from Kennedy. It was reported that, having voted off its first-ballot instructions, the delegation would vote on the second ballot 10½ for Kennedy, 11 each for Johnson and Symington, ½ for Stevenson, with 1 vote still undecided. Such wholesale defections would have been fatal to the Kennedy drive, but, as it turned out, there never was a second ballot.

With 761 votes needed for nomination, Kennedy reached the 100 mark with Idaho, the 200 mark with Indiana, and passed 300 with Massachusetts. The vote of Pennsylvania put him within 80 votes of victory, and the bandwagon continued to roll. By the time Vermont had cast its votes, Kennedy had 698½, and Robert Kennedy realized that, if Wyoming's 15 votes were cast for Kennedy, he would have the nomination. Wyoming intended to give Kennedy 8½ of its votes, but, while West Virginia and Wisconsin were balloting, the candidate's brother moved into the Wyoming delegation, calling upon them to achieve the distinction of ensuring the nomination. When the clerk called Wyoming, all 15 votes went to Kennedy, who had the nomination by a 2-vote margin. The results of the ballot finally stood: Kennedy 806, Johnson 409, Symington 86, Stevenson 79½, Meyner 43, Humphrey 41½, Smathers 30, Governor Ross Barnett of Mississippi 23, Loveless 1½, and Governors Faubus of Arkansas, Brown of California, and Rosellini of Washington ½ each.

Following his nomination, the candidate appeared before the convention and began his remarks, "Under the official procedures of this convention it is not possible for me to give you an answer to your nomination until Friday night. But I think you can guess what the answer will be."

After adjournment, speculation turned inevitably to the vice-presidency. The Kennedy forces had been very free in offering the hope of the nomination to various favorite sons, and Los Angeles that night was filled with men who thought that they had received the Kennedy blessing. It was generally assumed that the vice-presidency would go either to Senator Henry M. Jackson of Washington or to Senator Symington. But the candidate had plans of his own. On the Sunday before the convention, he had casually remarked to a friend of Senator Johnson that he might offer the vice-presidency to the Senator if he would accept. Johnson's reaction was a particularly pungent expletive.

At eight o'clock Thursday morning, Kennedy called Johnson's suite and arranged a meeting. The two men met at 10:15 a.m. What was actually said at that meeting would no doubt make interesting reading, but the result was that Lyndon Johnson was offered, and agreed to accept, the vice-presidential nomination. When warned by friends that he would have far less power as vice-president than as majority leader, Johnson replied, mistakenly as it turned out, "Power is where power goes."

Johnson's acceptance of the offer apparently surprised everyone in Los Angeles except Kennedy and Johnson themselves, and some members of the Kennedy staff believed even the candidate was surprised. But the choice was a logical one. Roosevelt, Truman, and Stevenson had all run with southerners on the ticket, and the mathematics of the electoral college made a vice-presidential candidate who could carry the South almost a necessity. Beside, Johnson would be strong in those areas where Kennedy's Catholicism might be expected to do the ticket the most harm. Over the strong opposition of the liberals and labor, Johnson was Kennedy's choice, and the convention dutifully placed the Texan on the ticket.

"We collected every political
IOU we held in the country"

THE TWENTY-SEVENTH REPUBLICAN
NATIONAL CONVENTION
Los Angeles, July 25, 1960

Out of the disasters of the mid-term elections of 1958, the Republicans had salvaged one bright victory and a new hero. Nelson Rockefeller was elected governor of New York by better than a half-million-vote margin over incumbent Averell Harriman and began immediately to run for the Republican presidential nomination. The new Governor and his staff began to survey party leaders, assessing potential delegate strength, and to sound out the financial contributors who would be necessary to finance the pre-convention campaign. Rockefeller himself made several trips around the country to gauge popular sentiment. The results of these surveys came as a distinct shock.

All doors, Rockefeller found, were closed to him. He was cheered by crowds wherever he went, but the party leaders were frosty at best. Rockefeller, the newcomer to elective politics, was considered too new, too independent for their taste. Beside they had commitments elsewhere. It was the same with the big contributors. They were polite to Rockefeller—no businessman in his right mind would be anything but polite to a Rockefeller—but there were no offers of support. They, too, had previous commitments.

The man to whom the Republican leaders were committed was, of course, the Vice-President of the United States, Richard M.

507

Nixon. The political leaders were especially in his debt. Through good years and bad, it had been Nixon who had done the campaigning that Eisenhower found distasteful. It had been Nixon who had performed all the multitude of tasks necessary to keep a national political party operating and who had carried the load in the off-year elections. That he had been unable to help his party to victory in those elections was less important than that he had given all he had, regardless of the odds. For seven years, Nixon had been working for his party, and it was time to reward him. The leaders would go with Nixon, and Rockefeller could spend the next few years gaining experience in Albany.

By the end of 1959, Rockefeller understood that he had no chance for the nomination and announced, in December, that he would not be a candidate. He was careful, however, not to shut the door completely. Should conditions change, he might reconsider his decision.

In May, conditions did change, and Rockefeller did, indeed, reconsider. After the collapse of the summit conference, Rockefeller decided to speak out. It is open to question whether or not he actually believed that he could break Nixon's grip on the nomination, but the only way that he could even try was through ideas, not power plays. Accordingly, on June 8, 1960, he let loose a blast that, in effect, repudiated the entire program, foreign and domestic, of the Eisenhower administration. He was convinced, he said, of the failure of Republican leadership to make clear where it was leading the nation. "In this spirit, I am compelled to say two things bluntly. One: I find it unreasonable—in these times—that the leading Republican candidate for the Presidential nomination has firmly insisted upon making known his program and his policies, not before, but only after nomination by his party. Two: I find it reasonable—and urgently necessary—that the new spokesmen of the Republican Party declare now, and not at some later date, precisely what they believe and what they propose, to meet the great matters before the nation. . . ." Rockefeller then laid down his own nine-point platform, specific in detail, which was a repudiation of the entire Eisenhower policy.

A draft-Rockefeller movement was immediately set up, and Citizens for Rockefeller clubs were reactivated in twenty-nine states. On July 18, Rockefeller headquarters were established in the Conrad Hilton Hotel in Chicago, and appeals were made in newspaper advertisements and over television for Republicans to write, telephone, or wire their delegations to urge Rockefeller's nomination. The response was phenomenal. Within twenty-four hours, 260,000 pieces of mail had arrived at the Chicago convention, and two days later the volume of mail and telegrams had passed the million mark. It was an impressive display of popular support, but the major decisions of the convention had been settled long before the opening date of July 25.

If Rockefeller could not win the nomination, he could at least determine the platform. When the Governor saw the first draft of the platform that had been prepared in Chicago, he pronounced it unsatisfactory and let it be known that he intended a floor fight. Such a conflict would be awkward, to say the least. Nixon in his role of statesman wanted nothing to damage the image of a judicious convention solemnly deliberating and selecting the most experienced, most statesmanlike candidate. Never a man blindly devoted to specific principles, Nixon could, when called upon to preserve his image, accept whatever principles would be most useful.

The Vice-President arrived secretly in New York on the evening of Friday, July 22, and went into conference with the Governor at Rockefeller's apartment at 810 Fifth Avenue. After a discussion of several hours' length, the Vice-President and the Governor agreed on a platform embodying all Rockefeller's ideas —a compact that represented an even more sweeping surrender than the famous Eisenhower surrender to Taft in 1952.

The response was immediate, angry, and frenzied. In Chicago, the platform committee exploded, and, when Dwight Eisenhower read of the repudiation of his administration, so did he. It is an open question which explosion was the loudest. In Chicago, the angry Republicans revolted and released plank by plank the platform that they had already decided upon. One committee member proudly boasted that not one word of the national-defense plank had been influenced by the Rockefeller-Nixon compact.

Nixon arrived in Chicago on Monday afternoon to quell the revolt. He concluded that much of the original platform could go through as scheduled if Rockefeller's recommendations for strong civil-rights and defense planks were incorporated into it. Nixon employed all his excellent tactical skills in bringing the party round. As one of his aides put it, "We collected every political IOU we held in the country that night." The civil-rights plank was accepted over anguished warnings that Nixon was throwing away his chance to carry the South, and, after a day of delicate negotiations among the committee, Rockefeller, and President Eisenhower, a mutually satisfactory plank was written on national defense. Rockefeller was satisfied and informed the New York delegation that there would be no floor fight and that he was definitely not a candidate for the nomination.

On Wednesday evening, July 27, Richard Nixon realized his long-held ambition by receiving the Republican presidential nomination, and, at the nominee's recommendation, Ambassador to the United Nations Henry Cabot Lodge was named by the convention as the running mate.

BIBLIOGRAPHY

PRIMARY SOURCES

Bancroft, Frederic, ed. *Speeches, Correspondence and Political Papers of Carl Schurz.* Vol. III. New York: G. P. Putnam's Sons, 1913.

Beale, Harriet S. Blaine, ed. *Letters of Mrs. James G. Blaine.* Vol. I. New York: Duffield & Co., 1908.

Bigelow, John, ed. *Letters and Literary Memorials of Samuel J. Tilden.* New York: Harper & Row, Publishers, 1908.

Blaine, James G. *Twenty Years of Congress.* Norwich: The Henry Bill Publishing Company, 1886.

Bryan, William Jennings. *Memoirs.* Philadelphia: John C. Winston Company, 1925.

————. *A Tale of Two Conventions.* New York: Funk & Wagnalls Co., Inc., 1912.

Butler, Nicholas Murray. *Across the Busy Years.* Vol. I. New York: Charles Scribner's Sons, 1939.

Clark, Champ. *My Quarter Century of American Politics.* Vol. II. New York: Harper & Row, Publishers, 1920.

Cox, James M. *Journey Through My Years.* New York: Simon and Schuster, Inc., 1946.

David, Paul T., Malcolm Moos, and Ralph M. Goldman, eds. *Presidential Nominating Politics in 1952.* Baltimore: The Johns Hopkins Press, 1954.

Daniels, Josephus. *Editor in Politics*. Chapel Hill: University of North Carolina Press, 1941.

DePew, Chauncey M. *My Memories of Eighty Years*. New York: Charles Scribner's Sons, 1924.

Farley, James A. *Behind the Ballots*. New York: Harcourt, Brace & World, Inc., 1938.

Flynn, Edward J. *You're the Boss*. New York: The Viking Press, Inc., 1947.

Foraker, Joseph B. *Notes of a Busy Life*. Cincinnati: Stewart and Kidd Co., 1917.

Gresham, Matilda. *Life of Walter Quintin Gresham*. Chicago: Rand, McNally & Co., 1919.

Hancock, Almira Russell. *Reminiscences of Winfield Scott Hancock*. New York: C. L. Webster & Co., 1887.

Hoar, George F. *Autobiography of Seventy Years*. New York: Charles Scribner's Sons, 1903.

Hoover, Herbert C. *Memoirs, The Cabinet and the Presidency, 1920-1933*. New York: The Macmillan Company, 1952.

Hudson, William C. *Random Recollections*. New York: Cupples & Leon Company, 1911.

Julian, George W. *Political Recollections 1840-1872*. Chicago: Jansen, McClurg & Co., 1884.

Johnson, Walter. *How We Drafted Adlai Stevenson*. New York: Alfred A. Knopf, Inc., 1955.

McAdoo, William Gibbs. *Crowded Years*. Boston: Houghton Mifflin Company, 1931.

Martin, Joseph W., Jr. *My First Fifty Years in Politics*. New York: McGraw-Hill Book Co., Inc., 1960.

Mullen, Arthur F. *Western Democrat*. New York: W. Wilfred Funk, Inc., 1940.

Nevins, Allan, ed. *Letters of Grover Cleveland, 1850-1908*. New York: Houghton Mifflin Company, 1933.

Official Proceedings Democratic National Convention 1868-1960.

Official Proceedings Liberal Republican National Convention 1872.

Official Proceedings Republican National Convention 1868-1960.

Platt, Thomas C. *Autobiography*. New York: Dodge Publishing Company, 1910.

Redding, Jack. *Inside the Democratic Party*. Indianapolis: The Bobbs-Merrill Company, Inc., 1958.

Roosevelt, Elliott, ed. *F.D.R. His Personal Letters 1928-1945*. Vol. I. New York: Duell, Sloan & Pearce, Inc., 1950.

Roper, Daniel C. *Fifty Years of Public Life.* Durham: Duke University Press, 1941.

Rosewater, Victor. *Backstage in 1912.* Philadelphia: Dorrance & Company, Inc., 1932.

Sherman, John. *Recollections of Forty Years in the House, Senate and Cabinet.* Chicago: The Werner Co., 1895.

Smith, Alfred E. *Up to Now.* New York: The Viking Press, Inc., 1929.

Stevenson, Adlai E. *Major Campaign Speeches.* New York: Random House, Inc., 1953.

Storke, Thomas M. *California Editor.* Los Angeles: Westernlore Press, 1958.

Tillett, Paul, ed. *Inside Politics: The National Conventions, 1960.* Dobbs Ferry: Oceana Publications, Inc., 1962.

Truman, Harry S. *Memoirs.* Vol. II. New York: Doubleday & Company, Inc., 1956.

Vanderberg, Arthur, Jr., ed. *The Private Papers of Senator Vanderberg.* Boston: Houghton Mifflin Company, 1952.

Watson, James E. *As I Knew Them.* Indianapolis: The Bobbs-Merrill Company, Inc., 1936.

Watterson, Henry. *"Marse Henry," An Autobiography.* New York: George H. Doran Co., 1919.

White, William Allen. *Autobiography.* New York: The Macmillan Company, 1946.

Williams, Charles Richard. *Diary and Letters of Rutherford Birchard Hayes.* Vol. III. Columbus: The Ohio State Archaeological and Historical Society, 1924.

SECONDARY SOURCES

Bagby, Wesley M. *The Road to Normalcy.* Baltimore: The Johns Hopkins Press, 1962.

Baker, Ray Stannard. *Woodrow Wilson, Life and Letters.* Vol. III. New York: Doubleday & Company, Inc., 1922.

Barnard, Harry. *"Eagle Forgotten" The Life of John Peter Altgeld.* Indianapolis: The Bobbs-Merrill Company, Inc., 1938.

———. *Rutherford B. Hayes and His America.* Indianapolis: The Bobbs-Merrill Company, Inc., 1954.

Barnes, James A. *John G. Carlisle, Financial Statesman.* New York: Dodd, Mead & Co., 1931.

Barnes, Joseph. *Willkie*. New York: Simon and Schuster, Inc., 1952.

Bigelow, John. *The Life of Samuel J. Tilden*. New York: Harper & Row, Publishers, 1895.

Browne, Waldo R. *Altgeld of Illinois*. New York: B. W. Huebsch, Inc., 1924.

Caldwell, Robert Granville. *James A. Garfield, Party Chieftain*. New York: Dodd, Mead & Co., 1931.

Chidsey, Donald Barr. *The Gentleman from New York: A Life of Roscoe Conkling*. New Haven: Yale Uinversity Press, 1935.

Childs, Marquis. *Eisenhower: Captive Hero*. New York: Harcourt, Brace & World, Inc., 1958.

Coleman, Charles H. *The Election of 1868*. New York: Columbia University Press, 1933.

Conkling, Alfred R. *The Life and Letters of Roscoe Conkling*. New York: C. L. Webster & Co., 1889.

Cramer, C. H. *Newton D. Baker*. New York: Harcourt, Brace & World, Inc., 1961.

Dillon, Mary E. *Wendell Willkie*. Philadelphia: J. B. Lippincott Co., 1952.

Dunn, Arthur Wallace. *From Harrison to Harding*. Vol. I. New York: G. P. Putnam's Son's, 1922.

Eckenrode, H. J. *Rutherford B. Hayes, Statesman of Reform*. New York: Dodd, Mead & Co., 1930.

Ellis, Elmer. *Henry Moore Teller*. Idaho: The Caxton Printers, Ltd., 1941.

Foulke, William Dudley. *Life of Oliver P. Morton*. Indianapolis: The Bobbs-Merrill Company, Inc., 1899.

Freidel, Frank. *Franklin D. Roosevelt, The Ordeal*. Boston: Little, Brown & Co., 1954.

————. *Franklin D. Roosevelt, The Triumph*. Boston: Little, Brown & Co., 1956.

Fuess, Claude Moore. *Carl Schurz, Reformer*. New York: Dodd, Mead & Co., 1932.

Gilmore, Jesse Lee. "The Political Emergence of William Jennings Bryan." Unpublished Master's thesis, University of California, Berkeley, 1948.

Goodrich, Frederick E. *The Life and Public Services of Winfield Scott Hancock*. Boston: Lee and Shepard, 1880.

Gosnell, Harold F. *Champion Campaigner, Franklin D. Roosevelt*. New York: The Macmillan Company, 1952.

Goss, Hilton P. "The Pre-Convention Presidential Campaign of 1912." Unpublished Ph.D. dissertation, University of California, Berkeley, 1942.

Hagedorn, Hermann. *Leonard Wood.* Vol. II. New York: Harper & Row, Publishers, 1931.

Hamilton, Gail. *Biography of James G. Blaine.* Norwich: The Henry Bill Publishing Co., 1895.

Hart, Albert Bushnell. *Salmon Portland Chase.* Boston: Houghton Mifflin Company, 1899.

Haworth, Paul Leland. *The Hayes-Tilden Disputed Presidential Election of 1876.* Cleveland: Burrows Bros. Co., 1906.

Hesseltine, William B. *Ulysses S. Grant, Politician.* New York: Dodd, Mead & Co., 1935.

Hirsch, Mark D. *William C. Whitney, Modern Warwick.* New York: Dodd, Mead & Co., 1948.

Holcombe, John W. and Hubert M. Skinner. *Life and Public Services of Thomas A. Hendricks.* Indianapolis: Carlton & Hollenbeck, 1886.

Holzman, Robert S. *Stormy Ben Butler.* New York: The Macmillan Company, 1954.

Howe, George Frederick. *Chester A. Arthur, A Quarter-Century of Machine Politics.* New York: Dodd, Mead & Co., 1934.

Hutchinson, William T. *Lowden of Illinois.* Vol. II. Chicago: University of Chicago Press, 1957.

Jessup, Phillip C. *Elihu Root.* Vol. II. New York: Dodd, Mead & Co., 1938.

Johnson, Allen, ed. *Dictionary of American Biography.* New York: Charles Scribner's Sons, 1928-1936.

Johnson, Donald Bruce. *The Republican Party and Wendell Willkie.* Urbana: University of Illinois Press, 1960.

Lambert, John R. *Arthur Pue Gorman.* Baton Rouge: Louisiana State University Press, 1953.

Link, Arthur S. Wilson, *The Road to the White House.* Princeton: Princeton University Press, 1947.

Lyons, Maurice F. *William F. McCombs, The President Maker.* Cincinnati: The Bancroft Co., 1922.

McClure, A. K. *Our Presidents and How We Make Them.* New York: Harper & Row, Publishers, 1902.

———. *Recollections of Half a Century.* Salem, Mass.: The Salem Press Co., 1902.

McElroy, Robert. *Grover Cleveland, The Man and the Statesman.* New York: Harper & Row, Publishers, 1923.

———. *Levi Parsons Morton.* New York: G. P. Putnam's Sons, 1930.

McKenna, Marian C. *Borah.* Ann Arbor: The University of Michigan Press, 1961.

Merriam, George S. *The Life and Times of Samuel Bowles*. Vol. II. New York: The Century Co., 1885.

Mitchell, Stewart. *Horatio Seymour of New York*. Cambridge: Harvard University Press, 1938.

Moore, J. Hampton. *Roosevelt and the Old Guard*. Philadelphia: Macrae Smith Co., 1925.

Muzzey, David Saville. *James G. Blaine*. New York: Dodd, Mead & Co., 1934.

Nash, Howard P., Jr. *Third Parties in American Politics*. Washington: Public Affairs Press, 1959.

Nevins, Allan. *Grover Cleveland, A Study in Courage*. New York: Dodd, Mead & Co., 1932.

Palmer, George Thomas. *A Conscientious Turncoat, The Story of John M. Palmer*. New Haven: Yale University Press, 1941.

Paxson, Frederic L. *American Democracy and the World War, Pre-War Years*. Boston: Houghton Mifflin Company, 1936.

Peel, Roy V. and Thomas C. Donnelly. *The 1932 Campaign*. New York: Farrar & Rinehart, Inc., 1935.

Pepper, Charles M. *The Life and Times of Henry Gassaway Davis*. New York: The Century Co., 1920.

Pringle, Henry F. *The Life and Times of William Howard Taft*. Vol. II. New York: Farrar & Rinehart, Inc., 1939.

Pusey, Merlo J. *Charles Evans Hughes*. Vol. I. New York: The Macmillan Company, 1951.

Rhodes, James Ford. *History of the United States from Hayes to McKinley*. New York: The Macmillan Company, 1919.

Richardson, Leon Burr. *William E. Chandler, Republican*. New York: Dodd, Mead & Co., 1940.

Ross, Earle Dudley. *The Liberal Republican Movement*. New York: The Rumford Press, 1919.

Rovere, Richard. *The Eisenhower Years*. New York: Farrar, Straus & Cudahy, Inc., 1956.

Russell, Charles Edward. *Blaine of Maine*. New York: Cosmopolitan Book Corp., 1931.

Schuckers, J. W. *The Life and Public Services of Salmon Portland Chase*. New York: Appleton-Century-Crofts, 1874.

Sievers, Harry J., S.J. *Benjamin Harrison, Hoosier Statesman*. New York: University Publishers Inc., 1959.

Simkins, Francis Butler. *Pitchfork Ben Tillman*. Baton Rouge: Louisiana State University Press, 1944.

Smith, Theodore Clarke. *The Life and Letters of James Abram Garfield*. Vol. II. New Haven: Yale University Press, 1925.

Smith, Willard H. *Schuyler Colfax, The Changing Fortunes of a Political Idol.* Indianapolis: The Indiana Historical Bureau, 1952.

Smith, William Ernest. *The Francis Preston Blair Family in Politics.* Vol. II. New York: The Macmillan Company, 1933.

Stanwood, Edward. *James Gillespie Blaine.* Boston: Houghton Mifflin Company, 1905.

Stebbins, Homer A. *A Political History of the State of New York 1865-1869.* Studies in History, Economics and Public Law, Vol. 55. Columbia University, 1913.

Steinberg, Alfred. *The Man from Missouri.* New York: G. P. Putnam's Sons, 1962.

Stephenson, Nathanial Wright. *Nelson W. Aldrich.* New York: Charles Scribner's Sons, 1930.

Stiles, Lela. *The Man Behind Roosevelt.* New York: Harcourt, Brace & World, 1954.

Sullivan, Mark. *Our Times, 1900-1925.* New York: Charles Scribner's Sons, 1937-1940.

Tansill, Charles Callan. *The Congressional Career of Thomas Francis Bayard.* Washington: Georgetown University Press, 1946.

Timmons, Bascom N. *Garner of Texas.* New York: Harper & Row, Publishers, 1948.

Vallandigham, Rev. James L. *A Life of Clement L. Vallandigham.* Baltimore: Turnbull Bros., 1872.

Van Deusen, Glyndon G. *Horace Greeley, Nineteenth-Century Crusader.* Philadelphia: University of Pennsylvania Press, 1953.

Wall, Joseph Frazier. *Henry Watterson, Reconstructed Rebel.* New York: Oxford University Press, 1956.

Warner, Emily Smith. *The Happy Warrior.* Garden City: Doubleday & Company, Inc., 1956.

White, Horace. *The Life of Lyman Trumbull.* Boston: Houghton Mifflin Company, 1913.

White, Theodore H. *The Making of the President 1960.* New York: Atheneum Publishers, 1961.

White, William Allen. *Politics: The Citizen's Business.* New York: The Macmillan Company, 1924.

Williams, Robert L. "The Presidential Election of 1904." Unpublished Master's thesis, University of California, Berkeley, 1937.

ARTICLES

Arvey, Jacob M., as told to John Madigan. "The Reluctant Candidate—An Inside Story." *The Reporter,* Nov. 24, 1953.

Dilla, Harriette M. "The Politics of Michigan, 1865-1878." *Studies in History, Economics and Public Law,* Vol. 47. Columbia University, 1912.

Hatch, Alden. The "Men Around Deewy." *Harpers,* October, 1948.

Moore, Clifford H. "Ohio in National Politics, 1865-1896." *Ohio Archaeological and Historical Quarterly,* Vol. XXXVII, Nos. 2 & 3, April—July, 1928.

Thomas, Harrison Cook. "The Return of the Democratic Party to Power in 1884." *Studies in History, Economics and Public Law,* Vol. 89. Columbia University, 1919.

Walters, Everett. "The Ohio Delegation at the National Republican Convention of 1888." *The Ohio State Archaeological and Historical Quarterly,* Vol. 56, No. 3., July, 1947.

Woods, George B. "The New York Convention." *North American Review,* Vol. CVII, No. 221, October, 1868.

PERIODICALS

Collier's
Harper's Weekly
McClure's Magazine
The Nation
The New Republic
Newsweek

The New York Times
The North American Review
The Reporter
The Saturday Evening Post
Time